DATE DUE

			PRINTED IN U.S.A.

SOMETHING ABOUT THE AUTHOR

ISSN 0276-816X

something ABOUT THE AUTHOR

**Facts and Pictures about Authors
and Illustrators of Books for Young People**

EDITED BY
ANNE COMMIRE

VOLUME 53

Gale Research Inc.
Book Tower • Detroit, Michigan 48226

Editor: Anne Commire

Associate Editors: Agnes Garrett, Helga P. McCue

Senior Assistant Editor: Dianne H. Anderson

Assistant Editors: Elisa Ann Ferraro, Eunice L. Petrini, Linda Shedd

Sketchwriters: Marguerite Feitlowitz, Rachel Koenig

Researcher: Catherine Ruello

Editorial Assistants: Catherine Coray, Joanne J. Ferraro, Marja T. Hiltunen,
Evelyn Johnson, June Lee, Dieter Miller

Permissions Assistant: Susan Pfanner

In cooperation with the staff of *Something about the Author Autobiography Series*

Editor: Joyce Nakamura

Assistant Editors: Carolyn Chafetz, Laurie Collier

Research Assistants: Shelly Andrews, Kristin R. Dittmeier, Carolyn Kline

Production Manager: Mary Beth Trimper

External Production Assistants: Linda Davis, Patty Farley

Internal Production Associate: Louise Gagné

Layout Artist: Elizabeth Lewis Patryjak

Art Director: Arthur Chartow

Special acknowledgment is due to the members of the *Contemporary Authors* staff
who assisted in the preparation of this volume.

Library of Congress Catalog Card Number 72-27107
ISBN 0-8103-2263-3
ISSN 0276-816X

Computerized photocomposition by
Typographics, Incorporated
Kansas City, Missouri

Printed in the United States

Contents

Introduction   ix   Acknowledgments   xv
Illustrations Index   195   Author Index   215

A

Adair, Ian   1942- 1

Adams, Lowell
see Joseph, James (Herz) 87

Alajalov, Constantin   1900-1987
Obituary Notice... 3

Allen, Laura Jean
Brief Entry.. 4

Alzada, Juan Sanchez
see Joseph, James (Herz) 87

Anderson, Leone Castell   1923-   4

B

Bedoukian, Kerop   1907-1981 6

Bond, B.J.
see Heneghan, James 63

Brady, Esther Wood   1905-1987
Obituary Notice... 6

Brennan, Gale Patrick   1927-
Brief Entry.. 6

Brightfield, Richard   1927-
Brief Entry.. 7

Brightfield, Rick
see Brightfield, Richard 7

Britton, Kate
see Stegeman, Janet Allais................... 140

Brooks, Bruce
Brief Entry.. 7

Brown, Drollene P.   1939-   7

Brown, Marc (Tolon)   1946-   9

Bumstead, Kathleen (Mary)   1918-1987.............. 18

C

Campling, Elizabeth   1948-   19

Carlstrom, Nancy White   1948-   19

Caseley, Judith   1951-
Brief Entry.. 21

Caulfield, Peggy F.   1926-1987
Obituary Notice... 21

Chute, B(eatrice) J(oy)   1913-1987
Obituary Notice... 21

Colman, Hila 22

Cosgrove, Stephen E(dward)   1945-   31

Crayder, Teresa
see Colman, Hila 22

Cummings, Parke   1902-1987
Obituary Notice... 37

D

Daniel, Alan   1939-
Brief Entry.. 37

Drackett, Phil(ip Arthur)   1922-   38

E

Esbensen, Barbara Juster
Brief Entry.. 38

F

Fitzgerald, Merni I(ngrassia)   1955-   39

Frank, Hélène
see Vautier, Ghislaine 172

Frasconi, Antonio   1919-   40

G

Gammell, Stephen   1943-   50

Gennaro, Joseph F(rancis), Jr.   1924-   58

Graham-Cameron, M.
  see Graham-Cameron, M(alcolm) G(ordon)...... 59

Graham-Cameron, M(alcolm) G(ordon)
  1931- 59

Graham-Cameron, Mike
  see Graham-Cameron, M(alcolm) G(ordon)...... 59

Green, Roger (Gilbert) Lancelyn   1918-1987
  Obituary Notice.................................... 62

H

Hardy, Jon   1958- 62

Harris, Robie H.
  Brief Entry.. 62

Henderson, Gordon   1950- 62

Henderson, Kathy   1949-
  Brief Entry.. 63

Heneghan, James   1930- 63

Hill, Eric   1927-
  Brief Entry.. 64

Hind, Dolores (Ellen)   1931- 64

Holt, Stephen
  see Thompson, Harlan (Howard) 147

Hunkin, Tim(othy Mark Trelawney)   1950- 65

J

Jackson, Geoffrey (Holt Seymour)   1915-1987
  Obituary Notice.................................... 65

Janeczko, Paul B(ryan)   1945- 66

Johnson, Harriett   1908-1987
  Obituary Notice.................................... 67

Jones, Charles M(artin)   1912- 67

Jones, Chuck
  see Jones, Charles M(artin) 67

Joseph, James (Herz)   1924- 87

K

Kennedy, Dorothy M(intzlaff)   1931- 89

King, Paul
  see Drackett, Phil(ip Arthur)....................... 38

Kingston, Maxine (Ting Ting) Hong   1940- 91

Koertge, Ronald   1940- 95

Krupp, E(dwin) C(harles)   1944- 96

Krupp, Robin Rector   1946- 97

Kunhardt, Dorothy (Meserve)   1901-1979 99

Kunz, Roxane (Brown)   1932-
  Brief Entry....................................... 103

L

Lamb, Harold (Albert)   1892-1962..................... 103

Lawford, Paula Jane   1960-
  Brief Entry....................................... 109

Lesser, Rika   1953- 110

M

Mabery, D. L.   1953-
  Brief Entry....................................... 111

Marrin, Albert   1936- 112

Marsoli, Lisa Ann   1958-
  Brief Entry....................................... 112

McKissack, Frederick L(emuel)   1939-
  Brief Entry....................................... 112

Morgan, Ellen
  see Bumstead, Kathleen (Mary)..................... 18

Munthe, Nelly   1947- 113

N

Nerlove, Miriam   1959- 113

O

Oana, Katherine D.   1929- 114

Oana, Kay D.
  see Oana, Katherine D. 114

O'Brien, Anne Sibley   1952- 115

P

Paterson, Katherine (Womeldorf)   1932- 118

Pearson, Gayle   1947- 128

Perez, Walter
  see Joseph, James (Herz). 87

Purtill, Richard L.   1931- 129

R

Reese, Bob
  see Reese, Robert A. 130

Reese, Robert A. 1938-
  Brief Entry... 130

Rich, Mark J. 1948-
  Brief Entry... 130

Robbins, Ken
  Brief Entry... 130

Roberson, John R(oyster) 1930- 130

Ross, Pat(ricia Kienzle) 1943- 132

Russell, James 1933- 133

Russell, Jim
  see Russell, James... 133

S

Schur, Maxine 1948- 135

Snellgrove, L(aurence) E(rnest) 1928- 136

Stanley, George Edward 1942- 137

Stegeman, Janet Allais 1923- 140

Stewart, W(alter) P. 1924- 140

Strauss, Joyce 1936- 141

Stubbs, Joanna 1940-
  Brief Entry... 141

Swayne, Sam(uel F.) 1907- 141

Swayne, Zoa (Lourana) 1905- 144

Symons, Stuart
  see Stanley, George Edward 137

T

Tang, You-Shan 1946- 146

Thompson, Harlan (Howard) 1894-1987
  Obituary Notice.. 147

U

Uchida, Yoshiko 1921- 147

Ulmer, Louise 1943- 157

Underhill, Liz 1948- 158

V

Van Allsburg, Chris 1949- 160

Vautier, Ghislaine 1932- 172

Velthuijs, Max 1923- 173

W

Wainscott, John Milton 1910-1981 174

Walker, Lou Ann 1952-
  Brief Entry... 175

Wallace, Bill
  see Wallace, William Keith 178

Wallace, Ian 1950- 175

Wallace, William Keith 1947- 178

Walsh, George Johnston 1889-1981 180

Warriner, John 1907(?)-1987
  Obituary Notice.. 180

Weston, Martha 1947- 180

Williams, Vera B. 1927- 185

Wolny, P.
  see Janeczko, Paul B(ryan).............................. 66

Wood, Esther
  see Brady, Esther Wood 6

Y

Youngs, Betty 1934-1985 191

Introduction

As the only ongoing reference series that deals with the lives and works of authors and illustrators of children's books, *Something about the Author (SATA)* is a unique source of information. The *SATA* series includes not only well-known authors and illustrators whose books are most widely read, but also those less prominent people whose works are just coming to be recognized. *SATA* is often the only readily available information source for less well-known writers or artists. You'll find *SATA* informative and entertaining whether you are:

—a student in junior high school (or perhaps one to two grades higher or lower) who needs information for a book report or some other assignment for an English class;

—a children's librarian who is searching for the answer to yet another question from a young reader or collecting background material to use for a story hour;

—an English teacher who is drawing up an assignment for your students or gathering information for a book talk;

—a student in a college of education or library science who is studying children's literature and reference sources in the field;

—a parent who is looking for a new way to interest your child in reading something more than the school curriculum prescribes;

—an adult who enjoys children's literature for its own sake, knowing that a good children's book has no age limits.

Scope

In *SATA* you will find detailed information about authors and illustrators who span the full time range of children's literature, from early figures like John Newbery and L. Frank Baum to contemporary figures like Judy Blume and Richard Peck. Authors in the series represent primarily English-speaking countries, particularly the United States, Canada, and the United Kingdom. Also included, however, are authors from around the world whose works are available in English translation, for example: from France, Jean and Laurent De Brunhoff; from Italy, Emanuele Luzzati; from the Netherlands, Jaap ter Haar; from Germany, James Krüss; from Norway, Babbis Friis-Baastad; from Japan, Toshiko Kanzawa; from the Soviet Union, Kornei Chukovsky; from Switzerland, Alois Carigiet, to name only a few. Also appearing in *SATA* are Newbery medalists from Hendrik Van Loon (1922) to Russell Freedman (1988). The writings represented in *SATA* include those created intentionally for children and young adults as well as those written for a general audience and known to interest younger readers. These writings cover the spectrum from picture books, humor, folk and fairy tales, animal stories, mystery and adventure, science fiction and fantasy, historical fiction, poetry and nonsense verse, to drama, biography, and nonfiction.

Information Features

In *SATA* you will find full-length entries that are being presented in the series for the first time. This volume, for example, marks the first full-length appearance of Nancy White Carlstrom, Stephen E. Cosgrove, Chuck Jones, Maxine Hong Kingston, Dorothy Kunhardt, Harold Lamb, and Vera B. Williams.

Brief Entries, first introduced in Volume 27, are another regular feature of *SATA*. Brief Entries present essentially the same types of information found in a full entry but do so in a capsule form and without illustration. These entries are intended to give you useful and timely information while the more time-consuming process of compiling a full-length biography is in progress. In this volume you'll find Brief Entries for Barbara Juster Esbensen, Robie H. Harris, Kathy Henderson, Lisa Ann Marsoli, Ken Robbins, and Joanna Stubbs, among others.

Obituaries have been included in *SATA* since Volume 20. An Obituary is intended not only as a death notice but also as a concise view of a person's life and work. Obituaries may appear for persons who have entries in earlier *SATA* volumes, as well as for people who have not yet appeared in the series. In this volume Obituaries mark the recent deaths of Esther Wood Brady, B. J. Chute, Roger Lancelyn Green, Harriett Johnson, Harlan Thompson, John Warriner, and others.

Revised Entries

Since Volume 25, each *SATA* volume also includes newly revised and updated entries for a selection of *SATA* listees (usually four to six) who remain of interest to today's readers and who have been active enough to require extensive revision of their earlier biographies. For example, when Beverly Cleary first appeared in *SATA* Volume 2, she was the author of twenty-one books for children and young adults and the recipient of numerous awards. By the time her updated sketch appeared in Volume 43 (a span of fifteen years), this creator of the indefatigable Ramona Quimby and other memorable characters had produced a dozen new titles and garnered nearly fifty additional awards, including the 1984 Newbery Medal.

The entry for a given biographee may be revised as often as there is substantial new information to provide. In this volume, look for revised entries on Marc Brown, Hila Colman, Antonio Frasconi, Katherine Paterson, Yoshiko Uchida, and Chris Van Allsburg.

Illustrations

While the textual information in *SATA* is its primary reason for existing, photographs and illustrations not only enliven the text but are an integral part of the information that *SATA* provides. Illustrations and text are wedded in such a special way in children's literature that artists and their works naturally occupy a prominent place among *SATA*'s listees. The illustrators that you'll find in the series include such past masters of children's book illustration as Randolph Caldecott, Walter Crane, Arthur Rackham, and Ernest H. Shepard, as well as such noted contemporary artists as Maurice Sendak, Edward Gorey, Tomie de Paola, and Margot Zemach. There are Caldecott medalists from Dorothy Lathrop (the first recipient in 1938) to John Schoenherr (the latest winner in 1988); cartoonists like Charles Schulz ("Peanuts"), Walt Kelly ("Pogo"), Hank Ketcham ("Dennis the Menace"), and Georges Rémi ("Tintin"); photographers like Jill Krementz, Tana Hoban, Bruce McMillan, and Bruce Curtis; and filmmakers like Walt Disney, Alfred Hitchcock, and Steven Spielberg.

In more than a dozen years of recording the metamorphosis of children's literature from the printed page to other media, *SATA* has become something of a repository of photographs that are unique in themselves and exist nowhere else as a group, particularly many of the classics of motion picture and stage history and photographs that have been specially loaned to us from private collections.

Indexes

Each *SATA* volume provides a cumulative index in two parts: first, the Illustrations Index, arranged by the name of the illustrator, gives the number of the volume and page where the illustrator's work appears in the current volume as well as all preceding volumes in the series; second, the Author Index gives the number of the volume in which a person's biographical sketch, Brief Entry, or Obituary appears in the current volume as well as all preceding volumes in the series. These indexes also include references to authors and illustrators who appear in *Yesterday's Authors of Books for Children* (described in detail below). Beginning with Volume 36, the *SATA* Author Index provides cross-references to authors who are included in *Children's Literature Review*.

Starting with Volume 42, you will also find cross-references to authors who are included in the *Something about the Author Autobiography Series* (described in detail below).

Character Index—New Feature

If you're like many readers, the names of fictional characters may pop more easily into your mind than the names of the authors or illustrators who created them: Snow White, Charlotte the Spider, the Cat in the Hat, Peter Pan, Mary Poppins, Winnie-the-Pooh, Brer Rabbit, Little Toot, Charlie Bucket, Lassie, Rip Van Winkle, Bartholomew Cubbins—the list could go on and on. But who invented them? Now these characters, and several thousand others, can lead you to the *SATA* and *YABC* entries on the lives and works of their creators.

First published in Volume 50, the Character Index provides a broad selection of characters from books and other media—movies, plays, comic strips, cartoons, etc.—created by listees who have appeared in all the published volumes of *SATA* and *YABC*. This index gives the character name, followed by a *"See"* reference indicating the name of the creator and the number of the *SATA* or *YABC* volume in which the creator's bio-bibliographical entry can be found. As new *SATA* volumes are prepared, additional characters will be included in the cumulative Character Index and published annually in *SATA*. (The cumulative Illustrations and Author Indexes will continue to appear in each *SATA* volume.)

It would be impossible for the Character Index to include every important character created by *SATA* and *YABC* listees. (Several hundred important characters might be taken from Dickens alone, for example.) Therefore, the *SATA* editors have selected those characters that are best known and thus most likely to interest *SATA* users. Realizing that some of your favorite characters may not appear in this index, the editors invite you to suggest additional names. With your help, the editors hope to make the Character Index a uniquely useful reference tool for you.

What a *SATA* Entry Provides

Whether you're already familiar with the *SATA* series or just getting acquainted, you will want to be aware of the kind of information that an entry provides. In every *SATA* entry the editors attempt to give as complete a picture of the person's life and work as possible. In some cases that full range of information may simply be unavailable, or a biographee may choose not to reveal complete personal details. The information that the editors attempt to provide in every entry is arranged in the following categories:

1. The "head" of the entry gives

   —the most complete form of the name,
   —any part of the name not commonly used, included in parentheses,
   —birth and death dates, if known; a (?) indicates a discrepancy in published sources,
   —pseudonyms or name variants under which the person has had books published or is publicly known, in parentheses in the second line.

2. "Personal" section gives

   —date and place of birth and death,
   —parents' names and occupations,
   —name of spouse, date of marriage, and names of children,
   —educational institutions attended, degrees received, and dates,
   —religious and political affiliations,
   —agent's name and address,
   —home and/or office address.

3. "Career" section gives

   —name of employer, position, and dates for each career post,
   —military service,
   —memberships,
   —awards and honors.

4. "Writings" section gives

—title, first publisher and date of publication, and illustration information for each book written; revised editions and other significant editions for books with particularly long publishing histories; genre, when known.

5. "Adaptations" section gives

—title, major performers, producer, and date of all known reworkings of an author's material in another medium, like movies, filmstrips, television, recordings, plays, etc.

6. "Sidelights" section gives

—commentary on the life or work of the biographee either directly from the person (and often written specifically for the *SATA* entry), or gathered from biographies, diaries, letters, interviews, or other published sources.

7. "For More Information See" section gives

—books, feature articles, films, plays, and reviews in which the biographee's life or work has been treated.

How a *SATA* Entry Is Compiled

A *SATA* entry progresses through a series of steps. If the biographee is living, the *SATA* editors try to secure information directly from him or her through a questionnaire. From the information that the biographee supplies, the editors prepare an entry, filling in any essential missing details with research. The author or illustrator is then sent a copy of the entry to check for accuracy and completeness.

If the biographee is deceased or cannot be reached by questionnaire, the *SATA* editors examine a wide variety of published sources to gather information for an entry. Biographical sources are searched with the aid of Gale's *Biography and Genealogy Master Index*. Bibliographic sources like the *National Union Catalog*, the *Cumulative Book Index*, *American Book Publishing Record*, and the *British Museum Catalogue* are consulted, as are book reviews, feature articles, published interviews, and material sometimes obtained from the biographee's family, publishers, agent, or other associates.

For each entry presented in *SATA*, the editors also attempt to locate a photograph of the biographee as well as representative illustrations from his or her books. After surveying the available books which the biographee has written and/or illustrated, and then making a selection of appropriate photographs and illustrations, the editors request permission of the current copyright holders to reprint the material. In the case of older books for which the copyright may have passed through several hands, even locating the current copyright holder is often a long and involved process.

We invite you to examine the entire *SATA* series, starting with this volume. Described below are some of the people in Volume 53 that you may find particularly interesting.

Highlights of This Volume

MARC BROWN......"preferred the company of adults to that of other children" during his childhood in Erie, Pennsylvania. Although his parents had "more 'respectable' ambitions" than art school for their son, Brown "majored in painting at the Cleveland Institute of Arts." The Boston-bound young artist found work there as a mechanical drawing teacher at a junior college and as an illustrator of reading primers for Houghton Mifflin ("the work was steady, but the process stultifying"). His first non-textbook illustration was for Asimov's *What Makes the Sun Shine?* in 1970. Since then, Brown has illustrated numerous books besides his own, including the "Arthur Adventure" stories for children. When not working, Brown restores old houses. He is currently living in two: one in Hingham, Massachusetts, the other on Martha's Vineyard.

HILA COLMAN......was born and raised in New York City where she "led the life of an over-protected girl from a well-to-do Jewish family." As the daughter of an "early feminist," Colman and her sister were prepared to assume full careers. Her first published article offered a vindication of the rights of women and was well received even in 1947 "when...[traditional] sex roles were clearly defined." From feminism to stories for *True Confessions,* Colman progressed steadily until her first book ws published in 1957. Her stories for young adults reflect her confidence in teenagers. "There is nothing new to write about," says Colman. "What counts is your way of writing."

STEPHEN COSGROVE......"was one of seven males admitted" to Stevens College for Women on a drama scholarship, where he wrote plays, a short film, and a children's play. "The school's television program helped me to see things in picture frames," he said. This helped him later on as a writer of children's books. Today he is founder and president of Serendipity Communications Ltd., a company that produces inexpensive fantasy books for children. Among his series are the "Bumble B. Bear" series, the "Baby Bunny" series, and the "Whimsie Storybooks."

ANTONIO FRASCONI......was born in Argentina, the son of Italian parents. As a child, he cherished books and painting; as a teenager, he drew political cartoons. He came to the United States as the recipient of an Inter-American fellowship, with aspirations of becoming a painter, but found that "painting limits," and turned instead to woodcuts—"an exciting medium...[and] most satisfying to me." Through the years he has worked as a teacher and artist using simple tools and an ancient technique to create a diversity of work.

CHUCK JONES......"read Dickens and Twain and Trollope and Dumas before I even went to school." He also drew pictures: "Everybody in the family drew," he said. Graduating from art school during the Depression, Jones was lucky to get a job in animation "as a cel washer," working his "miserable way up" the career ladder. In his long and distinguished career as an animator, he has created Elmer Fudd, Bugs Bunny, Tweetie Bird, Porky Pig, the Road Runner, Pépé le Pew, and other noteworthy comic heroes. "Most of my characters are failures...wimps and nerds...and fighters," says Jones.

KATHERINE PATERSON......grew up in China, the daughter of "Southern Presbyterian missionary parents." Her first language was Chinese, although she quickly became bilingual. She describes herself as having been "a weird little kid," and notes that these qualities are sound preparations for becoming a writer. Reading and writing stories as a child were also helpful activities. She is an award-winning writer and Newbery Medal winner whose aim is to "uncover a story that children will enjoy."

YOSHIKO UCHIDA......was a "child of frugal immigrant parents" who grew up writing stories and keeping a journal which she began "the day I graduated from elementary school." She and her Japanese American family were incarcerated in a concentration camp in the Utah desert during World War II. The experience left Uchida with a "tremendous sense of responsibility to make good...for all Japanese Americans." Today she is the author of books about children of Japan, Japanese folktales, and her experiences as a Japanese American. "I think...freedom is a luxury to be cherished," she said.

CHRIS VAN ALLSBURG......was born in Michigan "sometime in the middle of the twentieth century." He had great enthusiasm for art, but was unsure what he would do when he grew up. In college, however, he began his career "as a sculptor and went into painting almost accidentally." He has become a well-known illustrator with numerous books to his credit, including the Caldecott winners, *Jumanji* and *The Polar Express.* "For me books are very compelling," he says. "I instantly get into their worlds, visualizing the place, the room, the people."

Yesterday's Authors of Books for Children

In a two-volume companion set to *SATA, Yesterday's Authors of Books for Children (YABC)* focuses on early authors and illustrators, from the beginnings of children's literature through 1960, whose books are still being read by children today. Here you will find "old favorites" like Hans Christian Andersen, J. M. Barrie, Kenneth Grahame, Betty MacDonald, A. A. Milne, Beatrix Potter, Samuel Clemens, Kate Greenaway, Rudyard Kipling, Robert Louis Stevenson, and many more.

Similar in format to *SATA, YABC* features bio-bibliographical entries that are divided into information categories such as Personal, Career, Writings, and Sidelights. The entries are further enhanced by book illustrations, author photos, movie stills, and many rare old photographs.

In Volume 2 you will find cumulative indexes to the authors and to the illustrations that appear in *YABC*. These listings can also be located in the *SATA* cumulative indexes.

By exploring both volumes of *YABC*, you will discover a special group of more than seventy authors and illustrators who represent some of the best in children's literature—individuals whose timeless works continue to delight children and adults of all ages. Other authors and illustrators from early children's literature are listed in *SATA*, starting with Volume 15.

Something about the Author Autobiography Series

You can complement the information in *SATA* with the *Something about the Author Autobiography Series (SAAS)*, which provides autobiographical essays written by important current authors and illustrators of books for children and young adults. In every volume of *SAAS* you will find about twenty specially commissioned autobiographies, each accompanied by a selection of personal photographs supplied by the authors. The wide range of contemporary writers and artists who describe their lives and interests in the *Autobiography Series* includes Joan Aiken, Betsy Byars, Leonard Everett Fisher, Milton Meltzer, Maia Wojciechowska, and Jane Yolen, among others. Though the information presented in the autobiographies is as varied and unique as the authors, you can learn about the people and events that influenced these writers' early lives, how they began their careers, what problems they faced in becoming established in their professions, what prompted them to write or illustrate particular books, what they now find most challenging or rewarding in their lives, and what advice they may have for young people interested in following in their footsteps, among many other subjects.

Autobiographies included in the *SATA Autobiography Series* can be located through both the *SATA* cumulative index and the *SAAS* cumulative index, which lists not only the authors' names but also the subjects mentioned in their essays, such as titles of works and geographical and personal names.

The *SATA Autobiography Series* gives you the opportunity to view "close up" some of the fascinating people who are included in the *SATA* parent series. The combined *SATA* series makes available to you an unequaled range of comprehensive and in-depth information about the authors and illustrators of young people's literature.

Please write and tell us if we can make *SATA* even more helpful to you.

Acknowledgments

Grateful acknowledgment is made to the following publishers, authors, and artists for their kind permission to reproduce copyrighted material.

ATHENEUM PUBLISHERS. Illustration by Antonio Frasconi from "Weeping Mulberry" in *Monkey Puzzle and Other Poems* by Myra Cohn Livingston. Text copyright © by Myra Cohn Livingston. Illustrations copyright © 1984 by Antonio Frasconi./ Jacket illustration by Kinuko Craft from *The Happiest Ending* by Yoshiko Uchida. Copyright © 1985 by Yoshiko Uchida./ Jacket illustration by Kinuko Craft from *A Jar of Dreams* by Yoshiko Uchida. Copyright © 1981 by Yoshiko Uchida./ Jacket illustration by Kinuko Craft from *The Best Bad Thing* by Yoshiko Uchida. Copyright © 1983 by Yoshiko Uchida./ Illustration by Charles Robinson from *Journey Home* by Yoshiko Uchida. Text copyright © 1978 by Yoshiko Uchida. Illustrations copyright © 1978 by Charles Robinson./ Illustration by Ian Wallace from *Chin Chiang and the Dragon's Dance* by Ian Wallace. Copyright © 1984 by Ian Wallace./ Illustration by Ian Wallace from *Very Last First Time* by Jan Andrews. Text copyright © 1985 by Jan Andrews. Illustrations copyright © 1985 by Ian Wallace. All reprinted by permission of Atheneum Publishers.

THE ATLANTIC MONTHLY PRESS. Jacket illustration by Marc Brown from *Arthur's Tooth* by Marc Brown. Copyright © 1985 by Marc Brown. Reprinted by permission of The Atlantic Monthly Press.

AVON BOOKS. Cover illustration from *Angels and Other Strangers: Family Christmas Stories* by Katherine Paterson./ Illustration by Haru Wells from *The Master Puppeteer* by Katherine Paterson. Copyright © 1975 by Katherine Paterson./ Illustration by Peter Landa from *The Sign of the Chrysanthemum* by Katherine Paterson. Copyright © 1973 by Katherine Paterson./ Cover illustration from *The Codebreaker Kids* by George Edward Stanley. Copyright © 1987 by George Edward Stanley./ Illustration from *The Italian Spaghetti Mystery* by George Edward Stanley. Copyright © 1987 by George Edward Stanley. All reprinted by permission of Avon Books.

BALLANTINE/DEL REY/FAWCETT BOOKS. Cover illustration from *China Men* by Maxine Hong Kingston. Copyright © 1977, 1978, 1979, 1980 by Maxine Hong Kingston. Reprinted by permission of Ballantine/Del Rey/Fawcett Books.

BELITHA PRESS LTD. Illustration by Jim Russell from *Noah and His Ark* by Catherine Storr. Text copyright © 1982 by Catherine Storr and Belitha Press Ltd. Illustrations copyright © 1982 by Jim Russell. Reprinted by permission of Belitha Press Ltd.

CAMBRIDGE UNIVERSITY PRESS. Illustration by Hilary Abrahams from *The Farmer* by M. Graham-Cameron. Text copyright © 1975 by M. Graham-Cameron and Dinosaur Publications Ltd. Illustrations copyright © 1975 by Hilary Abrahams. Reprinted by permission of Cambridge University Press.

COLLIER MACMILLAN LTD. Illustration by Robin Rector Krupp from *The Comet and You* by E. C. Krupp. Copyright © 1985 by Edwin C. Krupp and Robin Rector Krupp. Reprinted by permission of Collier Macmillan Ltd.

CREATIVE ARTS BOOK CO. Illustration by Donald Carrick and Sidelight excerpts from *Journey to Topaz* by Yoshiko Uchida. Text copyright © 1971 by Yoshiko Uchida. Prologue copyright © 1984 by Yoshiko Uchida. Reprinted by permission of Creative Arts Book Co.

THOMAS Y. CROWELL, INC. Illustration by Glo Coalson from *That's the Way It Is, Amigo* by Hila Colman. Copyright © 1975 by Hila Colman./ Jacket illustration by Fred Marcellino from *The Great Gilly Hopkins* by Katherine Paterson. Copyright © 1978 by Katherine Paterson./ Illustration by Donna Diamond from *Bridge to Terabithia* by Katherine Paterson. Copyright © 1977 by Katherine Paterson./ Illustration by Haru Wells from *Of Nightingales That Weep* by Katherine Paterson. Copyright © 1974 by Katherine Paterson./ Jacket illustration by Kinuko Craft from *Jacob Have I Loved* by Katherine Paterson. Copyright © 1980 by Katherine Paterson. All reprinted by permission of Thomas Y. Crowell, Inc.

CROWN PUBLISHERS, INC. Jacket illustration by John Wallner from *Tell Me No Lies* by Hila Colman. Copyright © 1978 by Hila Colman./ Illustration by John Wallner from *Ethan's Favorite Teacher* by Hila Colman. Text copyright © 1975 by Hila Colman. Illustrations copyright © 1975 by John Wallner./ Illustration by Chuck Jones from *William the Backwards Skunk* by Chuck Jones. Copyright © 1986 by Chuck Jones Enterprises. All reprinted by permission of Crown Publishers, Inc.

DODD, MEAD & CO. Illustration by James Joseph from *Better Water Skiing for Boys* by James Joseph. Copyright © 1964 by James Joseph./ Illustration by Paul O. Zelinsky from *Hansel and Gretel,* retold by Rika Lesser. Text copyright © 1984 by Rika Lesser. Illustrations copyright © 1984 by Paul O. Zelinsky. Both reprinted by permission of Dodd, Mead & Co.

DOUBLEDAY & CO., INC. Frontispiece illustration from *The Crusades* by Harold Lamb. Copyright 1930, 1931 by Harold Lamb./ Illustration from *The March of Muscovy: Ivan the Terrible and the Growth of the Russian Empire, 1400-1648* by Harold Lamb. Copyright 1948 by Harold Lamb. Both reprinted by permission of Doubleday & Co., Inc.

E. P. DUTTON, INC. Illustration by Marc Brown from *Hand Rhymes* by Marc Brown. Copyright © 1985 by Marc Brown./ Sidelight excerpts from *Gates of Excellence: On Reading and Writing Books for Children* by Katherine Paterson./ Illustration by Kinuko Craft from *Rebels of the Heavenly Kingdom* by Katherine Paterson. Copyright © 1983 by Katherine Paterson./ Illustration by Deborah Chabrian from *Come Sing, Jimmy Joe* by Katherine Paterson. Copyright © 1985 by Katherine Paterson. All reprinted by permission of E. P. Dutton, Inc.

FARRAR, STRAUS & GIROUX, INC. Illustration from *Some of Us Survived: The Story of an Armenian Boy* by Kerop Bedoukian. Copyright © 1978 by Kerop Bedoukian./ Illustration by Antonio Frasconi from "Sands at Seventy" in *Overhead the Sun: Lines from Walt Whitman.* Copyright © 1969 by Antonio Frasconi. Both reprinted by permission of Farrar, Straus & Giroux, Inc.

FOUR WINDS PRESS. Illustration by Stephen Gammell from *Once upon MacDonald's Farm* by Stephen Gammell. Copyright © 1981 by Stephen Gammell./ Illustration by Robin Rector Krupp from *Get Set to Wreck* by Robin Rector Krupp. Copyright © 1988 by Robin Rector Krupp. Both reprinted by permission of Four Winds Press.

DAVID R. GODINE, PUBLISHERS, INC. Illustration by Liz Underhill from *Jack of All Trades* by Liz Underhill. Copyright © 1985 by Liz Underhill. Reprinted by permission of David R. Godine, Publishers, Inc.

HARPER & ROW, PUBLISHERS, INC. Illustration by Stephen Gammell from *A Furl of Fairy Wind* by Mollie Hunter. Text copyright © 1977 by Maureen Mollie Hunter McIlwraith. Illustrations copyright © 1977 by Stephen Gammell. Reprinted by permission of Harper & Row, Publishers, Inc.

HODDER & STOUGHTON LTD. Sidelight excerpts from an article "Harold Lamb and Historical Romance," March, 1930 in *The Bookman.* Reprinted by permission of Hodder & Stoughton Ltd.

HOLT, RINEHART & WINSTON GENERAL BOOK. Cover illustration by Anne Sibley O'Brien from *I'm Not Tired* by Anne Sibley O'Brien. Copyright © 1985 by Anne Sibley O'Brien./ Illustration by Anne Sibley O'Brien from *Where's My Truck?* by Anne Sibley O'Brien. Copyright © 1985 by Anne Sibley O'Brien. Both reprinted by permission of Holt, Rinehart & Winston General Book.

THE HORN BOOK, INC. Sidelight excerpts from *Newbery and Caldecott Medal Books, 1976-1985,* edited by Lee Kingman. Copyright © 1986 by The Horn Book, Inc. Reprinted by permission of The Horn Book, Inc.

HOUGHTON MIFFLIN CO. Jacket illustration by Chris Van Allsburg from *The Polar Express* by Chris Van Allsburg. Copyright © 1985 by Chris Van Allsburg./ Illustration by Chris Van Allsburg from *The Z Was Zapped* by Chris Van Allsburg. Copyright © 1987 by Chris Van Allsburg./ Detail of jacket illustration by Chris Van Allsburg from *Ben's Dream* by Chris Van Allsburg. Copyright © 1982 by Chris Van Allsburg./ Illustration by Chris Van Allsburg from *The Mysteries of Harris Burdick* by Chris Van Allsburg. Copyright © 1984 by Chris Van Allsburg./ Illustration by Chris Van Allsburg from *The Stranger* by Chris Van Allsburg. Copyright © 1986 by Chris Van Allsburg./ Illustration by Chris Van Allsburg from *Jumanji* by Chris Van Allsburg. Copyright © 1981 by Chris Van Allsburg./ Illustrations by Chris Van Allsburg from *The Garden of Abdul Gasazi* by Chris Van Allsburg. Copyright © 1979 by Chris

Van Allsburg./ Illustration by Chris Van Allsburg from *The Wreck of the Zephyr* by Chris Van Allsburg. Copyright © 1983 by Chris Van Allsburg. All reprinted by permission of Houghton Mifflin Co.

IDEALS PUBLISHING CORP. Illustration by Chuck Jones from *Cricket in Times Square* by George Selden. Copyright © 1984 by Chuck Jones Enterprises. Reprinted by permission of Ideals Publishing Corp.

ALFRED A. KNOPF, INC. Jacket illustration by Elias Dominguez and Sidelight excerpts from *The Woman Warrior: Memoirs of a Girlhood among Ghosts* by Maxine Hong Kingston. Copyright © 1975, 1976 by Maxine Hong Kingston. Both reprinted by permission of Alfred A. Knopf, Inc.

LEGACY HOUSE. Illustrations by Sam and Zoa Swayne from *Great-Grandfather in the Honey Tree* by Sam and Zoa Swayne. Copyright 1949 by Sam and Zoa Swayne. Copyright renewed © 1977 by Sam and Zoa Swayne. Both reprinted by permission of Legacy House.

J. B. LIPPINCOTT CO. Illustrations by Stephen Gammell from *Scary Stories to Tell in the Dark: Collected from American Folklore* by Alvin Schwartz. Text copyright © 1981 by Alvin Schwartz. Illustrations copyright © 1981 by Stephen Gammell. Both reprinted by permission of J. B. Lippincott Co.

LITTLE, BROWN & CO., INC. Illustration by Marc Brown from *One Two Three: An Animal Counting Book* by Marc Brown. Copyright © 1976 by Marc Brown./ Illustration by Marc Brown from *I Found Them in the Yellow Pages* by Norma Farber. Text copyright © 1973 by Norma Farber. Illustrations copyright © 1973 by Marc Brown./ Illustration by Stephen Gammell from *Thaddeus* by Alison Cragin Herzig and Jane Lawrence Mali. Text copyright © 1984 by Alison Cragin Herzig and Jane Lawrence Mali. Illustrations copyright © 1984 by Stephen Gammell./ Illustration by Karen Ann Weinhaus from "A Word Is Dead" in *Knock at a Star: A Child's Introduction to Poetry* by X.J. Kennedy and Dorothy M. Kennedy. Illustrations copyright © 1982 by Karen Ann Weinhaus./ Illustration by Martha Weston from *The Book of Think; or, How to Solve a Problem Twice Your Size* by Marilyn Burns. Copyright © 1976 by The Yolla Bolly Press. All reprinted by permission of Little, Brown & Co., Inc.

LOTHROP, LEE AND SHEPARD BOOKS. Illustration by Stephen Gammell from *Git Along, Old Scudder* by Stephen Gammell. Copyright © 1983 by Stephen Gammell./ Illustration by Martha Weston from *Lizzie and Harold* by Elizabeth Winthrop. Text copyright © 1986 by Elizabeth Winthrop Mahony. Illustrations copyright © 1986 by Martha Weston. Both reprinted by permission of Lothrop, Lee and Shepard Books.

MACMILLAN PUBLISHING CO. Illustration by Jerry Pinkney from *Wild Wild Sunflower Child Anna* by Nancy White Carlstrom. Text copyright © 1987 by Nancy White Carlstrom. Illustrations copyright © 1987 by Jerry Pinkney./ Sidelight excerpts from the introduction to *Frasconi against the Grain: The Woodcuts of Antonio Frasconi* by Nat Hentoff./ Jacket illustration by Robert J. Blake from *Bridges to Cross* by Paul B. Janeczko. Text copyright © 1986 by Paul B. Janeczko. Illustrations copyright © 1986 by Macmillan Publishing Co./ Illustration by Robin Rector Krupp from *The Comet and You* by E.C. Krupp. Copyright © 1985 by Edwin C. Krupp and Robin Rector Krupp./ Illustration by Margot Zemach from *The Two Foolish Cats* by Yoshiko Uchida. Text copyright © 1987 by Yoshiko Uchida. Illustrations copyright © 1987 by Margot Zemach. All reprinted by permission of Macmillan Publishing Co.

WILLIAM MORROW & CO., INC. Jacket illustration by Jane Sterret from *Rachel's Legacy* by Hila Colman. Copyright © 1978 by Hila Colman./ Illustration by Leonard Weisgard from *Peter's Brownstone House* by Hila Colman./ Illustration by Suekichi Akaba from *The Crane Wife,* retold by Sumiko Yagawa. Translation from the Japanese by Katherine Paterson. Text copyright © 1979 by Sumiko Yagawa. Illustrations copyright © 1979 by Suekichi Akaba. English translation copyright © 1981 by Katherine Paterson./ Illustration by Vera B. Williams from *A Chair for My Mother* by Vera B. Williams. Copyright © 1982 by Vera B. Williams./ Illustration by Vera B. Williams from *Something Special for Me* by Vera B. Williams. Copyright © 1983 by Vera B. Williams./ Illustration by Vera B. Williams from *Cherries and Cherry Pits* by Vera B. Williams. Copyright © 1986 by Vera B. Williams./ Illustration by Vera B. Williams from *Music, Music for Everyone* by Vera B. Williams. All reprinted by permission of William Morrow & Co., Inc.

PRICE/STERN/SLOAN PUBLISHERS, INC. Illustration by Charles Reasoner from *Shutterbugg* by Stephen Cosgrove. Copyright © 1984 by Price/Stern/Sloan Publishers, Inc./ Illustration by Robin James from *Tee-Tee* by Stephen Cosgrove. Copyright © 1978 by

Price/Stern/Sloan Publishers, Inc./ Illustration by Robin James from *Crickle-Crack* by Stephen Cosgrove. Copyright © 1987 by Price/Stern/Sloan Publishers, Inc./ Illustration by Robin James from *Buttermilk Bear* by Stephen Cosgrove. Copyright © 1987 by Price/Stern/ Sloan Publishers, Inc./ Illustration by Robin James from *Morgan Mine* by Stephen Cosgrove. Copyright © 1982 by Price/Stern/Sloan Publishers, Inc./ Illustration by Charles Reasoner from *Katy-Didd* by Stephen Cosgrove. Copyright © 1984 by Price/Stern/Sloan Publishers, Inc. All reprinted by permission of Price/Stern/Sloan Publishers, Inc.

RANDOM HOUSE, INC. Illustration by Marc Brown from *Little Witch's Big Night* by Deborah Hautzig. Text copyright © 1984 by Random House, Inc. Illustrations copyright © 1984 by Marc Brown./ Illustration by Charles Reasoner from *Gimme* by Stephen Cosgrove. Copyright © 1985 by Jomega, Inc./DreamMakers./ Sidelight excerpts from *My Father's House* by Philip B. Kunhardt. All reprinted by permission of Random House, Inc.

ROLLING STONE PRESS. Illustration by Maxine Hong Kingston from "Small Kid Time" in *Wonders: Writings and Drawings for the Child in Us All,* edited by Jonathan Cott and Mary Gimbel. Copyright © 1980 by Rolling Stone Press. Reprinted by permission of Rolling Stone Press.

SCHOLASTIC, INC. Cover illustration from *Sometimes I Don't Love My Mother* by Hila Colman. Copyright © 1977 by Hila Colman. Reprinted by permission of Scholastic, Inc.

THE SCRIBNER BOOK CO., INC. Illustration by Martha Weston from *My Garden Companion: A Complete Guide for the Beginner* by Jamie Jobb. Copyright © 1977 by Jamie Jobb./ Illustration by Martha Weston from *The Long Ago Lake: A Child's Book of Nature Lore and Crafts* by Marne Wilkins. Copyright © 1978 by Marne Wilkins. Both reprinted by permission of The Scribner Book Co., Inc.

STEMMER HOUSE PUBLISHERS, INC. Illustration by Antonio Frasconi from *The Little Blind Goat* by Jan Wahl. Text copyright © 1981 by Jan Wahl. Illustrations copyright © 1981 by Antonio Frasconi. Reprinted by permission of Stemmer House Publishers, Inc.

UNIVERSITY OF WASHINGTON PRESS. Photographs and Sidelight excerpts from *Desert Exile: The Uprooting of a Japanese American Family* by Yoshiko Uchida. Copyright © 1982 by Yoshiko Uchida. All reprinted by permission of University of Washington Press.

USBORNE PUBLISHING LTD. Illustration by Colin King from *The Knowhow Book of Jokes and Tricks* by Heather Amery and Ian Adair. Copyright © 1977 by Usborne Publishing Ltd. Reprinted by permission of Usborne Publishing Ltd.

WALKER & CO. Illustration by Antonio Frasconi from *How the Left-Behind Beasts Built Ararat* by Norma Farber. Text copyright © 1966 by Norma Farber. Illustrations copyright © 1978 by Antonio Frasconi. Reprinted by permission of Walker & Co.

FREDERICK WARNE LTD. Illustration by Stephen Gammell from *Where the Buffaloes Begin* by Olaf Baker. Text copyright © 1981 by Frederick Warne and Co., Inc. Illustrations copyright © 1981 by Stephen Gammell. Reprinted by permission of Frederick Warne Ltd.

WESTERN PUBLISHING CO., INC. Cover illustration by Dorothy Kunhardt from *Pat the Bunny* by Dorothy Kunhardt. Copyright by Dorothy Kunhardt./ Illustration by Lucinda McQueen from *Kitty's New Doll* by Dorothy M. Kunhardt. Text copyright © 1984 by The Estate of Dorothy M. Kunhardt. Illustrations copyright © 1984 by Lucinda McQueen./ Illustration by Kathy Wilburn from *The Scarebunny* by Dorothy Kunhardt. Copyright © 1985 by The Estate of Dorothy M. Kunhardt. Illustrations copyright © 1985 by Kathy Wilburn. All reprinted by permission of Western Publishing Co., Inc.

WEYBRIGHT & TALLEY, INC. Illustration by Sally Trinkle from *Something Out of Nothing* by Hila Colman. Copyright © 1968 by Hila Colman. Reprinted by permission of Weybright & Talley, Inc.

ALBERT WHITMAN & CO. Illustration by Irene Trivas from *The Wonderful Shrinking Shirt* by Leone Castell Anderson. Text copyright © 1983 by Leone Castell Anderson. Illustrations copyright © 1983 by Irene Trivas./ Illustration by Margot Apple from *Sybil Rides for Independence* by Drollene P. Brown. Text copyright © 1985 by Drollene P. Brown. Illustrations copyright © 1985 by Margot Apple. Both reprinted by permission of Albert Whitman & Co.

Sidelight excerpts from an article "Chuck Jones Interviewed," by Joe Adamson in *The American Animated Cartoon,* edited by Gerald Peary and Danny Peary. Copyright © 1980 by E. P. Dutton. Reprinted by permission of American Film Institute./ Sidelight excerpts from

The Complete Guide to Writing Non-Fiction, edited by Glenn Evans. Reprinted by permission of American Society of Journalists and Authors./ Sidelight excerpts from an article "Can a Man Have a Career and a Family, Too?" by Hila Colman, April 30, 1947 in *The Saturday Evening Post.* Reprinted by permission of Hila Colman./ Illustration by Antonio Frasconi from *The Face of Edgar Allan Poe: With a Note on Poe by Charles Baudelaire.* Reprinted by permission of Antonio Frasconi./ Sidelight excerpts from an article "Chuck Jones," by Greg Ford and Richard Thompson, January-February, 1975 in *Film Comment.* Copyright © 1975 by The Film Society of Lincoln Center. Reprinted by permission of The Film Society of Lincoln Center.

Illustration of Bugs Bunny as "cover boy" of a special animation issue, January-February, 1975 of *Film Comment.* Reprinted by permission of Chuck Jones./ Illustration by Antonio Frasconi from "The Flattered Raven and the Crafty Fox" in *12 Fables of Aesop.* Reprinted by permission of The Museum of Modern Art./ Sidelight excerpts from an article "Newbery Award Acceptance," by Katherine Paterson, August, 1978 in *Horn Book.* Reprinted by permission of Katherine Paterson./ Sidelight excerpts from an article "Sounds in the Heart," by Katherine Paterson, December, 1981 in *Horn Book.* Reprinted by permission of Katherine Paterson./ Sidelight excerpts from an article "Newbery Medal Acceptance," by Katherine Paterson, August, 1981 in *Horn Book.* Reprinted by permission of Katherine Paterson./ Sidelight excerpts from an article "Interview with Antonio Frasconi," by Jane Sterrett, number 16-17, 1982 in *Print Review.* Reprinted by permission of *Print Review.*

Sidelight excerpts from an article "A Conversation with Antonio Frasconi," by Don Cyr, February, 1968 in *School Arts.* Reprinted by permission of *School Arts./* Sidelight excerpts from an article "An Interview with Antonio Frasconi," by Louise Elliott Rago, September, 1961 in *School Arts.* Reprinted by permission of *School Arts./* Sidelight excerpts from an article "The Aim of the Writer Who Writes for Children," by Katherine Paterson in *Theory into Practice,* Volume XXI, number 4, 1982. Copyright © 1982 by College of Education, The Ohio State University. Reprinted by permission of *Theory into Practice./* Sidelight excerpts from an article "Caldecott Medal Acceptance," by Chris Van Allsburg, August, 1986 in *Horn Book.* Reprinted by permission of Chris Van Allsburg.

PHOTOGRAPH CREDITS

Ian Adair: A. C. Littlejohns, A.M.P.A.; Marc Brown: Alison Shaw; Nancy White Carlstrom: Tony Blanchett; Hila Colman: Noah Barysh; Antonio Frasconi: Beth Shepherd; Joseph F. Gennaro, Jr.: Eugenia Ames; Dolores Hind: Gerald Campbell Studios; Paul B. Janeczko: Nadine Edris; Chuck Jones: copyright © Ottawa Karsh; Rika Lesser: Suzanne Kolare; Anne Sibley O'Brien: Robert O'Brien; Katherine Paterson: Jill Paton Walsh; John R. Roberson: Marian Davis; Pat Ross: Erica Ross; L.E. Snellgrove: Mary Allen; Sam Swayne: Tom Hasenyager; Zoa Swayne: Tom Hasenyager; Vera B. Williams: Susan Hirschman.

SOMETHING ABOUT THE AUTHOR

ADAIR, Ian 1942-

PERSONAL: Born December 20, 1942, in Scotland; son of John (a manager) and Isabell (a tracer; maiden name, Henderson) Adair; married Susan Ann Becraft, September 17, 1975; children: Kylie, Antony. *Education:* Educated at private academy in Scotland. *Home and office:* 20 Ashley Ter., Bideford, Devonshire, England.

CAREER: Children's entertainer, 1954—; magician and writer, 1960—. Partner in Supreme Magic Company Ltd., (theatrical suppliers), Bideford, Devonshire, England, 1965-73. Has also worked as a shoemaker, 1957, a television presenter, 1959, and a free-lance scriptwriter, 1960. Active in Round Table movement. *Member:* International Brotherhood of Magicians, Associated Wizards of the South (England; honorary vice-president), India Ring (Calcutta; honorary member), Magic Circle (London). *Awards, honors:* Invention awards from U.S. branch of International Brotherhood of Magicians, 1962, 1975, and 1976; Gold Medal from Magic Circle, 1974.

WRITINGS—Published by Supreme Magic Co. Ltd., except as indicated: *Adair's Ideas,* 1957, 3rd edition, 1970; *Entertaining Children,* 1960; *Magical Menu,* three volumes, 1960-63; *Encyclopaedia of Dove Magic,* four volumes, 1961-76; *Mental Magic,* 1962; *Dove Magic,* Part I, 1962, Part II, 1962; *Dove Magic Finale,* 1962; *Television Dove Magic,* 1963; *Illusions,* 1963; *My Card, Sir!,* 1963; *Twenty-One,* 1963; *Dove Magic Encore,* 1963; *Television Dove Steals,* 1964; *Doves in Magic,* 1964; *Doves from Silks,* 1964; *New Doves from Silks Methods,* 1964; *Dove Classics,* 1964.

Further Dove Classics, 1965; *More Modern Dove Classics,* 1965; *Stunners with Stamps,* 1965; *Television Card Manipulations,* 1966; *Classical Dove Secrets,* 1966; *Diary of a Dove Worker,* 1966; *Magic on the Wing,* 1966; *Cabaret Dove Act,* 1966; *A La Zombie Plus,* 1967; *Pot Pourri,* 1967; *Balloon-o-*

Dove, 1967; *Spotlight on Doves,* 1967; *Watch the Birdie,* 1967; *Rainbow Dove Routines,* 1967; *Heads Off!,* 1967; *Tricks and Stunts with Rubber Doves,* 1967; *Magic with Doves,* 1968; *Dove Dexterity,* 1968; *Twin Dove Production,* 1968; *Magic with Latex Budgies,* 1968; *Paddle Antics,* 1969; *Television Puppet Magic,* 1969.

Conjuring as a Craft (self-illustrated), A. S. Barnes, 1970; *Party Planning and Entertainment* (self-illustrated), A. S. Barnes, 1971; *Magic Step by Step,* Arco, 1972; *Papercrafts,* Arco, 1975; *Complete Guide to Conjuring,* A. S. Barnes, 1977; (with Heather Amery) *The Knowhow Book of Jokes and Tricks* (juvenile; illustrated by Colin King), Usborne, 1977; *The Complete Party Planner,* A. S. Barnes, 1978; *The Complete Guide to Card Conjuring* (self-illustrated), A. S. Barnes, 1979.

Swindles: The Cheating Game, A. S. Barnes, 1980; *Mini Magic Book* (juvenile), Usborne, 1981; (ghost writer) Paul Daniels, *The Paul Daniels Magic Book,* Piccolo Books, 1981; *Novel Notions,* 1981; *Do It Yourself Magic,* Pan Books, 1981; (with Ken De Courcy) *The Magical Jumbo Chinese Coin,* 1984.

Author of "Adair's Ideas" and "The Dove Column," monthly columns in *Magigram,* and of "The Fun Column," a self-illustrated weekly newspaper column. Contributor of more than three thousand articles to more than thirty-five magic journals in the United States and England.

WORK IN PROGRESS: A Chance in a Lifetime, and *Encyclopaedia of Dove Magic,* Volume V, both for Supreme Magic Co. Ltd.; *Now You See It.*

SIDELIGHTS: "I can still see myself as seven years old, waiting patiently, in front of the old television set ready for 'Whirligig,' a BBC programme. Only one section really interested me, and that was the 'magic' presented by Geoffrey Robinson.

1

Each week I would look, and wonder, and wish that I could be a magic man just like Mr. Robinson.''

One Christmas, Adair's grandmother presented him with a box of magic tricks. ''Within one day I had learnt and practiced all of the tricks in the box. I presented my first show for friends and relations the next day and became quite enthusiastic over this magic lark. The bug was there, and it was biting me. I performed shows at church gatherings, at schools and scouts and, in fact, any show that I was lucky to be asked to appear in. I loved doing magic—I loved fooling people and most of all, wanted to be the centre of attraction wherever I went. I was no good at telling jokes, dancing or reciting poems like some of my other friends at school. Conjuring and magic seemed to suit me quite well. I simply wanted to be 'on the stage.'

''I wasn't particularly bright in school, rather 'fair,' to say the least, and I admit this. English and composition were my worst subjects and I couldn't understand why there weren't lessons in 'conjuring!' I just wish my old primary teacher were alive to see my eighty published books on magic. I'm certain he would simply not believe it, considering the reports he used to give me.

''In fact, I wrote my first book when I was fourteen years of age, and sent it to a publisher who returned it. He told me he thought the ideas were good, very good, in fact, but advised that certain changes be made for publishing. He asked to make those changes on my behalf, and I accepted. One year later, my first book, *Adair's Ideas*, came out, and is now in its seventh edition.

''At eighteen years of age I was writing books as quickly as I could. I supplied not only the secrets, but the text, the illustrations and the photographs, and often the cover design for the dust jacket. I must admit that I have credit for some five

hundred dust jackets from books published throughout the world, not all dealing with my craft. Some of these books ranged from fifty to eighty pages, while others were larger, often consisting of several hundred fully illustrated pages and, on occasions, included full colour illustrations and photographs. Some thirty or more have been bound in leather, the spine and frontispiece stamped in gold, and laminated jackets.

''Of the eighty books I have written, possibly the most exciting, was *The Knowhow Book of Jokes and Tricks* in collaboration with Heather Amery. This is the most comprehensive of all books on magic for children, printed in colour, with hundreds of illustrations in a rather comic style. The design was intended for children ages seven to eleven.''

Of their collaborative effort, Adair wrote, ''I thought up a number of tricks for the planned book and so did Amery. We worked closely together. In the end we had quite a collection, and I was starting to submit the manuscript, using the planned characters who were illustrated to show each item page by page. The book was riddled with drawings of two characters, rather humorously dressed throughout. Those large and fancy words were omitted from the text, realising that although eleven-year-olds were going to read it, so, too, were seven-year-olds. The main illustrator, Colin King, took over, designing the entire book in comic strip fashion. It was easy to read, easy to learn and easy to put to practice, and this is what the publishers wanted. The hard work and effort was worth it in the end, for the book has been reprinted several times and has come out in many other countries. A smaller version, consisting of fewer pages on smaller sheets, came out one year later. Actually I bought quite a number of them to give away during my shows at children's parties.''

Some of Adair's books are published by specialized dealers and publishers intended specifically for magicians. His *Encyclopaedia of Dove Magic,* deals with the secrets of three thousand tricks using the white dove. ''Writing books can be easy if you know your subject well, and also have new and novel ideas to introduce. My main object is to ensure that the tricks I describe really work. I normally devise a trick, work on it and then present it before an audience. If it becomes popular with an audience, I will use it in one of my books.

'' 'Patter' or words spoken during the show mean so much to the magician. His patter makes his presentation good or bad. Even in books, one should also include the possible patter lines which should be delivered. A good book on magic should never simply expose, but should teach those who are fast becoming new students of the craft. Often people ask me 'Are you not exposing when you write books on your secret craft?' My answer is 'no.' I teach and hope that new blood will enter our craft as fine magicians, to keep the secrets of magic and share them with those who are genuinely interested.

''It is a great pleasure and honour to have many of my inventions and effects used by leading magicians, often at most important places, such as Buckingham Palace before Her Majesty the Queen and the royal children. I never dreamt that the tricks I was devising would be seen by Prince Charles, when he was younger, of course, and to other members of the royal family. Sitting in my little flat I never dreamt that a great many of my originations would be used on stage, screen and numerous television shows by top performers of the day.

''My magical world has taken me almost everywhere I could possibly want to go. I have entertained on stage before thousands, in people's homes for birthday parties, at holiday camp, at Buckingham Palace, and at open outdoor fetes.

IAN ADAIR

(From *The Knowhow Book of Jokes and Tricks* by Heather Amery and Ian Adair. Illustrated by Colin King.)

"When you are under contract and have to be there on time, every day, every week, entertaining people while you are ill, feeling bad, sad or otherwise, or when someone in the family has passed away suddenly, the show must go on. It's part of the scene. It's part of growing up into the show-business profession. It's magic-land!"

ALAJALOV, Constantin   1900-1987

OBITUARY NOTICE: Born November 18, 1900, in Rostov-na-Donu, Russia (now U.S.S.R.); immigrated to the United States, 1923; died after a long illness, October 24, 1987, in Amenia, N.Y. Painter, illustrator, and cartoonist. Alajalov started his artistic career with the Soviet government, painting murals and portraits of Communist leaders such as Nikolai Lenin and Leon Trotsky. In 1920 he traveled to Persia (now Iran) where he painted portraits for a provincial ruler until the fighting between British and Soviet forces in the area forced him to flee to Constantinople (now Istanbul). There he worked

as a sign painter to keep from going hungry. Eventually Alajalov began to get commissions painting pictures of film stars for motion picture theatres, and he saved up enough money to immigrate to the United States in 1923. A few years later a friend suggested that he submit his line drawings to the *New Yorker*, and he soon became a regular cover artist for that publication. His watercolor magazine covers are highly esteemed and memorable to American readers. Alajalov also contributed drawings to *Vogue*, was a sports cartoonist for the *New York Evening Post*, and was chosen to create murals for the oceanliner *S.S. America*. In addition, he illustrated books, including Cornelia Otis Skinner's *Our Hearts Were Young and Gay* and, for children, Alice Duer Miller's *Cinderella*. His artwork is displayed in many museums such as the Museum of Modern Art and the Brooklyn Museum in New York.

FOR MORE INFORMATION SEE: Illustrators of Children's Books, 1744-1945, Horn Book, 1947; *World Encyclopedia of Cartoons,* Gale, 1980; *Who's Who in American Art,* 17th edition, Bowker, 1986. Obituaries: *New York Times,* October 28, 1987.

ALLEN, Laura Jean

BRIEF ENTRY: Born in Collingswood, N.J. Artist, author and illustrator of books for young readers. A graduate of Philadelphia College of Art, Allen has contributed art work to magazines, designed fabrics, and created greeting cards. In addition, she has illustrated a number of books for early school age children, including *Little Hippo, The Secret Christmas,* and *The Witches' Secret,* all written by Frances C. Allen; *Lots and Lots of Candy,* by Carolyn Meyer; and *Sing Hey for Christmas Day!,* a collection of poems edited by Lee Bennett Hopkins. Allen has also written and illustrated her own works, such as *Ottie and the Star, Rollo and Tweedy and the Case of the Missing Cheese, Where Is Freddy?, A Fresh Look at Flowers,* and *Mr. Jolly's Sidewalk Market. Home:* 223 East 72nd St., New York, N.Y. 10021.

FOR MORE INFORMATION SEE: Contemporary Authors, Volume 110, Gale, 1984.

ANDERSON, Leone Castell 1923-

PERSONAL: Born August 12, 1923, in Los Angeles, Calif.; daughter of Carl A. (a painter) and Elsa (a homemaker; maiden name, Berggren) Castell; married J. Eric Anderson (an architect), August 17, 1946; children: Jon Scott, James Eric, Paul Lawrence. *Education:* Attended Austin Academy of Music, 1942-43. *Home:* 13115 E. Chelsea Rd., Stockton, Ill. 61085. *Office:* 127 S. Main, Stockton, Ill. 61085.

CAREER: Hope Publishing Co., Chicago, Ill., secretary, 1939-1940; Educational Screen, Chicago, Ill., secretary, 1940-41; Simpson Electric Co., Chicago, Ill., secretary, 1942-43; Russell Seeds, Chicago, Ill., advertising copywriter, 1944-46; freelance writer, 1946—; Elmhurst Public Library, Elmhurst, Ill., staff member, 1969-74; Lee's Booklover's Shop, Stockton, Ill., owner, 1979—. Speaker at schools, particularly for the Young Authors program; guest author, Illinois Young Authors Conference at Illinois State University, 1985. *Member:* Soci-

"Land-a-mighty," said Sarah. "It shrunk again!" ■ (From *The Wonderful Shrinking Shirt* by Leone Castell Anderson. Illustrated by Irene Trivas.)

ety of Children's Book Writers (Midwest representative, 1981-87), Children's Reading Round Table (Chicago), Authors Guild (New York), Off-Campus Writer's Workshop (Winnetka, Ill.).

WRITINGS: It's O.K. to Cry (illustrated by Richard Wahl), Child's World, 1979; *Glendenna's Dilemma* (play; first performed in Chicago at Performance Community of Chicago, 1979), Contemporary Drama, 1980; *Learning about Towers and Dungeons* (illustrated by Joe Van Severen), Childrens Press, 1982; *The Wonderful Shrinking Shirt* (illustrated by Irene Trivas), A. Whitman, 1983; *My Friend Next Door* (illustrated by Pat Karch), Dandelion House, 1983; *Surprise at Muddy Creek* (illustrated by Helen Endres), Dandelion House, 1984; *Christmas Handbook* (illustrated by Gwen Connelly), Child's World, 1984; *The Good-by Day* (illustrated by Eugenie), Golden Press, 1984; *Come-Uppance at Concord* (readers' theatre play), Worship Arts Clearing House (Boston, Mass.), 1986; *How Come You're So Shy?* (illustrated by J. Ellen Dolce), Golden Books, 1987.

Contributor of stories and articles to children's magazines and adult publications, including *Burlington Northern Railroad Commuter News*. Columnist for *Elmhurst Press* (Ill.) and *Stockton Herald News* (Ill.). Also contributor to "Josef's Restaurant Newsletter."

WORK IN PROGRESS: Take Up the Tomahawk (working title), a children's book about the Blackhawk War in 1832 and its effect on the Jo Davies County area and people; *My Own Grandpa* for Western; picture books for Whitman; *No Bears There*, a picture book wherein Boris takes measure to distract the bears, both in the woods and at his sister's wedding, despite being assured that there are 'no bears there.'

SIDELIGHTS: "I was the youngest in our family of four girls—until my brother came along five years later. As I tell children when I give talks in schools, it was a great position to be in. My sisters read to me, and when they tired of that, they taught me the letters and words, so I was beginning to read long before I started school. My oldest sister shared her stories written for school assignments, which inspired me to begin to write my own when I was about eight. And there was my little brother, just right to try them out on. The dull chore of doing the dishes together went more quickly, and I had an appreciative and uncritical audience.

"When I graduated from high school in 1939, it was the tag end of the Depression. To help out the family finances, as had my three sisters before me, I went to work. By the time I married in 1946, I'd worked in such diverse fields as hymn book publishing, educational movie review, magazine publishing, electrical meter manufacturing (this was during the war), and in advertising, where I was a copywriter.

"After marriage and babies, I stayed at home and free-lanced until the feminist movement, and the fact that my sons were capable of being on their own inspired my return to the workplace. The young people's department of the library was my choice, synchronous with my decision to concentrate on writing for children. And there I stayed for five years, interacting with the children, absorbing their ideas, learning what they liked to read, sharing thoughts and feelings. And writing.

"After moving to the country twelve years ago, to a one-hundred-year-old school house renovated by my architect husband, I found I needed the stimulation of people contact. So for the past eight years I've run my own paperback bookstore, open from twelve noon to four p.m. The morning hours are given to my writing, in an office behind the store. It's effective; eight books have resulted.

LEONE CASTELL ANDERSON

"Although music was once a primary interest—I was a student of piano at the Austin Academy of Music, and I studied voice with a private teacher—it remains an avocation which I pursue when time allows. But I'd like to think that a kind of rhythm, a sense of melodic line, comes through in my writing, which I attribute to my feel for music.

"My affinity for the theater—I've performed frequently in community theaters—plays a part in my writing, too. It's helped me to visualize and 'hear' the scenes of my books, almost as if on a stage. Then I try to convey this through dialogue and narrative.

"I don't think I've ever really stopped 'going to school' because I'm always learning—through omnivorous reading and through more structured studies as well as being open to all the experiences that life offers. And it's my hope that I distill these 'life experiences' into the books I write, whether humorous or serious, fiction or nonfiction. With the hope, too, that my books will strike a responsive chord in my readers, as did the books I read in my childhood."

HOBBIES AND OTHER INTERESTS: Gardening, crewel embroidery, reading.

My castle has a lot of doors;
Each one is numbered too.
No matter which you open first,
Two pages wait on you.

        —L.J. Bridgman

BEDOUKIAN, Kerop 1907-1981

PERSONAL: Born October 15, 1907, in Sivas, Turkey; died July 24, 1981; came to Canada, 1926; naturalized Canadian citizen, 1931; son of Haroutune (a grocer) and Serpoughi (der Mesrobian) Bedoukian; married Marjorie Hayey Clark (a social worker), June 21, 1935; children: Marian Bedoukian Sinn, Harold, Peter. *Politics:* None. *Religion:* Armenian Orthodox. *Residence:* Montreal, Quebec, Canada.

CAREER: Operated rug cleaning plant in Vancouver, British Columbia; dealer in Oriental rugs in Montreal, Quebec, 1935-81. President of Armenian General Benevolent Union, 1956-74. *Member:* Canadian Authors Association (vice-president), Armenian Congress (vice-president, 1960-64). *Awards, honors:* Centennial Medal from Government of Canada, 1967; Queen's Jubilee Medal, 1977; *Some of Us Survived: The Story of an Armenian Boy* was selected one of *School Library Journal*'s Best Books for Spring, 1979, named to the 1980 Fifty Books of the Year list by the American Institute of Graphic Arts, and selected one of New York Public Library's Books for the Teen Age, 1982.

WRITINGS: The Urchin: An Armenian's Escape, J. Murray, 1978, published as *Some of Us Survived: The Story of an Armenian Boy*, Farrar, Strauss, 1979.

(From *Some of Us Survived: The Story of an Armenian Boy* by Kerop Bedoukian.)

WORK IN PROGRESS: Biographies of remaining survivors of Turkish massacres, 1915-18; and a sequel to *The Urchin*, which was finished before Bedoukian's death, but has not been published.

SIDELIGHTS: ''My schooling had started when the war began in 1915 but it ended abruptly because of the general deportation and systematic killings of the Armenian population all over Turkey. From 1915 until my arrival in Canada in 1926, the story is of day-to-day survival; just to be able to exist was quite an achievement. It was only after my arrival in Canada that I could give some thought to my education, well-being, and the future.

''The first two years in Canada were spent on a farm in Ontario, a period of adjustment and building up my health. In 1931, I became a Canadian citizen and also got involved in the needs of the Armenian community. In 1952, upon request of the Canadian Council of Churches and with the help of the World Council of Churches, I sponsored and brought to Canada 750 Armenian refugees from Greece, remnants of the victims of Turkish atrocities.

''The immigrant assistance endeavor never stopped and the number of assisted immigrants grew to over two thousand in the next twenty years. I give most of my time to community service.''

BRADY, Esther Wood 1905-1987
(Esther Wood)

OBITUARY NOTICE—See sketch in *SATA* Volume 31: Born August 24, 1905, in Akron, N.Y.; died of cancer, June 30, 1987, in Bethesda, Md. Editor and author. From 1928 to 1932 Brady worked as an editor for the Women's Foreign Mission Society. Years later, after marrying and raising two children, she did volunteer tutoring in public schools, taking a particular interest in helping children with reading disabilities. Brady wrote several historical books for children, including *Pedro's Coconut Skates, Pepper Moon, The House in the Hoo, Toliver's Secret,* and *The Toad on Capitol Hill,* some of which were published under her maiden name, Esther Wood. An avid traveler, Brady gleaned some of the material for her writing from experiences she had while in Europe and the Orient.

FOR MORE INFORMATION SEE: Contemporary Authors, Volumes 93-96, Gale, 1980. Obituaries: *Washington Post,* July 2, 1987.

BRENNAN, Gale Patrick 1927-

BRIEF ENTRY: Born March 12, 1927, in Manitowoc, Wis. Brennan received his postgraduate degree in journalism from Marquette University in 1951. Among the occupations he has held since then are publications director of the Miller Brewing Co., president of Communications, Inc., and author and editor at Reiman Publications, Inc. In 1958 he founded Gale Brennan & Associates, a writing, advertising, and public relations firm, of which he is currently president. Brennan has written a number of books for children, including *Elihu the Elephant, Dugan the Duck, Emil the Eagle,* and *Freddie the Frog,* during the early to middle 1970s. Later he collaborated with author Tom LaFleur on more animal stories, all published by Brennan Books, including *Bingo the Bear, Isadore the Dinosaur, Woolly the Wolf, Tuffy the Tiger,* and *Henry the Hound.* In addition, Brennan has produced guides on vegetable gardening, family first aid, and energy conservation, as well as two books on the 1980 Olympics and, in 1987, a work entitled *About Alcohol and Alcoholics*. In his spare time, he enjoys golf, curling, politics, antique furniture. *Home and office:* 8419 Stickney Ave., Wauwatosa, Wis. 53226.

BRIGHTFIELD, Richard 1927- (Rick Brightfield)

BRIEF ENTRY: Born September 28, 1927, in Baltimore, Md. Graphic designer and artist, author. Brightfield worked as a graphic designer of university publications for Columbia University from 1964 to 1976, after which time he did free-lance graphic design until 1982. With his wife, Glory, he wrote a number of books under the name Rick Brightfield, including *Amazing Mazes, Outer Space Mazes, More Amazing Mazes,* and *Amazing Circle Mazes,* all published by Harper in the early to middle 1970s. "Finding your way through a Brightfield maze is almost a new kind of cerebral experience," remarked the *New York Times Book Review,* who commended the husband-and-wife team for creating the "best of all unorthodox maze books." The Brightfields also collaborated with Mary Orser on several titles, such as *Instant Astrology, Predicting with Astrology,* and *What's My Sign?*. Brightfield later produced a number of science fiction and fantasy books for young readers, including *Phantom Submarine, The Dragon's Den, The Secret Treasure of Tibet, The Castle of Doom, Island of Fear, The Deadly Shadow,* and *The Battle of the Dragons*. *Home:* 366 Libertyville Rd., New Paltz, N.Y. 12561.

FOR MORE INFORMATION SEE: Contemporary Authors, Volume 118, Gale, 1986.

BROOKS, Bruce

BRIEF ENTRY: Brooks, who graduated from the University of North Carolina, has worked as a letterpress printer, a newspaper and magazine reporter, and a teacher. His highly-acclaimed first novel for young adults, *The Moves Make the Man* (Harper, 1984), tells the story of Jerome Foxworthy, a black junior high-school student in a predominantly white school who excels in both academics and basketball. Jerome befriends Bix, a white athlete whose ability equals his own, and the two boys, through their experiences gain greater self-insight. According to Christine McDonnell of *Horn Book,* the qualities which distinguish Brooks' writing include a "confident, intense first-person voice . . . insightful probing into characters' complicated lives . . . [and] imaginative metaphors, often funny, always fresh." In 1984 the *New York Times* named this work a Notable Book of the Year and *School Library Journal* included it on its Best Books list. The following year it was selected as a Newbery Honor Book and received the *Boston Globe-Horn Book* Award. Brooks has also written *Midnight Hour Encores* (Harper, 1986), in which the protagonist seeks out her mother whom she has not seen since birth. *Residence:* Washington, D.C.

FOR MORE INFORMATION SEE: Horn Book, March/April, 1987.

The children in Holland take pleasure
    in making
What the children in England take
    pleasure in breaking.

                   —Nursery rhyme

BROWN, Drollene P. 1939-

PERSONAL: Born September 24, 1939, in South Charleston, W.Va.; daughter of Wilson William (a fireman and carpenter) and Evelyn (a church treasurer; maiden name, McClure) Plattner; married Charles R. Tittle, August 29, 1961 (divorced, May 21, 1975); married Albert J. Brown, Jr. (an airlines consultant), May 28, 1982; children: (first marriage) Mark Alan, Shauna Kay. *Education:* Ouachita Baptist University, B.A., 1961; University of Texas at Austin, M.A., 1963, graduate study, 1963-65. *Residence:* Boca Raton, Fla.

CAREER: Indiana University, Bloomington, Ill., research assistant and associate, 1965-70; College of Boca Raton, Boca Raton, Fla., assistant professor of sociology, 1973-78; American Savings and Loan Association, Boca Raton, branch manager, 1979-81; A. J. Brown, Inc. (consulting firm), Boca Raton, vice-president, 1981—. Director of Professional Arts Program, Wilmington College Extension at College of Boca Raton, 1978; chairperson of International Playwriting Competition at Boca Raton's Caldwell Playhouse, 1981-84. *Awards, honors:* Fellow of National Endowment for the Humanities, 1977; *Sybil Rides for Independence* was chosen one of Child Study Association of America's Children's Books of the Year, 1985.

WRITINGS: Sybil Rides for Independence (juvenile; illustrated by Margot Apple), A. Whitman, 1985; *Belva Lockwood Wins Her Case* (juvenile biography; illustrated by James Watling), A. Whitman, 1987. Columnist for *Boca Raton News* and *News of Delray,* both 1984-86. Contributor of articles and reviews

DROLLENE P. BROWN

"You're late again, Sybil," nine-year-old Archie declared. "Mother wants you to go straight into the house." ■ (From *Sybil Rides for Independence* by Drollene P. Brown. Illustrated by Margot Apple.)

to magazines and newspapers, including *Spanish River Papers* and *Cobblestone*.

WORK IN PROGRESS: A screenplay about a woman who was a jungle adventurer in the early twentieth century.

SIDELIGHTS: "When I was growing up, I used to write for the fun of it. From the age of seven, I would join my friends in organizing clubs in the neighborhood, then proceed to put a damper on their purely social intentions by insisting upon writing a constitution or—at the very least—a statement of purpose.

"I wasn't at all popular with my classmates in fifth and sixth grade when I submitted unassigned essays for my teachers' perusal. Observations would rumble around in my brain for a spell, then seemingly force themselves out through my fingers as I wrote them down. I don't remember showing these essays to my parents. I suppose I thought they'd praise me without bringing any critical powers to bear. I must have driven my already overworked teachers 'nuts' with my extra papers.

"Later I was able to channel my interest in writing to the 'Simmerings,' the high school newspaper. And even though I was editor-in-chief of that paper in my senior year, it didn't occur to me that I would ever be a writer or have anything to do with the writing field. I wanted to change lives—indeed, change the world—and I thought I knew the best way to do it. I would become a Christian missionary.

"In the middle of my sophomore year in college, I switched from a major in religion to one in sociology. I still wanted to change lives, but I thought a knowledge of sociology would help me do that. After college, I studied sociology for four more years in graduate school. My writing changed during this period, for professional training taught me to do careful research, to back up all information, and to be able to 'prove' everything I said. (In many cases, such writing can be very dull. Mine, I fear, was no exception.)

"Somewhere along the way, I came to believe that life as a private citizen would give me opportunities to make an impact on the world. I had married a fellow sociologist between college and graduate school. When we left the University of Texas for my husband's full-time teaching job at Indiana University, I got a part-time job in sociological research. My desire to change the world was channeled into volunteer work in the new Headstart program in Bloomington, Indiana. That work came to an end when my son was born in 1969. After we had moved to Florida and a baby girl joined our family, my volunteer work was with teenagers in trouble with drugs.

"Two years later I began to teach sociology at a local college. Preparing courses and developing ways to open the minds of my students was exciting. Many of my students came to my home and met my family. And partly because of my influence, many of them changed the direction of their lives. This is the kind of impact I had wanted to make when I was a young girl dreaming of becoming a missionary.

"But since the day I left my parents' home, outside elements haven't stayed the same for me for long periods. Soon I was no longer married and no longer teaching. I managed a bookstore for awhile, giving me time to read, to think, and to begin to write again without the proofs and rhetoric necessary for sociological writing. I wrote poems, short stories, and an adult novel.

"Some poems appeared in anthologies; the short stories made their rounds and then settled into a file drawer; the novel had a brief fling with an agent and a few publishers before coming to rest on a shelf in my closet.

"Deciding that I needed a total career change, I went into banking. But my old self showed through. I thought too much. I taught too much. I wrote too much. Customers told me that my explanation of financial matters and bank policies helped them understand such business more clearly than they ever had before. I wrote memos to my supervisors about such matters as the competition in the area or the feasibility of being open on Saturdays. I was trying to make changes in a business that doesn't welcome change. Within two years, I was promoted rapidly, then fired.

"I remarried, and at age forty-two began a new career. My husband and I started a consulting firm in an office at home. Although I had to learn about legalities that were new to me, in addition to checking out library books that would teach me accounting skills, I could now squeeze in time to write in earnest. At my husband's suggestion, I enrolled in a correspondence course on writing for children. Before the course was completed, I sold an article to *Cobblestone*. Soon I sold my first book. I also landed a job as a newspaper columnist. I found myself in the middle of two new careers, one as office manager and the other as writer.

"Much of my thrill in writing newspaper columns came when readers reported that I had told them something they hadn't known. There's contentment in seeing my words set down just so on a printed page. I've worried them and nudged them until I can do no more. I can feel pride then, too, but to know those words made a difference to someone—that's joy.

"I think it's important to show strong female role models, not only for the benefit of girls, but also for boys. Women won't have full equality until men, as well as women, expect and accept nothing else. *Sybil Rides for Independence* retells the story of a sixteen-year-old girl who rode through the night on April 26, 1777, to awaken minutemen to fight the British in the Battle of Ridgefield. *Belva Lockwood Wins Her Case* is a biography of the woman lawyer who ran for president of the United States in 1884 and 1888. A contemporary of Susan B. Anthony and Elizabeth Cady Stanton, Lockwood was a stalwart feminist and indefatigable worker for world peace.

"But in my basic outlook on life, I haven't changed. Out of my writing comes the opportunity to visit schools. When children ask me how to go about writing books and getting them published, I think my answers may help them. And by telling them about the historic characters who appear in my books, I try to give my listeners ideas for their own lives."

BROWN, Marc (Tolon)　1946-

PERSONAL: Born November 25, 1946, in Erie, Pa.; son of LeRoy Edward and Renita (Toulon) Brown; married Stephanie Marini (a ballet dancer and college teacher), September 1, 1968 (marriage ended, 1977); married Laurene Krasny (a psychologist and writer), September 11, 1983; children: (first marriage) Tolon Adam, Tucker Eliot; (second marriage) Eliza Morgan. *Education:* Cleveland Institute of Art, B.F.A., 1969. *Home and studio:* 562 Main St., Hingham, Mass. 02043; South Rd., Gay Head, Martha's Vineyard, Mass. 02535.

CAREER: WICU-TV (NBC affiliate), Erie, Pa., television art director, 1968-69; Garland Junior College, Boston, Mass., assistant professor, 1969-76; author and illustrator of children's books, 1976—. *Exhibitions:* Work exhibited widely in the U.S. and abroad, including numerous one-man shows. *Member:* Authors Guild.

AWARDS, HONORS: What Makes the Sun Shine? was selected one of Child Study Association of America's Children's Books of the Year, 1971, *One Two Three: An Animal Counting Book,* 1976, and *What's So Funny, Ketu?,* *Hand Rhymes,* and *The Banza,* 1986; *Arthur's Nose* was selected as a Children's Choice by the Children's Book Council and the International Reading Association, 1976, *Arthur's Eyes,* 1980, *Arthur's Valentine,* 1981, *The True Francine, Arthur's Halloween* and *Arthur Goes to Camp,* all 1982, and *Arthur's April Fool,* 1983; *There Goes Feathertop!* was selected for the American Institute of Graphic Arts Book Show, 1980; *Boston Globe-Horn Book* Honor Award for Illustration, 1980, for *Why the Tides Ebb and Flow; The True Francine* was selected a Notable Children's Trade Book in the Field of Social Studies by the joint committee of the National Council for Social Studies and the Children's Book Council, 1982, and *Oh Kojo! How Could You!,* 1985; *Swamp Monsters* was chosen one of Library of Congress' Books of the Year, 1985; *Hand Rhymes* was chosen one of *Booklist*'s Children's Editors' Choices, and one of New York Public Library's Children's Books, both 1985.

WRITINGS—Self-illustrated; all published by Atlantic-Little, Brown, except as noted: *One Two Three: An Animal Counting Book,* 1976; *Marc Brown's Full House,* Addison-Wesley, 1977; *Lenny and Lola,* Dutton, 1978; *Moose and Goose,* Dutton, 1978; *The Cloud over Clarence,* Dutton, 1979.

Pickle Things, Parents Magazine Press, 1980; *Finger Rhymes,* Dutton, 1980; *Witches Four,* Parents Magazine Press, 1980;

MARC BROWN

Your First Garden Book, 1981; *The True Francine,* 1981; *Wings on Things,* Random House, 1982; *Count to Ten,* Golden Press, 1982; *Marc Brown's Boat Book,* Golden Press, 1982; (with Stephen Krensky) *Dinosaurs, Beware! A Safety Guide* (ALA Notable Book), 1982; *The Silly Tail Book,* Parents Magazine Press, 1983; *Spooky Riddles,* Random House, 1983; (with S. Krensky) *Perfect Pigs: An Introduction to Manners,* 1983; *What Do You Call a Dumb Bunny? And Other Rabbit Riddles, Games, Jokes, and Cartoons,* 1983; *There's No Place Like Home,* Parents Magazine Press, 1984; (with wife, Laurene Krasny Brown) *The Bionic Bunny Show* (Reading Rainbow selection), 1984.

Hand Rhymes (Junior Literary Guild selection), Dutton, 1985; (with L. K. Brown) *Dinosaurs Divorce: A Guide for Changing Families,* 1986; (with L. K. Brown) *Visiting the Art Museum,* Dutton, 1986; *D. W. Flips!,* 1987; *Play Rhymes,* Dutton, 1987.

"Arthur Adventure" series; all self-illustrated; all published by Atlantic-Little, Brown: *Arthur's Nose,* 1976; *Arthur's Eyes* (Reading Rainbow selection), 1979, large print edition, 1986; *Arthur's Valentine,* 1980; *Arthur Goes to Camp,* 1982; *Arthur's Halloween,* 1982; *Arthur's April Fool,* 1983; *Arthur's Thanksgiving,* 1983; *Arthur's Christmas,* 1984; *Arthur's Tooth: An Arthur Adventure,* 1985; *Arthur's Teacher Trouble,* 1986; *Arthur's Baby,* 1987; *Arthur's Birthday Wish,* 1988.

Illustrator: Isaac Asimov, *What Makes the Sun Shine?,* Little, Brown, 1970; Norma Farber, *I Found Them in the Yellow Pages,* Little, Brown, 1972; Peter Dickinson, *The Iron Lion,* Allen & Unwin, 1972; Ted Clymer, *The Four Corners of the Sky: Poems, Chants and Oratory,* Little, Brown, 1975; (with Tom Cooke) Doug Morse, *Little Green Thumb's Window Garden,* Storyfold, 1975; Laurence White, *Science Games/Puzzles/Tricks/Toys* (4 books), Addison-Wesley, 1975, new edition, *Science Games and Puzzles,* Lippincott, 1979, and *Science Toys and Tricks,* Lippincott, 1980; Patty Wolcott, *Super Sam and the Salad Garden,* Addison-Wesley, 1975; Louise Moeri, *How the Rabbit Stole the Moon,* Houghton, 1977; Kathleen Daly, *My Doctor Bag Book,* Golden Press, 1977; Janwillem Van de Wetering, *Little Owl: An Eight-fold Buddhist Admonition,* Houghton, 1978; Joan Chase Bowden, *Why the Tides Ebb and Flow* (ALA Notable Book; *Horn Book* honor list), Houghton, 1979; N. Farber, *There Goes Feathertop!,* Dutton, 1979.

Judy Delton, *Rabbit's New Rug,* Parents Magazine Press, 1980; Diane Wolkstein, *The Banza: A Haitian Story,* Dial, 1981; Verna Aardema, adapter, *What's So Funny, Ketu?,* Dial, 1982; Mary Blount Christian, *Swamp Monsters,* Dial, 1983; Deborah Hautzig, *Little Witch's Big Night,* Random House, 1984; V. Aardema, *Oh, Kojo! How Could You!* (ALA Notable Book), Dial, 1984; M. B. Christian, *Go West, Swamp Monsters,* Dial, 1985; Jack Prelutsky, selector, *Read-Aloud Rhymes for the Very Young* (*Horn Book* honor list), Knopf, 1986; John T. McQueen, *A World Full of Monsters,* Crowell, 1986.

ADAPTATIONS—All produced by Random House, except as noted: "The True Francine" (read-along cassette), 1982; "Arthur's Valentine" (read-along cassette; filmstrip with cassette; videocassette), 1983; "Arthur's Halloween" (read-along cassette; filmstrip with cassette; videocassette), 1983; "Arthur's April Fool" (read-along cassette; filmstrip with cassette; videocassette), 1983; "Arthur's Thanksgiving" (read-along cassette; filmstrip with cassette; videocassette), 1983; "Arthur Goes to Camp" (read-along cassette; filmstrip with cassette), 1983; "Dinosaurs, Beware!" (filmstrip with cassette; with teacher's guide), 1984; "Arthur's Christmas" (read-along cassette; filmstrip with cassette; videocassette), 1985; "Arthur's

Finally, Arthur had a loose tooth. ■ (Jacket illustration by Marc Brown from *Arthur's Tooth* by Marc Brown.)

Tooth'' (read-along cassette; filmstrip with cassette), 1986; ''Oh Kojo! How Could You!'' (filmstrip with cassette), 1986.

WORK IN PROGRESS: A series featuring D. W., Arthur's [of *Arthur's Nose*] little sister—*D. W. Flips, D. W. All Wet; Party Rhymes;* with wife, *Visiting the Aquarium,* based on a trip to the Monterey Aquarium; *Dinosaur Travel: A Guide for Families on the Go.*

SIDELIGHTS: As a child, Brown spent a lot of time with his grandmother and uncle, who provided him with great quantities of paper, pens, and pencils. ''I spent as much time living in a fantasy world as in the so-called real one, and preferred the company of adults to that of other children. How lucky I was to have my grandmother as a support system. Her trust in my instincts made it possible for me to push myself.

''There weren't many museums in Erie, Pennsylvania, but a couple of family trips took us to the Chicago Art Institute. Peak experiences, particularly if you like the Impressionists view that a museum is heaven on earth. I remember the first time I saw Seurat's 'Afternoon on the Grande Jatte.' I was amazed at his craftsmanship and at his range of expression. After that Chicago trip, I began, with the encouragement of Nancy Bryan, my high school art teacher, to work in watercolor. She recognized that I was serious about developing my talent and worked closely with me.

''Through art books I discovered the work of Marc Chagall, and was so impressed, I changed my name from Mark to Marc. A light went on with Sendak's *Where the Wild Things Are.* I

had no idea the potential the field of children's books held. Sendak may well have determined the course of my life. Recently I was looking through my high school yearbook and noticed that under my picture, in the blank after the word 'ambition,' I wrote illustrator—I'm sure a 'post-Sendak' ambition.

''It was pretty clear that my parents were not going to send me to art school. They would have preferred more 'respectable' ambitions. If I wanted to get there, I'd have to do it on my own. I did, for the most part, with help from my grandmother.

''I majored in painting at the Cleveland Institute of Art. In those days illustration was considered a poor stepchild to Art with a capital 'A.' The temptation to experiment in various mediums was overpowering—I studied printmaking, photography, textile and graphic design in addition to painting. My work consisted of large figurative paintings in acrylic and mixed media. When I let my interest in children's book illustration known, I got the definite message that the field was absolutely the lowest rung on the artistic ladder. I was insecure enough to care what my peers thought of me. Everyone assumed I would win the Institute's drawing award. When I submitted my portfolio, I included my children's illustrations and was told that their presence cost me the award I, otherwise, would have won. I was angry and disappointed at the faculty's narrow-mindedness in choosing to ignore the scope of my work.

''After graduation I received a scholarship to attend Syracuse University. I went to Boston for the summer to earn some

Merry little snowflakes
Falling through the air.

■ (From *Hand Rhymes* by Marc Brown. Illustrated by the author.)

money before starting school in the fall. I was getting tired of the starving artist scene. I had held several odd jobs from delivery truck driver (I kept getting lost) to short-order cook. The lingo in the latter was unique. 'Catch a fish, hit it with rye, put a pair of shoes on it,' meant a tuna fish sandwich on rye bread to go. 'Throw a bull in the ring, crown it and let it bite,' meant hamburger with onion, very rare.

"'Don't call us, we'll call you,' was the greeting I received at Houghton Mifflin. Lo and behold, they called a few days later and offered me about five thousand dollars worth of free-lance work. I then learned about other publishers who hired illustrators for picture books. So I decided to settle in, apply for teaching jobs, and point myself toward a career in illustration. This was 1969 when the only way you could get a

teaching job in Boston was if someone died. And that is ex-actly what happened to me. I was hired to fill in for the me-chanical drawing teacher at a junior college (I'd never studied mechanical drawing!). Before the term began, he died, and the job landed in my lap.

"In terms of illustration, I worked on reading primers, the basic bread-and-butter stuff most illustrators start out with. The work was steady, but the process stultifying. Textbook publishers in the late sixties and early seventies were obsessed with the avoidance of racial and sexual stereotyping. Illustra-tors were given immutable directions for each picture. A three-inch-square airport scene would go like this: The airplane has just landed, the stairway is pushed up to the door and standing ready to deplane are three stewardesses, one black, one Asian-

"You made your bed again!" screeched Mother Witch. "Sorry Mother. I forgot," said little Witch. ■ (From *Little Witch's Big Night* by Deborah Hautzig. Illustrated by Marc Brown.)

American and one Spanish-American. The publishers would tell you how old each stewardess was supposed to be. It was inhibiting and demeaning. I wanted out.

"My first non-textbook illustration was *What Makes the Sun Shine?* by Isaac Asimov. I was a little nervous because Asimov was so famous, but I had no contact with him while I was doing the illustrations. After the book was done he wrote saying that at first he wasn't sure about the art work, until he looked through the eyes of a six-year-old child, then enjoyed it very much. I think that was a compliment.

"Norma Farber's *I Found Them in the Yellow Pages* was my next job. For an illustrator just starting out, it was a rare privilege to have access to someone like Norma. She lived in a high-rise overlooking Harvard. Her home was filled with all sorts of books, art work—interesting, interesting things. She would sit me down in one of her big old chairs and bring out stacks of manuscripts. She was incredibly prolific. She would hand me papers, saying things like, 'Oh, here's one, if you read Chinese.'

"I was also blessed with Emilie McLeod of Atlantic Monthly Press, a very talented editor. It was she who encouraged me to write, as well as illustrate, children's books and contracted *Arthur's Nose*. I think of my work as telling stories in words and pictures. When I get an idea for a book, the language and images happen simultaneously. First I must make the story work—the hardest aspect of doing a book. The text goes through many revisions. The two most troublesome parts are staying on a straight line and coming to a satisfying conclusion. If I don't watch it, I can digress and never find my way back. Stories have a way of spawning other stories, which in its way is wonderful, but I do like to have a sense of closure.

"My ideas have to germinate a long time before they come together in a book. I depend on an idea drawer full of scraps of stories, bits of dialogue, quick drawings, titles, concepts. At any one time there are probably one hundred ideas in the drawer, not all of them good. Sometimes just one small part of a drawing, one line of a vignette is usable. Often I scramble elements of a number of ideas and come up with something totally unexpected. A lot of my stories derive from things that have happened to me. *Arthur's Baby,* for example, sprang from our new baby.

"The art work is generally easier for me than the writing. Drawings need far fewer revisions than stories. Images tend to come to me in their entirety; stories piecemeal. My favorite medium is pencil with watercolor. I recently switched to Fabriano, the most exquisite Italian watercolor paper. The surface is so sensitive and responsive to the pressure of the pencil

(From the filmstrip "Arthur's Halloween." Produced by Random House/Miller-Brody Productions, 1983.)

(From *One Two Three: An Animal Counting Book* by Marc Brown. Illustrated by the author.)

that I can get an extraordinary variety of line quality. It is a huge change from Strathmore, another high-quality paper, but comparatively hard and thin. Fabriano, which is one hundred percent cotton is much softer and has more body. You pretty much lay your line on top of Strathmore; Fabriano, on the other hand, yields more layers to the pencil. Windsor Newton are my favorite watercolors. I mix them in American antique boxes on a white metal tray I got from a local butcher.

''*Arthur's Nose* was a breakthrough. I concentrated on the characters' expressions and finally succeeded in stripping away the stylish art school veneer. For the first time I thought more deeply about the kids who would read the book by wedding my concerns to my readers' interests. I became more consciously narrative in my drawings. I wanted to make sure my drawings succeeded in doing what language could not do.

''In terms of my artistic development another important book was *Why the Tides Ebb and Flow* by Joan Chase Bowden. Walter Lorraine, who edited the title, was the first to give me a chance to draw people. Before that, I did animals, animals and more animals. I began to rely on them years ago as a way of getting around the strictures of textbook illustration. Kids love animals, so it livened up those dull books; and you don't have to worry about racial and sexual stereotyping. The kids could relate to all the animals without having to think about what color they happened to be. Animals helped to save my

sanity while I illustrated textbooks, but unfortunately I was typecast.''

To illustrate Diane Wolkstein's *The Banza: A Haitian Story*, Brown traveled to Haiti. ''I took a lot of photographs and made a lot of sketches. I was overwhelmed by the texture of the place—beautiful patterns on the stones, walls, gates, fabrics, and the Victorian architecture was splendid everywhere. I was invited to stay with local artists on a small mountaintop farm.

''I used an overlay process to do the illustrations. I made a black draftboard plate and drew on it with a very fine-pointed permanent marker. With three-ply drafting paper I did pencil, watercolor and marker overlays. So I made blue, red and yellow plates as well. I would have preferred the art in black and white, but the publisher was committed to four colors. The plates are photographed separately and then the colors are brought together mechanically in production.

''I am continually amazed that publishers try to keep authors and illustrators apart. I have had wonderful experiences when I have had access to authors. Diane Wolkstein was most enthusiastic about my trip to Haiti and furnished me with many introductions. Verna Aardema was also extremely forthcoming and helpful. Norma Farber was a major influence.

''I met my wife, Laurene, on a book project. She was a researcher at Harvard exploring the importance of illustrations on children's imaging processes while reading picture books.

(From *I Found Them in the Yellow Pages* by Norma Farber. Illustrated by Marc Brown.)

Interestingly enough, no one had ever attempted to quantify the importance of illustrations in picture books. I was fascinated and worked with them for a while, giving talks and administering tests in schools. I would read a story to one group of kids and show them illustrations. As we finished different parts of the story, I would ask them to draw pictures. With the next group of kids I just read the story and asked them to draw pictures without showing them illustrations. The experiment revealed that the kids who had been shown illustrations drew more sophisticated pictures by tackling more difficult perspectives, using more intricate borders and incorporating more language into their drawings.

"When Laurie and I do a book together we work in our separate studios—she on the text, I on the pictures. But we consult often, contributing ideas to every aspect of the book. Laurie is an expert nonfiction writer, researcher and organizer. I generally cede all those responsibilities to her, although I suggest particular lines of dialogue or individual episodes. Of course changes in the text usually require changes in the illustrations, so it's important for us to be in touch every step of the way.

"A book on which Laurie was absolutely indispensable was *Dinosaurs Divorce: A Guide for Changing Families*. When I went through a divorce about ten years ago, I went to the library hoping to find books to help my two young sons through the experience. I found little information, and what there was was very sexist, depicting children living with the mother and the father living in a depressing residential hotel. Our experience was different: my sons lived with me. I started keeping a file for a book I had in mind to write one day. This file became so enormous, I couldn't face it any longer. Years later, Laurie organized it.

"Kids of picture-book age generally receive the least information when parents divorce. And that's a serious problem. Not only do they have a lot of questions, but they're in a lot of pain as well. I wanted to write a book that would give practical information and explain the many ways there are of solving a problem. Every family divorces differently. Some ways, of course, are better than others, but there's no one right way.

"It may sound like it, but I don't work *all* the time! I love to read books by my favorite authors: F. Scott Fitzgerald, John Cheever, Robert Louis Stevenson, Thomas Wolfe, Nathaniel Hawthorne, Charles Dickens, Eugene Field, Edward Lear and Hans Christian Andersen. Among my favorite artists are Brueghel, Dürer, Edward Hicks, Mark Rothko, Arthur Rackham, and the early works of Norman Rockwell. I also love Persian miniatures and collect early American and Haitian folk art.

"My hobby is restoring antique houses. I just finished the fifth, and I hope, last one. The house we live in now was originally built in 1799, but most of the L's emanating from the center were added in 1929. When the stock market crashed, the owners lost everything and the house was empty for years. For a while it was a girl's school. By the time we got it it was in awful shape. There is something about old houses—when they need help, they seem to cry out to me. We also have a house on Martha's Vineyard, circa 1835. We stripped it down to the bone and lived with it that way until we could afford to put everything back. This small farm house had never had heating. I shudder to think how cold it must have been.

"Laurie and I also like to garden. In Hingham our garden is mostly ornamental flowers, shrubs and fruit trees. On Martha's Vineyard, where we spend the summer, we grow our vege-

tables, herbs and berries. Incidentally, my red raspberry pie may well be the best in the world."

—*Based on an interview by Marguerite Feitlowitz*

Four Corners of the Sky: Poems, Chants, and Oratory was a Caldecott Award consideration, 1975.

BUMSTEAD, Kathleen (Mary)   1918-1987 (Ellen Morgan)

PERSONAL: Born September 20, 1918, in Knutsford, England; died March 29, 1987 of liver cancer; daughter of Edward (a salesman) and Margaret Ellen (a teacher; maiden name, Morgan) Lowe; married Roy Bumstead (a civil servant), December 21, 1942 (died, 1952); children: Christopher, David, Nathaniel. *Education:* Lady Margaret Hall, Oxford, B.A. (with honors), 1941; Cambridge Training College for Women, Certificate of Education, 1943. *Religion:* Church of England. *Home:* Dalton Lodge, Dallowgill, Ripon, North Yorkshire HG4 3QY, England.

CAREER: Head teacher at village schools in West-on-Trent, Derbyshire, England, and Kirkby Malzeard, North Yorkshire, England, 1953-64; College of Ripon, Ripon, North Yorkshire, England, senior lecturer in history, 1964-77; York St. John, Ripon, senior lecturer in history, 1964-77; writer, 1977-87. Chairman of local parish council; member of local Women's Institute and Mechanics' Institute. *Member:* Yorkshire Archaeological Society, Wensleydale History Society, Ramblers' Association, Highside Tennis Club (president).

WRITINGS: (Under pseudonym Ellen Morgan) *The New Anne Moby* (juvenile), Heinemann, 1985; *Another Winter's Tale* (juvenile), Heinemann, 1987. Contributor to periodicals, including *Yorkshire Archaeological Society Journal* and *Dalesman*.

KATHLEEN BUMSTEAD

WORK IN PROGRESS: Research on the local history of Dallowgill; *Summer Holiday.*

SIDELIGHTS: ''I have been writing ever since I was a child, but I did not try for publication. During the Second World War my husband fought in Burma, and I worked. When he came home I had a family of young children. I had to go back to teaching to raise my sons when my husband was killed in a climbing accident. I wrote two children's books and a novel, but had little time to try methodically for their publication. It was only when I retired to an isolated house in the Dales that I began to take my writing seriously. My life has been spent largely with children and young people, so it has seemed natural to write about and for them.''

The New Anne Moby is set in the 1890s. It is the story of a ten-year-old girl, who is abandoned by her parents in the city. She finds a home with an elderly rural woman, who may be her grandmother, and slowly begins a new way of life.

CAMPLING, Elizabeth 1948-

PERSONAL: Born July 2, 1948, in London, England; daughter of Frederick George (an accountant) and Peggy (a housewife; maiden name, Giles) May; married J. Robert Campling (a college lecturer), March 7, 1970; children: Eleanor, Rebecca. *Education:* University of Exeter, B.A. (with honors), 1969; University of Sussex, M.A., 1977. *Politics:* ''Democratic Socialist.'' *Home:* 17 Church Lane, Pagham, Bognor Regis, West Sussex PO21 4NS, England.

CAREER: Chichester College of Technology, Chichester, England, part-time lecturer in history, 1974-85; writer, 1980—.

WRITINGS—Of interest to young people: Africa in the Twentieth Century, Batsford, 1980; *Kennedy,* Batsford, 1980; (with husband, James Campling) *Living through History: The French Revolution,* Batsford, 1984; *Living through History: The Russian Revolution,* Batsford, 1985; *How and Why: The Russian Revolution,* Dryad Press, 1986; *Living through History: The 1960s,* Batsford, 1987; *The Modern World: The U.S.A. after 1945,* Batsford, 1988.

WORK IN PROGRESS: Portrait of a Decade: The 1970s and *Portrait of a Decade: 1900-1909,* both to be published by Batsford.

SIDELIGHTS: ''As a teacher, I think it is important that textbooks should not only present facts, but also teach students how to interpret or evaluate evidence, to look at issues from the perspective of the people who lived at the time, to place historical events in a larger context, and so on. The series for which I write aim to do this.

''The books are designed primarily for the fifteen to sixteen year olds who are studying modern history for the English general certificate of secondary education. However, they are just as suitable for readers of all ages who want a readable, clearly-illustrated introduction to the issues of the modern world. They are stocked by public as well as school libraries. As far as possible, the text is compiled from first-hand sources such as newspaper and magazine reports, speeches, diaries, etc.— always, of course, giving due attention to problems of bias. My collection of English-language journals, stretching back to the 1960s, threatens to take the house over!

''A year spent in the United States from 1985 to 1986 has given me a particular interest in the forces that shaped American history in those years.

''As part of Batsford's new 'Reputations' series, I have plans to write a high-school level textbook evaluating the career of Richard M. Nixon.''

CARLSTROM, Nancy White 1948-

PERSONAL: Born August 4, 1948, in Washington, Pa.; daughter of William J. (a steel mill worker) and Eva (a homemaker; maiden name, Lawrence) White; married David R. Carlstrom (in marketing), September 7, 1974; children: Jesse David, Joshua White. *Education:* Wheaton College, Wheaton, Ill., B.A., 1970; also studied at Harvard Extension and Radcliffe, 1974-76. *Religion:* Christian. *Home:* 2731 Alaska Range La., Fairbanks, Alas. 99709. *Agent:* Marilyn Marlow, Curtis Brown Ltd., 10 Astor Pl., New York, N.Y. 10003.

CAREER: A. Leo Weil Elementary School, Pittsburgh, Pa., teacher, 1970-72; Plum Cove Elementary School, Gloucester, Mass., teacher, 1972-74; Secret Garden Children's Bookshop, Seattle, Wash., owner and manager, 1977-83; writer, 1983—. Worked with children in West Africa and the West Indies; worked at school for children with Down's Syndrome in Mérida, Yucatán, Mexico. *Member:* Society of Children's Book Writers.

Nancy White Carlstrom with sons Jesse and Joshua.

WRITINGS—Juvenile: *Jesse Bear, What Will You Wear?* (Junior Literary Guild selection; illustrated by Bruce Degen), Macmillan, 1986; *The Moon Came, Too* (Junior Literary Guild selection; illustrated by Stella Ormai), Macmillan, 1987; *Wild Wild Sunflower Child Anna* (illustrated by Jerry Pinkney), Macmillan, 1987; *Better Not Get Wet, Jesse Bear* (illustrated by B. Degen), Macmillan, 1988; *Where Does the Night Hide?*, Macmillan, 1988; *Blow Me a Kiss Miss Lilly* (illustrated by Amy Schwartz), Harper, 1989; *Heather Hiding*, Macmillan, 1989; *Graham Cracker Animals 1-2-3*, Macmillan, 1989.

WORK IN PROGRESS: Four books dealing with the unique changes of the seasons as experienced in the Far North: *When the Night Is Bright Like Day*, about the Alaskan summer; *Goodbye Geese*, about the Alaskan autumn; *The Snow Garden*, about the Alaskan winter; *Greeting Songs*, about the Alaskan spring; *Northern Lullaby* to be illustrated by Leo Dillon and Diane Dillon for Philomel.

SIDELIGHTS: An editor of her high school newspaper and yearbook, Carlstrom also worked in the children's department of the local library during her high school years. "That's where my dream of writing children's books was born."

After receiving her B.A. from Wheaton College, she taught first and second grades from 1970-74. She then studied art and children's literature.

Carlstrom opened the Secret Garden Children's Bookshop in 1977. "As owner and manager of the bookshop I was constantly surrounded by children's books and spent a good portion of my time promoting quality children's literature through book fairs, presentations at churches and parent groups, and in our shop newsletter. In 1981 the urge to write resurfaced and I participated in a two-week workshop led by children's book author Jane Yolen. I greatly benefited from her expertise and encouragement and consider that time to be a real turning point in my writing career. During the workshop I wrote a picture book manuscript, *Wild Wild Sunflower Child Anna*, from beginning to end. It's a poem, really, that celebrates the joy of living through a little girl's exploration of the natural world around her. *Wild Wild Sunflower Child Anna* is still my favorite book of all that I have written.

Lifting up the pressing stone
beetles rushing giddy.

■ (From *Wild Wild Sunflower Child Anna* by Nancy White Carlstrom. Illustrated by Jerry Pinkney.)

"In 1982 our first child, Jesse, was born and the following year I sold my bookshop in order to devote my time to mothering and writing. My husband and I often called our son Jesse Bear, and the book *Jesse Bear, What Will You Wear?* began as a little song which I sang while dressing him. I finished the picture book text for Jesse's first birthday and on his second birthday received word from Macmillan that they would publish it. This, my first acceptance, came after eighty-two rejections on a number of other stories. Persistence is definitely a big part of getting published.

"I was pleased to hear that Bruce Degen would be *Jesse Bear*'s illustrator, as his own *Jamberry* was my son's current favorite. It was exciting to see Mr. Degen's illustrations and satisfying to realize that the book has taken on a life of its own, bigger than the one I first gave it.

"I am especially glad that *Jesse Bear* is my first published book, as it symbolizes where I am right now—the integration of my life as mother and writer.

"One dark night when Jesse was two-and-a-half, we drove to the library. Getting out of the car, he looked up at the sky and said, 'Mommy, the moon came, too!' The rhymed text of the *The Moon Came, Too* tells the story of a little girl who is going to grandma's house and wants to take all of her favorite toys, stuffed animals, and a different hat for each anticipated adventure. After arriving at grandma's she looks up into the sky and discovers one more treasure that came. I tried to write *The Moon Came, Too* in prose, but it wanted to be in rhyme and wouldn't work until I cooperated. Sometimes a story has a mind of its own.

"Kornei Chukovsky, who was called the dean of Russian children's literature, wrote a fascinating book called *From Two to Five,* about the language of young children. In it he said that poetry is their natural language. I keep this in mind when writing for the preschool child. Rhythm and rhyme are very important to me; I want the words of my books to flow off the page and be easy for young children to repeat. It seems to me that their participation is the final step in this creative process.

"A picture book, like a poem, is what I call a bare bones kind of writing. Usually I start with many more words than I need or want. I keep cutting away until I am down to the bare bones of what I want to say. It is then up to the illustrator to create pictures that will enlarge and enhance the text. If pictures and words work together well, the final book is much greater than either author or illustrator first conceived. That is how I felt when I held a finished copy of *Jesse Bear* in my hands.

"Often a title of a story will come first. I write it down and tend to think about it for a long time before actually sitting down to work on it. Sometimes I just get a few pieces of the story and they have to simmer on the back burner, like a good pot of soup. When the time is right, the writing of the story usually comes easily. Then I read it to my husband and members of my writing group and find out that I still have more work to do.

"Writing children's books is tremendously satisfying. But some days it seems like a great juggling act as I seek to balance my roles as mother, wife, and writer. My writing is often done in bits and pieces, fitting around preschool car pools and taking a backseat to sick kids. It helps to be reminded that not only are these interruptions my work and life, but it is within these relationships and experiences that I have found a wealth of ideas and images—seeds for my books.

"In January of 1987, my family and I moved to Fairbanks, Alaska, where we are presently enjoying the unique experiences of the far north—freely wandering moose, northern lights, and extreme seasonal changes to name a few. Poetry of the landscape and customs of its native peoples have become a part of my own writing. My first Alaskan book is *Northern Lullaby* which is illustrated by Leo and Diane Dillon."

HOBBIES AND OTHER INTERESTS: Reading, drawing, cross-country skiing, canoeing, early childhood education, peace and justice issues, especially as they relate to children of our world, and Christian meditation and prayer journal.

CASELEY, Judith 1951-

BRIEF ENTRY: Surname is pronounced *Case*-ley; born October 17, 1951, in Rahway, N.J. Artist, author and illustrator. Caseley graduated cum laude with a B.F.A. from Syracuse University in 1973. She has presented her art work in group and solo exhibitions in New York, New Jersey, and London, and her paintings are part of private collections in several countries, including France, Spain, England, Germany, the Soviet Union, and the United States. Although Caseley has designed and sold greeting cards and has received a number of awards for her tiny watercolors, she finds writing and illustrating children's books more fulfilling. In 1986 the New Jersey Writers Conference gave her an Author's Citation for *Molly Pink* and its sequel, *Molly Pink Goes Hiking.* Other books she wrote and illustrated include *When Grandpa Came to Stay, My Sister Celia,* and *Apple Pie and Onions.* In *When Grandpa Came to Stay,* Caseley depicts the relationship of a young boy and his grandfather shortly after the death of the boy's beloved grandmother. According to *School Library Journal,* the author's "presentation is honest and forthright, without sentimentality, and with light, humorous touches and an upbeat ending." Caseley is a member of the Society of Children's Book Writers. *Home:* 211-06 75th Ave., Bayside, N.Y. 11364.

FOR MORE INFORMATION SEE: Contemporary Authors, Volume 121, Gale, 1987.

CAULFIELD, Peggy F. 1926-1987

OBITUARY NOTICE: Born April 10, 1926, in Hartford, Conn.; died after a long illness, September 18, 1987, in New York, N.Y. Literary agent and author. Beginning in 1955 Caulfield worked as a literary agent with the A. Watkins Agency, whose clients have included Roald Dahl, Sinclair Lewis, and Edith Wharton. Her book, *Leaves,* which features photographic illustrations by her, was written for pre-teens. In addition, she wrote articles for *Mademoiselle* magazine.

FOR MORE INFORMATION SEE: Contemporary Authors, Volumes 5-8, revised, Gale, 1969. Obituaries: *Publishers Weekly,* October 23, 1987.

CHUTE, B(eatrice) J(oy) 1913-1987

OBITUARY NOTICE—See sketch in *SATA* Volume 2: Born January 3, 1913, in Minneapolis, Minn.; died of a heart attack, September 6, 1987, in New York, N.Y. Secretary, educator, and author. After working as her father's secretary for ten years, Chute first became known as an author of children's books and later wrote successful novels for adults as well. She authored *Blocking Back, Shattuck Cadet,* and *Camp Hero* for young readers as well as a number of sports stories, many of which were published in *Boys' Life.* For adults, Chute wrote works such as *Greenwillow, The Fields Are White,* and *The Good Woman* and contributed short fiction to several national magazines. As an established author she taught creative writing at Barnard College and served as director of Books across the Sea, an organization promoting American books abroad.

FOR MORE INFORMATION SEE: Contemporary Authors, Volumes 1-4, revised, Gale, 1962; *International Authors and Writers Who's Who,* 9th edition, Melrose, 1982. Obituaries: *New York Times,* September 15, 1987; *Chicago Tribune,* September 17, 1987; *Facts on File,* September 18, 1987.

COLMAN, Hila
(Teresa Crayder)

PERSONAL: Born in New York, N.Y.; daughter of Harris (a manufacturer) and Sarah (a designer; maiden name, Kinsberg) Crayder; married Louis Colman (a medical writer; deceased); children: Jonathan, James. *Education:* Attended Radcliffe College, two years. *Politics:* Democrat. *Residence:* Hemlock Rd., Bridgewater, Conn. 06752; Florida.

CAREER: National War Relief Agency, New York, N.Y., publicity and promotion work, 1940-45; Labor Book Club, New York, N.Y., executive director, 1945-47; free-lance writer, 1949—. Member of Democratic Town Committee, Bridgewater, Conn.; former member of Bridgewater Board of Education; chairperson of Zoning Board of Appeals, Bridgewater, Conn. *Awards, honors:* Child Study Association of America's Wel-Met Children's Book Award, 1962, for *The Girl from Puerto Rico;* Garden State Children's Book Award from the New Jersey Library Association, 1979, for *Nobody Has to Be a Kid Forever.*

*WRITINGS—*Juvenile, except as indicated; all published by Morrow, except as indicated: *The Big Step,* 1957; *A Crown for Gina,* 1958; *Julie Builds Her Castle,* 1959; *Best Wedding Dress,* 1960; (with husband, Louis Colman) *The Country Weekend Cookbook* (adult nonfiction), Barrows, 1961; *The Girl from Puerto Rico,* 1961; *Mrs. Darling's Daughter,* 1962; *Watch That Watch,* 1962; *Phoebe's First Campaign,* 1963; *Peter's Brownstone House* (illustrated by Leonard Weisgard), 1963; *Classmates by Request,* 1964.

Christmas Cruise, 1965; *The Boy Who Couldn't Make Up His Mind,* Macmillan, 1965; *Bride at Eighteen,* 1966; *Thoroughly Modern Millie* (novelization of screenplay), Bantam, 1966; *Car-Crazy Girl,* 1967; *Mixed-Marriage Daughter,* 1968; *Something out of Nothing,* Weybright, 1968; *A Career in Medical Research,* World, 1968; *Dangerous Summer,* Bantam, 1968;

Hila Colman with husband, Limey.

I'm almost thirteen years old and I know how to take care of myself. ■ (Jacket illustration by John Wallner from *Tell Me No Lies* by Hila Colman.)

Beauty, Brains, and Glamour: A Career in Magazine Publishing, World, 1968; *Claudia, Where Are You?,* 1969; *Making Movies: Student Films to Features,* World, 1969; *Andy's Landmark House,* Parents Magazine Press, 1969.

The Happenings at North End School, 1970; *End of the Game,* World, 1971; *Daughter of Discontent,* 1971; *City Planning: What It's All About—In the Planners' Own Words,* World, 1971; *The Family and the Fugitive,* 1972; *The Diary of a Frantic Kid Sister,* Crown, 1973; *Benny the Misfit,* Crowell, 1973; *Chicano Girl,* 1973; *Friends and Strangers on Location,* 1974; *After the Wedding,* 1975; *That's the Way It Is, Amigo,* Harper, 1975; *Ethan's Favorite Teacher* (illustrated by John Wallner; Junior Literary Guild selection), Crown, 1975.

Nobody Has to Be a Kid Forever, Crown, 1976; *The Amazing Miss Laura,* 1976; *The Case of the Stolen Bagels* (illustrated by Pat Grant Porter), Crown, 1977; *Sometimes I Don't Love My Mother,* 1977; *Hanging On* (adult), Atheneum, 1977; *Tell Me No Lies,* Crown, 1978; *The Secret Life of Harold the Bird Watcher* (illustrated by Charles Robinson), Harper, 1978; *Rachel's Legacy,* 1978; *Ellie's Inheritance,* 1979.

What's the Matter with Dobsons?, Crown, 1980; *Accident,* 1980; *Confessions of a Storyteller,* 1981; *The Family Trap,* 1982; *Girl Meets Boy,* Scholastic, 1982; *Not for Love,* 1983; *My Friend, My Love,* Archway, 1983; *Don't Tell Me That You Love Me,* Archway, 1983; *Just the Two of Us,* Scholastic, 1984; *Nobody Told Me What I Need to Know,* 1984; *Weekend Sisters,* 1985; *A Fragile Love,* Pocket Books, 1985; *Triangle*

of Love, Pocket Books, 1985; *Happily Ever After,* Scholastic, 1986; *Suddenly,* 1987; *Remind Me Not to Fall in Love,* Archway, 1987; *Rich and Famous Like My Mom,* Crown, 1988; *Double Life of Angela Jones,* 1988.

Under pseudonym Teresa Crayder: *Sudden Fame,* Macmillan, 1966; *Kathy and Lisette,* Doubleday, 1966; *Cleopatra,* Coward, 1969.

Contributor of short stories and articles to *McCall's, Saturday Evening Post, Ingenue, Ladies' Home Journal, Seventeen, Redbook,* and *Today's Woman.*

ADAPTATIONS: "Unforgivable Secrets," based on *Tell Me No Lies,* ABC Afterschool Special, February 10, 1982; "Sometimes I Don't Love My Mother," starring Patricia Elliott and Melinda Culea, ABC Afterschool Special, October 13, 1982.

WORK IN PROGRESS: "I have just signed a contract with Crown Publishing for a new book, but have not started on it yet."

SIDELIGHTS: "I have drawn a good deal on my own upbringing and background for my writing. Readers of *Rachel's Legacy* and *Ellie's Inheritance* have some very good clues as to where, when and how I grew up.

"I was born and raised in New York City and in many ways led the life of an over-protected girl from a well-to-do Jewish family. Rachel of *Rachel's Legacy* is based loosely on my mother, who came to this country from Russia as a child, around the turn of the century. She worked in sweatshops in the garment district and by dint of extremely hard work, became a designer of children's clothing and the partial owner (with my father, her sister and brother-in-law) of a very successful business. Their line consisted exclusively of white dresses for special occasions. 'Getting out the line' was a phrase we heard constantly in our house.

"I didn't realize we were rich until I was an adolescent. I saw my mother go to work each morning in a Cadillac driven by a chauffeur, but for some reason this didn't make an impression on me. Perhaps because my mother worked so very hard. Our household was austere in many ways. Oh, we lived in a beautiful apartment in a fancy neighborhood and summered on Long Island, but as children we were not given a lot in the way of personal luxuries. Work not privilege was the dominant theme in our house. My mother was an early feminist and raised my sister and me with the clear expectation that we would prepare ourselves for a profession. We were never imbued with the idea that as girls we could expect one day to be 'taken care of.' We were raised to assume we would have to earn our living. My mother wanted me to be an attorney. There was never any pressure on either of us to continue the business she had begun. I think she wanted us to create something for ourselves, not step into a situation that already existed.

"I remember my mother as a great reader. One of her favorite authors was George Eliot, all of whose books she owned. My father was the more political of the two. He was quick to spot contradictions between political theory and practice, and had no patience whatsoever for hypocrisy."

Unionizing textile workers is one theme in *Rachel's Legacy*, another is a tense mother/daughter relationship, again reflecting Colman's own situation. "I was definitely much closer to my father than to my mother. I was his 'darling,' no doubt about it. But I was jealous of the closeness between my mother and sister, and often felt hurt by what I perceived as my mother's coldness. Like so many who had worked in sweatshops and factories in the garment center, my mother died of tuberculosis at a young age. I was fifteen at the time of her death, but she was sick for a substantial part of my growing up. TB is a highly contagious disease. Her seeming undemonstrativeness toward me was born out of fear for my health. My father, neurotic about disease generally, denied her illness. He was a very affectionate person, and I felt much more comfortable with him than with my mother. In fact, I generally preferred being with men than women.

"My sister and I both attended the Calhoun School in Manhattan, an all-girl, fashionable private school. I was a good student. It would have been better had my sister and I gone to different schools, however. I was too prone to depend on an older sister—her ideas prevailed over mine. It got to the point where I hardly bothered coming up with my own ideas for things to do. It wasn't until I went to college that I tasted social independence."

(From "Sometimes I Don't Love My Mother," an "ABC Afterschool Special," starring Patricia Elliott and Melinda Culea. First broadcast October 13, 1982.)

The people who built the house wanted it to last for many, many years. ■ (From *Peter's Brownstone House* by Hila Colman. Illustrated by Leonard Weisgard.)

With help from her aunt, Colman was accepted into Radcliffe. "The school assumed its students were adult enough to handle themselves with little supervision. No one made sure you attended classes. I needed more structure than Radcliffe provided. Socially, too, I felt like a fish out of water. Everyone seemed much more sophisticated than I was.

"It never occurred to me to drop out, but, as it turned out, I did leave after my second year due to unforeseen circumstances. According to the terms of my mother's will, her business was to be liquidated within two years of her death. This was for two reasons: its success depended on her designs; and my father was far from a financial wizard. Her idea was that the liquidation would provide income for us for the rest of our lives. However, my father and my cousin, executors of the will, disregarded her wishes and mismanaged the business. On top of that, my father made some bad real estate investments. That was that—suddenly we were broke.

"My sister and I enrolled in a six-week secretarial course. I took my first job with the Philippine Mahogany Association. I worked for a very nice Pennsylvania Dutchman whose main responsibility was research. My shorthand was terrible, my typing was probably worse, but my boss was extremely patient and sweet. Also, he didn't generate that much work, so there was minimal pressure."

The sudden change in financial status did not change Colman's life style dramatically. "There is a big difference between being 'poor' and being 'broke.' We were *broke*. I could scrape together enough money for a movie, or get cheap tickets to a concert or play. Instead of buying a bottle of Scotch, I bought two bottles of sherry. I still had the same friends I had always had. I had the same books, the same music. In no way could our situation be likened to that of people who are truly impoverished. I never had the sense that the better things in life were unavailable to me because I didn't have a lot of money. I may have been living in a crummy apartment above a bar in Greenwich Village, but it was exactly where I wanted to be.

"The late 1930s/early 1940s represented a period of enormous growth for me. I had 'come of age' politically. My milieu was much like Ellie's in *Ellie's Inheritance*. I was meeting people who were politically savvy and dedicated to left-wing causes.

Betty was the smartest girl in the class. "Four times four is sixteen," she said promptly. ■ (From *Ethan's Favorite Teacher* by Hila Colman. Illustrated by John Wallner.)

The business prospered. By another year, we hired some Italian girls to work on the machines. ■ (Jacket illustration by Jane Sterret from *Rachel's Legacy* by Hila Colman.)

I knew people who went off to fight and die in the Spanish Civil War. Lionel, in *Ellie's Inheritance,* is based on someone I knew (although not as intimately as Ellie).

"During the late 1930s, I worked on the staff of *TAC,* a magazine published by the Theatre Arts Committee. We covered theatre, dance and music off the beaten track. We were a small staff, everyone pitched in and did a little bit of everything. I worked mostly with the editor, doing rewrites and line edits, although I also did paste-up and mechanicals as well. Soon after the Second World War broke out, *TAC* folded."

During the war years, Colman held a position with the Russian War Relief Agency. "There was a huge effort in this country to get medical supplies, clothing and so on to Russia. Eleanor Roosevelt was one of our volunteers, one of many luminaries from the arts, Wall Street and various professions who gave of their talents to our cause. I was responsible for printed material for fundraising effort. It was very exciting, I could call up the top art directors at the most prestigious advertising agencies and ask them for a layout, and they were more than happy to donate one. The finest painters of the day, among them Phillip Evergood, did posters for us. We had hundreds, if not thousands, of fundraising dinners, benefits and functions. It was a heady time—we were doing something we believed in.

"From 1945 until 1947 I was executive director of the Labor Book Club, sponsored by Reynal & Hitchcock. It was their belief that the end of the war would see a great resurgence of culture among the working classes. They couldn't have been more wrong. This laudable project, unfortunately, turned out to be somewhat of a fiasco. Most of the union rank and file weren't reading their union newsletters, let alone literature. But it was fun, nonetheless. Arthur Miller was one of our authors, as was Howard Fast. We would make the circuit addressing union locals. I remember Phillip Evergood and I went to Pittsburgh to talk with a mining union. I spoke and Phillip made drawings. Unfortunately, not many people joined the Club. After about two years, the operation folded.

"One evening in 1947 my husband and I both wished to attend a political meeting. For some reason we were unable to get a babysitter, and my husband took for granted that he would go out and I would stay home with the children. I did stay home, but was so furious that I sat down and wrote an article called 'Can a Man Have a Career and a Family, Too?', a spoof on similarly-titled articles directed at women.

"I gave the article to a writer friend a few days later. He offered to give it to Edith Haggert, his agent at Curtis Brown. Three days later, Haggert called with the news that she had sold my piece to the *Saturday Evening Post.* They not only sent me a nice, fat check, but did a big promotion for the piece. They put my name on the cover and had one of their staff writers do a rebuttal. There was a lavish double-spread with drawings, and to top it all off, advertisements for the article on the radio. Not a bad debut—especially for a piece I had written in one draft in a single evening!"

"One of my concoctions," Martha said. ■ (From *Something out of Nothing* by Hila Colman. Illustrated by Sally Trinkle.)

Colman's article was controversial not so much because it offered a 'vindication of the rights of women,' but because it attributed the traditional husband-and-father's minimal involvement with the day-to-day activities of his own home to male arrested development. In her piece, Colman introduces the Clark family—Helen, Joe and their two sons. Joe Clark is a middle-class 'Everyman' professional; he is good at what he does; he enjoys his job as an engineer; he earns a good salary; he doesn't drink; and for all appearances is devoted to his family. Yet not only does he not help cook and clean, but he is often emotionally unavailable to his family. When he comes home, he does not want to be *disturbed*. [Based on an interview by Marguerite Feitlowitz for *Something about the Author*.[1]]

"When Joe gets off the train at 5:30, he is bushed. His dream of home is the same as it had been in his nursery-school days, with a few variations. When he was five it was a warm bath, mamma giving him a good supper, a story and bed. Now it is a lukewarm shower, a stiff drink, Helen giving him dinner, reading a story all by himself, and bed. The fact that Helen had made the jump from her nursery-school haven to the awful reality that the hours between 5:30 and 8:30 were the busiest, most unrelaxed time of her harried day was something that just never occurred to him—or to her either, for that matter. They both took it for granted." [Hila Colman, "Can a Man Have a Career and a Family, Too?" *Saturday Evening Post*, April 30, 1947.[2]]

Colman attributes the roots of such male arrested development to the way that boys are raised. "Somehow or other, he and his friends grew up with the impression—maybe it's our mothers-in-law that did it—that all a man has to do is bring home a steady income to guarantee his wife's happiness and his children's welfare and security. It never dawned on anyone that he might become so engrossed in the business of his career that at home his personality would become nil, and emotionally he would be about as invigorating as last night's drink left on the kitchen table."[1]

Society as a whole, Colman argued, was organized so that women could take up the slack left by men. "Let's face it. All the microscopes, of late, have been turned on the women. Can a woman have a career and still be a good wife and mother? Can a woman be a housewife and still remain interesting, stimulating and glamorous to her husband and children? The best brains of our country have been turned to this question. Our magazines, writers, college professors and research institutions have been helping the little woman adjust to a full-time job and still smilingly face the thousand-and-one demands made of her at home by the family, emotionally and physically. Our leading industrialists have been busy inventing machines and gadgets to keep her from being a drudge; and if she is a housekeeper, she is constantly being impressed with the necessity of being witty, scintillating, relaxed, calm, well-read and emotionally stable, and with plenty of leisure time for all."[2]

"To look at the article today in the wake of the feminist movement of the 1960s and 1970s, it may not seem very extreme. But in 1947 when the country was focused on a conservative 'return to normalcy' following World War II, which meant that sex roles were clearly defined, the piece was radical in its outspokenness and 'sassy' tone. That the *Post* printed it with a staff rebuttal proved that they considered that my views went against the grain. Also, they didn't want my arguments in the air without counterarguments nearby.

"Even after that heady entrance into publishing, I still wasn't considering becoming a writer. Shortly after my *Post* article appeared, we bought a little summer house in Bridgewater, Connecticut. My husband, who had had a routine writing job in an office, was then offered a book contract. After much debate about finances and cultural development in our children, we gave in to our fantasy of moving to the country for a year while Louis wrote his book.

"We fell in love with Bridgewater and did not want to return to New York City too quickly. The only problem confronting us was earning a living here. So I decided to start writing. For the first two years, I wrote confessions for publications like *True Romance* and *True Confessions*. Confessions were quite lucrative and because they were anonymous, I could have several in a single issue of a given magazine.

"People often look down on that kind of writing I was doing, but I learned a lot. Confessions are always first-person narratives, which require that the piece sound authentic. The reader must absolutely believe that the person telling the story actually experienced it. The irony was that you had to sign a statement that the story you had written was *not* true—the publishers were afraid of libel suits. I also learned a lot about concision and pacing.

"Some articles were written in an interesting way. Most confession magazines ran contests every year as a way of getting material. Generally there was a grand prize of $10,000, and many smaller prizes of $25 or $50. Contest entrants generally scribbled their ideas on sheets of yellow lined paper. These 'germs' for stories were then turned over to a professional writer who would turn them into full-blown 'confessions.'

"In many ways, the stories in *True Confessions* were more realistic than what you read in the slick magazines. In the slicks, everybody had a house with a two-car garage and all the latest conveniences. I did stories about alcoholics, people who were out of work, kids who lived in foster homes, and teenage girls who had retarded babies out of wedlock. One piece I was particularly proud of was about anti-semitism, and centered on a young couple who on their honeymoon couldn't get into a hotel because they were Jewish. I admit that doing these pieces could get depressing. Stylistically, the one bad thing about them was that they lacked humor.

"Eventually I started writing for *McCall's, Redbook, Woman's Day, Today's Woman* and *Ingenue*."[1] Colman continued to write in favor of families devoted to the well-being of the family *as a whole* as opposed to that of one or two privileged members. In a piece entitled "We Stopped Sacrificing for Our Children," *Redbook*, June, 1962, she wrote of her and her husband's hard decision to move their family to Bridgewater from New York City. Their life in Manhattan had become focused almost entirely on their children. Not only had they moved to a neighborhood that required a different and lengthy commute for her husband because it was in a good school district, but she and her husband had given up theatre, concerts and entertaining so that they could provide music lessons, private school and other cultural advantages for their sons.[1]

". . . Somehow the quality of our own lives had changed to such a degree that our sacrifices, once freely made, were now increasingly tinged with resentment. More and more . . . I wondered whether the advantages we were giving our children would be important enough to justify our own constricted existence." [Hila Colman, "We Stopped Sacrificing for Our Children," *Redbook*, June, 1962.[3]]

Colman, after much introspection, concluded, "[Didn't our] kids deserve parents who [were] happy and fulfilled and fun to be with? And [didn't] we deserve to be happy too?"[3]

Country living, as described in this article, surprised Colman in a number of positive ways. "I found that mothers in the country were not as frenetic about their children as those I had known in the city or even in the suburbs. The two-room school had limitations . . . but it also had a great deal to offer . . . [Our sons'] intellectual interests did not suffer or disappear, but they had plenty to learn from country boys and girls with a background different from their own. We discovered that catering to children is not always the wisest way to help them develop into rich, well-rounded human beings. The greatest gift came to me—the time and right atmosphere to start working at home myself."[3]

"Underlying the positive feelings [of successful magazine articles] was a vague dissatisfaction I couldn't quite name. Close friends of ours, who had done a number of successful children's books, began good-naturedly to nag me, 'You'll never make a name for yourself doing articles, magazines will get you nowhere.' They suggested I write a book for adolescent girls, building on my experience with *Ingenue*. So I did a chapter and an outline. My friend took me to William Morrow and introduced me to the children's editor. I think I had to rewrite the chapter and outline five or six times, but finally they gave me a contract. I have been doing a book a year for Morrow ever since.

"Women writers have a lot of problems male writers do not have. Many of my close men friends are writers, so I am in a position to know. Male writers are completely protected by their wives from social engagements, housework, child care, marketing, anything that might interrupt their work. Women generally don't have that, and must be much more disciplined about their writing. My husband was completely supportive of me and my work, but still, it was hard. He had his profession, after all. I was constantly juggling. I would hire a babysitter to be in the house with my children when I needed to go into my study and work. And many women have a hard time taking themselves seriously until they start making a lot of money."[1]

The Big Step, Colman's first book, came out in 1957. "The idea for this book came from a family I knew. A man with two teen-age daughters married a woman with one teen-age girl; suddenly the three girls were thrown into one household together. While my book has little to do with that particular family, the situation intrigued me." [Lee Bennett Hopkins, *More Books by More People*, Citation, 1974.[4]]

She generally bases her books on people and places she has known, as is the case with *The Girl from Puerto Rico*. "I was living in New York City at the time in what is called a 'mixed neighborhood.' With that exposure, it would seem to me almost impossible for a writer not to become involved in the plight of the Puerto Rican families coming North in search of 'the good life.' A book about the situation seemed natural to me."[4]

Colman concentrates her writing for an adolescent audience because "the feelings one has as an adolescent are so intense, they never quite disappear, nor are they forgotten. Although today's generation is different from mine, basic emotional relationships and feelings remain consistent—and these are the important ingredients of a novel.

"The time of adolescence is in itself a wonderful age to write about. It combines an idealism and honesty and a wily sophistication that no other time of life enjoys. The teenager has vitality and enjoys life although he sees the ugliness and absurdities as well as the joys.

"Adolescents are also engaged in some of the most important 'work' they will ever do. It is the time when one establishes one's identity and comes of age in a number of critical areas—social, political, cultural, sexual. Conflict prevails during these years with one's parents, teachers, peers, and, most painfully, with oneself."

Her novels reflect confidence in young people. Her characters routinely confront extremely tough problems—divorced, alcoholic and/or psychotic parents, for example—and suggest ways to cope. In *The Family Trap*, fifteen-year-old Becky is left in the care of her eighteen-year-old sister Nancy after their father is killed in an industrial accident and their mother, who for years had been of fragile mental health, becomes psychotic and institutionalized. Nancy's way of handling their stressful situation is to impose strict rules to govern Becky's behavior and to maintain order in their lives. Nancy becomes so rigid that Becky resolves to file with the courts for the status of "emancipated minor," as soon as she turns sixteen. As an "emancipated minor," she would be responsible for herself financially, educationally, socially and emotionally. Nancy opposes this plan and fights Becky in court with the help of her attorney-fiancé. But Becky, who has found a job and a nice place to live, convinces the judge and wins her case.

"I had never heard of the concept of 'emancipated minor,' until I read about it in the newspaper. It seemed like a very good, but sobering, idea. Why should an adolescent with the ambition, commitment and ability to care for herself be required to live according to someone else's rules, even if that person is next-of-kin? In doing this book, I was also interested in the tense and competitive relationship between the two sisters, and in exploring the personality of Nancy's character. Nancy had a pretty rigid personality to begin with, but this was intensified because she felt overwhelmed with the responsibility of 'being in charge' of her younger sister. She may have appeared to enjoy wielding authority, but she resented it, too. I think that Nancy and Becky, after separating, have a much better chance for a good relationship. Living together as they were, each was the 'captive' of the other."[1]

One of Colman's best-received novels is *Claudia, Where Are You?* (1969), about a sixteen-year-old girl who runs away from her parents' well-appointed suburban home to the 'psychedelic' East Village of the late 1960s. The book, which is written in alternating chapters from Claudia's and then her mother's point of view, deals with intense parent-child conflict. Colman was praised for presenting both "the mortification and anguish of the parents and the trials and perils (and the perils are not minimized) of East Village life." [Patience M. Canham, "Teens Tuned In," *Christian Science Monitor*, November 6, 1969.[5]]

"I had a lot of fun researching *Claudia* in the East Village with my younger son and his friends. And I was very pleased to write both from the mother and daughter's viewpoints—technically, that was something of a 'coup' for me."

Colman's *Sometimes I Don't Love My Mother* was also highly praised for its exploration of a troubled mother/daughter relationship. In this novel, Dallas must try to establish a new closeness with her mother after the sudden death of her beloved father. She must deal not only with her own lacerating grief, but try to keep her equilibrium in the face of her mother falling to pieces and becoming pathologically dependent on her.

"'Sometimes I don't love my mother'—is something most kids feel at one time or another, and when they do, many are convinced that they're committing a crime. In any extremely close relationship, such as that between parents and children, emotions tend to run high. That's normal, particularly during the teenage years. During adolescence, kids need to break away from their parents. If parents try to hold on in a way that is unhealthy, kids are justified in feeling angry. Both sides have to give, which is not necessarily easy.''[1]

''Torn between protective pity and strong resentment, Dallas finds it hard to declare her independence,'' writes *Bulletin of the Center for Children's Books,* December, 1977 about *Sometimes I Don't Love My Mother.* ''She eventually does so, in logical fashion, but not before both mother and daughter have explored the intricacies of a taut emotional conflict. Colman, while sympathetic toward her young protagonist, makes the reader see clearly the internal conflict of each, and, while they are reacting to a stress situation, there is enough that is universal so that any reader can identify with the typical identity search of adolescence.''

In *Not for Love* Colman focuses on sixteen-year-old Jill, the pretty, rather pampered and only daughter of conservative parents. After meeting and falling in love with Toby, a political activist, Jill is swept up in a flurry of anti-nuclear activity. Her initial enthusiasm for the group opposing the building of a local nuclear power plant derives from her feelings for Toby. Because she has not yet thoroughly thought through the issues on her own, Jill is ill-equipped to combat her father's sarcastic disapproval of her position. When Toby, whose family is not as financially advantaged as Jill's, tells her that he is forced to take a summer job at the power plant in order to pay his college tuition, Jill is so disillusioned she ends their relationship as well as her own political involvement. Over the course of a lonely summer, Jill reflects on nuclear issues and her own political participation, and decides for herself that she opposes the plant. At summer's end, on the day of an anti-nuke demonstration, Jill not only is able effectively to rebut her father's criticism, but by her example convinces Toby to put down his shovel and hop the fence to join the picket line.

''Political activities can be complicated dynamics. People get involved for all sorts of reasons—because they believe strongly in a cause, because they yearn for solidarity with others, because they want to change the world. It's important to be clear on what you believe and why, and to consider wisely your means of protest. You can't act on the basis of someone else's reasons. In *Not for Love,* Jill is exposed for the first time not only to political activists, but to Toby's truly charismatic personality. Jill expects Toby to be perfect. Well, nobody is. This may well be a cliche, but it's a hard lesson to learn.

''I am particularly pleased that *Not for Love* is being translated for publication in Japan, which knows far better than any other country the horrors of nuclear war. My other titles have appeared in French, Italian, German and the Scandinavian languages, but not Japanese.

''I go up and down [on the nuclear issue]. Of course, I am absolutely terrified at the possibility of another disaster like Hiroshima, Nagasaki, or Chernobyl. Then I think, 'How could anyone let that happen *again*?' But I am very worried. There is no good leadership in the American Democratic party. And leaders all over the world are using nuclear warheads like so many bargaining chips—an *incredibly* dangerous game.

''I think the 1980s is a difficult decade in which to come of age politically. Civil Rights and the Viet Nam War were polarizing issues during the '60s. The lines could be clearly drawn—you were for or against. And there were charismatic

leaders—Martin Luther King, Jr., the Kennedys, JFK in particular, the student activists. There was communal activity and comradeship. I recently visited one of my granddaughters at a prestigious Eastern college. She was bemoaning the fact that there wasn't much in the way of political activism on her campus, and wished she could find a group to join. This speaks volumes about the times in which we are living. But I told her, 'You can still be involved. Getting someone elected to Congress is very important, as are local elections.' The 1960s were about big, national issues and widespread mobilization. The 1980s are quieter, but there is still work to be done and ways to do it.''

Every book begins with an idea and then an outline. ''On that basis I'm able to get a contract. Most books take me three or four months. The completed manuscript I show to my editor is pretty close to a first draft. I tend to write the story straight through, revising a little as I go along. I think I should spend more time polishing, but I am an impatient writer, eager to get on with my story. I am by no means my best editor. I can read a passage over and over and see no problems with it. But when my editor suggests that this or that should be developed further, or this part be tightened, I'm often in agreement.

''I have *great* respect for talented editors. Many trade books suffer from a lack of good editing. I am tired of reading rave reviews, and finding the book boring. Most writers profit with an expert 'outside eye,' telling them when to pick up the pace, sharpen a character, make something happen.

''One of my strengths as a writer is a good ear. If you're writing about adolescents, you have to be very careful with language. It must be contemporary without being too trendy, or it would have no shelf life at all. There is another consideration regarding language. I am told by librarians that older women like to read my books because they don't have too much sex in them by today's standards. A number of my books are for reluctant readers and are used in literacy programs. So while I may think about adolescent readers primarily, I am aware that they are not my only readers.''

One of Colman's books has been subject to some problems with censorship. ''*The Diary of a Frantic Kid Sister* piqued the ire of a Florida superintendent of schools. He wrote in response to a favorable review in *School Library Journal* advocating that my book be removed from school libraries. He was affronted by my use of the word 'boobs,' and contended that I also used the Lord's name in vain. In any case, *School Library Journal* wrote a favorable response to the gentleman's assertion and invited me to do the same. I wrote of my surprise at the superintendent's inability to judge the difference between profanity and vulgarity. I put forward my view that words are only 'dirty' in people's minds. *The Diary of a Frantic Kid Sister* has been one of my most popular books.

''I have also received letters from kids and parents complaining that I write so much about divorce. 'Why do families in your books have so many problems? Why do you use such vulgar language?' I always write back, explaining that we all need books to help us figure out the world as it really is. I deal with contemporary issues and contemporary problems because my readers do. Pretending the world is devoid of problems doesn't do anyone any favors.''

Colman's works include nonfiction as well. ''My nonfiction has been mostly of a journalistic nature. Doing research and talking with different kinds of people is very stimulating for me. It also affords me the opportunity to capitalize on interests that wouldn't normally find an outlet in fiction. For example,

It seemed to David they examined every part of the engine, but he couldn't catch their rapid Spanish. ∎ (From *That's the Way It Is, Amigo* by Hila Colman. Illustrated by Glo Coalson.)

my husband and I collaborated on *The Country Weekend Cookbook*.

"A book that means a lot to me is *Hanging On* about my husband's final illness and death. I did not necessarily want to write it, but had to in order to go on.

"After my husband died, I lived alone for eight years, wishing often that I had had a different profession, allowing me to be with people during the day. Not too long ago, I began living with a dear friend of forty years, who is also widowed. We met through the Russian War Relief Agency—he had one of the finest print shops in New York and I would buy printing from him. He tells everyone we are married, and we did have a private ceremony, but it's not official."

Winters are spent on one of the keys off the western coast of Florida, and summers in Bridgewater. "We have a pretty little house on a canal to spend winters in. I have fixed up a marvellous studio for myself, so my work goes on no matter where we are.

"Our family is very close. When my sons were growing up, I loved to have the house full of young people. That hasn't changed at all since I've become a grandmother to seven grandchildren."

Colman advises aspiring writers to: "Just sit down and write. I remember when I was in high school I tried to write stories like Kathryn Mansfield. I let myself be intimidated by the world's great writers. In fact, I know that this is the reason I haven't written an adult novel. Don't give in to the feeling that if you don't write something tremendous and special, it won't be worth it. And don't think you have to do something new. There is nothing new to write about, everything has already been written about. What counts is your way of writing it, your voice, your insight. That is what makes it unique."[1]

HOBBIES AND OTHER INTERESTS: Traveling, sunshine, tennis, walking, reading, movies, cooking, gardening.

FOR MORE INFORMATION SEE: Hila Colman, "Can a Man Have a Career and a Family, Too," *Saturday Evening Post,* April 30, 1947; H. Colman, "We Stopped Sacrificing for Our Children," *Redbook,* June, 1962; H. Colman, "Before the Weekend," *American Home,* June, 1964; *New York Times Book Review,* September 24, 1967; *Best Sellers,* October 1, 1967; *Christian Science Monitor,* November 2, 1967, November 6, 1969; *Young Readers Review,* December, 1968; Martha E. Ward and Dorothy A. Marquardt, *Authors of Books for Young People,* Scarecrow, 1971; Doris de Montreville and Donna Hill, editors, *Third Book of Junior Authors,* H. W. Wilson, 1972; *Horn Book,* April, 1973; Lee Bennet Hopkins, *More Books by More People,* Citation, 1974; *Bulletin of the Center for Children's Books,* December, 1977; *English Journal,* January, 1979, December, 1981, 1986; *Voya,* February, 1981, 1983, December, 1984; *Catholic Library World,* December, 1984; *School Library Journal,* February, 1984, December, 1985; *Publishers Weekly,* May 8, 1987.

COSGROVE, Stephen E(dward)   1945-

PERSONAL: Born July 26, 1945, in Spokane, Wash.; son of Patrick R. and Edith M. (a secretary; maiden name, Townsend) Cosgrove; married Joanne Ferrante, January 18, 1969 (divorced, March, 1977); married Shaerie A. Grames (a teacher), November 30, 1985; children: (first marriage) Jennifer Joanne, Julie Ann. *Education:* Attended Stephen's College for Women, 1963-64, Everett Community College, and University of Washington. *Religion:* Christian. *Studio:* The DreamMaker, W/C 50000, Woodinville, Wash. 98072.

CAREER: C-Star Concrete, Everett, Wash., assistant manager, 1964-68; Fleet Investment, Seattle, Wash., vice-president, 1968-74; Serendipity Communications, Ltd., Bothell, Wash., founder and president, 1974-79; author, 1974—.

WRITINGS—All juvenile fantasies; all illustrated by Robin James, except as noted; all published by Serendipity Press, except as noted: *The Muffin Muncher,* 1974; *Tail of Three Tales,* 1974; *Wheedle on the Needle,* 1974; *Serendipity,* 1974; *The Dream Tree,* 1974; *In Search of the Saveopotamas,* 1975; *Little Mouse on the Prairie,* Price Stern, 1975; *Morgan and Me,* 1975; *Cap'n Smudge,* 1975; *The Gnome from Nome,* 1975; *Jake O'Shawnasey,* 1976; *Kartusch,* Price Stern, 1976; *Hucklebug,* 1976; *Creole,* 1976; *Bangalee,* 1976; *Leo the Lop,* 1977; *Gabby,* 1977; *Leo the Lop: Tail Two,* Price Stern, 1977; *Leo the Lop: Tail Three,* Price Stern, 1977; *Flutterby,* 1978; *Catundra,* Price Stern, 1978; *Feather Fin,* 1978; *Snaffles,* Price Stern, 1978; *Shimmeree,* Price Stern, 1979; *Grampa-Lop,* 1979.

Trafalgar True, Price Stern, 1980; *Trapper,* 1980; *Raz-Ma-Taz,* 1980; *Nitter Pitter,* Price Stern, 1980; *Maui-Maui,* Price Stern, 1981; *Tee-Tee,* 1981; *Ming Ling,* 1981; *Morgan and*

STEPHEN E. COSGROVE

Yew, 1982; *Morgan Mine,* 1982; *Morgan Morning,* 1983; *Flutterby Fly,* 1983; *Kiyomi,* 1984; *Dragolin,* 1984; *Minikin,* 1984; *Crabby Gabby,* Price Stern, 1985; *Jingle Bear,* 1985; *Glitterby Baby,* 1985; *Squeakers,* Price Stern, 1985; *Buttermilk,* Price Stern, 1986; *Fanny,* Price Stern, 1986; *Mumkin,* Price Stern, 1986; *Pish-Posh,* Price Stern, 1986; *Crickle-Crack,* Price Stern, 1987; *Memily,* Price Stern, 1987; *Buttermilk Bear,* Price Stern, 1987; *Misty Morgan,* Price Stern, 1987; *Bundla Joy the Christmas Story* (illustrated by Louise Zingarelli), RainForest, 1987; *Serendipity Classic Adventure: Giggle-snitcher,* Price Stern, 1987; *Sassafras,* Price Stern, 1988; *Rhubarb,* Price Stern, 1988; *Persnickity,* Price Stern, 1988; *Sniffles,* Price Stern, 1988.

"Bugg" series; all juvenile; all illustrated by Charles Reasoner; all published by Price Stern, except as noted: *The Bugglar Brothers,* 1983; *Dune Bugg,* 1983; *Eevil Weevil,* 1983; *Glance,* 1983; *Humbugg,* 1983; *Lord and Lady Bugg,* 1983; *Vee-Dubb,* 1983; *Love Bugg,* 1983; *Snugg,* 1983; *Tik Tok,* 1983; *June Bugg,* 1984; *Jitterbugg,* 1984; *Crick-ette,* 1984; *Cooty-Doo,* 1984; *Snugg and Shoe Fly Flu,* 1984; *Shutterbugg,* 1984; *Katy-Didd,* 1984; *Doodle Bugg,* 1984; *BBOC,* 1988; *Buggly,* 1988; *Ugly Bugg,* 1988; *Bee Bopp,* 1988; *Scribble,* 1988; *Shrugg,* 1988; *Buzz,* 1988; *Chugga,* 1988; *Hugga Bugg,* 1988; *Barley,* 1988; *Betterfly,* 1988; *The Bigg Family,* 1988; *Brush Buggs,* 1988; *Bubble Bugg,* 1988; *Bubba Bugg,* 1988; *Bugg Off,* 1988; *Buggaboo!,* 1988; *Buggita,* 1988; *Button,* 1988; *Chubba,* 1988; *Dragon Fly,* 1988; *Fibber Bugg,* 1988; *Firefly,* 1988; *Flea Flicker,* 1988; *Flitterfly,* 1988; *Fly Baby Fly,* 1988; *Fuss E. Bugg,* 1988; *Hocus Locust,* 1988; *Little Buggaroo,* 1988; *Lullafly,* 1988; *Melody Moth,* 1988; *Merry Widow,* 1988; *Mizz Buggly,* 1988; *Popp Fly,* 1988; *Skeeter,* 1988.

"Bumble B. Bear" board books; all illustrated by C. Reasoner; all published by Price Stern, 1984: *Bumble B. Bear:*

The Christmas Tree; . . . *Takes a Walk;* . . . *Rides in a Car;* . . . *in the Garden;* . . . *Cleans Up;* . . . *: A Gift for the Giving.*

"Baby Bunny" series; all illustrated by C. Reasoner; all published by Price Stern: *Bunny's Playtime,* 1984; *Sleepy Time Bunny,* 1984; *Bunny's Busy Day,* 1984; *Bunny Goes to Market,* 1984; *Bunny Bakes a Cake,* 1986.

"Whimsie Storybooks"; all illustrated by C. Reasoner; all published by Random House, 1985: *Gimme; Tattletale; Gobble and Gulp; Cranky; Chatterbox; Giggle.*

"Old Fashion Stories from the DreamMaker" series; juvenile fantasy; all illustrated by W. Edelson; all published by Ideals, 1988: *Goldilocks, Billy Goats Gruff, Three Blind Mice, Humpty Dumpty.*

"The Books from Barely There" series; all illustrated by Wendy Edelson; all published by Multnomah, 1988: *Fiddler; Shadow Chaser; Gozzamer; Derby Downs.*

"The Simple Folk" series; all illustrated by Ilona Steelhammer; all published by Ideals, 1988: *Picnic; Kind and Gentle Ladies; Chores; Nosey Birds.*

"The Snuffin Chronicles" series; all illustrated by Richard McNatt; all published by Ideals, 1988: *Snarly Snuffin; Rooty Tooty Snooty; Snively Snuffin; The Gruffins.*

The egg crickled and cracked. ■ (From *Tee-Tee* by Stephen Cosgrove. Illustrated by Robin James.)

The presses would begin to roll and everybugg rushed to put out the morning edition. ■ (From
Shutterbugg by Stephen Cosgrove. Illustrated by Charles Reasoner.)

ADAPTATIONS: ''Catundra'' (cassette), Society for Visual
Education, 1979; ''Kartusch'' (cassette), Society for Visual
Education, 1979; ''Little Mouse on the Prairie'' (cassette),
Society for Visual Education, 1979; ''Nitter Pitter'' (cassette),
Society for Visual Education, 1979; ''Misunderstood Mon-
sters'' (16mm film or videocassette; contains *Creole* by S.
Cosgrove, *The Reluctant Dragon* by Kenneth Grahame, and
Beauty and the Beast by Marianna Mayer), Bosustow Enter-
tainment, 1981; ''More and More Bugg Adventures'' (six cas-
settes; includes *Snugg and Shoe-Fly Flu, Doodle Bugg, Katy-
Didd, Cooty-Doo, Jitterbugg,* and *Shutterbugg*), Society for
Visual Education, 1986.

Cassettes; all produced by Price Stern, 1984: ''The Bugglar
Brothers''; ''Crick-ette''; ''Dune Bugg''; ''Eevil Weevil'';
''Flutterby''; ''Gabby''; ''Glance''; ''Grampa-Lop''; ''Hum-

bugg''; ''June Bugg''; ''Leo the Lop''; ''Leo the Lop: Tail
Two''; ''Little Mouse on the Prairie''; ''Lord and Lady Bugg'';
''Love Bugg''; ''Ming Ling''; ''Morgan and Me''; ''Morgan
and Yew''; ''Morgan Mine''; ''Morgan Morning''; ''Snugg'';
''Tik Tok''; ''Vee-Dubb.''

WORK IN PROGRESS: Song of the Sea, an adult fantasy, and
The Dream Stealer, illustrated by Wendy Edelson, both to be
published by Ideals.

SIDELIGHTS: ''I am what I am today because of what I was
yesterday.

''I was born in Spokane, Washington, but didn't grow up
there. My father's job as troubleshooter for Boise Cascade
Corporation uprooted us constantly. We would live someplace

fifth grade, I 'caught myself' shoplifting, and returned what I had stolen. I didn't get caught by anyone else, but made myself return the merchandise.

''There were two places, Kennewick, Washington and Boise, Idaho, that I vividly recall. In Kennewick, I was very young and very sick, but my imagination was extremely fertile then. In Boise, I was encouraged to be creative at the high school and became very active in theater. If you are too introspective, a tremendous inner pressure builds up which must be vented in one way or another. I chose acting.''

Attended Stevens College for Women on a drama scholarship. ''I was one of seven males admitted with twenty-five hundred females. I wrote a play and produced a short film as projects, and also wrote a children's play that eventually became my first book. The college had a tremendous drama program. Many influential people, including George C. Scott and Maggie Smith, had studied there. The school's television program helped me to see things in picture frames, very helpful to me as a writer today, since I write for illustrators. I have to direct an illustrator through a story so he may see it exactly as I do.''

Opting for a business career, Cosgrove briefly abandoned his love for writing. ''I was vice-president of an investment company. I wore a three-piece suit, made lots of money, and was

"I am so sorry, Mother!" ■ (From *Crickle-Crack* by Stephen Cosgrove. Illustrated by Robin James.)

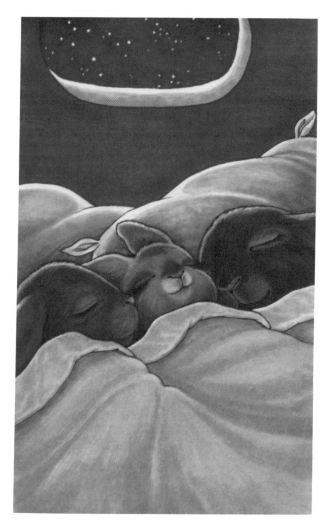

for a year, maybe two, and move again. I learned to entertain myself. When you move you don't have friends, so my friends became books. From the age of five or six I read a great deal of fantasy, including Grimm and Andre Norton. I was asthmatic and not really well when I was little and had to rely on myself because I couldn't go out and play. So I stayed inside and played. Being trapped in a bed all summer, you just let your mind exercise for you.

''I had two older brothers and a younger sister, but I felt isolated. I was the little kid brother nobody wanted around. It was actually a benefit since my imaginative friends and my imaginative relatives were the real thing to me.

''I had this very personal relationship with God that overpowered everything. God let me do things and guided me, which I accepted wholeheartedly. My brothers and sister called me the preacher, not because I quoted biblical passages, but because I preached about honesty. I would be as strict with myself as I was with them. I always had a sense of right and wrong and fair play. That's not to say I was the perfect child. I could be a real brat. I used to chase my brothers around the house with a bible shouting, 'God will get you if you aren't good!' That would scare them usually until they realized I was holding a book of Aesop's fables and not the Bible. Then, I would usually get pounded into the ground. When I was in

Then, because it was late, the three of them curled up beneath quilts of eiderdown. ■ (From *Buttermilk Bear* by Stephen Cosgrove. Illustrated by Robin James.)

very successful. My wife at the time (we were subsequently divorced), asked me to go to a bookstore and buy a book for my daughter. I picked up two textbooks, some Golden Books, and Dr. Seuss' *Cat in the Hat,* which I had never seen before. The cat, I felt, looked like it had been run over by a Mack truck and I couldn't understand the nonsensical lines. That's not to say there's anything wrong with Dr. Seuss or his books, but it wasn't what I was looking for. I was looking for something that I thought I may have read as a child, or may have imagined. I literally sat down that night, took an old play that I had called 'Barnaby Bumble,' and turned it into a book by the same title. It was hideous, but I discovered that I had a gift—the gift of telling stories. I am not talented, that is to say, I didn't learn that which I do. Rather my story telling boils from the inside. As is the responsibility of all gifts, they have to be given back in form. Within days I started telling anyone who would listen, 'I'm going to be an author; I'm going to write children's books.' They all thought I was nuts.''

Before he left his position with the investment company, Cosgrove met Robin James, who became the illustrator for his children's books. ''Our meeting was an act of serendipity. During a meeting with a client, a man stuck his head in the door of my office and asked me if I was looking for an illustrator. He gave me Robin's name.''

Serendipity Communications Ltd. was formed because Cosgrove could not agree with the editorial and creative policies of the New York publisher who wanted the books. He believed it was possible to create inexpensive fantasy books for children without giving up the quality of production. Since then, the books have been distributed in Canada, Africa, Australia, and Europe, and published in Spanish, German, French, Japanese, and Italian. ''Originally we sent our manuscripts to several publishers. One came back to us and offered us a very large contract with a very strong advance, but they wanted to make changes in the art work and take the morals out of the stories. They wanted to turn them into nonsensical rhymes with a Dr. Seuss approach. I refused to imitate.

''Originally everything we did, or at least Serendipity did, was only in paperback form and to the retail trade. Hardcover books were only bought through book clubs. Libraries were ignored, although there are library editions of our books now available.

''Today Serendipity books have sold over one hundred million copies. The books are highly illustrated fantasies, very metaphorical, since each one of them has a basic moral to it. Whether it is a simple thing like cleaning up your room or a complex understanding of death, which we did in *The Dream Tree,* we do have a broad philosophical approach to basic human values.

''I didn't sit down and consciously decide to write books with intrinsic morals. My imprint is on every book because of the way I write—flowery and moralistic. They are all fantasies with high adventure and although written in prose, they have rhythm. What I try to teach children is not only basic moral values, but the fact that no matter what they read, whether it be my book, a science-fiction book, or a romantic novel, they are going to gain something from it. Mine are a little more blatant.

''The first time that I actually took a central idea and a basic location and expanded it was with the 'Buggs' series. Like the 'Serendipity' books, each book has a separate title, with individual characters doing unique things. Presently, Chuck Reasoner, the illustrator, and I have done eighteen books, with thirty-five more scheduled for 1988.

The princess had the very good fortune of catching her dress on a limb. ■ (From *Morgan Mine* by Stephen Cosgrove. Illustrated by Robin James.)

''The 'Bumble B. Bear' series originated with a request from Price Stern asking for a pre-reader series with a central character. I conceived the 'Bumble B. Bear' series and the 'Baby Bunny' books with characters that could deal with simple things that kids that age deal with, like taking a bath, getting dirty, working in the garden, going with Dad in the car—very elementary things.

''I now work with eight illustrators. I write the story, lay it out, and then read it to them. As soon as I am sure they have the idea in their minds, I let them loose. I literally design the pages because I know what the art work should look like. I can see it, but I just can't draw it.

''Many times I spend days dreaming up titles. I will come up with characters that I like or titles that I like. The characters usually tell me great stories, but I am not writing at this point. It's a mental process—I will carry books for six or seven years in my mind before I am actually ready to sit down and do an outline. I may have a title; I may have simple episodes that I'll think about for years and years. When I do sit down to write, I'm ready. I do an outline first. Then I sit at my word processor and tell the story from the outline, which contains the pictures that I will break down page by page.''

Cosgrove's ideas come from common, everyday happenings. ''I live, I observe, I reflect. I never take myself seriously. I can't. There are stories everywhere. You don't have to go places. You can sit in your backyard or take a walk or go to a movie. Start observing, imagining and dreaming. I can't emphasize dreaming enough. That's why I call myself the 'DreamMaker' now. That's what I do—I make dreams. I never stop.

''When children don't understand what I am talking about, I ask them if they ever look out a window during school time, see a cloud gliding across the sky and wonder what it would be like to walk on it. I tell them to just sit and keep looking until they can almost do it. To me the game of 'what if' is the first step I take to begin the dream process. Sometimes I listen to music to build mood and suddenly the characters begin to dance and move around.''

Cosgrove has given seminars on motivating children for teachers. ''We are taught by our educational process, our parents, our peers, and our teachers, to shut off the subconscious and use only the conscious mind. When I talk to students, I usually do a closed seminar with their teachers to talk about daydreaming and tricks to stimulate it. I encourage teachers to use music in the classroom and to have a day-dreaming hour once a week where everybody in the class just sits back and does nothing but listen to music with a piece of blank paper on his table. They don't have to write if they don't want to, but if they see something they can jot it down.

''Adults need dreams, too. Right now television takes all the dreams away. It's a massive sponge that does all your thinking for you. At times we must turn it off. I'm as bad as everyone else. I love to watch certain shows. But if that is your only

Morethansmall. ■ (From *Katy-Did* by Stephen Cosgrove. Illustrated by Charles Reasoner.)

(From *Gimme* by Stephen Cosgrove. Illustrated by Charles Reasoner.)

form of entertainment, take it away. If that is the only way you dream, then you are losing something.''

The ''Serendipity'' series has been adapted for television as an animated program. Presently, one of Cosgrove's projects is working on developing a Saturday morning series. ''We did a library special with 'Misunderstood Monster' for CBS-TV, and are working with ABC-TV now to develop new programs. 'Serendipity,' I believe, is in development in Canada. We have also done a series in Japan. What I hope is that the characters that I develop will maintain a moral value rather than non-sensical violence during the half-hour of storytelling.

''Children are still children and we, as adults, have a responsibility to guide them. The big toy companies have a tendency to follow whatever is trendy. And violence right now is trendy. So there's this compelling desire to see violence on Saturday morning and that's wrong. Children need something much more fantasy-oriented.''

Since 1979, Serendipity Press has become an imprint of Price Stern. ''My choices were limited: be a publisher or an author, an empire builder or a dream maker. I couldn't be all. I chose to write and to dream. Although Price Stern publishes my books now, I still fight them over the morals and the values in my books. I think it's time that publishers realize that they are a public press and have a responsibility to give people something more than just the easy way out. I keep hoping that publishers will get to the point where they say that they are a public trust and have a responsibility to something more than selling a book. It's hard on a mass market level. You are dealing with an individual who rarely reads, who impulsively buys a book for his child, and grabs something that looks good. What he doesn't do is look at what's inside, and he must. He is allowing publishers to 'cop out.' If the buyer, the parents, would read these books, there would be more value in literature.''

Besides children's books, Cosgrove has recently written an illustrated adult novel. ''*Song of the Sea* is an adult fantasy about whales told from a whale's perspective of why they beach themselves. It's more than a metaphor, it's an allegory of man's inhumanity to man and his habit of allowing things to go on because they are a tradition. In this case, the whales beach themselves because it is an honor to die. It is a ritualistic suicide with one whale by the name of Harmony elected to record this 'song of the sea' as the others prepare to die. The final part of the story is concerned with Harmony's conflict over whether the story should be passed on.''

Cosgrove writes his stories at his twelve-acre farm in the state of Washington. ''I usually get up at three o'clock in the morning, seven days a week. I make a pot of coffee, toss it into a thermos bottle, and walk down to the barn with my dog. I have a big barn that has been converted into a massive studio. Now, the strange thing about this studio is that there are no windows. No light is allowed to come in. The reason is that I need, when I go in there, to dream and to manufacture my own environment. If I can see outside, I'm never going to work. What I did was to create a controlled studio environment. Usually I warm myself up by reading fan mail for thirty minutes or so, and by four o'clock I'm ready to begin working on whatever book or books I'm writing at the time. I usually work until ten o'clock. Then I stop, run my errands for the day, and work for two or three hours in the afternoon taking notes or dealing with publishers on the actual sales of my books. On weekends, I write until ten o'clock in the morning, and then 'goof off' for the rest of the day. I love what I do. My life, my hobby, my work is writing. I love to write.''

He advises young people who want to write to ''sit down in their chairs. That's it! It is just a matter of discipline. Discipline has to be learned. Even today I still fight it. I'd rather play.''

FOR MORE INFORMATION SEE: Judi Modie, ''Author: 'I'll Never Grow Old,' '' *Seattle Post-Intelligencer*, November 24, 1974; Barbara Nykoruk, editor, *Authors in the News*, Gale, 1976.

CUMMINGS, Parke 1902-1987

OBITUARY NOTICE—See sketch in *SATA* Volume 2: Born October 8, 1902, in West Medford, Mass.; died following a heart attack, July 1, 1987, in Westport, Conn. Author. Known for his humor, Cummings wrote the satirical *Whimsey Report; or, Sex Isn't Everything*, a parody of sex researcher Alfred Kinsey's famed report. His subsequent books include *The Dictionary of Sports*, *American Tennis: The Story of a Game and Its People*, and a collection of essays titled *The Fly in the Martini*. Cummings also wrote *I'm Telling You Kids for the Last Time*, a child care guide, and contributed humor and verse to *New Yorker*, *Esquire*, *Saturday Evening Post*, and other national magazines.

FOR MORE INFORMATION SEE: Contemporary Authors, Permanent Series, Volume 1, Gale, 1975; *Who's Who in America*, 44th edition, Marquis, 1986. Obituaries: *New York Times*, July 2, 1987.

DANIEL, Alan 1939-

BRIEF ENTRY: Born in 1939, in Ottawa, Canada. Illustrator of books for young readers. For over two decades Daniel has illustrated a wide range of children's books, including *In Praise of Cats* (Crown, 1974) compiled by Dorothy Foster; *The Mystery of the Plum Park Pony* (Garrard, 1980) by Lynn Hall;

Mr. Peeknuff's Tiny People (Atheneum, 1981) by Donna Hill; Beatrice Schenk de Regniers' collection of poems entitled *This Big Cat and Other Cats I've Known* (Crown, 1985); and James and Deborah Howe's *Bunnicula: A Rabbit Tale of Mystery* (Atheneum, 1979). In a review of Mark Rubin's book *The Orchestra* (Douglas & McIntyre, 1984), *Bulletin of the Center for Children's Books* said: ''Both audience and performers are multi-ethnic in [Daniel's] lively line and wash drawings, which have comic touches but are scrupulously realistic in the depiction of orchestral instruments.'' *Residence:* Kitchener, Ontario, Canada.

DRACKETT, Phil(ip Arthur) 1922-
(Paul King)

PERSONAL: Born December 25, 1922, in London, England; son of Arthur Ernest (a builder) and Mary Jane (a hotelier; maiden name, King) Drackett; married Joan Isobel Davies (a journalist), June 19, 1948. *Education:* University of London, general schools certificate, 1939. *Politics:* Conservative. *Religion:* Church of England. *Home and office:* 9 Victoria Rd., Mundesley, Norfolk NR11 8JG, England.

CAREER: Worked for local and national newspapers and magazines, 1939-56; actor, 1940-45; Royal Automobile Club, director of press and public relations, 1956-79; free-lance writer and broadcaster, 1979—. *Member:* Institute of Journalists, Guild of Motoring Writers, Sports Writers Association, British Ice Hockey Writers Association, Veteran Speedway Riders Association.

WRITINGS: Fighting Days, A-American, 1944; *Come Out Fighting*, A-American, 1945; *Speedway*, W. & G. Foyle, 1951; *Motor Racing*, W. & G. Foyle, 1952; *Motoring*, W. & G. Foyle, 1955; (with Leslie Webb) *You and Your Car*, W. & G. Foyle, 1957; (with A. Thompson) *You and Your Motor Cycle*, W. & G. Foyle, 1958; *Great Moments in Motoring*, Roy, 1958; *Automobiles Work Like This*, Phoenix House, 1958,

PHIL DRACKETT

Roy, 1960; *Veteran Cars*, W. & G. Foyle, 1961; *The Young Car Driver's Companion*, Sportshelf, 1961; *Vintage Cars*, W. & G. Foyle, 1962, Octopus, 1980; *Motor Rallying*, W. & G. Foyle, 1963; *Driving Your Car: Passing the Test and After*, Sportshelf, 1964; *Taking Your Car Abroad*, W. & G. Foyle, 1965; *International Motor Racing Book*, four volumes, Souvenir Press, 1967-70; *Let's Look at Cars*, Muller, 1967; *Slot Car Racing*, Souvenir Press, 1968; *Like Father, Like Son: The Story of Malcolm and Donald Campbell*, Clifton Books, 1969.

Rally of the Forests: The Story of the RAC International Rally of Great Britain, Pelham Books, 1970; *Motor Racing Champions*, two volumes, Purnell Books, 1971-72; *The Book of the Veteran Car*, Pelham Books, 1973; *Care for Your Car*, Kenneth Mason, 1973; *The Book of Great Disasters*, Purnell Books, 1978; *The Book of Dangerman*, Purnell Books, 1979; *The Encyclopedia of the Motor Car*, Octopus, 1979; *The All-Colour World of Cars*, Octopus, 1979; *Inns and Harbours of North Norfolk*, Royal Automobile Club, 1980; *The Car Makers*, Macdonald Educational, 1980; *The Story of the RAC International Rally*, Haynes, 1980; *The Classic Mercedes-Benz*, Bison Books, 1984; *Brabham: Story of a Racing Team*, Arthur Baker, 1985; *Flashing Blades*, Crowood, 1987. Contributor to programs of British Broadcasting Corp. and Independent Television; contributor of articles to many periodicals and newspapers.

SIDELIGHTS: ''I have been keen on reading and writing ever since I was a toddler. I came from a family who was very involved in sports—my great-uncle was a world heavyweight champion, my grandfather, a professional boxer, manager and promoter, and my father—was an amateur international footballer and keen cricketer—so writings tended towards sports and various newspaper staff jobs have all been concerned with sports or motoring. I had a brief fling on the professional stage (1940-45), but eventually had to choose between stage and writing.

''Although often referred to as an author of children's books, most of my books have been for adults. However, those children's books I have written (*The Car Makers* was the most recent; *Automobiles Work Like This*, the most successful) have been written in a straight-forward fashion and I make no conscious effort to write down to children. Providing the subject matter interests them and the writing is readable, I think most children can enjoy a higher level of writing than many adults appreciate. Being a great big (elderly) kid myself, I work on the basis that if it interests me it will interest an eleven year old.

''My wife and I left the big city of London years ago to concentrate on writing and broadcasting. We live in a village on the Norfolk coast, 200 yards from the shore, and there is nothing between us and the North Pole save the North Sea.''

ESBENSEN, Barbara Juster

BRIEF ENTRY: Educator and author of poetry for children. Esbensen majored in art at the University of Wisconsin, and then taught art for several years. Her poetry has appeared in a number of anthologies and journals and in 1965 Lerner published her first collection of poems for children, *Swing Around the Sun*, illustrated by Barbara Fumagalli. Esbensen's next work, *A Celebration of Bees: Helping Children Write Poetry* (Winston Press, 1975), inspires teachers to involve students in exploring their own creative minds. *English Journal* commended the book for its ''. . . love of language and love of children . . . and love of the excitement of bringing the two together in a classroom alive with language activity.'' In addition, Esbensen has written *Cold Stars and Fireflies: Poems of the Four Seasons* (Crowell, 1984) and *Words with Wrinkled Knees* (Crowell, 1986), a collection of animal poems. *Residence:* Edina, Minn.

FITZGERALD, Merni I(ngrassia) 1955-

PERSONAL: Born February 24, 1955, in Milwaukee, Wis.; daughter of Anthony F. (a government employee) and Eleanor M. (a homemaker; maiden name, Birkholz) Ingrassia; married David Fitzgerald, March 20, 1976 (divorced, 1986); children:

The children in the Central African Republic make toys from wire and old cans. ■ (From *The Peace Corps Today* by Merni Ingrassia Fitzgerald. Photograph courtesy of the Peace Corps.)

Toni Marie, Jaimi Michelle. *Education:* James Madison University, B.S., 1976. *Home:* 236 Irving St., Falls Church, Va. 22046. *Office:* Fairfax County Park Authority, 3701 Pender Dr. Fairfax, Va. 22030.

CAREER: U.S. Peace Corps, Washington, D.C., assistant to press officer, 1983-86: Fairfax County Park Authority, Fairfax, Va., public information officer, 1986—. Past member of Virginia Governor's Overall Advisory Council on the Needs of Handicapped Persons; member of board of directors of Falls Church Cable Access Corp. and Girl Scout Council of the Nation's Capital; member of Falls Church Community Education Advisory Commission. *Member:* National Association of County Information Officers, Northern Virginia Press Club, Washington Women in Public Relations. *Awards, honors:* Named an Outstanding Child Advocate by the Virginia Division for Children, 1984; *The Peace Corps Today* was named a Children's Book of Year by the Child Study Association, 1987.

WRITINGS: The Peace Corps Today (juvenile), Dodd, 1986; *Voice of America* (juvenile), Dodd, 1987.

SIDELIGHTS: "I have always wanted to be a writer. My father wrote a sports column in the *Milwaukee Sentinel* for many years, and I wanted to be like my dad. I don't remember doing a lot of writing outside of school during my childhood, but my brothers and sisters and I made up a lot of stories and characters when we played. I have three brothers and four sisters, so there was always someone to share games and fun. My older brother Mike and I created the 'Good Mike and Good Mern' stories. Many a snowy afternoon in Wisconsin would find us fighting the 'Big J' gang as our alter egos. The stories became quite involved, and eventually included 'Inspector Mike and Inspector Mern,' as well as 'Detective Mike and Detective Mern.' Despite this early experience in creativity, my two books are nonfiction.

"I enjoy writing for children because I know children so well. In addition to my experiences with my two daughters, I have been a Brownie Girl Scout Leader for the past eleven years. Every year, I have from twenty-three to twenty-eight little girls in my troop. I have learned a lot from my experiences with them; some things have gone very well, and some things have flopped, but it has always taught me something about what children like, hate and think.

"One year we entered a float in the Christmas parade in downtown Harrisonburg, Virginia where I lived for ten years. We were late to begin with, and Santa was impatiently waiting for us so that he could ride in the last float of the parade. Our float finally came; we managed in the snow to get all the little girls, dressed as toys, onto the flatbed truck. I started the taped holiday music, took a breath and began to relax. Then, one of the strangest happenings to ever occur in a parade occurred. Our wooden gingerbread house, the centerpiece of our toyland float, got tangled in the electrical wires above the street. The float could not move, and we looked back at a very upset Santa in the float behind us. He was already over a block behind the rest of the parade due to our tardy arrival, now he was delayed again. I can only imagine what all the children thought when they realized that we were holding up Santa Claus! We finally unceremoniously dumped the gingerbread house at the side of the street, and continued on our way. The girls had a grand time despite all!

"My Brownie experiences have taught me that children can do almost anything, and should certainly be allowed to at least try. My two books are both about U.S. government agencies.

But I knew that they would appeal to children. Children also benefit from *The Peace Corps Today.* The profit that would usually go to the author of that book (me), instead goes to the Peace Corps Partnership Program to help build schools and facilities for children and adults in the countries served by the Peace Corps.''

HOBBIES AND OTHER INTERESTS: "I collect wooden nutcrackers; I have over fifty, including the usual soldiers, and more unusual nutcrackers such as the Arabian nutcracker, the woman nutcracker, and the fox nutcracker dressed for the hunt.''

FRASCONI, Antonio   1919-

PERSONAL: Born April 28, 1919, in Buenos Aires, Argentina; came to United States in 1945; son of Franco (a chef) and Armida (a restauranteur; maiden name, Carbonai) Frasconi; married Leona Pierce (an artist), July 18, 1951; children: Pablo, Miguel. *Education:* Attended Círculo de Bellas Artes (Montevideo); studied at Art Students League (New York), 1945-46; studied mural painting at New School for Social Research, 1947-48. *Home and studio:* 26 Dock Rd., South Norwalk, Conn. 06854. *Agent:* Terry Dintenfass, Inc. Gallery, 50 West 57th St., New York, N.Y. 10019; Weyhe Gallery, 794 Lexington Ave., New York, N.Y. 10021; and Jane Haslem Gallery, 406 7th St. N.W., Washington, D.C. 20004. *Office:* Visual Arts Dept., State University of New York College at Purchase, Purchase, N.Y. 10577.

CAREER: Graphic artist and illustrator. *Marcha* and *La Linea Maginot* (weeklies), Montevideo, Uruguay, political cartoonist, 1940; New School for Social Research, New York, N.Y., member of art faculty, 1951-57; University of Hawaii, Honolulu, artist-in-residence, 1964; State University of New York College at Purchase, adjunct associate professor of visual arts, 1973-77, associate professor, 1977-79; professor of visual arts, 1979—. Has also taught at Vassar College, Brooklyn Museum, California State College at Hayward, University of California at Berkeley, and Carnegie-Mellon University; artist-

ANTONIO FRASCONI

(From *The Face of Edgar Allan Poe: With a Note on Poe by Charles Baudelaire.* Illustrated by Antonio Frasconi.)

in-residence, Dartmouth College, 1984, and Arizona State University, 1985; lecturer. Member of Mayor's Committee for Art in Public Places, Norwalk, Conn., 1978, and of Arts Review Committee, Westchester County, N.Y., 1980.

EXHIBITIONS: Ateneo de Montevideo, Uruguay, 1939, 1944; Santa Barbara Museum of Art, Calif., 1946, 1955, 1977; Brooklyn Museum of Arts and Sciences, New York, 1946; Weyhe Gallery, New York City, 1948-54, 1956, 1960-61, 1964-65, 1972.

San Francisco Museum of Art, Calif., 1950, 1975; Baltimore Museum of Art, Md., 1951, 1953, (retrospective) 1963; "The Work of Antonio Frasconi 1943-1952" (retrospective), Cleveland Museum of Art, Ohio, 1952; J. B. Speed Art Museum, Louisville, Ken., 1953; Los Angeles County Museum, Calif., 1953; Detroit Institute of Art, Mich., 1953; Smithsonian Institution, Washington, D.C., traveling exhibition, 1953-54, 1964; Minneapolis Institute of Arts, Minn., 1953-54; Fine Arts Center, Indiana University, 1953-54; Museum of Art, Rhode Island School of Design, 1953-54; Colorado Springs Fine Arts Center, Colo., 1953-54; School of Fine and Applied Arts, Ohio State University, 1953-54; Joslyn Art Museum, Omaha, Neb., 1953-54; Currier Gallery of Art, Manchester, N.H., 1955; Summit Art Association, Summit, N.J., 1955; Fort Worth Art Center, Tex., 1955; Chattanooga Art Association, George Thomas Hunter Gallery of Art, Tenn., 1955; University of Arkansas, 1955; University of Utah, 1955; Davison Art Cen-

ter, Wesleyan University, Middletown, Conn., 1956; University of Maine, Orono, 1956; Slater Memorial Museum, Norwich, Conn., 1957; Scripps College, Claremont, Calif., 1958; Berea College, 1958; Collectors Art Center, Tallahassee, Fla., 1958; Allegheny State College, 1959; Atlanta Art Institute, Ga., 1959; Carnegie College of Fine Arts, 1959; Marion Koogler McNay Art Institute, San Antonio, Tex., 1959.

(Retrospective) Salón Municípal, Montevideo, Uruguay, 1961; Terry Dintenfass Gallery, New York, N.Y., 1962, 1963, 1966, 1971, 1972, 1979, 1982, 1983; Print Club of Philadelphia, Pa., 1962; Pennsylvania State University, 1963; Ankrum Gallery, Los Angeles, Calif., 1963; "Antonio Frasconi Prints and Illustrated Books 1944-1964" (retrospective), Brooklyn Museum, 1964; "The Woodcuts of Antonio Frasconi," Penelope Galería d'Arte, Rome, Italy, 1967; Instituto General Electric, Montevideo, Uruguay, 1967; Salón Nacional de Bellas Artes, 1967; Galería Colibri, San Juan, Puerto Rico, 1967; Esposizione Biennale Internazionale d'Arte, Venice, Italy, 1968; Instituto de Cultura Puertorriqueña, San Juan, Puerto Rico, 1969, 1976.

Biennale of Latin American Graphic Art, Puerto Rico, 1974; "Recent Work," Esther Bear Gallery, Santa Barbara, Calif., 1975; International Biennial Exhibition of Prints, Tokyo, Japan, 1975; Museo de Arte Moderno, Cali, Colombia, 1976; (retrospective) Jane Haslem Gallery, Washington, D.C., 1976; La Casa del Libro, San Juan, Puerto Rico, 1976; Museum of Art, Fribourg, Switzerland, 1976; "Obra Grafica de Antonio Frasconi, 1943-1975" (retrospective), Museo del Grabado Latinoamericano, San Juan, Puerto Rico, 1976; American Institute of Graphic Arts, New York, N.Y., 1976, 1980; Austin Art Center, Trinity College, Hartford, Conn., 1976; Smithsonian Institution, 1976, 1986; "Woodcuts by Antonio Fras-

(From "Sands at Seventy" in *Overhead the Sun: Lines from Walt Whitman.* Edited and illustrated by Antonio Frasconi.)

coni, 1950-1975'' (traveling exhibition), Missouri State Council on the Arts, St. Louis, 1976-77; Neuberger Museum, State University of New York College at Purchase, N.Y., 1976-77; Cayman Gallery, New York, 1977; Zoller Gallery, Pennsylvania State University, University Park, 1977; Visual Images Art Gallery, Wellfleet, Mass., 1977; State University of New York College at Purchase, 1978, 1983; Annual Exhibition, National Academy of Design, New York, 1979, 1983, 1985.

International Biennial of Graphic Art, Ljubljana, Yugoslavia, 1980; Philadelphia Art Alliance, Pa., 1980; "Electroworks," Cooper-Hewitt Museum, N.Y., 1980; "Views of South Norwalk," Lockwood Mathews Mansion, South Norwalk, Conn., 1980; "Contemporary American Prints and Drawings 1940-1980," National Gallery of Art, Washington, D.C., 1981; "American Prints and Printmaking 1956-1981," Pratt Graphic Center, N.Y., 1981; "Printmakers' Prints," Amarillo Art Center, Tex., 1981; "20 X 20," Grace Borgenicht Gallery, N.Y., 1982; International Print Exhibit, Taipei Museum of Fine Arts, Taiwan, China, 1983; Biennale of Graphic Design, Brno, Czechoslovakia, 1983; "Portraits on a Human Scale," Whitney Museum of American Art, N.Y., 1983; "Prints from Blocks—Gauguin to Now," Museum of Modern Art, N.Y., 1983; Xylon International Triennial Exhibition of Woodcuts, Winterhur, Switzerland, 1983; "Woodcuts and Illustrated Books," Baker Library, Dartmouth College, 1984; Third International Biennial Exhibition of Drawings and Graphics, Tuzla, Yugoslavia, 1984; "Art against War: 400 Years of Protest Art," Parsons School Art Gallery, N.Y., 1984; Society of Wood Engravers, Bristol, England, 1985; "Books and Posters of Antonio Frasconi," State University of New York, Old Westbury, Long Island, N.Y., 1985; University of Puerto Rico Museum, San Juan, 1986; "Repression, Exilio y Democracia—La Cultura Uruguaya," University of Maryland, 1986; "1986 Biennial," Organization of International Biennial of Illustrations, Tokyo, Japan, 1986; "196 Fiera del Libro," Bologna, Italy, 1986; Museo d'Arte Contemporanea, Bologna, 1986; Museum of Contemporary Arts, N.Y., 1986; Commission on the Arts Showcase Gallery, Conn., 1987.

Work represented in many permanent collections, including Museum of Fine Arts, Boston, Mass.; Fogg Art Museum, Harvard University, Cambridge, Mass.; Bibliotheque National, Paris, France; Library of Congress, Washington, D.C.; Museum of Modern Art, New York, N.Y.; Metropolitan Museum of Art, New York, N.Y.; Art Institute of Chicago, Ill.; Detroit Institute of Arts, Mich.; Santa Barbara Museum of Art, Calif.; San Diego Museum of Art, Calif.; Brooklyn Museum, N.Y.; St. Louis Museum, Mo.; Casa Americas, Havana, Cuba; Museo Nacional de Bellas Artes, Montevideo, Uruguay; Museo Municipal Juan M. Blanes, Montevideo, Uruguay; Newark Museum, N.J.; Philadelphia Museum of Art, Penn.; Honolulu Academy of Arts, Hawaii; Akron Art Institute, Ohio; Cleveland Museum of Art, Ohio; Fort Worth Art Association, Tex.; Des Moines Art Center, Iowa; University of Notre Dame, Ind.; Joslyn Art Museum, Omaha, Neb.; Graphic Arts Collection, Princeton University, N.J.; Seattle Art Museum, Wash.; Springfield Art Museum, Mo.; University of Puerto Rico; Cincinnati Art Museum, Ohio; Fort Worth Art Association, Tex.; J. B. Speed Art Museum, Louisville, Ken.; New Britain Museum, Conn.; New York Public Library Collection, N.Y.; Wadsworth Atheneum, Hartford, Conn.; Baltimore Museum of Art, Md.; Arts Council of Great Britain, London, England; Museum of Art, Rhode Island School of Design, Providence; National Portrait Gallery, Washington, D.C.; Grunwald Center for the Graphic Arts, University of California, Los Angeles.

AWARDS, HONORS: Purchase Prize, Brooklyn Museum, 1946, and University of Nebraska, 1951; Philadelphia Print Club

Prize, 1951; Guggenheim Inter-American Fellowship in graphic arts, 1952; Erickson Award from the Society of American Graphic Artists, 1952; Yaddo scholarship, 1952; Joseph Pennell Memorial Medal from the Pennsylvania Academy of the Fine Arts, 1953; National Institute of Arts and Letters grant, 1954.

Twelve Fables of Aesop was chosen one of American Institute of Graphic Arts 50 Books of the Year, 1955, *Birds from My Homeland,* 1958, *The Face of Edgar Allan Poe,* 1959, *Known Fables,* 1964, and *The Cantilever Rainbow,* 1965; *See and Say* was selected one of *New York Times* Best Illustrated Books of the Year, 1955, *The House That Jack Built,* 1958, *The Snow and the Sun,* 1961, and *Monkey Puzzle and Other Poems,* 1985; First Prize for Book Illustration from the Limited Editions Club and the Society of American Graphic Artists, 1956; *The House That Jack Built* was selected one of the American Institute of Graphic Art's Children's Books, 1958-60 and *Unstill Life* and *Overhead the Sun,* 1970; Caldecott Honor Book from the American Library Association, 1959, for *The House That Jack Built.*

Grand Prix from the Venice Film Festival, 1960, for film, "The Neighboring Shore"; Tamarind Lithography Workshop grant, 1962; winner of competition to design postage stamp honoring National Academy of Science, 1963; Joseph H. Hirshorn Foundation Prize from the Society of American Graphic Artists, 1963; W. H. Walker Prize from Philadelphia Print Club, 1964; Le Prix du President du Comite National de la Region de la Moravie at the Second Biennale d'Art Graphique, Brno, Czechoslovakia, 1966; prize of Salón Nacional de Bellas Artes, Montevideo, Uruguay, 1967; Gran Premio from the Exposition de la Habana, Cuba, 1968; named National Academician by the National Academy of Design, N.Y., 1969.

Commissioned by the Metropolitan Museum of Art, N.Y., for a series of Christmas ornaments "Snow Flakes," 1972; *Crickets and Frogs* was included in the American Institute of Graphic Arts Children's Book Show, 1973-74; *The Elephant and His Secret* was selected one of Child Study Association's Children's Books of the Year, 1974; grant from the Connecticut Commission on the Arts, 1974; Prize of Ninth International Biennial of Arts, Tokyo, Japan, 1975; grant from the Xerox Corporation, 1978, for experimentation with the Xerox Color Copier; Cannon Prize from the National Academy of Design, N.Y., 1979.

Ralph Fabri Prize from the National Academy of Design, 1983; Chancellor's Award from the State University of New York, 1983, for excellence in teaching; Award from the Bienal de la Habana-Comision Nacional Cubana de la UNESCO, 1984; Meissner Prize from the National Academy of Design, 1985; *Monkey Puzzle and Other Poems* was included in the American Institute of Graphic Arts Book Show, 1985; Purchase Award from the American Academy and the Institute of Arts and Letters, 1986; Distinguished Teaching Professor from the State University of New York College at Purchase, 1986.

WRITINGS—All self-illustrated: See and Say: A Picture Book in Four Languages (ALA Notable Book), Harcourt, 1955; *The House That Jack Built: A Picture Book in Two Languages* (ALA Notable Book), Harcourt, 1958; *The Snow and the Sun/ La nieve y el sol: A South American Folk Rhyme in Two Languages* (ALA Notable Book; *Horn Book* honor list), Harcourt, 1961; *A Sunday in Monterey,* Harcourt, 1964; *See Again, Say Again: A Picture Book in Four Languages,* Harcourt, 1964; *Kaleidoscope in Woodcuts,* Harcourt, 1968; (editor) Walt Whitman, *Overhead the Sun: Lines from Walt Whitman* (ALA Notable Book), Farrar, Straus, 1969; (editor) Herman Mel-

Beneath him on the ground, a lean young fox crouched and watched and waited. ■ (From "The Flattered Raven and Crafty Fox" in *12 Fables of Aesop,* retold by Glenway Wescott. Illustrated by Antonio Frasconi.)

ville, _On the Slain Collegians: Selections from Poems_, Farrar, Straus, 1971; _Antonio Frasconi's World_, Macmillan, 1974; _Frasconi Against the Grain: The Woodcuts of Antonio Frasconi_, Macmillan, 1974.

Illustrator: Glenway Wescott, reteller, _12 Fables of Aesop_, Museum of Modern Art, 1954, revised edition, 1964; Jorge Luis Borges, _Dreamtigers_, University of Texas Press, 1964; Ruth Krauss, _The Cantilever Rainbow_, Pantheon, 1965; Pablo Neruda (pseudonym of Neftali R. R. Basulato), _Bestiary/Bestiario_ (verse), translated by Elsa Neuberger, Harcourt, 1965; Louis Untermeyer, editor, _Love Lyrics_, Odyssey, 1965; M. Benedetti, editor, _Unstill Life: An Introduction to the Spanish Poetry of Latin America_, Harcourt, 1969.

Isaac B. Singer, _Elijah the Slave: A Hebrew Legend Retold_, Farrar, Strauss, 1970; Gabriela Mistral (pseudonym of Lucila Godoy Alcayaga), _Selected Poems of Gabriela Mistral_, Johns Hopkins, 1970; G. Mistral, _Crickets and Frogs: A Fable in Spanish and English_, translation by Doris Dana, Atheneum, 1972; G. Mistral, _The Elephant and His Secret_, translation by D. Dana, Atheneum, 1974; Myra Cohn Livingston, editor, _One Little Room, an Everywhere: Poems of Love_, Atheneum, 1975; Penelope Farmer, compiler, _Beginnings: Creation Myths of the World_, Chatto & Windus, 1978, Atheneum, 1979; Norma Farber, _How the Left-Behind Beasts Built Ararat_, Walker, 1978; Jan Wahl, _The Little Blind Goat_, Stemmer House, 1981; Merce Rodereda, _The Salamander_, Red Ozier Press, 1982; I. B. Singer, _Yentl the Yeshiva Boy_, translated by Marion Magid and Elizabeth Pollet, Farrar, Straus, 1983; M. C. Livingston, _Monkey Puzzle and Other Poems_, Atheneum, 1984; Muso Soseki, _Sun at Midnight_ (poems), translated from Japanese by W. S. Merwin, Nadja, 1986.

Limited editions; all illustrated with woodcuts; all privately printed, except as noted: Aesop, _Some Well Known Fables_, 1950; _A Book of Vegetable Plants_, 1951; _Foothill Dairy_, 1951-52; _The World Upside Down_, 1952; _The Fulton Fish Market_, 1953; Federico García Lorca, _2 Poemas de Federico García Lorca: Romance de la luna, luna; Romance de la Guardia Civil Española_, 1953; _Outdoors_, 1953; _Plants, Ants and Other Insects_, 1953; _Santa Barbara_, 1953; _The Acrobats_, 1954; _El Camino Real_, 1954; _Lettuce Country_, 1954; _Printing with Dough_, 1954; _A Book of Many Suns_, 1955; _Fire Island Dunes_, 1955; _High Tide_, 1955; Abraham Lincoln, _The Fundamental Creed of Abraham Lincoln: A Selection from His Writings and Speeches_, edited by Earl Schenk Miers, 1956; _An Old Czech Carol_, Murray Printers, 1956; _Woodcuts 1957_, Spiral, 1957, also published as _Woodcuts: With Comments by Antonio Frasconi_, Weyhe, 1957; _Homage to Thelonious Monk_, 1958; _Birds from My Homeland: Ten Hand-Colored Woodcuts with Notes from W. H. Hudson's "Birds of La Plata"_, Roodenko, 1958; _A Calendar for 1960_, 1959; _The Face of Edgar Allan Poe: With a Note on Poe by Charles Baudelaire_, Roodenko, 1959.

Walt Whitman, _A Whitman Portrait_, Spiral, 1960; _Six Spanish Nursery Rhymes_, 1960; _American Wild Flowers_, 1961; Berthold Brecht, _Das Lied vom Sa-mann_, Spiral, 1961; _Oda a Lorca_, 1962; _Known Fables_, Spiral, 1964; _Six South American Folk Rhymes about Love: With Woodcuts_, Spiral, 1964; _An Appointment Calendar for 1966_, Baltimore Museum of Art, 1965; Henry David Thoreau, _A Vision of Thoreau_, Spiral, 1965; F. García Lorca, _Llanto por Ignacio Sanches Mejías_, 1967; _The Portrait_, 1967; _Quattro facciate_, 1967; _Viet Nam!_, 1967; Mario Benedetti, selector, _19 Poems de Hispano América_, 1969; _Vedute di Venezia_, Spiral, 1969.

Fourteen Americans, 1974; _Venice Remembered_, 1974; _A View_

of Tuscany, 1974; _Cantos a García Lorca_, 1974-75; _The Seasons on the Sound_, 1974-75; _The Sound_, 1974-75; _Frasconi's Composite Side Show_, 1978; _Frasconi's Night Creatures_, 1978; _The Tides at Village Creek_, 1979.

Monet Gardens, Giverny, 1980; _The USA from the San Francisco-Oakland Bay Bridge, California to the George Washington Bridge, New York, Every Six Miles_, 1982; _Ten Views of Rome_, 1983; Theodore Low De Vinne, _The First Editor: Aldus Pius Manutius_, 1983; _Los Desaparecidos_, 1984; Italo Calvino, _Prima che tu dica "Pronto"_, translated by William Weaver, Plain Wrapper Press, 1985; _Travels through Tuscany_, 1985; _Views of Venice by Day and Night_, 1986.

Film: "The Neighboring Shore" Sextant, 1960.

Contributor of illustrations to _New Republic_ and _Fortune_.

ADAPTATIONS: "See and Say" (sound filmstrip), Weston Woods, 1964. _Crickets and Frogs_ is available as a Braille book.

SIDELIGHTS: **April 28, 1919.** Born in Buenos Aires, Argentina, Frasconi was the son of Italian parents who had immigrated to South America five years before. When he was only two weeks old, he moved with his family to Uruguay. "Language was always a question (so I felt). At home our parents spoke Italian but outside we stumbled—at the beginning—with Spanish. Montevideo became our home, and Spanish our language, except for my mother who still speaks Italian."

Music, particularly opera, was a family interest. Frasconi's parents felt that drawing, however, was a waste of time. Frasconi, therefore, practiced his art without their approval, stealing free moments to develop his "hidden" talents. "I always liked to draw. That pleasure started so early I can't remember how old I was when it began. I remember my mother always urging me to go out and play, but my only sport was soccer, and we played that on Sunday. Much of the time, I was what I guess Americans would call a loner.

". . . My mother was born in Arezzo, in Tuscany, and Italians of that time—the 1890s, early 1900s—had an overrespect for art. They thought that art, in a sense, was made by the gods. Or rather, that artistic talent was some kind of divine gift. In Arezzo itself, in the church of San Francesco, there are Piero della Francesca's frescoes of _The Story of the True Cross_. But my mother couldn't conceive they had been done by a man who worked with paints, not by a god. She felt that if I had the divine gift, I wouldn't be where I was—part of a working class family that was in the restaurant business." [Nat Hentoff, "Introduction," _Frasconi Against the Grain: The Woodcuts of Antonio Frasconi_, Macmillan, 1974.[1]]

As a child, Frasconi cherished books and painting, taking his first job, at twelve, as a printer's apprentice. "There is always something to say about what is real in our lives. From the time I was a boy, I have had an idea of the immensity of the world in which an artist should function. I always wanted to communicate in my work what is dearest to me. Not death, but life itself, and the greatness of being alive."[1]

Always interested in politics and involved in his community, Frasconi was drawing political cartoons and, as a teenager, signing them "Chiquito." "There was a great deal of social awareness in Uruguay when I was growing up. We had a good popular press, and we read about everything that was going on in the world. The Spanish Civil War, for instance, affected us the way the Vietnam War affected many Americans during

(From "Weeping Mulberry" in *Monkey Puzzle and Other Poems* by Myra Cohn Livingston.
Illustrated by Antonio Frasconi.)

the 1960s. You had to take a position. If you were an artist you still had to take a position."[1]

Besides drawing posters and political caricatures, Frasconi assisted his family in their restaurant business, worked for the government drawing graphs, and studied at night at the Círculo de Belles Artes, the "official" fine arts academy of Uruguay. "I never really was a painter. In Uruguay, in Latin America in my time, there was a tradition of woodcuts and linoleum cuts. Artists also did murals for the schools, book illustrations, posters. The sense was that an artist should function within his society and should be aware of and try to fulfill some of the needs of that society."[1]

In Uruguay, Frasconi established a considerable reputation as both painter and printmaker, although by the early 1940s he had almost entirely abandoned painting for printmaking.

1945. Came to the United States as the recipient of an Inter-American fellowship from the Guggenheim Memorial Foundation. Frasconi had hoped to study under the German expressionist George Grosz, who taught at the Art Students League in New York City. "When I was growing up in Uruguay, the United States—culturally and even politically—was our vision of the New World. In old times, if you were something of an artist, you wanted to go to Paris or Rome. But I wanted to go to New York City. We had heard about La Guardia and Roosevelt and all the wonderful things that were happening in the United States. There was a sense of the brewing of a country—a culture in a state of ebullience.

"If there is one thing I am sorry about, it is that in some ways I came too late. Also my biggest frustration was that by the time I did come, George Grosz had left and had returned to Germany where he died. I never met him. As for the change in America itself from what I had imagined it to be, I arrived in 1945, just about the time the Cold War was beginning. I had a cartoon in the first issue of *The National Guardian*—Churchill of Fulton, Missouri, rattling the bomb. Then there was the McCarthy period, and the deadness of the 1950s."[1]

Instead of studying under the tutelage of Grosz, Frasconi studied art with the Japanese-born artist Yasuo Kuniyoshi at the Art Students League. "I learned from him what not to be. He was quite negative about me because I used bright colors, primary colors. In his own work, until four or five years before he died, Kuniyoshi used sepia, brown, black—very earthy colors. Later in life, he just used purple and orange. I was mystified that he would criticize me on the basis of what colors I used. I mean, you can criticize a piece of art on any number of grounds, but not for its colors. The colors you use are your way of seeing things."[1]

When Frasconi first came to the States, he was primarily concerned with being a painter. Gradually, however, he turned his attention to working with woodcuts. ". . . If you are an artist you must do what you really want to do, and now I find that doing woodcuts is not only an exciting medium but it is most satisfying to me. It is not the medium, it is the end result. Graphics does not limit me. Using different tools and different wood, and the problems presented by color overlay are most challenging to me. Doing woodcuts is a combination of all the media into one. I find painting limits me." [Louise Elliott Rago, "An Interview with Antonio Frasconi," *School Arts*, September, 1961.[2]]

1946. Held his first one-man American exhibition at the Santa Barbara Museum in California, followed by another at the Brooklyn Museum of Art.

1951. Married Leona Pierce, an artist whom he met at the Art Students League. During the early 1950s, Frasconi developed and refined his techniques, concentrating on his woodcuts. "No two pieces of wood are alike. Sometimes the wood gives you a break and matches your conception in the way it is grained. But often you must surrender to the grain, find the movement of the scene, the mood of the work, in the way the grain runs."[1]

Of his subject matter, Frasconi remarked, "We can respond to the beautiful, but the ugly things in life—these are life, too. You believe what you see—which makes you believe. You must be positive in your life-style. My straightjacket is to keep to reality, if that is the right word, and to translate my ideas into shapes, then make it all work as a piece to art. This is graphic satisfaction to me. Shapes must be related to reality, and the line between this and art for art's sake is a thin one."[1]

1952. A retrospective exhibition was held at the Cleveland Museum of Art. Thirty-four of the works from that exhibition were included in a year-long tour of twenty museums throughout the country that was sponsored by the Smithsonian Institution.

Recognized as one of America's foremost woodcut artists, Frasconi was selling his prints for $25 to $125 apiece. ". . . I do care about an audience and I do care about reactions to my work. Any creative medium communicates something. The so-called avant-garde is not avant-garde at all. It was born and already died. The faddism the museums are following has created a phony art and a phony intellectualism. The artist must portray good as well as evil. As Dostoevsky said, 'the artist cannot see life always black.'

". . . I feel admiration for the artist and for his work go hand in hand. I personally could not admire the artist's work without respecting him as a person. I not only admire the work of Picasso, Orozco and Grosz but I respect them as human beings. My son, Pablo, was named out of respect and admiration for Picasso."[2]

1955. In addition to his woodcuts, Frasconi illustrated his first book, *Twelve Fables of Aesop,* which was followed by a children's book *See and Say*. This book was written for Pablo, in an effort to teach him that there were many different languages and ways in which to say things. "I believe that children's literature should show a broader panorama: the diversity of other people, their culture, their language, etc. That should be the first step in the making of character—respect for other nationalities and the understanding of their cultures."

Several of Frasconi's books have been award winners, including *The House That Jack Built,* which was a runner-up for the Caldecott Medal in 1959. Sometimes using handletters, he prints his woodcuts by hand rubbing a spoon over a paper laid on an inked block. "The printmaker, above all, must be sensitive to his craft, must allow his medium to 'talk to him' while he is working, must seize and take advantage of all the possibilities that arise in the act of incising or printing of a woodcut." [Margit Varga, "Woodcuts by Antonio Frasconi," *American Artist,* October, 1974.[3]]

1960. Frasconi's film, "The Neighboring Shore," which was based on one hundred woodcuts that he made to accompany poems by Walt Whitman, won the Grand Prix in the International Film Festival at Venice, Italy.

1963. Chosen to design a postage stamp honoring the National Academy of Science. His design of a globe submounted by a

They raced back to the cave. ■(From *The Little Blind Goat* by Jan Wahl. Illustrated by Antonio Frasconi.)

star-filled horizontal panel was reproduced 120 million times. ''I am one who has always admired the printing qualities of the stamps issued by this country. They are probably not as 'sharp' as those printed in Europe but are of first-rate quality. Sometimes they achieve an almost relief feeling. Perhaps it is

because the design is so bad that the technical qualities come to the fore.

''How many times we pay (reluctantly) for the 'glorified eagles' or those 'fatherly portraits.' The object is not anymore

(From *How the Left-Behind Beasts Built Ararat* by Norma Farber. Illustrated by Antonio Frasconi.)

to portray historical figures or to commemorate events of the U.S.A. through an artistic eye, but to use the 'slick' or 'corn view' of the worst magazine illustration techniques. This 'portrait' of the United States is as deceiving as some manufactured by Hollywood and Madison Avenue. To make the matter even worse, the global distribution of American stamps is enormous.

"The problem as I see it, then, resides in the ratio of this distribution to the tastelessness of the stamps themselves due to the non-creative people who approve them." [Antonio Frasconi, "Stamps Designed by Fine Artists," *Art in America,* number 4, 1961.[4]]

Through the years, Frasconi has served as teacher and artist-in-residence at the New School for Social Research, the Brooklyn Museum, California State College at Haywood, Vassar College, the University of California at Berkeley, and the University of Hawaii. "Students should continually look at art originals by going to galleries and museums. By looking they will learn to see. I believe only mature people are ready to teach art. Too many teachers have personal problems which they impose upon their students. The main duty of a teacher is to help the student to learn to know himself."[2]

Using simple tools and an ancient technique, Frasconi has created a diversity of work. His woodcuts have been commissioned for advertising, magazine illustration, record covers, and Christmas cards. He works from his home in South Norwalk, Connecticut, which is hidden among trees on a hillside that overlooks Long Island Sound. About his working environment, he commented: "You have to have your table, your tools, your little radio. You have to have your environment. It's your world. You try to know when you should shut off the radio and eliminate the bad news of the day, but your studio is your own world. Without that, I think, it's an uphill battle to work in another kind of environment.

"My morning is really the most productive part of the day. I work steady for four or five hours and if I have a good morning's work that's all I really expect from myself. I sometimes work in the afternoon and also in the evening, too, but I find that the morning is really my best time.

"Inspiration or motivation is something that has to be in you if you are to do anything. Many times, you're going to get stuck and not know what to do next. But, when that time comes, you just knock it off and go for a long walk or go and see other people work. The heavy cloud eventually goes away. I don't believe in inspiration; it's just purely hard work.

"In order to make a good piece of art work, it has to be your own personality. You don't have to show off; you don't have to do anything other than your work. It is what you show the world you are that really counts. That's why the artist must *really* like his work." [Don Cyr, "A Conversation with Antonio Frasconi," *School Arts,* February, 1968.[5]]

1980. Professor at State University of New York College at Purchase. Frasconi perceives the future role of the artist in American society as one of political and social involvement and communication. ". . . If artists want to be part of society, they have to be aware of society. They should not only paint for it, they should *think* about it. One reason the graphic-art media have been so influential is that they can reach more people. The role of art is not just to end up on a museum wall. How is it possible to ask people who work all day long to go to a museum and see masterpieces? It's a big demand. An artist should be aware that there are people out there.

". . . We are artists. We have to express both our hatred and our love. Is our work only a play of color and shape? Certainly, we have to know our materials, but how are we going to use them? How can we not be aware of the things that surround us? Right or wrong, artists have to stand up and be counted. If you get mad at something you read in the paper, are you supposed not to react in your studio? React to all the awful things going on today . . . and to all the wonderful things, too? If I were a writer I'd probably be a pamphleteer. I don't know, maybe I'm a pamphleteer in my own work. But that doesn't bother me, because I don't really try to make art. I try to communicate something that bothers me. It may not interest you, but I don't care—I still have to tell you. If you want to understand me and know me, just look at my work. I don't think the artist's role in society is to decorate the walls of corporations or museums. That doesn't make any sense to me. I love to do record covers and book covers—anything that can be viewed by a large audience. Is it art? I really don't care. It's up to the viewer to judge. Judging is not my job." [Jane Sterrett, "Interview with Antonio Frasconi," *Print Review,* number 16-17, 1982.[6]]

Frasconi's works are included in the de Grummond Collection at the University of Southern Mississippi.

FOR MORE INFORMATION SEE: New York Times, March 19, 1950; *Print,* winter, 1950-51, August, 1955; *Fortune,* September, 1951; *Newsweek,* March 17, 1952, April 5, 1954; *Time,* June 15, 1953, December 20, 1963; *Life,* October 18, 1954; A. Salsamendi, "Lively Art of Antonio Frasconi," *Américas,* May, 1957; Betha M. Miller and others, compilers, *Illustrators of Children's Books: 1946-1956,* Horn Book, 1958; *Graphis,* May/June, 1958, March/April, 1962, Volume 23, number 134, 1967, March/April, 1983; "Frasconi's Brio with a Book," *Horizon,* March, 1961; Antonio Frasconi, "Stamps Designed by Fine Artists," *Art in America,* number 4, 1961, October, 1964; *School Arts,* September, 1961, May, 1966, February, 1968; Kim Taylor, "The Woodcuts of Antonio Frasconi," *Texas Quarterly,* autumn, 1962; F. Getlein, "Frasconi the Printmaker," *New Republic,* February 29, 1964; Fritz Eichenburg, "Frasconi: Artist, Printmaker, Designer, Publisher," *Artist's Proof,* Volume VI, number 9-10, 1966; Diana Klemin, *The Art of Art for Children's Books,* C. N. Potter, 1966; Lee Kingman and others, compilers, *Illustrators of Children's Books: 1957-1966,* Horn Book, 1968; Bettina Hürlimann, *Picture-Book World,* World, 1969.

D. Klemin, *The Illustrated Book: Its Art and Craft,* C. N. Potter, 1970; Martha E. Ward and Dorothy A. Marquardt, *Authors of Books for Young People,* 2nd edition, Scarecrow, 1971; *Graphis 155,* Volume 27, Graphis Press, 1971-72; *Current Biography,* H. W. Wilson, 1972; Doris de Montreville and Donna Hill, editors, *Third Book of Junior Authors,* H. W. Wilson, 1972; Donnarae MacCann and Olga Richard, *The Child's First Books,* H. W. Wilson, 1973; Margit Varga, "Woodcuts by Antonio Frasconi," *American Artist,* October, 1974; *Contemporary American Illustrators of Children's Books,* Rutgers University Art Gallery, 1974; A. Frasconi, *Frasconi Against the Grain,* Macmillan, 1974; "Antonio Frasconi—Graphic Artist" (film), Pablo Frasconi, 1976; Barbara Bader, *American Picture Books from Noah's Ark to the Beast Within,* Macmillan, 1976; Henry C. Pitz, *200 Years of American Illustration,* Clibborn, 1977; *Gebrauchs Graphik,* May 5, 1978; *The Illustrator's Notebook,* Horn Book, 1978; L. Kingman and others, compilers, *Illustrators of Children's Books: 1967-1976,* Horn Book, 1978; Jane Sterrett, "Interview with Antonio Frasconi," *Print Review,* number 16-17, 1982; Jim Roginski, compiler, *Newbery and Caldecott Medalists and Honor Book Winners,* Libraries Unlimited, 1982; "The Woodcuts of Antonio Frasconi" (film), American Federation of Art, 1985.

GAMMELL, Stephen 1943-

PERSONAL: Born February 10, 1943, in Des Moines, Iowa; married Linda (a photographer). *Education:* Attended schools in Des Moines, Iowa. *Residence and studio:* St. Paul, Minn.

CAREER: Author and illustrator of books for children. Also worked as a free-lance illustrator for various periodicals in New York, N.Y., during the early 1970s. *Awards, honors: The Hawks of the Chelney* was named one of American Library Association's Best Books for Young Adults, 1978; *Stonewall* was named one of *New York Times* Outstanding Books of the Year, 1979, and was chosen a *Boston Globe-Horn Book* Award Honor Book, 1980; *Meet the Vampire* was named a Children's Choice by the joint committee of the International Reading Association and Children's Book Council, 1980; *Where the Buffaloes Begin* was chosen a *Boston Globe-Horn Book* Award Honor Book for Illustration, one of *New York Times* Best Illustrated Books, one of *New York Times* Outstanding Books of the Year, and received the Parent's Choice Award from Parents' Choice Foundation, all 1981, Caldecott Honor Book, and nominated for the American Book Award, Picture Book category, both 1982; *Wake-Up, Bear—It's Christmas!* was selected a Children's Choice, 1982; *The Old Banjo* was selected one of New York Public Library's Children's Books, 1983; *The Relatives Came* was chosen one of *New York Times* Best Illustrated Books of the Year, and one of Child Study Association of America's Children's Books of the Year, both 1985, and Caldecott Honor Book, 1986; *Thanksgiving Poems* was selected one of Child Study Association of America's Children's Books of the Year, 1985; *Boston Globe-Horn Book* Award Honor Book for Illustration, 1987, for *Old Henry.*

WRITINGS—All juvenile fiction; all self-illustrated: *Wake-Up, Bear—It's Christmas!,* Lothrop, 1981; *Once upon MacDonald's Farm,* Four Winds, 1981; (adapter) *The Story of Mr.*

STEPHEN GAMMELL

and Mrs. Vinegar, Lothrop, 1982; *Git Along, Old Scudder,* Lothrop, 1983.

Illustrator; all juvenile fiction, except as indicated: Ida Chittum, *A Nutty Business,* Putnam, 1973; Sara Newton Carroll, *The Search: A Biography of Leo Tolstoy,* Harper, 1973; Paul Zindel, *Let Me Hear You Whisper* (play), Harper, 1974; Ramona Maher, *The Glory Horse: A Story of the Battle of San Jacinto and Texas in 1836,* Coward, 1974.

Patricia L. Gauch, *Thunder at Gettysburg,* Coward, 1975; Miriam A. Bourne, *Nabby Adams' Diary,* Coward, 1975; Seymour Simon, *Ghosts,* Lippincott, 1976; Georgess McHargue, *Meet the Werewolf,* Lippincott, 1976; Mollie Hunter (pseudonym of Maureen M. Hunter McVeigh McIlwraith), *The Kelpie's Pearls* (ALA Notable Book), Harper, 1976; M. Hunter, *A Furl of Fairy Wind: Four Stories,* Harper, 1977; R. Maher, *Alice Yazzie's Year* (poetry), Coward, 1977; Ellen Harvey Showell, *The Ghost of Tillie Jean Cassaway,* Four Winds, 1978; Marietta Moskin, *Day of the Blizzard,* Coward, 1978; Adrienne Jones, *The Hawks of Chelney,* Harper, 1978; Dilys Owen, *Leo Possessed,* Harcourt, 1979; Jean Fritz, *Stonewall* (biography; ALA Notable Book; *Horn Book* honor list), Putnam, 1979; Margaret Greaves, *A Net to Catch the Wind,* Harper, 1979; G. McHargue, *Meet the Vampire,* Lippincott, 1979; Eve Bunting, *Yesterday's Island,* Warne, 1979; Michael Fox, *Whitepaws: A Coyote-Dog,* Coward, 1979; David Seed, *Stream Runner,* Four Winds, 1979.

E. Bunting, *Terrible Things,* Harper, 1980; Malcolm Hall, *And Then the Mouse . . . : Three Stories* (folktales), Four Winds, 1980; Helen Reeder Cross, *The Real Tom Thumb* (biography), Four Winds, 1980; E. Bunting, *Blackbird Singing,* Macmillan, 1980; Ann Brophy, *Flash and the Swan,* Warne, 1981; Olaf Baker, *Where the Buffaloes Begin* (*Horn Book* honor list), Warne, 1981; Nathaniel Benchley, *Demo and the Dolphin,* Harper, 1981; Alvin Schwartz, compiler, *Scary Stories to Tell in the Dark* (folktales), Lippincott, 1981; Maggie S. Davis, *The Best Way to Ripton,* Holiday House, 1982; Dennis Haseley, *The Old Banjo,* Macmillan, 1983; A. Schwartz, compiler and reteller, *More Scary Stories to Tell in the Dark: Collected and Retold from Folklore,* Lippincott, 1984; Cynthia Rylant, *Waiting to Waltz: A Childhood* (poetry; ALA Notable Book), Bradbury, 1984; Alison C. Herzig and Jane L. Mali, *Thaddeus* (Junior Literary Guild selection), Little, Brown, 1984.

C. Rylant, *The Relatives Came,* (*Horn Book* honor list), Bradbury, 1985; Myra C. Livingston, editor, *Thanksgiving Poems,* Holiday House, 1985; Larry Callen, *Who Kidnapped the Sheriff? or, Tales from Tickfaw,* Atlantic, 1985; George Ella Lyon, *A Regular Rolling Noah,* Bradbury, 1986; Joan W. Blos, *Old Henry,* Morrow, 1987; Janet T. Lisle, *The Great Dimpole Oak,* F. Watts, 1987; Karen Ackerman, *Song and Dance Man,* Knopf, 1988.

ADAPTATIONS: ''Where the Buffaloes Begin'' (read-along cassette; filmstrip with cassette), Random House/Miller-Brody, 1982; ''The Old Banjo'' (filmstrip with cassette), Miller-Brody, 1984; ''The Relatives Came,'' (read-along cassette; filmstrip with cassette), Miller-Brody, 1986.

SIDELIGHTS: Gammell's father was an art editor with Meredith Publishing, creators of popular magazines, including *Better Homes and Gardens.* ''A big part of my childhood was spent drawing. Practically every night my father would being home a new variety of pencil and paper. These great piles of paper of many thicknesses and colors were better than any toy. Father also supplied me with magazines like *Colliers* and *Saturday Evening Post.* I remember being impressed by their il-

Long hair of palest gold flowed down her back, and it was from her that the light came. ■ (From *A Furl of Fairy Wind* by Mollie Hunter. Illustrated by Stephen Gammell.)

lustrations and cutting them up to make scrapbooks. While I had no notion of what an artist was, I did have an awareness of illustration from an early age. I knew these magazine illustrations went with a story, but I never read them. I was only interested in the art.

"I used to lie on my stomach on the floor of the solarium, and draw soldiers, airplanes, trains and semaphores, as well as the usual cowboys and Indians. Now, that I'm older, I stand up, use a drawing board, have better paper and pencils, and throw more drawings than I used to, but it's still just as much fun as ever. Drawing, that is.

"My favorite illustrations were of cowboys and Indians. Although I didn't know their names at the time, I now recognize them as the work of Harold von Schmidt, Frank Schoonover, Dean Cornwell, Frederic Remington and Charles Marion Russell. I wasn't interested then in who did the illustration, I only considered the subject matter, and if it was Western, it was just fine with me. I also remember liking the paintings and romantic illustrations of Robert Fawcett. I was interested in the detail of his work, the particular way he drew a dress, a window curtain, a chair.

"I hardly ever went to art museums as a child, but I recall visiting the historical museums near my house. I loved the stuffed animals, the American Indian artifacts and memorabilia of the West. The exhibitions about the settling of Iowa were fascinating to me.

"My father was very encouraging. He would help me draw, supply the paper and pencils, but he would never coach me or tell me how to work. I picked up the interest on my own; my parents never pushed me. It got me through elementary school. If you could draw, the big kids were more hesitant about beating you up. I tried to make this work for me.

"As years go by, you retain what is interesting from childhood and toss out the rest. Somehow the memorabilia and romance of Western history has always stayed with me. I suppose part of the lasting appeal is that artifacts are just plain fun to draw. I like the line and the form of the objects. An arrowhead, for instance, is fun to pick up, to play with, to touch, to draw. Tomahawks, hatchets, old revolvers, boots, and leather all have a certain sensual, visual appeal for me, and they, consequently, turn up in my illustration."

Attended high school and college in Iowa. "I tried to get through high school by drawing, too. I'd turn in book reports with illustrations, thinking the teachers would be impressed, but, of course, they weren't.

"After college, I drifted about for nine years. All through the sixties, I did odd jobs and continued to draw, but I never thought of myself as an artist. I wasn't intelligent enough to think about making a living at anything, much less art. I just fooled around.

"During the late sixties, while I was living in Minneapolis, I began to draw little ads for friends who ran neighborhood bookshops and record stores. They were published in local magazines and newspapers. I did a few poster jobs for music stores, signs for regional colleges—little jobs around town. I also illustrated several articles for local magazines. I fell into this by accident and can't imagine what would be better suited to my personality and abilities than doing this for a living— stuck away safely in a second floor studio, out of public view and bothering no one, doing harmless drawings and paintings. Everyone's happy. Or relieved."

In the early seventies, Gammell visited New York. "Everything in my life has happened by accident. My roommate was an actor in a local theatre company which was about to put on a play in New York City. This friend asked whether I'd like to tag along, and I agreed. I knew there were publishing companies in New York and that children's books, which were beginning to interest me, came out of major New York publishers. I put together some of my drawings and sketches, as well as the ads and illustrations I had been doing in Minneapolis. My thought was to contact some people in publishing. I didn't want or expect to find a job, I was simply interested in getting a professional opinion of my work. I went around to several children's book publishers and asked for their criticism. One editor liked my work and gave me a sample manuscript. She suggested I take it home and make two or three drawings. She could see I knew how to draw, but was interested in whether I could maintain a sense of consistency and continuity from page to page. I made some drawings and brought

Little Wolf was only ten years old, but he could run faster than any of his friends. ■ (From *Where the Buffaloes Begin* by Olaf Baker. Illustrated by Stephen Gammell.)

"Aaaaaaaaaaah!" ■ (From *Scary Stories to Tell in the Dark: Collected from American Folklore* by Alvin Schwartz. Illustrated by Stephen Gammell.)

them back several days later. To my surprise she offered me a contract for that very book, *A Nutty Business*. For the first six or seven years I illustrated everything I was offered. I wasn't at all selective; I just kept working.''

The whimsical fantasy, *And Then the Mouse . . .* , was a turning point for Gammell. ''With it, I was finally able to get silly and free myself from inhibitions. *And Then the Mouse . . .* loosened me up—I quit taking myself so seriously. As a result, I felt better about my attitude, my drawings, *myself*. From then on, I only accepted books that I really wanted to illustrate, books I could enjoy. I stopped trying to make an 'artistic statement,' and freed myself from that restrictive, self-imposed seriousness.''

Gammell has also illustrated several of his own stories. ''I'm very uncomfortable having the word 'author' with my name. Yes, I have written a few books, but the words are really nothing more than something to keep the art flowing smoothly. I hope.

''I hate writing, and find it terribly difficult. I often come up with ideas, but I haven't done any writing in several years. It is such a chore; I guess I just can't face sitting down to do it. As long as I am given good manuscripts, I will be very happy to stick to illustration.

''The first time I read a manuscript I can immediately tell whether I want to illustrate it. I may not know how the illustrations will look, but I get a certain feeling from the text. I respond to the words, and, if I can respond to a story, I can illustrate it.

''My first concern is to serve the story. That is an illustrator's job. I don't research unless I have to because I prefer to draw from my imagination. I need to know whether a detail is anatomically correct before I can take liberties, however. If I must find out how something looks—what comes out of an animal's little paws, for instance, or which side of the face the trunk is on—I'll go to the library. But if I can get away with making up my own version, I will. It is more fun to work this way, and the illustrations are more expressive. Whatever I draw, whether it's a buffalo or a chair, I try to make it my own to satisfy myself.

''Much of my early work is done in pen and ink because I wasn't trained in color media. Water color is still difficult for me. My interest in book design has evolved over the years. I like to keep artistic control over design, especially type placement, and I often make suggestions concerning overall design, quality of paper, and format.

A boy was digging at the edge of the garden when he saw a big toe. ■ (From *Scary Stories to Tell in the Dark: Collected from American Folklore* by Alvin Schwartz. Illustrated by Stephen Gammell.)

(From *Once upon MacDonald's Farm* by Stephen Gammell. Illustrated by the author.)

"I prefer to work alone, without feedback from the author. I believe that once a manuscript is written and accepted, the writer's work is over. Unless you collaborate on a book from its inception, talking with authors can create problems over artistic interpretation. When I illustrate a story, I want to work with my ideas and my perception of the words, not with the author.

"I am inspired by a text which gives me the freedom to interpret. I don't like being tied to a specific historical time period, style of architecture or costume. I like texts which take place anytime, anywhere. For this reason, I enjoy elements of fantasy in a story, and turn down anything that is too literal. A careful look at my work tells the way I *interpret* a text. I take a poetic approach. The events I depict could easily be portrayed in a number of different ways.''

Gammell keeps a regular work schedule. "I work in my studio every day. Whether I accomplish any work or not, I am there. It's my job to show up, and because I like my work, I wouldn't have it any other way.

"I don't like to split my focus, and prefer to work on one book at a time. I would like to have the time to draw or paint outside of my illustration, but I'm at the mercy of a good manuscript. As long as they continue to come in, I will continue to work on them. I remember times when I would finish a book, turn it in, and have weeks of free time, but was so nervous about not having another book to do, that I had a hard time relaxing enough to do my own drawings.

"I haven't any general advice for young artists, but make myself accessible to them. On an individual basis, I'm glad

(From *Thaddeus* by Alison Cragin Herzig and Jane Lawrence Mali. Illustrated by Stephen Gammell.)

(From *Git Along, Old Scudder* by Stephen Gammell. Illustrated by the author.)

to be helpful and encouraging, but am cautious about giving advice. I found my own way, and I think that is the best way.''

Gammell enjoys solitude, and prefers camping vacations in the backwoods to urban travel. He is also a music lover, and plays several instruments. ''Music comes naturally to me, even more naturally than drawing. I play guitar, banjo, mandolin, piano—anything with strings. I've played instruments since I was a kid, and if I hadn't become an artist, I probably would have pursued music. I have music on all the time in the studio—jazz, classical, early mountain music, bluegrass, and country music from the forties and fifties. Down in Iowa people loved country music, I grew up with it, and it was part of my environment.

''I think of myself as an artist—admittedly a basic term that can mean almost anything. One of the forms that my art takes is book illustration. It is very fulfilling to me. I don't feel a need to get away from my studio to rejuvenate. I love my work. I love drawing, painting and making books. In a deep sense, I *am* my work—what you see on the page is really me.''

——Based on an interview by Rachel Koenig

HOBBIES AND OTHER INTERESTS: American history, music, camping, backpacking, canoeing, bicycling, traveling.

FOR MORE INFORMATION SEE: Sally Holmes Holtze, editor, *Fifth Book of Junior Authors and Illustrators,* H. W. Wilson, 1983.

GENNARO, Joseph F(rancis), Jr. 1924-

PERSONAL: Born April 9, 1924, in Brooklyn, N.Y.; son of Joseph F. (a surgeon) and Elizabeth (Klemper) Gennaro; married Doris E. Margolin (an electron microscopist), November 10, 1943; children: Joanne Gennaro Selin, Tina, Lucia Gennaro Tranel, Joseph F. III, Justin. *Education:* Fordham University, B.S., 1947; University of Pittsburgh, M.S., 1949, Ph.D., 1952. *Home:* 100 Bleecker St., New York, N.Y. 10012. *Office:* New York University, Department of Biology, 652 Brown Building, Washington Square, New York, N.Y. 10003.

CAREER: University of Pittsburgh, Pa., fellow, 1947, lecturer, 1948, instructor, 1950; St. John's University, assistant professor of biology, 1951-52; State University of New York, College of Medicine, instructor, 1953-56; University of Florida, College of Medicine, assistant professor of anatomy, 1956-64; University of Louisville, School of Medicine, associate professor of anatomy, 1964-69; New York University, New York, N.Y., associate professor of biology, 1969—, director,

Laboratory of Cellular Biology. Biological photographer for Photo-Researchers, 1978—; scientific director of American Institute for Toxin Research, 1974-84; member of Anatomical Science Training Program, New York University Dental School, 1974—; associate research scientist, Center for Neurochemistry, Rockland Research Institute, 1980—; research associate, Osborn Laboratories, New York Aquarium, 1980—. *Military service:* U.S. Army, 1943-46. *Member:* American Society for Cell Biology, American Physiological Society, American Association of Anatomists, American Microscopical Society, Biophysical Society, International Society of Toxinology (founding member; secretary-treasurer, 1965-69), Electron Microscopy Society of America, New York Society of Electron Microscopy (board of directors, 1982—), International Society of Cryptozoology (founding member; treasurer, 1982; board of directors, 1982—), Tissue Culture Association, Northeast Branch (founding member; board of directors, 1982—; treasurer, 1982-84; president, 1984-87), Royal Microscopical Society (fellow).

AWARDS, HONORS: Research fellow at Brookhaven National Laboratory, 1952-56, Harvard University, 1964-65, and Smith Kline & French Laboratories, 1986; Special Award from the American Academy of Orthopedic Surgeons, and the North Carolina State Medical Association, first prize from the Texas Medical Association, second prize from the Florida Medical Association, and honorable mention from the American Medical Association, all 1961, all for "An Evaluation of Extremity

JOSEPH F. GENNARO, JR.

Loss Due to Venomous Snakebite in the State of Florida"; American Medical Association Recognition Award, 1967, for consultation to the medical faculty of the University of Saigon; Gustav Ohaus Award from the National Science Teachers Association, 1976, for innovative approaches to science teaching; *Small Worlds Close Up* was named one of the Best Books of the Year by *School Library Journal,* one of Library of Congress' Children's Books of the Year, an Outstanding Science Trade Book for Children by the National Science Teachers Association, and one of Child Study Association of America's Children's Books of the Year, all 1978, a Children's Choice by the International Reading Association, 1979, and one of New York Public Library's Books for the Teen Age, 1980, 1981, and 1982.

WRITINGS: (With Lisa Grillone) *Small Worlds Close Up* (ALA Notable Book), Crown, 1978. Contributor of scientific articles to journals, and of articles to periodicals, including *Natural History, Nature and Science, Medical World News,* and *Argosy.*

WORK IN PROGRESS: A photographic view of the body as seen through the eyes of a five-year-old child, *Small Worlds of the Sea,* and a photographic view of the body of an adolescent as seen by the subject, all with Lisa Grillone, all for Crown.

SIDELIGHTS: "Much of contemporary research, especially in the area of cell biology, is lost to the public for want of interpreters. This occurs at a time when our need to understand the physical (and physiological) consequences of environmental conditions could not be greater. Our efforts, however, are directed not to popularization of conservation data, as has been done by many others, but toward the spread of basic information so that it can easily be comprehended, usually through the use of photographic material. It is our intention to deliver, especially to the youth of today, a simple and useful understanding of the complex scientific information which deals with the structure and function of the units of life."

FOR MORE INFORMATION SEE: Times Literary Supplement, March 28, 1980.

GRAHAM-CAMERON, M(alcolm) G(ordon) 1931- (M. Graham-Cameron, Mike Graham-Cameron)

PERSONAL: Born January 18, 1931, in London, England; son of Charles (a theater and cinema producer/director) and Beatrice Elizabeth (Edwards) Graham-Cameron; married Caroline Jean Harris (a playwright and author), 1951 (divorced, 1962); married Althea Mary Braithwaite (an author and illustrator), 1966 (divorced, 1973); married Helen Jean Howat (a painter and illustrator under name Helen Herbert), February 11, 1984; children: (second marriage) Duncan Charles. *Education:* Attended school in Chepstow, England. *Politics:* "None (well, not to any political party)." *Religion:* Agnostic. *Home and office:* 10 Church St., Willingham, Cambridge, CB4 5HT, England.

CAREER: Royal Air Force, served as flight sergeant assigned to special duties in secretarial branch, 1948-60; Lion Garages Ltd., Huntingdon, England, sales manager, 1960-61, marketing manager, 1961-64; Polyhedron Printers Ltd., Cambridge, England, managerial co-director, 1964-74; Dinosaur Publications Ltd., Cambridge, co-founder, managing co-director, and commissioning editor, 1969-84; Graham-Cameron & Braithwaite (design, advertising, and printing company), Cambridge, managing co-director, 1970-74; Graham-Cameron Publishing, Cambridge, co-founder and editor, 1984—. Lecturer and conductor of workshops on children's book writing and illustration. Consulting editor, William Collins Publishers and Cambridge University Press; external assessor, Cambridge School of Art, 1984—; lecturer, Cambridge College of Arts and Technology, and Eastern Arts Association. *Member:* Association of Independent Museums, Museums Association, Independent Publishers Guild, Cambridge Professional Book Association (chairman, 1984—). *Awards, honors:* Award from the United Kingdom Reading Association, for *Cage Birds, Life on a Country Estate,* and *Cats;* Award from the British Council, for *The Farmer,* and *Playing Football; Home Sweet Home* was selected a Children's Book of the Year by the National Book League, 1979.

WRITINGS—Juvenile; under name M. G. Graham-Cameron: *The Cambridge Scene* (illustrated by Colin King), Dinosaur, 1977; *Life on a Country Estate* (illustrated by wife, Helen Herbert), Dinosaur, 1978; *Home Sweet Home* (illustrated by H. Herbert), Dinosaur, 1979, Merrimack, 1980; *Up from the Country,* National Dairy Council, 1986; *On Your Doorstep,* National Dairy Council, 1986; *Good Food to Eat,* National Dairy Council, 1987.

Juvenile; under name M. Graham-Cameron: *The Farmer* (illustrated by Hilary Abrahams), Dinosaur, 1975, revised edition, Cambridge University Press, 1983; *Playing Football* (illustrated by C. King), Dinosaur, 1975.

Juvenile; under name Mike Graham-Cameron: *Catching a Burglar* (illustrated by Peter Welford), Dinosaur, 1975; *Cats* (illustrated by H. Herbert), Merrimack, 1978; *Cage Birds* (illustrated by H. Abrahams), Dinosaur, 1978; *Life in an Edwardian Country Household* (illustrated by H. Herbert), Cam-

bridge University Press, 1978; (with Tim Hunkin) *Steam Power: Colouring Book* (illustrated by T. Hunkin), Dinosaur, 1980; *Households through the Ages* (illustrated by H. Herbert), Dinosaur, 1984; *The Police at Work* (illustrated by Martin Salisbury), Cambridge University Press, 1984; *Rural Life in Roman Suffolk* (illustrated by H. Herbert), Graham-Cameron Publishing, 1984; *Shopping at the Co-Op* (illustrated by H. Herbert), Graham-Cameron Publishing, 1985.

Contributor of articles to *Museums Association Journal.*

WORK IN PROGRESS: "I am particularly interested in social history. I am pursuing research on the family mores of Victorian society with a view to editing an observation on the life of ordinary people during those times; a study of the association between words and images in illustrated books for children, for the professional reader."

SIDELIGHTS: "I suppose I got into publishing by accident. The idea of initiating publications, instead of merely assisting them on their way, came to a head in 1969, when I ran a design, advertising, and printing company with my then wife. A series of drawings associated with short stories which she had produced made me persuade her to agree to their publication. Thus was born Dinosaur Publications, which became a noted, if small, children's publisher. That company was taken over by a large publisher in 1984, at which time I founded a new company, Graham-Cameron Publishing, with my present wife, Helen Herbert.

"I was born in London of parents who were Scottish and Welsh. My father came from a family of Scottish lairds, and my mother's parents were Welsh landowners. The image this suggests is inaccurate, however, as the family was London-based, and, as my father was severally an actor, a film director, and theatrical producer and manager, our Hyde Park house was usually full of writers, actors, poets, and singers—in fact people from all sorts of areas of the arts and of politics. As a young child I was sometimes allowed to be present during dinner parties (or at least part of them) and to listen to the pronouncements of many family friends whom I subsequently realised were household names.

"I was at my boarding school for a year before war broke out with Germany. I recall spending the night of 2nd/3rd September 1939 curled up under the bedcovers in my dormitory, praying extremely hard that there would be no war. At 11 a.m. the next day (a Sunday) the school was assembled to hear Neville Chamberlain's announcement that 'a state of war existed between Great Britain and Germany.' I became an agnostic at the same moment!

"I think I must have been something of a trial at school, though why I cannot recall. Except, perhaps that I have often been a a rebel, especially against real (or perceived) injustice, whether to myself or others. My first job in a Dickensian-style advertising agency ended in my being fired when I delayed my return to the office by fifteen minutes—I had stopped off on some errand or other to sample an irresistible new kind of ice cream confection just in from America, and this led to a bout of fury on the part of my managing director, who obviously didn't like ice cream.

"In joining the Royal Air Force, I fulfilled two needs—the first was for a job and the second (and no whit less important) was to satisfy my latent feelings of inadequacy in having been too young to serve my country in the war. (We used to think like that in those days!)

M. G. GRAHAM-CAMERON

The whole of the wool coat is cleverly cut off in one piece. ■ (From *The Farmer* by M. Graham-Cameron. Illustrated by Hilary Abrahams.)

"I had chosen a period of service through which the 'Cold War' was intense, and I spent my time in many countries outside Britain employed on the special duties list. I spent three years in Africa, travelling through most of the central and southern areas, and another three years in Europe where I was attached to SHAPE near Paris. By 1960 the atmosphere between East and West had stabilized, and military life became less interesting.

"I left the service after a course in management which was designed to fit us for civilian employment. The offers of jobs which followed were in large companies, mostly manufacturers, but I was yearning for a change from the large organization. After spending a few years in sales, working among other things to successfully sell the idea of the 'new' Volkswagen Beetle to a still rather anti-German public, I joined a printing and design company as sales manager. Things were so bad for the firm in those days that we had to collect the paper for every job and pay cash on the nail. With my fellow manager we bought out the company. It took two or three years' hard work to reverse the decline but eventually we made it successful, introducing advertising and marketing services to our portfolio of activities. And we started making money.

The publishing company, as mentioned earlier, grew out of the original printing company.

"Children's books must be the most difficult area of publishing there is. If a biased, ill-informed, sexist, racially prejudiced book hits the adult market, people can choose to believe it or not. But children, with their lack of experience, must expect truth from what they read. What, exactly, the truth consists of is another problem entirely. Enough to say that what we tried to do was to produce books which, however superficially they had to treat a subject for a very young readership, got over the truth to children and helped in a small way to make them believe in the positive aspects of mankind.

"In spite of pressures of all kinds from every kind of activist group you can imagine and from inspired and/or nutty individuals, publishing for children is fun even if one sometimes forgets it in the welter of sheer hard work it takes."

A child is an island of curiosity surrounded by a sea of question marks.

—Shell Oil Company

GREEN, Roger (Gilbert) Lancelyn 1918-1987

OBITUARY NOTICE—See sketch in *SATA* Volume 2: Born November 2, 1918, in Norwich, England; died October 8, 1987, in London, England. Educator, editor, and author. Before pursuing a full-time writing career, Green worked briefly as a teacher, antiquarian bookseller, actor, and librarian at Oxford University's Merton College. He also edited journals on Kipling and Sherlock Holmes, assisted in editing the letters of Lewis Carroll, and translated works of Greek dramatists Sophocles and Euripides. Additionally, Green contributed articles to books and periodicals, among them *Books and Bookmen* and *Times Literary Supplement*, and he served as associate editor of the "Children's Illustrated Classics" series published by Dent.

Best known as a compiler and reteller of myths, legends, and fairy tales for children, Green was also a prolific author of books for young and old alike. His publications for adults include two volumes of verse, *The Lost July and Other Poems* and *The Singing Rose and Other Poems*, the novel *From the World's End: A Fantasy*, biographies of Andrew Lang, Lewis Carroll, J. M. Barrie, Rudyard Kipling, C. S. Lewis, and other authors of adventure stories and children's books. For children, he wrote original stories such as *The Theft of the Golden Cat* and *The Land of the Lord High Tiger* as well as three fictional narratives based on Greek legends, *Mystery at Mycenae: An Adventure Story of Ancient Greece*, *The Land Beyond the North*, and *The Luck of Troy*, and retellings of fairy tales and legends, including *King Arthur and His Knights of the Round Table*, *The Adventures of Robin Hood*, *Myths of the Norsemen*, and *Heroes of Greece and Troy*.

FOR MORE INFORMATION SEE: Contemporary Authors, New Revision Series, Volume 2, Gale, 1981; *Twentieth-Century Children's Writers*, 2nd edition, St. Martin's, 1983; *Who's Who*, 139th edition, St. Martin's, 1987. Obituaries: *Times* (London), October 12, 1987; *Los Angeles Times*, October 14, 1987; *Washington Post*, October 17, 1987.

JON HARDY

HARDY, Jon 1958-

PERSONAL: Born June 11, 1958, in Shrewsbury, England; son of William Humphrey (a clerk) and Kathleen (a nurse; maiden name, Baring-Rees) Hardy; married Lesley Stokes, December 1, 1978 (divorced); married Maggie Boyd (a television production assistant), April 25, 1986. *Education:* Loughborough University, B.A., 1977; Guildhall School of Music and Drama, L.G.S.M.D., 1981. *Politics:* None. *Home:* 23b Florence Rd., Chiswick, London W4 5DP, England. *Office:* BBC-TV, Union House, Shepherd's Bush, London W.12, England.

CAREER: BBC-TV, London, England, script editor for drama series and serials, 1985—. Worked as an actor, debt collector, trainee accountant, driving instructor, stage manager, and insurance assessor.

WRITINGS: Biker (juvenile), Oxford University Press, 1985.

WORK IN PROGRESS: Two novels: *Eddie's Adult Life (So Far)*, and *Webster's Boy*.

HARRIS, Robie H.

BRIEF ENTRY: Harris received a master's degree at the Bank Street College and afterward taught there for several years. She has also worked in films and television, designed parks for children, and presently serves as a consultant to the Children's Museum in Boston. An expert in child development, Harris collaborated with Elizabeth Levy on *Before You Were Three: How You Began to Walk, Talk, Explore, and Have Feelings* (Delacorte, 1977), which traces the growth of a boy and a girl through their first three years of life. Geared for children in grades four through nine, this book contains photographs by Henry Gordillo and is, according to *School Library Journal*, "a useful and absorbing account of the years most readers cannot remember from their own childhoods." In addition, Harris has written fiction for younger children, including titles such as *Don't Forget to Come* (1978), *Rosie's Double Dare* (1980), *I Hate Kisses* (1981), and *Rosie's Razzle Dazzle Deal* (1982), all published by Knopf. Her most recent works are *Hot Henry* and *Messy Jessie*, both illustrated by Nicole Hollander and published by St. Martin's in 1987. *Residence:* Cambridge, Mass.

HENDERSON, Gordon 1950-

PERSONAL: Born December 13, 1950, in Ottawa, Canada; son of Gordon F. (a lawyer) and Joan (Parkins) Henderson; married Pamela Spence (a school librarian), June 9, 1973; children: Stuart, Katherine, Elizabeth. *Education:* York University, Toronto, B.A. (with honors), 1973; Carleton University, Ottawa, B.J., 1974. *Religion:* United Church of Canada. *Home:* 280 Glencairn Ave., Toronto, Ontario, Canada M5N 1T9. *Office:* 90th Parallel Film and Television Productions Ltd., 70 the Esplande, Toronto, Ontario, Canada M5E 1R2.

CAREER: Global TV, Ottawa, Canada, parliamentary correspondent, 1974-79; CTV-W5, Toronto, Canada, producer, 1979-83, senior field producer, 1986-87; Canadian Broadcasting Corp., Toronto, documentary producer, 1983-86; 90th Parallel Film and Television Productions Ltd., Toronto, co-founder, 1987—.

GORDON HENDERSON

WRITINGS: Sandy Mackenzie, Why Look So Glum? Rhymes and Pictures about Our Prime Ministers (illustrated by Peter Pickersgill), Deneau & Greenburg, 1979.

WORK IN PROGRESS: Don't Go That Way, children's poems about Canadian explorers; an historical novel, time frame is Canadian confederation.

SIDELIGHTS: "My writing for children is a hobby. I've been a journalist and documentary producer for thirteen years chasing stories around the world. Recently I co-founded a production company and hope to produce television and feature film dramas. So, there hasn't been a lot of excess time for my own writing.

"But there are a few stories, rooted in Canadian history (a subject far too often ignored), that keep nagging at my subconscious. So, I'll keep pounding away at the keyboard when I can find time.

"Why history? I guess that's the simplest question of all: because I love it. In French the word 'histoire' means story. And that's how I've always seen it. History to me is a collection of stories. In history books we meet people who came before us and share distant events which helped shape our world today.

"I remember when I first heard the story—again that word, 'story'—about Marco Polo in school. I was surprised that some other people in the class thought it was boring. (Yuck, history!) I thought it was fascinating. Imagine his trip. Imagine living then. What an adventure. What a 'story.'

"Maybe there's something else, too. When your career is making television programs, it's kind of nice to work on the printed page. Books are still irreplaceable. For people of all ages there's nothing more magical than a good book."

HOBBIES AND OTHER INTERESTS: Skiing, canoeing, music.

HENDERSON, Kathy 1949-

BRIEF ENTRY: Born April 22, 1949, in Oxford, England. Editor, teacher, researcher, author of books for adults and young children. After completing her education at Oxford University, Henderson became a commissioning editor for Penguin Books in 1971. She returned to school three years later, this time attending the Centre for Science Education sponsored by London University. In 1974 Henderson began part-time work as an adult literacy teacher, a post she maintained even after she resumed editing the following year. Staying within the academic setting, she later held positions of research fellow for a medical school and consultant for Open University. Her professional career came full circle in 1984 when she became a commissioning editor for Frances Lincoln Ltd.

Henderson's first publication, *My Song Is My Own: One Hundred Women's Songs* (Pluto Press, 1979), was co-written with Frankie Armstrong and Sandra Kerr and caters to adult readers. Since then she has created books for children, some of which she illustrated herself. In regard to *Sam and the Big Machines* (Andre Deutsch, 1985), *Kirkus Review* commented that "any small child who shares Sam's enthusiasms . . . will recognize this tall tale for the fantasy that it is, delighting in Sam's adventure. . . ." A sequel, entitled *Sam and the Box,* appeared in print in 1987. All published by MacDonald in 1986, Henderson's other works include *15 Ways to Go to Bed* and "Where Does It Come From?" books such as *Water, Banana, Sweater,* and *Lego Brick. Home:* 69 Woodland Rise, London N10 3UN, England.

HENEGHAN, James 1930-
(B. J. Bond)

PERSONAL: Born October 7, 1930, in Liverpool, England; emigrated to Canada in 1957, became a citizen in 1963; son of John (a civil engineer) and Ann (Fitzgerald) Heneghan; children: Ann, Robert, John, Leah. *Education:* Simon Fraser University, British Columbia, B.A., 1971. *Home:* 407-527 Commodore Rd., Vancouver, British Columbia, Canada V5Z 4G5.

CAREER: Vancouver Police, Vancouver, British Columbia, Canada, fingerprint technician, 1959-70; Burnaby Central High School, Burnaby, British Columbia, teacher, 1972—. *Member:* West End Writers Society; Canadian Society of Children's Authors, Illustrators and Performers.

WRITINGS: (With Bruce McBay) *Puffin Rock* (illustrated by Vesna Krstanovich), Book Society of Canada, 1980; (with B. McBay under joint pseudonym B. J. Bond) *Goodbye, Carleton High,* Scholastic-TAB, 1983; *Promises to Come,* Overlea House, 1988. Contributor to periodicals, including *B. C. Runner.*

WORK IN PROGRESS: The Case of the Marmalade Cat, a detective-thriller novel for children; *On Lost Lagoon,* a verse narrative for children.

SIDELIGHTS: "Writing for teenagers started as a joint idea when a colleague and I saw a need for high-interest stories for our own English students who were reading at a low level and who needed motivation to read. Our early stories, unpublished, tried to include characters and settings and situations our students could recognize and identify with.

"I enjoy writing for children, but still regard myself as a beginner. One thing I *have* discovered is that children are

JAMES HENEGHAN

tough critics—they know what they like, and only your best will do.

"I'm just finishing a novel for ten year olds, and a story in verse for eight year olds. It seems that the younger they are, the harder you have to work to earn that elusive happy face."

HOBBIES AND OTHER INTERESTS: "I'm a compulsive jogger, the outdoors always beckons. I enter most of the local races and usually finish last. Being Irish I read a lot because I'm basically lazy, and reading is one of those things that demands a comfortable chair."

HILL, Eric 1927-

BRIEF ENTRY: Born in 1927, in London, England. Author and illustrator of books for children. Hill, who worked as a messenger and sweeper for a commercial art studio when he was fifteen, learned his artistic style from a newspaper cartoonist also employed there. He soon began creating cartoons and cartoon strips which were sold to magazines, and later joined the art staff of an advertising agency before devoting his efforts solely to free-lance art. A turning point occurred for Hill when both Heinemann and Putnam published his first children's book, *Where's Spot?*, in 1980. Designed specifically for his young son's enjoyment, this book incorporates lift-up flaps under which new and relevant illustrations appear. It was chosen as runner-up for the Mother Goose Award in 1981. Hill has since created a series consisting of over twenty-five "Spot" books. Titles such as *Puppy Love, Spot Goes to School, Spot's Birthday Party,* and *Sweet Dreams, Spot!* represent the body of work hailed by *School Library Journal* as "colorful, imaginative, and delightfully simple." Hill has also created the "Baby Bear Storybook" series, featuring the daily

activities of a young bear, and the "Peek-A-Book" series, which similarly employs the lift-up flap techique.

FOR MORE INFORMATION SEE: Horn Book, September/ October, 1987.

HIND, Dolores (Ellen) 1931-

PERSONAL: Born July 17, 1931, in Welland, Ontario, Canada; daughter of William Harold (a retired salesman) and Martha (a homemaker; maiden name, Winger) Patterson; married Donald Hind (an account executive), April 17, 1954; children: Mary Jo, Carrie, Tom. *Education:* University of Toronto, B.A., 1975, M.Ed., 1979. *Religion:* Anglican. *Home:* 60 Meadowvale Dr., Toronto, Ontario, Canada M8Z 5U1; (summer) "Hindsite," R.R. #4, Shelburne, Ontario, Canada L0N 1S0. *Office:* Peel Board of Education, Hurontario St., Mississauga, Ontario, Canada.

CAREER: Windsor Board of Education, Windsor, Ontario, Canada, music and kindergarten teacher, 1950-58; University of Toronto, Institute of Child Study, Toronto, Ontario, instructor at laboratory school, 1968-72; Peel Board of Education, Mississauga, Ontario, teacher, consultant, 1972—; writer, 1978—; York University, Toronto, faculty of education professor and program coordinator, 1980-82. *Awards, honors:* Federation of Women Teachers of Ontario Writer's Award, 1981, for *The Animals' Walk.*

WRITINGS: The Animals' Walk (illustrated by John Mc-Cullogh), D. Hind, 1978, Holt, 1983; *Two by Two* (illustrated

DOLORES HIND

by Pauline McGraw), Ginn (Canada), 1982; *So Can I* (illustrated by Marilyn Mets), Ginn (Canada), 1982. Contributor of poem ''Wishers,'' to anthology, *Impressions* (third-grade reader), Holt, 1985.

SIDELIGHTS: ''As a mother and educator I have been deeply concerned with children's creativity and curiosity, language and literature, and most of all appreciation of beauty. Whether teaching kindergarten children or university graduate students, I have tried to instill a love of language, a love of beauty, and a love of life. As a conference speaker and workshop leader I have tried to stimulate parents and teachers to encourage their children to be creative, imaginative, and appreciative.

''My writing has been influenced by the many wonderful experiences we have been fortunate enough to share with our children, travelling, skiing, building, collecting, etc. As a family we constructed a ski chalet for weekends out of a chicken coop, refinished furniture, collected antiques, and in the last ten years have restored a ninety-five-year-old farmhouse on a fifty-five acre site. This special home we have named 'Hindsite.' Over the years we have explored the woods, picked wild raspberries, watched deer eat apples in our small apple orchard, listened to the gurgling of our freshwater stream, enjoyed the colourful birds and celebrated special holidays and major family events together.

''I have made presentations at the Ontario Schools Library Association conferences, some librarian conferences, 'Reading for the Love of It' conference, York University's reading conference and others. I have also presented workshops throughout Ontario for the Federation of Women Teachers Association on observing children. I have given many storytelling and story writing workshops in and outside the region of Peel.

''We needed to buy a home in Toronto because of difficult commuting in the winter. As I write, the spring sun is pouring through the windows and I eagerly look forward to spending Easter and then the spring and summer months at my beloved 'Hindsite.' It is at this special place where I am renewed and where creative thoughts begin to flow.''

HOBBIES AND OTHER INTERESTS: ''Interior decorating, renovating old homes, creative cooking, cross country skiing, reading, gardening,—most of all I enjoy my family activities with my adult children and husband.''

HUNKIN, Tim(othy Mark Trelawney) 1950-

PERSONAL: Born December 27, 1950, in London, England; son of Oliver John Wellington (a television producer) and Frances Elizabeth (an artist; maiden name, Holmes) Hunkin. *Education:* Caius College, Cambridge, B.Sc., 1971. *Politics:* Socialist. *Home:* Bulcamp House, Blythburg, Suffolk, England. *Agent:* Rod Hall, A.P. Watt Ltd., 26-28 Bedford Row, London WC1R 4HL, England.

CAREER: Phlegethon Fireworks (display contractors), London, England, owner, 1969-80; *Observer,* London, England, cartoonist and author of cartoon strip, ''Rudiments of Wisdom,'' 1973-87. Creator of animation for television and clocks in Covent Garden, London and Liverpool Garden Festival. *Exhibitions:* ''Press View,'' Crafts Council, 1979; ''The Disgusting Spectacle,'' Institute of Contemporary Arts, 1981; ''The Art Gallery'' (touring exhibition), 1983.

TIM HUNKIN

WRITINGS: Mrs. Gronkwonk and the Post Office Tower (juvenile), Angus & Robertson, 1971; *Rudiments of Wisdom* (juvenile), Hutchinson, 1974; (with Mike Graham-Cameron) *Steam Power: Colouring Book* (self-illustrated), Dinosaur, 1980; *Almost Everything There Is to Know,* Octopus, 1988.

Illustrator: Althea Braithwaite, *Man in the Sky,* Paul Elek, 1978; A. Braithwaite, *Making a Road,* Dinosaur, 1978; A. Braithwaite, *Machines on a Farm,* Evans, 1979; A. Braithwaite, *Making a Book,* Dinosaur, 1980; Peter Wiltshire, *Making Television Programmes,* Cambridge University Press, 1980.

WORK IN PROGRESS: Television scripts for a film about rubbish and a series about machines in the home. Constructing a refrigerator clock with giant icicles.

SIDELIGHTS: ''Although I make most of my income from the 'Rudiments' and miscellaneous illustration and animation work, I spend most of my time making things, mostly furniture and mechanical sculptures. I am currently making clocks on commission for public places. Both the 'Rudiments' and the sculpture are just different ways of finding out about things (which is what I really enjoy), the 'Rudiments' by reading, and sculptures by doing.

''I think that it is sad that engineering (how things work and are made) is not taught to younger children. It should be a subject like nature—children are surrounded by as many man-made objects as natural objects. Such books as there are on the subject are mostly boring and condescending. I feel some missionary zeal to improve the standard.''

JACKSON, Geoffrey (Holt Seymour) 1915-1987

OBITUARY NOTICE: Born March 4, 1915, in Little Hulton, England; died October 1, 1987. Government official and author. During his long career in the British diplomatic service Jackson held posts in embassies around the world. He made headlines in 1971 when, as ambassador to Uruguay, he was kidnapped by Tupamaros urban guerillas and held prisoner for eight months. While in captivity Jackson wrote a collection of short stories for children, *The Oven-Bird and Some Others,* based on animals he had encountered on his various postings. In addition, Jackson authored *People's Prison,* also published as *Surviving the Long Night: An Autobiographical Account of a Political Kidnapping,* and *Concorde Diplomacy: The Ambassador's Role in the World Today,* a humorous reminiscence of life as a diplomat. Jackson was a frequent contributor to periodicals, including *Observer, Tablet, Listener,* and *Daily Telegraph,* and served on a United Kingdom delegation attached to the United Nations during the 1950s.

FOR MORE INFORMATION SEE: New York Times Biographical Edition, September 16, 1971; *Contemporary Authors,* Volumes 61-64, Gale, 1976; *Who's Who in the World,* 4th edition, Marquis, 1978; *International Who's Who 1983-1984,* 47th edition, Europa Publications, 1983; *The Writers Directory: 1986-1988,* St. James Press, 1986. Obituaries: *Times* (London), October 2, 1987.

JANECZKO, Paul B(ryan) 1945-
(P. Wolny)

PERSONAL: Born July 27, 1945, in Passaic, N.J.; son of Frank John and Verna (Smolak) Janeczko; married Nadine Edris. *Education:* St. Francis College, Biddeford, Maine, A.B., 1967; John Carroll University, M.A., 1970. *Home:* 44 Mary Carroll St., New Auburn, Me. 04210. *Office:* Department of English, Gray-New Gloucester High School, Gray, Me. 04039.

CAREER: Padua Franciscan High School, Parma, Ohio, English teacher, 1968-72; Masconomet Regional High School, Topsfield, Mass., English teacher, 1972-77; Gray-New Gloucester High School, Gray, Me., teacher of language arts, 1977—. *Member:* National Council of Teachers of English, Educators for Social Responsibility, New England Association of Teachers of English, Maine Teachers of Language Arts, Maine Freeze Committee. *Awards, honors: Postcard Poems* was selected one of New York Public Library's Books for the Teen Age, 1980 and 1981, and *Don't Forget to Fly,* 1982; *Don't Forget to Fly* was selected one of the American Library Association's Best Young Adult Books, 1981, *Poetspeak,* 1983, *Strings,* 1984, *Pocket Poems,* 1985, and *Going Over to Your Place,* 1987; *Don't Forget to Fly* was selected one of *School Library Journal*'s Best Books, 1981, and *Poetspeak,* 1983; English-Speaking Union Books-across-the-Sea Ambassador of Honor Book, 1984, for *Poetspeak; Pocket Poems* was chosen one of Child Study Association of America's Children's Books of the Year, 1985.

*WRITINGS—*Young adult: (Editor) *The Crystal Image* (poems), Dell, 1977; (editor) *Postcard Poems: A Collection of Poetry for Sharing,* Bradbury, 1979; (editor) *It's Elementary* (detective stories), Bantam, 1981; *Loads of Codes and Secret Ciphers* (nonfiction), Simon & Schuster, 1981; (compiler) *Don't Forget to Fly: A Cycle of Modern Poems,* Bradbury, 1981; (editor) *Poetspeak: In Their Work, about Their Work,* Bradbury, 1983; (compiler) *Strings: A Gathering of Family Poems,* Bradbury, 1984; (compiler) *Pocket Poems: Selected for a Journey,* Bradbury, 1985; *Bridges to Cross* (novel; illustrated by Robert J. Blake), Macmillan, 1986; (editor) *Going Over to Your Place: Poems for Each Other,* Bradbury, 1987; *This Delicious Day,* F. Watts, 1987; *The Music of What Happens,* F. Watts, 1988.

Contributor: Lou Willett Stanek, editor, *Censorship: A Guide for Teachers, Librarians, and Others Concerned with Intellectual Freedom,* Dell, 1976; Jana Varlejs, editor, *Young Adult Literature in the Seventies,* Scarecrow, 1978; Gerard J. Senick, editor, *Children's Literature Review,* Volume III, Gale, 1978. Author of "Back Pages," a review column in *Leaflet,* 1973-76; guest editor, spring, 1977. Author of numerous articles, stories, poems (under pseudonym P. Wolny), and reviews to newspapers, professional journals, and popular magazines, including *Armchair Detective, New Hampshire Profiles, Modern Haiku, Dragonfly, Friend, Child Life,* and *Highlights for Children.*

WORK IN PROGRESS: A second novel for children; two poetry anthologies, one for children and one for young adults.

SIDELIGHTS: "I started teaching because I wanted to be the teacher I never had. I've been teaching since 1968 and have found it to be a demanding profession, yet satisfying because I enjoy working with young people and their language.

"Although I wrote some poetry and short stories for my college literary magazine, I started writing for wider publication when, after I'd been teaching for a few years, I began writing for educational journals. About this time I met Jerry Weiss who encouraged me to put together an anthology of the poems I'd been teaching. That collection turned out to be *The Crystal Image.* That book gave me the confidence to develop other anthologies. I'm especially pleased with my poetry anthologies *Postcard Poems* and *Don't Forget to Fly* because they are unique. *Postcard Poems* contains poems for sharing; poems

PAUL B. JANECZKO

Paul B. Janeczko

BRIDGES TO CROSS

I felt as if it were the bottom of the ninth and we were losing by ten runs. ■ (Jacket illustration by Robert J. Blake from *Bridges to Cross* by Paul B. Janeczko.)

short enough to fit on a postcard. *Don't Forget to Fly* breaks away from the traditional anthology arrangement and provides a wider poetic experience for the reader, and I'm delighted with the humorous poetry I was able to include in that book.

"My next collection, *Poetspeak*, was different from the other collections because it not only contained poems, it also included brief essays by the poets about their work and work habits. What is exciting about this book is that, with the exception of a few pieces, all the essays were written specifically for my book. *Strings*, a collection of poems about family, came next. That book has a special place in my heart because of the feelings and ties I have to my own family. *Pocket Poems* is a pocket-sized book filled with poems you can take with you on a journey. *Going Over to Your Place* contains some wonderful poems. I'm proud of that book because it contains so many different poets, many of whom do not get the recognition they deserve.

"When I'm developing an anthology, I keep my ears open for a poem that moves me. That's the first rule for developing a good anthology: the material must move you. It can anger you, delight you, make you cry, but you must be moved by it.

"I've always been fascinated by cloaks, daggers, spies, and secrets, so I wrote *Loads of Codes and Secret Ciphers*, a handbook for young people interested in secret writing.

"Even though I teach full time, I usually manage to write for an hour or two each day. This is not nearly as much time as

I would like to spend writing, but for the time being I will have to be satisfied with that. I wrote my first novel that way, so I guess I had the time I needed. That first novel, *Bridges to Cross*, is about a young boy who must reconcile a strict set of rules and his own freedom. Like many first novels, it is autobiographical in a number of ways. But it *IS* fiction.

"As more and more people read my books, I find myself being invited to educational conferences to speak to English teachers and librarians. Also, I've traveled to quite a few schools to be part of writing conferences for young authors. It's satisfying for me to help young people discover the challenge and fun in writing poetry. Writing poetry shouldn't be drudgery. It should be electric, exciting. So it's great fun for me to work with young writers and feel their energy as they work on a poem.

"Maine is a beautiful place to live and work. But like many beautiful places, it is threatened by the insanity of nuclear power. I work with people who are committed to putting an end to this threat to our planet. I also work with the Maine Freeze Committee and the local chapter of Educators for Social Responsibility to try to focus attention on the insanity of the arms race. During the last six years, we have moved closer to the brink of destruction and young people must be aware of that, and work for a future—their future—that will reduce that risk."

HOBBIES AND OTHER INTERESTS: Studying, baseball, cooking vegetarian meals, biking, working with wood, tending to his black dog, Ed.

JOHNSON, Harriett   1908-1987

OBITUARY NOTICE: Born August 31, 1908, in Minneapolis, Minn.; died of cancer, June 26, 1987, in La Jolla, Calif. Educator, music composer, music critic, editor, and author. Johnson served as head of the music department at Foxcroft School in Middleburg, Virginia, and taught layman's music courses in New York City and at the Berkshire Symphonic Festival in Lenox, Massachusetts. In 1943 she joined the staff of the *New York Post*, working as a music critic for the next forty-three years. Johnson wrote music herself, some of it for young people, including "Chuggy and the Blue Caboose," "Five Preludes for String Quartet and Wind Instruments," and "Three Questions." In addition, she edited *Billboard Music Yearbook* in 1945, contributed to music periodicals, and wrote *Your Career in Music*.

FOR MORE INFORMATION SEE: Who's Who in America, 42nd edition, Marquis, 1982. Obituaries: *New York Times*, July 2, 1987.

JONES, Charles M(artin)   1912-
(Chuck Jones)

PERSONAL: Born September 21, 1912, in Spokane, Wash.; son of Charles Adams and Mabel (Martin) Jones; married Dorothy Webster, January 31, 1935 (died, 1978); married Marian Dern (a writer), January 14, 1983; children: Linda Jones Clough. *Education:* Chouinard Art Institute (now California Institute of the Arts), diploma, 1931. *Politics:* Democrat. *Religion:* Unitarian. *Office:* 789 West 20th St., Costa Mesa, Calif. 92627.

CAREER: Began career working as a seaman and portrait painter, among other posts; worked as animator, director, and scenario writer for Ub Iwerks, Charles Mintz, and Walter Lantz, beginning in the early 1930s; Warner Bros., Inc., animator, 1933-38, director of numerous animated films featuring "Daffy Duck," "Bugs Bunny," "Sylvester," "Porky Pig," and others, 1938-63, co-creator of cartoon characters "Road Runner," "Wile E. Coyote," "Pepé le Pew," and "Snafu"; co-producer, writer, and director of "The Bugs Bunny Show," ABC-TV, 1960-62, and "The Bugs Bunny/Road Runner Hour," CBS-TV, 1968-71; writer, producer, and director of television specials, 1962—, including "How the Grinch Stole Christmas," 1970, "The Cricket in Times Square," ABC-TV, 1973, "Rikki-Tikki-Tavi," CBS-TV, 1975, "Bugs Bunny in King Arthur's Court," CBS-TV, 1978, "Raggedy Ann and Andy in the Great Santa Claus Caper," CBS-TV, 1978, and "The Pumpkin Who Couldn't Smile," 1979; Metro-Goldwyn-Mayer, Inc., Hollywood, Calif., producer of "Tom and Jerry" cartoon series, beginning 1963, head of animation department, beginning 1966; founder, Tower Twelve Productions, 1965; American Broadcasting Companies, Inc., vice-president of children's programming, beginning 1970, creator of program "The Curiosity Shop," 1971-73; founder, Chuck Jones Enterprises (motion picture company); creator of syndicated comic strip "Crawford," beginning 1978. Teacher and lecturer at various colleges and universities in the United States and abroad.

EXHIBITIONS: Gallery Lainzberg, 1976; Circle Fine Art Galleries, 1984. Film retrospectives: Museum of Modern Art, New York; British Film Institute at National Film Theater, London; American Film Institute at Kennedy Center, Washington, D.C.; New York Cultural Center; Harvard University, Cambridge, Mass.; Ottawa Art Center; London Film School; Filmex Festival, Hollywood; Deauville Festival of American Films (France); Moscow Film Festival; Montreal Film Festival. *Wartime service:* Worked on training films for the U.S. Army during World War II. *Member:* Academy of Motion Picture Arts and Sciences, Screen Writers Guild, Academy of Television Arts and Sciences, National Council on Children and Television, Screen Actors Guild.

AWARDS, HONORS: Newsreel Theatre's Award for the Best Animated Cartoon of the Year, 1940, for "Old Glory"; Academy Award from the Academy of Motion Picture Arts and Sciences for Best Animated Cartoons, 1950, for "For Sentimental Reasons," and 1965, for "The Dot and the Line," and for Best Documentary Short Subject, 1950, for "So Much for So Little"; CINE (Council on International Nontheatrical Events) Eagle Certificates for animated films, 1966, for "The Dot and the Line," 1973, for "The Cricket in Times Square," 1976, for "Rikki-Tikki-Tavi," and "The White Seal," and 1977, for "Mowgli's Brothers"; Peabody Award for Television Programming Excellence, 1971, for "How the Grinch Stole Christmas" and "Horton Hears a Who"; American Film Institute Tribute, 1975, 1980; Best Educational Film Award from the Columbus (Ohio) Film Festival, 1976; first prize at the Tehran Festival of Films for Children, 1977; British Film Institute Tribute, 1979; New York Film Festival Tribute, 1979; Parents' Choice Award for videos from the Parents' Choice Foundation, 1985, for "Rikki-Tikki-Tavi" and "Mowgli's Brothers"; Great Director Award from the USA Film Festival, 1986.

WRITINGS—Juvenile; all under name Chuck Jones; all self-illustrated; all published by Ideals Publishing, except as noted: (Adapter) Rudyard Kipling, *Rikki-Tikki-Tavi* (based on feature film of same title), 1982; (editor) R. Kipling, *The White Seal* (based on feature film of same title), 1982; (adapter) George Selden, *A Cricket in Times Square* (based on feature film of same title), 1984; *William the Backwards Skunk*, Crown, 1987. Also author of articles in the field of animation.

Director; all produced by Warner Bros.: "Night Watchman," 1938; "Dog Gone Modern," 1938; "Robin Hood Makes Good," 1939; "Presto Change-O," 1939; "Daffy Duck and the Dinosaur," 1939; "Naughty but Mice," 1939; "Old Glory," 1939; "Snowman's Land," 1939; "Little Brother Rat," 1939; "Little Lion Hunter," 1939; "The Good Egg," 1939; "Sniffles and the Bookworm," 1939; "Curious Puppy," 1939.

"Mighty Hunters," 1940; "Elmer's Candid Camera," 1940; "Sniffles Takes a Trip," 1940; "Tom Thumb in Trouble," 1940; "The Egg Collector," 1940; "Ghost Wanted," 1940; "Good Night Elmer," 1940; "Bedtime for Sniffles," 1940; "Elmer's Pet Rabbit," 1940; "Sniffles Bells the Cat," 1940; "Toy Trouble," 1941; "The Wacky Worm," 1941; "Inki and the Lion," 1941; "Snow Time for Comedy," 1941; "Joe Glow the Firefly," 1941; "Brave Little Bat," 1941; "Saddle Silly," 1941; "The Bid Came C.O.D.," 1941; "Porky's Ant," 1941; "Conrad the Sailor," 1941; "Porky's Prize Pony," 1941; "Dog Tired," 1941; "The Draft Horse," 1941; "Hold the Lion Please," 1941; "Porky's Midnight Matinee," 1941; "The Squawkin' Hawk," 1942; "Fox Pop," 1942; "My Favorite Duck," 1942; "To Duck or Not to Duck," 1942; "The Dover Boys," 1942; "Case of the Missing Hare," 1942; "Porky's Cafe," 1942; "Flop Goes the Weasel," 1943; "Super Rabbit," 1943; "The Unbearable Bear," 1943; "The Aristo Cat," 1943; "Wackiki Wabbit," 1943; "Fin 'n Catty," 1943; "Inki and the Mynah Bird," 1943; "Tom Turk and Daffy," 1944; "Angel Puss," 1944; "From Hand to Mouse," 1944; "The Odor-able Kitty," 1944; "Bugs Bunny and the Three Bears," 1944; "The Weakly Reporter," 1944; "Lost and Foundling," 1944.

"Trap Happy Porky," 1945; "Hare Conditioned," 1945; "Hare Tonic," 1945; "Hush My Mouse," 1945; "Fresh Airedale," 1945; "Quentin Quail," 1945; "Hair Raising Hare," 1945; "The Eager Beaver," 1945; "Roughly Squeaking," 1946; "Scent-Imental Over You," 1946; "Fair and Worm-er," 1946; "A Feather in His Hare," 1946; "Little Orphan Airedale," 1947; "What's Brewin' Bruin," 1947; "House Hunting Mice," 1947; "Haredevil Hare," 1947; "Inki at the Circus," 1947; "A Pest in the House," 1947; "Rabbit Punch," 1947; "You Were Never Duckier," 1948; "Mississippi Hare," 1948; "Mouse Wreckers," 1948; "Scaredy Cat," 1948; "My Bunny Lies over the Sea," 1948; "Awful Orphan," 1948; "The Bee-Deviled Bruin," 1948; "Daffy Dilly," 1948; "Long-Haired Hare," 1948; "Frigid Hare," 1949; "Rabbit Hood," 1949; "Often an Orphan," 1949; "Fast and Furry-Outs," 1949; "For Scenti-mental Reasons," 1949; "Bear Feat," 1949; "Homeless Hare," 1949; "So Much for So Little," 1949.

"The Hypochodri-Cat," 1950; "Dog Gone South," 1950; "The Scarlet Pumpernickel," 1950; "Eight-Ball Bunny," 1950; "The Ducksters," 1950; "Rabbit of Seville," 1950; "Caveman Inki," 1950; "Two's a Crowd," 1951; "A Hound for Trouble," 1951; "Rabbit Fire," 1951; "Chow Hound," 1951; "The Wearing of the Grin," 1951; "A Bear for Punishment," 1951; "Bunny Hugged," 1951; "Scent-imental Romeo," 1951; "Cheese Chasers," 1951; "Drip-Along Daffy," 1951; "Operation: Rabbit," 1952; "Water, Water Every Hare," 1952; "The Hasty Hare," 1952; "Mousewarming," 1952; "Don't Give up the Sheep," 1952; "Feed the Kitty," 1952; "Little Beau Pepe," 1952; "Beep Beep," 1952; "Going! Going! Gosh!," 1952; "Terrier Stricken," 1952; "Rabbit Seasoning," 1952; "Kiss Me Cat," 1952; "Forward March Hare," 1953; "Wild over You," 1953; "Bully for Bugs," 1953; "Duck Amuck," 1953; "Much Ado about Nutting," 1953; "Duck Dodgers in the 24 ½ Century," 1953; "Zipping Along," 1953; "Feline Frame-Up," 1953; "Punch Trunk," 1954; "From A to ZZZZ," 1954; "Bewitched Bunny," 1954; "Duck! Rabbit!"

CHUCK JONES

Duck!,'' 1954; ''No Barking,'' 1954; ''Stop, Look, and Hasten!,'' 1954; ''Sheep Ahoy,'' 1954; ''My Little Duckaroo,'' 1954.

''The Cat's Bah,'' 1955; ''Claws for Alarm,'' 1955; ''Lumberjack Rabbit'' (3-D), 1955; ''Ready, Set, Zoom!,'' 1955; ''Rabbit Rampage,'' 1955; ''Double or Mutton,'' 1955; ''Baby Buggy Bunny,'' 1955; ''Beanstalk Bunny,'' 1955; ''Past Performance,'' 1955; ''Jumpin' Jupiter,'' 1955; ''Guided Muscle,'' 1955; ''Knight-Mare Hare,'' 1955; ''Two Scents' Worth,'' 1956; ''One Froggy Evening,'' 1956; ''Bugs' Bonnets,'' 1956; ''Rocket Squad,'' 1956; ''Heaven Scent,'' 1956; ''Rocket-Bye-Baby,'' 1956; ''Broomstick Bunny,'' 1956; ''Gee-Whizzzz,'' 1956; ''Barbary Coast Bunny,'' 1956; ''Deduce, You Say,'' 1957; ''There They Go-Go-Go!,'' 1957; ''Scrambled Aches,'' 1957; ''Go Fly a Kite,'' 1957; ''Steal Wool,'' 1957; ''Zoom and Bored,'' 1957; ''To Hare Is Human,'' 1957; ''Ali Baba Bunny,'' 1957; ''Boyhood Daze,'' 1957; ''What's Opera, Doc?,'' 1957; ''Touche and Go,'' 1957; ''Hare-Way to the Stars,'' 1958; ''Hook, Line, and Stinker,'' 1958; ''Robin Hood Daffy,'' 1958; ''Whoa, Be Gone!,'' 1958; ''To Itch His Own,'' 1958; ''Baton Bunny,'' 1959; ''Hot Rod and Reel,'' 1959; ''Cat Feud,'' 1959; ''Hip Hip—Hurry!,'' 1959; ''Really Scent,'' 1959.

''Fastest with the Mostest,'' 1960; ''Who Scent You?,'' 1960; ''Rabbit's Feat,'' 1960; ''Wild about Hurry,'' 1960; ''Ready, Woolen and Able,'' 1960; ''High Note,'' 1961; ''Hopalong Casualty,'' 1961; ''The Abominable Snow Rabbit,'' 1961; ''A Scent of the Matterhorn,'' 1961; ''Lickety Splat,'' 1961; ''Zip 'n Snort,'' 1961; ''The Mouse on 57th Street,'' 1961; ''Compressed Hare,'' 1961; ''Louvre Come Back to Me,'' 1962; ''Beep Prepared,'' 1962; ''A Sheep in the Deep,'' 1962;

''Nelly's Folly,'' 1962; ''Zoom at the Top,'' 1962; ''Martian thru Georgia,'' 1963; ''Now Hear This,'' 1963; ''Hare-Breadth Hurry,'' 1963; ''I Was a Teenage Thumb,'' 1963; ''Woolen Under Where,'' 1963; ''War and Pieces,'' 1964; ''Transylvania 6-5000,''; ''Mad as a Mars Hare,'' 1964; ''To Beep or Not to Beep,'' 1964.

Director; all produced by Metro-Goldwyn-Mayer: ''Penthouse Mouse,'' 1963; ''The Cat Above and the Mouse Below,'' 1964; ''Is There a Doctor in the Mouse,'' 1964; ''Much Ado about Mousing,'' 1964; ''Snowbody Loves Me,'' 1964; ''Unshrinkable Jerry Mouse,'' 1964; ''The Dot and the Line,'' 1965; ''Ah Sweet Mouse-Story of Life,'' 1965; ''Tom-ic Energy,'' 1965; ''Bad Day at Cat Rock,'' 1965; ''Brothers Carry Mouse Off,'' 1965; ''Haunted Mouse,'' 1965; ''I'm Just Wild about Jerry,'' 1965; ''Of Feline Bondage,'' 1965; ''Year of the Mouse,'' 1965; ''Cat's Me-Ouch,'' 1965; ''Duel Personality,'' 1966; ''Jerry Jerry Quite Contrary,'' 1966; (with Ben Washam) ''Love Me, Love My Mouse,'' 1966; ''The Bear That Wasn't,'' 1967; ''Cat and Duplicat,'' 1967.

Feature films and television specials; producer and director: (Also author) ''Gay Purr-ee,'' UPA, 1962; ''How the Grinch Stole Christmas,'' 1970; (co-author of screenplay) ''The Phantom Toll Booth,'' Metro-Goldwyn-Mayer, 1971; ''Horton Hears a Who,'' 1971; ''The Pogo Special Birthday Special,'' 1971; (executive producer) ''A Christmas Carol,'' 1973; ''The Cricket in Times Square,'' ABC-TV, 1973; ''A Very Merry Cricket,'' ABC-TV, 1973; ''Yankee Doodle Cricket,'' ABC-TV, 1974; ''The White Seal,'' CBS-TV, 1974; ''Rikki-Tikki-Tavi,'' CBS-TV, 1975; ''Carnival of the Animals,'' CBS-TV, 1976; ''Mowgli's Brothers,'' CBS-TV, 1976; ''Bugs Bunny in King Arthur's Court,'' CBS-TV, 1978; ''Raggedy Ann and Andy

(From *William the Backwards Skunk* by Chuck Jones. Illustrated by the author.)

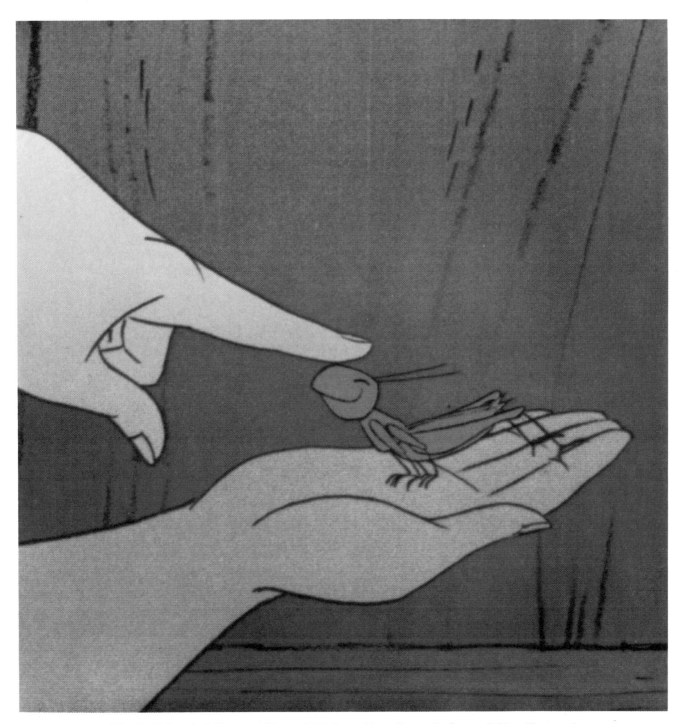

Mrs. Bellini stroked Chester. ■ (From *A Cricket in Times Square* by George Selden. Illustrated by Chuck Jones.)

in the Great Santa Claus Caper,'' CBS-TV, 1978; ''The Bugs Bunny/Road Runner Movie,'' 1979; ''Daffy Duck's Thanks for Giving Special,'' CBS-TV, 1979; ''Bugs Bunny's Looney Christmas Tales,'' 1979; ''The Pumpkin Who Couldn't Smile,'' CBS-TV, 1979; ''Bugs Bunny's Bustin' Out All Over,'' CBS-TV, 1980; ''Duck Dodgers and the Return of the 24 ½ Century,'' CBS-TV, 1980.

Also director of ''Hell Bent for Election,'' 1945, for Stephen Bosustow and co-creator of the ''Private Snafu'' series of cartoons for the U.S. Army.

ADAPTATIONS: ''A Very Merry Cricket'' (filmstrip with record or cassette), Miller-Brody, 1975; ''Rikki-Tikki-Tavi'' (filmstrip with cassette), Xerox Films, 1976; ''The White Seal'' (filmstrip with cassette), Xerox Films, 1976; ''The Cricket in Times Square'' (motion picture), Xerox Films, 1976; ''Yankee Doodle Cricket'' (motion picture; with teacher's guide), Xerox Films, 1976; ''Mowgli's Brothers'' (filmstrip with cassette; with teacher's guide), 1977.

Videocassettes: ''Bugs Bunny's Wacky Adventures'' (Beta, VHS; contains ''Long-Haired Hare,'' ''Bunny Hugged,'' ''Bully

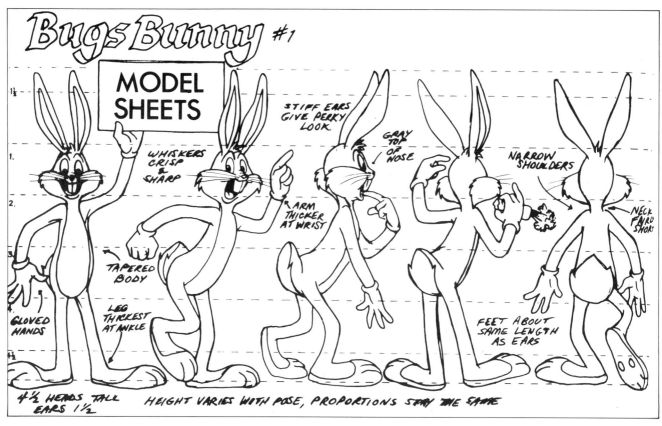

Model sheet of Bugs. (Courtesy of Warner Communications, Inc.)

for Bugs,'' ''Ali Baba Bunny,'' and ''Duck! Rabbit! Duck!''), Warner; ''Daffy Duck: The Nutiness Continues'' (Beta, VHS; contains ''Duck Amuck,'' ''Beanstalk Bunny,'' ''Deduce You Say,'' ''Rabbit Fire,'' ''Dripalong Daffy,'' and ''The Scarlet Pumpernickel''), Warner; ''Looney Toons Video Show #1-#7'' (Beta, VHS; #1 contains ''The Ducksters'' and ''Zipping Along,'' #2 contains ''Two Scents Worth,'' #3 contains ''Double or Mutton,'' ''Feline Frameup,'' ''Eight-Ball Bunny,'' ''Scaredy Cat,'' and ''Louvre Come Back to Me,'' #4 contains ''Heaven Scent'' and ''Don't Give Up the Sheep,'' #5 contains ''Fastest with the Mostest'' and ''Forward March Hare,'' #6 contains ''Lickety Splat'' and ''Scent of the Matterhorn,'' and #7 contains ''Beep Beep''), Warner; ''Porky Pig's Screwball Comedies'' (Beta, VHS; contains ''Often an Orphan'' and ''Wearing of the Grin''), Warner; ''Classic Chase'' (Beta, VHS), Warner; ''A Salute to Chuck Jones'' (Beta, VHS), Warner; ''The Bugs Bunny/Road Runner Show'' (Beta, VHS); ''Warner Bros. Cartoons'' (Beta, VHS; contains ''Case of the Missing Hare'' and ''Daffy Duck and the Dinosaur''), Yesteryear; ''The Best of Bugs Bunny and Friends'' (Beta, VHS; contains ''Bedtime for Sniffles'' and ''The Little Lion Hunter''), MGM/UA; ''Looney Tunes and Merrie Melodies 3'' (Beta, VHS; contains ''To Duck or Not to Duck''), Yesteryear; ''A Cricket in Times Square'' (Beta, VHS), Family; ''Horton Hears a Who'' (Beta, VHS).

SIDELIGHTS: Born in Spokane, Washington, September 21, 1912. ''My first ten years were spent in Ocean Park on Washington Street, off the old Speedway. A vacant lot separated our house from the ocean. We became students of the ocean and were wild young things.

''My father taught us an important lesson. 'The ocean doesn't care,' he used to say. 'It's not out to kill you or to save you.

It just doesn't care.' We always swam together, and wore a string with a small lead weight around our necks. If you got caught in a big wave and tossed around and the little weight hung against your chest, you were pointing up and if it hung in front of your nose, you were facing down. 'Chance favors the prepared mind,' according to my father. Swimming, he said, was a form of transportation, not a sport. To swim for sport was ridiculous in his mind. Why, there are so many creatures who swim faster than man, why would he bother?

''He also taught us to read. I read at four years of age, but lagged behind my sister who read at three. My father liked children but didn't want to amuse them. He figured the best way to get us out of his hair was to teach us to read. He never allowed us to talk at the breakfast table. 'It's no time to talk,' he'd say. 'It's too early in the day. If you can't think of anything better, read the cereal box.' He didn't care what we read, he just wanted us to read. He was right. You can't get an education by following a prescribed route for reading. I once protested. I memorized all the cereal boxes. When his inevitable, 'Read the cereal box,' comment was made one morning, I quipped, 'I've already read them.' 'Do you have a rubber heel?' he asked. 'Well, take off your shoe and read *that*.' My habits continue. I still can't speak at breakfast, and a book with lunch is wonderful.

''I read Dickens and Twain and Trollope and Dumas before I even went to school. You see, in those days it was common to rent houses with the owner's belongings still in them—sheets, dishes, and of course, books. Books were in when we were kids. There was no radio, no television. Motion pictures were a once-a-week deal if we were lucky, so we read books and magazines. Father always looked for a house full of books to rent, and we'd get straight to reading the minute we moved

© Warner Bros. Inc. 1980

Bugs Bunny on the move. (Courtesy of Warner Communications, Inc.)

in. By the time the last of us had finished the last of the books, we'd move on to a new house. I recall the owner of one house was the world's leading expert on the island of Guam. There must have been fifty books on Guam, and I still know quite a bit about it.

"I was always at war with my schools because they tried to teach me things I already knew, or to make me read things I already read, or worse, to read something I didn't want to read. A librarian once told me of a little girl who came in to tell her that she had just finished reading *Alice in Africa.* 'Oh, would you like another book about Africa?' asked the librarian. 'No,' said the little girl, 'I'm not reading about Africas, I'm reading about Alices. I would like another book on Alice.' I had a similar experience as a child. I read *Uncle Vanya,* figuring it would be a sequel to *Uncle Wiggly.* I found it very boring and was very upset that Alexander was spelled, 'Alexandr.' It was an outrage that the writer couldn't even spell.

"My father never allowed us to go to church on Sunday, because the scriptures declared Sunday a day of rest. Raised a Baptist, he knew the Bible by heart. Then he became an atheist. He'd approach the most intelligent of clergymen and try to convert them to atheism. He actually succeeded with one Catholic priest. He likened the Pope to a dishonest insurance agent who was publicly betting his clients would not die, when his company knew damn well they would.

"We always had a lot of paper around the house. Everybody in the family drew. My father encouraged us. 'Draw only on one side,' he used to say, 'and maybe you'll do something right. What if da Vinci had painted "The Last Supper" on one side of the paper and the "Mona Lisa" on the other?' He was appalled that other children used both sides of paper.

"Mother had the facility for drawing and was a gentle critic. She was a fine dollmaker, as well. The night before she died, there on her worktable was an unfinished doll, and two books: *Peter Rabbit* and Thomas Mann's *The Magic Mountain.* You see, she could enjoy the whole realm of books; her taste was universal. Never did she over criticize or over praise to the extent that we might lose respect for her opinion. She always made comments that we could understand. In one way or another, all four of us children went into graphics. My sister is a weaver and a teacher, my other sister a sculptress and a painter, and my brother, a painter and photographer, is now in audio-visual education.

"[Our progression] followed the usual path of copying things and making wonderful changes. But we kept drawing, which most people don't. I remember a teacher in art school telling us, 'You have a hundred thousand bad drawings in you, and the sooner you get rid of them, the better.' It didn't bother me, because by that time, I was already on my three hundred thousandth drawing. Parents, and people in general, don't understand the number of errors you have to make in any line of work.

"Growing up in Los Angeles we were very much aware of films. It was, after all, the city's industry. We used to go up to the Hollywood Hotel and watch the stars sitting out on the porch. The 160th Infantry in California with Mary Pickford as mascot used to parade on horses down Sunset Boulevard to cheering crowds. We'd squat on our front porch and watch. Cowboy actors would fist fight from one saloon to the next. I don't think they ever hurt each other much, but they knew how to tumble. Eucalyptus trees and big red flowers ran up the hills where the Hollywood freeway is now on a pass of winding road that followed the contour of the hills.

"I was a victim of the I.Q. Aptitude Test from Stanford University. My score moved me from fourth to seventh grade. At twelve I entered high school, a small, skinny kid, socially out of the picture. I was transparent, which is worse than being disliked. When you're disliked, at least you exist. I was invisible. Aside from social hardships, it was very difficult for me to keep up, especially with subjects like algebra, which I really wasn't ready for. My father, who had turned down a full scholarship to Carnegie Tech had high expectations and demanded straight A's. I didn't get them. I learned instead to forge his name on report cards. After three years, he finally realized that I wasn't going to school. He decided I was a failure, but came up with the idea of art school as a last resort. Art school was the best thing that ever happened to me.

"What was important at Chouinard was not the individual teachers but the character of the school itself. In the classical tradition, the school offered painting and drawing and anatomy. Chouinard did not teach cartooning, it taught the human figure. The feeling was that if you can draw the human figure, you can draw any vertebrate because all the vertebrates have the same bones and the same muscles. The big difference is head structure.

"A large number of people who went to work with Disney came from Chouinard, because they knew the human figure. A comic strip artist can find a style and go on with it forever. But the animator may have to draw a white seal one day and Bugs Bunny the next. Of course, animators have signature type touches, but the truth is that you cannot recognize a *bad* animator's work; you can only recognize the work of a good one. A bad animator tends to imitate other people's work, and not very well at that. A good animator can take the same scene, and bring his personality to the animation, not in a heavy way, but more like an actor who must put aside his personality to play a part, but whom we nevertheless recognize.

"I never decided on animation; circumstances decided. I came out of art school into the Depression. I considered myself lucky doing anything. Unemployment stood at about fifteen percent. I didn't know anything about animation, and neither did the people who did it. I started as a cel washer and worked my miserable way up.

"I always did the storyboards first, which consisted of about 150 drawings. I would lay each picture out and then write dialogue. I made about 300 drawings total for each six-minute cartoon. Then I would have someone type the dialogue directly from the drawings.

"With Bugs and Daffy, I always knew exactly what I wanted them to say. I worked with the actors to get a precise intonation and timing. Mel Blanc did both Bugs and Daffy, and I would read through the script with him. It must all be planned before it goes to the animator. The dialogue is in your head so clearly, and occasionally, when a line is spoken by an actor, you get a glimpse of something you did not foresee. Then you might change it. The pictures were laid out in musical terms. We'd go to the director and work out the tempo. The accent would always go on the down beat. The director had to time the entire picture. There's no room for method acting. We never overshot a film; we couldn't afford to. Our producer, Leon Schlesinger, was bright enough to figure out that if salaries went up because of demand, it would be cheaper to produce a shorter picture. He'd have made them two minutes long, if he'd had his druthers. Thankfully, the exhibitors insisted on six minutes, so our pictures averaged about 540 feet. Each unit made ten pictures a year. The directors had to learn to time the pictures before it went into animation, well within a few feet

(From the animated cartoon "Duck Dodgers in the 24½th Century." Copyright 1953 by Warner Bros., Inc.)

Wile E. Coyote and the Road Runner. (Copyright © by Warner Bros., Inc.)

Bugs, the nonchalant rabbit with the Brooklyn accent, along with his stablemates Daffy Duck, Porky Pig, etc. (Copyright © by Warner Bros., Inc.)

of sixty minutes. I got so much experience that I am now able to time a half hour of film within two or three seconds. You learn a rhythm of working and begin to recognize when to speed something up.

"I had no knowledge of music before I began to work in animation, but toward the end of my career with Warner Bros., I was able to read a piano score. I would suggest pieces of music, and basic notes were written out for me. I would make the characters move to the notes. We always played the music straight, even in something like 'What's Opera Doc?' where we squashed the entire fourteen-hour 'Ring of Nibelung' into six minutes. The music was honest.

"[Comparing animated humor] with Chaplin films, the same holds true. It all comes down to the most profound statement I've ever heard about humor. It was Ed Wynn who said, 'A comedian is not someone who opens a funny door, he's someone who opens a door funny.' That is an important distinction. Our characters are not funny to look at, they are not like comic-strips, they are personalities who evoke humor by the way they move. Even when people see a static image of one of our characters, they find it funny because they remember how the character moved, and they remember the funny things that character did. Would I be interested in a photograph of Chaplin if I'd never seen his work? It's a trick of memory.

"A professor of neurology at University of California, San Diego, recently wrote to me, 'I've watched with fascination

Daffy's growth from his earliest haphazard plural personality, through adolescence, to the splendid maturity in the fifties. Daffy has become a spokesman for the egoist in everyone, but he remains undaunted by the fear of consequences and is as cowardly as the rest of us.' That's what Daffy is about. There is a Daffy in all of us, just as there is a Grinch in all of us. Believability invokes sympathy, and if you don't have sympathy, you can't have humor.

"Most of my characters are failures, as are Chaplin's. They are wimps and nerds, and regardless of how kind and decent they are, they are fighters. They fight to get something to eat, they fight to win the girl. They are trying to live within the establishments of 'City Lights,' and 'Modern Times,' to maintain dignity in dehumanizing environments. From ancient comedy to Robin Williams and Richard Pryor, comic characters have fought to maintain their dignity.

"Elmer Fudd is funny for several reasons. First, he is very much afraid someone is going to interrupt him in his pursuit of his sport, hunting. Second, his voice is funny, because he always sounds as if he is about to cry. He wants to be understood, and his way of getting attention is by crying. Well, what do kids do when they want mommy's attention, when they want the candy that mommy is dead set against? They cry. But Elmer is a grown man and he cries. Everything he says is related to that little sob.

"Porky Pig started out as a juvenile character. His debut was in a little picture called, 'I Haven't Got a Hat,' in which he

The Chuck Jones version of Tom and Jerry. (Copyright 1940 by Loews.)

recites the 'Midnight Ride of Paul Revere,' while fending off his need to go to the bathroom. In his race to get through the recitation, he begins to stutter, and that was the birth of Porky's speech characteristic. Porky continued to stutter, until I directed a few episodes. Stuttering just didn't work for me; I don't find it funny. So I transformed his stutter from a speech impediment to an exaggerated form of what we all go through when we are searching for a word we can't find.

"Bugs Bunny, Tweetie Bird, and Pepé le Pew are comic heroes. Comic heroes are actually quite rare; we tend rather to turn ineptitude, inefficiencies, and defects into humor. Bugs, on the other hand, manages to make *success* funny—and that's not easy. In order to accomplish that, he's got to take a few lumps himself. And, while a character like [Walter Lantz's] Woody Woodpecker goes out and intentionally bedevils people, Bugs simply fights back. He is a counterrevolutionary, but does not aggress people without provocation. That would make him a wise-ass, and that would get tiring.

"My reason for using animals is very simple. Human beings are very complex. You have to work at getting a person to strike a general attitude. With an animal, you start from scratch. You can say, 'I want Daffy to be like "x."' But we are too familiar with human behavior to ever have such freedom to create. Take Disney's 'The Seven Dwarfs.' The picture began with complex characters. The queen is evil, but has the human attribute of fear that someone might be more beautiful than her. If she did not have this frailty, she wouldn't be believable.

"Like La Fontaine, you can assign human characteristics to animals. And you can play with people's assumptions about

animals. For instance, people assume that gorillas are evil because they find them ugly. We assume that snakes are bad, but the chances of being bit by a rattlesnake are the same as being hit by lightning. We admire bees, though they hurt us. We hate flies and they are harmless. These clichés open up animation to new areas of comedy—one must simply contradict the general assumption to get a laugh.

"Pepé le Pew would never work as a real skunk. He works because he is a black cat with a white stripe on his back. The humor that arises from the situation of his desire for a female is legitimate.

"Most characters start out one way and then evolve into more sophisticated behavior. Yosemite Sam is a victim of his own inability to control his bad temper. Daffy Duck believes the world owes him a living.

"I recall how on my sixth birthday I got a big cake. As I result I figured I was being initiated into manhood. After blowing out the candles, my mother gave me a knife and told me to cut as big a piece as I wanted. I gave her the knife back and said I had no interest in sharing the cake. I was a man, and it was my cake. There is the origin of Daffy Duck's obstinate behavior. I said I did not want to share, I was fed up with sharing, I had shared enough in my life to that point. Then my father came in. He seemed to be nine feet tall and looked like a moose without antlers. He took me to my room and revealed to me a word I had never heard before: Selfish. I then discovered, as Daffy did once, that in order to survive, you must learn certain rules. That in a cake—even your own birthday cake—there is a piece that is completely surrounded

The many faces of Porky Pig. (Courtesy of Warner Communications, Inc.)

The official Loony Tunes sign-off.

by corporal punishment. If you deviate, even one thousandth of an inch, *you're in trouble*. And this also relates to timing films; I have a great respect for that thousandth of an inch.

"Porky is an observer. In pictures like 'Buck Rogers' he watches with a kind of amused intelligence and comments on what is happening around him. Daffy as Buck Rogers started out as a third string, sub-Boy Scout type, but evolved into an interesting character. Sylvester and Coyote represent the fanatic type who becomes so obsessed that he doubles his effort and forgets his aim.

"The Road Runner has no meaning at all. He is simply a *force;* he is something to eat. The Road Runner ignores the Coyote. He just goes along on his way. We made structural rules about how the Coyote and Road Runner could behave. The Road Runner could never personally harm the Coyote; the Coyote being a victim of his own ineptitude and inability in getting the right product from the 'ACME' company. The Road Runner must stay on the road unless he is lured off by something relevant like a 'detour' sign or a white line. The Coyote is only after the Road Runner. The landscape was always the southwestern American desert. As Don Graham of Cal Arts pointed out, the Road Runner is the only character in the film who establishes himself as a form moving in deep space. You always know how deep the space is by the way the Road Runner moves, and *not* by what the background tells you.

"Jam sessions were unique at Warner Bros. I don't know who started them, but the way it worked was that after you came

up with a story or an idea for an animated picture, the director and writer would call in other directors, usually six or seven, as well as the production crew, and the producer (a spector at the feast). We'd come together for a two-hour session to decide if the idea might work. It was not like brain storming where anyone can say anything. In our jam sessions you could only say something of a contributory nature. You had to think in terms of the word, *yes*. No one was allowed to say anything negative whatsoever. It really worked.

"It wasn't long before everyone realized that if you began to horde ideas in the jam session, everyone else would horde, too. This realization fostered a more open atmosphere. Ideas began to pour in, and sometimes, you could almost write the entire story after one session. We worked on what we called character 'business' rather than on story structure.

"Some ideas did not catch fire. The director who brought in the original idea was the monitor. As director, you could detect an embarrassing silence or a futile effort on everyone's part to get the idea up and working. If it didn't begin to fatten up after half an hour, it was back to the drawing board. There was never any embarrassment involved in leaving the session with a failed idea.

"There are only two really bad words in the English language. One is 'no,' and the other is 'why.' How the baby ever survives the first 'no' is beyond my comprehension. Everything has been going very smoothly, milk and mommy and all that great stuff, and then suddenly he tips over a wastebasket and somebody screams 'No!' at him. He stops what he's doing. He feels bad; he is free no longer. He suddenly knows what life's about, and damn it, he has to start obeying the rules. It's awful.

"'Why' is such a perfect word to ask yourself. 'Why did I do that? Why can't I write better? Why don't you like me?' Kids often ask, 'Why did you spill the ink?' There's no answer to that. I could invent a myth, say that something happened to my ancestors eons ago that cause me to spill the ink. But it would be false. But if someone asks 'What happened?' Well, you can answer in honest detail. 'I was playing around, and spilt the ink, period.' We connect everything to motivation, even when it's completely nonexistent or irrelevant.''

Approaches to animating the same characters are uniquely different. ''Humphrey Bogart once said that the Academy Awards were nonsense because if you *really* wanted to judge acting, you should get five actors and have them all play one role, like Hamlet, and then decide. In terms of animation, I could see subtle differences between the Bugs Bunny cartoons that others directed and those that I did. The action would vary a bit; Fritz Freleng broadened what Bugs could do, and the character grew that way, which is only right. We had to be consistent, but characters nevertheless developed through accidents of style and creativity by mutation. Most mutations are bad—in animation, in drawing, in anything, but you still must constantly be on the alert for the good ones, and use them.

''The half-closed eyes of my characters are very important to me. Daffy laughed with his mouth and the front of his eyes. The contradiction worked very well. The half-glance of the

Coyote also worked well—he did not want the audience to see his disgrace. John Singer Sargent was once asked the difference between a portrait and a painting, 'A portrait is a picture in which something is wrong with the eyes.' We expect to see eyes moving. When painting, it is very difficult to portray where the eyes have been and where they will go. It's a problem of starting point. Lautrec and other painters came up against the same problem when portraying action. When does the horse jump? When does the discus thrower let go? Either it's ready to happen, or it has already happened—there is no in between. We used to start with that old hand on the hip. Things could go anywhere from there. You'd look at Bugs and think, 'What'll he do next?' The hip is a natural place for the hand to rest.

''Nobody performs an action immediately. If you pull a bow and arrow, you may not be aware of it, but you bring it back, hesitate ever so slightly and let it go. That is a 'field of action.' None of us are so damn confident that we execute an action without some hesitation. It's not intellectual, it's just natural, and probably a function of our eye movement. So to portray character, it is essential not to mechanize such nuances of action. None of us know precisely what we are going to do at any time, whether we are making love or eating cake or driving home. Watching my wife eat a plate of scrambled eggs is fascinating to me; she does all sorts of rearranging before she ever gets to the first bite. I am more direct than she. I eat what comes next. But still I hesitate. A bad director flattens out such characteristic behavior.

''Gesture is very important. For instance, Bugs eats his carrot with his pinky extended. It's a contradiction, and its funny. It's not like eating caviar, it's like eating a hot dog with your pinky extended.

Bugs and Daffy reach new heights as "cover boys" for *Film Comment*.

Sylvester and Tweety are featured stars of "The Bugs Bunny/Road Runner Hour" which debuted on CBS-TV, September 14, 1968 and is still running.

(From the television special "Rikki-Tikki-Tavi." Presented on CBS-TV, 1975.)

(From the award-winning animated special "How the Grinch Stole Christmas." Broadcast on CBS-TV, 1970.)

(From the animated special "The White Seal," which aired on CBS-TV, 1976.)

(From the television special "Mowgli's Brothers." Broadcast on CBS-TV, 1976.)

"At Warner Bros. the director was the composer and the performer. We had a great deal of artistic freedom and control, not because we were given it, but because we *demanded* it. The absolute control of the director was a vital factor.

"We never wrote for a 'target' audience. We never made pictures for children or for adults; we made them for ourselves. We couldn't know what an audience would react to because we were not allowed to preview. We made the pictures for ourselves, and if we kept our jobs we took it as an indication that we were doing something right. The only response we ever got was not from the front office or the distributors but from the exhibitors. It took about two years from the time we began an animated cartoon until the time it hit the screen. That's one reason why our pictures have no temporal connotations or references. We knew that that would date the pictures and so avoided it."

The directors who worked at Warner Bros. with Jones shared a diverse background. "Friz was raised in a middle-class Kansas City neighborhood; McKimson was from a ranch family in Denver; Carl Stallings was an organist from Kansas City; Ken Harris was a race track driver; Ben Washman was a short order cook; Tex Avery was raised in the middle of Texas and had all the prejudices that went with it. But we all drew. And so we were able to live together and to work.

"We learned from each other. It was like playing tennis. You can't play without an opponent. We never tried to beat each other. Competition never played any part. There was a spirit of intense cooperation in all the animation units.

"We had very little to do with each other socially. We were one wonderful head at work, but after work, we went our separate ways. Because our lives were so different, we maintained distinct points of view, and that, of course, enriched our work.

"In terms of editing, we worked more like Alfred Hitchcock, who said that his films were finished when he started shooting them. [For us, too] everything was timed and ready by the time it went to the animator."

Sketching animals at the zoo is one of his enjoyments. "Show me the skeleton of an animal and I'll show you how it must move. You could take two men, put them in a perfect horse suit, and they may actually look like a horse as long as they stand still. But the minute they move they will look like two men in a horse suit, because you can't move any differently. Years after I'd left Warner Bros. I met a girl who was the world's leading expert on road runners. She told me that our animation was actually accurate, with a slight difference in the shape of the head."

Jones feels that perspective affects the accuracy of a drawing. "We don't see the way we think we do. We don't see in perspective, we *can't*. Motion pictures give you a sense of vertigo because the whole image is in focus; our eyes don't work that way. Look at a Native American, African, or Middle Eastern painting and the perspective will be much more accurate than the so-called Italian masters. In Japanese erotic art, the sexual organs are magnified—nobody has sexual organs like that, except perhaps the horse! But the artists convey what they feel is important. Think of the reverse; Chinese culture is much older, and they diminish the centrality of the sexual organ in their art, and opt to portray an overall feeling. In African painting, if a lion is in the landscape, no matter how far away, it will be emphasized. But no matter how close you are to an elk or an elan, it will appear very small because these gentle creatures are not dangerous.

"Likewise, if something was dangerous in our cartoon, we'd emphasize it by using a close up. Proportion of sound was also important. When we first started making cartoons, the sound effects were all hugely exaggerated. Then one day we were dubbing a Road Runner cartoon and the Coyote fell off a cliff. I felt that one or two frames could make the difference in the gag. He'd go off the cliff and fall for thirty-two frames and then disappear for eighteen. I felt in twenty-four frames, it wouldn't be as funny. While we were working on the timing, the sound editor accidentally left the sound down. When the Coyote hit the ground, instead of a big 'PLOP' we heard a little 'plip.' Well, we never laughed so hard. Then the mixer shook his head, wiped his tears away and said, 'Well, we'd better fix that.' 'Bob,' I said, 'if you fix that I will stuff your shirt in your mouth. I will give you writer's cramp. . . . What the hell were you just doing?' 'Laughing,' he said. 'Why?' I asked. 'Because it was funny.' 'Why should we change it, then?' He said, 'Well, it's not the way we do things.' 'It's the way we do things from now on,' I said.

"Animation is a uniquely American art form. You see, people like Chaplin, Buster Keaton, and Laurel and Hardy made short subjects until 1930. When sound came in, they began to make features. The Keystone Cops faded out because they couldn't sustain feature length. Around 1930, there was suddenly an opening for short subjects. That is why animation took off. It's always that way—animation came into its own because there was a place for it to fit into. Exhibitors needed something of entertainment quality that was six minutes long and so animation became big.

"When Disney made 'The Three Little Pigs' it was a turning point for all of us. Up until then, good characters were cute and sweet, and evil characters were ugly and bad. The only way you could tell who the characters were was by their appearance. Character animation was born with 'The Three Little Pigs,' in which three characters with completely different personalities looked exactly alike. It was their movement and their personalities that distinguished one from the other, not their appearance.

"Voice has surprisingly little to do with character. If voice makes the character, why isn't Barney Rubble as famous as Bugs Bunny? Both are portrayed by the same voice actor. It is the quirky action that contributes to character, the funny visual effects like the dancing mushroom in *Fantasia* or the weird way that Goofy walks.

"The Warner Bros. cartoons became popular after World War II. Up until then, we were learning our trade. We weren't imitating Disney, but we were struggling with character. Then we realized that personalities were important. Our cartoons are more insouciant than those of the other studios. We seldom made pictures that were cute or pretty. Because after the war, everybody was saying, 'The hell with it, let's go do things.' We were an impertinent generation. We didn't believe in patriotism or ideology. Bugs, Daffy, and all the rest of our characters reflected that spirit of the post-war period. You cannot ignore the place or the time you live in.

"I am the only one of my generation of animation directors who refused to compromise. After Warner Bros. [disbanded], the characters were farmed out and they were cheapened. They were poorly animated and unprofessional. The tool of my trade is character animation. I left Warner Bros. in 1963 after thirty

years. I didn't know what I would do. I decided to pursue Dr. Seuss to see if he'd allow me to make *How the Grinch Stole Christmas* into an animated picture. It took some persuasion.

"That led to doing 'Horton Hears a Who,' 'The Cricket in Times Square,' 'Yankee Doodle Cricket,' 'A Very Merry Cricket,' and three stories from Rudyard Kipling's *The Jungle Book*.

"Every Disney film I've seen has had something of interest to me. An animator can always watch another's work with confidence that he will learn something. But the Disney Studio's respect for authors was very thin. Their 'Jungle Book' had zero to do with Kipling. I remember being so surprised by their pronunciation of 'Mowgli.' My father had always said, 'M*ow*gli' as in 'how' yet the Disney characters said, 'Mogli' as in 'toe.' When it came time to do my own work on *The Jungle Book,* I called up Kipling's daughter, who was eighty-five years old. I introduced myself and told her what we were working on. Finally I confessed that I was calling to find out how to pronounce, 'Mowgli.' After a pause, this lovely old English lady said, 'M*ow*gli.' Then she added, 'And I hate Walter Disney.' I had never heard anybody call him Walter before.

"We used the dialogue exactly as written in the original text. I wrote a few bridges to connect the material, because the actual 'Jungle' stories are very short. Orson Welles did the narration. I sent the script to him with an invitation to do a recording session, and what came back was a cassette tape of his reading. There were several things I didn't like, so I made a tape, sent it back to him, and I later got a new reading with all the corrections I had requested. Unfortunately, the tape was made in San Francisco, and I could hear lots of trolley bells in the background. I sent the tape back, and received his answer from Spain. He had recorded this second try on a machine that was not standard. I managed to transfer it, and sent it back for final corrections to an address in Paris. June Foray did the female voices. June is my all-purpose female voice, she is as versatile as Mel Blanc.

"I believe in my characters. As far as I'm concerned, they're alive. Tom Sawyer is not an illusion to me, he is not simply an image. He is vivid and alive. I feel the same about Daffy as I do about Tom Sawyer.

"It's very difficult for young artists to understand that every artist must have an audience, and that he may not get it in his own lifetime. Van Gogh, Gaugin did not live to see their work find an audience. Very few artists have been as lucky as I. The public is there, it is just a question of when the artist will make contact. The best analogy is the bullfighter, who can spend hours in the pasture, but he does not become a matador until he performs for an audience. Now that doesn't mean he has to fight the bull in a way that pleases the audience. But he does require an audience. What the bullfighter—or the artist for that matter—supplies to the audience is courage. Audiences are cowards. People would love to have the courage of a matador, or even the courage of Daffy or Bugs.''

Jones' advice to young would-be animators is to "learn the anatomy of vertebrates. As one great animator once said, '[You] should have at least two thousand tools.' By tools he meant, for instance, the gait of a horse, the amble of a dog. Once you learn these tools and the laws of movement, you will gain a lot of independence. Learn as many simple truths as you can—how *not* to use perspective, for instance. And don't tell the story with the background, tell the story with the action. Action is one's relation to the environment.''

—Based on an interview by Rachel Koenig

Pépé le Pew. (Copyright © by Warner Bros.)

FOR MORE INFORMATION SEE: Daily News, March 3, 1970, May 31, 1984, September 8, 1985; Alan Bunce, "ABC-TV Planning 'Sesame Street' Rival," *Christian Science Monitor,* November 2, 1970; Tom Mackin, "Don't Call This 'Kid Vid,'" *Newark Evening News,* January 12, 1971; "An Interview with Chuck Jones," *Funnyworld,* spring, 1971; *Dictionary of Film Makers,* University of California Press, 1972; *World Encyclopedia of Film,* A. & W. Visual Library, 1972; J. Cocks, "World Jones Made," *Time,* December 17, 1973, September 9, 1985; *Film Comment,* January/February, 1975, December, 1985; Chuck Jones, "Diary of a Mad Cel Washer," Program Book to the Third International Animation Festival in New York, 1975; *New York Times,* February 8, 1976, October 7, 1979; Richard Koszarski, *Hollywood Directors, 1941-1976,* Oxford University Press, 1977; Wayne Warga, "Chuck Jones—Director behind the Animated Stars," *Los Angeles Times,* August 27, 1978; C. Jones, "Confessions of a Cel Washer," *Take One,* September, 1978; William Scobie, "Animal Crackers," *Observer,* April 8, 1979; Jeff Millar, "The Biggest Laugh," *Houston Chronicle,* April 15, 1979; *Film Encyclopedia,* Crowell, 1979; *World Encyclopedia of Cartoons,* Volume 1, Gale, in association with Chelsea House, 1980; Joe Adamson, "Chuck Jones Interviewed," in *The American Animated Cartoon,* edited by Danny Peary and Gerald Peary, Dutton, 1980; John Lewell, "The Art of Chuck Jones," *Films and Filming,* September, 1982; *Atlantic,* December, 1984; *International Motion Picture Almanac, 1984,* Quigley, 1984; "Animator Chuck Jones in Conversation with David Colker and Chris Gulker," *Los Angeles Herald Examiner,* January 21, 1985; Leonard Maltin, "What's Up, Doc?" *American Film,* July-August, 1985; Ron Givens, "Honoring a Daffy Auteur," *Newsweek,* October 21, 1985; Timothy Onosko, "The Rise and Fall of the Classic Cartoon," *Video,* March, 1986.

JOSEPH, James (Herz) 1924-
(Lowell Adams, Walter Perez, Juan Sanchez Alzada)

PERSONAL: Born May 12, 1924, in Terre Haute, Ind.; son of Lawrence Herz (an accountant) and Lucille (a housewife; maiden name, Liberman) Joseph; married Marjorie Helen Waterman (divorced); children: Nancy Lee, James Jay. *Education:* Stanford University, B.A., 1949. *Home:* Los Angeles, Calif. *Agent:* Arthur Pine, Arthur Pine Associates, 1780 Broadway, New York, N.Y. 10019. *Office:* P.O. Box 24678, Los Angeles, Calif. 90024.

CAREER: Free-lance magazine, book and television writer, 1949—, primarily a writer-photographer in nonfiction ranging from family adventure pieces to technical industrial reporting. Taught first American college-level course on newsletters, California State University, Northridge, fall, 1977. Publisher, co-publisher of numerous newsletters. Consultant, former editor-in-chief, Kessler & Associates (business consultants), Los Angeles, Calif. *Military service:* U.S. Army Air Forces, 1942-46; instructor in radar. *Member:* Authors Guild, American Society of Journalists and Authors (chairman, Southern California chapter), Newsletter Association of America, Newspaper Features Council.

WRITINGS: How to Start a Successful Small Business, Science and Mechanics Publishing Company, 1956; *Income Opportunities,* Science and Mechanics Publishing Company, 1957, third edition, 1963; *Careers Outdoors,* T. Nelson, 1962; *Poolside Living,* Doubleday, 1963; *Better Water Skiing for Boys,* Dodd,

JAMES JOSEPH

1964; *You Fly It,* Dodd, 1965; (with William Divale) *I Lived inside the Campus Revolution,* Cowles, 1970; *Here Is Your Hobby: Snowmobiling,* Putnam, 1972; *The Complete Out-of-Doors: Job, Business and Profession Guide,* Contemporary, 1974; *Chilton's Diesel Guide,* Chilton, 1980; *The Car-Keeper's Guide,* Contemporary, 1982.

Columnist: "Quick Stops" (weekly travel column), Universal Press Syndicate; "Road to Discovery . . . in America" (monthly travel column), self-syndicated in twenty nations; "Doing Business Abroad" (weekly feature), self-syndicated in North America; "You in Sports" (weekly feature), self-syndicated in North America.

Regular contributor to more than fifty national consumer and industrial magazines; contributor of over 3500 articles to over 500 magazines and newspapers. West coast editor for various industrial magazines; editor of numerous newsletters. President and founder of World Reach, global marketing communications specialists. Conducts frequent seminars at major universities, especially in University of California and California State University systems. Seminar subjects include: "Inside the GLOBAL Writer's Market," "High-Tech Writing for Business," and "How to Write, Edit, Publish—and Profit from—Newsletters," among others.

WORK IN PROGRESS: A guide to interstate highway travel based on his syndicated weekly feature, "Quick Stops."

SIDELIGHTS: "Obviously, many of today's established nonfiction writers not only look back fondly on their career-establishing business writing days—but enthusiastically continue to write for business. I am one of those free-lance veterans. My own venture into nonfiction article writing and into business writng may be one of the more unusual demonstrations of career building existent. Quite literally, I launched my career as a lifetime nonfiction freelancer in a single momentous, adventurous, hardworking year—in the 'trades' (business trade journals).

"Now, more than thirty years later, I have written and photo-illustrated more than thirty-five hundred magazine articles. They have been published by leading magazines around the world (I self-syndicate my major articles globally, in some forty nations and twenty-five languages). I have written twenty-one books, the latest an alternate feature selection for Book-of-the-Month Club and Quality Paperback Book Club. I have done

Even boys who may not be good at football or baseball become first-rate water skiers. ■ (From *Better Water Skiing for Boys* by James Joseph. Illustrated by the author.)

major assignments for business and industry, including a number of respected business newsletters.

"Long before graduating from Stanford University, I made two basic decisions: I would pursue freelancing as a lifelong career. And I would *not* begin by making the novice freelancer's numerous errors—the worst among them being to aim, still green as I was at the writing craft, at the major general magazines (which, in those days, included the *Saturday Evening Post, Collier's,* and *American Magazine,* for all of which I eventually wrote).

"Instead, not a month out of college, I began as a business writer. And in a most unorthodox way. I loaded my car with typewriter, camera, and luggage, and headed into the Intermountain states (Utah, Montana, Wyoming, and Idaho).

"There, I reasoned—in the boondocks, if you will, but exhilarating country—were thriving local businesses and ranches with innovative concepts and methods—business innovations seldom explored and never put to paper. For while most of the few writers I then knew congregated in the major cities (New York, Chicago, Washington, Los Angeles), as did most business-magazine staffers; the fertile hinterlands lay seldom or seriously 'business-reported.' I decided to report from the hinterlands.

"For that full year—my first as a free-lance nonfiction writer-photographer—I roamed the business back country. I knew not a single magazine editor. I had not a single cashable contract, but I had what every successful nonfiction writer must have: an astute and developing sense of 'story'—an instinct for the truly innovative and newsworthy.

"I was also, even then, a middling good photographer (I'd been campus news photographer for such national photo feature syndicates as Acme Newspictures and the NEA—Newspaper Enterprise Association). And I was a good writer. All through college I had written and sold articles, some of them to national magazines. I also wrote and self-syndicated a western weekly newspaper column, 'Western Round-up.'

"As a hinterlands business writer, I was the equivalent of a traveling salesman. I would drive into a town, ride around eyeing its businesses, and then head for the office of the local (usually weekly) paper. To its editor I would . . . explain my mission: to find good local business articles for business magazines. Most of the editors were extremely helpful. Many suggested local business stories. All turned their back-copy files over to me.

"Usually, before day's end—every day, seven days a week and across thousands of miles of the West—I had at least one story researched and photographed.

"That night, in my motel room, I wrote the article and sometimes, with a portable developing kit, even processed the films (all black and white in those days). I had photo prints made at the local print shop. And, packaging my text and art, often by late next day I had the article in the mail to an editor I didn't know (but who shortly, I was confident, would be reading an article of business interest to his specialized readers) from an area seldom covered by the magazine or its staff.

"In one year I wrote and photographed nearly a hundred hinterland business articles. Even at the then-going poverty rates paid by the then-fledgling business press, I earned more than ten thousand dollars my first free-lance 'year on the road.' And in those days—the early 1950s—ten thousand dollars, while perhaps not a bushel, was a peck of money.

"And I had done it without magazine or editor contacts, and with only passing knowledge of the many business and agri-subjects I researched, photographed, and wrote about during that busy-as-thrashing-time year.

"I had found a lifelong career in free-lancing, in writing for business." [Glenn Evans, editor, *The Complete Guide to Writing Non-Fiction,* Writer's Digest Books, 1983.]

HOBBIES AND OTHER INTERESTS: Traveling (has been in the Arctic, Alaska, Mexico, South and Central America, Europe, and elsewhere), fishing, sailing, home do-it-yourself work.

KENNEDY, Dorothy M(intzlaff) 1931-

PERSONAL: Born March 8, 1931, in Milwaukee, Wis.; daughter of Henry Carl and Clara Anna (Lange) Mintzlaff; married Joseph C. Kennedy (a writer, under pseudonym X. J. Kennedy), January 31, 1962; children: Kathleen Anna, David Ian, Matthew Devin, Daniel Joseph, Joshua Quentin. *Education:* Milwaukee-Downer College (now Lawrence University of Wisconsin), B.A. (magna cum laude), 1953; University of Michigan, M.A., 1956, further graduate study, 1956-57, 1959-62. *Politics:* Independent. *Religion:* Protestant. *Home and office:* 4 Fern Way, Bedford, Mass. 01730. *Agent:* Curtis Brown Ltd., 575 Madison Ave., New York, N.Y. 10022.

CAREER: High school teacher of English and Spanish in Milledgeville, Ill., 1953-55; Ohio University, Athens, instructor in English, 1957-59; University of Michigan, Ann Arbor, teaching fellow, 1960-62; writer, 1977—. *Member:* National Council of Teachers of English, Phi Beta Kappa. *Awards, honors:* In 1983 *Knock at a Star* was named a choice book by National Council of Teachers of English and a book of the year by *School Library Journal.*

WRITINGS: All with X. J. Kennedy: *Knock at a Star: A Child's Introduction to Poetry* (illustrated by Karen A. Weinhaus),

DOROTHY M. KENNEDY

Little, Brown, 1982; *The Bedford Reader,* Bedford Books, 1982, 3rd edition, 1988; *The Bedford Guide for College Writers,* Bedford Books, 1987.

Contributor of articles and reviews to magazines, including *Michigan Quarterly Review.* Co-editor of *Counter Measures,* 1972-74; member of editorial board of *Cuyahoga Review.*

WORK IN PROGRESS: Talking Like the Rain, an introduction to poetry for the very young, with X. J. Kennedy.

SIDELIGHTS: "Even though nowadays I visit classrooms only sporadically—to talk about writing or, more usually, to have a conference about one of my children—I suppose that basically I'm a teacher. Of the books I've co-authored so far, even *Knock at a Star* does some teaching. To X. J. Kennedy and me, the way a poem is put together is immensely interesting. We thought that children would find it so, too. Consequently, in *Knock at a Star* we present not only good poems by good poets but also some opportunity to look closely at poems, to see what they're made of. We encourage children to write poems of their own, too—but not because we look upon every child as a budding poet. A very few are, of course. But even the others can probably acquire a great deal of respect for poets

and poetry by writing poems of their own and trying them out on an audience of their peers.

"It seems to me that the younger children are, the more open they are to the delights of poetry. That's one reason we're putting together *Talking Like the Rain.* We aim to include in it poetry that adults will like well enough to read to very small children.

"As a child in Milwaukee, I longed to see the world. To some extent, I have done so. In early days I travelled through space and time with enthralling books: *Little Women, Heidi, The Wonderful Adventures of Nils, Alice's Adventures in Wonderland* and *Through the Looking Glass, Hans Brinker, Caddie Woodlawn,* and many more. In high school, college, and graduate school I learned Spanish and French. As a college senior I translated, with Professor Gladys Calbick, Lorca's *The House of Bernarda Alba* for presentation by the college's drama club the following spring. During our twenty-five years of marriage my husband and I, with our growing family, have lived in North Carolina, in Southern California, and in Massachusetts; in London and in Yorkshire, England. From those home bases we have ventured into many other cities, states, and countries, as wonderful to me as Oz to that other, more famous Dorothy.

**A word is dead
When it is said,
Some say.**

—Emily Dickinson

■ (From "A Word Is Dead" in *Knock at a Star: A Child's Introduction to Poetry* by X. J. Kennedy and Dorothy M. Kennedy. Illustrated by Karen Ann Weinhaus.)

"Like most families during the Depression, mine had too little money and almost no technology. But children in that faraway time were offered something that seems too rare now: a chance to grow up slowly, at their own pace—not trouble free, certainly, but with their sense of wonder preserved at least until puberty. I can't help thinking that today's children, prematurely exposed as they are—to television, to problem novels written for the young, in unstable family lives, to adult frailty— are systematically denied something very precious: their innocence.

"As a writer I bloomed late—maybe because I can't seem to bloom in more than one area at a time. First teaching and then childrearing took priority, and I enjoyed both. In 1977 or 1978, when our youngest child started school, I began to work on instructor's manuals, and one thing led to another—specifically to college textbooks and to children's books. Now I write more than I do other things. Sitting down at my desk (or at the kitchen table, where I can watch the birds who come to the feeder outside) to put words together is always a high point of my day. I expect to do more and more of it."

KINGSTON, Maxine (Ting Ting) Hong 1940-

PERSONAL: Born October 27, 1940, in Stockton, Calif.; daughter of Tom (owner of New Port Laundry) and Ying Lan (a practitioner of medicine and midwifery, a cannery worker and a laundry worker; maiden name, Chew) Hong; married Earll Kingston (an actor), November 23, 1962; children: Joseph Lawrence Chung Mei. *Education:* University of California, Berkeley, A.B., 1962, teaching certificate, 1965. *Home:* Oakland, Calif. *Agent:* John Schaffner Literary Agency, 114 East 28th St., New York, N.Y. 10016.

CAREER: Writer. Sunset High School, Hayward, Calif., teacher of English, 1965-67; Kahuku High School, Kahuku, Hawaii, teacher of English, 1967; Kahaluu Drop-In School, Kahaluu, Hawaii, teacher, 1968; Honolulu Business College, Honolulu, Hawaii, teacher of English as a second language, 1969; Kailua High School, Kailua, Hawaii, teacher of language arts, 1969; Mid-Pacific Institute, Honolulu, teacher of language arts, 1970-77; University of Hawaii, Honolulu, visiting associate professor of English, 1977-78; Eastern Michigan University, Ypsilanti, Mich., distinguished professor, 1986.

AWARDS, HONORS: National Book Critics Circle Award for nonfiction, 1976, *Mademoiselle* Magazine Award, 1977, Ainsfield-Wolf Race Relations Award, 1978, named one of the top ten nonfiction works of the decade by *Time* magazine, 1979, and chosen one of New York Public Library's Books for the Teen Age, 1980, 1981, and 1982, all for *The Woman Warrior: Memoirs of a Girlhood among Ghosts;* NEA Award, 1977; National Education Association writing fellow, 1980; Guggenheim fellowship, 1980; named "Living Treasure of Hawaii," 1980; American Book Award for general nonfiction, chosen one of New York Public Library's Books for the Teen Age, and Pulitzer Prize runner-up, all 1981, all for *China Men;* Stockton (Calif.) Arts Commission Award, 1981, for contribution to the arts; Hawaii Writers Award, 1983.

WRITINGS: (Contributor) Jerry Walker, editor, *Your Reading,* National Council of Teachers of English, 1975; *The Woman Warrior: Memoirs of a Girlhood among Ghosts,* Knopf, 1976, large print edition, J. Curley, 1978; *China Men* (ALA Notable Book), Knopf, 1980; *Hawaii One Summer,* Meadow Press, 1987; *Tripmaster Monkey: His Fake Book,* Knopf, 1988.

MAXINE HONG KINGSTON

Contributor to anthologies, including *Wonders: Writings and Drawings for the Child in Us All,* edited by Jonathan Cott and Mary Gimbel, Rolling Stone, 1983; Geoff Hancock and Rikki Ducornet, editors, *Shoes and Shit,* Aya Press, 1984; Mark Schorer, *Harbrace College Reader,* 6th edition, Harcourt, 1984; Sandra Gilbert and Susan Gubar, editors, *The Norton Anthology of Literature by Women,* Norton, 1985; *Hers,* Time-Life, 1985; Scott Walker, editor, *Buying Time,* Graywolf Press, 1985; *Essay 2: Reading with the Writer's Eye,* Wadsworth, 1987. Also contributor of stories and articles to periodicals, including *New York Times Magazine, Ms., New Yorker, New West, New Dawn, American Heritage, Iowa Review, New York Times Book Review* and *Washington Post.*

ADAPTATIONS: "China Men" (cassette), American Audio Prose Library; "The Woman Warrior" (recording), Green Island Productions.

SIDELIGHTS: **October 27, 1940.** Named Maxine by her Chinese-American father who had known a blond American lady gambler, Kingston grew up in Stockton. She was always conscious of conflicting cultural ties, which later inspired her writing. "I come from the tradition of storytellers, and that tradition is thousands of years old; but I'm different from the others in that I write, whereas the rest of them used memory and the moods of the audience. Storytelling is communal, whereas writing is solitary and intellectual—and inflexible in a way. Tellers' stories change from telling to telling and from the storyteller to the listener, but when you write them down, there's a permanence." [Maxine Kingston, *The Woman Warrior: Memoirs of a Girlhood among Ghosts,* Knopf, 1976.[1]]

1945. Difficulties with the English language and with American gestures, which her parents made no effort to teach, kept Kingston and her younger sister silent for many years at school. "When I went to kindergarten and had to speak English for the first time, I became silent. My silence was thickest—total—during the three years that I covered my school paintings with black paint. I painted layers of black over houses and flowers and suns, and when I drew on the blackboard, I put a layer of chalk on top. I was making a stage curtain, and it was the moment before the curtain parted or rose. The teachers called my parents to school, and I saw they had been saving my pictures, curling and cracking, all alike and black. The

People you don't see so much when you grow up:

man with turtle growing on his back (not true)

Harry the Half-Man Half-Woman Handyman

Spastic man walking his cat

witch ladies

Detail of a playful cartoon by Maxine Hong Kingston. ■ (From "Small Kid Time" by Maxine Hong Kingston in *Wonders: Writing and Drawings for the Child in Us All,* edited by Jonathan Cott and Mary Gimbel.)

teachers pointed to the pictures and looked serious, talked seriously too, but my parents did not understand English. ('The parents and teachers of criminals were executed,' said my father.) My parents took the pictures home. I spread them out (so black and full of possibilities) and pretended the curtains were swinging open, flying up, one after another, sunlight underneath, mighty operas.

"During the first silent year I spoke to no one at school, did not ask before going to the lavatory, and flunked kindergarten. My sister also said nothing for three years, silent in the playground and silent at lunch. There were other quiet Chinese girls not of our family, but most of them got over it sooner than we did. I enjoyed the silence. At first it did not occur to me I was supposed to talk or to pass kindergarten. I talked at home and to one or two of the Chinese kids in class. I made motions and even made some jokes. I drank out of a toy saucer when the water spilled out of the cup, and everybody laughed, pointing at me, so I did it some more. I didn't know that Americans don't drink out of saucers.

"I liked the Negro students (Black Ghosts) best because they laughed the loudest and talked to me as if I were a daring talker too. One of the Negro girls had her mother coil braids over her ears Shanghai-style like mine; we were Shanghai twins except that she was covered with black like my paintings. Two negro kids enrolled in Chinese school, and the teachers gave them Chinese names.

"Some Negro kids walked me to school and home, protecting me from the Japanese kids, who hit me and chased me and stuck gum in my ears. The Japanese kids were noisy and tough.

They appeared one day in kindergarten, released from concentration camp, which was a tick-tac-toe mark, like barbed wire, on the map.

"It was when I found out I had to talk that school became a misery, that the silence became a misery. I did not speak and felt bad each time that I did not speak. I read aloud in first grade, though, and heard the barest whisper with little squeaks come out of my throat. 'Louder,' said the teacher, who scared the voice away again. The other Chinese girls did not talk either, so I knew the silence had to do with being a Chinese girl.

"Reading out loud was easier than speaking because we did not have to make up what to say, but I stopped often, and the teacher would think I'd gone quiet again. I could not understand 'I.' The Chinese 'I' has seven strokes, intricacies. How could the American 'I,' assuredly wearing a hat like the Chinese, have only three strokes, the middle so straight? Was it out of politeness that this writer left off strokes the way a Chinese has to write her own name small and crooked? No, it was not politeness; 'I' is a capital and 'you' is lower-case. I stared at that middle line and waited so long for its black center to resolve into tight strokes and dots that I forgot to pronounce it. The other troublesome word was 'here,' no strong consonant to hang on to, and so flat, when 'here' is two mountainous ideographs. The teacher, who had already told me every day how to read 'I' and 'here,' put me in the low corner under the stairs again, where the noisy boys usually sat.

"When my second grade class did a play, the whole class went to the auditorium except the Chinese girls. The teacher, lovely and Hawaiian, should have understood about us, but instead left us behind in the classroom. Our voices were too soft or nonexistent, and our parents never signed the permission slips anyway. They never signed anything unnecessary. We opened the door a crack and peeked out, but closed it again quickly. One of us (not me) won every spelling bee, though.

"I remember telling the Hawaiian teacher, 'We Chinese can't sing "land where our fathers died."'" She argued with me about politics, while I meant because of curses. . . .

"After American school, we picked up our cigar boxes, in which we had arranged books, brushes, and an inkbox neatly, and went to Chinese school, from 5:00 to 7:30 P.M. There we chanted together, voices rising and falling, loud and soft, some boys shouting, everybody reading together, reciting together and not alone with one voice. When we had a memorization test, the teacher let each of us come to his desk and say the lesson to him privately, while the rest of the class practiced copying or tracing. Most of the teachers were men. The boys who were so well behaved in the American school played tricks on them and talked back to them. The girls were not mute. They screamed and yelled during recess, when there were no rules; they had fist-fights. Nobody was afraid of chil-

(Cover illustration from *China Men* by Maxine Hong Kingston.)

dren hurting themselves or of children hurting school property. The glass doors to the red and green balconies with the gold joy symbols were left wide open so that we could run out and climb the fire escapes.

"We played capture-the-flag in the auditorium, where Sun Yat-sen and Chiang Kai-shek's pictures hung at the back of the stage, the Chinese flag on their left and the American flag on their right. We climbed the teak ceremonial chairs and made flying leaps off the stage. One flag headquarters was behind the glass door and the other on stage right. Our feet drummed on the hollow stage. During recess the teachers locked themselves up in their office with the shelves of books, copybooks, inks from China. They drank tea and warmed their hands at a stove. There was no play supervision. At recess we had the school to ourselves, and also we could roam as far as we could go—downtown, Chinatown stores, home—as long as we returned before the bell rang.

"At exactly 7:30 the teacher again picked up the brass bell that sat on his desk and swung it over our heads, while we charged down the stairs, our cheering magnified in the stairwell. Nobody had to line up.

"Not all of the children who were silent at American school found voice at Chinese school. One new teacher said each of

(Cover illustration from *The Woman Warrior* by Maxine Hong Kingston.)

us had to get up and recite in front of the class, who was to listen. My sister and I had memorized the lesson perfectly. We said it to each other at home, one chanting, one listening. The teacher called on my sister to recite first. It was the first time a teacher had called on the second-born to go first. My sister was scared. She glanced at me and looked away; I looked down at my desk. I hoped that she could do it because if she could, then I would have to. She opened her mouth and a voice came out that wasn't a whisper, but it wasn't a proper voice either. I hoped that she would not cry, fear breaking up her voice like twigs underfoot. She sounded as if she were trying to sing though weeping and strangling. She did not pause or stop to end the embarrassment. She kept going until she said the last word, and then she sat down. When it was my turn, the same voice came out, a crippled animal running on broken legs. You could hear splinters in my voice, bones rubbing jagged against one another. I was loud, though. I was glad I didn't whisper. . . .

". . . We American-Chinese girls had to whisper to make ourselves American-feminine. Apparently we whispered even more softly than the Americans. Once a year the teachers referred my sister and me to speech therapy, but our voices would straighten out, unpredictably normal, for the therapists. Some of us gave up, shook our heads, and said nothing, not one word. Some of us could not even shake our heads. At times shaking my head no is more self-assertion than I can manage. Most of us eventually found some voice, however faltering. We invented an American-feminine speaking personality. . . ."[1]

We could be heroines, swordswomen. . . . A swordswoman got even with anybody who hurt her family. ■ (Jacket illustration by Elías Dominguez from *The Woman Warrior: Memoirs of a Girlhood among Ghosts* by Maxine Hong Kingston.)

Years later, conversing with people still makes Kingston anxious. "A dumbness—a shame—still cracks my voice in two, even when I want to say 'hello' casually, or ask an easy question in front of the check-out counter, or ask directions of a bus driver. I stand frozen, or I hold up the line with the complete, grammatical sentence that comes squeaking out at impossible length. 'What did you say?' says the cab driver, or 'Speak up,' so I have to perform again, only weaker the second time. A telephone call makes my throat bleed and takes up that day's courage. It spoils my day with self-disgust when I hear my broken voice come skittering out into the open. It makes people wince to hear it. I'm getting better, though. Recently I asked the postman for special-issue stamps; I've waited since childhood for postmen to give me some of their own accord. I am making progress, a little every day."[1]

1951. "We have so many secrets to hold in. Our sixth grade teacher, who liked to explain things to children, let us read our files. My record shows that I flunked kindergarten and in first grade had no IQ—a zero IQ. I did remember the first grade teacher calling out during a test, while students marked X's on a girl or a boy or a dog, which I covered with black. First grade was when I discovered eye control; with my seeing I could shrink the teacher down to a height of one inch, gesticulating and mouthing on the horizon. I lost this power in sixth grade for lack of practice, the teacher a generous man. 'Look at your family's old addresses and think about how you've moved,' he said. I looked at my parents' aliases and their birthdays, which variants I knew. But when I saw Father's occupations I exclaimed, 'Hey, he wasn't a farmer, he was a . . . .' He had been a gambler. My throat cut off the word—silence in front of the most understanding teacher. There were secrets never to be said in front of the ghosts, immigration secrets whose telling could get us sent back to China.

"Sometimes I hated the ghosts for not letting us talk; sometimes I hated the secrecy of the Chinese. 'Don't tell,' said my parents, though we couldn't tell if we wanted to because we didn't know. Are there really secret trials with our own judges and penalties? Are there really flags in Chinatown signaling what stowaways have arrived in San Francisco Bay, their names, and which ships they came on? . . .

"They would not tell us children because we had been born among ghosts, were taught by ghosts, and were ourselves half ghosts. They called us a kind of ghost."[1]

1962. After receiving a degree from the University of California, Berkeley, Kingston taught English and creative writing. Although she has taught several courses in writing, she is not convinced that writing courses are necessary for the development of a writer. ". . . I didn't take very many creative writing courses. I took one in college, and it was mostly a reading course: we just read and discussed the books. Also I began writing when I was a child, and so it seems to me that there is a lot of desire and ability that one is born with. A creative writing class can perhaps shorten the amount of time it takes to start putting things together or start publishing. Also it helps discipline, and it gives a certain amount of encouragement so that a person can keep going. But I don't know whether it can instill that great desire and obsession. Maybe you have to be born with that. And the love of words: that's probably something you're born with. You see little kids that hear very well and repeat sounds and have a good time making up words and stories, and then you see other little kids that don't do that. Maybe writing classes can refine and help the process along, but not begin it."

1967. Moved to Hawaii with her husband, Earll, whom she had married in 1962. Kingston held various high school and college teaching positions there, until the publication of her first book. The sources for her first novel, *The Woman Warrior: Memoirs of a Girlhood among Ghosts,* were tales told to her by her Chinese mother and other Chinese storytellers during her youth. "... Some of the things that happen to us in life seem to have no meaning, but when you write them down you find the meanings for them; or, as you translate life into words, you force a meaning. Meaning is intrinsic in words and stories.

"One of the themes in *The Woman Warrior* is: what is it that's a story and what is it that's life? Sometimes our lives have plots like stories; sometimes we're affected by the stories or we try to live up to them, or the stories give a color and an atmosphere to life. So sometimes the boundaries are very clear, and sometimes they interlace and we live out stories.

"In *The Woman Warrior* I was telling that the attitude towards women in China was very puzzling because on the one hand there was this slavery, which is so weird—I mean, I can almost understand better how white people can enslave black people than how men can enslave women. But at the same time they had these heroic stories about the women warriors, so there were two traditions going at once—about powerful fighters and poets and rulers that were women, and on the other hand, enslavement. So I think that women's liberation was already a tradition in China. . . ."

Kingston's second book, *China Men* (1977), was a companion volume to her first one. It used myths, memories, facts and stories to tell the story of her male ancestors in China and America. "I feel I have a task to recreate the way the people actually talk; and I try to hear as keenly as possible the way people talk in real life, which means that I have to figure out some kind of orthography or rhythm to transcribe and to translate dialect and accents. And sometimes, since I am writing in English, if people are speaking Chinese I have to find the most correct rhythm and translation. Sometimes people are speaking in English, but they speak with an accent, so I have to figure out the right way to do that without making it really clumsy and using strange misspellings that make people sound stupid. I think that I'm constantly looking for ways of doing those tasks, because they're not solved once and for all.

"I find that when Mark Twain does that strange spelling, it's really hard to read. If the reader comes from the Mississippi River area, then Twain is not hard to read because the reader has heard those dialects. But if you're not familiar with them, like me, a reader from the West, you have to try to recreate them from his orthography. And I think that's impossible. So I want to work more the way Gertrude Stein did in 'Melanctha,' where she doesn't fool around with the spelling; she plays with syntax and rhythm rather than weird spelling and apostrophes and all that.

"I've read *Orlando* by Virginia Woolf many times trying to understand how she works so well with time, the big expanses of time and the little moments. She can do a whole story in one paragraph and then she'll zip out of that and be in a different story in another century with different people. I try to figure out how she does that; I want to do that too. Orlando's mind has hundreds of years of knowledge; she can juxtapose something that happened four hundred years ago with something that happened today, and Woolf can make that dramatic and not a history lesson. I was trying for that too, in *China Men* especially."

Kingston described her own writing process as an emotional task that becomes an intellectual one as the process progresses.

"... When I first set something down I feel the emotions I write about. But when I do second draft, third draft, ninth draft, then I don't feel very emotional. The rewriting is very intellectual; all my education and reading and intellect are involved. The mechanics of sentences, how one phrase or word goes with another one—all that happens in later drafts. There's a very emotional first draft and a very technical last draft.

"What I have at the beginning of a book is not an outline. I have no idea of how stories will end or where the beginning will lead. Sometimes I draw pictures. I draw a blob and then I have a little arrow and it goes to this other blob, if you want to call that an outline. It's hardly even words; it's like a doodle. Then when it turns into words, the words lead me to various scenes and stories which I don't know about until I get there. I don't see the order until very late in the writing and sometimes the editing just comes. I just run up against it. All of a sudden the book's over and I didn't know it would be over. I could wake up in the morning and not know that that was the day the story was going to end. So it's a surprise for me too. . . ."

FOR MORE INFORMATION SEE: Maxine Hong Kingston, *The Woman Warrior: Memoirs of a Girlhood among Ghosts,* Knopf, 1976; *America,* February 26, 1976; *New York Times,* September 17, 1976, June 3, 1980; *Harper's,* October, 1976, August, 1980; *Washington Post Book World,* October 10, 1976, June 22, 1980; *Newsweek,* October 11, 1976, June 16, 1980; *New York Times Book Review,* November 7, 1976, June 15, 1980; *New Yorker,* November 15, 1976; *Time,* December 6, 1976, June 30, 1980; *Ms.,* January, 1977, August, 1980; *New York Review of Books,* February 3, 1977, August 14, 1980; *New York Times Biographical Service,* February, 1977; Susan Brownmiller, "Susan Brownmiller Talks with Maxine Hong Kingston," *Mademoiselle,* March, 1977; *International Fiction Review,* January, 1978; *Times Literary Supplement,* January 27, 1978; *Southwest Review,* spring, 1978; Edith Blicksilver, *The Ethnic American Woman: Problems, Protests, Lifestyle,* Kendall-Hart, 1978.

M. H. Kingston, *China Men,* Knopf, 1980; *New Republic,* June 21, 1980; *Los Angeles Times Book Review,* June 22, 1980; *Washington Post,* June 26, 1980; *Saturday Review,* July, 1980; Timothy Pfaff, "Whispers of a Literary Explorer," *Horizon,* July, 1980; *Christian Science Monitor,* August 11, 1980; *San Francisco Review of Books,* September 2, 1980; *Contemporary Literary Criticism,* Gale, Volume XII, 1980, Volume XIX, 1981; *Dictionary of Literary Biography Yearbook: 1980,* Gale, 1981; Marilyn Yalom, *Women Writers of the West Coast: Speaking of Their Lives and Careers,* Capra, 1983; Catherine Rainwater and William J. Scheick, *Contemporary American Women Writers: Narrative Strategies,* University Press of Kentucky, 1985; Barbara Ann Porte, *The Kidnapping of Aunt Elizabeth,* Greenwillow, 1985; Paul John Eakin, *Fiction in Autobiography,* Princeton University Press, 1986; James D. Houston, *West Coast Fiction,* Bantam, 1986; Robert R. Potter, *The American Anthology,* Globe, 1987; Roberta Rubenstein, *Boundaries of the Self: Gender, Culture, Fiction,* University of Illinois Press, 1987.

KOERTGE, Ronald 1940-

PERSONAL: Surname is pronounced *Kur*-chee; born April 22, 1940, in Olney, Ill.; son of William Henry and Bulis Olive (Fiscus) Koertge; married Cheryl Vasconcellos (a teacher). *Education:* University of Illinois, B.A., 1962; University of Arizona, M.A., 1965. *Home:* 1115 Oxley, South Pasadena,

Calif. 91030. *Agent:* William Reiss, Paul R. Reynolds, Inc., 12 East 41st St., New York, N.Y. 10017. *Office:* Department of English, Pasadena City College, 1560 Colorado Blvd., Pasadena, Calif. 91106.

CAREER: Pasadena City College, Pasadena, Calif., professor of English, 1965—.

WRITINGS: Meat: Cherry's Market Diary, Mag Press, 1973; *The Father Poems,* Sumac Press, 1974; *The Hired Nose,* Mag Press, 1974; *My Summer Vacation,* Venice Poetry Co., 1975; *Men under Fire,* Duck Down Press, 1976; *Twelve Photographs of Yellowstone,* Red Hill Press, 1976; *How to Live on Five Dollars a Day,* Venice Poetry Co., 1976; *Cheap Thrills,* Wormwood Review Press, 1976; *Sex Object,* Little Caesar Press, 1979; *The Boogeyman* (novel), Norton, 1980; *The Jockey Poems,* Maelstrom Press, 1980; *Diary Cows,* Little Caesar Press, 1982; *Life on the Edge of the Continent: Selected Poems,* University of Arkansas Press, 1982; *Where the Kissing Never Stops* (young adult), Atlantic Monthly, 1987; *The Arizona Kid,* Little, Brown, 1988.

WORK IN PROGRESS: One Hundred Things to Write About, a textbook.

KRUPP, E(dwin) C(harles) 1944-

PERSONAL: Born November 18, 1944, in Chicago, Ill.; son of Edwin F. (an engineer) and Florence Ann (Olander) Krupp; married Robin Suzanne Rector (an artist and teacher), December 31, 1968; children: Ethan Hembree. *Education:* Pomona College, B.A., 1966; University of California, Los Angeles, M.A., 1968, Ph.D., 1972. *Agent:* Jane Jordan Browne Multimedia Product Development, Inc., 410 S. Michigan Ave., Suite 724, Chicago, Ill. 60605. *Office:* Griffith Observatory, 2800 East Observatory Rd., Los Angeles, Calif. 90027.

CAREER: Griffith Observatory, Los Angeles, Calif., curator, 1972-74, director, 1974—. Member of faculty at University of California, El Camino College, and University of Southern California. Host of ''Project: Universe,'' a television series of Public Broadcasting Service. *Member:* American Astronomical Society (chairman, Historical Astronomy Division, 1984-86), Astronomical Society of the Pacific (board member, 1983-87), Sigma Xi, Explorers Club (fellow). *Awards, honors:* Science Writing Award from the American Institute of Physics and U.S. Steel Foundation, 1978, for *In Search of Ancient Astronomies;* Science Writing Award from the American Institute of Physics, and selected one of Child Study Association

The mailman comes by almost every day. Your birthday comes but once a year. Halley's Comet comes by every 76 years. That's a long time to wait. ■ (From *The Comet and You* by E. C. Krupp. Illustrated by Robin Rector Krupp.)

E. C. Krupp at Zoser's Step Pyramid, Mt. Saqqara, Egypt.

of America's Children's Books of the Year, and Outstanding Science Trade Book for Children from the National Science Teachers Association and the Children's Book Council, all 1985, and received the Notable Work of Nonfiction Award from the Southern California Council on Literature for Children and Young People, 1986, all for *The Comet and You.*

WRITINGS: (Editor and contributor) *In Search of Ancient Astronomies, Stonehenge to von Daniken: Archaeoastronomy Discovers Our Sophisticated Ancestors,* Doubleday, 1978; (contributor) Joe Goodwin and others, editors, *Fire of Life: Smithsonian Book of the Sun,* Smithsonian Exposition Books, 1981; (contributor) George O. Abell and Barry Singer, editors, *Science and the Paranormal,* Scribner, 1981; *Echoes of the Ancient Skies: The Astronomy of Lost Civilization,* Harper, 1983; (editor and contributor) *Archaeoastronomy and the Roots of Science,* Westview, 1984; *The Comet and You* (illustrated by wife, Robin Rector Krupp), Macmillan, 1985; *The Big Dipper and You* (illustrated by R. R. Krupp), Morrow, 1989; *Beyond the Blue Horizon: Sky Tales and Why We Tell Them,* Harper, 1989.

Also author of sound recordings "Ancient Astronomy," American Chemical Society, 1979, and "Archaeoastronomy: Sky and Culture," American Chemical Society, 1980. Editor in chief, *Griffith Observer,* 1974—.

SIDELIGHTS: "I have traveled to, photographed, and studied more than seven hundred ancient and prehistoric sites throughout the world, including England, Scotland, Wales, Ireland, France, Malta, Corsica, Sardinia, Greece, Egypt, Central America, Mexico, Peru, Colombia, Chile, Bolivia, India, Indonesia, Australia, New Zealand, Canada, the United States, and the People's Republic of China.

"I am interested in science as one route to entertainment, and entertainment is for me a vehicle for sharing the experience of science. Rational thought and imaginative thought are tools for survival. Anyone with a Darwinian outlook will recognize that misleading oneself with pseudoscientific notions is a misuse of a valuable tool. It could cost us plenty.

"The interaction of the brain with the sky is a universal and fundamental human experience. What we make of the sky determines how we think of ourselves and how we behave. Traveling to faraway places with strange-sounding names in pursuit of this experience puts one at the heart of human nature. Of course, it's also present back in your own backyard—provided the sky is dark."

In Search of Ancient Astronomies has been translated into German and Portugese.

HOBBIES AND OTHER INTERESTS: Comic books, especially "Uncle Scrooge" and "Dr. Strange"; ghost stories and supernatural tales of terror; running around the block.

FOR MORE INFORMATION SEE: New Scientist, September 13, 1979; *New West,* October 8, 1979; *Times Literary Supplement,* May 16, 1980.

KRUPP, Robin Rector   1946-

PERSONAL: Surname rhymes with "up"; born March 29, 1946, in Brooklyn, N.Y.; daughter of Robert Wayman (a mathematician) and Margaret (a playwright; maiden name, Hayden) Rector; married Edwin Charles Krupp (an astronomer), December 31, 1968; children: Ethan Hembree. *Education:* Pomona College, Claremont, Calif., B.A. (cum laude), 1968; California State University at Northridge, M.A., 1970. *Home and office:* 5208 Mt. Royal Dr., Eagle Rock, Calif. 90041. *Agent:* Jane Jordan Browne, Multimedia Product Development, Inc., 410 S. Michigan Ave., Suite 724, Chicago, Ill. 60605.

CAREER: Free-lance artist, 1970—; Pierce College, Woodland Hills, Calif., part-time instructor, 1971-85; Fashion In-

ROBIN RECTOR KRUPP

"Use my imagination? That works for vowels? Well, I don't think so," he said, "but I'll try it. Short **A**, short **A**, what does it sound like? I need three words for short **A**." Curtis closed his eyes.

(From *Get Set to Wreck* by Robin Rector Krupp. Illustrated by the author.)

stitute of Design and Merchandising, Sherman Oaks, Calif., part-time instructor, 1979—; California State University at Northridge, instructor, 1988—. Lecturer; workshop leader. Member of planning committee for ''Save the Books'' fundraiser for the Los Angeles Public Library, member of the steering committee for the Year of the Young Reader. *Exhibitions*—Solo: California State University of Northridge, 1970; Brand Library Art Center, Glendale, Calif., 1973; Villa Montalvo, Saratoga, Calif., 1974. Group shows: Running Ridge Gallery, Ojai, Calif.; Cedar Street Gallery, Santa Cruz, Calif.; Wexler-Weiss Gallery, Encino, Calif.; Los Angeles Art Association, Calif.; Downey Museum of Art, Calif., 1971; San Pedro Municipal Gallery, Calif., 1972; Brand Library Art Center, Glendale, 1974; Los Angeles Institute of Contemporary Art, Calif., 1975; Pierce College, Woodland Hills, Calif., 1975, 1977, 1981; Richard Mann Gallery, Calif., 1977; California State University at Los Angeles, 1978.

MEMBER: Society of Children's Book Writers (co-chairman for San Gabriel area), Women in Design, Southern California Children's Booksellers Association, Southern California Council on Literature for Children and Young People. *Awards, honors:* Notable Work of Nonfiction Award from the Southern California Council for Literature for Children and Young People, 1986, for *The Comet and You.*

WRITINGS: Get Set to Wreck! (self-illustrated), Four Winds Press, 1988.

Illustrator: E. C. Krupp, *The Comet and You,* Macmillan, 1985; E. C. Krupp, *The Big Dipper and You,* Morrow, 1989.

Contributor of drawings and photographs: E. C. Krupp, *In Search of Ancient Astronomies,* Doubleday, 1978; E. C. Krupp, *Echoes of the Ancient Skies,* Harper, 1983; E. C. Krupp, editor, *Archaeoastronomy and the Roots of Science,* American Association for the Advancement of Science, 1983. Also contributor of illustrations to *Griffith Observer, Boogie Woogie Review* and *Scriblerus Papers, Archaeoastronomy, U.S.-China Review,* and of photographs to *Fire of Life: The Smithsonian Book of the Sun,* Smithsonian, 1981.

WORK IN PROGRESS: I Hold My Heart, visual love poems; a novel.

SIDELIGHTS: ''First, I'm an artist. One of those people who always drew as a child. My mother said it was never a question of whether or not I would draw. It was just whether or not she would supply the paper. Luckily, she supplied lots of paper and I've always received family encouragement. It is a real pleasure to dedicate my first illustrated book *The Comet and You* to my parents.

''My educational background in art includes a B.A. in painting from Pomona College and a M.A. in painting from California State University at Northridge. Additional art study was completed at Otis/Parsons, University of California at Los Angeles, University of California at Santa Barbara, El Camino College, and John Wallis' Stained Glass Studio. I studied painting in Paris, France with College Art Study Abroad. For seven years I took weekly lessons in Japanese Tea Ceremony from Sosei Matsumoto and, in 1974, I studied Tea Ceremony for a month in Kyoto, Japan.

''Since 1970 I have exhibited my art work in galleries in group and solo shows. Round paintings and colorful collages make up most of my exhibited work. My interest in composition led me to use large quilting hoops as a stretching structure for my round paintings. Using handmade and commercial patterned papers, I produced a set of twelve zodiac collages, one for every constellation of the zodiac. Presently, I am working on a series of pastel portraits. Most of my time now is spent illustrating children's books.

''Like many artists, I find it hard to describe my art. Wit, diversity, and sensual stimulus are usually present. I like the challenge of solving complex problems from putting together a jigsaw puzzle to illustrating children's books.

''My work for children seems always to be a blend of education and entertainment. I am a teacher at heart and like to help people get started doing things they love. I often write to find out what I am thinking. Often I am surprised and I like that. I would love to do more work for adults as well. I am working on some visual love poems, *I Hold My Heart,* and a novel at present. I am intrigued by designing books. I often tell myself 'Someday, this will be a *real* book' and that helps this impatient person get through all that stuff that takes patience.

''If I am an artist first, I am a teacher too. I taught art at Pierce College in Woodland Hills from 1971 to June, 1985. I have taught at the Fashion Institute of Design and Merchandising since 1979. I encourage art students to use their imaginations through unusual assignments. Students studying surrealism are asked to make incongruous works of edible art. Students studying perspective are asked to use an ant's or a bird's eye view. Interior design students are asked to build room models inspired by existing design traditions. I hope that my enthusiasm for art is contagious.

''My husband, Dr. E. C. Krupp, is an astronomer, director of Griffith Observatory, and the author of *The Comet and You.* He received the American Institute of Physics Best Science Writing Award for 1985 for *The Comet and You.* This was the first time a children's book had ever received the award.

''While this is our first children's book, Ed and I have collaborated on many projects since our marriage in 1968. First and foremost, we've collaborated on our son, Ethan. Ethan helped us by doing all the notes written by a child in *The Comet and You.* Ed and I have also carved and painted seventeen Halloween pumpkins, doubled the size of our 1913 California bungalow, been involved with Cub Scouts, and traveled the world over, visiting ancient and prehistoric sites. We've taken over 60,000 slides for Ed's work in achaeoastronomy, and led UCLA Extension tours to Egypt, China, Mexico, South America, etc.''

FOR MORE INFORMATION SEE: Christian Science Monitor, November 1, 1985; Ellen Perry, ''Authors Perform Stories for Glendale Students,'' *News-Press,* January 7, 1988.

KUNHARDT, Dorothy (Meserve) 1901-1979

PERSONAL: Born in 1901 in New York, N.Y.; died December 23, 1979, in Beverly, Mass.; daughter of Frederick Hill and Edith (Turner) Meserve; married Philip B. Kunhardt (an executive; died, 1963); children: Nancy, Philip, Kenneth, Edith. *Education:* Received degree from Bryn Mawr College. *Residence:* New York, N.Y.; and Morristown, N.J.

CAREER: Author and illustrator of children's books, 1932-77. *Awards, honors: New York Herald Tribune*'s Children's Spring Book Festival honor book, 1948, for *Tiny Animal Stories.*

WRITINGS—Juvenile: Junket Is Nice (self-illustrated), Harcourt, 1933, published as *Rennet Dessert Is Nice,* Forbes Lith-

Dorothy Kunhardt with daughter, Edith, in 1940.

ograph, 1947, published as *Pudding Is Nice*, Bookstore Press, 1975; *Now Open the Box*, Harcourt, 1934, published as *Little Peewee; or, Now Open the Box* (illustrated by J. P. Miller), Simon & Schuster, 1948; *Little Ones* (illustrated by Kurt Wiese), Viking, 1935; *Lucky Mrs. Ticklefeather*, Harcourt, 1935, new edition (illustrated by J. B. Miller), Simon & Schuster, 1951; *Brave Mr. Buckingham*, Harcourt, 1935; *Wise Old Aard-vark*, Viking, 1936.

David's Birthday Party (illustrated by Dorothea Warren), Rand McNally, 1940; *Pat the Bunny* (self-illustrated), Simon & Schuster, 1940, new edition, Golden Press, 1962; *Once There Was a Little Boy* (illustrated by Helen Sewell), Viking, 1946; *Billy the Barber* (illustrated by William Pene du Bois), Harper, 1961; *Dr. Dick* (illustrated by Fritz Siebel), Harper, 1962; *Gas Station Gus* (illustrated by Janina Domanska), Harper, 1962; *Tickle the Pig*, Golden Press, 1965; *The Telephone Book* (self-illustrated), Western, 1975; *Kitty's New Doll* (illustrated by Lucinda McQueen), Western, 1984; *The Scarebunny* (illustrated by Kathy Wilburn), Western, 1985, new edition published as *The Friendly Bunny*, 1987; *Pat the Bunny Book and Bunny*, Golden Books, 1987.

Omnibus volumes: *Lucky Mrs. Ticklefeather and Other Funny Stories: The Best of Dorothy Kunhardt* (illustrated by Garth Williams), Western, 1975.

Other; nonfiction; with son Philip B. Kunhardt, Jr.: *Twenty Days: A Narrative in Text and Pictures of the Assassination of Abraham Lincoln and the Twenty Days That Followed—The Nation in Mourning, the Long Trip Home to Springfield*, foreword by Bruce Catton, Harper, 1965; (with the editors of

Time-Life Books) *Mathew Brady and His World: Produced from Pictures in the Meserve Collection*, Time-Life, 1977.

Also author of *Feed the Animals*, and "Tiny" series; published by Simon & Schuster; illustrated by Garth Williams: *Tiny Animal Stories; Tiny Nonsense Stories*.

SIDELIGHTS: Kunhardt's career as an author and illustrator of children's books began in 1932 with the publication of *Junket Is Nice* and spanned three decades. A *New York Herald Tribune* columnist compared her first work in its simplicity and imagination with *Little Black Sambo* and *Alice in Wonderland*. Her stories for very young children continued with such works as *Now Open the Box, Lucky Mrs. Ticklefeather*, and *Brave Mr. Buckingham*.

She wrote her stories from her large Victorian home in Morristown, New Jersey, surrounded by her family: husband Philip, an executive in the woolens business, sons Philip Jr. and Kenneth, and daughters Nancy and Edith. Within this busy environment, Kunhardt wrote her stories undaunted by the responsibilities that a young and large family bring. Much later, son Philip Jr. described his mother in his memoir: "My mother despised the outside just as much as my father loved it. She liked being boxed in by house or city. Fresh country air just didn't agree with her, she always claimed. She told us if she had her wish she would live in one of those little cubbyholes in Grand Central Station where you can lock your bag for twenty-five cents. She said she'd just climb in there and close the door and be extremely happy with those close walls and no weather at all to worry about.

"My mother and father found out how different they were in this respect on their honeymoon when he chose to take her to a small woodsy camp near Monticello in Virginia where she watched him lie and splash like a huge white tadpole in an outsize brook, where they had bad food and rode old jogging plugs of horses through the woods. They had spent one night en route in a hotel in Washington, D.C., and my mother had longed to stay there, in an exciting and interesting city, not the horrible woods. But my father had hated the hotel, the city, had longed to get to the real heart of his week's honeymoon, in the woods and fields.

"Later on, as their marriage settled into a tacit agreement, each to give in to the other on the little things that did not matter, they let their sense of humor enter into the problems of daily life. She would sit upstairs in the window backed by her thousands of Civil War books calling to my father down in the garden with his roses, 'Come in, come in!' And he would smile and call back, 'Come out, come out!' with no resulting change in their positions.

"Of all the children my mother was closest to Nancy, although you wouldn't have known it. They both cared so much about every little thing, and that made them clash all the time, and a good clash meant going at each other like crazy people. About any subject at all. Little finicky subjects usually. Squabbling and squawking about practically nothing, practically anything. There were times when one just couldn't say or do anything that didn't aggravate the other.

"My mother could get angry at my brother and me, too. Especially if her concentration was suddenly broken by some lavish, wiseacre noise of ours. Other transgressions that brought on varying degrees of recrimination might include making rabbit ears or nose-thumbs behind the backs of aunts or other guests; whipping the thermometer from under our tongues to the steaming radiator to force it up to 102 and keep us out of school for the day; burning a cousin at the stake; bringing home boys whom my mother considered sneaks or bad-mouths, and that included practically all my friends; dragging our feet like cripples in the market; spitting; teasing; having blasting gunfights all over the house, using pointed fingers for pistols. . . . Those are just a few of maybe five or six thousand little tricks we had.

"'Let the punishment fit the crime,' proclaimed my mother. 'If you want to thumb your nose at Auntie, come out from behind her back and do it to her face.' Or, 'Spit! Go out and spit behind the house to your heart's content until you'll never want to spit again.' And, if it were too much yelling and yapping and screeching we were doing, she might, if she were in the mood, set up the worst din you ever heard, yelling and yapping and screeching louder even than we had been doing, so that we just stopped and looked at her in amazement and with a little fear. And when she was done with her act, she'd ask us how we'd like that kind of racket going on all the time, and we'd get the point.

"My father kept peace in the house. He would settle arguments, calm people down, quiet rough waters. He could put an arm around one of us and comfort tears away.

"And after my father got home from work, if we or something else had upset my mother during the day, he would soothe her down too, do the coping, set a course, give her strength. He seemed to have the patience of Job. But that patience broke down over a couple of subjects. One of them was money. My mother's extravagances drove him to distraction, even though they were practically penny extravagances in those days. But things were tight in the thirties and pennies meant everything.

"On long car rides, my mother would keep my father happy and amused. She would try to make him promise not to punish any more drivers, and she would tell him odd little stories and observations that only her strange, nonsensical mind, that always seemed to end up making sense, could have thought up. Day and night that mind of hers gobbled up quantities of information on every conceivable subject. She could read a page at a single glance and remember everything on it. He marveled at her, he even put up with orders to stop the car this minute, there's a turtle on the road that had to be moved over to the side by hand or somebody's cruel old tire is going to squash him flat, and she'd be out of the car, lifting the turtle to the bank in the direction he was heading and talking to the turtle and telling him not to be naughty again by going out on any more highways. My father even put up with my mother's sense of direction, which was nonexistent, and whenever he let her have the wheel to spell him, which was not very often, he'd give her five minutes before she was dead lost.

". . . My mother was the best spree person in the world. She worked terribly hard at everything she did, but I don't think she did anything better than giving sprees. Just as in the children's books she wrote, she seemed to know exactly what each of us liked and how we liked it, exactly how our minds worked and what got each one of us excited or left us bored. A spree day was a magical journey into that mysterious city where my father disappeared five days a week. It was his city, to me, in those days, although I never visited his office and know that he disliked being interrupted there by a phone call from my mother." [Philip B. Kunhardt, Jr., *My Father's House*, Random House, 1970.[1]]

Kunhardt's most famous book, *Pat the Bunny*, was known by generations of parents who introduced books to their preschool children. Written in 1940, the book sold in the millions and

(Cover illustration by Dorothy Kunhardt from *Pat the Bunny* by Dorothy Kunhardt.)

Once there was a little boy named Tam, who lived with his mother and father in a nice house that had roses climbing up the porch.

(From *The Scarebunny* by Dorothy Kunhardt. Illustrated by Kathy Wilburn.)

has been on the best-selling list of children's classics ever since. The book urged young children to stroke the furry characters represented in it.

In later years, Kunhardt, who was an acclaimed Lincoln scholar, collaborated with her son Philip Jr. on a study of the assassination of President Lincoln and on a book of Mathew Brady's civil war photographs, drawn largely from the collection of her father, who was a renowned collector of Lincoln memorabilia. Philip Jr. recalled: ''. . . My mother was always acquiring huge stacks of old books. Her interest, inherited from her father who was a pioneer collector of early American photographs, was the Civil War and especially Abraham Lincoln and everything about his times. She would go two and three times a week to a secondhand book shop in town which got very good collections from the libraries of the big old houses all over the East, and each time she would come home with at least half a dozen books, and sometimes the whole back seat of the car would be full of them. The library downstairs, which was also the back living room, was already full, so first of all a lot of old standing bookcases were bought and placed along the walls of the back hall; when they were full, additional stacks of books were piled up on top until they reached the ceiling, and other stacks on the floor in front of the cases soon grew, so that pretty soon it was worth your life to use that hallway. First of all you had to turn sideways and suck gut to get through at all, but the danger was that if you happened to hit a key book with an elbow, you might get a landslide of a ton of them on your head.

''When the back hall was full, then books started to wander up to the front hall and pretty soon my mother's clothes closet was full of books, and then my father's, and finally even the space between the two closets, the space in front of the window that used to give us all such a nice view of the garden before it got its book barrier. Soon they began to creep into my father's and mother's bedroom, too, in great stacks against the wall, in swiveling bookshelves, then underneath the beds, finally even on top. For that was where my mother did a lot of her researching and reading and notetaking and work. She would sit on her own bed and she would lay out the books she wanted to read and to refer to on my father's bed, and by the end of the day his bed had at least a foot deep of books and notes spread over it. When he got home, he would make jokes about Mr. Lincoln being in his bed, and she would take the books off and make a swaying skyscraper of them in the last open corner of the room, but they were back on his bed again the next morning as soon as he was out of it.

''My mother didn't stop with books for her researching. She doted on strange and fascinating and minuscule information of all kinds. She drove with the garbage man in his truck to see how delicious garbage was and to find out exactly what he thought about the garbage and how he could tell whose garbage it was without even looking at the house it came from, just by inspecting what was in the cans. She sat in the barber shop for hours to see all the things Mr. DeFalco did to people's hair. She went to farms and zoos and studied each animal, how they looked and walked and ate and licked themselves and how they used their tails and ears.

''The amount of paper that was used in our house was extraordinary, first of all because my mother was constantly taking notes on all these things for her children's books, plus notes on every member of the family, what he or she was like, what they said, what they did, over the years. . . .''[1]

Kunhardt died on **December 23, 1979** in Beverly, Massachusetts, at the age of seventy-eight.

(From *Kitty's New Doll* by Dorothy Kunhardt. Illustrated by Lucinda McQueen.)

FOR MORE INFORMATION SEE: Martha Kieffer, "A Best Seller for Baby," *Chicago Tribune,* September 24, 1972; M. Kieffer, "Mitey Masterpiece, *Pat the Bunny* Is Baby's Best-Seller," *Detroit Free Press,* October 21, 1972; *Saturday Review,* November 29, 1975; Barbara Bader, *American Picturebooks from Noah's Ark to the Beast Within,* Macmillan, 1976; *New Republic,* December 3, 1977; *New York Times Book Review,* December 4, 1977; *Time,* December 12, 1977; Martha E. Ward and Dorothy A. Marquardt, *Authors of Books for Young People,* supplement to the 2nd edition, Scarecrow, 1979.

Obituaries: *New York Times,* December 25, 1979; *Publishers Weekly,* January 18, 1980.

KUNZ, Roxane (Brown) 1932-

BRIEF ENTRY: Born July 29, 1932, in Jamestown, N.Y. Kunz, who received both a B.A. and an M.A. from Arizona State University, has taught elementary school, special reading, and learning disabled children. Since 1976 she has worked as a psychologist for the Washington Elementary School District in Phoenix, and is also a certified reality therapist with a part-time practice in individual and family counseling. The philosophy behind this therapy, to aid clients in taking effective control of their lives, reflects itself in the nonfiction books Kunz and co-author Judy Harris Swenson have written for children. Titles such as *Cancer: The Whispered Word, Feeling Down: The Way Back Up,* and *Stress and Pressure,* all published by Dillon, are designed to help children deal with stressful occurrences in their lives. *No One Like Me* discusses the personal differences which make individuals unique and special, and, according to *Science Books and Films,* ". . . offers each child reassurance of self while laying the foundation for sensitivity to others. . . ." In addition, the authors have collaborated on *What Should I Do? Learning to Make Choices* and *Learning My Way: I'm a Winner!* Kunz belongs to several

organizations, including the National Writers Club, the American Association of School Psychology, and the Arizona Association for Children and Adults with Learning Disabilities. *Office:* Washington Elementary School District, 8610 North 19th Ave., Phoenix, Ariz. 85021.

FOR MORE INFORMATION SEE: Contemporary Authors, Volume 121, Gale, 1987.

LAMB, Harold (Albert) 1892-1962

PERSONAL: Born September 1, 1892, in Alpine, N.J.; died of cancer, April 9, 1962, in Rochester, Minn.; buried at Brookside Cemetery, Englewood, N.J.; son of Frederick Stymetz (a businessman) and Nellie (Albert) Lamb; married Ruth Lemont Barbour, June 14, 1917; children: Cary, Frederick Stymetz II. *Education:* Columbia University, B.A., 1916. *Politics:* Republican. *Residence:* Beverly Hills, Calif.

CAREER: Historian; writer of historical articles and stories. Prior to World War I, worked as a make-up man for a motor trade weekly and as a financial writer for the *New York Times;* scriptwriter in Hollywood, Calif. *Military service:* U.S. Army, infantryman, World War I; Office of Strategic Services, World War II. *Member:* P.E.N., Authors' League, American Oriental Society, American Geographical Society, American Friends of the Middle East, Near East College Association, Institute of Turkish Studies, Los Angeles County Museum, California Writers' Club, St. Anthony Club (New York). *Awards, honors:* Guggenheim fellowship, 1929; Second Order of "Elmi" from the Persian Government, 1933, for *The Crusades;* Silver Medal from the Commonwealth Club of California, 1933, for *Nur Mahal,* and 1940; Rupert Hughes Award from the Commonwealth Club, 1950.

WRITINGS: Marching Sands (juvenile), Appleton, 1920, reissued with introduction by L. Sprague de Camp, Hyperion Press,

HAROLD LAMB

1974; *The House of the Falcon* (juvenile), Appleton, 1921; *White Falcon*, McBride, 1926; *Genghis Khan, the Emperor of All Men* (biography), McBride, 1927, published as *Genghis Khan, the Conqueror, the Emperor of All Men*, Bantam, 1963; *Tamerlane, the Earth Shaker* (biography), McBride, 1928, reissued with *The March of the Barbarians* (see below) under title *The Earth Shakers*, Doubleday, 1956.

The Boy's Genghis Khan (edited by James Gilman; illustrated by William Siegel), McBride, 1930; *The Crusades*, Doubleday, Volume I: *Iron Men and Saints*, 1930, Volume II: *The Flame of Islam*, 1931, reissued in one volume as *The Crusades: The Whole Story of the Crusades*, Doubleday, 1962; *Durandal: A Crusader in the Horde* (juvenile; illustrated by

Allan McNab; Junior Literary Guild selection), Doubleday, 1931; *Nur Mahal* (novel), Doubleday, 1932; *Kirdy: The Road Out of the World* (juvenile; illustrated by Boris Artzybasheff; Junior Literary Guild selection), Doubleday, 1933; *Omar Khayyam: A Life* (historical novel), Doubleday, 1934, reissued, Pinnacle Books, 1978.

The March of the Barbarians, Doubleday, 1940; *Persian Mosaic: An Imaginative Biography of Omar Khayyam Based Upon Reality, in the Oriental Manner*, Hale, 1943; *Alexander of Macedon: The Journey to World's End*, Doubleday, 1946, reissued, Pinnacle Books, 1976; *A Garden to the Eastward* (novel), Doubleday, 1947; *The City and the Tsar: Peter the Great and the Move to the West, 1648-1762*, Doubleday, 1948; *The March of Muscovy: Ivan the Terrible and the Growth of the Russian Empire, 1400-1648*, Doubleday, 1948.

Suleiman, the Magnificent, Sultan of the East, Doubleday, 1951, reissued, Pinnacle Books, 1978; *Theodora and the Emperor: The Drama of Justinian*, Doubleday, 1952, reissued, Pinnacle Books, 1977; *Charlemagne: The Legend and the Man*, Doubleday, 1954; *Genghis Khan and the Mongol Horde* (juvenile: illustrated by Elton Fax), Random House, 1954, reissued, Pinnacle Books, 1976; *New Found World: How North America Was Discovered and Explored*, Doubleday, 1955; *Constantinople: Birth of an Empire*, Knopf, 1957; (wtih others) *Hannibal: One Man against Rome*, Doubleday, 1958, reissued, Pinnacle Books, 1976; *Chief of the Cossacks* (juvenile; illustrated by Robert Frankenberg), Random House, 1959.

Cyrus the Great, Doubleday, 1960, reissued, Pinnacle Books, 1976; *Babur the Tiger, First of the Great Monguls*, Doubleday, 1961, reissued, Pinnacle Books, 1979; *The Curved Saber: The Adventures of Khlit the Cossack* (short stories), Doubleday, 1964; *The Mighty Manslayer*, Doubleday, 1969.

Author of screenplays, "The Crusaders," Paramount, 1935; "The Plainsman," Paramount, 1936; "The Buccaneer," Paramount, 1938; "Samson and Delilah," Paramount, 1949. Contributor of articles and stories to magazines such as *National Geographic, Asia, Adventure, San Francisco Chronicle, Saturday Evening Post, Country Gentleman, Pictorial Review,* and *Collier's.*

Procession . . . at German court. ■ (From *The March of Muscovy: Ivan the Terrible and the Growth of the Russian Empire, 1400-1648* by Harold Lamb.)

(From the movie "The Crusades," starring Loretta Young. Copyright 1935 by Paramount Productions, Inc.)

(From the movie "The Buccaneer," starring Fredric March and Akim Tamiroff. Screenplay co-written by Harold Lamb. Produced by Paramount, 1938.)

(From the movie "Samson and Delilah," starring Victor Mature and Hedy Lamarr. Copyright 1949 by Paramount Pictures, Inc.)

(From the remake of the film "The Buccaneer," starring Yul Brynner and Charlton Heston. Screenplay co-written by Harold Lamb. Produced by Paramount, 1958.)

(From the movie "The Plainsman," starring Gary Cooper and Jean Arthur. Produced by Paramount, 1937.)

SIDELIGHTS: Lamb, whose father and grandfather were both artists, spent his early education at Friends' Seminary in New York City, where he rebelled against academic studies. He eventually received his degree from Columbia, but only after failing general history. "I was born in Alpine, New Jersey, with damaged eyes, ears, and speech, and grew up so. For some twenty years it was an ordeal to meet people, and I am still uncomfortable in cities or crowds, although by now the damages of childhood have nearly righted themselves. 'To build up,' I was sent from the gymnasium to the open country; but all my free time was spent in my grandfather's library, to my huge satisfaction and to the detriment of my eyes. School was torment, and college—Columbia—was worse. The hours that really counted were spent in the library at Columbia." ["Harold Lamb," *Twentieth Century Authors*, H. W. Wilson, 1942.[1]]

Lamb left Columbia in 1914 to take jobs as a make-up man for a trade publication and later as a financial writer for the *New York Times*. In his off hours he continued to study and write, and his stories were first published by *Adventure* magazine. He attributed his eventual success to *Adventure*'s editor, Arthur Sullivant Hoffman, who allowed him to write on subjects of his own choosing. Hoffman later recalled his early association with Lamb: "Back in 1917 . . . there came to me, following a sea story (historical, by the way), a fiction tale about Khlit, an old Cossack of the sixteenth and seventeenth centuries, and I published it in *Adventure*. That magazine during my years as editor ran strongly to reliable historical settings for its fiction; the readers followed it with interest and they at once took Khlit to their bosoms.

"For nearly eleven years there was a steady flow of stories, novelettes and serials—fifty-two of them—all dealing with Asia of the past. There were only four laid elsewhere, and none after 1920. Asia had [Harold Lamb]. There was a dearth of sources to draw on in the English language; in addition to several European languages, he learned to read Arabic, Chinese and a third that I've forgotten, besides something of various other Asiatic tongues, for European sources, too, were scarce and second-hand and he wanted the ultimate facts.

"In 1926 he took the rather inchoate mass of the *Babar Nameh* ('The Book of the Tiger'), and condensed its 160,000 words into a smooth flowing narrative of 22,000. It is the actual autobiography of Babar, Moghul (Turco-Mongol) conqueror of India, a great-great-grandson of Tamerlane, acknowledged by European scholars as deserving a place beside the confessions of Rousseau and Cellini, yet practically unknown in this country. Mr. Lamb was the first to make it available as a continuous, unified narrative.

"For eleven years before he wrote *Genghis Khan* he lived with these people, saturated himself with their histories and civilizations, the homely details of their daily lives. Always he was the scholar first, the good fictionist second. Rarely did a story appear without his historian's letter of comment for the magazine's department in which the authors chatted with the readers—letters meticulous as to every least variation from established historical fact, carefully balanced, ripe, fairly bursting with intimate knowledge of the broad and only partially explored field that had become his specialty. And very human letters—it was not dry bones and dusty records that interested him; he wanted to find out what kind of men these had been and what manner of life they led. In the beginning he couldn't. Nobody else had; there was no one to whom he could turn. He must pioneer. So he pioneered. And when Harold Lamb sets himself to a task it gets done. Concentration? Thoroughness? Gentle persistence? Irresistible driving power? Harold

Lamb. The task, while a stupendous labor, was in this case only a joyful obsession.

"He writes me from Rome, busily at work on the second volume of *The Crusades:* 'The work here is devilish—the Crusades loom up like a sea that drowns a chap—the mass of evidence buried in hundreds of old Latin records is appalling, and the controversies are frightful. I'm having a bully time.'

"But during the eleven years of the fifty-two pieces of fiction he was accomplishing much more than the building of broad, strong foundations as a historian. He was learning, through fiction, to make the ancient peoples as living, breathing and human to readers as they were to him.

"The road was not easy going. Aside from the one magazine there was no market for these stories—one of those curious editorial stone walls standing across his path. 'Mongols and such? Nobody writes about them; therefore nobody wants to read about them. Historical stuff, anyhow, and costume fiction is out of fashion now.' The dictum was the harder to bear because he knew that people did like to read about 'Mongols and such' if they were the right kind of Mongols and such. The popularity of his stories with the magazine's readers had been proving that to him for years and, later, the longer ones of these same stories, like *White Falcon* and *The House of the Falcon,* were to prove it still further in book form—not to mention the three books that have swept him into his place as a historian who is an acknowledged authority on both sides of the Atlantic and who can make his history as interesting as the most colorful fiction.

"But through those eleven years that stone wall stood, and there came a time when he questioned the sense of going on with the only kind of writing into which he could put his whole heart—questioned even his right to do so. He sent me the outline of a purely conventional story of the type that most magazines will buy and I sent it back to him, saying that thousands could do this kind of thing but that his own particular kind of work had never been done before, urging him to go ahead. I think his dogged fighting spirit needed no more than the reassurance of a single person in the 'writing game' who saw things as he did. There was nothing from then on but steady plugging at his chosen work." [Arthur Sullivant Hoffman, "Harold Lamb and Historical Romance," *Bookman*, March, 1930.[2]]

As an historical writer, Lamb needed to know the sounds and sights and to visualize the real people whom he wrote about. Perhaps this need to visualize—to see clearly the lives of ancient peoples—came from his artistic heritage. For whatever reason, Lamb's stories and articles were based on extensive travel and research. He travelled widely in the regions about which he wrote, even attempting to retrace the paths of men like Marco Polo, Genghis Khan, and Alexander the Great. For the most part, Lamb's books took the form of romantic-adventure stories, but never strayed from historical and cultural accuracy. "So much of our history and biography and fiction, too, has been written out of prejudice or a preconceived bias. 'Catherine the Great was one of the most gifted women of all time' *vs* 'Catherine the Great was one of the greatest wantons of all time.' 'Alexander of Macedonia was a superman' *vs* 'Alexander was mad.' You know how these things shape up.

"Nowadays one cannot enter a bookshop without seeing on all sides 'The Truth About This' or 'Outlines of That.' The desire of readers to learn is real enough. The fault is with the writers, who lack both scholarship and inclination to devote months or years to finding out the truth as nearly as possible.

"Blessing the Swords of the Crusades," painting by **Georges Clairin.** ■ (From *The Crusades* by Harold Lamb.)

The result is that the very modern histories are usually 'outlines' right enough.

"Scholarship seems to have died in the last century. Anyway, I'll wager you can't name a better story of the Crusades than Scott's *The Talisman*. Sir Walter admitted that he wrote from meagre information—there was little to be had in his day—but he was a scholar and a conscientious student of his epoch.

"History, our dictionaries say, is 'a narrative devoted to the exposition of the unfolding of events.' Discarding this husk of Latin phrasing the dictionary says that history is the story of what actually happened. By the way, it's interesting to notice that the dictionary ranks fiction equally with chronicle. And 'unfolding' is just the word. What is history but the uncovering or unfolding of the past? The story of what certain men did—their adventures—because it's more interesting to read about what they did than what they were. And easier to get at the truth that way.

"It's so absurd to sit down and start in to whitewash some individual or people and call it history. And equally absurd to assemble a few facts and draw personal conclusions from them without taking the trouble to get at *all* the facts."[2]

During a writing career that spanned a half century of research and travel, Lamb wrote for both adults and children, and his works were published in several different languages. Since many of his books were about the past in western Asia and Russia, several of them were translated in those countries. Several Russian stories were translated into Ukrainian, while other works were published in Urdu in northern India, in Turk-

ish, and in Finnish. His fifty-year interest in the East and Middle East "came out of an intense irritation over the fact that all history seemed to draw a north-south line across Europe, through Berlin and Venice, say. Everything was supposed to have happened west of that line, nothing to the east. Ridiculous, of course. I've been doing research and writing books about history east of that line ever since. Each book takes a good year of intense planning and research, and is then written in a matter of weeks...." [Nash K. Burger, "Talk with Harold Lamb," *New York Times Book Review*, August 10, 1952.[3]]

When not writing and traveling, much of Lamb's leisure time was devoted to book collecting, gardening, playing chess and tennis. He died of cancer at the age of sixty-nine in Rochester, Minnesota on April 9, 1962. "Life is good, after all, when a man can go where he wants to, and write about what he likes best and know that other men find pleasure in his work." [Stanley J. Kunitz and Howard Haycraft, editors, *Junior Book of Authors*, H. W. Wilson, 1934.[4]]

FOR MORE INFORMATION SEE: Bookman, March, 1930; *New York Times Book Review*, June 9, 1946, August 10, 1952, November 19, 1961; *Saturday Review of Literature*, March 6, 1948, March 17, 1951; Stanley J. Kunitz and Howard Haycraft, editors, *Junior Book of Authors*, H. W. Wilson, 1934, 2nd edition, 1951; J. K. Hutchens, "On an Author," *New York Herald Tribune Book Review*, August 3, 1952; S. J. Kunitz, editor, *Twentieth Century Authors*, H. W. Wilson, 1942, 1st supplement, 1955; Martha E. Ward and Dorothy A. Marquardt, *Authors of Books for Young People*, Scarecrow, 1964.

Obituaries: *New York Times*, April 10, 1962; *Time*, April 20, 1962; *Newsweek*, April 23, 1962; *Publishers Weekly*, April 23, 1962; *Encyclopedia Britannica Yearbook*, 1963.

LAWFORD, Paula Jane 1960-

BRIEF ENTRY: Born September 3, 1960, in Romford, England. Lawford, who graduated from the Reigate School of Art in 1981, married Andrew Martyr, an engineer and writer, two years later. Since then the husband-and-wife team have collaborated on several books for young children, including *Willisk's Tooth* (1985), *Winston's Ice Cream Caper* (1986), and *Patch the Pirate Cat* (1987). In *Willisk's Tooth*, a walrus visits the owl dentist in hopes of relieving a toothache, only to find himself in a situation which requires the aid of all his animal friends. *Junior Bookshelf* commended Lawford's "cheerful illustrations with their fresh attractive colours" and suggested that this lighthearted story "may perhaps make a visit to the dentist a matter of mirth instead of fear." Lawford also illustrated and co-wrote *Diz and the Big Fat Burglar* (Hamish Hamilton, 1987) with Margaret Stuart Barry. Presently, she and her husband are working on *Beeswax the Bad*, a story about a cat written entirely in rhyme. *Address:* c/o Hamish Hamilton Ltd., Garden House, 57-59 Long Acre, London WC2E 9JZ, England.

Lord, give to men who are old and rougher
The things that little children suffer,
And let keep bright and undefiled
The young years of the little child.

—John Masefield
(From *The Everlasting Mercy*)

RIKA LESSER

LESSER, Rika 1953-

PERSONAL: First syllable of given name is pronounced like "Rick"; born July 21, 1953, in Brooklyn, N.Y.; daughter of Milton S. (a teacher and editor) and Celia (Fogelhut) Lesser. *Education:* Yale University, B.A. (summa cum laude), 1974; attended University of Gothenburg, 1974-75; Columbia University, M.F.A., 1977. *Home and office:* 133 Henry St., No. 5, Brooklyn, N.Y. 11201.

CAREER: Barron's Business and Financial Weekly, New York City, news and graphics assistant, 1976-84; George Washington University, Washington, D.C., Jenny McKean Moore Visiting Lecturer in creative writing, 1985-86; Yale University, New Haven, Conn., visiting lecturer, 1987. Instructor of poetry workshops at Poetry Center of the Young Men's and Young Women's Hebrew Association (YM-YWHA) in New York City, 1982-85; governing board member, Translation Center at Columbia University; past member of faculty at Bernard M. Baruch College of the City University of New York. *Member:* American P.E.N.; Academy of American Poets; Poets and Writers; American Society of Composers, Authors and Publishers; Associated Writing Programs; American Literary Translations Association; Phi Beta Kappa.

AWARDS, HONORS: David Oliker Award from *American Review,* 1974, for poem "The Room"; Amy Lowell Poetry Traveling Scholarship, 1974-75; John Courtney Murray fellowship, 1974-75; Ingram Merrill Foundation Award, 1978-79, for poetry writing; grants from Swedish Institute and Finnish Literature Information Center, 1981, 1982; Harold Morton Landon Translation Prize for Poetry from the Academy of American Poets, 1982, for translation *Guide to the Underworld;* grants from Finnish Literature Information Center, Finnish Ministry of Education, Swedish Literary Society of Finland, and Swedish Institute, 1984; *Hansel and Gretel* was a Caldecott Honor Book from the American Library Association, 1985; grants from the Swedish Institute, 1985, 1987.

WRITINGS: (Translator) Rainer Maira Rilke, *Holding Out: Poems,* Abattoir, 1975, revised edition published as *Rilke:*

Between Roots, Princeton University Press, 1986; (translator) Hermann Hesse, *Hours in the Garden and Other Poems,* Farrar, Straus, 1979; (translator) H. Hesse, *Pictor's Metamorphoses and Other Fantasies,* Farrar, Straus, 1982; (translator) Gunnar Ekelöf, *Guide to the Underworld* (poem), University of Massachusetts Press, 1980; *Etruscan Things* (poems), Braziller, 1983; (reteller) *Hansel and Gretel* (illustrated by Paul O. Zelinsky), Dodd, 1984; (translator) Sigrid Heuck, *The Hideout* (young adult novel), Dutton, 1988; P. C. Jersild, *A Living Soul,* Norvik Press, 1988. Contributor to magazines and newspapers, including *New Yorker, New York Review of Books, Nation,* and *New Republic.*

ADAPTATIONS: "Hansel and Gretel" (read-along cassette; filmstrip with cassette), Random House, 1985.

WORK IN PROGRESS: A book of original poems; translations of selected poems of Goeran Sonnevi and Rabbe Enckell; translation of *Agnes Cecilia* by Maria Gripe, a young adult novel to be published by Harper.

SIDELIGHTS: "So far as I can remember I began to write in the fourth grade, when I was eight years old. I don't know why, but it was distinctly poetry. When I read it aloud in class, nobody could understand it. I don't remember it as being terribly symbolic or incomprehensible. I do remember that it was rhymed and metrical and contained foreign places. I believe we had to memorize 'In Flanders Field the Poppies Grow' that year as the class poem (quite a morbid poem for eight and nine-year-olds), so I couldn't understand why I couldn't use foreign places in my poems. Happily, at the end of that school year, we moved to another neighborhood ('we' includes my parents and two older sisters), one that was less hostile to poetry and less hostile in general.

"In my new school I was given lots of encouragement for writing poetry, especially from my fifth-grade teacher, Rhoda Goldstein—I wish I could find her now! I went on writing, even though in high school I was a science jock headed for a career in what I thought would be biochemistry. It wasn't my only interest—I was an editor of the school newspaper, published poems in the literary magazine, and was a serious student of the piano. At Yale I dropped all my science courses during my freshman year and went straight for literature and languages then.

"I had a lot of wonderful teachers at Yale. But it was Richard Howard, the poet/critic/translator, a visiting lecturer during my sophomore year, who had the greatest influence on me, who taught me more than anyone before or since about writing poems, who for years was my mentor and now is my friend. Only one teacher in graduate school (Columbia's School of the Arts) gave me as much, the late Howard Moss.

"Nobody ever questions my learning and translating German, but everybody asks about Swedish, particularly since I don't have a drop of Swedish blood in my veins. I began arbitrarily. I was a bit tired of German and one of my German professors said, 'Learn Swedish, there's such a marvelous literature.' After studying it for two years at Yale, I received some grants and lived in Gothenburg for a year, and I've bounced back and forth ever since. Since 1981 also to Finland—not many people seem to be aware that there's a whole branch of Swedish literature written in Finland; Tove Jansson's marvelous 'Moomintroll' books are a part of that literature.

"The first book I had published was a selection of Rilke's poems, beautifully hand set and printed by Harry Duncan; it was recently reprinted in a revised edition by Princeton—lovely,

They came upon a little house that was built out of bread. ■ (From *Hansel and Gretel*, retold by Rika Lesser. Illustrated by Paul O. Zelinsky.)

though less splendid, and certainly more available. It was sheer luck that Harry took the manuscript; in fact, he accepted it sight unseen on Richard Howard's recommendation. Strangely enough, my first commercial translation was also a book of poems, this time by Hermann Hesse, who, unfortunately, was no longer one of my favorite authors. I think I enjoyed translating a collection of his stories a few years later better than I had the poems; the stories were in several different styles and stretched me as a writer/translator.

"For several years, beginning when I lived in Sweden, I was working on a translation of a single book by the great Swedish poet, Gunnar Ekelöf. I'm sure that his widow and I exchanged a few hundred letters about the poems before the book was done and finally published. When I was notified by the Academy of American Poets that it had received the Landon Prize—but that I wasn't to speak of it before public notice had been made—I immediately phoned Ingrid Ekelöf. Even in translators' rather isolated and desk-chained existences there are moments of sheer joy.

"It was through Ekelöf's poems that I stumbled upon the Etruscans and spent several years with them, first in libraries, museums, and bookstores here, and later, after I'd learned a bit of Italian, *in situ*. No other body of art has ever spoken to me the way the Etruscan things did. I've been pleased to hear from some friends that they've taken my book of poems with them to Etruscan collections in museums. Right now I'm working on a long, perhaps book-length poem. And there's another manuscript of shorter poems I keep weeding.

"I look at poems as verbal objects of art and I am committed to poetry as an art form, whether I am writing my own poems or translating poems from German or Swedish. Of course, as a poet/translator I am often tormented by the *inexpressible,* by what the mind can grasp but not necessarily put into words. As someone who also simply enjoys learning languages—for about a year I was studying Finnish, the first non-Indo-European language I've tried to learn—I am fascinated by things

that seem more readily expressed in one language than another and by the relationship between human language and human thinking.

"Not all the translations I have done have been of my own choosing. But those that have been—notably Rilke, Ekelöf, Sonnevi, and Enckell—have been and are labors of love. It is not important *how* one chooses love but *that* one chooses it.

"In recent years, I suppose it started when my old friend Paul Zelinsky needed a text for a version of *Hansel and Gretel* he would be illustrating, I've gotten involved with children's literature, mainly with translating young adult novels. Except for Norton Juster's *The Phantom Tollbooth* and one or two of Astrid Lindgren's 'Pippi Longstocking' books (perhaps my first exposure to Swedish literature), I did not read children's books as a child, so I'm learning a lot. A lot about what I like—imaginative books that address children as human beings, and what I don't like—all sorts of books that are overly cute, patronizing, or condescending. Perhaps I'll write one someday."

HOBBIES AND OTHER INTERESTS: Music, visual arts.

MABERY, D. L. 1953-

BRIEF ENTRY: Born January 13, 1953, in Reading, Calif. In 1980 Mabery was awarded first place by the Rocky Mountain Collegiate Press Association for both a column entitled "On the Beat" and a critical review. The next year he received his B.S. from Utah State University, and then worked as typesetter and keyliner, copywriter, and magazine editor. From 1982 to 1985 he wrote a weekly music column in the *Twin Cities Reader* and since 1985 has edited the arts and entertainment section of the Minneapolis-based *Skyway News*. Mabery began producing books for young readers in 1984 when Lerner Publications asked him to write Michael Jackson's life story. Since then he has written several celebrity biographies, all published by Lerner, including *Prince* (1984), *Tina Turner* (1986), *Julian Lennon* (1986), *Steven Spielberg* (1986), and *George Lucas* (1987). *School Library Journal* commented that "even reluctant readers will be enticed to these brief but informative biographies." In addition, Mabery has written *Tell Me about Yourself: How to Interview Anyone from Your Friends to Famous People* (Lerner, 1985) and has contributed to a number of magazines and newspapers. *Home:* 3138 Girard Ave. S., Minneapolis, Minn. 55408.

FOR MORE INFORMATION SEE: Contemporary Authors, Volume 121, Gale, 1987.

MARRIN, Albert 1936-

PERSONAL: Born July 24, 1936, in New York, N.Y.; son of Louis and Frieda (Funt) Marrin; married Yvette Rappaport (a teacher), November 22, 1959. *Education:* City College (now City College of the City University of New York), B.A., 1958; Yeshiva University, M.S.Ed., 1959; Columbia University, M.A., 1961, Ph.D., 1968. *Home:* 750 Kappock St., Bronx, N.Y. 10463. *Agent:* Toni Mendez, Inc., 141 East 56th St., New York, N.Y. 10022. *Office:* Department of History, Yeshiva University, 500 West 185th St., New York, N.Y. 10033.

CAREER: William Howard Taft High School, New York, N.Y., social studies teacher, 1959-68; Yeshiva University, New York, N.Y., assistant professor of history, 1968-78, professor and chairman of history department, 1978—; author, 1968—. Visiting professor at Yeshiva University, 1967-68, and Touro College, 1972—. *Member:* American Historical Association,

ALBERT MARRIN

Phi Alpha Theta (president of Alpha Mu chapter, 1957-58). *Awards, honors: Boston-Globe Horn Book* Honor Book for Nonfiction, and chosen a Notable Children's Trade Book in the Field of Social Studies by the National Council for Social Studies and the Children's Book Council, both 1985, both for *1812: The War Nobody Won.*

WRITINGS: War and the Christian Conscience: Augustine to Martin Luther King, Jr., Regnery, 1971; *The Last Crusade: The Church of England in the First World War,* Duke University Press, 1973; *Nicholas Murray Butler,* Twayne, 1976; *Overlord: D-Day and the Invasion of Europe,* Atheneum, 1982; *The Airman's War: World War II in the Sky,* Atheneum, 1982; *Victory in the Pacific,* Atheneum, 1983; *War Clouds in the West: Indians and Cavalrymen, 1860-1890,* Atheneum, 1984; *The Sea Rovers: Pirates, Privateers, and Buccaneers,* Atheneum, 1984; *1812: The War Nobody Won,* Atheneum, 1985; *The Secret Armies: Spies, Counterspies, and Saboteurs in World War II,* Macmillan, 1985; *Aztecs and Spaniards: Cortés and the Conquest of Mexico* (illustrated by Richard Rosenblum), Atheneum, 1986; *The Yanks Are Coming: The United States in the First World War,* Atheneum, 1986; *Hitler: A Portrait of a Tyrant* (young adult), Viking, 1987; *Struggle for a Continent: The French and Indian Wars, 1690-1760,* Macmillan, 1987.

WORK IN PROGRESS: A book about Mao Tse-Tung.

HOBBIES AND OTHER INTERESTS: Travel (Europe).

MARSOLI, Lisa Ann 1958-

BRIEF ENTRY: Born November 4, 1958, in Providence, R.I. After receiving her B.A. from Barnard College in 1981, Marsoli became an editor for Tribeca Communications based in New York. A member of the Women's National Book Association, she has done free-lance work for Simon & Schuster and Intervisual Communications, and since 1985 has edited for Price/Stern/Sloan Publishers. Beginning in 1984, Marsoli created a "Look Before You Leap" series targeted for children in grades three through six. Some of the titles, all published by Silver Burdett, include: *Things to Know About Going to the Dentist* (1984), . . . *Before Going to Camp* (1984), . . . *About Babysitting* (1985), . . . *About Death and Dying* (1985), . . . *Before You Move* (1985), and . . . *Before You Take a Plane Trip* (1985). *School Library Journal* called the titles on babysitting and moving ". . . useful guides, offering practical, beneficial advice." In addition, Marsoli has collaborated with Mel Green on *Smart Women, Stupid Books: Stop Reading & Learn to Love Losers* (Price Stern, 1987). *Home:* 1709 North Fuller, Hollywood, Calif. 90046.

FOR MORE INFORMATION SEE: Contemporary Authors, Volume 120, Gale, 1987.

McKISSACK, Fredrick L(emuel) 1939-

BRIEF ENTRY: Born August 12, 1939, in Nashville, Tenn. McKissack attended what is now Tennessee State University and served in the U.S. Marine Corps from 1957 to 1960. He worked as a civil engineer for both city and federal governments between 1964 and 1974, after which time he owned his own general contracting company in St. Louis, Mo. Since 1982 McKissack has collaborated with his wife, Patricia, on a number of books for children, including *Abram, Abram, Where Are We Going?* (David Cook, 1984), which received a C. S. Lewis Award from the Christian Educators Association in 1985, *Look What You've Done Now, Moses* (David Cook, 1984), *When Do You Talk to God? Prayers for Small Children* (Augsburg, 1986), *All Paths Lead to Bethlehem* (Augsburg, 1987), and *My Bible ABC Book* (Augsburg, 1987). The McKissacks have also created the "Big Bug Books" series for preschoolers and have retold popular tales such as *Cinderella, The Little Red Hen, The King's New Clothes,* and *Three Billy Goats Gruff,* all published by Childrens Press. For older children, they have co-authored *The Civil Rights Movement in America from 1865 to the Present* (Childrens Press, 1985), which *Booklist* called a "well-defined overview of the subject," and *Frederick Douglass: The Black Lion* (Childrens Press, 1987). In addition, the husband-wife team has edited several children's books by other authors. *Home:* 5900 Pershing Ave., St. Louis, Mo. 63112.

FOR MORE INFORMATION SEE: Contemporary Authors, Volume 120, Gale, 1987.

MUNTHE, Nelly 1947-

PERSONAL: Surname is pronounced Moon-*teh;* born October 9, 1947, in Paris, France; daughter of Elie (a banker) and Liliane (Fould-Springer) Rothschild; married Adam-John Munthe (a writer and carpet dealer), January 1, 1975; children: Turi, Tobias. *Education:* Sorbonne, University of Paris, B.A., 1968; attended the Institute of Restoration of Paintings, Rome, Italy, 1973. *Religion:* Jewish. *Home:* 11 St. Mary Abbotts Place, London W8, England.

CAREER: Worked at Instituto Centrale del Restauro, Rome, Italy, 1969-73; International Centre for the Study of the Preservation and the Restoration of Cultural Property, Rome, Italy, assistant of restoration mission in Turkey, 1974, assistant teacher of fresco restoration, 1973-74; Louvre Museum, Paris, France, restorer, 1974; restorer in London, England, 1976—. *Member:* London College of Storytellers.

WRITINGS: Meet Matisse (self-illustrated), Little, Brown, 1983.

WORK IN PROGRESS: With husband, Adam-John Munthe, a children's book based on a manuscript of Renaissance painter and theorist Cennino Cennini; books and games on art in museums; a studio for teaching children.

NELLY MUNTHE

SIDELIGHTS: "After four years of studying art, I felt I had lost touch with the magic of paintings and was wandering around art galleries looking at the name on the frames and worrying that I would not know the painting or painter. I went to Italy and learned how to become a restorer of paintings, and became closer to appreciating the beauty again. I feel that the frustration first and the satisfaction of understanding them has helped me a great deal.

"I think that what pushed me to write the book on Henri Matisse was the memory of my frustration at not understanding how to look at paintings, and also, the questions that my sons asked needed answers. It is the craftsman that interests me, the effort, the humility, and the content. I hope to help my children and others to use their eyes with freedom and confidence and acquire more understanding of their surroundings.

"My family and my interest in education led me to experiment with teaching art appreciation to nursery school children. At present I have various ideas for books for children about a treatise of paintings of the fourteenth century and maybe Van Gogh. Also possibly taking children, ages four to twelve, to museums."

HOBBIES AND OTHER INTERESTS: Travel (including Turkey and Egypt), storytelling, textiles, carpets.

NERLOVE, Miriam 1959-

PERSONAL: Born July 24, 1959, in Minneapolis, Minn.; daughter of Marc Leon (a professor) and Mary Ellen (a teacher; maiden name, Lieberman) Nerlove; married Howard Tushman (a cantor), June 17, 1984; children: Eleanor Sarah. *Education:* Oberlin College, B.A., 1979; Pratt Institute, M.F.A., 1982. *Home and office:* Evanston, Ill.

CAREER: Metropolitan Museum of Art, New York, N.Y., assistant in photographic library, 1982-84; writer and freelance illustrator, 1984—. *Member:* Children's Reading Round Table. *Awards, honors: I Made a Mistake* was selected one of Child Study Association of America's Children's Books of the Year, 1985.

WRITINGS—Juvenile; self-illustrated: *I Made a Mistake,* Atheneum, 1985; *I Meant to Clean My Room Today,* McElderry Books, 1988.

Illustrator: Evelyn Nerlove, *Who Is David? A Story of an Adopted Adolescent and His Friends,* Child Welfare League of America, 1985; Marilyn Singer, *Lizzie Silver of Sherwood Forest* (Junior Literary Guild selection), Harper, 1986; Marya Dantzer-Rosenthal, *Some Things Are Different, Some Things Are the Same,* A. Whitman, 1986.

WORK IN PROGRESS: Just One Tooth, self-illustrated.

SIDELIGHTS: "I started out primarily as an illustrator, but I've found additional and challenging rewards in creating my own text. I find it more difficult to write for children than to illustrate for them. Finding a topic that children can recognize and relate to and creating a unique presentation of that topic is something I'm still experimenting with. I find that I do my best writing when I don't make a studied effort at determining what I think children will like. For me the best has always been spontaneous, something that sparked the child within.

MIRIAM NERLOVE

"I enjoy illustrating other people's work and hope to do more of this. It adds variety and dimension to try to interpret what someone else has written and felt.

"Illustrating my own text is the most fun—I don't worry about the author's intentions being misinterpreted. As I mentioned above, however, trying to interpret someone else's text can be wonderfully challenging. Being able to choose and change what I'm going to draw is a delightful luxury."

OANA, Katherine D. 1929-
(Kay D. Oana)

PERSONAL: Born August 29, 1929, in Akron, Ohio; daughter of William (a tire builder) and Florence (a homemaker; maiden name, Yuhacs) Deme; married Larry Oana, Jr. (a buyer and engineer), July 1, 1954; children: Patty. *Education:* University of Akron, B.S., 1951, M.S., 1956. *Residence:* Akron, Ohio. *Office:* Riedinger Middle School, Akron, Ohio 44311.

CAREER: University of Akron, Akron, Ohio, special instructor, 1951-60, part-time instructor, 1960—; Akron Public Schools, Akron, teacher and counselor, 1960—; Oddo Publishing, Inc., Fayetteville, Ga., associate editor, 1982—. *Member:* American Personnel and Guidance Association, Society of Children's Book Writers, Authors Guild, Authors League of America, National Education Association, Akron Education Association, Ohio Education Association.

WRITINGS—Juvenile, except as noted: *The Little Dog Who Wouldn't Be,* Oddo, 1978; *Robbie and Raggedy Scarecrow* (illustrated by Jacquelyn S. Stephens), Oddo, 1978; *Shasta and the Shebang Machine* (illustrated by J. S. Stephens), Oddo, 1978; *Opportunities in Counseling and Guidance* (adult), National Textbook Co., 1979.

Timmy Tiger and the Masked Bandit, Oddo, 1980; *Bobbie Bear Goes to the Beach,* Oddo, 1980; *Bobbie Bear and the Blizzard,* Oddo, 1980; *Timmy Tiger and the Butterfly Net,* Oddo, 1981; *Women in Their Own Business* (adult), National Textbook Co., 1982; *Leonard the Leopard,* Ideals, 1982; *Harry the Horse,* Ideals, 1982; *Gertrude the Goat,* Ideals, 1982; *Potter the Otter,* Ideals, 1982; *Bertrand the Bull,* Ideals, 1982; (with others) *Holiday Finger Plays, Worksheets and Paper Plate Art Projects* (illustrated by Patti Carson and Janet Dellosa), Carson-Dellos, 1983, published as *Finger Fun, Worksheets and Paper Plate Art Project,* 1984; *Holiday Thank You Notes to Write and Color,* Carson-Dellos, 1983; *How to Write Notes* (illustrated by P. Carson and J. Dellosa), Carson-Dellos, 1984; *Zoo Fun Book* (illustrated by Joan Clapsadle), Carson-Dellos, 1984; *The Sporting Way to Reading Comprehension* (illustrated by Dorathye Shuster), University Classics, 1984.

Kippy Koala (illustrated by Lyn M. Butrick), University Classics, 1985; *Spacebear Lands on Earth* (illustrated by Dorathye B. Wallace), University Classics, 1986; *Chirpy Chipmunk* (illustrated by L. M. Butrick), University Classics, 1986; *Learning Words of Color* (illustrated by D. B. Wallace), University Classics, 1987.

WORK IN PROGRESS: Additional books in the "Bobbie Bear" series; book reviews for *Akron Beacon Journal, West Side Leader,* and other periodicals. "As a compulsive worker, I am always writing something, somewhere, somehow."

SIDELIGHTS: "Even as a child, I had the compulsion to put words down on paper. I kept a diary, made notes, wrote letters. At twelve I was writing stories and poems for a Sunday school newspaper. My pen name was Kay Davis, using my original initials.

"Throughout my school years teachers asked if I 'really wrote that story' myself. I didn't think I had any unusual talent at writing. I was feature editor of my high school paper and wanted to become a newspaper reporter. My father wanted me to be a school teacher and I followed his advice. He also wanted me to teach business skills such as typing, shorthand,

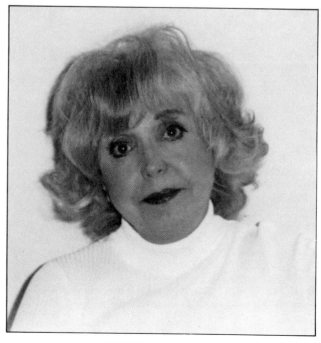

KATHERINE D. OANA

and accounting because he thought they were practical. He was a dear, practical man.

"Since I was not wild about business subjects (I was wild about the kids and still am), my masters degree was in guidance counseling. Being so enthusiastic about counseling, my first book was *Opportunities in Counseling and Guidance* published by National Textbook Company. I was so carried away with my ebullience, I overwrote the format by about 20,000 words. *Women in Their Own Business* is about successful women most of whom started penniless and eventually became millionaires.

"Five of my children's books have been translated into French. I speak frequently to manuscript clubs, schools, writers' workshops and authors' conferences. I divide my talk into two sections: writing and getting published. Writing is a skill that can be learned, acquired, polished, improved. I believe that almost anyone can become a fairly decent writer if one wishes to put in the time, effort and energy.

"Getting published? That is another story. Getting published is extremely difficult, more difficult than learning to write. I would think it easier to swim the English Channel than it is trying to get one's manuscripts published. And I'm not even a swimmer. When people ask, 'Then, how did you get published?' I answer, 'Just lucky, I guess.'

"Being a guidance counselor is the most gratifying work I have ever done. Helping another person is more rewarding than financial remuneration. Young people are 'my thing' and I have established countless scholarships for them. (Monies from books go into helping young people further their education.)"

HOBBIES AND OTHER INTERESTS: "Working is my main hobby. In addition to that, I write, read voraciously, bike, like to dance and keep active. I seldom enjoy television, shopping, talking on the phone, small talk, lunches, teas and trivia."

O'BRIEN, Anne Sibley   1952-

PERSONAL: Born July 10, 1952, in Chicago, Ill.; daughter of John Rawson (a medical missionary) and Jean Lee (a missionary; maiden name, Butler) Sibley; married Robert Rogers O'Brien (an elementary school librarian), August 13, 1977; children: Perry Edmond, Yunhee Marie. *Education:* Attended Ewha Woman's University, Seoul, Korea, 1973-74; Mount Holyoke College, B.A. (cum laude), 1975. *Politics:* Democrat. *Religion:* United Methodist. *Home:* Maple St., Peaks Island, Me. 04108.

CAREER: Kojedo Community Health Project, Koje Island, Korea, designer of visual aids for health education, 1976-77; Community SEED Center (resource center), Shelburne Falls, Mass., teacher and assistant director, 1977-78; free-lance artist, 1978-80, 1982-84; Community Intertainment Agency (provider of free entertainment for the institutionalized), Portland, Me., director, 1980-82; author and illustrator of children's books, 1984—. Chairperson of Commission on Religion and Race, Maine Annual Conference of the United Methodist Church, 1984-88. *Member:* Society of Children's Book Writers. *Awards, honors: Come Play with Us, I'm Not Tired, I Want That!,* and *Where's My Truck?* were all selected one of Child Study Association of America's Children's Books of the Year, 1985, and *Jamaica's Find,* 1987; International

ANNE SIBLEY O'BRIEN

Reading Association's Children's Choice, 1986, for *Jamaica's Find.*

WRITINGS—Self-illustrated children's books: *Come Play with Us,* Holt, 1985; *I'm Not Tired,* Holt, 1985; *Where's My Truck?,* Holt, 1985; *I Want That!,* Holt, 1985; *I Don't Want to Go,* Holt, 1986; *It's Hard to Wait,* Holt, 1986; *It Hurts!,* Holt, 1986; *Don't Say No!,* Holt, 1986.

Illustrator: Juanita Havill, *Jamaica's Find* (Reading Rainbow selection), Houghton, 1986; Judy Delton, *The Mystery of the Haunted Cabin,* Houghton, 1986.

Contributor to periodicals, including *Korea Quarterly, Korea Journal,* and *This Month in Korea.*

WORK IN PROGRESS: Finding My Way Home, a novel for the eight- to twelve-year-old reader, about a Hmong refugee child who comes to an American school; a picture book for younger childern, about the feelings of an older sibling on the arrival of his adopted baby sister, a Korean folktale, *The Princess and Pabo Ondal;* a picture book about nighttime fears, *Just the Wind.*

SIDELIGHTS: "For as long as I can remember, I have loved to draw. My mother has a drawing of a bird I did when I was three years old which she thought was remarkable and kept. Drawing was always fun, and since I did a lot of it, soon I became pretty good at it. As the pleasure of drawing was increased by the admiration of people around me, I was hooked.

"I was one of those kids who was considered 'the artist' in my elementary classes. Other kids used to ask me to make pictures for them, usually of cute toddlers or babies with huge eyes and long eyelashes. I was a constant doodler, sometimes to the frustration of my teachers, and to this day the margins of my note papers are filled with doodles.

"One problem with getting approval from other people for what came easily to me was that I didn't have to work at it, and I got lazy. My education in international schools in Korea was excellent in most respects, but there wasn't any real art training. I took art classes in the U.S. during junior high in perspective and poster making. It was very technical, and I was very messy. I think I got a 'C' for seventh-grade art, much to the amusement of my parents. They arranged for me to have private art lessons with a tutor every Saturday. The lessons were quite serious: still-lifes and tie-dye are two things I remember most. I think I was a little bored, maybe because I was too young for that approach. I still have a pastel still-life I did which is excellent, so I must have been learning something.

"Other than those two years, I went for nineteen years with no real art training. In late high school, and during the year I spent on a Korean island with my parents' medical project after graduation, I began to take my drawing seriously, and kept sketchbooks of people's faces, done mostly from my imagination. I was still doing what came easily. But it was in college as a studio art major that I really began to see, and an explosion of new awareness took place. It only took a few suggestions from my professors, and I began to see things about light and tone and space and line which had been there all along but I'd never noticed. I was just waiting for that basic instruction so that I could take off. I spent my junior year back in Korea where I studied Oriental painting, and watercolor joined pencil as my favorite medium.

"In college I also took the few opportunities that came my way to study anything I could about children's books, such as, an evening presentation by Uri Shulevitz, and a workshop led by a student on illustrating. So it is clear to me now that I was steadily moving in the direction of a career in children's books even if I didn't realize it at the time.

"The real decision came in 1978 when, as the assistant director of a teacher-community center, I had the privilege of setting up a course on writing and illustrating childen's books with the reknowned Eric Carle, who lived in the Western Massachusetts region served by the center. I participated in the course as a student also, and during that time became absolutely certain that this was what I wanted to do, no matter what it took. I made a commitment that I would learn everything I could, even if it took ten years. It ended up taking seven.

"Along with this life-long love of drawing, I have also always loved children's books. My mother read to us frequently, and we received beautiful picture books, new and classic, for our birthdays and Christmas, so we were surrounded by great literature. I still have my childhood copies of *Blueberries for Sal* and many other favorites. I recently had the pleasure of reading *The Cricket in Times Square* to my five-year-old son. The last time I had encountered it was when it was read to me as a child, and I still remembered the feel of the book so clearly thirty or so years later. Unlike many people who love children's books only when they are young, I never grew out of them. I was an avid reader, still remembering my seventh-grade favorite, *Tatsinda* by Elizabeth Enright, and the exquisite pictures by Irene Haas are still full of things for me to learn as an illustrator.

"I've always recognized myself as a reader as well as artist. One surprise recently has been the realization that while I was drawing, I was also writing. Now that I go into schools and work with students on their own writing, I've had to think back to remember myself in school. From third to ninth grade writing stories was one of my chief pleasures. I now find many of those earlier stories terrible for the most part, but lots of fun to read and to see what I was thinking about at the time. I find writing harder work, because I haven't put in as much time as I have on illustration.

"The most profound influence on my life and work is the time I spent growing up in South Korea as the daughter of medical

"Where's my truck?" he asked his mother.

(From *Where's My Truck?* by Anne Sibley O'Brien. Illustrated by the author.)

I'm Not Tired

Anne Sibley O'Brien

(Cover illustration by Anne Sibley O'Brien from *I'm Not Tired* by Anne Sibley O'Brien.)

missionaries. I am actively bilingual and bicultural, and again and again, I find myself wanting to tell the stories of people who are caught between cultures. My life has come full circle with the recent adoption of our daughter from Korea. My commitment to books with a multiracial perspective is now intensified by my hope that as Yunhee grows, she will be able to find images of herself in books.

''My series of eight toddler board books deals with everyday conflicts experienced by toddlers and their parents. Designed for parents to read with their children, these books encourage children to initiate their own solutions without parental pressure. In this way they offer support to parents, reassurance to

children that their troubles are normal, and help for the whole family in coping with the often frustrating toddler years.

''Though serious in subject, the tone of these board books is light, with some humorous details. Realistic full-color paintings depict toddlers in everyday surroundings, reacting expressively to everyday conflicts and resolutions. My editor suggested the concept, and the specific stories came directly out of my husband's and my experiences with our then two-and-a-half-year-old son.

''In preparing my illustrations, I spend a lot of time developing the plan for the book, using storyboards and dummies, which are models of the book showing what would go on each page. Then I choose my models, take lots and lots of photographs of them in different poses and with different expressions. I then use the photographs as references when I'm doing the final paintings. None of the illustrations turn out like the photographs; they're more like collages: I get a gesture from one photo, an expression from another, part of the background from another, and so on. I enjoy using my family, friends and neighbors as models, and sometimes I end up making new friends when I have to look for the perfect model, like Brandy, who posed for the pictures of Jamaica in *Jamaica's Find.*''

PATERSON, Katherine (Womeldorf)   1932-

PERSONAL: Born October 31, 1932, in Qing Jiang, Jiangsu, China; daughter of George Raymond (a clergyman) and Mary (Goetchius) Womeldorf; married John Barstow Paterson (a clergyman), July 14, 1962; children: Elizabeth Po Lin, John Barstow, Jr., David Lord, Mary Katherine. *Education:* King College, A.B. (summa cum laude), 1954; Presbyterian School of Christian Education, M.A., 1957; Naganuma School of the Japanese Language, Kobe, Japan, 1957-59; Union Theological Seminary, New York, N.Y., M.R.E., 1962. *Politics:* Democrat. *Religion:* Presbyterian. *Residence:* Vermont. *Address:* c/o Crowell Junior Books, 10 East 53rd St., New York, N.Y. 10022.

CAREER: Lovettsville Elementary School, Lovettsville, Va., teacher, 1954-55; Presbyterian Church in the U.S., Board of World Missions, Nashville, Tenn., missionary in Japan, 1957-

KATHERINE PATERSON

61; Pennington School for Boys, Pennington, N.J., teacher of sacred studies and English, 1963-65; author of materials for church use and novels for young people, 1964—. *Member:* Author's Guild, Children's Book Guild (Washington, D.C.; president, 1978).

AWARDS, HONORS: Of Nightingales That Weep was chosen one of Child Study Association of America's Children's Books of the Year, 1974, and one of New York Public Library's Books for the Teen Age, 1980, 1981, and 1982; *The Master Puppeteer* was chosen one of *School Library Journal*'s Best of the Best, 1966-78, received the National Book Award for children's literature, and Edgar Allan Poe Award runner-up from Mystery Writers of America, both 1977, and finalist, American Book Award, 1982; *Bridge to Terabithia* was selected one of *School Library Journal*'s Best Books, 1977, received the Newbery Medal from the American Library Association, and Lewis Carroll Shelf Award, both 1978, Michigan Young Reader's Award runner-up from the Michigan Council of Teachers of English, 1980, Janusz Korcazk Medal (Poland), 1981, and the Colorado Blue Spruce Young Adult Book Award, and Le Grand Prix des Jeunes Lecteurs (France), both 1986; D.Litt., King College, 1978, Saint Mary-of-the-Woods College, Indiana, 1981, University of Maryland, and Washington and Lee University, both 1982; Christopher Award, and selected one of *School Library Journal*'s Best Books, both 1978, National Book Award for Children's Literature, Newbery Honor Book, Jane Addams Peace Association Children's Book Award Honor Book, and CRABbery Award Honor Book from Oxon Hill Branch of Prince George's County Library (Md.), all 1979, finalist, American Book Award, 1980, Garden State Children's Book Award for younger fiction from the New Jersey Library Association, Georgia Children's Book Award from the College of Education of the University of Georgia, Iowa Children's Choice Award from Iowa Educational Media Association, Massachusetts Children's Book Award from the Education Department of Salem (Mass.) State College, and William Allen White Children's Book Award from the William Allen White Library at Emporia State University (Kansas), all 1981, all for *The Great Gilly Hopkins.*

Finalist, American Book Award (hardcover category), and one of *New York Times* Outstanding Books of the Year, one of the American Library Association's Best Books for Young Adults, and one of *School Library Journal*'s Best Books, all 1980, received the Newbery Medal, and CRABbery Award Honor Book, both 1981, one of New York Public Library's Books for the Teen Age, 1981 and 1982, and finalist, American Book Awards (paperback category), 1982, all for *Jacob Have I Loved;* United States nomination for the Hans Christian Andersen Award, 1980; D.H.L., Otterbein College, 1980; *The Crane Wife* was chosen one of *New York Times* Best Illustrated Books of the Year, and one of *New York Times* Outstanding Books of the Year, both 1981; Kerlan Sword, 1983; Silver Medallion from the University of Southern Mississippi, 1983, for outstanding contributions to the field of children's literature; Parents' Choice Award for Literature from the Parents' Choice Foundation, 1983, and selected a Notable Children's Trade Book in the Field of Social Studies by the National Council for Social Studies, one of Child Study Association of America's Children's Books of the Year, and one of Library of Congress' Books of the Year, all 1985, all for *Rebels of the Heavenly Kingdom.*

Come Sing, Jimmy Jo was selected one of Child Study Association of America's Children's Books of the Year, an International Reading Association/Children's Book Council Children's Choice, one of *Booklist*'s Children's Editors' Choices, and one of *School Library Journal*'s Best Books of

(Cover illustration from *Angels and Other Strangers: Family Christmas Stories* by Katherine Paterson.)

the Year, all 1985; *Consider the Lilies* was selected one of Child Study Association of America's Children's Books of the Year, 1986; Children's Literature Festival Award from Keene State College, 1987, for her body of work in recognition of continuing distinguished contributions in the field of children's literature; Adolescent Literature Assembly Award from the National Council of Teachers of English, 1987, for her contribution to young adult literature.

WRITINGS: Who Am I? (illustrated by David Stone), John Knox Press, 1966; *Justice for All People,* Friendship Press, 1973; *To Make Men Free,* John Knox Press, 1973; *The Sign of the Chrysanthemum* (illustrated by Peter Landa), Crowell, 1973; *Of Nightingales That Weep* (ALA Notable Book; *Horn Book* honor list; illustrated by Haru Wells), Crowell, 1974; *The Master Puppeteer* (ALA Notable Book; *Horn Book* honor list; illustrated by H. Wells), Crowell, 1976; *Bridge to Terabithia* (ALA Notable Book; *Horn Book* honor list; illustrated by Donna Diamond), Crowell, 1977; *The Great Gilly Hopkins* (ALA Notable Book; *Horn Book* honor list), Crowell, 1978, large print edition, ISIS, 1987; *Angels and Other Strangers: Family Christmas Stories,* Crowell, 1979, published in England as *Star of Night,* Gollancz, 1980.

Jacob Have I Loved (ALA Notable Book; *Horn Book* honor list), Crowell, 1980; (translator) Sumiko Yagawa (reteller), *The Crane Wife* (ALA Notable Book; illustrated by Suekichi Akaba), Morrow, 1981; *Gates of Excellence: On Reading and Writing Books for Children* (adult), Elsevier/Nelson, 1981;

Rebels of the Heavenly Kingdom (young adult), Dutton, 1983; *Come Sing, Jimmy Jo* (ALA Notable Book; Junior Literary Guild selection), Dutton, 1985; (with husband, John Paterson) *Consider the Lilies: Plants of the Bible* (illustrated by Anne Ophelia Dowden), Crowell, 1986; (contributor) *Once Upon a Time: Celebrating the Magic of Children's Books in Honor of the Twentieth Anniversary of Reading Is Fundamental,* Putnam, 1986; (translator) Momoko Ishii (reteller), *The Tongue-Cut Sparrow* (illustrated by S. Akaba), Dutton, 1987; *Park's Quest,* Dutton, 1988.

Reviewer, *Washington Post Book World,* 1975—; member of editorial board, *Writer,* 1987—. Contributor to journals.

ADAPTATIONS: "Bridge to Terabithia" (listening record or cassette; filmstrip with cassette), Miller-Brody, 1978, (filmstrip), Random House/Miller-Brody, 1980, (film), PBS-TV, 1985; "The Great Gilly Hopkins" (film), Hanna-Barbera, 1980, (listening record or cassette; filmstrip with cassette), Random House; "Angels and Other Strangers" (cassette), Random House; "Jacob Have I Loved" (listening cassette; filmstrip with cassette), Random House, 1982; "Getting Hooked on Books: Challenges" (filmstrip with cassette; with teacher's guide; contains "The Great Gilly Hopkins"), Guidance Associates, 1986.

WORK IN PROGRESS: The Mandarin Ducks, to be illustrated by Diane Dillon and Leo Dillon; *The Spying Heart* (tentative title), short pieces on reading and writing for children.

It was some moments before he became aware of another presence in the room. ■ (From *The Sign of the Chrysanthemum* by Katherine Paterson. Illustrated by Peter Landa.)

SIDELIGHTS: **October 21, 1932.** Born in the Jiangsu Province of China in the city of Qing Jiang. "If I tell you that I was born in China of Southern Presbyterian missionary parents, I have already given away the three chief clues to my tribal memory.

"Let me start at the end and work backward through the description. Missionary parents. I have discovered as I have gone out into the world that most people do not regard missionary work as a respectable occupation. And I'm sure that many of us 'mish kids' would argue whether having been born one was a plus or a minus for the living of this life. There is no way to escape a certain peculiarity of personality. . . .

"The most basic and most lasting gift of this parentage was a total identification with the children of Israel. The stories of the Bible were read to us, not to make us good but to tell us who we were. It seems a bit strange to me, as I look back, that my feeling of kinship was not with the early Christian Church but with the Hebrew people. In fact, it was years later, after considerable study of Paul's Epistles, that I had to come to the conclusion that *gentile,* after all, was not a dirty word.

"It is still hard for me to accept as fact that my blood ancestors were gentiles and were until fairly recently painting themselves blue and running around naked. My real ancestors left Ur of the Chaldees with Abraham and wandered in the wilderness with Moses. Add to this strong Biblical heritage the interpretation of it by Calvin, Knox, and the Westminster divines, and you have got one sure foundation beneath your feet. Again, it

was amazing to me to learn that to most people Calvinism seems more like the foundations which ladies of my mother's generation used to wear—squeezing all the breath out of you and poking into you every step you take. This, of course, was not my experience. . . .

"My father was raised a farmer in the Shenandoah Valley of Virginia. His people never owned slaves, although they were farming the valley before the Revolutionary War. They were a combination of German peasant and Scotch-Irish rock, fiercely independent, glorying in God and in their own strong backs. My father went from Washington and Lee University to join the French as an ambulance driver before America entered the First World War. He left his right leg in France and brought home a Croix de Guerre and a dose of poisonous gas. He was, I believe, as ideally suited as any Westerner to go to China. He was intelligent, hard-working, almost fearless, absolutely stoical, and amazingly humble, with the same wonderful sense of humor found in many Chinese. Not only was he capable of learning the language and enduring the hardships of his chosen life, but he was also incapable of seeing himself in the role of Great White Deliverer.

"We lived, unlike most foreigners of that era, in a Chinese house in a school complex where all of our neighbors were Chinese. My father's coworker and closest friend was the first son of a first son, a well-born man who was not only a recognized scholar, but was also eligible for official positions which would have brought him even more wealth and prominence. He chose, instead, to become a Christian pastor. He

The music was inside her—Takiko. . . . She was a maker of music. ■(Jacket illustration by Haru Wells from *Of Nightingales That Weep* by Katherine Paterson.)

and my father traveled together, riding donkeys from village to village, sleeping on the straw in flea-ridden pigsties because they were the best accommodation some friendly farmer could offer. Where there was famine—as there too often was—they went with food, and where there was plague or disease, they went with medicine. . . .

"What this meant for me was that when I went to Japan many years later, I had, through no virtue of my own, an attitude towards the Orient that most Westerners, especially the Americans I met there, seemed to lack. I knew that I had come to a civilization far older than my own, to a language that after a lifetime of study I would still be just beginning to grasp, to a people whose sense of beauty I could hope only to appreciate but never to duplicate." [Katherine Paterson, "Sounds in the Heart," *Horn Book,* December, 1981.[1] Amended by Katherine Paterson.]

1937. "Chinese was my first language, although I quickly became bilingual. When I was five, we were refugeed to the United States for the first time, and even though we returned to China the following year, only my father got back to our home in Hwaian. The rest of us lived among foreigners, mostly in the British sector of Shanghai, so my fluency in Chinese disappeared. I have forgotten Chinese almost entirely, but I believe and I hope it is still there, bred into my bones along with steamed pork dumplings."[1]

Paterson's childhood included some frightening and lonely experiences. From the ages of five to eighteen, she moved more than fifteen times. "Among the more than twice-told tales in my family is the tragic one about the year we lived in Richmond, Virginia, when I came home from first grade on February 14 without a single valentine. My mother grieved over this event until her death, asking me once why I didn't write a story about the time I didn't get any valentines. 'But, Mother,' I said, '*all* my stories are about the time I didn't get any valentines.'

"When people ask me what qualifies me to be a writer for children, I say I was once a child. But I was not only a child, I was, better still, a weird little kid, and though I would never choose to give my own children this particular preparation for life, there are few things, apparently, more helpful to a writer than having once been a weird little kid.

"An earnest mother asked me last year how she could encourage her son to become a writer. I couldn't imagine what to say in reply. Have him born in a foreign country, start a war that drives him, not once, but twice like a refugee to another land, where his clothes, his speech, his very thoughts will cut him off from his peers; then, perhaps, he will begin to read books for comfort and invent elaborate fantasies inside his head for entertainment. You will be glad to know that I kept my mouth shut. I do not believe for one minute that her son needs to experience what I've experienced in order to write books. I'm sure there are plenty of fine writers who have overcome the disadvantages of a normal childhood and have gone on to do great things. It's just that we weird little kids do seem to have a head start." [Katherine Paterson, *Gates of Excellence: On Reading and Writing Books for Children,* Elsevier/Nelson, 1981.[2]]

Reading and writing stories are among Paterson's pleasant childhood remembrances. ". . . We didn't have many books when I was little. There were no libraries or bookstores with English books in Hwaianfu, China. But the books we had, my mother read to us over and over. There was *Jo Boy.* I've never met anyone outside my family who has ever heard of [this

Make him hear us this time. ■ (From *The Master Puppeteer* by Katherine Paterson. Illustrated by Haru Wells.)

book]. But the reason I don't kill spiders is because of *Jo Boy*—that goes for sweeping down cobwebs, too, in case some acquaintance thinks it's poor housekeeping. I can almost recite from heart the poems and stories of A. A. Milne, and I loved *The Wind in the Willows* almost as fanatically as the youth of the sixties loved Tolkien."[2]

An avid reader, it was only natural that Paterson would also enjoy writing stories.

> "Pat! Pat! Pat!
> "There is the cat.
> "Where is the rat?
> "Pat, pat, pat.

"As well as I can determine, this is my first published work. It appeared in the *Shanghai American,* our school newspaper, when I was seven years old. I cannot believe that any teacher or any parent, however doting, having read my early works, would have singled me out for a literary career.

"From such primitive beginnings, I progressed by the age of eight to imitations of Elsie Dinsmore. Elsie, for those of you fortunate enough never to have been exposed to her, was a pious Victorian child whose mother was dead and whose father was an unfeeling unbeliever.

"Imagine, if you can without damaging the mind, imitations of Elsie Dinsmore written by an eight-year-old. Compared to these early prose efforts, 'Pat! Pat! Pat!' was a literary gem."[2]

I love Rass Island, although for much of my life, I did not think I did. ∎ (Jacket illustration by Kinuko Craft from *Jacob Have I Loved* by Katherine Paterson.)

1941. "When I enrolled in the Calvin H. Wiley School in Winston-Salem, North Carolina, I was nine years old, small for my age, and unbelievably timid. I had only recently gotten off a boat that had brought us refugeeing from China. I spoke English with a British accent and wore clothes out of a missionary barrel. Because children are somewhat vague about geography, my classmates knew only that I had come from somewhere over there and decided I was, if not a Japanese spy, certainly suspect, so they called me, in the friendly way that children have, 'Jap.' The only thing I could do anything about was the accent. Although I have since that time lived in five states and one foreign country, I still speak like a North Carolinian.

"My accent is not the only thing I owe to Calvin H. Wiley School. The school stood 'on a hill above a meadow,' as the school song had it, and on the hills and playgrounds of Wiley School were spent some of the most miserable hours of my life. When I read about children who had to pay protection money in the blackboard jungles of today, my thoughts fly back fondly to Pansy and her gang of seventh-grade Amazons who used to roam the playground, 'seeking whom they might devour.' I suppose they regarded me as a bit of delicious fun. On the other hand, I couldn't have been much of a challenge. They never had to lay a finger on me. I could spot them coming across the entire width of the school grounds and would be reduced to jelly on the spot.

"I can't remember at what point I discovered the library. But I do not think it would be hyperbolic to say that it saved my sanity. That's where, of course, I first heard of the Newbery Medal, for I read everything of Kate Seredy and Robert Lawson and Rachel Fields that the shelves contained. And the daydreamer that I was, it never occurred to me that someday there would be a book bearing that wonderful gold seal which would have my name on its cover.

"I wish the librarian at Wiley School could know, but even if she is still alive, she's not likely to remember me. I was just one of her library aides. We shelved the books and read stories to the younger classes. I don't remember her name. I remember her manner, which was cheerful and precise. As I got to the sixth or seventh grade I was arranging cards in the card catalog, opening the new books, carefully, a bit at a time and gently pressing back the pages, pasting the pockets in the back. I was, before I left, even allowed to mend books. Do librarians mend books anymore? I hope so. What a loving, caring task. And even though I cannot remember her name or her face, I do remember how the librarian taught me to put on the double cloth binding, dipping the brush into the large pot of glue, pulling it against the edge of the pot, first one side of the brush, then the other, so that no errant drops would remain to fall upon the precious book. Years later it is a scene that found its way tranformed into the opening pages of *The Master Puppeteer*. I still marvel at this woman, as fastidious as she was, entrusting us children with the care of her books. I have never taken more pride in any job I have held than I took in being a library aide at Calvin H. Wiley School. And I am sure that my sensuous love for books as paper, ink, and binding, treasures to be respected and cherished, is in large part due to the Wiley School librarian."[2]

1950-1954. ''By the time I got to college I had apparently read enough so that it was beginning to rub off a bit on my work. Indeed, an English professor once noted my chameleonic tendency to adopt the style of whatever literary figure I happened to be doing a paper on. I am grateful that he encouraged me to write papers on only the best. An apprenticeship imitating the masters of the English language was bound to have a beneficial effect.

''. . . In college I discovered Gerard Manley Hopkins and John Donne and made friends with Shakespeare and Sophocles. The Narnia books were being published then, and I lost my voice reading *The Lion, the Witch and the Wardrobe* aloud on the tour bus that was taking the college choir to Atlanta to sing. The list is not endless. I have read far more since I left school than I ever did in school.''[2]

Following graduation from King College in Bristol, Tennessee, Paterson taught elementary school in Lovettsville, a small rural town in Virginia for one year before getting her masters degree in Christian education from the Presbyterian School of Christian Education in Richmond, Virginia. ''In graduate school a favorite professor stopped me in the hall one day to ask if I had ever thought of becoming a writer. 'No,' I replied, swelling with twenty-four-year-old pomposity. 'I wouldn't want to add another mediocre writer to the world.' 'But maybe that's what God is calling you to be.' She meant, of course, that if I wasn't willing to risk mediocrity, I'd never accomplish anything. . . .''[2]

1957. Served as a missionary in Japan—an experience that had a profound effect on her writing. ''. . . The only Japanese I had known as a child were enemy soldiers. What made it possible for me to go to Japan at all was a close friend I had in graduate school, a Japanese woman pastor who persuaded me that despite the war, I would find a home in Japan, if I would give the Japanese people a chance. And she was right. In the course of four years I was set fully free from my deep childish hatred. I truly loved Japan, and one of the most heartwarming compliments I ever received came from a Japanese man I worked with who said to me one day that someone had told him I had been born in China. Was that true? I assured him it was. 'I knew it,' he said. 'I've always known there was something Oriental about you.' ''[1]

1961. ''. . . After four years in Japan, I boarded a jet in Tokyo and landed about twenty hours later in Baltimore. I was met by my parents and one of my sisters and taken home to Virginia. Every night for many weeks I would get out of the bed, which was killing my back, and lie sleepless on the floor. I was utterly miserable. 'These people,' I would say to myself, meaning my own family, 'these people don't even know me.' The reason I thought my family didn't know me was that they didn't know me in Japanese.

''You see, in those four years I had become a different person. I had not only learned new ways to express myself, I had new

The sun was high in the summer heaven, burning Wang Lee's back. ■ (Jacket illustration by Kinuko Craft from *Rebels of the Heavenly Kingdom* by Katherine Paterson.)

thoughts to express. I had come by painful experience to a conclusion that linguists now advance: language is not simply the instrument by which we communicate thought. The language we speak will shape the thoughts and feelings themselves.''[2]

Paterson accepted a fellowship at Union Theological Seminary in New York where she met—and married in 1962—John Barstow Paterson, a Presbyterian minister. She began a new career as wife and eventually mother to four children: two sons and two adopted daughters. ''Because I remembered so well what it was like not to have words, it was easy for me to imagine, when I at last became a mother, what my children were going through when they were first learning to speak. In my great and just possibly superfluous concern I determined to help them all I could. I spoke to them from the first in complete English sentences, just as though they could take in every word I was saying. I read to them poems and wonderful books, far before an educator, indeed before any sensible person would think they could be ready to understand the words. But in the midst of this richness, when one of them would stand before me, the little cords straining in his neck, as he sought to express the still inexpressible, I would wait with totally uncharacteristic patience, reasoning that if they were to learn to speak freely and comfortably to me, I must be willing to listen. Nor would I correct their mistakes. It is rude, I thought, to correct the grammar of someone who is trying his best to tell you something, no matter how tall the person might happen to be. And if it was rude for me, it was certain to be frustrating and discouraging to the speaker. They would learn quite soon enough, I reasoned, the difference between the singular and plural form of the verb. All they had to do was listen. If not to me, to their father.''[2]

Paterson's children have had a profound influence on her writing, and have supplied rich source material for her books. She began writing when she was pregnant with her first son and awaiting the arrival of her first daughter from a Hong Kong orphanage.

1964. Accepted her first professional writing assignment—formulating curriculum. ''I became a writer, then, . . . without ever really formulating the ambition to become one. When the curriculum assignment was completed, I turned to fiction, because that is what I most enjoy reading.

''I had no study in those days, not even a desk or file or bookcase to call mine alone. I was, I must admit, doing a lot of mediocre work, but with the encouragement, not to say nagging, of my husband, I was writing—learning and growing along with the children—until eventually I was writing fiction worthy of publication. It might have happened sooner had I had a room of my own and fewer children, but somehow I doubt it. For as I look back on what I have written, I can see that the very persons who have taken away my time and space are those who have given me something to say.

''Now I have a study with bookcases, files, and an oversized wooden desk. Taped above the desk is a three-by-five card on which I have hand-printed a Greek saying that I borrowed from an Edith Hamilton book. In letters large enough to be read without my glasses, it says:

The very idea of singing in front of people made him want to heave his breakfast. ■ (Jacket illustration by Deborah Chabrian from *Come Sing, Jimmy Joe* by Katherine Paterson.)

She blew until she could barely see the shape of the social worker's head through the pink bubble. ■ (Jacket illustration by Fred Marcellino from *The Great Gilly Hopkins* by Katherine Paterson.)

BEFORE THE GATES OF EXCELLENCE
THE HIGH GODS HAVE PLACED SWEAT

''I always type with my back to it. Also out of my line of vision as I work is a 'Peanuts' sequence that my typist in Maryland had mounted for me. Snoopy and typewriter are on the roof of the doghouse. 'It,' says the first frame. Then follow two frames of Snoopy pacing the roof. 'It was'—pace. 'It was a dark'—two more frames of pacing. 'It was a dark and stormy night.' In the final frame Snoopy looks up from the machine to observe: 'Good writing is hard work.'

''They are both right, the Greek and the beagle. Even if in my terror of the specter of mediocrity I keep my back to them, I still believe in the sweat theory of good writing. In addition, they serve to remind me that we writers are not a breed apart, a privileged aristocracy doling out gifts to less fortunate mortals, but rather that we are, like the majority of the human race, day laborers. And if we marvel at the artist who has written a great book, we must marvel more at those people whose lives are works of art and who don't even know it, who wouldn't believe it if they were told. However hard work good writing may be, it is easier than good living.

''And finally, no matter how good the writing may be, a book is never complete until it is read. The writer does not pass through the gates of excellence alone, but in the company of readers. Most of my readers are young, storming the gates for a good story, always hopeful that the next book they pick up

will be the best they have ever read. It is a joy to write fiction for such readers. . . .''[2]

Paterson's first editor was her husband who also started the custom of having her write a Christmas story each year for the Christmas service at the Takoma Park Presbyterian Church.

1973. After writing for nine years, Paterson had her first novel, *The Sign of the Chrysanthemum,* published. Drawing on the interest in Japanese culture and history, she used Japan as the setting for her first three novels.

''There is as much loose talk these days about creativity as there is about self-expression. But those of us who are mortal do not create *ex nihilo*—out of nothing—any more than we simply express ourselves. We seek, in Madeleine L'Engle's phrase, to 'serve the work. . . .'

''The gift, you see, is possibility. The aim of the writer is, like Michaelangelo's, to chip away at the block of marble to reveal the statue within it.

''It is a humbling experience to be at the service of a work. It reminds me of the feeling I remember when holding my firstborn, who was a tiny, beautiful baby. I said to myself when I was going through that proverbial second day low in the hospital: 'Here he is, perfect, and I'm going to ruin him.' Well, of course, that was a delusion of grandeur on my part. I have had some power over his life, but not really so much as I feared. He was much too intelligent and humorous and strong-willed to be ruined by the likes of me. On the other hand, it would be silly to say that stories cannot be ruined by writers; they can be and have been. But the marvelous thing to behold in your own work or the work of other writers is the story that overcomes the weakness of the writer.

"Story tellers and artists are very unsatisfactory creatures to the bulk of society. The more faithful they are to serving the work they have been given, the less receptive they are to advice on how the world is to be served by this work. I am blessed in that I have an editor who likes what I do, who never tries to tell me how to do my job, but who also never hesitates to point out those instances when it appears to her I have not done what I set out to do.

"After I had written *The Sign of the Chrysanthemum* . . ., one of my good friends who is an ardent feminist asked me to make my next book about a girl, a strong person who overcomes many odds, because, she said, her daughter needed such a book. . . . I thought I could do just that, write a book about a strong girl who overcomes many odds and who would serve as a role model for my friend's daughter and maybe my own two daughters as well. It started out all right, but the more I

Then, stomach down on the bed, he began to draw. ■ (From *Bridge to Terabithia* by Katherine Paterson. Illustrated by Donna Diamond.)

listened to the story, the more I realized that my strong girl was also selfish and vain and would be brought low by her flaws as well as exalted by her strengths. She turned, you see, in the course of the story, into a human being, set in a specific time in history and in an actual geographical location, both of which conspired against her budding feminism. By the time I'd finished, I thought I'd written a pretty good story, but I knew my friend was going to be sadly disappointed.

"I am sure I am not the only writer who can't understand sometimes what a reviewer means, and I think this is often because a writer can no more separate setting, characterization, plot, and theme in her own books than a mother, looking at a beloved child, breaks him down into bone structure, muscular system, psychological development, etc. Now, of course, there are occasions when some part of the child demands particular attention. I've been asked to direct my attention to vast expanses of adolescent skin lately. But even while I'm obediently looking at the skin, there is a voice coming out from under it, crying: 'Why me? Why not John? Why do I always get zits just before a party? Never John.' And I'm not even allowed to study the skin objectively and in peace." [Katherine Paterson, "The Aim of the Writer Who Writes for Children," *Theory into Practice,* autumn, 1982.[3]]

1977-1979. After thirteen years in Takoma Park, Maryland, the family moved to Norfolk, Virginia. "It was the fall of 1977. *The Great Gilly Hopkins* (Crowell) was at the printers, the hoopla following the National Book Award for *The Master Puppeteer* (Crowell) was over, and I had finished the curriculum unit on the Shang and Chou Dynasties of ancient China. I could no longer put it off. I must face the beast in its den, or, what was worse, that stack of blank paper beside my typewriter.

"How do you begin a book? People always want to know how you begin. If only I knew. Think of all the agonizing days and weeks I could have spared myself, not to mention my long-suffering family. They know better than to ask me about my work when I'm trying to start all over again. My replies are never gracious. There must be a better way. My way is to write whatever I can, hoping against hope that with all the priming the pump will begin to flow once more." [Katherine Paterson, "Newbery Medal Acceptance," *Horn Book,* August, 1981.[4]]

1978. Awarded her first Newbery Medal for *Bridge to Terabithia,* a powerful novel that was written as an attempt to face the issue of death after her son's best friend was killed. "I have been afraid of death since I was a child—lying stiffly in the dark, my arms glued to my sides, afraid that sleep would seduce me into a land of no awakening or of wakening into judgment.

"As I grew up, the fear went underground but never really went away. Then I was forty-one years old with a husband and four children whom I loved very much, my first novel published, a second soon to be and a third bubbling along, friends I cared about in a town I delighted to live in, when it was discovered that I had cancer.

"But even though the operation was pronounced successful and the prognosis hopeful, it was a hard season for me and my family, and just when it seemed that we were all on our feet again and beginning to get on with life, our David's closest friend was struck and killed by lightning.

"We listened to him and cried with him, but we could not give Lisa back to him, these mere mortals that he now knew his parents to be.

"Ah!" came a voice from within. At the same time Yohei cried out in horror and fell back from the doorway.

What Yohei saw was not human. It was a crane, smeared with blood, for with its beak it had plucked out its own feathers to place them in the loom.

At the sight Yohei collapsed into a deep faint.

(From *The Crane Wife* by Sumiko Yagawa. Translated from the Japanese by Katherine Paterson. Illustrated by Suekichi Akaba.)

"In January I went to a meeting of the Children's Book Guild of Washington at which Ann Durell of Dutton was to speak. By some chance or design, depending on your theology, I was put at the head table. In the polite amenities before lunch someone said to me: 'How are the children?'—for which the answer, as we all know, is 'Fine.' But I botched it. Before I could stop myself I began really to tell how the children were, leading my startled tablemates deep into the story of David's grief.

"No one interrupted me. But when I finally shut up, Ann Durell said very gently, 'I know this sounds just like an editor, but you should write that story.'

"I thought I couldn't write it. That I was too close and too overwhelmed, but I began to try to write. It would be a kind of therapy for me, if not for the children. I started to write in pencil on the free pages of a used spiral notebook so that when it came to nothing I could pretend that I'd never been very serious about it.

"After a few false starts, thirty-two smudged pages emerged, which made me feel that perhaps there might be a book after all. In a flush of optimism I moved to the typewriter and pounded out a few dozen more, only to find myself growing colder and colder with every page until I was totally frozen. The time had come for my fictional child to die, and I could not let it happen.

"I caught up on my correspondence, I rearranged my bookshelves, I even cleaned the kitchen—anything to keep the inevitable from happening. And then one day a friend asked, as friends will, 'How is the new book coming?' and I blurted out—'I'm writing a book in which a child dies, and I can't let her die. I guess,' I said, 'I can't face going through Lisa's death again.'

"'Katherine,' she said, looking me in the eye, for she is a true friend, 'I don't think it's Lisa's death you can't face. I think it's yours.'

"I went straight home to my study and closed the door. If it was my death I could not face, then by God, I would face it. I began in a kind of fever, and in a day I had written the chapter, and within a few weeks I had completed the draft, the cold sweat pouring down my arms.

"I have never been happier in my life than I was those weeks I was revising the book. It was like falling happily, if a little crazily, in love. I could hardly wait to begin work in the morning and would regularly forget about lunch. The valley of the shadow which I had passed through so fearfully in the spring had, in the fall, become a hill of rejoicing.

"I have never ceased to love the people of this book—even the graceless Brenda and the inarticulate Mrs. Aarons. And, oh, May Belle, will you ever make a queen? I still mourn for Leslie, and when children ask me why she had to die, I want to weep, because it is a question for which I have no answer." [Katherine Paterson, "Newbery Award Acceptance," *Horn Book,* August, 1978.[5]]

1981. A novel for young adults and adults about sibling rivalry, *Jacob Have I Loved,* gave Paterson her second Newbery Medal. "The conflict at the core of *Jacob Have I Loved* began east of Eden, in the earliest stories of my heritage. Cain was jealous of his brother, and, we are told, 'Cain rose up against Abel his brother and slew him.' If, in our Freudian orientation we speak of the basic conflict as that between parent and child, the Bible, which is the earth from which I spring, is much more concerned with the relationships among brothers and sisters. 'A friend loveth at all times,' says the writer of Proverbs, 'but a brother is born for adversity.' They never taught us the second half of that verse in Sunday School.

"I was the middle child of five, swivel position, the youngest of the three older children and the oldest of the three younger. Although I can remember distinctly occasions when I determined that someday I would show my older brother and sister a thing or two, and I have no recollection that my two younger sisters were plotting to do me in, still the stories in which the younger by meanness or magic or heavenly intervention bested the elder always bothered me. They simply weren't fair. The divine powers, whether the Hebrew God or the European fairy, always weighted the contest. And although the civilized Calvinist part of my nature spoke in quiet tones about the mystery of divine election, there was a primitive, beastly part, a Caliban, that roared out against such monstrous injustice. Novels, I have learned, tend to come out of the struggle with the untamed beast.

"... I have learned, for all my failings and limitations, that when I am willing to give myself away in a book, readers will respond by giving themselves away as well, and the book that I labored over so long becomes in our mutual giving something far richer and more powerful than I could have ever imagined."[4]

In a speech given at Simmons College, Paterson described the three major influences in her own life that dominated her writing: her experiences in China and Japan, her adolescence in the American South, and her strong biblical heritage. "The way a writer shapes human experience depends to a great extent on her history—all those forces, most of which she had nothing to do with, that made her what she is. In speaking of those forces, we are speaking of our human heritage, our particular family history, and our individual past experience. These are the memories which we call up, consciously or unconsciously, as we write."[4]

After her 1981 Newbery Medal, Paterson was asked what her future plans were. She answered: "... The implication seemed to be that I had done children's books and ought to be moving on. I began to feel that the medal was becoming a fiery sword expelling me from the garden and barring my return. I wanted to cry out to somebody: 'Why do I have to stop doing what I most want to do?'

"If my aim as a writer had been to gain recognition or to win a prize, well, then, those aims had been reached, and I could and should go on to something else; but my aim, like that of most writers of fiction, is to tell a story. My gift seems to be that I am one of those fortunate people who can, if she works hard at it, uncover a story that children will enjoy."[3]

HOBBIES AND OTHER INTERESTS: Reading, swimming, tennis, sailing.

FOR MORE INFORMATION SEE: Horn Book, October, 1973, February, 1975, August, 1978, August, 1979, August, 1981, December, 1981, September, 1984, May/June, 1986; *Book World,* February 8, 1976; *Writer,* December, 1978, December, 1980, October, 1984, April, 1987; Martha E. Ward and Dorothy A. Marquardt, *Authors of Books for Young People,* supplement to the second edition, Scarecrow, 1979; Jacqueline S. Weiss, "Katherine Paterson" (videocassette), Profiles in Literature, Temple University, 1979; Katherine Paterson, *Gates of Excellence: On Reading and Writing Books for Children* (adult), Elsevier/Nelson, 1981; K. Paterson, "The Aim of the Writer Who Writes for Children," *Theory into Practice,* autumn, 1982; M. Sarah Smedman, "'A Good Oyster': Story and Meaning in *Jacob Have I Loved,*" *Children's Literature in Education,* autumn, 1983; D. L. Kirkpatrick, editor, *Twentieth-Century Children's Writers,* St. Martin's, 1983; Sally Holmes Holtze, editor, *Fifth Book of Junior Authors and Illustrators,* H. W. Wilson, 1983; "Meet the Newbery Author: Katherine Paterson" (filmstrip with cassette), Miller-Brody/Random House, 1983; *Publisher's Weekly,* February 26, 1988.

Collections: Kerlan Collection at the University of Minnesota.

PEARSON, Gayle 1947-

PERSONAL: Born July 12, 1947, in Chicago, Ill.; daughter of Wallace J. (a civil service employee) and Frances (an artist and homemaker; maiden name, Bjornson) Pearson. *Education:* Northern Illinois University, B.S., 1970; San Jose State University, graduate study, 1976-77. *Home:* 533-A Diamond St., San Francisco, Calif. 94114.

CAREER: Vance Publications, Chicago, Ill., assistant news editor, 1970-71; Elign State Hospital, Chicago, social worker, 1971-73; Ming Quong Children's Center, Los Gatos, Calif., child care worker, 1973-75; Santa Clara County Information and Referral, San Jose, Calif., area director, 1977-81; author, 1978—; University of California, San Francisco, administrative assistant, 1982—. *Member:* Society of Children's Book Writers; National Writers Union. *Awards, honors:* Best Children's Book from the Bay Area Reviewer's Association, 1986, for *Fish Friday.*

WRITINGS: Fish Friday (juvenile), Atheneum, 1986. Contributor of articles and stories to magazines and newspapers, including *Ms., California Living,* and *Highlights for Children.*

WORK IN PROGRESS: An historical novel for young adults set in the early 1930s to be published by Atheneum.

SIDELIGHTS: "The interplay of fiction and history is of particular interest to me. Going back in time is a common fantasy. For the writer, historical fiction provides a way to do that. My own perspectives on past events shape the story and characters. I love digging up obscure facts and weaving them into a story. If history is meant to teach us how to live in the present better than we do, then serious historical fiction is one more way in which to learn.

"I began putting stories on paper when I was about ten, but didn't have one officially published until I was thirty. I did win a writing contest in high school for which I was promised a fifty dollar award. The day after I learned I'd won, a woman called to tell me there had been a small mistake. The prize offer was five dollars, not fifty dollars! I was disappointed, of

GAYLE PEARSON

course. My grandmother, feeling sorry for me, gave me fifty dollars of her own money, so I came out five dollars ahead. I'd like to find an agent like that.

"I didn't work on my high school newspaper or the yearbook, because I didn't have enough confidence in my writing ability during my teens. In college, I began as a journalism major, but I suppose I switched to English so I could teach. It seemed a choice many women were making, and I was strongly influenced by what everyone else was doing. But I didn't like student teaching, and got my first job as an assistant editor with a hair salon magazine in Chicago. When I tired of reading and writing about Mrs. So-and-So opening her beauty salon in Springfield and Detroit, etc., I embarked on a series of jobs in mental health and community service settings.

"But I never forgot about writing. I was always thinking of stories, and sometimes wrote things about patients or kids that I worked with. I wrote my first children's story on my way to California in a van in 1973, but didn't do another for several years.

"I can't think of any other work that's both so entertaining and demanding. Perhaps acting is like that, because an actor becomes someone else, too.

"Now that I live on the West Coast, I find I'm often writing about my midwestern roots, sometimes longing for the cohesive, working class neighborhood of my childhood. As a kid, I often pretended to be an explorer, going off alone or with a friend to discover or create adventure in a grassy field on the other side of the railroad tracks, a dark closet with a crawl space. I'm still an explorer, not knowing for certain what I'll find when a character in a story takes me by the hand, leads me into an abandoned building, an unfamiliar city, through another chapter. . . ."

PURTILL, Richard L.   1931-

PERSONAL: Born March 12, 1931, in Chicago, Ill.; son of Joseph T. (a businessman) and Bertha (a housewife; maiden name, Walker) Purtill; married Elizabeth Banks (a statistician), June 20, 1959; children: Mark, Timothy, Steven. *Education:* University of Chicago, B.A., 1958, M.A., 1960, Ph.D., 1965; University of California, Los Angeles, postgraduate study, 1960-62. *Politics:* Independent. *Religion:* Roman Catholic. *Home:* 1708 Douglas Ave., Bellingham, Wash. 98225. *Agent:* Ruth Cantor, 156 Fifth Ave., New York, N.Y. 10010. *Office:* Department of Philosophy, Western Washington University, Bellingham, Wash. 98225.

CAREER: Western Washington University, Bellingham, instructor, 1962-65, assistant professor, 1965-68, associate professor, 1968-72, acting chairman of department, 1970-71, professor of philosophy, 1972—. Visiting lecturer, San Francisco State College, 1968-69. *Military service:* U.S. Army, 1949-52; became sergeant. *Member:* American Philosophical Association, American Association of University Professors, Sierra Club. *Awards, honors:* National Endowment for the Humanities summer grant, 1970.

WRITINGS: Logic for Philosophers, Harper, 1971; *Logical Thinking,* Harper, 1972; *Philosophically Speaking,* Prentice-Hall, 1975; *Thinking about Ethics,* Prentice-Hall, 1976; *Thinking about Religion,* Prentice-Hall, 1978; *Logic: Argument, Refutation, and Proof,* Harper, 1979; *The Golden Gryphon Feather,* DAW, 1979; *The Stolen Goddess,* DAW, 1980; *C.*

RICHARD L. PURTILL

S. Lewis's Case for the Christian Faith, Harper, 1981; *Murdercon,* Doubleday, 1982; *J.R.R. Tolkien: Myth, Morality, and Religion,* Harper, 1983; *The Mirror of Helen,* DAW, 1983; *The Parallel Man,* DAW, 1984; *Reason to Believe,* Eerdmans, 1984; *Lord of the Elves and Eldils: Fantasy and Philosophy in C. S. Lewis and J.R.R. Tolkien,* Zondervan, 1984; *Enchantment at Delphi* (young adult), Harcourt, 1986. Contributor of articles to philosophy journals.

WORK IN PROGRESS: A Logical Introduction to Philosophy, Letters to Telemachus, Murder Must Travel.

SIDELIGHTS: "The two sides of my life might be symbolized by the owl, a symbol of wisdom, and the mythological gryphon, a symbol of fantasy. My owl side led me to study philosophy at the University of Chicago where I received my Ph.D. in 1965 and to make a career as a professional philosopher. It may also help to account for the facts that I have been married to the same person since 1959, and have lived in the same town and taught at the same university since 1962. My 'owl' writing consists of six textbooks in philosophy, four non-fiction trade books and numerous articles in professional journals.

"My more fantastic and adventurous gryphon side may account for my decision to join the U.S. Army and see something of the world after graduating from high school and before going on to college. It may also help to explain my enjoyment of travel. The Army took me to England and to other parts of Europe, and some years ago my wife and I took a second honeymoon in Greece, which has fascinated me ever since; my 1986 trip to Greece was my sixth. My 'gryphon' writing consists of three fantasy novels based on Greek mythology, a science-fiction novel, a mystery story, and various short stories in the area of fantasy, science fiction and mystery.

"Our three sons have probably inherited some of both sides, but the eldest is a mathematician and the second son is an artist. The youngest is only ten, so it's a bit early to predict what he will be. *Enchantment at Delphi,* a time-travel fantasy is, of course, mainly a 'gryphon' book, but it is firmly based on our archeological and historical knowledge of Delphi and its oracle, so it has its 'owl' element too."

HOBBIES AND OTHER INTERESTS: Reading, food and wine.

Here I possess—what more should I require?
Books, children, leisure,—all my heart's desire.
                                        —Robert Southey

REESE, Robert A. 1938-
(Bob Reese)

BRIEF ENTRY: Born August 15, 1938, in Hollywood, Calif. Reese, who worked as an artist for Walt Disney Studios between 1956 and 1959, later attended Brigham Young University where he received his B.S. in 1963. For the next two years, he remained on campus to supervise the university's graphic arts department, and from 1965 to 1973 worked as a free-lance artist in Provo. Since then he has written and illustrated books for Aro Publishing, in addition to serving as company president. In Reese's own words, his self-illustrated children's stories are "an attempt to capture and recreate . . . the happiness of my own youth." Under the name Bob Reese, he collaborated with others on the "Holiday Series" which consists of ten books for young readers featuring prominent holidays like Christmas, Easter, Halloween, and Thanksgiving. He has also created, either singly or with others, a multitude of other children's books, including titles such as *Crab Apple, Little Dinosaur, Sunshine, Lactus Cactus, Calico Jack and the Desert Critters, The Critter Race, Huzzard Buzzard, Coral Reef, Scary Larry, the Very, Very Hairy Tarantula, Dale the Whale,* and *Wellington Pelican.* Most of Reese's works are contained in sets like the "Critterland Reader" series or the "I Can Read Underwater" series. Works he illustrated include a six-volume "Funny Farm" series written by Wendy Kanno. *Home:* 2376 East Dimple Dell Rd., Sandy, Utah 84092.

FOR MORE INFORMATION SEE: Contemporary Authors, Volume 114, Gale, 1985.

RICH, Mark J. 1948-

BRIEF ENTRY: Born November 23, 1948, in Ray, Ariz. In 1952 Rich's family left the small, copper-mining town of Ray and moved to the Los Angeles area. He later enrolled at Arizona State University where he received a B.A. in 1970 and an M.A. in 1972, both in elementary education; since then he has taught fourth through six grades in Phoenix. For young readers, Rich has written several nonfiction books, all published by Childrens Press, including three titles for which he also provided the photographs: *Diesel Trucks* (1978), *Earth Movers* (1980), and *Custom Vans* (1981). In its review of *Earth Movers, Appraisal* commented that "the subject is irresistible, the format inviting, and the author . . . manages to present a substantial amount of information. . . ." His other books include *Custom Cars and Trucks* and *Custom Cycles,* and two titles written with Tyrone Malone, *The Million Dollar Truck Display* and *Super Boss: King of Diesel Truck Drag Racing.* In his spare time, he enjoys traveling, writing, tennis, golf, and photography.

ROBBINS, Ken

BRIEF ENTRY: Editor, photographer, author of nonfiction books for children. Robbins, who graduated from Cornell University and formerly edited books, now devotes his time to writing and free-lance photography. Fascinated by trucks ever since he was young, Robbins spent several months traveling throughout New York and New Jersey in order to observe and photograph trucks in operation. The result was *Trucks of Every Sort* (Crown, 1981), his first picture book for children. His next work, *Tools* (Four Winds, 1983), evolved from watching his small nephew point at various tools in a workshop and learn their names with apparent enjoyment. In 1983 *Tools* was named a New York Times Best Illustrated Children's Book of the Year and in 1984 it was featured in the American Institute of Graphic Arts Book Show. According to *Horn Book,* "the photographs are clear and unadorned, and the tools as artistic forms are successful, even excellent, examples of the beauty to be found in homely objects." Robbins has used this picture book format to create other titles for young readers, including *Building a House* (Four Winds, 1984), *City/Country: A Car Trip in Photographs* (Viking, 1985), and *Beach Days* (Viking, 1987). *Kirkus Review* called this last work, which depicts the simple pleasures of a day at the beach, "reminiscent . . . of 1940s picture post cards whose . . . lovely, subtle colors are muted and seem illuminated by a strange light source." *Residence:* East Hampton, N.Y.

ROBERSON, John R(oyster) 1930-

PERSONAL: First syllable of surname rhymes with "Bob"; born March 7, 1930, in Roanoke, Va.; son of Zebulon Vance (a Presbyterian minister) and Irving Claire (a homemaker; maiden name, Royster) Roberson; married Charlene Grace Hale (an executive secretary), September 17, 1966; children: David Hale, Kathryn Grace. *Education:* University of Grenoble, certificate of French studies, 1st degree, 1951, 2nd degree, 1952; University of Virginia, B.A., 1950, M.A., 1953, graduate study, 1953-55; Army Language School, diploma in Mandarin Chinese, 1956; City University of the City University of New York, graduate study, 1979. *Politics:* Liberal Democrat. *Religion:* Presbyterian. *Home:* 16 Hassake Rd., Old Greenwich, Conn. 06870. *Office:* Reader's Digest Condensed Books, Pleasantville, N.Y. 10570.

CAREER: University of Maryland Far East Program, Okinawa, Japan, instructor in English composition, 1957-58; *Hol-*

JOHN R. ROBERSON

iday (magazine), Philadelphia, Pa. and New York, N.Y., senior editor, 1959-70; N. W. Ayer (advertising agency), New York City, copywriter, 1971-76; Reader's Digest Condensed Books, Pleasantville, N.Y., senior editor, 1976—. Member, National Council of Churches task force on leisure, 1965; deacon and elder in several churches, 1965—; delegate to Vatican Congress on spiritual values of tourism, 1967; secretary and director of publications, Science Education Center, Fairfield County, 1980—. *Military service:* U.S. Army, 1955-58, specialist 5, Chinese linguist. *Member:* International House of Japan, U.S.-China Peoples Friendship Association, Colonial Philadelphia Historical Society, Elfreth's Alley Association (secretary, 1961-63). *Awards, honors: China from Manchu to Mao, 1699-1976* was selected one of the New York Public Library's Books for the Teen Age, 1981 and 1982, *Japan from Shogun to Sony, 1543-1984,* 1986.

WRITINGS—For young adults: *China from Manchu to Mao, 1699-1976,* Atheneum, 1980; *Japan from Shogun to Sony, 1543-1984,* Atheneum, 1985. Contributor of a poem to *Seventeen,* and of articles to periodicals, including *Atlantic, Reader's Digest, Gentleman's Quarterly,* and others.

WORK IN PROGRESS: A book on Russian history, for young adults; (with Phillip Snyder) a book of Christmas memories.

SIDELIGHTS: "My primary interest throughout my career has been international understanding. My bachelor's degree is in international relations. I have always sought opportunities to study languages, to improve my communications—Latin, Greek, French, Italian, German, Chinese, Japanese, and Russian. The Rotary International Foundation gave me the opportunity to study for a year at the University of Grenoble in France and to travel all over western Europe. That showed me there are many ways of living. The U.S. Army was kind enough to teach me Chinese and station me in the Far East.

"In Philadelphia I lived in 'the oldest continuously-inhabited-on-both-sides street in America,' Elfreth's Alley, and worked in 'America's most historic square mile,' just opposite Independence Hall. This environment combined with my Virginian heredity to develop an interest in history.

"When an editor friend suggested I write a book on Chinese history for the high school age, many of my interests seemed to come together, and I agreed. The most difficult part of that writing was deciding what to leave out from such a long, rich story. I tried very hard to look at the events included from the point of view of the Chinese as well as that of the Westerner, to achieve the objectivity necessary if the book was to make a contribution to international understanding. I also knew it was necessary to keep a strong story line going, to maintain the reader's interest. And I was careful to include only the most essential Chinese proper names, which are difficult for Westerners to hold in mind. Eventually, *China from Manchu to Mao* was completed.

"Other friends suggested I follow *China* with Japan, which I did. The story line in both books grew out of the interaction between an ancient civilization and new Western ideas. I was fascinated to see how the same stimulus—the arrival of European merchants and, later, Western military forces—produced such a different response in China and Japan. I am also intrigued by the way attitudes in the United States toward both China and Japan have swung back and forth through the years, from offers of friendship to bitter denunciation and back again.

"In my book of Russian history, I will be looking for the same themes—modern European influence on an ancient society,

Matsuo Munefusa, called Basho, was born in 1644 into a samurai family, but he chose to write instead of fight. ■ (From *Japan from Shogun to Sony, 1543-1984* by John R. Roberson. Illustration courtesy of the New York Public Library Picture Collection.)

from the time of Peter the Great, and alternating American attitudes. During World War II, I wrote an article for our high school magazine on the contribution of Russian children to the fight against our common enemy. I hope all my books can make a contribution to the fight against the common enemies of all mankind: nations' misguided self-interest, man's destruction of the environment, the waste of war.

"In Philadelphia my neighbor in Elfreth's Alley was a wonderful man named Phillip Snyder. His particular historic interest was collecting old Christmas ornaments. When he tried to do research about the orgins of the ornaments in his growing collection, he found that the only thorough book on the subject was in German. With characteristic energy, he traveled to Germany, talked with the author and resolved to write a book for Americans. Since I was a writer/editor, he asked for my help polishing the manuscript, which I gladly gave. Viking published *The Christmas Tree Book* in 1976. Next came *December 25th* (Dodd, Mead, 1985), a history of the American observance of Christmas. He still has a wealth of material for a book of Christmas memories, the recollections of people young and old he has interviewed. And he dreams of someday having a Christmas museum in New York City.

"In 1963 I moved to New York City, and there I found my wonderful wife Charlene.

''Much of my spare time has been taken up with an organization called the Science Education Center. In 1980 a group of parents, educators, and businessmen banded together to provide students keenly interested in science and mathematics opportunities for study and exploration beyond their schools' curriculum. I was elected secretary of the group. We have expanded now into four communities, offering courses in subjects from space travel to the electron microscope and field trips to research laboratories, a nuclear submarine base, and so on. My in-house science advisor is son David, who entered M.I.T. in the fall of 1985 to prepare for a career in aerospace.

''I have very itchy feet—that is, I love to travel, as do all the Robersons, especially daughter Kathryn. Working as an editor of *Holiday* provided many pleasant trips. My score to date is fourteen countries in Europe, eight in South America, five in Asia, plus Australia, New Zealand, and Egypt. I also love taking photographs and listening to operas—and, as must be obvious by now, talking about myself.''

FOR MORE INFORMATION SEE: Philadelphia Bulletin Sunday Magazine, January 21, 1962.

ROSS, Pat(ricia Kienzle)   1943-

PERSONAL: Born February 4, 1943, in Baltimore, Md.; daughter of Eugene (a business owner) and Anita (Baseman) Kienzle; married Joel R. Ross (an investment banker), February 10, 1968; children: Erica Hope. *Education:* Hood College, A.B., 1965. *Home:* 130 East End Ave., New York, N.Y. 10028. *Agent:* Amy Berkower, Writers House, 21 W. 26th St., New York, N.Y. 10010. *Office:* Sweet Nellie, 1262 Madison Ave., New York, N.Y. 10128.

CAREER: Humpty Dumpty's Magazine, New York, N.Y., assistant, 1965-67; David White (publisher), New York, N.Y., assistant, 1967-68; Random House, Knopf-Pantheon Books for Young Readers division, New York, N.Y., assistant editor, 1968-70, associate editor, 1970-74, senior editor, 1974-80, editor-in-chief and division vice-president, 1980-84; Sweet

PAT ROSS

Nellie, New York, N.Y., president/owner, 1984—; Sweet Nellie Designs Corp., New York, N.Y., president, 1987—. *Member:* Children's Book Council (board member, 1975-76); Feminists on Children's Media (founding ''mother''). *Awards, honors: M and M and the Big Bag* was selected a Children's Choice by the International Reading Association, 1982.

WRITINGS: Hi, Fly (illustrated by John Wallner), Crown, 1971; (editor) *Young and Female: Turning Points in the Lives of Eight American Women,* Random House, 1972; *What Ever Happened to the Baxter Place?* (illustrated by Roger Duvoisin), Pantheon, 1975; *Gloria and the Super Soaper* (illustrated by Susan Paradis), Little, Brown, 1982; *Molly and the Slow Teeth* (illustrated by Jerry Milord), Lothrop, 1980; (with Joel Ross) *Your First Airplane Trip* (illustrated by Lynn Wheeling), Lothrop, 1981; *The Bandbox Baker,* Viking, 1988.

''M and M'' series; all illustrated by Marylin Hafner: *Meet M and M,* Pantheon, 1980; *M and M and the Haunted House Game,* Pantheon, 1980; *M and M and the Big Bag,* Pantheon, 1981; *M and M and the Bad News Babies* (Junior Literary Guild selection), Pantheon, 1983; *M and M and the Mummy Mess* (Junior Literary Guild selection), Viking, 1985; *M and M and the Santa Secrets,* Viking, 1985; *M and M and the Superchild Afternoon,* Viking, 1987.

ADAPTATIONS: ''Young and Female'' (cassette), Caedmon; ''Meet M and M'' (read-along cassette), Random House; ''M and M and the Haunted House Game'' (read-along cassette), Random House.

SIDELIGHTS: ''When I applied for my first job in publishing—as an assistant on *Humpty Dumpty's Magazine,* which I landed—I carried along with me a portfolio of children's book manuscripts that I had written and illustrated in college. Those rather sad works never did see the light of day (a later relief to me, and, I'm sure, to the publishing industry), but they were a beginning. My first book, *Young and Female,* was a compilation for young adults of turning points in the lives of eight young American women, as seen through their autobiographical accounts. This book was published in the mid-seventies when I was actively involved with Feminists on Children's Media, an organization dedicated to changing the image of girls and women in children's literature.

''In the late 70s, I began writing about two young girls who were constantly in and out of 'funny troubles,' and who lived in a large city. Their amusing adventures have taken the two (and me!) through seven beginning-reader books since that first *Meet M and M.* Marylin Hafner has joyfully illustrated all the books, and our combination of words and art has been a happy one.

''For eighteen years I worked in publishing. After three years with *Humpty Dumpty's Magazine,* I moved into book publishing, spending twelve years at Random House in the Knopf-Pantheon Books for Young Readers department. I began there as an assistant editor in 1968, and was editor-in-chief and vice-president of the department when I 'retired' from publishing in 1984 to begin my own business.

''In the winter of 1984, I opened a shop on Madison Avenue, combining my long-time interest in antiques and American crafts. The shop is called Sweet Nellie, and it has made it through four wonderful and challenging years. In 1988 Sweet Nellie Designs, a licensing business for our original fabric, wallcovering, tableware and book designs, was born.

''Writing for children and young people has never been my main vocation, yet it is such an important part of my life and my well-being that it has endured through two careers. Writing for children puts me in touch with a part of myself and in touch with a kind of creativity that I don't seem to find anywhere else. Although writing is always hard work, it is never a chore. Escape to my typewriter becomes a kind of 'vacation' from the business world. Getting in touch with a character fills me with energy; it makes me laugh; it touches deep. I know the characters in the 'M and M' series—Mandy and Mimi—like the back of my hand, yet their adventures are still a challenge. After all this time, you'd think it would be easier with those two!

"My latest book, *The Bandbox Maker*, is the fictionalized account of the 'invention' of the nineteenth century bandbox. I sell these beautiful boxes at Sweet Nellie, covered with romantic and lyrical vintage wallpapers; and so I was inspired to think about how the first bandbox came about. The life of bandbox-maker Hannah Davis was a jumping-off point, and an inspiration for my story. So my past life and my present life work together well. . . .

"My daughter, Erica, who is now a teenager, has been a constant inspiration. I shamelessly eavesdropped on her at age six, and *Molly and the Slow Teeth* as well as the 'M and M' series resulted. The wit and cleverness of six- and seven-year-olds cannot be understated, and I am grateful for all her fine qualities that went from life to the pages of my books. Some day, she will thank me!"

HOBBIES AND OTHER INTERESTS: Attending opera, traveling in the United States and Europe, collecting historical boxes.

FOR MORE INFORMATION SEE: Jim Roginski, *Behind the Covers*, Libraries Unlimited, 1985.

RUSSELL, James 1933-
(Jim Russell)

PERSONAL: Born June 30, 1933, in Walsall, Staffordshire, England; son of Ronald James (an architect) and Violet (a teacher; maiden name, Allen) Russell; married Emily Rebecca Cook (a junior school head teacher), December 19, 1959; children: John Allen, Katharine Rebecca. *Education:* Birmingham College of Arts and Crafts, N.D.D., 1955, A.T.D., 1958. *Home and office:* 10 Milton Rd., London SE24 0NP, England.

CAREER: Free-lance artist and illustrator, 1960—; St. Martin's Art College, London, England, part-time lecturer, 1961-70; Young Vic Theatre, London, England, artist, 1980—. *Exhibitions*—One-man shows: William Ware, London, 1967, 1969; Drian, London, 1974; Amalgam Barnes, London, 1976, 1978, 1980, 1982, 1985, 1988; Young Vic Theatre, London, 1981; Froebel Institute, London, 1982; National Theatre, London, 1987. Group shows: Royal Academy, London, 1959—; John Moore's, Liverpool, 1972; Drawing Bienale, Middlesborough, England, 1975; Royal Watercolour Society, London, 1984. *Military service:* Army National Service, 1955-57; became sergeant. *Member:* Chelsea Art Society. *Awards, honors:* City of London Mayor's Award, 1970, 1971, 1972, for paintings; Chelsea Art Society Award for watercolors, 1984.

ILLUSTRATOR: Eileen Thompson (pseudonym of Eileen Thompson Panowski) *The Blue-Stone Mystery*, Abelard, 1963; E. Thompson, *The Spanish Deed Mystery*, Abelard, 1964; E. Thompson, *The Apache Gold Mystery*, Abelard, 1965; E. Thompson, *The Dog Show Mystery*, Abelard, 1966; Don Byrne, *Down the River*, 1967.

Bruce Carter, *Kick Back,* Longman, 1970; Marjorie Darke, *Mike's Bike,* Kestrel, 1974; Mabel Esther Allan, *The Secret Players,* Brockhampton, 1974; Margaret Mahy, *David's Witch Doctor,* F. Watts, 1975; Petronella Breinburg, *What Happened at Rita's Party,* Kestrel, 1976; (under name Jim Russell) Robert Leeson, *Demon Bike Rider,* Collins, 1976; (under name Jim Russell) Jan Mark, *Thunder and Lightnings,* Kestrel, 1976, Harper, 1979; Patrick Rutland, *Kites and Gliders,* F. Watts, 1977; R. Leeson, *Challenge in the Dark,* Collins, 1978; James Webster, *Missing! The Secret Wish,* Hart-Davis, 1978; *Pups,* Hart-Davis, 1979; *Copper,* Hart-Davis, 1979.

Helen Morgan, *The Sketchbook Crime,* Wheaton, 1980; (under name Jim Russell) Catherine Storr, reteller, *Noah and His Ark,* Raintree, 1982; (under name Jim Russell) C. Storr, reteller, *Moses of the Bulrushes,* Raintree, 1984; (under name Jim Russell) C. Storr, *Moses and the Plagues,* Raintree, 1985; *Reader's Digest Field Guide,* six books, Reader's Digest, 1981; *Story Line: Scotland,* Oliver & Boyd, 1984; *Wildlife,* Reader's Digest, 1987; Brigitte Tilleray, *East Anglian Food and Wine,* Partners, 1987.

Also illustrator of numerous other books, including *Adam and Eve,* retold by C. Storr, F. Watts; *A Real Beauty, A Man in the Mist, Poached Eggs, Pups!* Contributor of illustrations to "Jackanory," BBC-TV, 1976-87, and to *Punch.*

WORK IN PROGRESS: A series of drawings and paintings of productions at the Young Vic Theatre in London; drawings for the London Wine Society.

JAMES RUSSELL

A week later, Noah sent the dove out again. ■ (From *Noah and His Ark* by Catherine Storr. Illustrated by Jim Russell.)

SIDELIGHTS: "I am a compulsive painter and the location is not, in itself, important. In England or in France (where we mostly spend our holidays), in the towns or in the countryside, I find subjects to draw or paint. I paint in water colour and oils—the former on the spot and the latter from drawings.

"With book illustration I am happier with contemporary subjects. The recent books of Bible stories for Franklin Watts are, of course, not of today, but the treatment of the drawings (and the writing) is directed at the present day child, and I found the project very interesting.

"I enjoy the combination of painting and book illustration. The freedom of one and the discipline of the other, and hope that the same qualities are found in both.

"In my paintings—the successful ones at least—there is a sense of mystery. The pictures are 'figurative' but, I hope, hint at possible discordancies. Illustrations, of course, depend more on the writing and the descriptions therein, but I hope a general style is apparent in all that I do."

"I have recently become involved with the Young Vic Theatre, drawing actors in rehearsal. Two years work, including large oil paintings based on my drawings and prints resulted in a large exhibition at the National Theatre in London in 1987 which has led to other commissions.

"I have become increasingly interested in the traditional role of the artist (pre-photography) recording incidents and occasions. I am doing a series of drawings of work at Thames News Television following reporters and cameramen on their assignments—drawing in the cutting room and at meetings, and attempting to show the full range of activities at a major British television news station."

HOBBIES AND OTHER INTERESTS: "A player of various sports in youth, retain interest as an adult, now as a spectator! Reading and theatre are main interests and, of course, visiting art galleries."

FOR MORE INFORMATION SEE: Lee Kingman and others, compilers, *Illustrators of Children's Books: 1967-1976,* Horn Book, 1978.

SCHUR, Maxine 1948-

PERSONAL: Born October 21, 1948, in San Francisco, Calif.; married Stephen Schur (a systems analyst); children: Aaron, Ethan. *Education:* Received B.A. from University of California at Berkeley. *Home:* 736 28th Ave., San Mateo, Calif. 94403.

CAREER: New Zealand National Film Unit, Wellington, New Zealand, film editor, 1972-75; actress in television program "Close to Home," New Zealand Broadcasting Corp.; writer; writer for Addison-Wesley Publishing Co., 1978-80; educational software designer for Wordwright, 1981-84. *Member:* Society of Children's Book Writers, Jewish Arts Community of the Bay Area, Northern California Women's Film Network, Bay Area Writer's Network. *Awards, honors:* Work-in-Progress Grant from the Society of Children's Book Writers, 1981, for *The Circlemaker;* Foster City Seventh Annual Writers Contest, first place in fiction and nonfiction, 1982, for an article "The Long-Tailed Imagination."

WRITINGS: Weka Won't Learn (illustrated by Victor Ambrus), Viking/Sevenseas (New Zealand), 1977; *The Witch at*

the Wellington Library (illustrated by V. Ambrus), Viking/ Sevenseas, 1978; *Shnook the Peddler* (illustrated by Dale Redpath), Dillon, 1985; *Hannah Szenes: A Song of Light* (illustrated by Donna Ruff), Jewish Publication Society, 1986; *Gullible Gregory* (juvenile), Little, Brown, 1986; *Day of Delight* (juvenile), Melton Research Institute, 1986; *Samantha's Surprise: A Christmas Story* (illustrated by Nancy N. Lusk), Pleasant, 1986. Also author of *The Circlemaker* (juvenile novel), 1986.

Author of preschool television shows for British Broadcasting Company's "Playschool": "Mr. Snoops New Hat," "The Best Disguise of All," "Grandma's Birthday Present." Contributor to *San Francisco Magazine.*

ADAPTATIONS: "Samantha's Surprise: A Christmas Story" (cassette), Pleasant, 1986.

WORK IN PROGRESS: The Earth Speaks, a biblical archaeology for young people to be published by Behrman House.

SIDELIGHTS: Schur was born in San Francisco, California. After attending the University of California at Berkeley she set out with her husband to travel the world. At the end of two years they had journeyed by bus, train, car, plane, donkey, truck and tramp steamer to more than forty countries, and had lived briefly in three of them, Switzerland, Turkey and Australia. In 1972 they settled in Wellington, New Zealand where Schur became a film editor and actress. "My mind though was haunted by exotic scenes, unforgettable people and incredible anecdotes, 'traveller's tales.' I began to write of our adventures in southern Turkey as a way of remembering, but soon sold them to the New Zealand Department of Education to be made into storybooks for the schoolchildren. These first

MAXINE SCHUR

autobiographical stories were illustrated by the Caldecott Award winning illustrator Victor Ambrus. These first small beginnings got me hooked on writing as a means of remembering and communicating. I've been hooked ever since. Much of my writing is still drawing inspiration from that journey (for example, 'A Memory of Herat' an autobiographical article on Afghanistan), but much also takes its inspiration from the journeys I made in distance . . .and time in my own mind.''

HOBBIES AND OTHER INTERESTS: Reading, traveling, visiting art museums.

SNELLGROVE, L(aurence) E(rnest) 1928-

PERSONAL: Born Feburary 2, 1928, in Woolwich, London, England; son of Ernest George and Emily (Wren) Snellgrove; married Jean Hall, April 5, 1951; children: Peter Laurence. *Education:* Culham College, Oxford, 1948-50, Associate of College of Preceptors, 1953. *Religion:* Church of England. *Home:* 23 Harvest Hill, East Grinstead, Sussex, England.

CAREER: Assistant master of Rose Hill School, Oxford, England, 1950-53, Cheshunt County Secondary School, Hertfordshire, England, 1953-55, and Yaxley School, Huntingdonshire, England, 1955-57; Caterham Valley County Secondary School, Surrey, England, head of history department, 1957-66; de Stafford Comprehensive School, Caterham, Surrey, head of history department, 1966-73; writer and lecturer, 1973—. *Military service:* Royal Air Force, 1945-48; became leading aircraftsman. *Member:* World Literary Academy (fellow).

L. E. SNELLGROVE

WRITINGS—All published by Longmans, Green through 1970 and by Longman after 1970, except as indicated: *From Kitty Hawk to Outer Space,* 1960; *From Steam Carts to Minicars,* 1961; *From Coracles to Cunarders,* 1962; *From ''Rocket'' to Railcar,* 1963; *Suffragettes and Votes for Women,* 1964, 1984; *Franco and the Spanish Civil War,* 1965, McGraw, 1968; *The Modern World since 1870,* 1968, 1984; (with Richard J. Cootes) *The Ancient World,* 1970; *Early Modern Age,* 1971, new edition, 1988; *Hitler,* 1974; *World War II,* 1974; (with J.R.C. Yglesias) *Mainstream English,* five volumes, 1974-75; (with R. Sandford) *Picture the Past,* five volumes, 1974-81; *Wide Range History* (juvenile readers), four volumes, Oliver & Boyd, 1978; *History around You,* Book 2, 1982, Book 4, 1983; *Britain since 1700,* 1985; *Storyline History,* four volumes, Oliver & Boyd, 1985.

WORK IN PROGRESS: Rewriting and reorganizing *The Ancient World* with R. J. Cootes.

SIDELIGHTS: ''A large market square, flanked by the imposing gates of the Royal Arsenal, cobbled stones stained with rotting vegetables and other garbage, stalls manned by cockneys shouting their wares, peddlers of 'wonder' cures, men escaping from straight jackets, fire-eaters, jugglers, soap-box orators ranting about politics or religion, a shop which sold hot milk from a barrel, another where you could buy eels, live and wriggling on small mountains of ice. It sounds like a scene from a Dickens' novel. Yet this was Beresford Square, Woolwich, the focus of my childhood in the 1930s.

''Three miles away, across a hilly, wind-swept Common, I grew up on a public housing estate. This was Royal Eltham, so named because William the Conqueror took it as his own domain after the Norman victory at Hastings. We lived near large parks, within sight of a medieval palace where English kings and queens held court until Tudor times. The High Street was still countrified, although suburbia had started to disfigure it. To cycle in any direction, perhaps racing the trams on a bike, was to go on a history tour. Two miles to the north was Blackheath, where Wat Tyler camped with his rebel peasants in 1381. Nearby, sprawled in majestic beauty along the side of the Thames, was Christopher Wren's masterpiece, now the Naval Academy and Maritime Museum. Behind it, facing Greenwich Park with its famous Observatory, was the exquisite 'Queen's House,' built by order of Charles I for Henrietta Maria. Woolwich itself had been a military town for three centuries, the headquarters of the Royal Artillery. Barracks were dotted all over the town, and, as a boy, I was used to seeing eighteen-pounder guns with their limbers being driven through the streets by teams of six horses and three riders.

''This was the history of the history books. In 1940 came fifty-two consecutive nights of bombing by the Luftwaffe, and in 1944-45 further pounding from Hitler's V1 and V2 weapons. Adolescence, of course, is a time of vivid and lasting impressions. There can be few impressions more lasting than the noise of sirens, guns and bombs, and the sight of wrecked houses, bombers caught in searchlights and homeless people. Gaping holes in streets, gaps, too, in bereaved families became part of everyday life. Even so, the homely lived side by side with the dramatic: hot-chestnut and ice-cream vans near ruins, dripping toast beside a warm fire as well as the drone of bombers.

''My own 'military' life had no set pattern. The Royal Air Force was in transition from war to peace. Thousands of recruits were pouring into over-crowded camps, whilst thousands of war veterans were marking time with 'fill-in' jobs until their demobilisation. There were shortages of everything, particularly food which seemed to be available only for cooks!

When I was called up it took the authorities three weeks to find an ill-fitting uniform for me. During that time we recruits were confined to barracks in case the locals in a north of England town wondered where all the strangely-spoken 'civilians' came from. Most camps were run down, some were make-shift. One had no hot water supply at all; another was taken down whilst I was stationed there! I recall a hut which had grass growing through cracks in the floor and we were ordered to cut it before polishing. But here, also, were links with the recent past. I served with men who had fought the Germans in mere 'kites' during the First World War, and others who had put down Arab revolts in the twenties simply by flying over armies of warriors who ran away because they had never seen an aeroplane.

"Within three weeks of 'demob' I was walking amongst the architectural beauties of Oxford. It was a move from hell to heaven, from mud to magic. The college towers and spires really did seem to float in the mists of that first autumn term. The feeling of being human again, instead of a name, rank and number, was enhanced by contact with educated minds. There was a link with what had gone before. It was peripheral but unique—we were all ex-servicemen. We were all glad to be out but we spoke the same language, shared the same pedigree. All of us had tales to tell, some humourous, some tragic. We were all men mature beyond our years. Even the younger lecturers were ex-servicemen. Our Chaplain had been captured by the Japanese and forced to work on the infamous Burma Road. The diary he kept then is even now being printed by a Japanese publisher from a copy which turned up at the Imperial War Museum in London. I remember him telling me that some months he averaged fourteen burials a day.

"When I became a teacher the schools I worked in were a link with those I had known as a child and the comprehensive 'glasshouses' and 'education factories' of today. We began with solid walls, small windows, desks and pen and ink, blackboards and easels. When I retired in order to devote my time to full-time writing in 1973, we were working in imitation office-blocks, with built-in furniture, xerox machines, tape recorders, television and even rumours of computers. I tried to guide youngsters through the 'Rock and Roll' fifties—one of my pupils now calls himself Cliff Richard—the 'Swinging' sixties and the early seventies. Britain had an Empire when I began teaching; it was part of the European Common Market when I finished. Schools grew larger, examinations, at least in my own subject, less literary, and old-style classes gave way to subject groups and 'sets.' At first I was just a teacher. By the time I retired I was a counsellor and even in one advanced school, a 'father' to a miscellaneous group of all ages and both sexes. The kids, despite superficial fashions, remained like kids in most countries and, I suspect, most ages. They were ready to behave and work when forced to do so; they could only learn from those they respected. Most of them laughed at the wilder absurdities wished on them by the media and commercial pressures. Drugs were known but drink was the most common vice. Relations between the sexes were relaxed and pleasant. I knew some older pupils who were more sensible about love and marriage than some of their teachers!

"As the years went by my own youth became history. It was part of the subject I was teaching. Dates on examination papers were no longer always the years before I was born. Questions were no longer dry-as-dust, at least not to me. For example, 'Discuss the Labour Party victory in 1945. What were its chief causes?' To me, that victory evokes one enduring memory—my father entering the house with the news. He was crying with joy. The party he had supported for nearly forty years, the party for which he had suffered dismissal and unemploy-

ment, was in power at last. The 'Brave New World' had dawned. Now it was just a question to be answered by quaking examination candidates. 'What was it like, sir?' became a common question, and once the questioners grasp of time and geography was so weak that I was being asked about the American Civil War!

"My wife Jean was born on the Suffolk coast at Aldeburgh, the little town Benjamin Brittan made famous with his Festival. The sea she swam in as a girl inspired the 'Seascapes' in 'Peter Grimes.' In 1940 she was taken to live in Oxford where we met in the late forties. I had been brought up to love the theatre in London; she grew to love it at the 'Playhouse' and 'New' theatres in the university city. This is one of the many tastes we share, and we have been lucky enough to indulge it at the New York 'Met' as well as London's National Theatre, the Paris L'Opera, Stratford-upon-Avon, the Vienna Staatsoper and the Chichester Festival Theatre. Oxford we still love and visit regularly. Aldeburgh we go to each year to relax. Time seems to have stood still in this Suffolk town which is difficult to 'develop' because it has sensible residents and is enclosed by sea and river.

"As a lover of history, I am glad I was alive in 1940, the year Churchill called 'Our Finest Hour.' Many of my younger friends are glad they were young when Elvis Presley and the Beatles 'made history.' I find this faintly amusing. Give or take a hundred years, I doubt whether people will remember the latter, even though they gave pleasure instead of horror to millions. But they will be taught about 1940, when the fate of a large part of the civilised world hung in the balance. However humbly, I walked the dusty, bomb-scarred streets during that famous year, I saw the spitfires and hurricanes and Messerschmidts wheel and turn and burn in the sky. If there have to be wars, and of course, we all wish there did not, what more could an historian ask for?"

HOBBIES AND OTHER INTERESTS: Music, theatre, swimming, and sitting in a deckchair during the short English summer.

STANLEY, George Edward 1942-
(Stuart Symons)

PERSONAL: Born July 15, 1942, in Memphis, Tex.; son of Joseph (a farmer) and Cellie (a nurse; maiden name, Lowe) Stanley; married Gwen Meshew (a Slavic specialist), June 29, 1974; children: James Edward, Charles Albert Andrew. *Education:* Texas Tech University, B.A., 1965, M.A., 1967; University of Port Elizabeth, D.Litt., 1974. *Politics:* Democrat. *Religion:* Baptist. *Home:* 5527 Eisenhower Dr., Lawton, Okla. 73505. *Office:* Department of Languages and Communication, Cameron University, 2800 West Gore, Lawton, Okla. 73505. *Agent:* Susan Cohen, Writers House, Inc., 21 West 26th St., New York, N.Y. 10010.

CAREER: East Texas State University, Commerce, instructor in English as a foreign language, 1967-69; University of Kansas, Lawrence, instructor in English as a foreign language, 1969-70; Cameron University, Lawton, Okla., instructor, 1970-73, assistant professor, 1973-76, associate professor, 1976-79, professor of German and Dutch, 1979—, chairman of department of languages and communication, 1984—, director of creative writing program. Fulbright lecturer at University of Chad, 1973. Director, annual Writers of Children's Literature Conference co-sponsored by Cameron University and the Society of Children's Book Writers; member of faculty, Institute of Children's Literature, Redding Ridge, Conn., 1986—.

GEORGE EDWARD STANLEY

Member: Mystery Writers of America, Crime Writers Association of Great Britain, Society of Children's Book Writers. *Awards, honors:* Distinguished Faculty Award from Phi Kappa Phi, 1974; Member of the Year Award from the Society of Children's Book Writers, 1979.

WRITINGS—Juvenile: *Mini-Mysteries,* Saturday Evening Post Co., 1979; *The Crime Lab* (illustrated by Andrew Glass), Avon, 1980; *The Case of the Clever Marathon Cheat,* Meadowbrook, 1985; *The Ukrainian Egg Mystery,* Avon, 1986; *The Codebreaker Kids!,* Avon, 1987; *The Italian Spaghetti Mystery,* Avon, 1987; *The New Bobbsey Twins: The Case of the Runaway Money,* Simon & Schuster, 1988; *The Mexican Tamale Mystery,* Avon, 1988; *The Codebreaker Kids Return,* Avon, 1989.

Other: *Writing Short Stories for Young People,* Writer's Digest, 1987.

Radio plays; all produced by British Broadcasting Corporation: "The Reclassified Child," March, 1974; "Another Football Season," November, 1974; "Better English," September 14, 1975.

Also author of "Mini-Mystery Series," a monthly short story in *Child Life Mystery and Science Fiction,* 1977—. Contributor of short stories under pseudonym Stuart Symons to *Espionage.* Also contributor of articles, stories, and reviews to scholarly journals and popular magazines for adults and children, including *Texas Outlook, English Studies in Africa, Linguistics, Bulletin of the Society of Children's Book Writers,*

Darling, Women's Choice, Children's Playmate, Health Explorer, Junior Medical Detective, and *Jack and Jill.*

WORK IN PROGRESS: Hershell Cobwell and the Miraculous Tattoo. "In order to be distinctive, sixth-grader Hershell Cobwell decides to get a tattoo on his chest. But things don't work out exactly as Hershell had planned. This book explores the superficiality of some childhood relationships."

SIDELIGHTS: "When I was growing up in the small town of Memphis, Texas, in the late 40s and early 50s, I discovered that I had two passions: mysteries and movies. I read all the mysteries in the public library and went to all the Saturday afternoon matinees, mainly to see the serials. There were two movie houses in Memphis and I would walk to town several times a week just to see the new movie posters. Since I was allowed to go to the movies only on Saturday afternoons, I missed a lot of the great films of those years, but have since been able to buy video tapes of most of the ones that I never got to see and can now watch them anytime I want to! (I also collect movie posters!) Two of my favorite movies from that period are 'The Bat' and 'Home Sweet Homicide,' because they both have mystery writers as the main characters.

"As I grew older, my interests broadened, of course, and I began studying foreign languages. (Actually, I have always liked anything 'foreign.') In college, I majored in French and

The International Italian Spaghetti Summit Meeting is about to begin! ■ (Cover illustration from *The Italian Spaghetti Mystery* by George Edward Stanley.)

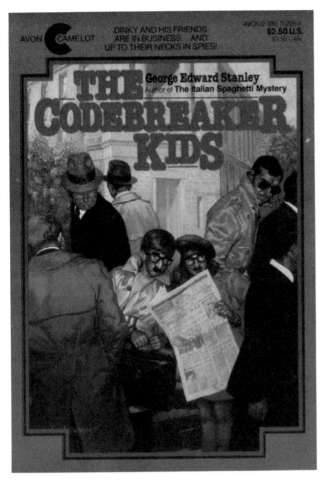

(Cover illustration from *The Codebreaker Kids!* by George Edward Stanley.)

Portugese and minored in German, and I went the route of the typical college professor as far as writing is concerned: I began writing very esoteric articles about linguistics that I doubt many people read.

"When it came time to work on my doctorate, I decided to follow another one of my dreams: going to Africa. I went to South Africa, to the University of Port Elizabeth, to research the problems the Xhosa have learning English and Afrikaans. Following my work in South Africa, I accepted a Fulbright professorship to the University of N'Djamena in Chad, Central Africa. It was there that I began writing fiction (something else I had always wanted to do) and I sold my first radio play to the British Broadcasting Corporation World Service in London.

"I grew up reading mysteries and wanting to write mysteries. I never got over Nancy Drew, the Dana Girls, or the Hardy Boys. If Nancy Drew had been a forensic scientist, I might be in a different occupation today. But she wasn't and that's why I created Dr. Constance Daniels, head of the Forensic Science Laboratory of the Bay City Police Department. Dr. Daniels first appeared in *Child Life* magazine. Later, I introduced a new, younger character in the series, Marie-Claire Verlaine, and moved the locale to Paris, but the forensic science solutions remained. If I had known someone like Dr. Daniels, or Marie-Claire when I was studying biology, chemistry, and physics, I might have excelled in science.

"There was a long period of time in my life when I wrote only one short story a month. Looking back on that period

now, I can't honestly tell you why that's all I did, but it was, and I was perfectly satisfied. It filled my need to be a published writer, but the need then probably wasn't as great as it has since become, and I think that's a normal development. We develop into writers. For some of us it's absolutely necessary that we take it easy and let ourselves evolve into writers. I used to wonder how some of my friends wrote several different stories and books at the same time. I thought I'd never be able to do that, but I was able, and I am able.

"As I developed, I got to the point where I began getting ideas for other stories and other series and other characters. I'd been working long enough with some of my editors that I felt quite comfortable in suggesting these new ideas to them. Some of them were accepted. Some weren't. Some even became the basis for entire magazines. At one time, I had seven series running at the same time (some stayed longer in the magazines than others), but soon the evolutionary process took over and I got to the point where I wanted to write books, too.

"Writing for young people carries with it a great responsibility. Some young person is actually going to read what you've written and be influenced by it. Keeping this in mind can be helpful, because it makes you want to put your best foot forward and produce not only something that you'll be proud of, but something that the young reader will never forget, whether it carries a lesson for life or simply recounts an exciting adventure.

"It's very important that you perceive yourself as a young person; this is one of the secrets of writing for them. You have to live what he is living and feel what he is feeling. You have to understand a young person's emotions, fears, disappointments, triumphs. You have to understand what it means to score that soccer goal or not to score it. You have to understand what it means to make one hundred percent on a spelling quiz. You have to understand what it means not to understand math. You have to understand what it means not to be able to play football, either because you're too small or because your parents won't let you. You have to understand what it means to have to wait for Christmas or a birthday party. You almost have to become the character you're writing about.

"One of the great things about writing for young people is that they're interested in learning about everything. This can't help but inspire the writer to reach greater heights. You want to teach them, to entertain them, to make them read what you've written. It's quite mind-boggling, frankly, when they come up to you and tell you that they really enjoy reading your stories.

"I very much dislike a lot of what is being written today for children. I think most children are looking for something that will excite them and carry them off to other worlds. They can see enough realism on the nightly news to last them a lifetime. Give them something they can look forward to, something that will stir their sense of adventure and make them want to become the best in whatever they finally end up doing. But don't forget to make them laugh!

"I am married, and my wife (who has taught German and Russian) and I have two wonderful boys, James and Charles. They are the delights of our lives. I think that I would probably have written for children anyway because I seem to have a fixation for the eight- to twelve-year-old period of my life, but having children makes writing for them that much more exciting for me. I am not, however, my sons' favorite author! (I'm working on that!)

"I spend my spare time reading, studying the grammars of such languages as Catalan and Basque, going to soccer games, doing church work, P.T.A. work, and just trying to keep my head above the water. My wife tells me that I can't relax; actually, I'm relaxing when I'm busy. It's when I'm not busy that I start getting uptight!"

STEGEMAN, Janet Allais 1923- (Kate Britton)

PERSONAL: Born October 18, 1923, in Oak Park, Ill.; daughter of John Robert (an executive) and Elizabeth (a teacher, maiden name, Spence) Allais; married John Foster Stegeman (a retired physician), March 20, 1942; children: Herman James, Paul Allais (deceased), Ann Allais Scott. *Education:* Attended Northwestern University, 1941-42, Emory University, 1942, Agnes Scott College, 1942-43, and Emory School of Medical Technology, 1943. *Politics:* "I vote for policies, not parties." *Religion:* "I am religious, but not affiliated." *Home and office:* 120 Greenbriar Ct., Athens, Ga. 30606. *Agent:* Curtis Brown Ltd., 10 Astor Place, New York, N.Y. 10003.

CAREER: Emory School of Medicine, Atlanta, Ga., medical researcher, 1943-44; writer, 1954—. Has done volunteer work in Athens, Ga. for the Heart Association Clinic, as a special education tutor with Family Counseling Service and the Department of Offender Rehabilitation Services, and Recording for the Blind. Has also helped start a community theater, hosted a public television interview program for WGTV, has been a "Great Books" leader, an officer and board member of Boys' Club, and a workshop leader for fiction writers. Member of several Athens Mayors' Citizens Advisory Committees; president, League of Women Voters, Athens, Ga., 1952-53. *Awards, honors:* South Carolina Association of School Librarians nominated *Last Seen on Hopper's Lane* as one of Twenty Best Young Adult Books of the Year, 1985-86; several small or regional prizes for short stories.

WRITINGS: (With husband, John F. Stegeman) *Caty: A Biography of Catharine Littlefield Greene*, Rhode Island Bicentennial Foundation, 1977, reissued, University of Georgia Press,

JANET ALLAIS STEGEMAN

1985; (under pseudonym, Kate Britton) *Nightmare at Lilybrook* (young adult), Bouregy, 1979; *Last Seen on Hopper's Lane* (young adult), Dial, 1982, revised edition, Scholastic, 1985.

Contributor of poems, articles and short stories to *Georgia Review, Toronto Star Weekly, American History Illustrated, Atlanta Journal-Constitution Magazine*, and local newspapers.

WORK IN PROGRESS: The Summer They Kicked Pete Out, a new children's book; *New Beginning* (tentative title), a young adult book.

SIDELIGHTS: "I did most of my growing up before I was ten, I think. We lived as part of a farming community near Wheeling, Illinois, a philanthropic enterprise of Frances Crane Lillie for widows and children. My mother and sister were given 'twin acres' on which to build a duplex for their families if they would agree to teach in the 'farm' school and help with supervising the enterprise. My father, a rising executive with Sears, commuted to Chicago. My uncle served in various capacities on the farm. Although we were considered 'different' because we had fathers, my cousins and my brother, sisters and I were definitely a part of the gang. Many a night, when my weary father returned from the city, there would be a knock at the door and some group of children would push a spokesman forward to ask, 'Can Mr. Allais come out and play!'

"When we moved to Atlanta, I was lost. Although I had some various undiagnosed congenital defects, my many illnesses after the move away from that huge family and country life were considered 'all in your head.' But I became too ill to go to school, and I think that was when I began to write 'seriously.' I made up fantastic plots to be acted out by my sister and all the neighbors when school was out. (Perhaps my mother had some reason to consider malingering when she saw the energy I put into production of these play/stories complete with costumes and props.)

"Another transfer sent us to Cincinnati where my health improved and I spent a different sort of happy time. I was in school and loving it! My teachers were outstanding and several of them urged me to write. I was singled out, for some reason, to help the school counselors with various problems with kids— one or two of them my friends, which gave me an enormously tricky thing to handle. With their guidance, I found myself growing interested in the workings of other people's minds, their attitudes, their reasons and choices. No angel myself, I could put myself in the place of someone who just needed a nudge to go see the counselor and talk out a problem. All of this has had a great influence on my writing, as well as on me as a person. I rather think the counselors saw that *I* needed to be close to them, and that some of these 'assignments' were to help involve me with them so that they could get to know me better, too. Without realizing it, I was gathering material and characters for future stories, all to become composites as I was exposed to other persons and situations.

STEWART, W(alter) P. 1924-

PERSONAL: Born July 31, 1924, in Melfort, Saskatchewan, Canada; son of James Mitchell and Sarah (Pendlebury) Stewart. *Education:* Concordia University, Montreal, Quebec, B.A., 1958; University of Minnesota, M.A., 1988. *Politics:* "Strictly neutral." *Home:* Big Island, P.O. Box 496, Kenora, Ontario, Canada P9N 3X5. *Office:* Butterfly Books Ltd., CPO 2234, Winnipeg Manitoba, Canada R3C 3R5.

CAREER: Butterfly Books Ltd., Winnipeg, Manitoba, Canada, president, 1982—. Arctic Geo-Tech Data Resource, Inc., Winnipeg and Denver, Colo., president, 1982-87.

WRITINGS—All published by Butterfly: *The Ten Premiers of Canada,* 1976; *The Village of Rockcliffe Park,* 1976; *Town of Maple Creek, Saskatchewan,* 1978; *The Growth of Western Canada Nationalism,* 1978; *The City of Regina, Saskatchewan,* 1979; *Eagle Feathers in the Dust,* 1979; *My Name Is Piapot,* 1981; *G-5: Fictional Artificial Intelligence in 1992,* 1984.

SIDELIGHTS: In his youth, Stewart liked writing themes about international peace. He studied English, philosophy and religion in college because of "public concern for international peace."

Stewart's career is writing—"book publishing is merely an aspect of it." His Indian series is directed "at a youthful appreciation of native people. I write to *sell,* not to relate personal experiences."

HOBBIES AND OTHER INTERESTS: Reading.

FOR MORE INFORMATION SEE: Canadian Children's Literature, number 26, 1982.

STRAUSS, Joyce 1936-

PERSONAL: Born August 12, 1936, in Los Angeles, Calif.; daughter of Benjamin and Pearl Strauss; children: Beverly, Karen, Dan. *Education:* International College, M.A., 1982. *Home:* 6050 Canterbury Dr., #E-119, Culver City, Calif. 90230.

CAREER: Works in public relations. *Awards, honors:* Christopher Award for *Imagine That!!! Exploring Make-Believe,* 1984.

WRITINGS: How Does It Feel . . .? (illustrated by Sumishta Brahm), Velvet Flute Books, 1979; *Imagine That!!! Exploring Make-Believe* (illustrated by Jennifer Barrett), Human Sciences Press, 1984.

SIDELIGHTS: "My intention is to aid people of all ages, in a most gentle way, to reach out and touch, examine, and play with feelings, and risk exposing themselves to themselves, to each other, and to their children.

JOYCE STRAUSS

"Feelings come in all sizes and shapes, as well as combinations of them mixed together. Good and bad feelings can be felt simultaneously and can be recalled in the same instance.

"Sharing goes on constantly, especially between peers, but adults sometimes fail to realize the importance of *sharing feelings* with children. Children can grow up barely realizing that adults have, and have had, some of those same feelings that the children are currently experiencing. Sharing instances is one thing. Adding the feelings surrounding those instances is another, each equally important. Sharing feelings also adds a special quality to the closeness that a child and an adult are attempting to reach, and that is what *How Does It Feel . . .?* is about. It is intended to increase greater awareness by stimulating more means of communication on levels that everyone can identify with.

Imagine That!!! Exploring Make Believe helps children to feel the 'oneness' that connects all that is, which, consequently, helps to develop the humility, appreciation, and understanding that is needed by each human being. Imagining stimulates children's minds so that limitations can be minimized, and expanded possibilities, maximized. *Imagine That!!!* allows the spirit its freedom."

STUBBS, Joanna 1940-

BRIEF ENTRY: Born April 20, 1940, in London, England. Artist, author and illustrator of books for young readers. Having spent her childhood in England, Trinidad, and Germany, Stubbs relied heavily on books to compensate for missed schooling. She eventually attended St. Martin's School of Art in London and Maidstone College of Art in Kent, where she specialized in technical aspects of book production. Since then Stubbs has written and illustrated several books for children, which reflect her own girlhood preoccupations as well as the perspectives of the five children she and husband, William Stobbs, have raised. Some of these titles include *The Forest and the Bulldozer, Shetland Peg, The Tree House, Hannah, Happy Bear's Day, Weather Witch,* and *With Cat's Eyes You'll Never Be Scared of the Dark. Junior Bookshelf* observed that in *Hannah* ". . . the illustrations alternate delightfully between close-ups and long shots, in delicate yet firm colours or interesting textures of grey and white." Over the last two decades, Stubbs has also illustrated over thirty children's books by various authors.

FOR MORE INFORMATION SEE: Illustrators of Children's Books: 1967-1976, Horn Book, 1978.

SWAYNE, Sam(uel F.) 1907-

PERSONAL: Born December 22, 1907, in Paulding County, Ohio; son of James Park (a teacher) and Marion (a homemaker; maiden name, Stoddart) Swayne; married Zoa Shaw (a teacher, author and artist), June 2, 1934; children: David, James, John, Mark. *Education:* Attended College of Idaho, 1926-27; University of Idaho, B.S., 1930, Juris Doctor, 1934. *Politics:* Democrat. *Religion:* Protestant. *Home:* Swayne Lane, Orofino, Idaho 83544. *Office:* Legacy House, Inc., P.O. Box 786, Orofino, Idaho 83544.

CAREER: Clearwater County, Idaho, prosecuting attorney, pro-tem judge, general, civil and criminal practice, 1934-85; Legacy House, Inc. (publishers), Orofino, Idaho, president, 1982—. President of J. Miles Realty Company, 1958-72, and Riverview Development Company, 1963—. President, Orofino Chamber of Commerce, 1938; State Committeeman, Clearwater County, 1963; trustee of land owned by local scout group, 1938—. *Member:* Idaho State Bar, Clearwater Bar Association, Clearwater Historical Society, Banner Grange.

WRITINGS: Great Grandfather in the Honey Tree (Junior Literary Guild selection; illustrated by wife, Zoa Swayne), Viking, 1949, reissued, Legacy House, 1982.

WORK IN PROGRESS: Editing *The Joy of Knowledge* by Lewis Kelly, a digest of the history of old cultures; *Freddie*, the adventures of a boy, for grade school level; *For Brides*, the essence of fifty years of divorce law practice; *Sewel Stories*, tales of the first homesteaders; *Lumberjacks*, stories of the Clearwater lumberjacks; *The Gone Forest*, early adventures in the National Forests; *Woodrat Fire*, story of a forest fire; *Swayne Tribunes*, a compilation of forty-odd years of letters.

SIDELIGHTS: "I well remember when my father moved his family by wagon to a homestead in Battle River Valley in Alberta, Canada in 1910. The wheel tracks in the deep prairie grass wound through low rolling hills dotted with clumps of aspen and willow in the low places, or skirted along side hills so steep I was in terror lest the wagon tip over. After leaving Lloyminister, the railhead town, I do not remember seeing a house or fence until we reached the place, later called Paradise Valley, which was to be our home for the next fifteen years.

"There were no improvements on the land except a board shack sixteen-feet square built in a burned spot about four acres in extent with a fireguard plowed around it. This was to protect the house from fires which frequently swept across the country.

SAM SWAYNE

"Buffalo trails criss-crossed our land in straight lines from water holes to wallows. Buffalo bone, some with parts of the hide still intact, lay scattered over the prairie. We children played with several skulls in our sand pile; and later, when the men insulated the house with a wall of sod around it, they put three, big, wide-horned skulls under the eaves at the right of the door.

"The country settled up rapidly. About half was fenced, and houses began to replace the sod or log homestead shacks. The government built telephone lines, but I was thirteen or fourteen when, on a trip to town with my father, I learned how to turn on electric lights. Our living was primitive but we were healthy and happy.

"In due course, I attended the one room school which served all nine grades but rarely had more than ten students. In summer we walked and in the winter we skied the two miles to school.

"After school chores were parcelled among the four children. At first it was getting in the wood, gathering the eggs and feeding chickens and pigs; but as we became older our duties included the whole spectrum of farm activities—milking, driving teams, and handling range stock.

"The severe winter chill kept parents alert to protect their offspring from freezing when going to or from school or going about necessary feeding and recreation. On occasions, it would get to sixty or sixty-five below zero at night and would not warm up to much above forty below zero in the day. These cold snaps would sometimes last for several weeks.

"At such times, the family stayed in bed to keep warm and passed the time by reading, singing or hollering through the partitions at one another. Frost balls, the size of hen's eggs, would collect on the heads of the nails in the ceiling. At noon everyone got up; the men went to feed and turn the stock out to water and get them back into shelter. At night the family stayed up until around midnight and stoked the fires so it could be done again next day. When the weather warmed to twenty below or warmer, normal life would resume. The farmers prepared for winter weather from October to April, but hoped that a month of cold would be cut off of one end or the other.

"The boys soon got big enough to ride all over the hills in the summer and go skiing or skating in the winter. We hunted the year round with twenty-two rifles. We hunted rabbits, gophers, coyotes, and ducks in the summer and rabbits and prairie chickens in the winter. For that matter, we hunted almost anything that moved.

"Through the mists of sixty-five to seventy years, several events of pioneer life shine out. When going for a load of wood with my father, I killed my first coyote with my single shot twenty-two rifle while I rode on the back axle of the running gears of a wagon. Another time a sudden blizzard whipped up the snow in thirty below weather, and the team I was driving would not willingly face it, so I had to stand up and drive instead of squatting in the shelter of the wagon box. I drove a mile out of the most direct route home to take some younger children to their lane, because I didn't think they could make it through the drifts. It was a close squeak; and that night I came down with double pneumonia. Then there was the night of the longest day when I drove a load of hogs to market, starting at midnight so they would stay cool. The pink glow of sunset was visible all night, until, the sun popped up in the morning. I remember roping the calves in the corral so the men could brand, dehorn and castrate them, and seeing men

She salted down the fish and preserved all the turkeys and wild geese, half cooked, in the bear grease.

(From *Great-Grandfather in the Honey Tree* by Sam and Zoa Swayne. Illustrated by the authors.)

gallop their horses from the fields to fight a prairie fire which threatened the community. I remember the feeling of apprehension and surge of patriotism as the young men went off to World War I; the sorrow caused by the numerous deaths from the 1918 flu epidemic; the hard time the men had digging graves in soil frozen six feet deep; the amazement at seeing geese flying north in flocks that stretched from the east horizon to the west, each flock following another before the forest was out of sight and continuing day and night for several days, are misty memories.

"World War I had a traumatic impact on the community. Many of the young men never returned. High prices, shortages of almost everything, a very severe winter with such shortage of cattle feed that Mounties came out and shot several starving herds, and the flu epidemic, and finally, low prices and collapse of farm markets, devastated the economy.

"In October, 1924, my father received a letter from his brother in Idaho, urging him to send me to the States so I could finish my high school education. The next day my father drove me to town, and with all my possessions (and some borrowed from my brother) in one small suitcase, started me on a new and different existence. Because I could not remember riding on a trail, Dad went with me as far as Edmonton, and put me on the train for Nampa, Idaho, where my uncle met me.

"The new surroundings were exciting. For the first time I associated with many students of my own age on a daily basis. Instead of working stock or pitching wheat bundles, the teen-agers pitched alfalfa hay and picked Idaho potatoes. I had expected to return to Alberta during the school summer vacation, but my uncle persuaded my father to sell out and move to the States. After I finished high school at Melba, I entered the College of Idaho, at Caldwell, Idaho.

"Other than making life-long friends, taking up wrestling to combat the damage done to my lungs in the Canadian blizzard was the most important event in my freshman year at the College of Idaho.

"The following year I transferred to the University of Idaho at Moscow and continued to turn out for wrestling and earned a letter in the sport in 1930. This effort gave me enough notice on campus to enable me to get some of the few available jobs and to graduate from the school of business administration. This was at the height of the Great Depression. In spite of the best efforts of my dean and the American Bankers scholarship, no job was available.

"With a friend also out of work, we hitchhiked to Seattle and tried to ship out on a freighter. Thousands of men lined up for each possible job. After a week or so we joined the gang in the 'hobo jungles' and hopped a freight back home. I hitchhiked to the Musselshell Ranger Station in Clearwater National Forest, where I had worked during previous summers. Because fire season was at its height, I got a job for the rest of the summer. When rain ended that job, I hitchhiked back to Moscow and entered law school. By working in the forest during the summer and at various other jobs, I managed to graduate, Juris Doctor, in 1934. I almost didn't make it though, because I had vexed the dean by skipping the last week of regular classes to appear at a Forest Service job in order to hold it for the summer. He relented finally, and I received the degree and was permitted to write the State Bar exam.

"On June 2, 1934 I wrote the final section of the Bar exam, borrowed ten dollars from my mother and hitchhiked with the preacher to Spokane, Washington where I was married, according to plan, to Zoa Shaw in the home of her second grade teacher. After the wedding we rode with the preacher back to Moscow. My father took us on to Pierce, Idaho with some other foresters and deposited us at a little cabin I had previously rented. Next morning I shouldered my packsack and headed for a Blister Rust Camp leaving my bride to spend her honeymoon alone in a strange logging town full of lumberjacks, Forest Service men and CCC boys. She reported good reception by the local women and no problems other than being a bit lonely.

"At the end of the summer we had saved most of the fabulous salary of $200 per month which I had earned as checking supervisor for nine Blister Rust camps. In October, 1934, we opened a law office in Orofino, Idaho.

"With heat and light furnished, the office rent was ten dollars per month. My desk was a homemade table and my library was a set of Codes borrowed from a legislator. My typewriter was a portable borrowed from my sister-in-law.

"My gross receipts were about twenty-five dollars a month, at first. My wife got a job in a doctor's office as receptionist for $35 per month, which kept us going until I had a trial defending a case. The prosecuting attorney, a fine old gentleman, dropped dead in the middle of the trial. I was appointed to fill his place.

"The prosecutor's salary was $1200 a year. With this financial boost we were able to buy a new Hudson for $900 and begin to raise a family. With the usual ups and downs we have managed to get along. In 1970 we completed our honeymoon with a sixty-day cruise to the Mediterranean.

"By 1984 I had completed fifty years in law practice and retired to operate Legacy House, Inc., our publishing corporation, and to oversee our 300-acre ranch. Legacy House was organized as a convenient vehicle to conduct the compilations of our manuscripts for printing and to isolate that enterprise from our other business affairs.

"My recreation has been hunting every fall for elk and deer; but the climax of all the hunts was the shooting of a big bull moose in 1984, a once-in-a-lifetime experience in Idaho."

The idea for *Great Grandfather in the Honey Tree* came out of Swayne's childhood. "At milking time my father used to tell his children 'great-grandfather stories.' He would milk a cup of milk into each child's cup; and as we sat around the cow, he would tell various episodes of a tale. When my boys wanted a story, I cemented the more exciting episodes together in narrative form with just enough embellishment to make them plausible. After many tellings the boys recited the stories to their classes in school. This response prompted me to dictate the story to my secretary. My wife illustrated it and sent it off to the Viking Press."

HOBBIES AND OTHER INTERESTS: Oil painting (mainly of old lumberjacks), grafting fruit and nut trees, hunting big game, camping, and prospecting for gold.

FOR MORE INFORMATION SEE: Oxen Tales to Jet Trails, Inter-Collegiate Press of Canada, 1981.

Collections: De Grummond Collection, University of Southern Mississippi.

SWAYNE, Zoa (Lourana) 1905-

PERSONAL: Born December 23, 1905, in Torrington, Wyo.; daughter of Raphael Leonard (a farmer) and Bertha May (a farmwife; maiden name, Toman) Shaw; married Samuel F. Swayne (an attorney), June 2, 1934; children: David, James, John, Mark. *Education:* Attended Albion State Normal, Idaho, 1923-24; University of Idaho, B.S., 1931. *Politics:* Republican. *Religion:* United Methodist. *Home and office:* P.O. Box 786, Orofino, Ida. 83544.

ZOA SWAYNE

CAREER: Chimney Creek School, Corral, Ida., teacher, 1924-26; Washington Avenue Summer School, Fairfield, Ida., teacher, 1928; teacher in Harrison, Ida., 1928-29, Hill City, Ida., 1931-33, and Fairfield, Ida., 1933-34, principal in Fairfield, 1933-34; artist and author, 1947—. State art chairman, Idaho Territorial Centennial Commission, 1959; chairman, Community Buildings sub-committee, Nez Perce Development Advisory Committee, 1962-64. *Member:* American Association of University Women (honorary life member), Clearwater Art Association, Clearwater Historical Society. *Awards, honors:* First and Best of Show, National Grange Art Contest, 1970, for oil painting ''Threshing Bee''; Governor's Award, White House Conference on Aging, 1971, for oil painting ''Gammy''; First and Best of Show, Valley Art Center, Clarkston, Wash., 1976, for oil painting ''Mother's Day.''

ILLUSTRATOR: Sam Swayne (husband), *Great-Grandfather in the Honey Tree* (Junior Literary Guild selection), Viking, 1949, reissued, Legacy House, 1982. Also illustrator of book jacket of *Idaho Reader* by Grace Jordan, Syms-York, 1963.

WORK IN PROGRESS: Do Them No Harm, a book about the Lewis and Clark Party and the Nez Perce Indians of Clearwater Valley in Idaho.

SIDELIGHTS: ''My first four years were spent on my parents' homestead, during the period when the open rangeland of that area was being put under irrigation. Memories of wolfhounds, windmills, cactus, horses, cattle and sand hills contrast sharply with memories of lady-slippers in the woods, fog horns on the Sound, and a Christmas with no snow on Whidby Island in Puget Sound, where we lived for the next three years.

''A move to Curlew in northeastern Washington necessitated my riding horseback to school through grade school years—3,240 miles in six years. We then made a five-hundred-mile

The terrified bear tore out of the tree trunk, dragging Great-grandfather with him. ■ (From *Great-Grandfather in the Honey Tree* by Sam and Zoa Swayne. Illustrated by the authors.)

trip by covered wagon to a wheat ranch in southern Idaho—possibly the last family to arrive on Camas Prairie in that fashion. How we worked to farm hundreds of acres of wheatland with horse-drawn equipment! My job one summer was to drive eight horses pulling a combine.

"I left for school that fall as strong as a boy. In 1923 I graduated from Gooding High School, and after a year at Albion State Normal I taught my first school. Study at the University of Idaho was interrupted by teaching, but finally I graduated in 1931 with a major in art.

"In 1934 Sam Swayne, a young attorney, and I were married, and eventually became the parents of four boys for whom and with whom I have drawn pictures, and from whom I have often sought escape through drawing pictures. When I draw I find myself calling upon my observations made from nature, memories of childhood experiences, of my father's response to beauty, and of my mother's ability to find fun in everyday events." [B. M. Miller and others, compilers, *Illustrators of Children's Books, 1946-1956*, Horn Book, 1958.]

"*Great-Grandfather in the Honey Tree* is a folk tale which was handed down in my husband's family. When our children were young, they demanded it every night for their bedtime story.

"We finally decided, 'If these boys enjoy it so much, let us write it as a book for other children to enjoy.' My husband dictated the story to his secretary in one half hour. It took me a year to do the illustrations."

Swayne commented on her work in progress. "I have been enchanted by the stories Nez Perce Indians have told about their ancestor's reaction to the coming of Lewis and Clark. For the past fifty years I have been gathering this information and am now in the process of putting everything together. *Do Them No Harm* is an interpretation of the relationship established between the Lewis and Clark Party and the Nez Perce Indians of the Clearwater Valley in Idaho. The narrative is based on the daily entries in the Lewis and Clark journals from September 20, 1805 to October 10, 1805 and from May 5, 1806 to July 4, 1806, and wherever appropriate, stories that have come down through oral histories of the Nez Perces have been interwoven.

"I have traveled over the Lolo Trail (the Lewis and Clark Trail over the Bitterroot Mountains) and visited their campsites. Many Nez Perces have shared their stories and lore. I have read books and articles pertaining to the subject as references. The identities of some Nez Perce of Lewis and Clark's time, which have puzzled historians, have been revealed.

"The reader will derive information, entertainment, a deeper appreciation for the Nez Perce people, and a higher regard for the quality of young men in the Lewis and Clark party. While the book has been written with the general reader in mind, serious historians will find new light on the identities of some Nez Perces mentioned in the journals, and young people, ages twelve and up, will find the book readable."

FOR MORE INFORMATION SEE: B. M. Miller and others, compilers, *Illustrators of Children's Books, 1946-1956*, Horn Book, 1958; Martha E. Ward and Dorothy A. Marquardt, *Illustrators of Books for Young People*, Scarecrow, 1975.

Come, my best friends, my books, and lead me on.
—Abraham Cowley

YOU-SHAN TANG

TANG, You-Shan 1946-

PERSONAL: Born January 10, 1946, in China; married Fang Chang (a fashion designer) December 3, 1981. *Education:* Peking University, B.A. 1970; Central Academy of Fine Arts, Beijing, China, M.A., 1980. *Home and office:* 734 Bush St., #43, San Francisco, Calif. 94108.

CAREER: Kweichow Cultural Center, Kweichow, China, art teacher, 1970-78; Peking Artists' Publishing House, Beijing, China, art director, 1978-80; free-lance graphic artist and illustrator, 1980—. *Exhibitions:* Art Museum of China, Beijing, 1979; Central Academy of Fine arts, Beijing, 1979; China Books Co., San Francisco, Calif., 1983; B. Dalton Book Co., San Francisco, 1983; Santa Cruz Book Co., Calif., 1983. *Awards, honors:* Central Academy of Fine Arts, Beijing, China, first prize for painting, 1979; American Book Award, 1984, for *Pie-Biter*.

ILLUSTRATOR: Ruthanne Lum McCunn, *Pie-Biter*, Design Enterprises, 1983.

SIDELIGHTS: "A firm believer that an alliance between Western and Chinese art will lead to new artistic dimensions, I blend Asian and Occidental techniques into a harmonious fusion. Though *Pie-Biter* is predominantly Western in tone, traditional Chinese techniques can be seen in the bold expressive strokes, fine line drawings and decorative motifs."

FOR MORE INFORMATION SEE: Chung PAO Monthly (China), February, 1983; "*Pie-Biter* Gives Readers a Chinese American Folk Hero," *East/West*, July 27, 1983; *World Journal*, July 28, 1983; "San Francisco County Fair Has Some Charms Uniquely Its Own," *San Francisco Examiner*, July

30, 1983; *Montana Standard* (Butte), July 31, 1983; *Centre Daily News* (San Francisco, Calif.), August 1, 1983, August 13, 1983; *San Francisco Journal,* August 14, 1983; *Publishers Weekly,* August 19, 1983; *San Francisco Chronicle,* September 21, 1983, December 11, 1983; "*Pie-Biter* Gives Kids History, Entertainment," *Asian Week,* October 14, 1983.

THOMPSON, Harlan (Howard)   1894-1987 (Stephen Holt)

OBITUARY NOTICE—See sketch in *SATA* Volume 10: Born December 25, 1894, in Brewster, Kan.; died October 9, 1987, in Pasadena, Calif. Rancher and author. Thompson, who was raised on a ranch in Canada, turned to writing after an injury forced him to abandon his strenuous life-style. He wrote a number of books for children based on his experiences as a rancher, many of which were published under the pseudonym Stephen Holt. His works include *Wild Palimino, Phantom Roan, Stormy, Prairie Colt,* which was awarded a Boys' Club of America gold medal in 1948, and *Spook, the Mustang,* which received a Commonwealth Club juvenile silver medal in 1957. Thompson's novel *Silent Running* was adapted for film in 1972.

FOR MORE INFORMATION SEE: Contemporary Authors, Permanent Series, Volume 1, Gale, 1978; *Who's Who in the West,* 18th edition, Marquis, 1982. Obituaries: *Los Angeles Times,* October 14, 1987.

UCHIDA, Yoshiko   1921-

PERSONAL: Surname is pronounced "Oo-*chee*-dah"; born November 24, 1921, in Alameda, Calif.; daughter of Dwight Takashi (a businessman) and Iku (a poet; maiden name, Umegaki) Uchida. *Education:* University of California, Berkeley, A.B. (cum laude), 1942; Smith College, M.Ed., 1944. *Politics:* Democrat. *Religion:* Protestant. *Residence:* Berkeley, Calif.

YOSHIKO UCHIDA

CAREER: Elementary school teacher in Japanese relocation center in Utah, 1942-43; Frankford Friends' School, Philadelphia, Pa., teacher, 1944-45; Institute of Pacific Relations, New York City, membership secretary, 1946-47; United Student Christian Council, New York City, secretary, 1947-52; full-time writer, 1952-57, 1962—; University of California, Berkeley, secretary, 1957-62. *Exhibitions:* Oakland Museum, 1972.

AWARDS, HONORS: Ford Foundation Foreign Study and Research Fellowship to Japan, 1952; *New York Herald Tribune*'s Children's Spring Book Festival Honor Book, 1955, for *The Magic Listening Cap;* Silver Medal for Best Juvenile Book by a California Author from the Commonwealth Club of California, 1972, for *Samurai of Gold Hill* and 1982, for *A Jar of Dreams;* Award of Merit from the California Association of Teachers of English, 1973, for her body of work; citation from the Contra Costa Chapter of Japanese American Citizens League, 1976, for outstanding contribution to the cultural development of society; *Journey Home* was selected one of International Reading Association's Children's Choices, 1979, and *The Happiest Ending,* 1985; *Journey Home* was selected as a Notable Children's Trade Book in the Field of Social Studies by the National Council for Social Studies and the Children's Book Council, 1979, *A Jar of Dreams,* 1982, and *The Happiest Ending,* 1985.

Morris S. Rosenblatt Award from the Utah State Historical Society, 1981, for article, "Topaz, City of Dust"; University of Oregon's Distinguished Service Award, 1981, for "a significant contribution to the cultural development of society"; *The Best Bad Thing* was selected as one of *School Library Journal*'s Best Books of the Year, and one of New York Public Library's Children's Books, both 1983; Award from the Berkeley Chapter of the Japanese American Citizens League, 1983, for "her many books which have done so much to better the understanding of Japanese culture and Japanese American experiences in America"; *The Happiest Ending* was chosen one of Child Study Association of America's Children's Books of the Year, 1985; Young Authors' Hall of Fame Award from the San Mateo and San Francisco Reading Associations, 1985; Bay Area Book Reviewers Association Book Award for Children's Literature, 1986, for *The Happiest Ending;* Friends of Children and Literature Award, 1987, for *A Jar of Dreams.*

WRITINGS—For young people, except as noted: *The Dancing Kettle and Other Japanese Folk Tales* (illustrated by Richard C. Jones), Harcourt, 1949, new edition, Creative Arts, 1986; *New Friends for Susan* (illustrated by Henry Sugimoto), Scribner, 1951; *We Do Not Work Alone: The Thoughts of Kanjiro Kawai* (adult nonfiction), Folk Art Society (Japan), 1953; *The Magic Listening Cap: More Folk Tales from Japan* (self-illustrated), Harcourt, 1955, new edition, Creative Arts, 1987; *The Full Circle* (self-illustrated; junior high school study book), Friendship Press, 1957; *Takao and Grandfather's Sword* (illustrated by William M. Hutchinson), Harcourt, 1958; *The Promised Year* (illustrated by W. M. Hutchinson), Harcourt, 1959.

Milk and the Prowler (illustrated by W. M. Hutchinson), Harcourt, 1960; (translator of English portions) Soetsu Yanagi, editor, *Shoji Hamada* (adult), Asahi Shimbun, 1961; *Rokubei and the Thousand Rice Bowls* (illustrated by Kazue Mizumura), Scribner, 1962; *The Forever Christmas Tree* (illustrated by K. Mizumura), Scribner, 1963; *Sumi's Prize* (illustrated by K. Mizumura), Scribner, 1964; *The Sea of Gold and Other Tales from Japan* (illustrated by Marianne Yamaguchi), Scribner, 1965, new edition, Creative Arts, 1988; *Sumi's Special Happening* (illustrated by K. Mizumura), Scribner, 1966;

In-Between Miya (illustrated by Susan Bennett), Scribner, 1967; *Hisako's Mysteries* (illustrated by S. Bennett), Scribner, 1969; *Sumi and the Goat and the Tokyo Express* (illustrated by K. Mizumura), Scribner, 1969.

Makoto, the Smallest Boy: A Story of Japan (illustrated by Akihito Shirakawa), Crowell, 1970; *Journey to Topaz: A Story of the Japanese-American Evacuation* (ALA Notable Book; illustrated by Donald Carrick), Scribner, 1971, revised edition, Creative Arts, 1985; *Samurai of Gold Hill* (illustrated by Ati Forberg), Scribner, 1972, new edition, Creative Arts, 1985; *The History of Sycamore Church* (adult nonfiction), privately printed, 1974; *The Birthday Visitor* (illustrated by Charles Robinson), Scribner, 1975; *The Rooster Who Understood Japanese* (illustrated by C. Robinson), Scribner, 1976; *Journey Home* (sequel to *Journey to Topaz*; Junior Literary Guild selection; illustrated by C. Robinson), McElderry Books, 1978.

A Jar of Dreams (Junior Literary Guild selection), McElderry Books, 1981; *Desert Exile: The Uprooting of a Japanese American Family* (adult nonfiction), University of Washington Press, 1982; *The Best Bad Thing* (sequel to *A Jar of Dreams*; ALA Notable Book; Junior Literary Guild selection), McElderry Books, 1983; *Tabi: Journey through Time, Stories of the Japanese in America*, United Methodist Publishing House, 1984; *The Happiest Ending* (sequel to *The Best Bad Thing*; ALA Notable Book; Junior Literary Guild selection), McElderry Books, 1985; (reteller) *The Two Foolish Cats* (Junior

How did I ever let Mama talk me into this. . . . ■
(Jacket illustration by Kinuko Craft from *The Happiest Ending* by Yoshiko Uchida.)

Literary Guild selection; illustrated by Margot Zemach), McElderry Books, 1987; *Picture Bride* (adult novel), Northland, 1987.

Contributor of juvenile short stories: *Flight Near and Far*, Holt, 1970; *Scribner Anthology for Young People*, Scribner, 1976; *Arbuthnot Anthology of Children's Literature*, 4th edition, Scott, Foresman, 1976; *Courage to Adventure*, Crowell, 1976; *Sense*, Scott, Foresman, 1977; *Sharing Literature with Children*, D. McKay, 1977; *Image*, Scott, Foresman, 1977; *Clues and Clocks*, Harper, 1977; *Echoes of Time: A World History*, McGraw, 1977; *The Secret Life of Mr. Mugs*, Ginn, 1978; *With the Works*, Scott, Foresman, 1978; *Riding Rainbows*, Allyn & Bacon, 1978; *Handstands*, Allyn & Bacon, 1978; *The Big Ones 2*, Allyn & Bacon, 1978; *Standing Strong*, Allyn & Bacon, 1978; *Literature and Life*, Scott, Foresman, 1979; *Changing Scenes*, Harcourt, 1979; *And Everywhere Children*, Greenwillow, 1979; *Many Voices*, Harcourt, 1979; *Tell Me How the Sun Rose*, Ginn, 1979; *Question and Form in Literature*, Scott, Foresman, 1979; *Japan: Change and Continuity*, Rigby, 1980; *Full Circle*, Macmillan, 1980; *Fairy Tales of the Sea*, Harper, 1981; *Here and There*, Holt, 1981; *Spinners*, Houghton, 1981; *Banners*, Houghton, 1981; *The Abracadabras*, Addison-Wesley, 1981; *Wingspan*, Allyn & Bacon, 1981; *Another Earth, Another Sky*, Harcourt, 1982; *Understanding Literature*, Macmillan, 1983; *Anthology of Children's Literature*, Scott, Foresman, 1984; *Strategies for Reading*, Harcourt, 1984; *Exploration*, Houghton, 1986.

I never thought one small lady from Japan could make such a big difference in my life, but she did. ■
(Jacket illustration by Kinuko Craft from *A Jar of Dreams* by Yoshiko Uchida.)

Contributor to exhibit catalogue, *Margaret da Patta*, of Oakland Museum, 1976. Contributor of adult stories and articles to newspapers and periodicals, including *Woman's Day, Gourmet, Utah Historical Quarterly, Far East, Craft Horizons, Nippon Times* (Tokyo), *Motive,* and *California Monthly.*

ADAPTATIONS: "The Old Man with the Bump" (cassette; based on a story from *The Dancing Kettle*), Houghton, 1973; "The Two Foolish Cats" (filmstrip with cassette; based on a story from *The Sea of Gold*), Encyclopedia Britannica Educational, 1977; "The Fox and the Bear" (cassette; based on a story from *The Magic Listening Cap*), Science Research Associates, 1979.

WORK IN PROGRESS: A poetry collection; a picture book interpretation of a Japanese folk tale.

SIDELIGHTS: **November 24, 1921.** Born in Alameda, California. "Whenever I am in the neighborhood, I find myself drawn back to Stuart Street [Berkeley], to drive once more past the stucco bungalow just above Grove, where my older sister Keiko, and I grew up.

"I remember the sunny yard in back with the peach and apricot and fig trees. I remember the sweetpeas that grew higher than my head, and the enormous chrysanthemums that measured seventeen inches around. . . . I remember my father in his gardening clothes, raking the yard and filling the dusky evening air with the wonderful smell of burning leaves, and my mother standing at the back porch, wearing her big apron, ringing a small black bell because she didn't like calling out to bring us in for supper.

"It was a sunny, pleasant three-bedroom house we rented, and there was nothing particularly unusual about our living there except that we were Japanese Americans. And in those days before the Second World War, few Japanese families in Berkeley, California, lived above Grove Street with the exception of some early settlers. . . .

"Because my father was a salaried man at Mitsui, our lives were more secure and somewhat different from many of our Japanese friends, especially those whom we knew at the small Japanese church we attended. For them life in the 1930s was a dark desperate struggle for survival in a country where they could neither become citizens nor own land. Many spoke little English. Some of the mothers took in sewing or did work in white homes. . . . Most of the fathers struggled to keep open such small businesses as dry cleaners, laundries, groceries, or shoe repair shops, and they sometimes came to ask my father for advice and help.

"My father understood their struggles well, for he too had grown up in poverty in Japan. His father, a former samurai turned teacher, had died when he was ten. His mother, married at sixteen and widowed at thirty, sent her five children to live with various relatives, and my father never forgot the sadness of those long snow-covered roads he walked to reach the home of the uncle who took him in.

"My father worked his way through Doshisha University by delivering milk in the mornings, working as a telephone operator at night, and later serving as a clerk in a bank.

"Because both my parents had learned to be frugal in their youth and had worked hard for a living, they were never wasteful or self-indulgent even when they had the means. They also felt much compassion for anyone in need. When one of our neighbors on Stuart Street lost his job during the Depression,

and his wife sold homemade bread, my mother not only bought her bread, but arranged to learn French from her as well, to give her the additional income. . . .

"My parents also provided solace and frequent meals to lonely homesick students from Japan who were studying at the University of California or the Pacific School of Religion. These students seemed to come to our home in an unending procession, much to the dismay of my sister and I who found them inordinately dull. . . . They crowded around our table on most holidays, on frequent Sundays, and they often dropped in uninvited for a cup of tea." [Yoshiko Uchida, *Desert Exile: The Uprooting of Japanese American Family*, University of Washington Press, 1982.¹]

"But now these people who were so dull and annoying to me as a child, provide wonderful material for my writing, and I remember them not only with fascination, but with some guilt for the shabby way I treated them. I also remember the laughter, the wonderful smell of *sukiyaki* cooking at the table, and the after-dinner singing around our piano, and realize that in spite of ourselves, Keiko and I often had good times at these gatherings."

"These students were only part of the deluge from Japan. There were also visiting ministers, countless alumni from Doshisha University, and sometimes the president of the university himself. I felt as though our house was the unofficial

The barn was filled with huge, bright-colored kites. ■
(Jacket illustration by Kinuko Craft from *The Best Bad Thing* by Yoshiko Uchida.)

alumni headquarters for Doshisha and I one of its most reluctant members.

"My mother was a giving and deeply caring person. 'Don't ever be indifferent,' she used to say to us. 'Indifference is the worst fault of all.' And she herself was never indifferent. She cared and felt deeply about everything around her. She could find joy in a drive to the park, a rainbow in the sky, a slim new moon, or an interesting weed appearing among the irises. . . .''[1]

"The written word was always important in our family, and my mother often wrote poetry—the thirty-one-syllable Japanese *tanka*. Like most women of her day, however, she focused her attention on her family, and her creativity existed on the fringes of her life. She wrote her poems on scraps of paper and the backs of envelopes, and they were published by a friend in a small Japanese newsletter.

"My mother also loved books, and our house was filled with them. Although she didn't find time to read much for herself, she often read Japanese stories to Keiko and me. Many of these were the Japanese folktales which I later included in my first published book, *The Dancing Kettle*.

"It seems to me I've been interested in books and writing for as long as I can remember. I was writing stories when I was ten, and being the child of frugal immigrant parents, I wrote them on brown wrapping paper which I cut up and bound into booklets, and because I am such a saver, I still have them. The first is titled, 'Jimmy Chipmonk and His Friends: A Short Story for Small Children.'

"I not only wrote stories, I also kept a journal of important events which I began the day I graduated from elementary school. Of course my saver self kept that journal as well, and even today I can read of the special events of my young life, such as the times my parents took us to an opera or concert in San Francisco, or the day I got my first dog, or the sad day it died, when I drew a tombstone for him in my journal and decorated it with floral wreaths.

"By putting these special happenings into words and writing them down, I was trying to hold on to and somehow preserve the magic as well as the joy and sadness of certain moments in my life, and I guess that's really what books and writing are all about."

1931. Throughout her childhood, Uchida longed to be accepted as an American. Although her family gave her much love and security, she felt intimidated by the outside community. "Our lives—my sister's and mine—were quite thoroughly infused with the customs, traditions, and values of our Japanese parents, whose own lives had been structured by the samurai code of loyalty, honor, self-discipline, and filial piety. Their lives also reflected a blend of Buddhist philosophy dominated by Christian faith. So it was that we grew up with a strong dose of the Protestant ethic coupled with a feeling of respect for

Uchida (left) about three years old with sister.

He just went right on, weighing and munching, weighing and munching, until at last he had eaten up both rice cakes. ■ (From *The Two Foolish Cats* by Yoshiko Uchida. Illustrated by Margot Zemach.)

our teachers and superiors; a high regard for such qualities as frugality, hard work, patience, diligence, courtesy, and loyalty; and a sense of responsibility and love, not only for our parents and family, but for our fellow man.

"My parents' Japaneseness was never nationalistic in nature. They held the Imperial family in affectionate and respectful regard, as did all Japanese of their generation. But their first loyalty was always to their Christian God, not the Emperor of Japan. And their loyalty and devotion to their adopted country was vigorous and strong. My father cherished copies of the Declaration of Independence, the Bill of Rights, and the Constitution of the United States, and on national holidays he hung, with great pride, an enormous American flag on our front porch, even though at the time, this country declared the first generation Japanese immigrants to be 'aliens ineligible for citizenship.'"[1]

When she was ten, Uchida's family took a trip to Connecticut, and the impression of being perceived as a foreigner remained with her throughout her lifetime. "We visited several eastern cities, but most important to my mother was a special trip we made to the small village of Cornwall, Connecticut, to visit one of her former Doshisha instructors . . . and to meet for the first time two white women pen pals with whom she had corresponded since college. Both my mother and father were great letter writers and kept up a voluminous correspondence. They cherished their many friends and I don't believe either of them ever lost one for neglect on their part.

"We were probably the first Asians ever to visit Cornwall and one of its residents, an elderly white woman, patted me on the head and said, 'My, but you speak English so beautifully.' She had looked at my Japanese face and addressed only my outer person, and although she had meant to compliment me, I was thoroughly abashed to be perceived as a foreigner. . . ."[1]

Family portrait, with Yoshiko Uchida second from left.

1934. "As I approached adolescence, I wanted more than anything to be accepted as any other white American. Imbued with the melting pot mentality, I saw integration into white American society as the only way to overcome the sense of rejection I had experienced in so many areas of my life. The insolence of a clerk or a waiter, the petty arrogance of a bureaucrat, discrimination and denial at many establishments, exclusion from the social activities of my white classmates— all of these affected my sense of personal worth. They reinforced my feelings of inferiority and the self-effacement I had absorbed from the Japanese ways of my parents and made me reticent and cautious.

"When I was in junior high school, I was the only Japanese American to join the Girl Reserve unit at our school and was accepted within the group as an equal. On one occasion, however, we were to be photographed by the local newspaper, and I was among the girls to be included. The photographer casually tried to ease me out of the picture, but one of my white friends just as stubbornly insisted on keeping me in. I think I was finally included, but the realization of what the photographer was trying to do hurt me more than I ever admitted to anyone.

"In high school, being different was an even greater hardship than in my younger years. In elementary school one of my teachers had singled out the Japanese American children in class to point to our uniformly high scholastic achievement. (I always worked hard to get A's.) But in high school, we were singled out by our white peers, not for praise, but for total exclusion from their social functions. . . .

"Unhappy in high school, I couldn't wait to get out. I increased my class load, graduated in two and a half years, and entered the University of California in Berkeley when I was sixteen, immature and naive. There I found the alienation of the Nisei [second generation Japanese] from the world of the white students even greater than in high school. Asians were not invited to join the sororities or fraternities, which at the time were a vital part of the campus structure. Most of the Nisei avoided general campus social events and joined instead the two Japanese American social clubs—the Japanese Women's Student Club and the Japanese Men's Student Club. We had our own dances, picnics, open houses, and special events in great abundance. These activities comprised my only social outlet and I had a wonderful time at them.

"For many years I never spoke to a white person unless he or she spoke to me first. At one of my freshman classes at the university, I found myself sitting next to a white student I had known slightly at high school. I sat silent and tense, not even turning to look at her because I didn't want to speak first and be rebuffed. Finally, she turned to me and said, 'Yoshi, aren't you going to speak to me?'

"Only then did I dare smile, acknowledge her presence, and become the friendly self I wanted to be. Now, my closest friend for the past twenty years has been a white person, but if I had met him in college, I might never have spoken to him, and I probably would not have gone out with him.''[1]

December 7, 1941. Uchida was busy studying for her final exams at the University of California when war between Japan and the United States was declared. When she returned home from the library, her father had been seized by the FBI and taken to the San Francisco Immigration Headquarters. "Executives of Japanese business firms, shipping lines, and banks, men active in local Japanese associations, teachers of Japanese language schools, virtually every leader of the Japanese Amer-

ican community along the West Coast had been seized almost immediately.

"Actually the FBI had come to our house twice, once in the absence of my parents and sister who, still not realizing the serious nature of the attack, had gone out to visit friends. Their absence, I suppose, had been cause for suspicion and the FBI or police had broken in to search our house without a warrant. On returning, my father, believing that we had been burglarized, immediately called the police. Two policemen appeared promptly with three FBI men and suggested that my father check to see if his valuables were missing. They were, of course, undisturbed, but their location was thereby revealed. Two of the FBI men requested that my father accompany them 'for a short while' to be questioned, and my father went willingly. The other FBI man remained with my mother and sister to intercept all phone calls and to inform anyone who called that they were indisposed.

"One policeman stationed himself at the front door and the other at the rear. When two of our white friends came to see how we were, they were not permitted to enter or speak to my mother and sister, who, for all practical purposes, were prisoners in our home.

"By the time I came home, only one FBI man remained but I was alarmed at the startling turn of events during my absence. In spite of her own anxiety, Mama in her usual thoughtful way was serving tea to the FBI agent. He tried to be friendly and courteous, reassuring me that my father would return safely in due time. But I couldn't share my mother's gracious attitude toward him. Papa was gone, and his abrupt custody into the hands of the FBI seemed an ominous portent of worse things to come. I had no inclination to have tea with one of its agents, and went abruptly to my room, slamming the door shut.''[1]

February 19, 1942. President Franklin D. Roosevelt issued an Executive Order imprisoning Japanese Americans in "relocation camps." Uchida's father was sent to a prisoner-of-war camp in Missoula, Montana. "Upon reaching Montana, my father wrote immediately, his major concern being whether we would have enough money for our daily needs. He and my mother were now classified as 'enemy aliens' and his bank account had been blocked immediately. For weeks there was total confusion regarding the amount that could be withdrawn from such blocked accounts for living expenses, and early reports indicated it would be only $100 a month.

"Both the Fifth and Fourteenth Amendments to the Constitution providing for 'due process of law' and 'equal protection under the law for all citizens,' were flagrantly ignored in the name of military expediency, and the forced eviction was carried out purely on the basis of race.

"Stunned by this unprecedented act of our government, we Nisei were faced with the anguishing dilemma of contesting our government's orders and risking imprisonment (as a few courageous Nisei did) or of complying with the government edict.

"Because the FBI had interned most of the Issei [first generation Japanese] leaders of the community, effectively decimating Issei organizations, the vacuum in leadership was filled by the Japanese American Citizens League, then led by a group of relatively young Nisei. The JACL met in emergency session attempting to arrive at the best possible solution to an intolerable situation. Perceiving that a compromise with the government was impossible, and rejecting a strategy of total opposition, because it might lead to violence and bloodshed, the

JACL leaders decided the only choice was to cooperate 'under protest' with the government.

"My sister and I were angry that our country could deprive us of our civil rights in so cavalier a manner, but we had been raised to respect and to trust those in authority. To us resistance or confrontation, such as we know them today was unthinkable and of course would have had no support from the American public. We naively believed at the time that cooperating with the government edict was the best way to help our country."[1]

"The world then was, of course, totally different from the one we know today. In 1942 the voice of Martin Luther King had not yet been heard and ethnic pride was yet unborn. There was no awareness in the land of civil rights, and there had yet been no freedom marches or demonstrations of protest. Most Americans, supporting their country in a war they considered just, did nothing to protest our forced removal, and might well have considered it treasonous had we tried to resist or protest.

"Told to demonstrate our loyalty by doing as our country asked, we had no choice but to trust our government leaders. We did not know then, as we do now, that they had acceded to political and economic pressure groups and imprisoned us with full knowledge that their action was not only unconstitutional, but totally unnecessary." [Yoshiko Uchida, *Journey to Topaz: A Story of the Japanese-American Evacuation,* revised edition, Creative Arts, 1985. Amended by the author.[2]]

April 21, 1942. Removal orders were issued for Uchida's family, as well as the other Japanese American families living in the area. . . . These families had ten days to dispose of their homes and personal possessions. "During the last few weeks on campus, my friends and I became sentimental and took pictures of each other at favorite campus sites. The war had jolted us into a crisis whose impact was too enormous for us to fully comprehend, and we needed these small remembrances of happier times to take with us as we went our separate ways to various government camps throughout California."[1]

May 1, 1942. Incarcerated in the Tanforan Race Track, which housed eight thousand uprooted Japanese Americans in its stables and barracks. The family lived for the next five months in a horse stall and the entire camp was surrounded by barbed wire. "When we reached stall number 40, we pushed open the narrow door and looked uneasily into the vacant darkness. The stall was about ten by twenty feet and empty except for three folded Army cots lying on the floor. Dust, dirt, and wood shavings covered the linoleum that had been laid over manure-covered boards, the smell of horses hung in the air, and the whitened corpses of many insects still clung to the hastily white-washed walls.

"High on either side of the entrance were two small windows which were our only source of daylight. The stall was divided into two sections by Dutch doors worn down by teeth marks, and each stall in the stable was separated from the adjoining one only by rough partitions that stopped a foot short of the sloping roof. That space, while perhaps a good source of ventilation for the horses, deprived us of all but visual privacy, and we couldn't even be sure of that because of the crevices and knotholes in the dividing walls.

"Our stable consisted of twenty-five stalls facing north which were back to back with an equal number facing south, so we were surrounded on three sides. Living in our stable were an assortment of people—mostly small family units—that in-cluded an artist, my father's barber and his wife, a dentist and his wife, an elderly retired couple, a group of Kibei bachelors (Japanese born in the United States but educated in Japan), an insurance salesman and his wife, and a widow with two daughters. . . ."[1]

The "prisoners" quickly organized schools, churches, and recreation centers. Uchida taught second grade. "I loved teaching and decided I would like to work for a teaching credential, for I now had received my degree from the university. My classmates and I had missed commencement by two weeks and my diploma, rolled in a cardboard container, had been handed to me in my horse stall by the Tanforan mailman.

"After three months of communal living, the lack of privacy began to grate on my nerves. There was no place I could go to be completely alone—not in the washroom, the latrine, the shower, or my stall. I couldn't walk down the track without seeing someone I knew. I couldn't avoid the people I didn't like or choose those I wished to be near. There was no place to cry and no place to hide. It was impossible to escape from the constant noise and human presence. I felt stifled and suffocated and sometimes wanted to scream. But in my family we didn't scream or cry or fight or even have a major argument, because we knew the neighbors were always only inches away. . . ."[1]

September, 1942. Sent to Topaz, a concentration camp located in the Utah desert. "In its frantic haste to construct this barrack city, the Army had removed every growing thing, and what had once been a peaceful lake bed was now churned up into one great mass of loose flour-like sand. With each step we sank two to three inches deep, sending up swirls of dust that crept into our eyes and mouths, noses and lungs. After two long sleepless nights on the train, this sudden encounter with the sun, the glaring white sand, and the altitude made me feel weak and light-headed. We were all worried about my mother, and I thought I might collapse myself, when we finally reached Block 7.

"Each barrack was one hundred feet in length, and divided into six rooms for families of varying sizes. We were assigned to a room in the center, about twenty by eighteen feet, designed for occupancy by four people. When we stepped into our room it contained nothing but four army cots without mattresses. No inner sheetrock walls or ceilings had yet been installed, nor had the black pot-bellied stove that stood outside our door. Cracks were visible everywhere in the siding and around the windows, and although our friends had swept out our room before we arrived, the dust was already seeping into it again from all sides."[1]

Dust continued to be a constant problem and the severe dust storms were particularly terrifying. "One day about noon, I saw gray-brown clouds massing in the sky, and a hot sultry wind seemed to signal the coming of another storm. I waited for word that schools would be closed for the afternoon, but none was forthcoming.

"I dreaded the long seven-block walk to school, but shortly after lunch, I set out with a scarf wrapped around my head so it covered my nose and mouth as well. By the time I was half way to Block 41, the wind grew so intense, I felt as though I were caught in the eye of a dust hurricane. Feeling panicky, I thought of running home, but realized I was as far from my own barrack now as I was from school, and it was possible some children might be at the school.

"Soon barracks only a few feet away were completely obscured by walls of dust and I was terrified the wind would knock me off my feet. Every few yards, I stopped to lean against a barrack to catch my breath, then lowering my head against the wind, I plodded on. When I got to school, I discovered many children had braved the storm as well and were waiting for me in the dust-filled classroom.

"I was touched, as always, to see their eagerness to learn despite the desolation of their surroundings, the meager tools for learning, and, in this case, the physical dangers they encountered just to reach school. At the time their cheerful resiliency encouraged me, but I've wondered since if the bewildering trauma of the forced removal from their homes inflicted permanent damage to their young psyches.

"Although I made an attempt to teach, so much dust was pouring into the room from all sides as well as the hole in the roof that it soon became impossible, and I decided to send the children home before the storm grew worse. 'Be very careful and run home as fast as you can,' I cautioned, and the other teachers of Block 41 dismissed their classes as well.

"That night the wind still hadn't subsided, but my father went out to a meeting he felt he shouldn't miss. As my mother, sister, and I waited out the storm in our room, the wind reached such force we thought our barrack would be torn from its feeble foundations. Pebbles and rocks rained against the walls, and the newspapers we stuffed into the cracks in the siding came flying back into the room. The air was so thick with the smoke-like dust, my mouth was gritty with it and my lungs seemed penetrated by it. For hours the wind shrieked around our shuddering barrack, and I realized how frightened my mother was when I saw her get down on her knees to pray at her cot. I had never seen her do that before."[1] But the barrack held.

"None of us felt well during our incarceration in Topaz. We all caught frequent colds during the harsh winter months and had frequent stomach upsets. Illness was a nuisance, especially after we began to work, for memos from a doctor were required to obtain sick leave. Much of our energy simply went into keeping our room dusted, swept, and mopped to be rid of the constant accumulation of dust, and in trying to do a laundry when the water was running."[1]

May, 1943. With the help of the Student Relocation Committee (administered by the American Friends Service Committee), Uchida was able to leave Topaz by obtaining a fellowship to do graduate work at Smith College, Northampton, Massachusetts. ". . . I had passed up an earlier opportunity to go to Smith College from Tanforan because I felt I should stay with my fellow internees and make some positive contribution to our situation. Now, however, I longed to get out of this dreary camp, return to civilization, and continue my education. I applied for enrollment in the Education Department at Smith College in Northampton, Massachusetts, but discovered the earlier opening there was no longer available. I also discovered that the process for obtaining a leave clearance was long and tedious. One did not decide to leave and simply walk out the gates. I waited impatiently and with increasing frustration as the weeks passed.

"Students were among the first internees to leave the camps, and others followed to midwestern and eastern cities where previously few Japanese Americans had lived. . . . The National Japanese American Student Relocation Council eventually assisted some three thousand students to leave the camps and enter over five hundred institutions of higher learning throughout the country.

"I left Topaz determined to work hard and prove I was as loyal as any other American. I felt a tremendous sense of

responsibility to make good, not just for myself, but for all Japanese Americans. I felt I was representing all the Nisei, and it was sometimes an awesome burden to bear.

"When the war was over, the brilliant record of the highly decorated Nisei combat teams, and favorable comments of the GIs returning from Japan, helped alleviate to some degree the hatred directed against the Japanese Americans during the war. Although racism had by no means been eliminated, new fields of employment, previously closed, gradually opened up for many Nisei. In time they were also able to purchase and rent homes without being restricted to ghetto areas as the Issei had been."[1]

"Today we know, in spite of the government claim at the time, that there was no military necessity for our imprisonment. Today we know this gross violation of our Constitution caused one of the most shameful episodes in our country's history. Our leaders betrayed not only the Japanese Americans, but *all* Americans, for by denying the Constitution, they damaged the very essence of our democratic beliefs.

"In 1976 President Gerald R. Ford stated, 'Not only was that evacuation wrong, but Japanese Americans were and are loyal Americans'. . . . In 1983 a Commission of Wartime Relocation and Internment of Civilians established by the United States Congress concluded that a grave injustice was done to Japanese Americans and that the causes of the uprooting were race prejudice, war hysteria and a failure of leadership."[2]

Uchida taught school in Philadelphia, Pennsylvania for a year and worked as a secretary in New York City for six years. In 1952 she was awarded a fellowship to study in Japan. "I spent two years in Japan as a Ford Foundation Foreign Area Fellow and became acquainted with the relatives and friends who until then had been only strangers to me. . . . I climbed to remote wooded temple cemeteries to pour water on the tombstones of my grandfathers and maternal grandmother 'to refresh their spirits,' and I traveled the countryside, finding it incredibly beautiful.

"Although I went primarily as a writer to collect more folktales, I became equally immersed in the magnificent arts and crafts of Japan. The strength and honesty of its folk art especially appealed to me, and I felt an immediate kinship with the Japanese craftsmen I met. I was privileged to become acquainted with the three founders of the Mingei (folk art) movement in Japan—the philosopher-writer Soetsu Yanagi, and the noted potters Shoji Hamada and Kanjiro Kawai. Their Zen-oriented philosophy, their wholeness of spirit, and their totality as human beings enriched me immeasurably and made a lasting impact on my thought and writing.

"My experience in Japan was as positive and restorative as the uprooting and imprisonment had been negative and depleting. I came home aware of a new dimension to myself as a Japanese American and with new respect and admiration for the culture that had made my parents what they were. The circle was complete. I feel grateful today for the Japanese values and traditions they instilled in me and kept alive in our home, and unlike the days of my youth, I am proud to be a Japanese American and am secure in that knowledge of myself."[1]

While in Japan, Uchida wrote articles on handcrafts and folk artists for the *Nippon Times*. Upon her return to the United States, she continued to write articles for *Craft Horizons* magazine, and studied weaving, pottery, and jewelry-making herself.

A man was shouting in angry and agitated tones. ■
(From *Journey to Topaz* by Yoshiko Uchida. Illustrated by Donald Carrick.)

1972. Awarded a silver medal for best juvenile book from the Commonwealth Club of California for *Samurai of Gold Hill*. Although Uchida's early books dealt with the children of Japan, she turned to writing about the Japanese American experience in the late 1960s. "I saw the need to reinforce the self-knowledge and pride of young Japanese Americans, to give them a remembrance of their culture and their own particular history."

"I feel that children need the sense of continuity that comes through knowing about the past. All of us must understand our own past in order to move ahead into the future. I feel it's so important for Japanese American—and all Asian American—children to be aware of their history and culture, and to understand some of the traditions, hopes, and values of the early immigrants. At the same time, I write for *all* children, and I try to write about values and feelings that are universal.

"I try to stress the positive aspects of life that I want children to value and cherish. I hope they can be caring human beings who don't think in terms of labels—foreigners or Asians or whatever—but think of people as human beings. If that comes across, then I've accomplished my purpose." [Catherine E. Studier Chang, "Profile: Yoshiko Uchida," *Language Arts*, February, 1984. Amended by the author.[3]]

1981. Received the University of Oregon's Distinguished Service Award for "a significant contribution to the cultural de-

velopment of society." "In *Desert Exile,* my non-fiction account for adults, I emphasized the dignity and strength with which most of the first generation Japanese endured that tragedy, for I felt this was truly a triumph of the human spirit. That same strength and spirit I hoped to evoke in my trilogy—*A Jar of Dreams, The Best Bad Thing,* and *The Happiest Ending.*

"Most of all, I wanted to convey in my trilogy the *values* that gave those early immigrant families their strength, and to convey the strong sense of family that sustained them. I always try to give young readers a sense of hope and affirmation and purpose in life, and the courage to dream big dreams.

"Although all my books have been about the Japanese people, my hope is that they will enlarge and enrich the reader's understanding, not only of the Japanese and the Japanese Americans, but of the *human condition.* I think it's important for each of us to take pride in our special heritage, but we must never lose our sense of connection with the community of man. And I hope our young people will, through the enriching diversity of the books they read, learn to celebrate our common humanity and the universality of the human spirit."

Uchida has written numerous children's books, including collections of Japanese folktales, stories of Japanese children living in Japan or the United States, and historical fiction about Japanese American children in America during the 1930s and 1940s. "Today as a writer of books for young people, I often speak at schools about my experiences as a Japanese American. I want the children to perceive me not as a foreigner, as some still do, or as the stereotypic Asian they often see on film and television, but as a human being. I tell them of my pride in being a Japanese American today, but I also tell them I celebrate our common humanity, for I feel we must never lose our sense of connection with the human race.

"The children ask me many questions, most of them about my wartime experiences. 'I never knew we had concentration camps in America,' one child told me in astonishment. 'I thought they were only in Germany and Russia.'

"And so the story of the wartime incarceration of the Japanese Americans, as painful as it may be to hear, needs to be told and retold and never forgotten by succeeding generations of Americans.

"I always ask the children why they think I wrote *Journey to Topaz* and *Journey Home,* in which I tell of the wartime experiences of the Japanese Americans. 'To tell about the camps?' they ask. 'To tell how you felt? To tell what happened to the Japanese people?'

"'Yes,' I answer, but I continue the discussion until finally one of them will say, 'You wrote those books so it won't ever happen again.'"[1]

1985. Wrote the award-winning children's book, *The Happiest Ending.* Uchida's books have been translated into German, Dutch, Japanese and Afrikaans.

1987. First novel for adults, *Picture Bride,* published. "This novel tells of the strength and courage of the early Japanese women immigrants and of one early Japanese American community in which they played a vital role.

"I . . . feel very lucky to be a writer, doing what I love best. I love the freedom of being able to structure my own days—to work or play or to see my friends or to travel when I please. I think that kind of freedom is a luxury to be cherished."

How can I pack our whole life into boxes and cartons in just ten days? ■ (From *Journey Home* by Yoshiko Uchida. Illustrated by Charles Robinson.)

When she is not writing, Uchida enjoys fine arts, folk crafts, the theater and visiting museums. She also enjoys walking and has developed a new interest in writing poetry. "Anything that isn't writing, I consider play. I seem to manage to play quite a lot!"

FOR MORE INFORMATION SEE: Muriel Fuller, editor, *More Junior Authors,* H. W. Wilson, 1963; *Young Readers' Review,* January, 1967; *Children's Book World,* November 5, 1967; Martha E. Ward and Dorothy A. Marquardt, *Authors of Books for Young People,* 2nd edition, Scarecrow Press, 1971; D. L. Kirkpatrick, *Twentieth-Century Children's Writers,* St. Martin's Press, 1978, 2nd edition, 1983; Catherine E. Studier Chang, "Profile: Yoshiko Uchida," *Language Arts,* February, 1984; *New York Times Book Review,* February 9, 1986.

Filmstrip: "What Makes a Story" (filmstrip and cassette), Filmedia, 1978.

Collections: Kerlan Collection at the University of Minnesota; University of Oregon Library, Eugene (manuscript collection prior to 1981); Bancroft Library, University of California, Berkeley (manuscripts, papers and all published materials since 1981).

All that mankind has done, thought, gained or been: it is lying as in magic preservation in the pages of books.
—Thomas Carlyle

ULMER, Louise 1943-

PERSONAL: Born January 11, 1943, in Fayetteville, Ark.; daughter of Virginia (a retired businesswoman; maiden name, Webb) Bradshaw; married Charles Alvin Ulmer, Jr., July 3, 1964; children: Jeffrey Todd, David, Dan. *Education:* Attended Johnson Bible College and North Arkansas Community College; Norwich University, Vermont College, B.A., 1987. *Politics:* Republican. *Religion:* Christian. *Home and office:* 803 Diamond, Williamsport, Penn., 17701. *Agent:* Elizabeth Burke, 10 Waterside Plaza, New York, N.Y. 10010.

CAREER: Writer. Ozark Bible College, Joplin, Mo., secretary to Academic Dean, 1972-74; worked as parent for teenage boys in Christian youth homes in Elizabethton, Tenn., 1974-77, and Fortville, Ind., 1977-79; secretary at Salem Lutheran Church, 1979-84; Williamsport Area Community College, Williamsport, Penn., adult education instructor (writing, word processing, and art history), 1985—; Institute of Children's Literature, Redding Ridge, Conn., instructor, 1987—. Drama coach for arts festival at Kentucky Christian College, 1983. Actress affiliated with Arts Center of the Ozarks, 1983. *Member:* Society of Children's Book Writers.

WRITINGS: (With Ruthild Kronberg and Lynn Rubright) *For the Bible Tells Me So: Bible Story-Plays with Puppets* (illustrated by Art Kirchoff), Concordia, 1979; *Teacher's Guide to Arch Books with Children* (illustrated by George Ibera), Concordia, 1982; *Bringing Bible People to Life,* CSS of Ohio, 1982; *The Bible That Wouldn't Burn: How the Tyndale English Version of the New Testament Came About,* Concordia, 1983;

LOUISE ULMER

Theatrecraft for Church and School, Contemporary Drama, 1983; *Who Are These Men?: A Study of the Apostles*, Contemporary Drama, 1983; *Help, I'm in Trouble: True-to-Life Stories for Young Teens*, Augsburg, 1986; *Let's Play a Bible Story*, Contemporary Drama, 1986; *Charity and the Great Adventure*, CSS of Ohio, 1987; (with M. Ali Baysinger), *Electrolysis and You*, Peach Blossom Publications, 1987.

"Arch Book" series; published by Concordia: *What's the Matter with Job?*, 1974; *Elijah and the Wicked Queen*, 1976; *The Man Who Learned to Give*, 1977; *The Son Who Said He Wouldn't*, 1981; *Jesus's Twelve Disciples*, 1982; *Adam's Story*, 1985; *Samuel, the Judge*, 1986.

Contributor of two short stories to anthology *Fifty-Two Bedtime Stories*, Concordia, 1987. Also contributor of articles to periodicals, including *Americana, Ministry, Christian Standard, Ozark Mountaineer*, and *Key to Christian Education*.

WORK IN PROGRESS: A Gothic romance set in Louisiana, *Serenade at Midnight; A Christmas College of Retold Legends, Stories; Crafts; Spinning, History and Hobby;* a collection of nursery rhymes.

SIDELIGHTS: "I am a mother, and children have always been my favorite people. Most of my stories have grown out of situations shared by my children and their friends. Nearly everything I write is for children or about them. When I learn something new myself, such as art technique, my first inclination is to share that new knowledge.

"I recently finished a course in art history and began a series of lessons to help young children understand the basic elements of art. I think it is sad that art concepts are not taught more often in elementary school. Appreciation for art should begin in kindergarten by calling attention to the many fine picture book illustrations and the wonderfully varied work they do.

"Writing for children is my first love, but I also write about American history, art, and antiques. My illustrated quizzes can be seen in *Americana* and other magazines.

"I'm delighted with the way the computer helps to get work done faster and easier. As a teacher of word processing, it gives me great pleasure to help beginners of all ages discover the world of computers. I believe their use in school is going to encourage creativity on all levels of learning, and that will be wonderful for everyone."

HOBBIES AND OTHER INTERESTS: Publishing books, poetry, photography, vintage houses, bird-watching.

FOR MORE INFORMATION SEE: Northwest Arkansas Times, June 4, 1983.

UNDERHILL, Liz 1948-

PERSONAL: Born March 18, 1948, in Worthing, England; daughter of Charles William (an officer in the Royal Air Force) and Ann Trewella (a housewife; maiden name, Harbut) Matten; married Graham Underhill (an author, painter, illustrator, and teacher), November 21, 1970; children: Emma Jane. *Education:* Portsmouth College of Art, B.A., 1970; Brighton Polytechnic, A.T.D., 1971. *Home:* 32 Abbey Rd., Bourne, Lincolnshire PE10 9EP, England. *Agent:* Jess Wilder, Portal Gallery, 16A Grafton St., Bond St., London W1, England.

Office: Methuen Children's Books Ltd., 11 New Fetter La., London EC4P 4EE, England.

CAREER: Wokingham College of Adult Education, Wokingham, Berkshire, England, tutor, 1972-74; Peele School, Long Sutton, Lincolnshire, England, art teacher 1974-77; artist, 1977-82; illustrator, and artist, 1982—.

WRITINGS—Juvenile; self-illustrated: *Pigs Might Fly*, Methuen, 1984; *Jack of All Trades*, David R. Godine, 1985; *The Town Cat's Christmas*, Holt, 1986; *This Is the House That Jack Built*, Holt, 1987.

WORK IN PROGRESS: The Lucky Coin; Pleasure Pursuits.

SIDELIGHTS: "I was definitely a late developer in the artistic field, not discovering the joys of creating things until almost through secondary school. Then, suddenly, art lessons became the highlight of a boarding school week. But imagination played a very big part in my early childhood, and I was never happier than when playing elaborate make-believe games with a huge collection of soft animal toys. I realize now that I was setting up the sort of visual situations that I now paint: a schoolroom of cats, a family of mice.

"Boarding school regime put a stop to such dreaming, and life became rather academic and serious until the art room in the upper school offered a delightful refuge and opened up the imagination again.

"At art college the first year was spent investigating all the different disciplines of art and choosing one for specialisation. Sculpture captivated me, and I spent the next three years buried under vast fiberglass constructions and plaster moulds. A far cry from the miniaturist paintings that I do today, but the intense satisfaction of seeing a tangible end product grow from an idea was just the same as it is now.

LIZ UNDERHILL

(From *Jack of All Trades* by Liz Underhill. Illustrated by the author.)

"Whilst at college I met and married a fellow student, the painter Graham Underhill. We both completed a year's post-graduate teacher training, but secretly hoped that we would be able to exist without it. However our daughter, Emma Jane, made her presence known soon after we qualified and with an

extra little body to support, Graham dutifully found himself a teaching job.

"I was the lucky one that stayed at home, and had a wonderful two years delving into the world of nursery rhymes and furry animals all over again, but with a very imaginative little play-mate this time. At this stage I started to paint: little nursery pictures illustrating the funny little anecdotes of a young child's world. Friends took an interest in these pictures and I started to sell them.

"After two years, Graham cut down his teaching time and I started to do some, so that we both had some studio time. We moved to an idyllic cottage in rural Lincolnshire, surrounded by tulip and wheat fields, the homes of many rabbits and mice. It was a very stimulating environment and we both had exhibitions anywhere that would show our paintings.

"Graham was offered a one-man exhibition at the prestigious Portal Gallery, London, and stopped teaching to prepare for it while I filled the teaching gap. The show was a great success, but it was becoming obvious that we both wanted to be full-time painters. So we sold just about everything we owned and moved to a tiny two-up, two-down cottage in a nearby village and I gave up my job. We had very few luxuries but were blissfully happy because we had the one important luxury: time. We painted all day every day whilst Emma went to the little village school.

"I followed Graham to the Portal Gallery and was introduced to Joy Backhouse of Methuen Children's Books. With her help I strung together twelve new animal paintings with a story, and *Pigs Might Fly* took off from there. A lot of my animal characters are based on people that I know who have particularly strong animal likenesses. In fact it is a favourite game of mine to study people's faces and mannerisms and think what animal they might be. This practice has given me a lot of ideas for painting and, therefore, for books.

"My paintings are often on wood, and Graham cuts the board to shape and hinges it at the side so that the painting will open. Instead of painting Mr. Owl busy at work, I paint Mr. Owl seen through the windows of his house and then the house can be opened up to show him at work inside. This rather unusual presentation has developed over the years, and with Graham's very patient cooperation, I have enjoyed painting a big wooden house full of cats for *The Town Cats Christmas,* and a wooden painting that opens up to reveal the strange occupants of each room: the rats, cat, dog and cow, and a few humans, too for *This Is the House That Jack Built.*

"I paint more ordinary pictures, too when Graham is involved with his own projects and does not have the time for my elaborate fretwork, but the subject matter tends to revolve around a world of animals going about their every day lives as if they behaved like humans. I hope though, that although they wore clothes and walk on their hind legs, that the animals retain the beauty and dignity that they have in their natural world, and I hope that portraying them indulging in human activities pokes fun at us rather than at them."

HOBBIES AND OTHER INTERESTS: Horse riding and keeping, walking, nature conservation, reading, clay model making, embroidery, listening to music (especially folk), learning to play the guitar.

FOR MORE INFORMATION SEE: Country Life, September, 1984.

Better to be driven out from among men than to be disliked of children.

—Richard Henry Dana

CHRIS VAN ALLSBURG

Van ALLSBURG, Chris   1949-

PERSONAL: Born June 18, 1949, in Grand Rapids, Mich.; son of Richard (a dairy owner) and Chris Van Allsburg; married Lisa Morrison (self-employed). *Education:* University of Michigan, B.F.A., 1972; Rhode Island School of Design, M.F.A., 1975. *Religion:* Jewish. *Home:* 114 Lorimer Ave., Providence, R.I. 02906. *Office:* c/o Houghton-Mifflin, 2 Park St., Boston, Mass. 02107.

CAREER: Artist; sculptor, author and illustrator of children's books. Rhode Island School of Design, Providence, R.I., teacher of illustration, 1977—. Has exhibited his work at Whitney Museum of American Art, New York, N.Y.; Museum of Modern Art, New York, N.Y.; Alan Stone Gallery, New York, N.Y.; Grand Rapids Art Museum, Grand Rapids, Mich. and Port Washington Public Library, N.Y.

AWARDS, HONORS: The Garden of Abdul Gasazi was one of *New York Times* Best Illustrated Children's Books, 1979, *Jumanji,* 1981, *Ben's Dream,* 1982, *The Wreck of the Zephyr,* 1983, *The Mysteries of Harris Burdick,* 1984, *The Polar Express,* 1985, and *The Stranger,* 1986; Caldecott Honor Book from the American Library Association, and *Boston Globe-Horn Book* Award for illustration, both 1980, and one of International Board on Books honor books for illustration, 1982, all for *The Garden of Abdul Gasazi;* Irma Simonton Black Award from Bank Street College of Education, 1980, for *The Garden of Abdul Gasazi,* and 1985, for *The Mysteries of Harris Burdick; Jumanji* was one of *New York Times* Outstanding Books, 1981, and *The Wreck of the Zephyr,* 1983; Caldecott Medal, 1982, for *Jumanji,* and 1986, for *The Polar Express; Boston Globe-Horn Book* Award honor book for illustration, 1982, for *Jumanji,* and 1986, for *The Polar Express;* Chil-

The B was badly Bitten. ■ (From *The Z Was Zapped* by Chris Van Allsburg. Illustrated by the author.)

dren's Choice from the International Reading Association, and American Book Award for illustration from Association of American Publishers, both 1982, Kentucky Bluegrass Award from Northern Kentucky University, and Buckeye Children's Book Award from Ohio State Library, both 1983, Washington Children's Choice Picture Book Award from the Washington Library Media Association, 1984, and West Virginia Children's Book Award, 1985, all for *Jumanji;* Parents' Choice Award for Illustration from the Parents' Choice Foundation, 1982, for *Ben's Dream,* 1984, for *The Mysteries of Harris Burdick,* 1985, for *The Polar Express,* and 1986, for *The Stranger;* Kentucky Bluegrass Award from Northern Kentucky University, 1987, for *Polar Express.*

Ben's Dream was included in the American Institute of Graphic Arts Book Show, 1983, *The Wreck of the Zephyr,* 1984, and *The Mysteries of Harris Burdick,* 1985; *The Wreck of the Zephyr* was chosen one of New York Public Library's Children's Books,

1983, and *The Polar Express,* 1985; *Boston Globe-Horn Book Award,* 1985, both for *The Mysteries of Harris Burdick; The Polar Express* was chosen one of *Redbook*'s Ten Best Picture Books for Kids, and one of Child Study Association's Children's Books of the Year, both 1985; *The Stranger* was chosen one of Child Study Association's Children's Books of the Year, 1987.

WRITINGS—Self-illustrated children's books; all published by Houghton: *The Garden of Abdul Gasazi* (ALA Notable Book), 1979; *Jumanji* (ALA Notable Book; *Horn Book* honor list), 1981; *Ben's Dream,* 1982; *The Wreck of the Zephyr* (ALA Notable Book; *Horn Book* honor list), 1983; *The Mysteries of Harris Burdick* (ALA Notable Book), 1984; *The Polar Express* (ALA Notable Book; *Horn Book* honor list), 1985; *The Stranger* (*Horn Book* honor list), 1986; *The Z Was Zapped: A Play in Twenty-Six Acts,* 1987.

(Detail of jacket illustration by Chris Van Allsburg from *Ben's Dream* by Chris Van Allsburg.)

ADAPTATIONS: ''The Garden of Abdul Gasazi'' (read-along cassette; filmstrip with cassette), Random House; ''Jumanji'' (cassette), Random House; ''Ben's Dream'' (cassette), Random House, (film), Library Productions, 1983; ''The Wreck of the Zephyr'' (cassette), Random House, 1985; ''The Polar Express'' (read-along cassette; filmstrip with cassette), 1986.

SIDELIGHTS: ''Sometime in the middle of the twentieth century—I like to be mysterious about my age—I was born in Grand Rapids, Michigan. Growing up, I liked to do normal kid things like playing baseball and building model cars, trucks, and planes. I also used to drive a go-cart on public streets, which was illegal. I lived in a growing suburb with half-built houses, great to spook around in, especially in those with only the stud work sticking out of the top of the foundations. We were not suppose to do this—it was taboo. Obviously parents were afraid we'd hurt ourselves.'' [Based on an interview by Catherine Ruello for *Something about the Author.*¹]

''The first book I remember reading is probably the same book many people my age recall as their first. It was profusely illustrated and recounted the adventures and conflicts of its three protagonists, Dick, Jane, and Spot. Actually, the lives of this trio were not all that interesting. A young reader's reward for struggling through those syllables at the bottom of

the page was to discover that Spot got a bath. Not exactly an exciting revelation. Especially since you'd already seen Spot getting his bath in the picture at the top of the page.

''The Dick, Jane, and Spot primers have gone to that book shelf in the sky. I have, in some ways, a tender feeling toward them, so I think it's for the best. Their modern incarnation would be too painful to look at. Dick and Jane would have their names changed to Jason and Jennifer. Faithful Spot would be transformed into an Afghan hound, and the syllables at the bottom of the page would reveal that the children were watching MTV.

''In third grade my class paid its first visit to the school library as prospective book borrowers. It was on this occasion that we learned about the fascinating Dewey decimal system. None of us really understood this principle of cataloging books, but we were inclined to favor it. Any system named Dewey was all right with us. We looked forward to hearing about the Huey and Louie decimal systems, too.

''The book I checked out on my first visit was the biography of Babe Ruth. I started reading it at school and continued reading it at home. I read till dinner and opened the book again after dessert, finally taking it to bed with me. The story of

(From *The Stranger* by Chris Van Allsburg. Illustrated by the author.)

Babe Ruth was an interesting one, but I don't think it was as compelling as that constant reading suggests. There was something else happening: I just simply did not know when to stop or why. Having grown up with television, I was accustomed to watching something until it was finished. I assumed that as long as the book was there I should read it to the end. The idea of setting the book aside uncompleted just didn't occur to me.

"This somewhat obsessive approach to reading manifested itself again during the summer after third grade. My neighbor had a collection of every Walt Disney comic book ever published. I took my little wagon to his house and hauled every issue to my bedroom. For a solid week I did nothing but read about Pluto, Mickey, Donald, and Daisy. It was spooky. By the sixth day they'd become quite real to me and were turning up in my dreams. After I returned the comics, I felt very lonely, as if a group of lively house guests had left suddenly." [Chris Van Allsburg, "Caldecott Medal Acceptance," *Horn Book*, July/August, 1986.[2]]

"In my elementary school we had art twice a week. I loved those days. Children often use a slight fever as an excuse to stay home from school, drink ginger ale, and eat ice cream in bed. Once, in the second grade, I felt feverish at breakfast but concealed it from my mother because it was an art day. Midway through the morning art class, my teacher noticed that I looked a little green. Ordinarily it wouldn't be unusual, but paint wasn't being used that day. She took me out into the hall where we children left our coats and boots and asked if I felt O.K. I said I felt fine and then threw up into Billy Marcus's boots. I was profoundly embarrassed. The teacher was very comforting. She took me to the nurse's office, and my mother was summoned. I went home, drank ginger ale, and ate ice cream in bed.

"There was another occasion when my physical health and my passion for art collided. When I was eight, my friend Russell and I became voracious stamp collectors. I loved those tiny little pictures. We wanted all our relatives to take a vacation in the Ukraine and write us lots of letters. After three weeks of looking at nothing but stamps, I got a fever—the flu again. In my delirium, all I could see was a stamp picturing the Lewis and Clark expedition. I was there, too, with Lewis and Clark, standing in front of a timber fort with our Indian guides, but we never went anywhere. When I pulled out of the fever, I gave all my stamps to Russell. To this day I'm a terrible letter-writer, no doubt because of my lasting aversion to stamps.

"There was a great deal of peer recognition to be gained in elementary school by being able to draw well. One girl could draw horses so well, she was looked upon as a kind of sorceress. (Everyone else's horses looked like water buffalo.) Being able to draw cartoon characters was a good trick, too. Pluto and Mickey always impressed friends. I specialized in Dagwood Bumstead, a little too sophisticated, perhaps, to be widely appreciated." [Lee Kingman, editor, *Newbery and Caldecott Medal Books, 1976-1985*, Horn Book, 1986[3]]

"Drawing was a child pleasure that faded away as I got older. By the time I was in fourth grade, I really didn't think much about myself as an artist. There were other social considerations and expectations. Little boys were supposed to spend their time and energy learning how to play baseball and football and becoming good little athletes. It wasn't a condition that had anything to do with the teachers at my school, or with my environment being prejudiced against art, or with my parents' attitude. It was just the condition of being a kid growing up.

"I had no idea what I wanted to be when I grew up. I thought I'd be a lawyer, mostly because I couldn't think of anything else. I thought about doing a few other things but never seriously. In high school it was thought okay to study art as a way of expanding cultural horizons, but it was not considered a legitimate career pursuit. So, I studied the usual college prep requirements as math, science, etc. . . . It was understood that I'd go to college, not a decision I had to make, because it was made for me. I still hadn't made a clear choice of what I wanted to do, had no portfolio, and I hadn't studied any of the subjects required for art school. However, because of a bureaucratic oversight, I was accepted into the art school at the University of Michigan. At first it was just a lark. I thought it would be a great way to earn a college degree by goofing around for four years."[1]

"At that time I was quite naive about the study of art. As a freshman I received a form that listed the courses I would have, their times and places, and the necessary materials. One course, described simply as 'Fgdrw,' met at eight o'clock in the morning. I did not know what Fgdrw meant, but the materials required were newsprint and charcoal. I went to the appointed room and was surprised to see an older woman wearing a terry-cloth robe and slippers. I thought, 'What? Does she live here or something? Maybe we're here too early, and she hasn't had time to dress.' Then she took off her bathrobe, and I deduced the meaning of Fgdrw."[3]

"The enthusiasm I had for art as a child was once again rekindled. The first thing I responded to was sculpture, because it was close to the pleasure I had gotten from making things (plastic cars etc.) with my hands, which I did quite a lot until I was eleven years old. I drew only to pass the required courses, spending all my time learning how to cast bronze, carve wood and work in ceramics.

"I began my career as a sculptor and went into painting almost accidentally. It wasn't that I was discouraged with my life as a sculptor. On the contrary, I had already had a couple of well-received shows in New York City. I started drawing in the evening as a hobby, and considered sculpture my real job. A friend of mine who illustrated books saw my drawings and encouraged me to consider illustrations. My wife, who also encouraged me taught elementary school at the time and occasionally brought home illustrated books. I spent some time working on a little story. My wife took it around to publishers who suggested that I develop it further. I did. The first verse was grim couplets which were a little silly. So, I decided to write prose, instead. That's something I've learned to do. I've only written a few books, and two of them aren't even books. *Harris Burdick* for example, is not, in a conventional sense, a book.

"When my first book, *The Garden of Abdul Gasazi*, was published, I had no expectations at all. I remember thinking, 'maybe a few copies will sell; I'll buy the remainder and give them to friends for Christmas.' But *The Garden of Abdul Gasazi* sold quite well. As a fine artist, you're used to an audience, which in a gallery is at best three to four hundred people in the course of a month. Out of those four hundred people, maybe fifteen are going to buy something. But with an illustrated book, the audience is immense. If 40,000 books are sold, a lot of those are going to be in elementary schools, and it's going to be seen by at least thirty kids every time it's used in class. That was appealing to me. Perhaps this is egotistical—it's one thing to have the impulse to make a piece of art, but quite another to want everyone to see it in order to confirm the feelings you have about it. I guess it's more insecurity, than egotism. Still, I like having a lot of people see what I do. There are dangers

(From *The Mysteries of Harris Burdick* by Chris Van Allsburg. Illustrated by the author.)

to this, too, however. Sometimes the reproduction of my illustrations makes me feel very bad. It takes a good piece of art to stand up to the rigors of reproduction. The disappointing thing is: I'll send out a piece of art and am not able to approve the reproduction process. It's going to go to the lowest-bid printer. Nobody is going to worry about it. They'll send me back a poster of the finished work, and it will look terrific. Then, I'll have a book project, like *The Polar Express,* and there will be eight people from production pulling their hair out, sending people to every pressroom, and making trips back and forth to the printer, getting the thing approved, and approved, and approved. It's like an unending nightmare. Either way it's almost out of your hands. It's like the gods of printing look down, and if they see that you care too much, they're going to stick it to you. But if you don't make a stink, they don't notice you, and they let it go by. That's the down side of being an illustrator. With fine artists, people only see what *you* have done. Your work never gets better with reproduction.

My feeling is, if in reproduction your work looks better, then it should not have looked like that in the first place.

''For *Ben's Dream,* I used scratchboard, drawing white lines into black, giving the suggestion of an engraving. In fact, this is one of the reasons this particular drawing style appeals to me. I have a strong prejudice against pen and ink style of crosshatching, where you merely weave lines. If you're trying to describe something with black lines, or trying to create value with black lines, it doesn't make sense to use the black line to describe a spherical or cylindrical shape, and then put straight crosshatch lines on it. The lines should bend around the cylindrical form to show that there's a cylinder.

''When I do a book, I follow my own reactions to what I've drawn or written. It would be inconceivable to draw something and say, 'A child will understand it, but it doesn't move me,' or 'I'm not moved by it, but I trust my audience.' I have never

They bolted out the door. ■ (From *Jumanji* by Chris Van Allsburg. Illustrated by the author.)

(One of Van Allsburg's signature elements is the small dog included in most of his books. From
The Garden of Abdul Gasazi by Chris Van Allsburg. Illustrated by the author.)

had that criteria. However, I do think about kids when I write, because regardless of the premise of the story, it must be accessible to a fairly early reader—maybe not a first-grade, but a second-grade reader.

"A book is a four-and-a-half month commitment, and the challenge is to actually finish it. My problem is maintaining self-motivation after the tenth drawing. There are fourteen to fifteen drawings in a conventionally laid-out book and by the tenth drawing I'm ready to start another project. I've got a 'sketchbook' in my head with thousands of pieces of sculpture and enough descriptions for ten books. But I let those things sit in the back of my mind whereby the weaker ideas settle out by themselves. I would like to be six people at once, so that I could get more of them out of the way.''[1]

In his approach to creating a book, Van Allsburg usually writes the story first. "However, it would probably be fair to say that I go through the story visually without really hearing the words. I see the whole, but it exists as a texture of story before I do any drawings. I might see the story three or four different ways—it's a little bit like making a film. A director has the choice of where to place the camera. Basically I have the same choice, and use it to try to create drama for a single drawing,

and create variety—sometimes the camera is high, sometimes low—so that there's not a static feeling for the reader.

"After I have the text and know essentially what has to be illustrated, I'll do a lot of crude thumbnail sketches which deal with one event at intervals of several minutes, or deal with point of view. The truth is, there are a number of ways to do an illustration. In terms of point of view and lighting alone, there are an infinite number of possibilities. Through sketching I narrow my choices. When I get one which I think is going to do the job, I work on the composition and perspective. I only use models for figures. Everything else is fabrication based on perspective. My drawings vary in size. The drawings for *Harris Burdick,* for example, were very large, about two-and-half feet tall. *The Polar Express* drawings were quite small, a little larger than in the actual book.

"Once I've created the space, I have to create the light. Light made up has a clarity that real light may not have. It has to do with things like atmosphere and perspective. In a real space light bounces off walls and is overall more diffuse. When you invent, you can't anticipate the subtle things that result within the space. Consequently, the light becomes a little simpler and a little starker and gives the space a kind of surrealistic quality.

Slowly he followed Fritz's tracks along a path that led into a forest. ■ (From *The Garden of Abdul Gasazi* by Chris Van Allsburg. Illustrated by the author.)

While it's real, it's not the way you could light a kitchen. In the cover of *Jumanji*, there's a fair amount of light in the kitchen, which suggests that there should be a lot of reflected light on other things. Very little is reflected on the monkeys, however, giving a sense of darkness over your left shoulder in front of the picture. That's the way it has to be in order to get that low level reflected light coming back on the monkeys. These aren't things you plan, they just happen.

"If I compressed all the time I've worked in color, it would probably amount to a year and a half. The desire to use color came from the need to experiment and from the stories themselves. Interiors can be handled easily in black and white, but there's something about landscape that seems to insist on a little bit of color. In dealing with color, the most difficult thing is not the decision about what color to use. It's easy to decide that someone is going to wear a green shirt. The problem is how that green changes as it passes from light to shadow. When you draw with value, it's just a matter of drawing it darker or lighter. With color it's not a matter of simply adding black or white to the pigment, but having to decide about such things as the temperature and saturation changes. When you do it with one color, you have to do it with all of them. You can't let the green go through a color change, and not the red, for example.

"My approach to color is a little bit like my approach to everything else: I intellectualize it. It's impossible for me to do a complicated set-up. I can't go out, for instance, and put a train in front of a house, but as a draftsman I can figure out what it would look like in perspective. Then I would have to anticipate what would happen with colors. And when you are trying to make things up, you can't be literal.

"I haven't painted a lot from life. I'm trying to do more of that. My ability to conjecture color is dependent on my continuing to work from life. Unless I learn the principles of light on color I cannot apply them to things I imagine. I go out to see what the grass looks like in shadow and then in light. Now, if you look at it long enough, you can actually sense some of the blue emanating from the shadow crest. Probably because it has the reflected light of the sky in it. You can also sense the yellowishness in the shadow. It is this experience that gets translated into a pigment decision. It's one thing to see that a particular shade is green, another to know which pigments to use to make the right green happen. I became more sensitive to color. I would look at things and wonder how I would try to render it. This did not happen so much with value drawings, when I tended to see the world in black and white.

"In doing my first pastel books I made some technical mistakes. I used pastels as though they were paints. With that medium you usually create colors by juxtaposing small pieces of various pigments. For example, if he wanted a particular kind of green sea, a pastel artist might put down a blue next to a yellow. But I always mixed the pigments just as a painter would. If you look closely at *Stranger,* you can see I was a little less concerned with mixing the bits of color in order to create a single color. I let the marks stay separate.

"If all artists were forced to wear a badge, I'd probably wear the badge of surrealism. I don't mean something as extreme as Salvador Dali's melting clocks, but a gentle surrealism with certain unsettling provocative elements. I'm pleased when my own drawings are a little mysterious to me. This happens rarely, since most of the time I'm aware of what I'm doing. I like to create a world where not everything is possible, but where strange things may happen. I try not to use fantasy as a self-serving way to make an interesting story. Fantasy as a way of revealing human psychological depth via goblins and dwarfs is not appealing to me. The demand I put on myself is that it be logical. Once I create a fantastic premise, I apply that premise consistently. For example, that boats can fly in *The Wreck of the Zephyr* has a visual reason behind it. If you look carefully, when the boats leave the water they are trimmed coincidently on port and starboard tack, which is something that can't happen. You *cannot* trim a boat that way. But I had a certain logic built into flying boats and I carried it to the end.''[1]

One of Van Allsburg's signature elements is the small dog included in most of his books. "With the last couple of books, before starting even the thumbnail sketches, I looked forward to placing the dog. It's a little game with me. I look forward to concealing him more and more, so that you might have to spend four or five hours looking for him. However, I always play fair. It's occurred to me that I could hide the dog in an abstract pattern in smoke, for example, which would be a rough outline of the dog. But that is so ambiguous, it seems like cheating. I haven't really challenged people very much in terms of the dog who will probably be the most difficult to find in *The Stranger*.

"I like the idea of withholding something, both in drawings and writing. I don't like to be too specific in a drawing. I like turning a face away a little bit, or cropping the drawing with part of a figure in the frame. I also like leaving something out of the story. There must be something to ponder at the end. My stories neither begin by posing nor end by solving a question. The reader has to resolve the book after he has read it. The book itself is merely chapter one.''[1]

"Over the years that have passed since my first book was published, a question I've been asked often is, 'Where do your ideas come from?' I've given a variety of answers to this question, such as: 'I steal them from the neighborhood kids,' 'I send away for them by mail order,' and 'They are beamed to me from outer space.'

(From *The Wreck of the Zephyr* by Chris Van Allsburg. Illustrated by the author.)

"It's not really my intention to be rude or smart-alecky. The fact is, I don't know where my ideas come from. Each story I've written starts out as a vague idea that seems to be going nowhere, then suddenly materializes as a completed concept. It almost seems like a discovery, as if the story was always there. The few elements I start out with are actually clues. If I figure out what they mean, I can discover the story that's waiting.

"When I began thinking about what became *The Polar Express,* I had a single image in mind: a young boy sees a train standing still in front of his house one night. The boy and I took a few different trips on that train, but we did not, in a figurative sense, go anywhere. Then I headed north, and I got the feeling that this time I'd picked the right direction, because the train kept rolling all the way to the North Pole. At that point the story seemed literally to present itself. Who lives at the North Pole? Undoubtedly a ceremony of some kind, a ceremony requiring a child, delivered by a train and would have to be named the Polar Express.

"These stray elements are, of course, merely events. A good story uses the description of events to reveal some kind of moral or psychological premise. I am not aware, as I develop a story, what the premise is. When I started *The Polar Express,* I thought I was writing about the train trip, but the story was actually about faith and the desire to believe in something. It's an intriguing process. I know if I'd set out with the goal of writing about that, I'd still be holding a pencil over a blank sheet of paper.

"Fortunately, or perhaps I should say necessarily, that premise is consistent with my own feelings, especially when it comes to accepting fantastic propositions like Santa Claus. Santa is our culture's only mythic figure truly believed in by a large percentage of the population. It's a fact that most of the true believers are under eight years old, and that's a pity. The rationality we all embrace as adults makes believing in the fantastic difficult, if not impossible. Lucky are the children who *know* there is a jolly fat man in a red suit who pilots a flying sleigh. We should envy them. And we should envy the

people who are so certain Martians will land in their back yard that they keep a loaded Polaroid camera by the back door. The inclination to believe in the fantastic may strike some as a failure in logic . . . but it's really a gift. A world that might have Bigfoot and the Loch Ness monster is clearly superior to one that definitely does not.

"I don't mean to give the impression that my own sense of what is possible is not shaped by rational, analytic thought. As much as I'd like to meet the tooth fairy on an evening walk, I don't really believe it can happen.

"When I was seven or eight, on the night before Easter, my mother accidentally dropped a basket of candy outside my bedroom door. I understood what the sound was and what it meant. I heard my mother, in a loud whisper, trying unsuccessfully to keep the cats from batting jelly beans across the wooden floor. It might have been the case that the Easter Bunny had already become an iffy proposition for me. In any event this was just the moment the maturing skeptic in me

was waiting for. I gained the truth, but I paid a heavy price for it. The Easter Bunny died that night."[2]

Van Allsburg teaches part time. "If I didn't teach, I'd never leave my studio, which would probably not be healthy in terms of mental hygiene. Teaching drawing made me discover the importance of composition earlier than I otherwise would have. When I first started drawing about six or seven years ago, I wasn't very sensitive to the placement of objects on a page or to the effects of composition on the mind. As a teacher I was forced to talk about this, and had to come to grips with principles of composition and why some drawings, though well drafted, lack power. When you critique students' work, you are forced to look again and again at a drawing, and to determine its failing. And because you're responsible for articulating what is wrong with it, your eyes improve and self realization becomes keener."[1]

The influences in Van Allsburg's life have been many. "If I were to name ten people who have influenced me, I would

(Jacket illustration by Chris Van Allsburg from *The Polar Express* by Chris Van Allsburg.)

feel that I've neglected the other fifty. Still, there are some like the German etcher Max Klinger who left a big impression on me. Also, something about the work of the painter Casper David-Friedrich moves me a lot. I like drawings and images in which the emotional content is not based on the subject matter. That may not be a fair evaluation of the work of Klinger and David-Friedrich, but I think some of their best work has a moody quality which is not dependent on subject matter. The feeling they create is not a consequence of content but of composition. It's easy to get an emotional response by doing a drawing of a little boy and a puppy dog. It's much more difficult to create sentiment by drawing a landscape or a still life.

"For me books are very compelling. I instantly get into their world, visualizing the place, the room, the people. I don't have to read too many lines to imagine a character's face. It's disconcerting when the author describes the character after I have already been reading description of his inner life and dialogues, when he is not at all what I pictured. The same holds true with a movie adaption—I usually have visualized the book differently than the filmmaker."[1]

"As years have passed, my taste in literature has changed. I do, however, still have obsessive reading habits. I pore over every word on the cereal box at breakfast, often more than once. You can ask me anything about Shredded Wheat. I also spend more time in the bathroom than necessary, determined to keep up with my *New Yorker* subscription.

"It seems strange now, considering my susceptibility to the power of the printed word, that I'd been reading for more than twenty years before I thought about writing. I had, by that time, staked out visual art as my form of self-expression. But my visual art was and is very narrative. I feel fortunate that I've become involved with books as another opportunity for artistic expression."[2]

"I get hundreds of letters from kids. Some want a picture of me, others want to invite me to dinner. They want to know if I like spaghetti. I got a lot of letters with stories that kids have written for the pictures in *Harris Burdick*. I remember the first letter was a strange kind of crank letter from an adult, written with red Magic Marker on tissue paper. He didn't want to know anything about the books I had written, he simply wanted to know if I thought the world would exist as we know it ten years from now.

"I answered the first hundred letters. But then my volume of mail became so great that it literally would take me four to five days a month to keep up with it. Every once in awhile I'll meet a librarian who will mention that I answered a letter five years ago, and that the children loved it so much they still talk about it. I think of all these kids I haven't done that for, and it's guilt-provoking. I still have a dream that one day I will answer all the letters written by kids on their own initiative. By then, they'll be eighteen years old, and it may be an even bigger treat for them to get a letter twelve years later."[1]

HOBBIES AND OTHER INTERESTS: "When I'm not drawing, I enjoy taking walks and going to museums. I play tennis a few times a week, like to sail—although I have fewer opportunities to do it now (I used to have more friends with boats). I read quite a lot."

FOR MORE INFORMATION SEE: New York Times Book Review, November 11, 1979, November 25, 1979, April 26, 1981, April 25, 1982, June 5, 1983, November 10, 1985, November 9, 1986; *Washington Post Book World,* November

11, 1979, July 12, 1981, May 9, 1982, October 14, 1984; *Time,* December 3, 1979, December 21, 1981, December 20, 1982; *Newsweek,* December 17, 1979; *Times Literary Supplement,* September 18, 1981; *New Yorker,* December 7, 1981; *School Library Journal,* May, 1982, March, 1983; *Chicago Tribune Book World,* August 1, 1982; *Los Angeles Times Book Review,* March 21, 1982, April 3, 1983; *Horn Book,* August, 1982, July/August, 1986, September/October, 1986; *Publishers Weekly,* April 9, 1983; *Children's Literature Review,* Gale, Volume 5, 1983, Volume 13, 1987; Sally Holmes Holtze, *Fifth Book of Junior Authors and Illustrators,* H. W. Wilson, 1983; Lee Kingman, editor, *Newbery and Caldecott Medal Books, 1976-1985,* Horn Book, 1986.

Collections: Kerlan Collection at the University of Minnesota.

VAUTIER, Ghislaine 1932-
(Hélène Frank)

PERSONAL: Born December 28, 1932, in New York, N.Y.; daughter of Paul (in publicity) and Laura (Murat) Frank; married Sylvestre Vautier (a professor), April 5, 1952; children: Nicole Brisa-Vautier, Antoine, Isabelle. *Education:* Attended San Francisco State College (now San Francisco State University), 1950-51, and University of Lausanne, 1951-53. *Politics:* None. *Religion:* Catholic. *Home and office:* Avenue de Rumine 51, CP22, CH-1000 Lausanne 5, Switzerland.

CAREER: Publisher and writer. Free-lance journalist for the *Toledo Blade* and several French-language magazines and newspapers, c. 1950-66; Editions Pierrot (publishers), Lausanne, Switzerland, founder and director, 1966-83; Editions les Quatre Saisons, Lausanne, Switzerland, founder and publisher, 1985—. Has hosted a monthly television program for children in Switzerland, 1971-73. *Member:* Zonta International, Swiss Association of French Language Publishers, Cantonal Commission for Cinema Control, Commission for Special Publications for the Deaf, SACD (Société des Auteurs et Compositeurs Dramatiques), Association Vaudoise des Ecrivains, Société Suisse des Ecrivains. *Awards, honors: The Shining Stars: Greek Legends of the Zodiac* was selected chil-

GHISLAINE VAUTIER

dren's book of the year by National Book League, England, 1982.

WRITINGS—All juvenile, except as noted; all first published in Switzerland by Editions Pierrot: *La toque du chef* (cookbook; title means "The Chef's Cap"), 1975; *Au fond du grenier* (title means "Up in the Attic"), 1976; (under pseudonym Hélène Frank) *Je te déteste* (title means "I Hate You"), 1979; *Quand brillent les etoiles*, 1980, translation by Kenneth McLeish published as *The Shining Stars: Greek Legends of the Zodiac* (illustrated by Jacqueline Bezencon), Cambridge University Press, 1981; *Les Lois du ciel*, 1982, translated by K. McLeish published as *The Way of the Stars: Greek Legends of the Constellations* (illustrated by J. Bezencon), Cambridge University Press, 1983; (under pseudonym H. Frank) *Je suce mon pouce* (title means "I Suck My Thumb"), 1983; (under pseudonym H. Frank) *Je déménage* (title means "I'm Moving"), 1983; *Tobor* (title means "Robot [written backwards]"), 1983; *Les Rebus* (title means "The Picture Puzzles"), 1984.

Author of books with records, published and produced by Editions Pierrot: *Un Ane de Bethleem* (title means "The Donkey from Bethlehem"), 1969; *Le Secret de Francois* (title means "Francis Has a Secret"), 1970; *Oncle Jacques et son péroquet* (title means "Uncle Jack and His Parrot"), 1971.

Editor of children's magazine *Mon Ami Pierrot*, 1966-83. Contributor of articles to magazines and newspapers. Adapter and translator of *Fingermath* by Edwin Lieberthal for Editions les Quatre Saisons, 1986.

WORK IN PROGRESS: Le Kaleidoscope, a collection of short stories for adults; a five-to-ten volume work concerning the history of the cantons of Switzerland as illustrated by their museums; *Numbers Galore*, a short history of man's discovery and use of the numbers, for children ages eight to twelve.

SIDELIGHTS: "Our children have done their best to teach me to try to never stop growing. It is through their eyes that I've learned to watch grass blades dance, freckles crinkle or storm clouds swell in wanderlust. To care and to share, if possible.

"I am a bilingual author, living and working in Switzerland, one of the most exceptionally privileged countries of the world. I just try, through my own writing and through the choice of the books our company publishes, to contribute one or two extra pebbles to building the road of international comprehension and sympathy. It appears vital to me to help young children realize that for the essentials of life, be it in the past, the present, or the future, there are no frontiers. 'Communication is possible' is my motto.

"I simply can't list the titles of all the children's stories I've written: to date, 565. Add different articles, for children or adults and we'll end up with the Manhattan directory and this is the sort of 'problem' best to be avoided for it's part of the job. A wonderful job, a game which I love to play every day. And if I'm especially lucky, someday, somewhere, just one little sentence will trigger off a new idea for somebody else and the game will continue."

Taped versions of issues of *Mon Ami Pierrot*, the children's magazine edited by Vautier, have been produced for blind children for the Foundation Laurent Bernat.

Just at the age 'twixt boy and youth,
When thought is speech, and speech is truth.
—Sir Walter Scott

VELTHUIJS, Max 1923-

PERSONAL: Born May 22, 1923, in The Hague, Netherlands; son of Johannes (a teacher) and Liesbeth (a teacher) Velthuijs; married second wife, Charlotte van Zadelhoff, 1985; children: (first marriage) one son; (second marriage) one son. *Education:* Studied art in the Netherlands. *Politics:* "Progressive-thinking," *Home and office:* Westerbaenstr. 27, 2513 GG Den Haag, Netherlands.

CAREER: Free-lance graphic designer. Political cartoonist, The Hague, Netherlands, 1945-50; illustrator of children's books, 1965—; author of children's books, 1967—; Art Academy, The Hague, Netherlands, teacher of graphic art, until 1987. Has had many one-man exhibitions in Dutch galleries. *Awards, honors:* Golden Apple Award Plaque from the Bienále Ilustrácií Bratislava, 1971, and Prix des Treize (France), both for *Der Junge und der Fisch; The Little Boy and the Big Fish* was included in Child Study Association of America's Children's Books of the Year, 1969; Grapic Art Award from the Society of Illustrators, 1975, included in the Children's Book Showcase of the Children's Book Council, 1976, and nominated for the Mildred L. Batchelder Award, 1977, all for *The Painter and the Bird;* Gouden Penseel from the Commission for the Promotion of the Dutch Book and the Professional Graphic Artists' Association, 1977, for *Het goedige monster en de rovers,* and 1986, for *Klein-Mannchen findt das glück;* Troisdorf Preis, 1985, for *Die ente und der fuchs.*

WRITINGS: For children; in German; all self-illustrated: *Der junge und der fisch*, Nord-Süd, 1967, translation published as

MAX VELTHUIJS

The Little Boy and the Big Fish, Platt & Munk, 1969; *Der arme holzhacker und die taube*, Nord-Süd, 1969, translation published as *The Poor Woodcutter and the Dove*, Delacorte, 1970; *Der maler und der vogel*, Nord-Süd, 1970, translation by Ray Broekel published as *The Painter and the Bird*, Addison-Wesley, 1975; *Das gutherzige ungeheuer* (title means ''The Good-Hearted Monster''), Nord-Süd, 1973; *Das gutherzige ungeheuer und die räuber* (title means ''The Good-Hearted Monster and the Robbers), Nord-Süd, 1976; *Klein-Mannchen hat kein haus*, Nord-Süd, 1983, published as *Little Man Finds a Home*, Abelard, (England), 1984, Holt, 1985; *Die ente und der fuchs* (title means ''The Duck and the Fox''), Maier, 1984; *Der bär und das schweinchen* (title means ''The Bear and the Little Pig''), Maier, 1985; *Klein-Mannchen findet das glück*, Nord-Süd, 1985, published as *Little Man's Lucky Day*, Holt, 1986; *Klein-Mannchen hilft ein freund*, Nord-Süd, 1986, published as *Little Man to the Rescue*, Holt, 1986; *Elefant und krokodil* (title means ''The Elephant and the Crocodile''), Maier, 1987.

Illustrator: Mischa Damjan (pseudonym) *Der wolf und das zicklein*, Nord-Süd, 1968, translation published as *The Wolf and the Kid*, McGraw, 1968 (published in England as *The Wolf and the Little Goat*, Abelard, 1968).

WORK IN PROGRESS: Little Bear's Birthday Cake for Nord-Süd; illustrations for *The Little Red Hen* for D.C. Heath.

SIDELIGHTS: ''My father and mother were both teachers. They collected antique furniture and paintings. I had three elder sisters. Music and drawing were very important in our family.

''I started my career at a studio drawing electrical illustrations when I was sixteen. During the war, I left the city and moved to Arnhem, where I studied at the academy until 1944 when the Battle of Arnhem forced me to hide from the Germans until the end of the war. I returned to The Hague and started working as a political cartoonist until 1950.

''During my career as a graphic designer I made all kinds of posters, announcements, cartoons, book jackets, animated films for television, etc. In 1965 I started drawing illustrations for children's books, and about 1967 I wrote and illustrated my first book, *The Little Boy and the Big Fish*. It was very successful, but I soon found that it was impossible to make a living doing only books.

''In 1983 I finally decided to give up my graphic design work in order to devote more time to picture books and in 1987 stopped teaching at the academy for the same reason.

''I begin my books with pictures living in my head. I can see them when I close my eyes, and I hear the voices. Writing comes second. I need a lot of time for my illustrations, because I work slowly and am seldom satisfied with the results. It is nearly impossible to realize the illustrations I see in my fantasy. Making children's books changed my life completely and I am very happy doing them.

''In 1985 I married for the second time and am the father of a young son.''

HOBBIES AND OTHER INTERESTS: Jazz, animals, sports, playing chess, skating, bicycling.

FOR MORE INFORMATION SEE: Graphic 155, Volume 27, 1971-72; Lee Kingman and others, compilers, *Illustrators of Children's Books: 1967-1976*, Horn Book, 1978.

JOHN MILTON WAINSCOTT

WAINSCOTT, John Milton 1910-1981

PERSONAL: Born April 26, 1910, in Belvedere, Alberta, Canada; died in September, 1981; son of Zorus (a farmer) and Madge Eliza (Bricka) Wainscott; married wife, Kathleen Nora Brunton, October 31, 1953. *Politics:* Socialist. *Religion:* Agnostic.

CAREER: Head greenskeeper at Gorge Vale Golf Course in Victoria, British Columbia, Canada. *Awards, honors:* Numerous prizes for woodworking, turnings, carving, and photography.

WRITINGS: Furred and Feathered People: Little Stories in Verse (self-illustrated), Vesta, 1977.

SIDELIGHTS: Wainscott's granddaughter writes: ''John Wainscott's family homesteaded in Belvedere, Alberta until the 1920s when they moved to Jordan River, British Columbia where his father was a beekeeper.

''John spent several years prospecting and gold panning. He was a union organizer and secretary of the Canadian Woodworkers Union. He went on the Unemployed Workers Trek to Ottawa in the 1930s.

''In the late 1940s John and his brother started construction on a log cabin on seven acres of wooded land. John and his wife, Nora, lived in this home until his death in 1981.

''His lifetime interest in outdoors and nature led to his writing poetry about the wildlife that lived in the woods surrounding his home.''

WALKER, Lou Ann 1952-

BRIEF ENTRY: Born December 9, 1952, in Blackwood County, Ind. A hearing child of deaf parents, Walker grew up in a warm and loving household. She attended Harvard University where she received her B.A. in comparative literature in 1976 and a Rockefeller Foundation fellowship in the humanities. That same year, she began a series of assistant and associate editor positions for magazines such as *New York, Diversion, Esquire,* and *Cosmopolitan.* She wrote articles for some of these periodicals, in addition to others, and edited *Direct* Magazine between 1981 and 1982. Walker also worked on a project coordinated by New York City's Museum of Modern Art for the Hearing-impaired. Her book for young readers, *Amy: The Story of a Deaf Child* (Lodestar, 1985), was photographed by Michael Abramson and depicts the life of a deaf girl who, with the help of hearing aids and sign language, leads an otherwise normal existence. According to *Appraisal,* the book's power "lies in the sincerity of Amy's own words and the outstanding photographs on each page." *A Loss for Words: The Story of Deafness in a Family* (Harper & Row, 1986) recounts Walker's own childhood, in which she acted as "translator between her parents and the hearing world. Referred to by *Publishers Weekly* as "beautifully written and deeply affecting," this work received a Christopher Award for its humanitarian portrayal. *Agent:* Liz Darhansoff, 1220 Park Ave., New York, N.Y. 10128.

FOR MORE INFORMATION SEE: New York Times Magazine, August 31, 1986; *Newsweek,* September 22, 1986; *People,* December 15, 1986.

WALLACE, Ian 1950-

PERSONAL: Born March 31, 1950, in Niagara Falls, Ontario, Canada; son of Robert Amiens (a sales manager) and Kathleen (a homemaker; maiden name, Watts) Wallace. *Education:* Attended Ontario College of Art, 1969-74. *Home and office:* 370 Palmerston Blvd., Toronto, Ontario, Canada M6G 2N6.

CAREER: Kids Can Press, Toronto, Ontario, staff writer and illustrator, 1974-76; free-lance artist and author, 1974—; Art Gallery of Ontario, Toronto, Ontario, information officer, 1976—. *Exhibitions:* Art Gallery of Ontario, 1986. *Member:* Writers Union of Canada, Author's Guild of America. *Awards, honors: Chin Chiang and the Dragon's Dance* received the Imperial Order of the Daughters of the Empire Book Award, 1984, Amelia Frances Howard-Gibbon Medal from the Canadian Association of Children's Librarians, 1985, and was included on the International Board on Books for Young People Honor List, 1986; *Very Last First Time* was exhibited at the Bologna International Children's Book Fair, and was chosen one of Child Study Association's Children's Books of the Year, both 1987.

WRITINGS—Juvenile: *Julie News* (self-illustrated), Kids Can Press, 1974; (with Angela Wood) *The Sandwich,* Kids Can Press, 1975, revised edition, 1985; *The Christmas Tree House* (self-illustrated), Kids Can Press, 1976; *Chin Chiang and the Dragon's Dance* (self-illustrated), Macmillan, 1984; *Sparrow's Song,* Viking, 1986; *Morgan the Magnificent* (self-illustrated), Macmillan, 1988.

Illustrator: Jan Andrews, *Very Last First Time* (Junior Literary Guild selection), Macmillan, 1985; J. Andrews, *Eva's Ice Adventure,* Methuen, 1986. Tim Wynne-Jones, *The Architect of* *the Moon,* Groundwood, 1988. Contributor to periodicals, including *Canadian Books for Young People.*

SIDELIGHTS: "Like most children growing up in Niagara Falls, Ontario in the 1950s, Sunday afternoons were spent with my family driving leisurely through the countryside counting cows, cars and the many species of trees that my brothers and I could see through the back window of our father's car. This activity was far removed from the one carried out by the fair percentage of large city dwellers of the 80s, many of whom bring their children indoors on Sunday afternoons to expansive spaces we know as art galleries and museums. Free to roam those hallowed halls children count the numbers of Renoirs and Modigliani's or the stuffed horn-rimmed owls and the variety and colour of rare duck's eggs to be found in a single glass case.

"My first exposure to the world of art came not through pictures hung on gallery and museum walls, but through the picture books my brothers and I carted out of our local library. Contained within the covers of each book were worlds so foreign and exciting that we marvelled at the daring of the characters, thrilled to their singular and collective bravery, and were often chillingly jerked back by great waves of fear that flushed through our veins. For children growing up in small-city Ontario, these books and their images carried us out of our sheltered environment to places we never imagined and only discovered within those treasured pages. Just as important they made us keenly aware of the fact that a painter was not merely someone who, like our father, picked up a brush or roller and stroked or rolled it over the walls of our house whenever the rooms had grown tired around the edges. But rather, an artist was someone who made dreams real.

"From those years there are three resonant images I carry around in my hip pocket like a child saving a dried worm for

IAN WALLACE

that special day. From Kenneth Grahame's *Wind in the Willows* comes the first two images. It is of Toad gleefully flying his bright orange bi-plane just seconds after a death defying crash into a now crumbling chimney. That image still delights me with the deliciousness of having achieved a feat of which my parents would NEVER HAVE APPROVED. My recklessness and independent abandon for property and propriety are abruptly brought into check by the second image that can still bring me into line: a repentent Toad having escaped from jail, ball and chain shackled to his ankle standing at the edge of freedom. The quiet solemnity of that moment in illustration and my life, glows as strongly today with the moonlit light it emitted three decades ago.

"The third image is taken from a book that has fallen from grace of late, *Little Black Sambo* by Helen Bannerman. As a child I was not aware of the racist tones educators today say are present in this cherished little book. I had not been exposed to racism, or to black people at that point in my life and I loved Sambo, his Momma and Papa, and was especially admiring and envious of his bright lime green umbrella, fine red jacket, short blue pants, and odd pointed shoes. A suit of such colour and quality I never imagined would be mine. But ohhhhh,

how I longed to have one just like Sambo's. Wouldn't I be grand when I walked around our neighborhood? Wouldn't everyone be envious of Me?

"The magic and power of that story, of course, is found in the act of the four tigers who having taken Little Black Sambo's clothes, grab hold of each others tails and quickly spin themselves into a frenzy, melting away 'and there was nothing left but a great big pool of melted butter (or ''ghi,'' as it is called in India) round the foot of a tree.' What delicious pancakes that butter made.

"Perhaps it was the power of those three images that captured my imagination as a child and forced me to draw the same magic with crayons and pencils over my bedroom walls, the sidewalk that ran from the front door of our house to the street, and even (sacrilege!) within the covers of books we had received as gifts. Certainly they were a catalyst. However, looking at the scenarios from a broader perspective, they allowed me the chance to emulate what I had seen, attempting to capture with my own hand the magic, the drama, and the excitement of those images. Imitating those characters and worlds would later enable me to look at my own world and describe

As the dance went on, Chin Chiang's feet moved more surely. ■ (From *Chin Chiang and the Dragon's Dance* by Ian Wallace. Illustrated by the author.)

Eva and her mother walked through the village. ■ (From *Chin Chiang and the Dragon's Dance* by Ian Wallace. Illustrated by the author.)

it through my own eyes as my talent emerged and developed. What better place to learn than at the feet of masters!

"My creative life hiccuped along dropping in and out with unpredictable regularity until the day at age thirteen when I gave up the notion of being a fireman and announced that I was going to be an artist. My parents' response was not surprising since they were consistently supportive of my brothers and me, no matter what wild dreams we espoused or what strange predicament we had managed to get ourselves into.

"'Of course you will,' they said.

"And that was that. The decision was made. And with it came the unconditional support of my parents, so crucial to anyone risking the possibility of living a creative life. This desire to become an artist did not diminish as my teenage years pro-

gressed, but helped to conquer those racing hormones, the battle against teenage angst and love, and the ability to pass countless hours alone in my room with only the sound of a pencil scratching over the surface of stacks of paper.

"My training has been mainly visual, but the single most important thing I've learned is that everything creative must have a purpose and a reason for its expression. My first three books were labors of love. Writing and illustrating do not come easily to me; the challenge is in the struggle. I have had the opportunity to read to 100,000 children across Canada, and I now understand how important books are to our lives. To watch children laugh or cry at a story with you is achieving a high level of communication."

Wallace wrote and illustrated *Chin Chiang and the Dragon's Dance* over a period of six years. "The first time I saw the dragon's dance I was overwhelmed by the dramatic images and exploding sounds. That New Year celebration felt as exciting that day as it must have been when first performed centuries ago. I decided then and there to tell a story encompassing this dance. Here was a tale steeped in tradition, passed down the generations. With every step, leap, twist, and curl of the dragon's tail those dancers breathed life into that mythic creature, bestowing favour on the Chinese community for the coming year. The animated faces of the crowd on that sunny February day told me not only was this an important celebration for the Chinese people, but also an expression of a universal human spirit.

"The task of creating this book was not completed in the short term, but over six years. Having endured that long gestation, I cannot stress enough the value of time—time to allow the right works to come forth, time to allow the drawings to formulate in the head before they appear on paper, and time to allow both to be as polished as a piece of rare jade.

"Visually, I wanted the illustrations to be the story's emotional barometer. This was achieved through the design, the changing perspectives, and the use of colour (watch the colour intensify toward the climax).

"This is a story with which people of all ages and races can identify. Remember, whether we are six or sixty-six we all have fears that must be overcome. If we can rid ourselves of those basic fears, anything becomes possible."

Illustrated *Very Last First Time* by Jan Andrews. "I could not believe my good fortune to have been presented with a story that captured my imagination so immediately, and would test my artistry and skill as an illustrator. Possessed by the sweeping grandeur and by an inherent fear of the under-ice world, I realized the necessity of portraying the young Inuit girl, Eva Padlyat, with dignity and respect due a race of people who live in harmony with the land. It was in the spirit world, as integral a part of the Tundra landscape as the ice, the snow and the animals found there, that I discovered the emotional link of illustrator to story, and the story to its reader.

"As much as I am in need of solitude when I am lost in the activity of writing or illustrating, I am also a social creature by nature, enjoying the comraderie of friends and people in general. Writing and illustrating provide me with the former while storytelling provides me with the latter. At times my life does appear somewhat schizophrenic, but for the most part, I love the balance of the two activities; writing and illustrating or storytelling.

"What a luxury it is to wake up each morning and know that this new day will not be the same as the one before and never the same as those that come after."

HOBBIES AND OTHER INTERESTS: Walking, movies, travel, dining out.

FOR MORE INFORMATION SEE: In Review, April, 1979; *Quill and Quire*, February, 1985; *Emergency Librarian*, February, 1985; *Canadian Children's Literature*, 48, 1987.

When I am grown to man's estate
I shall be very proud and great,
And tell the other girls and boys
Not to meddle with my toys.

—Robert Louis Stevenson

WALLACE, William Keith 1947- (Bill Wallace)

PERSONAL: Born August 1, 1947, in Chickasha, Okla.; son of Keith (retired from General Adjustment Bureau) and Mabel (a math teacher; maiden name, Burke) Wallace; married Carol Ann Priddle (an elementary school teacher), 1966; children: Laurie Beth, Amanda Nicole, Justin Keith. *Education:* Attended University of Oklahoma, 1965-69; University of Science and Arts of Oklahoma, B.A., 1971; South Western State University, M.S., 1974. *Politics:* Democrat. *Religion:* First Christian. *Home and Office:* Rte. 1, Box 91, Chickasha, Okla. 73018.

CAREER: Writer, 1971—; Lincoln Center School, Chickasha, Okla., teacher, 1971-76, assistant principal, 1972-76; Grand Avenue Elementary School, Chickasha, teacher, 1976-77; West School, Chickasha, principal, 1977-87. Lecturer at schools, libraries and universities. Member of Youth Services Advisory Council; member of Early Childhood Education Advisory Board, University of Science and Arts of Oklahoma. *Member:* Authors Guild, Cooperative Council of Oklahoma School Administrators. *Awards, honors:* Sequoyah Children's Book Award from the Oklahoma State Department of Education and Texas Bluebonnet Award from the Texas Library Association, both 1983, Central Missouri State University Award for Excellence in Children's Literature, 1984, Golden Sower Award from the Nebraska Library Association, 1985, all for *A Dog Called Kitty;* Central Missouri State University Award for Excellence in Children's Literature, 1984, and Pine Tree Book Award from West Bloomfield Public Schools, 1985, both for *Trapped in Death Cave.*

WRITINGS—Juvenile; all under name Bill Wallace; all published by Holiday House: *A Dog Called Kitty,* 1980; *Trapped in Death Cave,* 1984; *Shadow on the Snow,* 1985; *Ferret in the Bedroom, Lizards in the Fridge,* 1986; *Red Dog,* 1987; *Danger on Panther Peak,* Simon & Schuster, 1987.

Contributor of short stories to *Western Horseman, Hunting Dog,* and *Horse Lovers.*

WORK IN PROGRESS: Snot Stew.

SIDELIGHTS: "Although I hold the title 'Principal,' I consider myself first and foremost a *teacher*. I have had a few good teachers and they have been role models whom I have admired and strived to emulate. I hope I am a good teacher.

"As a teacher, I cannot overemphasize the importance of reading to the curriculum. In fact, as Jim Trelease stated, '. . . Reading is the curriculum.' I have found that reading aloud to students is one of the strongest motivational tools we have in creating a love of reading. The better job we do of teaching reading in the elementary schools, the better chance of success a student has—not only in school, but in life.

"I enjoyed reading good fiction to my fourth grade class. One year we had difficulty finding books to keep their attention. Since I had had some luck with articles and short stories, I decided to try my hand with a book for them to listen to. When I found how well they liked the stories, I decided to try them with various publishers. *Shadow on the Snow* was the first book I ever wrote for my students, and was the third to be published. *Trapped in Death Cave* was the second book I wrote for my class, and also the second to become a 'real book.' The third story, *A Dog Called Kitty* was the first one accepted for publication by Holiday House.

WILLIAM KEITH WALLACE

''When I left the classroom, and became a principal, I wrote for my third graders (who were the oldest students in my building). But, the fourth graders whom I taught never left me. They are still with me whenever I write.

''I get my ideas from combining childhood experiences with a *whole lot* of imagination. I also use ideas my students give me and try to keep my dialogue 'modern' by listening to them at school. I get ideas from my children at home, as well. *Snot Stew,* which is due for publication in spring of 1989, came from watching and listening to Nikki and Justin.

''Although I don't like flying, I enjoy traveling to new places and meeting new people. I bring my experience as a teacher with me when I do presentations to students or in-service activities for teachers and/or librarians. Due to these 'school experiences' I have a fabulous presentation which people familiar with school settings can quickly and easily relate to.

''I view my writing and my 'booktalk' presentations as extensions of my teaching. My books help students *want to* read. Some of the most gratifying letters I receive come from teachers who tell me that my stories have helped a student with reading problems become a reader.

''My family is very supportive and very loving. My wife always reads my stories to our children before we send them off to the publisher. Usually, she takes the manuscript to school and reads it to her kids, too, as do my teachers at West School.

''I enjoy hunting and fishing. I find myself much more at home in an outdoor setting than in a fancy French restaurant or a formal gathering.''

Wallace's works are included in the de Grummond Collection at the University of Southern Mississippi.

WALSH, George Johnston   1889-1981

PERSONAL: Born July 1, 1889, in Stormont, Nova Scotia, Canada; died in 1981; son of William (a miner) and Ester (a homemaker; maiden name, Hallet) Walsh; married Mamie Kathleen Hodgson, September 20, 1924; children: June, Huntley, Bloise, Irene. *Education:* Attended school in Stormont, Nova Scotia. *Politics:* Conservative. *Religion:* Methodist.

CAREER: Miner.

WRITINGS: Broad Horns, Lancelot, 1975.

WARRINER, John   1907(?)-1987

OBITUARY NOTICE: Born about 1907; died of cancer, July 29, 1987, in St. Croix, Virgin Islands. Educator and author. An instructor at both the college and high school levels, Warriner wrote two textbook series, ''Warriner's Handbook of English'' for grades nine and ten and ''Warriner's English Grammar and Composition'' intended for grades six through twelve. Together the two series have sold an estimated thirty million copies. In addition, he produced workbooks, test booklets, teachers' manuals, and compiled a short story anthology.

FOR MORE INFORMATION SEE: Obituaries: *New York Times,* August 8, 1987; *Chicago Tribune,* August 9, 1987; *Washington Post,* August 9, 1987.

MARTHA WESTON

WESTON, Martha   1947-

PERSONAL: Born January 16, 1947, in Asheville, N.C.; daughter of Nelson George (a professor) and Martha (a homemaker; maiden name, Patton) Hairston; married Richard Weston (a hospital consultant); children: Dory, Charley. *Education:* Attended University of North Carolina, Greensboro, 1965-66; University of Michigan, B.F.A., 1969. *Office:* P.O. Box 2544, San Anselmo, Calif. 94960. *Agent:* Dilys Evans, 1123 Broadway, Room 313, New York, N.Y. 10010.

CAREER: Free-lance illustrator, 1970—. Was a paste-up artist in Philadelphia, Pa., 1969-70. *Exhibitions:* Eagle Gallery, New York, N.Y., 1980, 1986. *Member:* Society of Children's Book Writers. *Awards, honors: The Book of Think; or, How to Solve a Problem Twice Your Size* was selected for the Children's Book Showcase, 1977; New York Academy of Sciences Children's Science Book Award, Younger Category, 1981, for *Bet You Can't; The Hanukkah Book* was selected a Notable Children's Trade Book in Social Studies, 1982; *Word Power* was selected one of Child Study Association's Children's Books of the Year, 1986, and *What Big Teeth You Have,* 1987.

WRITINGS: Peony's Rainbow (juvenile fiction; self-illustrated), Lothrop, 1981, published as *If I Only Had a Rainbow,* Xerox, 1982.

Illustrator; all juvenile: Jamie Jobb, *My Garden Companion: A Complete Guide for the Beginner* (nonfiction), Scribner, 1977; Em Riggs and Barbara Darpinian, *I Am a Cookbook* (nonfiction), St. Martin's, 1977 (Weston was not associated with earlier edition); Marne Wilkins, *The Long Ago Lake: A Child's Book of Nature Lore and Crafts* (nonfiction), Sierra Books, 1978.

Vicki Cobb and Kathy Darling, *Bet You Can't! Science Impossibilities to Fool You* (nonfiction; Junior Literary Guild selection), Lothrop, 1980; Miriam Schlein, *Lucky Porcupine!* (nonfiction), Four Winds Press, 1980; Stephen Manes, *The Hoople's Haunted House* (fiction), Delacorte, 1981; Dean Hughes, *Honestly, Myron* (fiction), Atheneum, 1982; Carl M. Wallace, *Should You Shut Your Eyes When You Kiss?; or, How to Survive "The Best Years of Your Life"* (nonfiction), Little, Brown, 1983; Pat Sharp, *Brain Power! Secrets of a*

Winning Team, Lothrop, 1984; Catherine B. Kaye, *Word Works: Why The Alphabet Is a Kid's Best Friend*, Little, Brown, 1985; Elizabeth Winthrop, *Lizzie and Harold*, Lothrop, 1985; *Esther Hautzig, Make It Special: Cards, Decorations, and Party Favors for Holiday and Other Celebrations*, Macmillan, 1986; Patricia Lauber, *What Big Teeth You Have!*, Harper, 1986; Norma Jean Sawicki, *Something for Mom*, Lothrop, 1987.

All written by Marilyn Burns: *The Book of Think; or, How to Solve a Problem Twice Your Size*, Little, Brown, 1976; *I Am Not a Short Adult! Getting Good at Being a Kid*, Little, Brown, 1977; *This Book Is about Time*, Little, Brown, 1978; *The Hanukkah Book*, Four Winds Press, 1981; *The Hink Pink Book;*

(From *The Book of Think; or, How to Solve a Problem Twice Your Size* by Marilyn Burns. Illustrated by Martha Weston.)

or, What Do You Call a Magician's Extra Bunny? (riddle book), Little Brown, 1981; *Math for Smarty Pants; or, Who Says Mathematicians Have Little Pig Eyes?*, Little, Brown, 1982.

WORK IN PROGRESS: Three books: one about maps and compasses, one about Valentine's Day, and one about adoption.

SIDELIGHTS: "As a kid I liked to play outside in the yard, not because I shared my parents' interest in gardening, but because I was looking for fairies under leaves. I felt sure they were living in the garden behind our house, but didn't know exactly where. So I searched and searched.

"For me the hardest thing about growing up was having to learn that make-believe wasn't true. When some older kids told me that Santa Claus didn't exist, I was shattered.

"I drew constantly and was often reprimanded in school for drawing pictures at the top of my spelling test instead of filling in the blanks with spelling words. Luckily, my parents were always encouraging, telling me my pictures were 'beautiful.' They were not artists themselves, but appreciated art and generally had the attitude that whatever career their children chose was okay. From the time I was very young I knew that I would be an artist when I grew up. I simply couldn't imagine another life.

"For the most part I grew up in Ann Arbor, Michigan, a college town where my father served as professor of zoology

The horse was bug-eyed at the strange creature on his back. ■ (From *The Long Ago Lake: A Child's Book of Nature Lore and Crafts* by Marne Wilkins. Illustrated by Martha Weston.)

at the University of Michigan. He told me once, 'You know, for years I thought I would have to do something serious, like chemistry. When I discovered I could make my living at something I loved, zoology, I was amazed and thrilled.' To have a father who loves his work was an important role model for me.

"From 1954 to 1956 we lived in the Philippines while my father worked for the World Health Organization. My mother educated my younger sister, brother and me with the Calvert System, a mail-order curriculum designed for Americans living abroad with no access to English-language schools. There was no television, which made books extremely important. Luckily, the Calvert Company sent lots of books for all reading levels and I devoured them all, reading many out loud to my younger brother and sister.

"When I was very young, I wanted all my books to be pretty. An imporant work for me was *The Faraway Tree*, which belonged to a neighbor of ours born and raised in India. In it, two children climb a magical tree. At the very top of the tree the clouds part and they find themselves in another world. *The Faraway Tree* was a series and in each trip to the top the children arrived in a different world. It was absolutely enchanting to me.

"Arthur Rackham's pictures gave me shivers. He was always true to the story. If the text said a witch was ugly, he made her ugly. If the text said someone was fat, he made the character fat. I mean, *The Ugly Duckling* makes no sense if the duckling is drawn to look cute! I was terribly sensitive to illustrators who 'cheated.' They destroyed the truth of the author's make-believe and I disliked them for it. Even as a budding artist, I preferred books with no pictures to one with bad pictures.

"When I was a junior in high school I went to Europe with a group from my French class. That summer I fell in love with cathedrals. And I looked at as many paintings as my eyes could bear. I also did things my parents would never have let me do, like eat lots of pastries and drink the water!

"Even though I knew I wanted to be an artist, I preferred to go to college for a liberal education. I was nervous about the prospect of being around artists all the time. The idea of dropping my French studies and never learning anything about history didn't appeal to me. The easy choice was the University of Michigan, but my parents insisted that all of us attend college out of state to get out on our own. I spent my freshman year at the University of North Carolina at Greensboro, which met my initial requirements—a fairly small school with a decent art department.

"The first semester I enrolled in an introduction to art course. The professor had us all go home and make an eight-and-a-half by eleven-inch collage constructed of magazine cut-outs. So we all went home and did that, turned in our work and waited for our grade. Next class he returned our collages, explaining that he had graded them by picking numbers out of a hat. 'I didn't so much as look at your collages,' he told us. We were outraged; he was nonplussed. 'I want you to understand that that is how the world is going to judge your art work. They're going to evaluate it by their own bizarre standards. Remember what it feels like, get used to it, and get on with your work.' Generally, we all felt crushed because we'd worked so hard. I think I was one of the few in class who caught on. I wanted to stand up and shout at my classmates, 'Don't you get it? This is terrific!' I could feel in my gut that I had learned a major lesson.

"My sophomore year I transferred to the University of Michigan. I think it is unfortunate that in our society we are expected to combine growing up with getting a college education. I hadn't had much of a social life in high school and wanted to make up for it in college (I was no longer the tallest person for miles around). I got involved with the campus Gilbert & Sullivan group, working on sets. The art department, which was separate from the rest of the campus, was like a world-within-a-world. I majored in printmaking because there was no drawing major. Etching was as close as I could get. The painting classes concentrated mostly on abstract work which didn't interest me too terribly much. I was a competent, but not a brilliant, printmaker. I wasn't sufficiently fascinated in the process, which is quite technical and complicated. I didn't like chemistry, and that's an important consideration in lithography, for example.

"I want immediacy in my work and so turned to water colors, but not with the idea of becoming an illustrator. Illustration was not something we even talked about. Great artists were *artists* not illustrators. I am amazed at the technical facility of young illustrators today who had benefit of bona fide illustration programs. I wish such a curriculum had existed when I was in school. As it was, I had only a vague idea of what I wanted to do, but no name for it. I knew I wanted to have a career where I could draw, but didn't have a clue where I might get work, what type of work I might do. My confusion was exacerbated by a teacher who apparently had failed to establish a commercial career and taught 'on the rebound,' so to speak. She had one message: 'It's a jungle out there.' In those days there was an unwritten, but uncontested, three-tier system. The real artists went to graduate school. The okay artists went into advertising and illustration. The dopes became art teachers.

"Of enormous help to me during my college years were two summer programs I participated in, one in Philadelphia, the other in Banff, Canada. It was important to work on ambitious, long-term projects rather than day-to-day assignments. In Philadelphia I worked in printmaking and drawing. In terms of my development, I did an important piece that summer—a series in which the work got physically bigger and bigger. That was really exciting. At Banff I studied painting, which never was my forte. But I learned a lot and got advice from my printing teacher that helped put my entire college career in perspective. 'Don't worry so much about *what* you study,' he said, 'but rather, find out who the best teachers are and study with them.'

"I went to New York after graduation. I found the city overwhelming and couldn't get a handle on how one could find a job, an apartment and a roommate all at once. When a friend who was starting graduate school in Philadelphia suggested I move in with her, I jumped at the chance. But I didn't have much luck finding a job. It was a vicious circle—no experience, no job; no job, how do you get experience? A printer I met suggested I apprentice myself to a design studio in order to learn paste-up and mechanicals. I did. For six weeks I worked for free and then was hired at a salary a friend called 'petty cash.' My take-home pay was fifty-six dollars a week. But it was enough; in fact, I had a savings account.

"Paste-up and mechanicals are dreary jobs to be sure, but in my opinion illustrators who have those skills are ahead of the game. It's extremely helpful to know what happens to drawings in reproduction.

"Not long afterward I moved to San Francisco where I found a job inking and painting for animation, many for 'Sesame Street.' I drove to an absolutely beautiful house in Mill Valley, drank tea and colored all day. I thought I'd died and gone to heaven for three-fifty an hour! Today a lot of animation is done on computer, but during the 70s more of the work was done by hand. The animator works from a cel, which is a piece of paper with register holes down one side and the drawing on it. A clear acetate is then laid down and registered on top of the drawing. You trace the drawing with ink. The painter will then turn over the acetate, check a color code and paint in the pigment.

"I was able to support myself with animation, paste-up and some illustration. The first book I did was for a series put out by Fearon Publishers for teachers in need of ideas for their bulletin boards. I got fifteen dollars a drawing. It was rather boring work—I shudder to think what those bulletin boards must have looked like—but I learned a lot about composition, page layout, design and working quickly!

"In 1972 I met Marilyn Burns with whom I collaborated on several books. She wrote and I illustrated *The I Hate Mathematics Book, The Book of Think; or, How to Solve a Problem Twice Your Size* among others. Our collaboration was very close, which is unusual since publishers generally keep the author and illustrator apart. Marilyn and I would sit down with the manuscript and go through it together talking about characters, situations, jokes. We spent a lot of time talking about her specific objectives for the book. I was the one who decided

(From *My Garden Companion: A Complete Guide for the Beginner* by Jamie Jobb. Illustrated by Martha Weston.)

$\mathbf{M}$ore than anything else, Lizzie wanted a best friend.

(From *Lizzie and Harold* by Elizabeth Winthrop. Illustrated by Martha Weston.)

where the text went and what the scale of the drawings and type would be. I had leeway to do crazy, off-the-wall stuff.

''Burns' philosophy is that anybody can solve problems if they are taught to think rather than memorize reams of materials. She also emphasizes an interdisciplinary approach to problem-solving, which I very much relate to. Just because you have to solve a physics problem doesn't mean you should tempo-

rarily forget everything you know about poetry, music and chemistry. The books I did with Marilyn Burns were extraordinarily satisfying.

''I think what I like best about being an illustrator is that one is called upon to solve a fixed problem. *Lizzie and Harold* is a good case in point. The manuscript provided no visual clues— no hints as to what the characters looked like, what they were wearing, what they do while they talk. The text is comprised almost completely of dialogue. So I had to make all those decisions as well as others, such as, what season it was. The first thing I did was to make thumbnail sketches of Lizzie and Harold. It took me a number of tries to get them to look exactly as I imagined. Then I did a spread, in pencil, so that the visual emphasis would remain on the characters. I was nervous at that early stage about being distracted by color. After I was secure that I wouldn't 'lose' Lizzie and Harold I addressed myself to color. I am generally unable to do one finished pencil sketch until I have roughed out the whole book with the typeface. I really need to feel the rhythm of the book before I can fill in details because the overall rhythm determines the 'weight' of each visual detail. A particularly wonderful challenge in *Lizzie and Harold* was to show the game of cat's cradle they play. I researched the game scrupulously and then drew in all the strings—madness! I did *Lizzie and Harold* in pencil and water color, which is now my favorite medium.

"For years I worked only in black and white since publishers rarely published full-color interior illustrations. Covers, maybe, but rarely an entire book. For covers I generally used color pencils although this sometimes posed problems in reproduction because colored pencils photograph rather weakly. Then in 1983 I was doing a book called *Brain Power: Secrets of a Winning Team* for Lothrop. I did a sketch, then colored it in colored pencil. The editor called to say, 'This is fine, but use paint instead.' Well, I was in total panic. I hadn't touched water colors since college, and I'm not a very confident painter. Not long before I had made the acquaintance of a water colorist whose work I admired enormously. I started taking lessons from her and was thrilled with the medium. I found that one can actually draw with a brush and render details too fine to be rendered with a graphite pencil.

"Among the most challenging problems facing an illustrator has to do with realism. I think I 'peaked' in realism in *What Big Teeth You Have!* For that book I did a tremendous amount of research, spending hours and hours poring over photographs of animals facing you with their mouths open. Not easy to come by. My main source was the picture file at the San Francisco Academy of Science.

"Although I consider myself first and foremost an illustrator, I really enjoyed writing *Peony's Rainbow*. I must say, however, that it was very difficult for me. The story originally came to me in an image rather than in words. I did a picture of Peony stuffing a rainbow in her pocket which I showed to my agent who immediately said, 'There's a book here. Why not go ahead and do it?' So I came up with a story to go with that picture by asking myself questions about the initial illustration. Why a rainbow? Why does Peony want it? Why does she want to put it in her pocket? What will happen to the rainbow? On the basis of my answers to those questions, I was able to do a draft of the whole story. It took me several drafts, each with fundamental changes, until I was satisfied. Sometimes a small revision in the form of a syllable, a sound, a shade of meaning makes a huge difference.

"One of the best things about being an illustrator is that you have a tangible record of your work. I can look at a book I did and remember all kinds of things that were happening in my life while I worked on it. My bookshelves hold more than just books, they hold my life."

—Based on an interview by Marguerite Feitlowitz

FOR MORE INFORMATION SEE: Marin Review, summer, 1987.

WILLIAMS, Vera B. 1927-

PERSONAL: Born January 28, 1927, in Hollywood, Calif.; daughter of Albert S. and Rebecca (Porringer) Baker; married Paul Williams (an architect, divorced, 1970); children: Sarah, Jennifer, Merce. *Education:* Black Mountain School, Black Mountain, N.C., graduated, 1949.

CAREER: Writer, graphic artist, educator, political activist. Gate Hill Cooperative Community, Stony Point, N.Y., co-founder, teacher, and member, 1953-70, and Collaberg School (alternative school for children), Stony Point, co-founder and teacher, 1960-69; Everdale School, Ontario, Canada, teacher and cook, 1970-73; author and illustrator of books for children, 1975—; Goddard College, Plainfield, Vt., instructor, 1980-82. Executive Committee War Register's League, 1984-87. *Member:* PEN, Author's Guild.

AWARDS, HONORS: Parents' Choice Award for illustrations in children's books from Parents' Choice Foundation, 1981, for *Three Days on a River in a Red Canoe; A Chair for My Mother* was selected one of *School Library Journal*'s Best Children's Books, 1982, and *Something Special for Me,* 1983; Caldecott Honor Book from the American Library Association, and *Boston Globe-Horn Book* Award for Illustration, both 1983, and Other Award from the *Children's Book Bulletin,* 1984, all for *A Chair for My Mother;* Jane Addams Children's Book Award Honor book from Jane Peace Association, 1985, for *Music, Music for Everyone;* Parents' Choice Award in Literature Notable Book, chosen one of Child Study Association of America's Children's Books of the Year, and one of *New York Times* Best Illustrated Books of the Year, all 1986, and *Boston Globe-Horn Book* Award Honor Book for illustration, 1987, both for *Cherries and Cherry Pits.*

WRITINGS—For children; all self-illustrated; all published by Greenwillow: *It's a Gingerbread House: Bake It, Build It, Eat*

VERA B. WILLIAMS

It!, 1978, large print edition, 1978; *The Great Watermelon Birthday*, 1980; *Three Days on a River in a Red Canoe* (Junior Literary Guild selection; Reading Rainbow selection), 1981, large print edition, 1981; *A Chair for My Mother* (ALA Notable Book; Reading Rainbow selection), 1982; *Something Special for Me* (sequel to *A Chair for My Mother*; ALA Notable Book), 1983, large print edition, 1983; *Music, Music for Everyone* (sequel to *Something Special for Me*; ALA Notable Book), 1984, large print edition, 1984; *Cherries and Cherry Pits* (ALA Notable Book; *Horn Book* honor list), 1986; *My Mother, Leah and George Sand*, 1986; (with daughter Jennifer) *Stringbean's Trip to the Shining Sea*, 1988. Also contributor of adult short story to *Tribe of Dina*.

Illustrator; for children: Remy Charlip and Lilian Moore, *Hooray for Me!*, Parents Magazine Press, 1975; Barbara Brenner, *Our Class Presents Ostrich Feathers: A Play in Two Acts*, Parents Magazine Press, 1978.

ADAPTATIONS: "A Chair for My Mother" (read-along cassette; filmstrip with cassette), Random House; "Something Special for Me" (cassette), Random House.

SIDELIGHTS: **January 28, 1927.** Born in California and grew up in New York City. "My parents were originally from Russia and Poland. My father arrived in this country when he was

sixteen, my mother as a small child. They met and married in America. Both raised in Orthodox Jewish families, they remained culturally Jewish though anti-religion. Politically they were left-wing, which is to say, they held dear the original socialist and community aspirations for a better life for the working class. I grew up in a hopeful climate.

"My mother started the parents association at P.S. 4, the Bronx and tried to make its work relevant to our depression times— food for kids who came to school hungry, medical, dental and psychological help. She campaigned to remove teachers who showed negative attitudes toward the children of the poor (which we all were at that time). One of my teachers, for instance, used to tell us, 'If your fathers got up earlier, they'd find jobs.' During the Depression she said this!

"Looking back, P.S. 4, the one of some nine or ten I went to the longest, was an O.K. school. It was originally a vocational school with sewing and cooking facilities. It had a swimming pool in the basement. We had a newly introduced 'activities program' with extra staff provided by the W.P.A. (Works Progress Administration). We had one black teacher, Mr. Lashley (the only one I can recall from any school I went to). Many teachers were imaginative and devoted to the children, but school was still regimented. And I hated keeping quiet and sitting still.

My mother works as a waitress in the Blue Tile Diner. ■ (From *A Chair for My Mother* by Vera B. Williams. Illustrated by the author.)

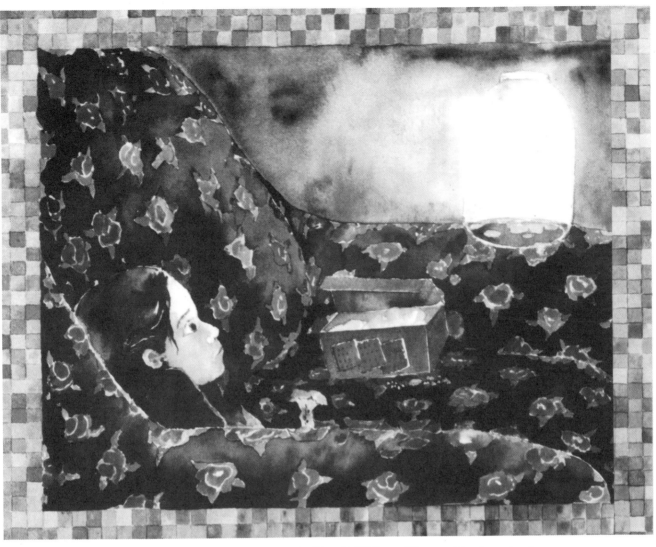

(From *Music, Music for Everyone* by Vera B. Williams. Illustrated by the author.)

"My parents half supported a certain amount of rebelliousness. They didn't think obedience was the end-all of growing up. I remember occasionally playing hooky. We had a cohort in the playground director across the street who also offered arts and crafts supplies and a place for projects.

"Our family, like thousands of others at the time, had a hard time making a living, staying together, paying rent, resisting despair. My sister Naomi, two years older, and I lived in several foster homes and in a Children's Home (of which I have vivid memories, some quite painful). We moved around a lot both in California and New York City. Part of this was the Depression with its plentiful empty apartments and shortage of rent payers; a lot was my father's restlessness.

"My parents encouraged my sister and me to be doing supervised, creative activities. They had their own ideas of culture completely different from the mainstream—penny candy, pop music, the Green Hornet, Superman, and hanging around the street were not for us. At one time, I grew tomatoes, peas and beets in a little plot in the neighborhood garden in Crotona Park. Our whole family belonged to the Bronx House, a settlement house, where we became involved with art, dramatics, crafts, games and dance with a student of Isadora Duncan.

"The Works Progress Administration sponsored an exhibit of art all over the country for adults and kids at the Modern Museum of Art in New York City. They entered my paintings called 'Yentas' (Jewish for busybodies). I stood beside it hoping to be asked about it. Eleanor Roosevelt visited the show and asked me, 'And what are Yen-tazz?' I would have talked with her all day if they would have let me. She and I and 'Yentas' were shown together in that weeks 'Movietone News' at the local cinemas." ("Yentas" was exhibited again in 1986 at the Bronx Museum's "Jewish Life in the First 50 Years of the Century.")

"My parents were convinced Naomi and I had special talents and were always on the lookout for educational opportunities. The school 'visiting' teacher, forerunner of the school psychologist, referred us to The Clinic for Gifted Children at New York University. Dr. Harvey Zorbaugh introduced us to the art classes of Florence Cane on the 24th floor of Rockefeller Center, later crammed into the psych offices at N.Y.U. and finally in Mrs. Crane's own studio on Fourth Street.

"We travelled downtown from the Bronx by ourselves on the subway every Saturday morning. I attended these art classes for eight or nine years, and must add, *always* without charge! Many times we went to the main children's room at the Forty-Second Street Library and to the zoo and carousel in Central Park afterwards. Often one of our parents would meet us. Both park and library were paradise.

First she makes a dot on the paper. Then she draws a line out from that dot. ■ (From *Cherries and Cherry Pits* by Vera B. Williams. Illustrated by the author.)

"Mrs. Crane was way ahead of her time as an art teacher. I didn't know it then but she was part of an avant garde circle close to the Alfred Stieglitz group. We would start many sessions with dance movement. 'Scribbles' were an art exercise designed to keep our work spontaneous. After a trip to India, she brought with her a new-found sense of sound and color interaction. She would have us make sounds of different pitches and timbres and while in the grip of that sound choose colors and do our work. We were shy and awkward about this. But her effort was always to free us from the habitual." In *The Artist in Each of Us* Cane writes about her methods, using case studies of her students, including Williams, who appears as Linda.

"We spent a lot of time outdoors on weekends. My father would hike with us from our home in central Bronx to Orchard

Beach, or to the Palisades, or Riverdale, etc. Often there wasn't money for two-way fares and treats. We didn't mind. We all loved to walk, to make little fires and picnic. One time my father swam across the Hudson at the George Washington Bridge. He was a strong swimmer but he was carried way down by the current until we lost sight of him—scary, but typical. He was a physically very active man. He loved to sing and to dance as much as he loved political argument. He was also reckless and inconsiderate at times. Our family life was intense with much love and caring, along with fighting, competition and worry. My mother held the family together but I was my 'father's girl.' Later, through the insights of the women's movement, I came to see that being daddy's girl had eclipsed my mother's strength and love.

"I followed my sister to the High School of Music and Art. It was new then, still small and with a special spirit. I was an art student, with a special interest in history, English, current affairs. I wrote a long research piece on how there was no real evidence to support racial inequality for this magazine.

"I was surprised at the number of boys, in particular, who were set upon an 'art career.' I'd never thought in those terms. I went on making things, assuming I'd always have creative solutions to problems set before me. I wrote, illustrated, and bound my first book at Music and Art about an enormous banana that feeds an entire family."

Attended Black Mountain College in North Carolina. "It was a nontraditional setting rooted in John Dewey and Bauhaus, a unique art school in Germany that has contributed much to modern art and architecture. Our time at Black Mountain was divided between liberal arts, art, and practical work. I worked in the milk room on the college farm, made butter and cottage cheese. As an art student, I painted, drew, studied color, did constructions, took weaving, set type along with my liberal arts classes. We had an old printing press that several students parleyed into a small production shop. I designed, set type and printed brochures and programs for the college as part of my graduation project. I was strongly drawn to black and white and to arts such as calligraphy, pen and ink and type design. I studied the history of type, and wrote one of my final papers on the color black. Black Mountain brought in outside examiners—in my case, sculptor Richard Lippold—to evaluate student work for graduation and to conduct oral exams and view the students work. It was a good system. It made you

feel that your work extended beyond the college and into the world."

Met and married Paul Williams while at college. The young couple settled in Boston to continue their education—he at Harvard; she at Boston Museum School. "I was free to do a lot more art than I actually did during that period, but I had a strong desire to be part of the community and also to teach children, and I had the confusions and lack of confidence so many women (with notable exceptions) had at that time about a career in the arts.

"I put a lot of artistic energy into cooking, sewing, rebuilding the basement in which we lived, and organizing free children's activities on my block. Children have always been a creative focus for me."

Founded, with husband and a group of friends from Black Mountain College, an intentional community at Stony Point, New York. "Most of the first members were artists, musicians, writers and craftspeople. My husband designed and built the houses but many of us also worked on some aspects of the building. (The houses and land were owned in common.) We shared some communal activities—day care, work on the property, decision making, meetings! meetings! There was much art and related creative activity in my daily life. I helped build our house, working on the stone floor and stone wall and laying tiles, painting walls, etc. I made a mosaic mural for one of the buildings. We held an annual picnic for which we

I tried on skates. ■ (From *Something Special for Me* by Vera B. Williams. Illustrated by the author.)

prepared weeks long transforming the grounds with our decorative works. I made drawings, paintings, took calligraphy lessons and did woodcuts at the Pratt Graphic Arts workshop. I kept notebooks of poetry and sketches. I cooked and baked for many people, worked with children and gardened. It took a long time to come to feel that a career in writing and art was also on my agenda.

"The gifts I offered were elaborate. I received much approval for these things, which rewarded my putting so much energy into them. I was raised progressively, but always assumed that a lot of my energy would go into homemaking. I moved quickly toward marriage and having children as everyone around us in 1949 was urging women to do.

"There were other factors involved in my not pursuing a career as well. For one thing, I was very much against doing anything commercial; to mix commerce and art, I believed was to violate arts. Also, my husband came from a wealthy family and we had a private income. We tried to live according to the ideal of communal anonymity with which we were imbued at Black Mountain. Gate Hill provided me with as many outlets as I could handle. The Barker School, founded by Robert Barker (later known as the Collaberg School), in which we were deeply involved was particularly important to me. I taught nature study, art, writing, cooking, a number of crafts. Having a lot of responsibility for a small, independent and struggling school, I was to learn, is a consuming activity.

"In 1970, the Collaberg School closed and my life in Stony Point came to a turning point. This was a definite demarcation in my life because I left much behind—drawings, paintings, objects, friends, a community. My plan was to go away for a year and give everything a rest. That one year stretched into nine. I went to Canada to become a cook in a school much like Collaberg. 'I won't get involved in running the school,' I thought, 'I'll do my work and sort out my goals.' But true to form, I ended up extremely busy: I cooked two meals a day for forty people, started a bakery, made butter, canned and froze vegetables, helped with the butchering. But I would also withdraw from this busy-ness and people-centered work to do my work. I would write and draw at a feverish pace sometimes writing and drawing simultaneously. I believe the two are very close, much more alike than different.

"It was during this time that I took up canoeing, making many trips on Ontario rivers with friends and finally a long trip on the Yukon river, Yukon Territory, Canada. These adventures led to *Three Days on a River in a Red Canoe.*

"I moved from my wonderful houseboat to Toronto after three years. I missed my family on the East Coast, but I wasn't yet ready to leave Canada, a wonderful country whose praises are not sung loud enough. I lived in Toronto in a cooperative household with two families and their children. We all helped with the children and household. I joined the Toronto Women's Writing Collective, wrote poetry, adult short stories, and continued with children's books. To me, all three have never been very separate or different.

"In 1979 I moved back to New York . . . this time into New York City."

Williams' illustrations have all the freshness of the paintings and drawings she did as a child. "When I first started doing my books for children, I tried to remember the pictures from my own childhood—how I did them, what I was feeling when I made them. In all of my children's books, I've worked from these early artistic impulses. Of course, it's not entirely the

same. Many of my illustrations appear to have been 'dashed off'—and so they were . . . some of them over and over. Sometimes I select one entire drawing from a number of attempts, sometimes, I cut and paste parts from various drawings. When the process is long, I try to stay faithful to my main intent, which is to capture some emotional essence from the story, usually rooted in my own life, and to keep the clarity of color and the spontaneity."

When asked about the research she does for her pictures, Williams answered, "Once in a while I have a child pose for some detail. For *Music, Music for Everyone,* I rented an accordion, got a book on how to play it and tried my hand slightly. That may have been a laborious way of going about things—but it helps me to know how it feels to hold an accordion (or in other cases a violin or to kneel and draw, etc.) However indirectly, I believe that knowledge shows up in the drawings. I also use books and pictures from the New York Public Library picture collection.

"I tend to revise my stories less than my drawings. It's mostly a specific section of a story, often the beginning and the end, for which I do many drafts and sometimes wait many weeks for the right solution. Here too, I work toward clarity and freshness and emotional candor."

Kindness, generosity, and adventure abound in Williams' stories. Her five-hundred-mile canoe trip on the Yukon River was the inspiration for *Three Days on a River in a Red Canoe,* in which two mothers take their son and daughter canoeing and camping. "My books are not 'political' in a preaching sense. They are, however, deliberately aware of the real life—varicolored peoples, women-centered families, people working for a living and worrying about money, neighborhood loyalties. I try not to write political tracts though I am very committed to ending militarism and to total equality for women and people of color. Even when I write leaflets, I try to write in a direct, fresh and personal way from experiences and feelings I have lived. I am thankful I grew up in a home where politics meant the politics of making a better life for everyone. Politics was not 'dirty' or merely electoral as many people see it. It was part of our daily lives as well as our dreams. It made us hopeful. I feel hopefulness has to be in children's literature."

A Chair for My Mother is about a girl who saves her money to help buy her mother a comfortable chair in which to relax after her day of work at the diner. "When I got the inspiration for the book, I had the wonderful feeling that I now had the power, as a writer and an illustrator, to change the past into something happier than it really was, and to offer it as a gift to my mother's memory. The image of that big, comfortable chair is, I think, a symbol of some great maternal force looking after Rosa, her mother and grandmother. I have done other drawings and paintings of chairs sometimes like the one in *A Chair for My Mother.* It's an important subject for me. At about the same time I wrote an adult story, *My Mother, Leah and George Sand,* also an exploration and a gift to my mother's memory.

Williams is a regular visiting writer/artist at elementary schools and librarians' and teachers' conferences. "When I illustrate in front of children, I draw the characters, black, tan, ivory—whatever. I don't say 'this is a black child, an Indian,' etc. just as we don't say 'this is a white child.' I talk with them about color for trees and sky—the colors you need for skin tones. 'What colors do we need for skin color?' I'll ask. The answer is almost always peach or pink. When that answer comes from a brown face, as it sometimes does, it breaks my heart. Then I ask, 'How am I going to paint the skin of these children,' pointing to a page in one of my books where four differently colored children sit together in the big chair? Finally, kids begin to see that you can't even paint a peach properly with just peach color, and that we along with everything else, are 'vari-hued.' Another thing I do is draw a face with them, trying to examine what makes it seem more a girl or more a boy to them. Along the way we look at some of the cliches they accept even though they can see how they themselves and the kids around them contradict those cliches. For instance, as soon as I put eyelashes on a drawing they all yell, 'it's a girl.'' Then I have to ask them if boys come without eyelashes. This always ends in laughter and, I trust, some new thoughts.''

Williams has consistently devoted time to the causes of nonviolence, children, women and the environment (not necessarily in that order). She serves on the executive committee of the War Resisters' League (a national secular pacifist organization). In 1981 she was one of some 250 women arrested for peacefully blocking the entrance to the Pentagon as part of a women's demonstration. She served a one-month prison term in Alderson Federal Penitentiary. ''I didn't 'like' it, but it was an important addition to my education. We mixed with the other prisoners. Some were there for violent acts. We were there for opposing violence. We got a glimpse of the pain and injustice of prison life. I had previously only been in jail overnight—in resistance to the 'pseudo' bomb shelter drills we used to have in New York state in the early 1950s and then to the war in Vietnam. In 1984 I was jailed with fifty-four other women in a junior high school in Seneca Falls, New York (no room in the jail). A walk I participated in from the several historical sites of the early women's movement to a woman's peace camp outside the gates of the Seneca Army Depot was blocked by local people. Arrested for our 'protection,' we were charged and held five days. The charges were later dismissed.

''I don't make a point of ending up in jail. But if you try to put your hopes and beliefs for a better life into effect, arrest *is* sometimes a hazard. I am asked if I think any of this helps or works. I say, in the short run, we can't know, but many things we take for granted have been gained by the similar actions of people like myself—the end of child labor, more rights for black people, the vote for women, the end of the Vietnam War are a few. As a person who works for children, who raised three children, who is about to have a grandchild, I have to be able to say I did something to try to save our planet from destruction. It is my faith that we will. I find living mysterious, difficult and wonderous. I hope that is in my books somehow.''

—Based on an interview by Marguerite Feitlowitz

HOBBIES AND OTHER INTERESTS: Art, teaching, parenting, food, nature, justice and social issues.

FOR MORE INFORMATION SEE: Sally Holmes Holtze, editor, *Fifth Book of Junior Authors and Illustrators*, H. W. Wilson, 1983.

YOUNGS, Betty 1934-1985

PERSONAL: Born October 1, 1934, in North Staffordshire, England; died January 3, 1985; married Edward G. Youngs (a research soil physicist), 1958; children: Richard. *Education:* Attended Chelsea School of Pharmacy, University of London.

BETTY YOUNGS

CAREER: Employed for some years as a hospital chief pharmacist; began creating fabric pictures, about 1969; author and illustrator of books for children.

WRITINGS—Picture books for children; self-illustrated; published by Bodley Head: *Farm Animals*, 1976; *Humpty Dumpty and Other First Rhymes*, 1977; *One Panda: An Animal Counting Book*, 1980; *Pink Pigs in Mud: A Colour Book*, 1982; *Two by Two*, 1985.

SIDELIGHTS: Following marriage and the birth of her son, Betty Youngs abandoned her career as a pharmacist and began to nurture a love for art that had existed since childhood. Her fabric pictures were sold privately, and then as greeting cards. In 1976 Bodley Head published her first book, *Farm Animals*, a board book for babies. Youngs won reviewers' praise for her imaginative use of textiles and needlecraft in all her children's books. Combining a variety of fabrics such as lace, wool, tweeds, and furs, as well as embroidery silks, her pictures have a ''touchable'' quality that is especially appealing to preschoolers.

FOR MORE INFORMATION SEE: Lee Kingman and others, compilers, *Illustrators of Children's Books: 1967-1976*, Horn Book, 1978. Obituaries: *Junior Bookshelf*, April, 1985.

Cumulative Indexes

Illustrations Index

(In the following index, the number of the volume in which an illustrator's work appears is given *before* the colon, and the page on which it appears is given *after* the colon. For example, a drawing by Adams, Adrienne appears in Volume 2 on page 6, another drawing by her appears in Volume 3 on page 80, another drawing in Volume 8 on page 1, and another drawing in Volume 15 on page 107.)

YABC

Index citations including this abbreviation refer to listings appearing in *Yesterday's Authors of Books for Children*, also published by the Gale Research Company, which covers authors who died prior to 1960.

Aas, Ulf, *5:* 174
Abbé, S. van. *See* van Abbé, S.
Abel, Raymond, *6:* 122; *7:* 195; *12:* 3; *21:* 86; *25:* 119
Abrahams, Hilary, *26:* 205; *29:* 24-25; *53:* 61
Abrams, Kathie, *36:* 170
Abrams, Lester, *49:* 26
Accorsi, William, *11:* 198
Acs, Laszlo, *14:* 156; *42:* 22
Adams, Adrienne, *2:* 6; *3:* 80; *8:* 1; *15:* 107; *16:* 180; *20:* 65; *22:* 134-135; *33:* 75; *36:* 103, 112; *39:* 74
Adams, John Wolcott, *17:* 162
Adamson, George, *30:* 23, 24
Adkins, Alta, *22:* 250
Adkins, Jan, *8:* 3
Adler, Peggy, *22:* 6; *29:* 31
Adler, Ruth, *29:* 29
Adragna, Robert, *47:* 145
Agard, Nadema, *18:* 1
Agre, Patricia, *47:* 195
Ahl, Anna Maria, *32:* 24
Aichinger, Helga, *4:* 5, 45
Aitken, Amy, *31:* 34
Akaba, Suekichi, *46:* 23; *53:* 127
Akasaka, Miyoshi, *YABC 2:* 261
Akino, Fuku, *6:* 144
Alain, *40:* 41
Alajalov, *2:* 226
Albrecht, Jan, *37:* 176
Albright, Donn, *1:* 91
Alcorn, John, *3:* 159; *7:* 165; *31:* 22; *44:* 127; *46:* 23, 170
Alda, Arlene, *44:* 24
Alden, Albert, *11:* 103
Aldridge, Andy, *27:* 131
Alex, Ben, *45:* 25, 26
Alexander, Lloyd, *49:* 34
Alexander, Martha, *3:* 206; *11:* 103; *13:* 109; *25:* 100; *36:* 131
Alexeieff, Alexander, *14:* 6; *26:* 199
Aliki. *See* Brandenberg, Aliki
Allamand, Pascale, *12:* 9
Allan, Judith, *38:* 166
Alland, Alexander, *16:* 255
Alland, Alexandra, *16:* 255
Allen, Gertrude, *9:* 6
Allen, Graham, *31:* 145
Allen, Pamela, *50:* 25, 26-27, 28
Allen, Rowena, *47:* 75

Allison, Linda, *43:* 27
Almquist, Don, *11:* 8; *12:* 128; *17:* 46; *22:* 110
Aloise, Frank, *5:* 38; *10:* 133; *30:* 92
Althea. *See* Braithwaite, Althea
Altschuler, Franz, *11:* 185; *23:* 141; *40:* 48; *45:* 29
Ambrus, Victor G., *1:* 6-7, 194; *3:* 69; *5:* 15; *6:* 44; *7:* 36; *8:* 210; *12:* 227; *14:* 213; *15:* 213; *22:* 209; *24:* 36; *28:* 179; *30:* 178; *32:* 44, 46; *38:* 143; *41:* 25, 26, 27, 28, 29, 30, 31, 32; *42:* 87; *44:* 190
Ames, Lee J., *3:* 12; *9:* 130; *10:* 69; *17:* 214; *22:* 124
Amon, Aline, *9:* 9
Amoss, Berthe, *5:* 5
Amundsen, Dick, *7:* 77
Amundsen, Richard E., *5:* 10; *24:* 122
Ancona, George, *12:* 11
Anderson, Alasdair, *18:* 122
Anderson, Brad, *33:* 28
Anderson, C. W., *11:* 10
Anderson, Carl, *7:* 4
Anderson, Doug, *40:* 111
Anderson, Erica, *23:* 65
Anderson, Laurie, *12:* 153, 155
Anderson, Wayne, *23:* 119; *41:* 239
Andrew, John, *22:* 4
Andrews, Benny, *14:* 251; *31:* 24
Angel, Marie, *47:* 22
Angelo, Valenti, *14:* 8; *18:* 100; *20:* 232; *32:* 70
Anglund, Joan Walsh, *2:* 7, 250-251; *37:* 198, 199, 200
Anno, Mitsumasa, *5:* 7; *38:* 25, 26-27, 28, 29, 30, 31, 32
Antal, Andrew, *1:* 124; *30:* 145
Apple, Margot, *33:* 25; *35:* 206; *46:* 81; *53:* 8
Appleyard, Dev, *2:* 192
Aragonés, Sergio, *48:* 23, 24, 25, 26, 27
Araneus, *40:* 29
Archer, Janet, *16:* 69
Ardizzone, Edward, *1:* 11, 12; *2:* 105; *3:* 258; *4:* 78; *7:* 79; *10:* 100; *15:* 232; *20:* 69, 178; *23:* 223; *24:* 125; *28:* 25, 26, 27, 28, 29, 30, 31, 33, 34, 35, 36, 37;

31: 192, 193; *34:* 215, 217; *YABC 2:* 25
Arenella, Roy, *14:* 9
Armer, Austin, *13:* 3
Armer, Laura Adams, *13:* 3
Armer, Sidney, *13:* 3
Armitage, David, *47:* 23
Armitage, Eileen, *4:* 16
Armstrong, George, *10:* 6; *21:* 72
Arno, Enrico, *1:* 217; *2:* 22, 210; *4:* 9; *5:* 43; *6:* 52; *29:* 217, 219; *33:* 152; *35:* 99; *43:* 31, 32, 33; *45:* 212, 213, 214
Arnosky, Jim, *22:* 20
Arrowood, Clinton, *12:* 193; *19:* 11
Arting, Fred J., *41:* 63
Artzybasheff, Boris, *13:* 143; *14:* 15; *40:* 152, 155
Aruego, Ariane, *6:* 4
See also Dewey, Ariane
Aruego, Jose, *4:* 140; *6:* 4; *7:* 64; *33:* 195; *35:* 208
Asch, Frank, *5:* 9
Ashby, Gail, *11:* 135
Ashby, Gwynneth, *44:* 26
Ashley, C. W., *19:* 197
Ashmead, Hal, *8:* 70
Assel, Steven, *44:* 153
Astrop, John, *32:* 56
Atene, Ann, *12:* 18
Atherton, Lisa, *38:* 198
Atkinson, J. Priestman, *17:* 275
Atkinson, Wayne, *40:* 46
Attebery, Charles, *38:* 170
Atwood, Ann, *7:* 9
Augarde, Steve, *25:* 22
Austerman, Miriam, *23:* 107
Austin, Margot, *11:* 16
Austin, Robert, *3:* 44
Auth, Tony, *51:* 5
Averill, Esther, *1:* 17; *28:* 39, 40, 41
Axeman, Lois, *2:* 32; *11:* 84; *13:* 165; *22:* 8; *23:* 49
Ayer, Jacqueline, *13:* 7
Ayer, Margaret, *15:* 12; *50:* 120

B.T.B. *See* Blackwell, Basil T.
Babbitt, Bradford, *33:* 158
Babbitt, Natalie, *6:* 6; *8:* 220
Bachem, Paul, *48:* 180

Back, George, *31:* 161
Bacon, Bruce, *4:* 74
Bacon, Paul, *7:* 155; *8:* 121; *31:* 55;
    50: 42
Bacon, Peggy, *2:* 11, 228; *46:* 44
Baker, Alan, *22:* 22
Baker, Charlotte, *2:* 12
Baker, Jeannie, *23:* 4
Baker, Jim, *22:* 24
Baldridge, Cyrus LeRoy, *19:* 69;
    44: 50
Balet, Jan, *11:* 22
Balian, Lorna, *9:* 16
Ballantyne, R. M., *24:* 34
Ballis, George, *14:* 199
Baltzer, Hans, *40:* 30
Bang, Molly Garrett, *24:* 37, 38
Banik, Yvette Santiago, *21:* 136
Banner, Angela. *See* Maddison, Angela
    Mary
Bannerman, Helen, *19:* 13, 14
Bannon, Laura, *6:* 10; *23:* 8
Baptist, Michael, *37:* 208
Bare, Arnold Edwin, *16:* 31
Bare, Colleen Stanley, *32:* 33
Bargery, Geoffrey, *14:* 258
Barker, Carol, *31:* 27
Barker, Cicely Mary, *49:* 50, 51
Barkley, James, *4:* 13; *6:* 11; *13:* 112
Barks, Carl, *37:* 27, 28, 29, 30-31, 32,
    33, 34
Barling, Tom, *9:* 23
Barlow, Perry, *35:* 28
Barlowe, Dot, *30:* 223
Barlowe, Wayne, *37:* 72
Barner, Bob, *29:* 37
Barnes, Hiram P., *20:* 28
Barnett, Moneta, *16:* 89; *19:* 142;
    31: 102; *33:* 30, 31, 32; *41:* 153
Barney, Maginel Wright, *39:* 32, 33,
    34; *YABC 2:* 306
Barnum, Jay Hyde, *11:* 224; *20:* 5;
    37: 189, 190
Barrauds, *33:* 114
Barrer-Russell, Gertrude, *9:* 65; *27:* 31
Barrett, Angela, *40:* 136, 137
Barrett, John E., *43:* 119
Barrett, Ron, *14:* 24; *26:* 35
Barron, John N., *3:* 261; *5:* 101;
    14: 220
Barrows, Walter, *14:* 268
Barry, Ethelred B., *37:* 79;
    YABC 1: 229
Barry, James, *14:* 25
Barry, Katharina, *2:* 159; *4:* 22
Barry, Robert E., *6:* 12
Barry, Scott, *32:* 35
Bartenbach, Jean, *40:* 31
Barth, Ernest Kurt, *2:* 172; *3:* 160;
    8: 26; *10:* 31
Barton, Byron, *8:* 207; *9:* 18; *23:* 66
Barton, Harriett, *30:* 71
Bartram, Robert, *10:* 42
Bartsch, Jochen, *8:* 105; *39:* 38
Bascove, Barbara, *45:* 73
Baskin, Leonard, *30:* 42, 43, 46, 47;
    49: 125, 126, 128, 129, 133
Bass, Saul, *49:* 192
Bassett, Jeni, *40:* 99

Batchelor, Joy, *29:* 41, 47, 48
Bate, Norman, *5:* 16
Bates, Leo, *24:* 35
Batet, Carmen, *39:* 134
Batherman, Muriel, *31:* 79; *45:* 185
Battaglia, Aurelius, *50:* 44
Batten, John D., *25:* 161, 162
Battles, Asa, *32:* 94, 95
Bauernschmidt, Marjorie, *15:* 15
Baum, Allyn, *20:* 10
Baum, Willi, *4:* 24-25; *7:* 173
Baumann, Jill, *34:* 170
Baumhauer, Hans, *11:* 218; *15:* 163,
    165, 167
Bayley, Dorothy, *37:* 195
Bayley, Nicola, *40:* 104; *41:* 34, 35
Baynes, Pauline, *2:* 244; *3:* 149;
    13: 133, 135, 137-141; *19:* 18,
    19, 20; *32:* 208, 213, 214;
    36: 105, 108
Beame, Rona, *12:* 40
Beard, Dan, *22:* 31, 32
Beard, J. H., *YABC 1:* 158
Bearden, Romare, *9:* 7; *22:* 35
Beardsley, Aubrey, *17:* 14; *23:* 181
Bearman, Jane, *29:* 38
Beaton, Cecil, *24:* 208
Beaucé, J. A., *18:* 103
Beck, Charles, *11:* 169; *51:* 173
Beck, Ruth, *13:* 11
Becker, Harriet, *12:* 211
Beckett, Sheilah, *25:* 5; *33:* 37, 38
Beckhoff, Harry, *1:* 78; *5:* 163
Beckman, Kaj, *45:* 38, 39, 40, 41
Beckman, Per, *45:* 42, 43
Bedford, F. D., *20:* 118, 122; *33:* 170;
    41: 220, 221, 230, 233
Bee, Joyce, *19:* 62
Beeby, Betty, *25:* 36
Beech, Carol, *9:* 149
Beek, *25:* 51, 55, 59
Beerbohm, Max, *24:* 208
Behr, Joyce, *15:* 15; *21:* 132; *23:* 161
Behrens, Hans, *5:* 97
Beisner, Monika, *46:* 128, 131
Belden, Charles J., *12:* 182
Belina, Renate, *39:* 132
Bell, Corydon, *3:* 20
Beltran, Alberto, *43:* 37
Bemelmans, Ludwig, *15:* 19, 21
Benda, Wladyslaw T., *15:* 256;
    30: 76, 77; *44:* 182
Bendick, Jeanne, *2:* 24
Bennett, F. I., *YABC 1:* 134
Bennett, Jill, *26:* 61; *41:* 38, 39;
    45: 54
Bennett, Rainey, *15:* 26; *23:* 53
Bennett, Richard, *15:* 45; *21:* 11, 12,
    13; *25:* 175
Bennett, Susan, *5:* 55
Bentley, Carolyn, *46:* 153
Bentley, Roy, *30:* 162
Benton, Thomas Hart, *2:* 99
Berelson, Howard, *5:* 20; *16:* 58;
    31: 50
Berenstain, Jan, *12:* 47
Berenstain, Stan, *12:* 47
Berg, Joan, *1:* 115; *3:* 156; *6:* 26, 58
Berg, Ron, *36:* 48, 49; *48:* 37, 38

Berger, William M., *14:* 143;
    YABC 1: 204
Bering, Claus, *13:* 14
Berkowitz, Jeanette, *3:* 249
Bernadette. *See* Watts, Bernadette
Bernath, Stefen, *32:* 76
Bernstein, Michel J., *51:* 71
Bernstein, Ted, *38:* 183; *50:* 131
Bernstein, Zena, *23:* 46
Berrill, Jacquelyn, *12:* 50
Berry, Erick. *See* Best, Allena.
Berry, William A., *6:* 219
Berry, William D., *14:* 29; *19:* 48
Berson, Harold, *2:* 17-18; *4:* 28-29,
    220; *9:* 10; *12:* 19; *17:* 45;
    18: 193; *22:* 85; *34:* 172; *44:* 120;
    46: 42
Bertschmann, Harry, *16:* 1
Beskow, Elsa, *20:* 13, 14, 15
Best, Allena, *2:* 26; *34:* 76
Bethers, Ray, *6:* 22
Bettina. *See* Ehrlich, Bettina
Betts, Ethel Franklin, *17:* 161,
    164-165; *YABC 2:* 47
Bewick, Thomas, *16:* 40-41, 43-45,
    47; *YABC 1:* 107
Bezencon, Jacqueline, *48:* 40
Biamonte, Daniel, *40:* 90
Bianco, Pamela, *15:* 31; *28:* 44, 45, 46
Bible, Charles, *13:* 15
Bice, Clare, *22:* 40
Biggers, John, *2:* 123
Bileck, Marvin, *3:* 102; *40:* 36-37
Bimen, Levent, *5:* 179
Binks, Robert, *25:* 150
Binzen, Bill, *24:* 47
Birch, Reginald, *15:* 150; *19:* 33, 34,
    35, 36; *37:* 196, 197; *44:* 182;
    46: 176; *YABC 1:* 84;
    YABC 2: 34, 39
Bird, Esther Brock, *1:* 36; *25:* 66
Birmingham, Lloyd, *12:* 51
Biro, Val, *1:* 26; *41:* 42
Bischoff, Ilse, *44:* 51
Bjorklund, Lorence, *3:* 188, 252;
    7: 100; *9:* 113; *10:* 66; *19:* 178;
    33: 122, 123; *35:* 36, 37, 38, 39,
    41, 42, 43; *36:* 185; *38:* 93;
    47: 106; *YABC 1:* 242
Blackwell, Basil T., *YABC 1:* 68, 69
Blades, Ann, *16:* 52; *37:* 213; *50:* 41
Blair, Jay, *45:* 46; *46:* 155
Blaisdell, Elinore, *1:* 121; *3:* 134;
    35: 63
Blake, Quentin, *3:* 170; *10:* 48; *13:* 38;
    21: 180; *26:* 60; *28:* 228; *30:* 29,
    31; *40:* 108; *45:* 219; *46:* 165,
    168; *48:* 196; *52:* 10, 11, 12, 13,
    14, 15, 16, 17
Blake, Robert J., *37:* 90; *53:* 67
Blake, William, *30:* 54, 56, 57, 58,
    59, 60
Blass, Jacqueline, *8:* 215
Blegvad, Erik, *2:* 59; *3:* 98; *5:* 117;
    7: 131; *11:* 149; *14:* 34, 35;
    18: 237; *32:* 219; *YABC 1:* 201
Bliss, Corinne Demas, *37:* 38
Bloch, Lucienne, *10:* 12

Bloom, Lloyd, *35:* 180; *36:* 149;
    47: 99
Blossom, Dave, *34:* 29
Blumenschein, E. L., *YABC 1:* 113,
    115
Blumer, Patt, *29:* 214
Blundell, Kim, *29:* 36
Boardman, Gwenn, *12:* 60
Bobri, *30:* 138; *47:* 27
Bock, Vera, *1:* 187; *21:* 41
Bock, William Sauts, *8:* 7; *14:* 37;
    16: 120; *21:* 141; *36:* 177
Bodecker, N. M., *8:* 13; *14:* 2;
    17: 55-57
Boehm, Linda, *40:* 31
Bohdal, Susi, *22:* 44
Bolian, Polly, *3:* 270; *4:* 30; *13:* 77;
    29: 197
Bolognese, Don, *2:* 147, 231; *4:* 176;
    7: 146; *17:* 43; *23:* 192; *24:* 50;
    34: 108; *36:* 133
Bond, Arnold, *18:* 116
Bond, Barbara Higgins, *21:* 102
Bond, Bruce, *52:* 97
Bond, Felicia, *38:* 197; *49:* 55, 56
Bonn, Pat, *43:* 40
Bonners, Susan, *41:* 40
Bonsall, Crosby, *23:* 6
Booth, Franklin, *YABC 2:* 76
Booth, Graham, *32:* 193; *37:* 41, 42
Bordier, Georgette, *16:* 54
Boren, Tinka, *27:* 128
Borja, Robert, *22:* 48
Born, Adolf, *49:* 63
Bornstein, Ruth, *14:* 44
Borten, Helen, *3:* 54; *5:* 24
Bossom, Naomi, *35:* 48
Boston, Peter, *19:* 42
Bosustow, Stephen, *34:* 202
Bottner, Barbara, *14:* 46
Boucher, Joelle, *41:* 138
Boulat, Pierre, *44:* 40
Boulet, Susan Seddon, *50:* 47
Bourke-White, Margaret, *15:* 286-287
Boutet de Monvel, M., *30:* 61, 62, 63,
    65
Bowen, Richard, *42:* 134
Bowen, Ruth, *31:* 188
Bower, Ron, *29:* 33
Bowser, Carolyn Ewing, *22:* 253
Boyd, Patti, *45:* 31
Boyle, Eleanor Vere, *28:* 50, 51
Bozzo, Frank, *4:* 154
Bradford, Ron, *7:* 157
Bradley, Richard D., *26:* 182
Bradley, William, *5:* 164
Brady, Irene, *4:* 31; *42:* 37
Bragg, Michael, *32:* 78; *46:* 31
Braithwaite, Althea, *23:* 12-13
Bram, Elizabeth, *30:* 67
Bramley, Peter, *4:* 3
Brandenberg, Aliki, *2:* 36-37; *24:* 222;
    35: 49, 50, 51, 52, 53, 54, 56, 57
Brandenburg, Jim, *47:* 58
Brandi, Lillian, *31:* 158
Brandon, Brumsic, Jr., *9:* 25
Bransom, Paul, *17:* 121; *43:* 44
Brenner, Fred, *22:* 85; *36:* 34; *42:* 34
Brett, Bernard, *22:* 54

Brett, Harold M., *26:* 98, 99, 100
Brett, Jan, *30:* 135; *42:* 39
Brewer, Sally King, *33:* 44
Brewster, Patience, *40:* 68; *45:* 22,
    183; *51:* 20
Brick, John, *10:* 15
Bridge, David R., *45:* 28
Bridgman, L. J., *37:* 77
Bridwell, Norman, *4:* 37
Briggs, Raymond, *10:* 168; *23:* 20, 21
Brigham, Grace A., *37:* 148
Bright, Robert, *24:* 55
Brinckloe, Julie, *13:* 18; *24:* 79, 115;
    29: 35
Brion, *47:* 116
Brisley, Joyce L., *22:* 57
Brock, Charles E., *15:* 97; *19:* 247,
    249; *23:* 224, 225; *36:* 88; *42:* 41,
    42, 43, 44, 45; *YABC 1:* 194,
    196, 203
Brock, Emma, *7:* 21
Brock, Henry Matthew, *15:* 81;
    16: 141; *19:* 71; *34:* 115; *40:* 164;
    42: 47, 48, 49; *49:* 66
Brodkin, Gwen, *34:* 135
Brodovitch, Alexi, *52:* 22
Bromhall, Winifred, *5:* 11; *26:* 38
Brooke, L. Leslie, *16:* 181-183, 186;
    17: 15-17; *18:* 194
Brooker, Christopher, *15:* 251
Broomfield, Maurice, *40:* 141
Brotman, Adolph E., *5:* 21
Brown, Buck, *45:* 48
Brown, David, *7:* 47; *48:* 52
Brown, Denise, *11:* 213
Brown, Ford Madox, *48:* 74
Brown, Judith Gwyn, *1:* 45; *7:* 5;
    8: 167; *9:* 182, 190; *20:* 16, 17,
    18; *23:* 142; *29:* 117; *33:* 97;
    36: 23, 26; *43:* 184; *48:* 201, 223;
    49: 69
Brown, Marc Tolon, *10:* 17, 197;
    14: 263; *51:* 18; *53:* 11, 12, 13,
    15, 16-17
Brown, Marcia, *7:* 30; *25:* 203;
    47: 31, 32, 33, 34, 35, 36-37, 38,
    39, 40, 42, 43, 44; *YABC 1:* 27
Brown, Margery W., *5:* 32-33; *10:* 3
Brown, Palmer, *36:* 40
Brown, Paul, *25:* 26; *26:* 107
Browne, Anthony, *45:* 50, 51, 52
Browne, Dik, *8:* 212
Browne, Gordon, *16:* 97
Browne, Hablot K., *15:* 65, 80;
    21: 14, 15, 16, 17, 18, 19, 20;
    24: 25
Browning, Coleen, *4:* 132
Browning, Mary Eleanor, *24:* 84
Bruce, Robert, *23:* 23
Brude, Dick, *48:* 215
Brule, Al, *3:* 135
Bruna, Dick, *43:* 48, 49, 50
Brundage, Frances, *19:* 244
Brunhoff, Jean de, *24:* 57, 58
Brunhoff, Laurent de, *24:* 60
Brunson, Bob, *43:* 135
Bryan, Ashley, *31:* 44
Brychta, Alex, *21:* 21

Bryson, Bernarda, *3:* 88, 146; *39:* 26;
    44: 185
Buba, Joy, *12:* 83; *30:* 226; *44:* 56
Buchanan, Lilian, *13:* 16
Bucholtz-Ross, Linda, *44:* 137
Buchs, Thomas, *40:* 38
Buck, Margaret Waring, *3:* 30
Buehr, Walter, *3:* 31
Buff, Conrad, *19:* 52, 53, 54
Buff, Mary, *19:* 52, 53
Bull, Charles Livingston, *18:* 207
Bullen, Anne, *3:* 166, 167
Burbank, Addison, *37:* 43
Burchard, Peter, *3:* 197; *5:* 35; *6:* 158,
    218
Burger, Carl, *3:* 33; *45:* 160, 162
Burgeson, Marjorie, *19:* 31
Burgess, Gelett, *32:* 39, 42
Burkert, Nancy Ekholm, *18:* 186;
    22: 140; *24:* 62, 63, 64, 65;
    26: 53; *29:* 60, 61; *46:* 171;
    YABC 1: 46
Burn, Doris, *6:* 172
Burnett, Virgil, *44:* 42
Burningham, John, *9:* 68; *16:* 60-61
Burns, Howard M., *12:* 173
Burns, Jim, *47:* 70
Burns, M. F., *26:* 69
Burns, Raymond, *9:* 29
Burns, Robert, *24:* 106
Burr, Dane, *12:* 2
Burra, Edward, *YABC 2:* 68
Burri, René, *41:* 143
Burridge, Marge Opitz, *14:* 42
Burris, Burmah, *4:* 81
Burroughs, John Coleman, *41:* 64
Burroughs, Studley O., *41:* 65
Burton, Marilee Robin, *46:* 33
Burton, Virginia Lee, *2:* 43; *44:* 49,
    51; *YABC 1:* 24
Busoni, Rafaello, *1:* 186; *3:* 224;
    6: 126; *14:* 5; *16:* 62-63
Butchkes, Sidney, *50:* 58
Butterfield, Ned, *1:* 153; *27:* 128
Buzonas, Gail, *29:* 88
Buzzell, Russ W., *12:* 177
Byard, Carole M., *39:* 44
Byars, Betsy, *46:* 35
Byfield, Barbara Ninde, *8:* 18
Byfield, Graham, *32:* 29
Byrd, Robert, *13:* 218; *33:* 46

Caddy, Alice, *6:* 41
Cady, Harrison, *17:* 21, 23; *19:* 57, 58
Caldecott, Randolph, *16:* 98, 103;
    17: 32-33, 36, 38-39; *26:* 90;
    YABC 2: 172
Calder, Alexander, *18:* 168
Calderon, W. Frank, *25:* 160
Caldwell, Doreen, *23:* 77
Caldwell, John, *46:* 225
Callahan, Kevin, *22:* 42
Callahan, Philip S., *25:* 77
Cameron, Julia Margaret, *19:* 203
Campbell, Ann, *11:* 43
Campbell, Rod, *51:* 27
Campbell, Walter M., *YABC 2:* 158

Camps, Luis, *28:* 120-121
Canright, David, *36:* 162
Caras, Peter, *36:* 64
Caraway, James, *3:* 200-201
Carbe, Nino, *29:* 183
Carigiet, Alois, *24:* 67
Carle, Eric, *4:* 42; *11:* 121; *12:* 29
Carlson, Nancy L., *41:* 116
Carr, Archie, *37:* 225
Carrick, Donald, *5:* 194; *39:* 97;
    49: 70; *53:* 156
Carrick, Malcolm, *28:* 59, 60
Carrick, Valery, *21:* 47
Carroll, Lewis. *See* Dodgson, Charles
    L.
Carroll, Ruth, *7:* 41; *10:* 68
Carter, Barbara, *47:* 167, 169
Carter, Harry, *22:* 179
Carter, Helene, *15:* 38; *22:* 202, 203;
    YABC 2: 220-221
Cartlidge, Michelle, *49:* 65
Carty, Leo, *4:* 196; *7:* 163
Cary, *4:* 133; *9:* 32; *20:* 2; *21:* 143
Cary, Page, *12:* 41
Case, Sandra E., *16:* 2
Cassel, Lili. *See* Wronker, Lili Cassel
Cassel-Wronker, Lili.
    See also Wronker, Lili Cassel
Cassels, Jean, *8:* 50
Castellon, Federico, *48:* 45, 46, 47, 48
Castle, Jane, *4:* 80
Cather, Carolyn, *3:* 83; *15:* 203;
    34: 216
Cauley, Lorinda Bryan, *44:* 135;
    46: 49
Cayard, Bruce, *38:* 67
Cazet, Denys, *52:* 27
Cellini, Joseph, *2:* 73; *3:* 35; *16:* 116;
    47: 103
Chabrian, Debbi, *45:* 55
Chabrian, Deborah, *51:* 182; *53:* 124
Chagnon, Mary, *37:* 158
Chalmers, Mary, *3:* 145; *13:* 148;
    33: 125
Chamberlain, Christopher, *45:* 57
Chamberlain, Margaret, *46:* 51
Chambers, C. E., *17:* 230
Chambers, Dave, *12:* 151
Chambers, Mary, *4:* 188
Chambliss, Maxie, *42:* 186
Chandler, David P., *28:* 62
Chapman, C. H., *13:* 83, 85, 87
Chapman, Frederick T., *6:* 27; *44:* 28
Chapman, Gaynor, *32:* 52, 53
Chappell, Warren, *3:* 172; *21:* 56;
    27: 125
Charles, Donald, *30:* 154, 155
Charlip, Remy, *4:* 48; *34:* 138
Charlot, Jean, *1:* 137, 138; *8:* 23;
    14: 31; *48:* 151
Charlton, Michael, *34:* 50; *37:* 39
Charmatz, Bill, *7:* 45
Chartier, Normand, *9:* 36; *52:* 49
Chase, Lynwood M., *14:* 4
Chastain, Madye Lee, *4:* 50
Chauncy, Francis, *24:* 158
Chen, Tony, *6:* 45; *19:* 131; *29:* 126;
    34: 160
Cheney, T. A., *11:* 47

Cheng, Judith, *36:* 45; *51:* 16
Chermayeff, Ivan, *47:* 53
Cherry, Lynne, *34:* 52
Chess, Victoria, *12:* 6; *33:* 42, 48, 49;
    40: 194; *41:* 145
Chessare, Michele, *41:* 50
Chesterton, G. K., *27:* 43, 44, 45, 47
Chestnutt, David, *47:* 217
Chevalier, Christa, *35:* 66
Chew, Ruth, *7:* 46
Chifflart, *47:* 113, 127
Chin, Alex, *28:* 54
Cho, Shinta, *8:* 126
Chodos, Margaret, *52:* 102, 103, 107
Chollick, Jay, *25:* 175
Chorao, Kay, *7:* 200-201; *8:* 25;
    11: 234; *33:* 187; *35:* 239
Christelow, Eileen, *38:* 44
Christensen, Gardell Dano, *1:* 57
Christiansen, Per, *40:* 24
Christy, Howard Chandler,
    17: 163-165, 168-169; *19:* 186,
    187; *21:* 22, 23, 24, 25
Chronister, Robert, *23:* 138
Church, Frederick, *YABC 1:* 155
Chute, Marchette, *1:* 59
Chwast, Jacqueline, *1:* 63; *2:* 275;
    6: 46-47; *11:* 125; *12:* 202;
    14: 235
Chwast, Seymour, *3:* 128-129; *18:* 43;
    27: 152
Cirlin, Edgard, *2:* 168
Clairin, Georges, *53:* 109
Clark, Victoria, *35:* 159
Clarke, Harry, *23:* 172, 173
Claverie, Jean, *38:* 46
Clayton, Robert, *9:* 181
Cleaver, Elizabeth, *8:* 204; *23:* 36
Cleland, T. M., *26:* 92
Clement, Charles, *20:* 38
Clevin, Jörgen, *7:* 50
Clifford, Judy, *34:* 163; *45:* 198
Coalson, Glo, *9:* 72, 85; *25:* 155;
    26: 42; *35:* 212; *53:* 31
Cober, Alan E., *17:* 158; *32:* 77;
    49: 127
Cochran, Bobbye, *11:* 52
CoConis, Ted, *4:* 41; *46:* 41; *51:* 104
Coerr, Eleanor, *1:* 64
Coes, Peter, *35:* 172
Cogancherry, Helen, *52:* 143
Coggins, Jack, *2:* 69
Cohen, Alix, *7:* 53
Cohen, Vincent O., *19:* 243
Cohen, Vivien, *11:* 112
Coker, Paul, *51:* 172
Colbert, Anthony, *15:* 41; *20:* 193
Colby, C. B., *3:* 47
Cole, Herbert, *28:* 104
Cole, Olivia H. H., *1:* 134; *3:* 223;
    9: 111; *38:* 104
Collier, David, *13:* 127
Collier, John, *27:* 179
Collier, Steven, *50:* 52
Colonna, Bernard, *21:* 50; *28:* 103;
    34: 140; *43:* 180
Cone, Ferne Geller, *39:* 49
Cone, J. Morton, *39:* 49
Conklin, Paul, *43:* 62

Connolly, Jerome P., *4:* 128; *28:* 52
Connolly, Peter, *47:* 60
Conover, Chris, *31:* 52; *40:* 184;
    41: 51; *44:* 79
Converse, James, *38:* 70
Cook, G. R., *29:* 165
Cookburn, W. V., *29:* 204
Cooke, Donald E., *2:* 77
Cooke, Tom, *52:* 118
Coomaraswamy, A. K., *50:* 100
Coombs, Charles, *43:* 65
Coombs, Patricia, *2:* 82; *3:* 52;
    22: 119; *51:* 32, 33, 34, 35, 36-
    37, 38, 39, 40, 42, 43
Cooney, Barbara, *6:* 16-17, 50; *12:* 42;
    13: 92; *15:* 145; *16:* 74, 111;
    18: 189; *23:* 38, 89, 93; *32:* 138;
    38: 105; *YABC 2:* 10
Cooper, Heather, *50:* 39
Cooper, Mario, *24:* 107
Cooper, Marjorie, *7:* 112
Copelman, Evelyn, *8:* 61; *18:* 25
Copley, Heather, *30:* 86; *45:* 57
Corbett, Grahame, *30:* 114; *43:* 67
Corbino, John, *19:* 248
Corcos, Lucille, *2:* 223; *10:* 27; *34:* 66
Corey, Robert, *9:* 34
Corlass, Heather, *10:* 7
Cornell, James, *27:* 60
Cornell, Jeff, *11:* 58
Corrigan, Barbara, *8:* 37
Corwin, Judith Hoffman, *10:* 28
Cory, Fanny Y., *20:* 113; *48:* 29
Cosgrove, Margaret, *3:* 100; *47:* 63
Costabel, Eva Deutsch, *45:* 66, 67
Costello, David F., *23:* 55
Courtney, R., *35:* 110
Couture, Christin, *41:* 209
Covarrubias, Miguel, *35:* 118, 119,
    123, 124, 125
Coville, Katherine, *32:* 57; *36:* 167
Cox, *43:* 93
Cox, Charles, *8:* 20
Cox, Palmer, *24:* 76, 77
Craft, Kinuko, *22:* 182; *36:* 220;
    53: 122, 123, 148, 149
Craig, Helen, *49:* 76
Crane, Alan H., *1:* 217
Crane, H. M., *13:* 111
Crane, Jack, *43:* 183
Crane, Walter, *18:* 46-49, 53-54,
    56-57, 59-61; *22:* 128; *24:* 210,
    217
Crawford, Will, *43:* 77
Credle, Ellis *1:* 69
Crews, Donald, *32:* 59, 60
Crofut, Susan, *23:* 61
Crowell, Pers, *3:* 125
Cruikshank, George, *15:* 76, 83;
    22: 74, 75, 76, 77, 78, 79, 80,
    81, 82, 84, 137; *24:* 22, 23
Crump, Fred H., *11:* 62
Cruz, Ray, *6:* 55
Cstari, Joe, *44:* 82
Cuffari, Richard, *4:* 75; *5:* 98; *6:* 56;
    7: 13, 84, 153; *8:* 148, 155; *9:* 89;
    11: 19; *12:* 55, 96, 114; *15:* 51,
    202; *18:* 5; *20:* 139; *21:* 197;
    22: 14, 192; *23:* 15, 106; *25:* 97;

27: 133; 28: 196; 29: 54; 30: 85; 31: 35; 36: 101; 38: 171; 42: 97; 44: 92, 192; 45: 212, 213; 46: 36, 198; 50: 164
Cugat, Xavier, 19: 120
Cumings, Art, 35: 160
Cummings, Chris, 29: 167
Cummings, Pat, 42: 61
Cummings, Richard, 24: 119
Cunette, Lou, 20: 93; 22: 125
Cunningham, Aline, 25: 180
Cunningham, David, 11: 13
Cunningham, Imogene, 16: 122, 127
Curry, John Steuart, 2: 5; 19: 84; 34: 36
Curtis, Bruce, 23: 96; 30: 88; 36: 22

Dabcovich, Lydia, 25: 105; 40: 114
Dain, Martin J., 35: 75
Daley, Joann, 50: 22
Dalton, Anne, 40: 62
Daly, Niki, 37: 53
Dalziel, Brothers, 33: 113
D'Amato, Alex, 9: 48; 20: 25
D'Amato, Janet, 9: 48; 20: 25; 26: 118
Daniel, Alan, 23: 59; 29: 110
Daniel, Lewis C., 20: 216
Daniels, Steve, 22: 16
Dann, Bonnie, 31: 83
Danska, Herbert, 24: 219
Danyell, Alice, 20: 27
Darley, F.O.C., 16: 145; 19: 79, 86, 88, 185; 21: 28, 36; 35: 76, 77, 78, 79, 80-81; YABC 2: 175
Darling, Lois, 3: 59; 23: 30, 31
Darling, Louis, 1: 40-41; 2: 63; 3: 59; 23: 30, 31; 43: 54, 57, 59
Darrow, Whitney, Jr., 13: 25; 38: 220, 221
Darwin, Beatrice, 43: 54
Darwin, Len, 24: 82
Dastolfo, Frank, 33: 179
Dauber, Liz, 1: 22; 3: 266; 30: 49
Daugherty, James, 3: 66; 8: 178; 13: 27-28, 161; 18: 101; 19: 72; 29: 108; 32: 156; 42: 84; YABC 1: 256; YABC 2: 174
d'Aulaire, Edgar, 5: 51
d'Aulaire, Ingri, 5: 51
David, Jonathan, 19: 37
Davidson, Kevin, 28: 154
Davidson, Raymond, 32: 61
Davis, Allen, 20: 11; 22: 45; 27: 222; 29: 157; 41: 99; 47: 99; 50: 84; 52: 105
Davis, Bette J., 15: 53; 23: 95
Davis, Dimitris, 45: 95
Davis, Jim, 32: 63, 64
Davis, Marguerite, 31: 38; 34: 69, 70; YABC 1: 126, 230
Davisson, Virginia H., 44: 178
Dawson, Diane, 24: 127; 42: 126; 52: 130
Dean, Bob, 19: 211
de Angeli, Marguerite, 1: 77; 27: 62, 65, 66, 67, 69, 70, 72; YABC 1: 166

Deas, Michael, 27: 219, 221; 30: 156
de Bosschère, Jean, 19: 252; 21: 4
De Bruyn, M(onica) G., 13: 30-31
De Cuir, John F., 1: 28-29
Degen, Bruce, 40: 227, 229
De Grazia, 14: 59; 39: 56, 57
de Groat, Diane, 9: 39; 18: 7; 23: 123; 28: 200-201; 31: 58, 59; 34: 151; 41: 152; 43: 88; 46: 40, 200; 49: 163; 50: 89; 52: 30, 34
de Groot, Lee, 6: 21
Delacre, Lulu, 36: 66
Delaney, A., 21: 78
Delaney, Ned, 28: 68
de Larrea, Victoria, 6: 119, 204; 29: 103
Delessert, Etienne, 7: 140; 46: 61, 62, 63, 65, 67, 68; YABC 2: 209
Delulio, John, 15: 54
Demarest, Chris L., 45: 68-69, 70
De Mejo, Oscar, 40: 67
Denetsosie, Hoke, 13: 126
Dennis, Morgan, 18: 68-69
Dennis, Wesley, 2: 87; 3: 111; 11: 132; 18: 71-74; 22: 9; 24: 196, 200; 46: 178
Denslow, W. W., 16: 84-87; 18: 19-20, 24; 29: 211
de Paola, Tomie, 8: 95; 9: 93; 11: 69; 25: 103; 28: 157; 29: 80; 39: 52-53; 40: 226; 46: 187
Detmold, Edward J., 22: 104, 105, 106, 107; 35: 120; YABC 2: 203
Detrich, Susan, 20: 133
DeVelasco, Joseph E., 21: 51
de Veyrac, Robert, YABC 2: 19
DeVille, Edward A., 4: 235
Devito, Bert, 12: 164
Devlin, Harry, 11: 74
Dewey, Ariane, 7: 64; 33: 195; 35: 208
See also Aruego, Ariane
Dewey, Kenneth, 39: 62; 51: 23
de Zanger, Arie, 30: 40
Diamond, Donna, 21: 200; 23: 63; 26: 142; 35: 83, 84, 85, 86-87, 88, 89; 38: 78; 40: 147; 44: 152; 50: 144; 53: 126
Dick, John Henry, 8: 181
Dickens, Frank, 34: 131
Dickey, Robert L., 15: 279
DiFate, Vincent, 37: 70
DiFiori, Lawrence, 10: 51; 12: 190; 27: 97; 40: 219
Di Grazia, Thomas, 32: 66; 35: 241
Dillard, Annie, 10: 32
Dillon, Corinne B., 1: 139
Dillon, Diane, 4: 104, 167; 6: 23; 13: 29; 15: 99; 26: 148; 27: 136, 201; 51: 29, 48, 51, 52, 53, 54, 55, 56-57, 58, 59, 60, 61, 62
Dillon, Leo, 4: 104, 167; 6: 23; 13: 29; 15: 99; 26: 148; 27: 136, 201; 51: 29, 48, 51, 52, 53, 54, 55, 56-57, 58, 59, 60, 61, 62
DiMaggio, Joe, 36: 22
Dinan, Carol, 25: 169
Dines, Glen, 7: 66-67
Dinesen, Thomas, 44: 37

Dinnerstein, Harvey, 42: 63, 64, 65, 66, 67, 68; 50: 146
Dinsdale, Mary, 10: 65; 11: 171
Disney, Walt, 28: 71, 72, 73, 76, 77, 78, 79, 80, 81, 87, 88, 89, 90, 91, 94
Dixon, Maynard, 20: 165
Doares, Robert G., 20: 39
Dobias, Frank, 22: 162
Dobrin, Arnold, 4: 68
Docktor, Irv, 43: 70
Dodd, Ed, 4: 69
Dodd, Lynley, 35: 92
Dodgson, Charles L., 20: 148; 33: 146; YABC 2: 98
Dodson, Bert, 9: 138; 14: 195; 42: 55
Dohanos, Stevan, 16: 10
Dolch, Marguerite P., 50: 64
Dolesch, Susanne, 34: 49
Dolson, Hildegarde, 5: 57
Domanska, Janina, 6: 66-67; YABC 1: 166
Dominguez, Elías, 53: 94
Domjan, Joseph, 25: 93
Donahue, Vic, 2: 93; 3: 190; 9: 44
Donald, Elizabeth, 4: 18
Donna, Natalie, 9: 52
Doré, Gustave, 18: 169, 172, 175; 19: 93, 94, 95, 96, 97, 98, 99, 100, 101, 102, 103, 104, 105; 23: 188; 25: 197, 199
Doremus, Robert, 6: 62; 13: 90; 30: 95, 96, 97; 38: 97
Dorfman, Ronald, 11: 128
Doty, Roy, 28: 98; 31: 32; 32: 224; 46: 157
Dougherty, Charles, 16: 204; 18: 74
Douglas, Aaron, 31: 103
Douglas, Goray, 13: 151
Dowd, Vic, 3: 244; 10: 97
Dowden, Anne Ophelia, 7: 70-71; 13: 120
Dowdy, Mrs. Regera, 29: 100.
See also Gorey, Edward
Doyle, Richard, 21: 31, 32, 33; 23: 231; 24: 177; 31: 87
Draper, Angie, 43: 84
Drath, Bill, 26: 34
Drawson, Blair, 17: 53
Drescher, Joan, 30: 100, 101; 35: 245; 52: 168
Drew, Patricia, 15: 100
Drummond, V. H., 6: 70
du Bois, William Pène, 4: 70; 10: 122; 26: 61; 27: 145, 211; 35: 243; 41: 216
Duchesne, Janet, 6: 162
Dudash, Michael, 32: 122
Duer, Douglas, 34: 177
Duffy, Joseph, 38: 203
Duffy, Pat, 28: 153
Duke, Chris, 8: 195
Dulac, Edmund, 19: 108, 109, 110, 111, 112, 113, 114, 115, 117; 23: 187; 25: 152; YABC 1: 37; YABC 2: 147
Dulac, Jean, 13: 64
Dumas, Philippe, 52: 36, 37, 38, 39, 40-41, 42, 43, 45

Dunn, Harvey, *34:* 78, 79, 80, 81
Dunn, Phoebe, *5:* 175
Dunn, Iris, *5:* 175
Dunnington, Tom, *3:* 36; *18:* 281;
    25: 61; *31:* 159; *35:* 168; *48:* 195
Dutz, *6:* 59
Duvoisin, Roger, *2:* 95; *6:* 76-77;
    7: 197; *28:* 125; *30:* 101, 102,
    103, 104, 105, 107; *47:* 205
Dypold, Pat, *15:* 37

E.V.B. *See* Boyle, Eleanor Vere
    (Gordon)
Eachus, Jennifer, *29:* 74
Eagle, Michael, *11:* 86; *20:* 9; *23:* 18;
    27: 122; *28:* 57; *34:* 201; *44:* 189
Earle, Olive L., *7:* 75
Earle, Vana, *27:* 99
Eastman, P. D., *33:* 57
Easton, Reginald, *29:* 181
Eaton, Tom, *4:* 62; *6:* 64; *22:* 99;
    24: 124
Ebel, Alex, *11:* 89
Ebert, Len, *9:* 191; *44:* 47
Echevarria, Abe, *37:* 69
Eckersley, Maureen, *48:* 62
Ede, Janina, *33:* 59
Edens, Cooper, *49:* 81, 82, 83, 84, 85
Edgar, Sarah E., *41:* 97
Edrien, *11:* 53
Edwards, Freya, *45:* 102
Edwards, George Wharton, *31:* 155
Edwards, Gunvor, *2:* 71; *25:* 47;
    32: 71
Edwards, Jeanne, *29:* 257
Edwards, Linda Strauss, *21:* 134;
    39: 123; *49:* 88-89
Eggenhofer, Nicholas, *2:* 81
Egielski, Richard, *11:* 90; *16:* 208;
    33: 236; *38:* 35; *49:* 91, 92, 93,
    95, 212, 213, 214, 216
Ehlert, Lois, *35:* 97
Ehrlich, Bettina, *1:* 83
Eichenberg, Fritz, *1:* 79; *9:* 54;
    19: 248; *23:* 170; *24:* 200;
    26: 208; *50:* 67, 68, 69, 70, 71,
    72, 73, 74, 75, 77, 79, 80, 81;
    YABC 1: 104-105; *YABC 2:* 213
Einsel, Naiad, *10:* 35; *29:* 136
Einsel, Walter, *10:* 37
Einzig, Susan, *3:* 77; *43:* 78
Eitzen, Allan, *9:* 56; *12:* 212; *14:* 226;
    21: 194; *38:* 162
Eldridge, Harold, *43:* 83
Elgaard, Greta, *19:* 241
Elgin, Kathleen, *9:* 188; *39:* 69
Ellacott, S. E., *19:* 118
Elliott, Sarah M., *14:* 58
Emberley, Ed, *8:* 53
Emberley, Michael, *34:* 83
Emery, Leslie, *49:* 187
Emmett, Bruce, *49:* 147
Engle, Mort, *38:* 64
Englebert, Victor, *8:* 54
Enos, Randall, *20:* 183
Enright, Maginel Wright, *19:* 240,
    243; *39:* 31, 35, 36

Enrique, Romeo, *34:* 135
Epstein, Stephen, *50:* 142, 148
Erhard, Walter, *1:* 152
Erickson, Phoebe, *11:* 83
Erikson, Mel, *31:* 69
Ernst, Lisa Campbell, *47:* 147
Escourido, Joseph, *4:* 81
Esté, Kirk, *33:* 111
Estoril, Jean, *32:* 27
Estrada, Ric, *5:* 52, 146; *13:* 174
Etchemendy, Teje, *38:* 68
Ets, Marie Hall, *2:* 102
Eulalie, *YABC 2:* 315
Evans, Katherine, *5:* 64
Ewing, Juliana Horatia, *16:* 92

Falconer, Pearl, *34:* 23
Falls, C. B., *1:* 19; *38:* 71, 72, 73, 74
Falter, John, *40:* 169, 170
Farmer, Andrew, *49:* 102
Farmer, Peter, *24:* 108; *38:* 75
Farquharson, Alexander, *46:* 75
Farrell, David, *40:* 135
Fatigati, Evelyn, *24:* 112
Faul-Jansen, Regina, *22:* 117
Faulkner, Jack, *6:* 169
Fava, Rita, *2:* 29
Fax, Elton C., *1:* 101; *4:* 2; *12:* 77;
    25: 107
Fay, *43:* 93
Federspiel, Marian, *33:* 51
Feelings, Tom, *5:* 22; *8:* 56; *12:* 153;
    16: 105; *30:* 196; *49:* 37
Fehr, Terrence, *21:* 87
Feiffer, Jules, *3:* 91; *8:* 58
Feigeles, Neil, *41:* 242
Feller, Gene, *33:* 130
Fellows, Muriel H., *10:* 42
Felts, Shirley, *33:* 71; *48:* 59
Fennelli, Maureen, *38:* 181
Fenton, Carroll Lane, *5:* 66; *21:* 39
Fenton, Mildred Adams, *5:* 66; *21:* 39
Ferguson, Walter W., *34:* 86
Fetz, Ingrid, *11:* 67; *12:* 52; *16:* 205;
    17: 59; *29:* 105; *30:* 108, 109;
    32: 149; *43:* 142
Fiammenghi, Gioia, *9:* 66; *11:* 44;
    12: 206; *13:* 57, 59; *52:* 126, 129
Field, Rachel, *15:* 113
Fine, Peter K., *43:* 210
Finger, Helen, *42:* 81
Fink, Sam, *18:* 119
Finlay, Winifred, *23:* 72
Fiorentino, Al, *3:* 240
Firmin, Charlotte, *29:* 75; *48:* 70
Fischel, Lillian, *40:* 204
Fischer, Hans, *25:* 202
Fisher, Leonard Everett, *3:* 6; *4:* 72,
    86; *6:* 197; *9:* 59; *16:* 151, 153;
    23: 44; *27:* 134; *29:* 26; *34:* 87,
    89, 90, 91, 93, 94, 95, 96;
    40: 206; *50:* 150; *YABC 2:* 169
Fisher, Lois, *20:* 62; *21:* 7
Fisk, Nicholas, *25:* 112
Fitschen, Marilyn, *2:* 20-21; *20:* 48
Fitzgerald, F. A., *15:* 116; *25:* 86-87

Fitzhugh, Louise, *1:* 94; *9:* 163;
    45: 75, 78
Fitzhugh, Susie, *11:* 117
Fitzsimmons, Arthur, *14:* 128
Fix, Philippe, *26:* 102
Flack, Marjorie, *21:* 67; *YABC 2:* 122
Flagg, James Montgomery, *17:* 227
Flax, Zeona, *2:* 245
Fleishman, Seymour, *14:* 232; *24:* 87
Fleming, Guy, *18:* 41
Floethe, Richard, *3:* 131; *4:* 90
Floherty, John J., Jr., *5:* 68
Flora, James, *1:* 96; *30:* 111, 112
Florian, Douglas, *19:* 122
Flory, Jane, *22:* 111
Floyd, Gareth, *1:* 74; *17:* 245; *48:* 63
Fluchère, Henri A., *40:* 79
Flynn, Barbara, *7:* 31; *9:* 70
Fogarty, Thomas, *15:* 89
Folger, Joseph, *9:* 100
Folkard, Charles, *22:* 132; *29:* 128,
    257-258
Foott, Jeff, *42:* 202
Forberg, Ati, *12:* 71, 205; *14:* 1;
    22: 113; *26:* 22; *48:* 64, 65
Ford, George, *24:* 120; *31:* 70, 177
Ford, H. J., *16:* 185-186
Ford, Pamela Baldwin, *27:* 104
Foreman, Michael, *2:* 110-111
Forrester, Victoria, *40:* 83
Fortnum, Peggy, *6:* 29; *20:* 179;
    24: 211; *26:* 76, 77, 78; *39:* 78;
    YABC 1: 148
Foster, Brad W., *34:* 99
Foster, Genevieve, *2:* 112
Foster, Gerald, *7:* 78
Foster, Laura Louise, *6:* 79
Foster, Marian Curtis, *23:* 74; *40:* 42
Foucher, Adèle, *47:* 118
Fowler, Mel, *36:* 127
Fox, Charles Phillip, *12:* 84
Fox, Jim, *6:* 187
Fracé, Charles, *15:* 118
Frame, Paul, *2:* 45, 145; *9:* 153;
    10: 124; *21:* 71; *23:* 62; *24:* 123;
    27: 106; *31:* 48; *32:* 159; *34:* 195;
    38: 136; *42:* 55; *44:* 139
Francois, André, *25:* 117
Francoise. *See* Seignobosc, Francoise
Frank, Lola Edick, *2:* 199
Frank, Mary, *4:* 54; *34:* 100
Franké, Phil, *45:* 91
Frankel, Julie, *40:* 84, 85, 202
Frankenberg, Robert, *22:* 116; *30:* 50;
    38: 92, 94, 95
Franklin, John, *24:* 22
Frascino, Edward, *9:* 133; *29:* 229;
    33: 190; *48:* 80, 81, 82, 83, 84-
    85, 86
Frasconi, Antonio, *6:* 80; *27:* 208;
    53: 41, 43, 45, 47, 48
Fraser, Betty, *2:* 212; *6:* 185; *8:* 103;
    31: 72, 73; *43:* 136
Fraser, Eric, *38:* 78; *41:* 149, 151
Fraser, F. A., *22:* 234
Frazetta, Frank, *41:* 72
Freas, John, *25:* 207

Freeman, Don, *2:* 15; *13:* 249; *17:* 62-63, 65, 67-68; *18:* 243; *20:* 195; *23:* 213, 217; *32:* 155
Fregosi, Claudia, *24:* 117
French, Fiona, *6:* 82-83
Friedman, Judith, *43:* 197
Friedman, Marvin, *19:* 59; *42:* 86
Frinta, Dagmar, *36:* 42
Frith, Michael K., *15:* 138; *18:* 120
Fritz, Ronald, *46:* 73
Fromm, Lilo, *29:* 85; *40:* 197
Frost, A. B., *17:* 6-7; *19:* 123, 124, 125, 126, 127, 128, 129, 130; *YABC 1:* 156-157, 160; *YABC 2:* 107
Fry, Guy, *2:* 224
Fry, Rosalie, *3:* 72; *YABC 2:* 180-181
Fry, Rosalind, *21:* 153, 168
Fryer, Elmer, *34:* 115
Fuchs, Erich, *6:* 84
Fuchshuber, Annegert, *43:* 96
Fufuka, Mahiri, *32:* 146
Fujikawa, Gyo, *39:* 75, 76
Fulford, Deborah, *23:* 159
Fuller, Margaret, *25:* 189
Funai, Mamoru, *38:* 105
Funk, Tom, *7:* 17, 99
Furchgott, Terry, *29:* 86
Furukawa, Mel, *25:* 42

Gaberell, J., *19:* 236
Gackenbach, Dick, *19:* 168; *41:* 81; *48:* 89, 90, 91, 92, 93, 94
Gaetano, Nicholas, *23:* 209
Gag, Flavia, *17:* 49, 52
Gág, Wanda, *YABC 1:* 135, 137-138, 141, 143
Gagnon, Cécile, *11:* 77
Gál, László, *14:* 127; *52:* 54, 55, 56
Galdone, Paul, *1:* 156, 181, 206; *2:* 40, 241; *3:* 42, 144; *4:* 141; *10:* 109, 158; *11:* 21; *12:* 118, 210; *14:* 12; *16:* 36-37; *17:* 70-74; *18:* 111, 230; *19:* 183; *21:* 154; *22:* 150, 245; *33:* 126; *39:* 136, 137; *42:* 57; *51:* 169
Gallagher, Sears, *20:* 112
Galloway, Ewing, *51:* 154
Galster, Robert, *1:* 66
Galsworthy, Gay John, *35:* 232
Gammell, Stephen, *7:* 48; *13:* 149; *29:* 82; *33:* 209; *41:* 88; *50:* 185, 186-187; *53:* 51, 52-53, 54, 55, 56, 57, 58
Gannett, Ruth Chrisman, *3:* 74; *18:* 254; *33:* 77, 78
Gantschev, Ivan, *45:* 32
Garbutt, Bernard, *23:* 68
Garcia, *37:* 71
Gardner, Earle, *45:* 167
Gardner, Joan, *40:* 87
Gardner, Joel, *40:* 87, 92
Gardner, John, *40:* 87
Gardner, Lucy, *40:* 87
Gardner, Richard. *See* Cummings, Richard, *24:* 119

Garland, Michael, *36:* 29; *38:* 83; *44:* 168; *48:* 78, 221, 222; *49:* 161
Garnett, Eve, *3:* 75
Garnett, Gary, *39:* 184
Garraty, Gail, *4:* 142; *52:* 106
Garrett, Agnes, *46:* 110; *47:* 157
Garrett, Edmund H., *20:* 29
Garrison, Barbara, *19:* 133
Gates, Frieda, *26:* 80
Gaughan, Jack, *26:* 79; *43:* 185
Gaver, Becky, *20:* 61
Gay, Zhenya, *19:* 135, 136
Geary, Clifford N., *1:* 122; *9:* 104; *51:* 74
Gee, Frank, *33:* 26
Geer, Charles, *1:* 91; *3:* 179; *4:* 201; *6:* 168; *7:* 96; *9:* 58; *10:* 72; *12:* 127; *39:* 156, 157, 158, 159, 160; *42:* 88, 89, 90, 91
Gehm, Charlie, *36:* 65
Geisel, Theodor Seuss, *1:* 104-105, 106; *28:* 108, 109, 110, 111, 112, 113
Geldart, William, *15:* 121; *21:* 202
Genia, *4:* 84
Gentry, Cyrille R., *12:* 66
George, Jean, *2:* 113
Gérard, Jean Ignace, *45:* 80
Gérard, Rolf, *27:* 147, 150
Geritz, Franz, *17:* 135
Gerlach, Geff, *42:* 58
Gerrard, Roy, *47:* 78
Gershinowitz, George, *36:* 27
Gerstein, Mordicai, *31:* 117; *47:* 80, 81, 82, 83, 84, 85, 86; *51:* 173
Gervase, *12:* 27
Getz, Arthur, *32:* 148
Gibbons, Gail, *23:* 78
Gibbs, Tony, *40:* 95
Gibran, Kahlil, *32:* 116
Giesen, Rosemary, *34:* 192-193
Giguère, George, *20:* 111
Gilbert, John, *19:* 184; *YABC 2:* 287
Gilbert, W. S., *36:* 83, 85, 96
Giles, Will, *41:* 218
Gill, Margery, *4:* 57; *7:* 7; *22:* 122; *25:* 166; *26:* 146, 147
Gillen, Denver, *28:* 216
Gillette, Henry J., *23:* 237
Gilliam, Stan, *39:* 64, 81
Gilman, Esther, *15:* 124
Giovanopoulos, Paul, *7:* 104
Githens, Elizabeth M., *5:* 47
Gladstone, Gary, *12:* 89; *13:* 190
Gladstone, Lise, *15:* 273
Glanzman, Louis S., *2:* 177; *3:* 182; *36:* 97, 98; *38:* 120, 122; *52:* 141, 144
Glaser, Milton, *3:* 5; *5:* 156; *11:* 107; *30:* 26; *36:* 112
Glass, Andrew, *36:* 38; *44:* 133; *48:* 205
Glass, Marvin, *9:* 174
Glasser, Judy, *41:* 156
Glattauer, Ned, *5:* 84; *13:* 224; *14:* 26
Glauber, Uta, *17:* 76
Gleeson, J. M., *YABC 2:* 207
Glegg, Creina, *36:* 100

Gliewe, Unada, *3:* 78-79; *21:* 73; *30:* 220
Glovach, Linda, *7:* 105
Gobbato, Imero, *3:* 180-181; *6:* 213; *7:* 58; *9:* 150; *18:* 39; *21:* 167; *39:* 82, 83; *41:* 137, 251
Goble, Paul, *25:* 121; *26:* 86; *33:* 65
Goble, Warwick, *46:* 78, 79
Godal, Eric, *36:* 93
Godfrey, Michael, *17:* 279
Goembel, Ponder, *42:* 124
Goffstein, M. B., *8:* 71
Golbin, Andrée, *15:* 125
Goldfeder, Cheryl, *11:* 191
Goldsborough, June, *5:* 154-155; *8:* 92, *14:* 226; *19:* 139
Goldstein, Leslie, *5:* 8; *6:* 60; *10:* 106
Goldstein, Nathan, *1:* 175; *2:* 79; *11:* 41, 232; *16:* 55
Goodall, John S., *4:* 92-93; *10:* 132; *YABC 1:* 198
Goode, Diane, *15:* 126; *50:* 183; *52:* 114-115
Goodelman, Aaron, *40:* 203
Goodenow, Earle, *40:* 97
Goodman, Joan Elizabeth, *50:* 86
Goodwin, Harold, *13:* 74
Goodwin, Philip R., *18:* 206
Goor, Nancy, *39:* 85, 86
Goor, Ron, *39:* 85, 86
Gordon, Gwen, *12:* 151
Gordon, Margaret, *4:* 147; *5:* 48-49; *9:* 79
Gorecka-Egan, Erica, *18:* 35
Gorey, Edward, *1:* 60-61; *13:* 169; *18:* 192; *20:* 201; *29:* 90, 91, 92-93, 94, 95, 96, 97, 98, 99, 100; *30:* 129; *32:* 90; *34:* 200. *See also* Dowdy, Mrs. Regera
Gorsline, Douglas, *1:* 98; *6:* 13; *11:* 113; *13:* 104; *15:* 14; *28:* 117, 118; *YABC 1:* 15
Gosner, Kenneth, *5:* 135
Gotlieb, Jules, *6:* 127
Gough, Philip, *23:* 47; *45:* 90
Gould, Chester, *49:* 112, 113, 114, 116, 117, 118
Govern, Elaine R., *26:* 94
Grabianski, *20:* 144
Grabiański, Janusz, *39:* 92, 93, 94, 95
Graboff, Abner, *35:* 103, 104
Graham, A. B., *11:* 61
Graham, L., *7:* 108
Graham, Margaret Bloy, *11:* 120; *18:* 305, 307
Grahame-Johnstone, Anne, *13:* 61
Grahame-Johnstone, Janet, *13:* 61
Grainger, Sam, *42:* 95
Gramatky, Hardie, *1:* 107; *30:* 116, 119, 120, 122, 123
Grandville, J. J., *45:* 81, 82, 83, 84, 85, 86, 87, 88; *47:* 125
Granger, Paul, *39:* 153
Grant, Gordon, *17:* 230, 234; *25:* 123, 124, 125, 126; *52:* 69; *YABC 1:* 164
Grant, (Alice) Leigh, *10:* 52; *15:* 131; *20:* 20; *26:* 119; *48:* 202
Graves, Elizabeth, *45:* 101

Gray, Harold, *33:* 87, 88
Gray, Reginald, *6:* 69
Green, Eileen, *6:* 97
Green, Michael, *32:* 216
Greenaway, Kate, *17:* 275; *24:* 180;
    26: 107; *41:* 222, 232;
    YABC 1: 88-89; *YABC 2:* 131,
    133, 136, 138-139, 141
Greenwald, Sheila, *1:* 34; *3:* 99; *8:* 72
Gregorian, Joyce Ballou, *30:* 125
Gregory, Frank M., *29:* 107
Greiffenhagen, Maurice, *16:* 137;
    27: 57; *YABC 2:* 288
Greiner, Robert, *6:* 86
Gretter, J. Clemens, *31:* 134
Gretz, Susanna, *7:* 114
Gretzer, John, *1:* 54; *3:* 26; *4:* 162;
    7: 125; *16:* 247; *18:* 117; *28:* 66;
    30: 85, 211; *33:* 235
Grey Owl, *24:* 41
Gri, *25:* 90
Grieder, Walter *9:* 84
Grifalconi, Ann, *2:* 126; *3:* 248;
    11: 18; *13:* 182; *46:* 38; *50:* 145
Griffin, Gillett Good, *26:* 96
Griffin, James, *30:* 166
Griffiths, Dave, *29:* 76
Gringhuis, Dirk, *6:* 98; *9:* 196
Gripe, Harald, *2:* 127
Grisha, *3:* 71
Gropper, William, *27:* 93; *37:* 193
Grose, Helen Mason, *YABC 1:* 260;
    YABC 2: 150
Grossman, Nancy, *24:* 130; *29:* 101
Grossman, Robert, *11:* 124; *46:* 39
Groth, John, *15:* 79; *21:* 53, 54
Gruelle, Johnny, *35:* 107
Gschwind, William, *11:* 72
Guggenheim, Hans, *2:* 10; *3:* 37;
    8: 136
Guilbeau, Honoré, *22:* 69
Gundersheimer, Karen, *35:* 240
Gusman, Annie, *38:* 62
Gustafson, Scott, *34:* 111; *43:* 40
Guthrie, Robin, *20:* 122
Gwynne, Fred, *41:* 94, 95
Gyberg, Bo-Erik, *38:* 131

Haas, Irene, *17:* 77
Hack, Konrad, *51:* 127
Hader, Berta H., *16:* 126
Hader, Elmer S., *16:* 126
Hafner, Marylin, *22:* 196, 216; *24:* 44;
    30: 51; *35:* 95; *51:* 25, 160, 164
Hague, Michael, *32:* 128; *48:* 98, 99,
    100-101, 103, 105, 106-107, 108,
    109, 110; *49:* 121; *51:* 105
Halas, John, *29:* 41, 47, 48
Haldane, Roger, *13:* 76; *14:* 202
Hale, Irina, *26:* 97
Hale, Kathleen, *17:* 79
Haley, Gail E., *43:* 102, 103, 104, 105
Hall, Chuck, *30:* 189
Hall, Douglas, *15:* 184; *43:* 106, 107
Hall, H. Tom, *1:* 227; *30:* 210
Hall, Sydney P., *31:* 89
Hall, Vicki, *20:* 24

Hallinan, P. K., *39:* 98
Halpern, Joan, *10:* 25
Halverson, Janet, *49:* 38, 42, 44
Hamberger, John, *6:* 8; *8:* 32; *14:* 79;
    34: 136
Hamil, Tom, *14:* 80; *43:* 163
Hamilton, Bill and Associates, *26:* 215
Hamilton, Helen S., *2:* 238
Hamilton, J., *19:* 83, 85, 87
Hammond, Chris, *21:* 37
Hammond, Elizabeth, *5:* 36, 203
Hampshire, Michael, *5:* 187;
    7: 110-111; *48:* 150; *51:* 129
Hampson, Denman, *10:* 155; *15:* 130
Hampton, Blake, *41:* 244
Handforth, Thomas, *42:* 100, 101,
    102, 103, 104, 105, 107
Handville, Robert, *1:* 89; *38:* 76;
    45: 108, 109
Hane, Roger, *17:* 239; *44:* 54
Haney, Elizabeth Mathieu, *34:* 84
Hanley, Catherine, *8:* 161
Hann, Jacquie, *19:* 144
Hannon, Mark, *38:* 37
Hanson, Joan, *8:* 76; *11:* 139
Hanson, Peter E., *52:* 47
Hardy, David A., *9:* 96
Hardy, Paul, *YABC 2:* 245
Harlan, Jerry, *3:* 96
Harnischfeger, *18:* 121
Harper, Arthur, *YABC 2:* 121
Harrington, Richard, *5:* 81
Harris, Susan Yard, *42:* 121
Harrison, Florence, *20:* 150, 152
Harrison, Harry, *4:* 103
Harrison, Jack, *28:* 149
Hart, William, *13:* 72
Hartelius, Margaret, *10:* 24
Hartshorn, Ruth, *5:* 115; *11:* 129
Harvey, Bob, *48:* 219
Harvey, Gerry, *7:* 180
Hassall, Joan, *43:* 108, 109
Hassell, Hilton, *YABC 1:* 187
Hasselriis, Else, *18:* 87; *YABC 1:* 96
Hauman, Doris, *2:* 184; *29:* 58, 59;
    32: 85, 86, 87
Hauman, George, *2:* 184; *29:* 58, 59;
    32: 85, 86, 87
Hausherr, Rosmarie, *15:* 29
Hawkinson, John, *4:* 109; *7:* 83;
    21: 64
Hawkinson, Lucy, *21:* 64
Haxton, Elaine, *28:* 131
Haydock, Robert, *4:* 95
Hayes, Geoffrey, *26:* 111; *44:* 133
Haywood, Carolyn, *1:* 112; *29:* 104
Healy, Daty, *12:* 143
Hearon, Dorothy, *34:* 69
Hechtkopf, H., *11:* 110
Hedderwick, Mairi, *30:* 127; *32:* 47;
    36: 104
Hefter, Richard, *28:* 170; *31:* 81, 82;
    33: 183
Heigh, James, *22:* 98
Heighway, Richard, *25:* 160
Heinly, John, *45:* 113
Hellebrand, Nancy, *26:* 57
Heller, Linda, *46:* 86
Hellmuth, Jim, *38:* 164

Helms, Georgeann, *33:* 62
Helweg, Hans, *41:* 118; *50:* 93
Henderson, Keith, *35:* 122
Henkes, Kevin, *43:* 111
Henneberger, Robert, *1:* 42; *2:* 237;
    25: 83
Henriksen, Harold, *35:* 26; *48:* 68
Henry, Everett, *29:* 191
Henry, Thomas, *5:* 102
Hensel, *27:* 119
Henstra, Friso, *8:* 80; *36:* 70; *40:* 222;
    41: 250
Hepple, Norman, *28:* 198
Herbert, Wally, *23:* 101
Herbster, Mary Lee, *9:* 33
Hergé. *See* Rémi, Georges
Hermanson, Dennis, *10:* 55
Herrington, Roger, *3:* 161
Heslop, Mike, *38:* 60; *40:* 130
Hess, Richard, *42:* 31
Hester, Ronnie, *37:* 85
Heustis, Louise L., *20:* 28
Heyduck-Huth, Hilde, *8:* 82
Heyer, Hermann, *20:* 114, 115
Heyman, Ken, *8:* 33; *34:* 113
Heywood, Karen, *48:* 114
Hickling, P. B., *40:* 165
Higginbottom, J. Winslow, *8:* 170;
    29: 105, 106
Higham, David, *50:* 104
Hildebrandt, Greg, *8:* 191
Hildebrandt, Tim, *8:* 191
Hilder, Rowland, *19:* 207
Hill, Gregory, *35:* 190
Hill, Pat, *49:* 120
Hillier, Matthew, *45:* 205
Hillman, Priscilla, *48:* 115
Himler, Ronald, *6:* 114; *7:* 162; *8:* 17,
    84, 125; *14:* 76; *19:* 145; *26:* 160;
    31: 43; *38:* 116; *41:* 44, 79;
    43: 52; *45:* 120; *46:* 43
Himmelman, John, *47:* 109
Hinds, Bill, *37:* 127, 130
Hines, Anna Grossnickle, *51:* 90
Hiroshige, *25:* 71
Hirsh, Marilyn, *7:* 126
Hitz, Demi, *11:* 135; *15:* 245
Hnizdovsky, Jacques, *32:* 96
Ho, Kwoncjan, *15:* 132
Hoban, Lillian, *1:* 114; *22:* 157;
    26: 72; *29:* 53; *40:* 105, 107, 195;
    41: 80
Hoban, Tana, *22:* 159
Hoberman, Norman, *5:* 82
Hockerman, Dennis, *39:* 22
Hodgell, P. C., *42:* 114
Hodges, C. Walter, *2:* 139; *11:* 15;
    12: 25; *23:* 34; *25:* 96; *38:* 165;
    44: 197; *45:* 95; *YABC 2:* 62-63
Hodges, David, *9:* 98
Hodgetts, Victoria, *43:* 132
Hofbauer, Imre, *2:* 162
Hoff, Syd, *9:* 107; *10:* 128; *33:* 94
Hoffman, Rosekrans, *15:* 133; *50:* 219
Hoffman, Sanford, *38:* 208
Hoffmann, Felix, *9:* 109
Hofsinde, Robert, *21:* 70
Hogan, Inez, *2:* 141
Hogarth, Burne, *41:* 58

Hogarth, Paul, *41:* 102, 103, 104;
    YABC 1: 16
Hogarth, William, *42:* 33
Hogenbyl, Jan, *1:* 35
Hogner, Nils, *4:* 122; *25:* 144
Hogrogian, Nonny, *3:* 221; *4:* 106-107;
    5: 166; *7:* 129; *15:* 2; *16:* 176;
    20: 154; *22:* 146; *25:* 217;
    27: 206; *YABC 2:* 84, 94
Hokusai, *25:* 71
Holberg, Richard, *2:* 51
Holdcroft, Tina, *38:* 109
Holder, Heidi, *36:* 99
Holiday, Henry, *YABC 2:* 107
Holl, F., *36:* 91
Holland, Brad, *45:* 59, 159
Holland, Janice, *18:* 118
Holland, Marion, *6:* 116
Holldobler, Turid, *26:* 120
Holling, Holling C., *15:* 136-137
Hollinger, Deanne, *12:* 116
Holmes, B., *3:* 82
Holmes, Bea, *7:* 74; *24:* 156; *31:* 93
Holmgren, George Ellen, *45:* 112
Holt, Norma, *44:* 106
Holtan, Gene, *32:* 192
Holz, Loretta, *17:* 81
Homar, Lorenzo, *6:* 2
Homer, Winslow, *YABC 2:* 87
Honigman, Marian, *3:* 2
Honoré, Paul, *42:* 77, 79, 81, 82
Hood, Susan, *12:* 43
Hook, Frances, *26:* 188; *27:* 127
Hook, Jeff, *14:* 137
Hook, Richard, *26:* 188
Hoover, Carol A., *21:* 77
Hoover, Russell, *12:* 95; *17:* 2;
    34: 156
Hoppin, Augustus, *34:* 66
Horder, Margaret, *2:* 108
Horen, Michael, *45:* 121
Horvat, Laurel, *12:* 201
Horvath, Ferdinand Kusati, *24:* 176
Hotchkiss, De Wolfe, *20:* 49
Hough, Charlotte, *9:* 112; *13:* 98;
    17: 83; *24:* 195
Houlihan, Ray, *11:* 214
Housman, Laurence, *25:* 146, 147
Houston, James, *13:* 107
How, W. E., *20:* 47
Howard, Alan, *16:* 80; *34:* 58; *45:* 114
Howard, J. N., *15:* 234
Howard, John, *33:* 179
Howard, Rob, *40:* 161
Howe, Stephen, *1:* 232
Howell, Pat, *15:* 139
Howell, Troy, *23:* 24; *31:* 61; *36:* 158;
    37: 184; *41:* 76, 235; *48:* 112
Howes, Charles, *22:* 17
Hubley, Faith, *48:* 120-121, 125, 130,
    131, 132, 134
Hubley, John, *48:* 125, 130, 131, 132,
    134
Hudnut, Robin, *14:* 62
Huffaker, Sandy, *10:* 56
Huffman, Joan, *13:* 33
Huffman, Tom, *13:* 180; *17:* 212;
    21: 116; *24:* 132; *33:* 154; *38:* 59;
    42: 147

Hughes, Arthur, *20:* 148, 149, 150;
    33: 114, 148, 149
Hughes, David, *36:* 197
Hughes, Shirley, *1:* 20, 21; *7:* 3;
    12: 217; *16:* 163; *29:* 154
Hugo, Victor, *47:* 112
Hülsmann, Eva, *16:* 166
Hummel, Berta, *43:* 137, 138, 139
Hummel, Lisl, *29:* 109;
    YABC 2: 333-334
Humphrey, Henry, *16:* 167
Humphreys, Graham, *25:* 168
Hunt, James, *2:* 143
Hurd, Clement, *2:* 148, 149
Hurd, Peter; *24:* 30, 31, *YABC 2:* 56
Hurd, Thacher, *46:* 88-89
Hugo, Victor, *47:* 112
Hürlimann, Ruth, *32:* 99
Hustler, Tom, *6:* 105
Hutchins, Pat, *15:* 142
Hutchinson, William M., *6:* 3, 138;
    46: 70
Hutchison, Paula, *23:* 10
Hutton, Clarke, *YABC 2:* 335
Hutton, Kathryn, *35:* 155
Hutton, Warwick, *20:* 91
Huyette, Marcia, *29:* 188
Hyman, Trina Schart, *1:* 204; *2:* 194;
    5: 153; *6:* 106; *7:* 138, 145; *8:* 22;
    10: 196; *13:* 96; *14:* 114; *15:* 204;
    16: 234; *20:* 82; *22:* 133; *24:* 151;
    25: 79, 82; *26:* 82; *29:* 83; *31:* 37,
    39; *34:* 104; *38:* 84, 100, 128;
    41: 49; *43:* 146; *46:* 91, 92, 93,
    95, 96, 97, 98, 99, 100, 101, 102,
    103, 104-105, 108, 109, 111, 197;
    48: 60, 61; *52:* 32

Ichikawa, Satomi, *29:* 152; *41:* 52;
    47: 133, 134, 135, 136
Ide, Jacqueline, *YABC 1:* 39
Ilsley, Velma, *3:* 1; *7:* 55; *12:* 109;
    37: 62; *38:* 184
Inga, *1:* 142
Ingraham, Erick, *21:* 177
Innocenti, Roberto, *21:* 123
Inoue, Yosuke, *24:* 118
Ipcar, Dahlov, *1:* 124-125; *49:* 137,
    138, 139, 140-141, 142, 143, 144,
    145
Irvin, Fred, *13:* 166; *15:* 143-144;
    27: 175
Irving, Jay, *45:* 72
Irving, Laurence, *27:* 50
Isaac, Joanne, *21:* 76
Isadora, Rachel, *43:* 159, 160
Ishmael, Woodi, *24:* 111; *31:* 99
Ives, Ruth, *15:* 257

Jackson, Michael, *43:* 42
Jacobs, Barbara, *9:* 136
Jacobs, Lou, Jr., *9:* 136; *15:* 128
Jacques, Robin, *1:* 70; *2:* 1; *8:* 46;
    9: 20; *15:* 187; *19:* 253; *32:* 102,
    103, 104; *43:* 184; *YABC 1:* 42

Jagr, Miloslav, *13:* 197
Jakubowski, Charles, *14:* 192
Jambor, Louis, *YABC 1:* 11
James, Derek, *35:* 187; *44:* 91
James, Gilbert, *YABC 1:* 43
James, Harold, *2:* 151; *3:* 62; *8:* 79;
    29: 113; *51:* 195
James, Robin, *50:* 106; *53:* 32, 34, 35
James, Will, *19:* 150, 152, 153, 155,
    163
Janosch. *See* Eckert, Horst
Jansons, Inese, *48:* 117
Jansson, Tove, *3:* 90; *41:* 106, 108,
    109, 110, 111, 113, 114
Jaques, Faith, *7:* 11, 132-33; *21:* 83,
    84
Jaques, Frances Lee, *29:* 224
Jauss, Anne Marie, *1:* 139; *3:* 34;
    10: 57, 119; *11:* 205; *23:* 194
Jeffers, Susan, *17:* 86-87; *25:* 164-165;
    26: 112; *50:* 132, 134-135
Jefferson, Louise E., *4:* 160
Jenkyns, Chris, *51:* 97
Jeruchim, Simon, *6:* 173; *15:* 250
Jeschke, Susan, *20:* 89; *39:* 161;
    41: 84; *42:* 120
Jessel, Camilla, *29:* 115
Joerns, Consuelo, *38:* 36; *44:* 94
John, Diana, *12:* 209
John, Helen, *1:* 215; *28:* 204
Johns, Jeanne, *24:* 114
Johnson, Bruce, *9:* 47
Johnson, Crockett. *See* Leisk, David
Johnson, D. William, *23:* 104
Johnson, Harper, *1:* 27; *2:* 33; *18:* 302;
    19: 61; *31:* 181; *44:* 46, 50, 95
Johnson, Ingrid, *37:* 118
Johnson, James David, *12:* 195
Johnson, James Ralph, *1:* 23, 127
Johnson, Jane, *48:* 136
Johnson, John E., *34:* 133
Johnson, Larry, *47:* 56
Johnson, Margaret S., *35:* 131
Johnson, Milton, *1:* 67; *2:* 71; *26:* 45;
    31: 107
Johnson, Pamela, *16:* 174; *52:* 145
Johnson, William R., *38:* 91
Johnston, David McCall, *50:* 131, 133
Johnstone, Anne, *8:* 120; *36:* 89
Johnstone, Janet Grahame, *8:* 120;
    36: 89
Jonas, Ann, *50:* 107, 108, 109
Jones, Carol, *5:* 131
Jones, Chuck, *53:* 70, 71
Jones, Elizabeth Orton, *18:* 124, 126,
    128-129
Jones, Harold, *14:* 88; *52:* 50
Jones, Jeff, *41:* 64
Jones, Laurian, *25:* 24, 27
Jones, Robert, *25:* 67
Jones, Wilfred, *35:* 115; *YABC 1:* 163
Joseph, James, *53:* 88
Joyner, Jerry, *34:* 138
Jucker, Sita, *5:* 93
Judkis, Jim, *37:* 38
Juhasz, Victor, *31:* 67
Jullian, Philippe, *24:* 206; *25:* 203
Jupo, Frank, *7:* 148-149
Justice, Martin, *34:* 72

Kahl, M. P., *37:* 83
Kahl, Virginia, *48:* 138
Kakimoo, Kozo, *11:* 148
Kalett, Jim, *48:* 159, 160, 161
Kalin, Victor, *39:* 186
Kalmenoff, Matthew, *22:* 191
Kalow, Gisela, *32:* 105
Kamen, Gloria, *1:* 41; *9:* 119; *10:* 178; *35:* 157
Kandell, Alice, *35:* 133
Kane, Henry B., *14:* 90; *18:* 219-220
Kane, Robert, *18:* 131
Kappes, Alfred, *28:* 104
Karalus, Bob, *41:* 157
Karlin, Eugene, *10:* 63; *20:* 131
Kasuya, Masahiro, *41:* 206-207; *51:* 100
Katona, Robert, *21:* 85; *24:* 126
Kauffer, E. McKnight, *33:* 103; *35:* 127
Kaufman, Angelika, *15:* 156
Kaufman, Joe, *33:* 119
Kaufman, John, *13:* 158
Kaufmann, John, *1:* 174; *4:* 159; *8:* 43, 1; *10:* 102; *18:* 133-134; *22:* 251
Kaye, Graham, *1:* 9
Kazalovski, Nata, *40:* 205
Keane, Bil, *4:* 135
Keats, Ezra Jack, *3:* 18, 105, 257; *14:* 101, 102; *33:* 129
Keegan, Marcia, *9:* 122; *32:* 93
Keely, John, *26:* 104; *48:* 214
Keen, Eliot, *25:* 213
Keeping, Charles, *9:* 124, 185; *15:* 28, 134; *18:* 115; *44:* 194, 196; *47:* 25; *52:* 3
Keith, Eros, *4:* 98; *5:* 138; *31:* 29; *43:* 220; *52:* 91, 92, 93, 94
Kelen, Emery, *13:* 115
Keller, Arthur I., *26:* 106
Keller, Dick, *36:* 123, 125
Keller, Holly, *45:* 79
Keller, Ronald, *45:* 208
Kelley, True, *41:* 114, 115; *42:* 137
Kellogg, Steven, *8:* 96; *11:* 207; *14:* 130; *20:* 58; *29:* 140-141; *30:* 35; *41:* 141; *YABC 1:* 65, 73
Kelly, Walt, *18:* 136-141, 144-146, 148-149
Kemble, E. W., *34:* 75; *44:* 178; *YABC 2:* 54, 59
Kemp-Welsh, Lucy, *24:* 197
Kennedy, Paul Edward, *6:* 190; *8:* 132; *33:* 120
Kennedy, Richard, *3:* 93; *12:* 179; *44:* 193; *YABC 1:* 57
Kent, Jack, *24:* 136; *37:* 37; *40:* 81
Kent, Rockwell, *5:* 166; *6:* 129; *20:* 225, 226, 227, 229
Kepes, Juliet, *13:* 119
Kerr, Judity, *24:* 137
Kessler, Leonard, *1:* 108; *7:* 139; *14:* 107, 227; *22:* 101; *44:* 96
Kesteven, Peter, *35:* 189
Ketcham, Hank, *28:* 140, 141, 142
Kettelkamp, Larry, *2:* 164
Key, Alexander, *8:* 99
Kiakshuk, *8:* 59

Kiddell-Monroe, Joan, *19:* 201
Kidder, Harvey, *9:* 105
Kidwell, Carl, *43:* 145
Kieffer, Christa, *41:* 89
Kiff, Ken, *40:* 45
Kilbride, Robert, *37:* 100
Kimball, Yeffe, *23:* 116; *37:* 88
Kincade, Orin, *34:* 116
Kindred, Wendy, *7:* 151
King, Colin, *53:* 3
King, Robin, *10:* 164-165
King, Tony, *39:* 121
Kingman, Dong, *16:* 287; *44:* 100, 102, 104
Kingsley, Charles, *YABC 2:* 182
Kingston, Maxine Hong, *53:* 92
Kipling, John Lockwood, *YABC 2:* 198
Kipling, Rudyard, *YABC 2:* 196
Kipniss, Robert, *29:* 59
Kirchhoff, Art, *28:* 136
Kirk, Ruth, *5:* 96
Kirk, Tim, *32:* 209, 211
Kirmse, Marguerite, *15:* 283; *18:* 153
Kirschner, Ruth, *22:* 154
Klapholz, Mel, *13:* 35
Kleinman, Zalman, *28:* 143
Kliban, B., *35:* 137, 138
Knight, Ann, *34:* 143
Knight, Christopher, *13:* 125
Knight, Hilary, *1:* 233; *3:* 21; *15:* 92, 158-159; *16:* 258-260; *18:* 235; *19:* 169; *35:* 242; *46:* 167; *52:* 116; *YABC 1:* 168-169, 172
Knotts, Howard, *20:* 4; *25:* 170; *36:* 163
Kobayashi, Ann, *39:* 58
Kocsis, J. C. See Paul, James
Koehn, Ilse, *34:* 198
Koering, Ursula, *3:* 28; *4:* 14; *44:* 53
Koerner, Henry. See Koerner, W.H.D.
Koerner, W.H.D., *14:* 216; *21:* 88, 89, 90, 91; *23:* 211
Koffler, Camilla, *36:* 113
Kogan, Deborah, *8:* 164; *29:* 238; *50:* 112, 113
Koide, Yasuko, *50:* 114
Komoda, Kiyo, *9:* 128; *13:* 214
Konashevicha, V., *YABC 1:* 26
Konigsburg, E. L., *4:* 138; *48:* 141, 142, 144, 145
Kooiker, Leonie, *48:* 148
Korach, Mimi, *1:* 128-129; *2:* 52; *4:* 39; *5:* 159; *9:* 129; *10:* 21; *24:* 69
Koren, Edward, *5:* 100
Kossin, Sandy, *10:* 71; *23:* 105
Kostin, Andrej, *26:* 204
Kovacević, Zivojin, *13:* 247
Krahn, Fernando, *2:* 257; *34:* 206; *49:* 152
Kramer, Anthony, *33:* 81
Kramer, Frank, *6:* 121
Krantz, Kathy, *35:* 83
Kraus, Robert, *13:* 217
Kredel, Fritz, *6:* 35; *17:* 93-96; *22:* 147; *24:* 175; *29:* 130; *35:* 77; *YABC 2:* 166, 300
Krementz, Jill, *17:* 98; *49:* 41
Kresin, Robert, *23:* 19

Krupp, Robin Rector, *53:* 96, 98
Krush, Beth, *1:* 51, 85; *2:* 233; *4:* 115; *9:* 61; *10:* 191; *11:* 196; *18:* 164-165; *32:* 72; *37:* 203; *43:* 57
Krush, Joe, *2:* 233; *4:* 115; *9:* 61; *10:* 191; *11:* 196; *18:* 164-165; *32:* 72, 91; *37:* 203; *43:* 57
Kubinyi, Laszlo, *4:* 116; *6:* 113; *16:* 118; *17:* 100; *28:* 227; *30:* 172; *49:* 24, 28
Kuhn, Bob, *17:* 91; *35:* 235
Kunhardt, Dorothy, *53:* 101
Künstler, Mort, *10:* 73; *32:* 143
Kurchevsky, V., *34:* 61
Kurelek, William, *8:* 107
Kuriloff, Ron, *13:* 19
Kuskin, Karla, *2:* 170
Kutzer, Ernst, *19:* 249

LaBlanc, André, *24:* 146
Laboccetta, Mario, *27:* 120
Laceky, Adam, *32:* 121
La Croix, *YABC 2:* 4
La Farge, Margaret, *47:* 141
Laimgruber, Monika, *11:* 153
Laite, Gordon, *1:* 130-131; *8:* 209; *31:* 113; *40:* 63; *46:* 117
Lamarche, Jim, *46:* 204
Lamb, Jim, *10:* 117
Lambert, J. K., *38:* 129; *39:* 24
Lambert, Saul, *23:* 112; *33:* 107
Lambo, Don, *6:* 156; *35:* 115; *36:* 146
Landa, Peter, *11:* 95; *13:* 177; *53:* 119
Landau, Jacob, *38:* 111
Landshoff, Ursula, *13:* 124
Lane, John, *15:* 176-177; *30:* 146
Lane, John R., *8:* 145
Lang, G. D., *48:* 56
Lang, Jerry, *18:* 295
Lange, Dorothea, *50:* 141
Langner, Nola, *8:* 110; *42:* 36
Lantz, Paul, *1:* 82, 102; *27:* 88; *34:* 102; *45:* 123
Larrecq, John, *44:* 108
Larsen, Suzanne, *1:* 13
Larsson, Carl, *35:* 144, 145, 146, 147, 148-149, 150, 152, 153, 154
Larsson, Karl, *19:* 177
La Rue, Michael D., *13:* 215
Lasker, Joe, *7:* 186-187; *14:* 55; *38:* 115; *39:* 47
Latham, Barbara, *16:* 188-189; *43:* 71
Lathrop, Dorothy, *14:* 117, 118-119; *15:* 109; *16:* 78-79, 81; *32:* 201, 203; *33:* 112; *YABC 2:* 301
Lattimore, Eleanor Frances, *7:* 156
Lauden, Claire, *16:* 173
Lauden, George, Jr., *16:* 173
Laune, Paul, *2:* 235; *34:* 31
Lauré, Jason, *49:* 53; *50:* 122
Lavis, Stephen, *43:* 143
Lawrence, John, *25:* 131; *30:* 141; *44:* 198, 200
Lawrence, Stephen, *20:* 195
Lawson, Carol, *6:* 38; *42:* 93, 131
Lawson, George, *17:* 280

Lawson, Robert, *5:* 26; *6:* 94; *13:* 39; *16:* 11; *20:* 100, 102, 103; *YABC 2:* 222, 224-225, 227-235, 237-241
Lazare, Jerry, *44:* 109
Lazarevich, Mila, *17:* 118
Lazarus, Keo Felker, *21:* 94
Lazzaro, Victor, *11:* 126
Lea, Tom, *43:* 72, 74
Leacroft, Richard, *6:* 140
Leaf, Munro, *20:* 99
Leander, Patricia, *23:* 27
Lear, Edward, *18:* 183-185
Lebenson, Richard, *6:* 209; *7:* 76; *23:* 145; *44:* 191
Le Cain, Errol, *6:* 141; *9:* 3; *22:* 142; *25:* 198; *28:* 173
Lee, Doris, *13:* 246; *32:* 183; *44:* 111
Lee, Manning de V., *2:* 200; *17:* 12; *27:* 87; *37:* 102, 103, 104; *YABC 2:* 304
Lee, Robert J., *3:* 97
Leech, John, *15:* 59
Leeman, Michael, *44:* 157
Lees, Harry, *6:* 112
Legènisel, *47:* 111
Legrand, Edy, *18:* 89, 93
Lehrman, Rosalie, *2:* 180
Leichman, Seymour, *5:* 107
Leighton, Clare, *25:* 130; *33:* 168; *37:* 105, 106, 108, 109
Leisk, David, *1:* 140-141; *11:* 54; *30:* 137, 142, 143, 144
Leloir, Maurice, *18:* 77, 80, 83, 99
Lemke, Horst, *14:* 98; *38:* 117, 118, 119
Lemke, R. W., *42:* 162
Lemon, David Gwynne, *9:* 1
Lenski, Lois, *1:* 144; *26:* 135, 137, 139, 141
Lent, Blair, *1:* 116-117; *2:* 174; *3:* 206-207; *7:* 168-169; *34:* 62
Leone, Leonard, *49:* 190
Lerner, Sharon, *11:* 157; *22:* 56
Leslie, Cecil, *19:* 244
Lester, Alison, *50:* 124
Le Tord, Bijou, *49:* 156
Levai, Blaise, *39:* 130
Levin, Ted, *12:* 148
Levine, David, *43:* 147, 149, 150, 151, 152
Levit, Herschel, *24:* 223
Levy, Jessica Ann, *19:* 225; *39:* 191
Lewin, Betsy, *32:* 114; *48:* 177
Lewin, Ted, *4:* 77; *8:* 168; *20:* 110; *21:* 99, 100; *27:* 110; *28:* 96, 97; *31:* 49; *45:* 55; *48:* 223
Lewis, Allen, *15:* 112
Lewis, Richard W., *52:* 25
Leydon, Rita Flodén, *21:* 101
Lieblich, Irene, *22:* 173; *27:* 209, 214
Liese, Charles, *4:* 222
Lightfoot, Norman R., *45:* 47
Lignell, Lois, *37:* 114
Lilly, Charles, *8:* 73; *20:* 127; *48:* 53
Lilly, Ken, *37:* 224
Lim, John, *43:* 153
Limona, Mercedes, *51:* 183
Lincoln, Patricia Henderson, *27:* 27

Lindberg, Howard, *10:* 123; *16:* 190
Linden, Seymour, *18:* 200-201; *43:* 140
Linder, Richard, *27:* 119
Lindman, Maj, *43:* 154
Lindsay, Vachel, *40:* 118
Line, Les, *27:* 143
Linell. *See* Smith, Linell
Lionni, Leo, *8:* 115
Lipinsky, Lino, *2:* 156; *22:* 175
Lippman, Peter, *8:* 31; *31:* 119, 120, 160
Lisker, Sonia O., *16:* 274; *31:* 31; *44:* 113, 114
Lisowski, Gabriel, *47:* 144; *49:* 157
Lissim, Simon, *17:* 138
Little, Harold, *16:* 72
Little, Mary E., *28:* 146
Livesly, Lorna, *19:* 216
Llerena, Carlos Antonio, *19:* 181
Lloyd, Errol, *11:* 39; *22:* 178
Lo, Koon-chiu, *7:* 134
Lobel, Anita, *6:* 87; *9:* 141; *18:* 248
Lobel, Arnold, *1:* 188-189; *5:* 12; *6:* 147; *7:* 167, 209; *18:* 190-191; *25:* 39, 43; *27:* 40; *29:* 174; *52:* 127
Loefgren, Ulf, *3:* 108
Loescher, Ann, *20:* 108
Loescher, Gil, *20:* 108
Lofting, Hugh, *15:* 182-183
Loh, George, *38:* 88
Lonette, Reisie, *11:* 211; *12:* 168; *13:* 56; *36:* 122; *43:* 155
Long, Sally, *42:* 184
Longtemps, Ken, *17:* 123; *29:* 221
Looser, Heinz, *YABC 2:* 208
Lopshire, Robert, *6:* 149; *21:* 117; *34:* 166
Lord, John Vernon, *21:* 104; *23:* 25; *51:* 22
Lorenz, Al, *40:* 146
Loretta, Sister Mary, *33:* 73
Lorraine, Walter H., *3:* 110; *4:* 123; *16:* 192
Loss, Joan, *11:* 163
Louderback, Walt, *YABC 1:* 164
Lousada, Sandra, *40:* 138
Low, Joseph, *14:* 124, 125; *18:* 68; *19:* 194; *31:* 166
Lowenheim, Alfred, *13:* 65-66
Lowitz, Anson, *17:* 124; *18:* 215
Lowrey, Jo, *8:* 133
Lubell, Winifred, *1:* 207; *3:* 15; *6:* 151
Lubin, Leonard B., *19:* 224; *36:* 79, 80; *45:* 128, 129, 131, 132, 133, 134, 135, 136, 137, 139, 140, 141; *YABC 2:* 96
Ludwig, Helen, *33:* 144, 145
Lufkin, Raymond, *38:* 138; *44:* 48
Luhrs, Henry, *7:* 123; *11:* 120
Lupo, Dom, *4:* 204
Lustig, Loretta, *30:* 186; *46:* 134, 135, 136, 137
Luzak, Dennis, *52:* 121
Lydecker, Laura, *21:* 113; *42:* 53
Lynch, Charles, *16:* 33
Lynch, Marietta, *29:* 137; *30:* 171
Lyon, Elinor, *6:* 154

Lyon, Fred, *14:* 16
Lyons, Oren, *8:* 193
Lyster, Michael, *26:* 41

Maas, Dorothy, *6:* 175
Maas, Julie, *47:* 61
Macaulay, David, *46:* 139, 140-141, 142, 143, 144-145, 147, 149, 150
Macdonald, Alister, *21:* 55
MacDonald, Norman, *13:* 99
Macdonald, Roberta, *19:* 237; *52:* 164
Mace, Varian, *49:* 159
Macguire, Robert Reid, *18:* 67
Machetanz, Fredrick, *34:* 147, 148
MacInnes, Ian, *35:* 59
MacIntyre, Elisabeth, *17:* 127-128
Mack, Stan, *17:* 129
Mackay, Donald, *17:* 60
MacKaye, Arvia, *32:* 119
MacKenzie, Garry, *33:* 159
Mackinlay, Miguel, *27:* 22
MacKinstry, Elizabeth, *15:* 110; *42:* 139, 140, 141, 142, 143, 144, 145
Maclise, Daniel, *YABC 2:* 257
Madden, Don, *3:* 112-113; *4:* 33, 108, 155; *7:* 193; *YABC 2:* 211
Maddison, Angela Mary, *10:* 83
Maestro, Giulio, *8:* 124; *12:* 17; *13:* 108; *25:* 182
Magnuson, Diana, *28:* 102; *34:* 190; *41:* 175
Maguire, Sheila, *41:* 100
Mahony, Will, *37:* 120
Mahood, Kenneth, *24:* 141
Maik, Henri, *9:* 102
Maisto, Carol, *29:* 87
Maitland, Antony, *1:* 100, 176; *8:* 41; *17:* 246; *24:* 46; *25:* 177, 178; *32:* 74
Makie, Pam, *37:* 117
Malsberg, Edward, *51:* 175
Malvern, Corinne, *2:* 13; *34:* 148, 149
Mandelbaum, Ira, *31:* 115
Manet, Edouard, *23:* 170
Mangurian, David, *14:* 133
Manham, Allan, *42:* 109
Manniche, Lise, *31:* 121
Manning, Samuel F., *5:* 75
Maraja, *15:* 86; *YABC 1:* 28; *YABC 2:* 115
Marcellino, Fred, *20:* 125; *34:* 222; *53:* 125
Marchesi, Stephen, *34:* 140; *46:* 72; *50:* 147
Marchiori, Carlos, *14:* 60
Margules, Gabriele, *21:* 120
Mariana. *See* Foster, Marian Curtis
Mariano, Michael, *52:* 108
Marino, Dorothy, *6:* 37; *14:* 135
Markham, R. L., *17:* 240
Marokvia, Artur, *31:* 122
Marriott, Pat, *30:* 30; *34:* 39; *35:* 164, 165, 166; *44:* 170; *48:* 186, 187, 188, 189, 191, 192, 193
Mars, W. T., *1:* 161; *3:* 115; *4:* 208, 225; *5:* 92, 105, 186; *8:* 214;

9: 12; *13:* 121; *27:* 151; *31:* 180;
38: 102; *48:* 66
Marsh, Christine, *3:* 164
Marsh, Reginald, *17:* 5; *19:* 89;
22: 90, 96
Marshall, Anthony D., *18:* 216
Marshall, James, *6:* 160; *40:* 221;
42: 24, 25, 29; *51:* 111, 112, 113,
114, 115, 116, 117, 118, 119,
120, 121
Martchenko, Michael, *50:* 129, 153,
155, 156, 157
Martin, David Stone, *23:* 232
Martin, Fletcher, *18:* 213; *23:* 151
Martin, René, *7:* 144; *42:* 148, 149,
150
Martin, Richard E., *51:* 157
Martin, Ron, *32:* 81
Martin, Stefan, *8:* 68; *32:* 124, 126
Martinez, John, *6:* 113
Martucci, Griesbach, *52:* 106
Marx, Robert F., *24:* 143
Masefield, Judith, *19:* 208, 209
Mason, George F., *14:* 139
Massie, Diane Redfield, *16:* 194
Massie, Kim, *31:* 43
Mathewuse, James, *51:* 143
Mathieu, Joseph, *14:* 33; *39:* 206;
43: 167
Matsubara, Naoko, *12:* 121
Matsuda, Shizu, *13:* 167
Matte, L'Enc, *22:* 183
Mattelson, Marvin, *36:* 50, 51
Matthews, F. Leslie, *4:* 216
Matulay, Laszlo, *5:* 18; *43:* 168
Matus, Greta, *12:* 142
Mauldin, Bill, *27:* 23
Mawicke, Tran, *9:* 137; *15:* 191;
47: 100
Max, Peter, *45:* 146, 147, 148-149,
150
Maxie, Betty, *40:* 135
Maxwell, John Alan, *1:* 148
Mayan, Earl, *7:* 193
Mayer, Marianna, *32:* 132
Mayer, Mercer, *11:* 192; *16:* 195-196;
20: 55, 57; *32:* 129, 130, 132,
133, 134; *41:* 144, 248, 252
Mayhew, Richard, *3:* 106
Mayo, Gretchen, *38:* 81
Mays, Victor, *5:* 127; *8:* 45, 153;
14: 245; *23:* 50; *34:* 155; *40:* 79;
45: 158
Mazal, Chanan, *49:* 104
Mazza, Adriana Saviozzi, *19:* 215
Mazzetti, Alan, *45:* 210
McBride, Angus, *28:* 49
McBride, Will, *30:* 110
McCaffery, Janet, *38:* 145
McCann, Gerald, *3:* 50; *4:* 94; *7:* 54;
41: 121
McCay, Winsor, *41:* 124, 126, 128-
129, 130-131
McClary, Nelson, *1:* 111
McClintock, Theodore, *14:* 141
McCloskey, Robert, *1:* 184-185;
2: 186-187; *17:* 209; *39:* 139,
140, 141, 142, 143, 146, 147, 148
McClung, Robert, *2:* 189

McClure, Gillian, *31:* 132
McConnel, Jerry, *31:* 75, 187
McCormick, A. D., *35:* 119
McCormick, Dell J., *19:* 216
McCrady, Lady, *16:* 198; *39:* 127
McCrea, James, *3:* 122; *33:* 216
McCrea, Ruth, *3:* 122; *27:* 102;
33: 216
McCully, Emily Arnold, *2:* 89;
4: 120-121, 146, 197; *5:* 2, 129;
7: 191; *11:* 122; *15:* 210; *33:* 23;
35: 244; *37:* 122; *39:* 88; *40:* 103;
50: 30, 31, 32, 33, 34, 35, 36-37;
52: 89, 90
McCurdy, Michael, *13:* 153; *24:* 85
McDermott, Beverly Brodsky, *11:* 180
McDermott, Gerald, *16:* 201
McDonald, Jill, *13:* 155; *26:* 128
McDonald, Ralph J., *5:* 123, 195
McDonough, Don, *10:* 163
McEntee, Dorothy, *37:* 124
McFall, Christie, *12:* 144
McGee, Barbara, *6:* 165
McGregor, Malcolm, *23:* 27
McHugh, Tom, *23:* 64
McIntosh, Jon, *42:* 56
McKay, Donald, *2:* 118; *32:* 157;
45: 151, 152
McKeating, Eileen, *44:* 58
McKee, David, *10:* 48; *21:* 9
McKie, Roy, *7:* 44
McKillip, Kathy, *30:* 153
McKinney, Ena, *26:* 39
McLachlan, Edward, *5:* 89
McLean, Sammis, *32:* 197
McLoughlin, John C., *47:* 149
McMahon, Robert, *36:* 155
McMillan, Bruce, *22:* 184
McMullan, James, *40:* 33
McNaught, Harry, *12:* 80; *32:* 136
McNaughton, Colin, *39:* 149; *40:* 108
McNicholas, Maureen, *38:* 148
McPhail, David, *14:* 105; *23:* 135;
37: 217, 218, 220, 221; *47:* 151,
152, 153, 154, 155, 156, 158-159,
160, 162-163, 164
McPhee, Richard B., *41:* 133
McQueen, Lucinda, *28:* 149; *41:* 249;
46: 206; *53:* 103
McVay, Tracy, *11:* 68
McVicker, Charles, *39:* 150
Mead, Ben Carlton, *43:* 75
Mecray, John, *33:* 62
Meddaugh, Susan, *20:* 42; *29:* 143;
41: 241
Melo, John, *16:* 285
Menasco, Milton, *43:* 85
Mendelssohn, Felix, *19:* 170
Meng, Heinz, *13:* 158
Mero, Lee, *34:* 68
Merrill, Frank T., *16:* 147; *19:* 71;
YABC 1: 226, 229, 273
Meryman, Hope, *27:* 41
Meryweather, Jack, *10:* 179
Meth, Harold, *24:* 203
Meyer, Herbert, *19:* 189
Meyer, Renate, *6:* 170
Meyers, Bob, *11:* 136
Meynell, Louis, *37:* 76

Micale, Albert, *2:* 65; *22:* 185
Middleton-Sandford, Betty, *2:* 125
Mieke, Anne, *45:* 74
Mighell, Patricia, *43:* 134
Mikolaycak, Charles, *9:* 144; *12:* 101;
13: 212; *21:* 121; *22:* 168;
30: 187; *34:* 103, 150; *37:* 183;
43: 179; *44:* 90; *46:* 115, 118-119;
49: 25
Miles, Jennifer, *17:* 278
Milhous, Katherine, *15:* 193; *17:* 51
Millais, John E., *22:* 230, 231
Millar, H. R., *YABC 1:* 194-195, 203
Millard, C. E., *28:* 186
Miller, Don, *15:* 195; *16:* 71; *20:* 106;
31: 178
Miller, Edna, *29:* 148
Miller, Frank J., *25:* 94
Miller, Grambs, *18:* 38; *23:* 16
Miller, Jane, *15:* 196
Miller, Marcia, *13:* 233
Miller, Marilyn, *1:* 87; *31:* 69; *33:* 157
Miller, Mitchell, *28:* 183; *34:* 207
Miller, Shane, *5:* 140
Mills, Yaroslava Surmach, *35:* 169,
170; *46:* 114
Millsap, Darrel, *51:* 102
Minor, Wendell, *39:* 188; *52:* 87
Mitsuhashi, Yoko, *45:* 153
Miyake, Yoshi, *38:* 141
Mizumura, Kazue, *10:* 143; *18:* 223;
36: 159
Mochi, Ugo, *8:* 122; *38:* 150
Modell, Frank, *39:* 152
Mohr, Nicholasa, *8:* 139
Moldon, Peter L., *49:* 168
Momaday, N. Scott, *48:* 159
Montresor, Beni, *2:* 91; *3:* 138;
38: 152, 153, 154, 155, 156-157,
158, 159, 160
Moon, Carl, *25:* 183, 184, 185
Moon, Eliza, *14:* 40
Moon, Ivan, *22:* 39; *38:* 140
Moore, Agnes Kay Randall, *43:* 187
Moore, Mary, *29:* 160
Mora, Raul Mina, *20:* 41
Mordvinoff, Nicolas, *15:* 179
Morgan, Tom, *42:* 157
Morrill, Les, *42:* 127
Morrill, Leslie, *18:* 218; *29:* 177;
33: 84; *38:* 147; *44:* 93; *48:* 164,
165, 167, 168, 169, 170, 171;
49: 162
Morris, *47:* 91
Morrison, Bill, *42:* 116
Morrow, Gray, *2:* 64; *5:* 200; *10:* 103,
114; *14:* 175
Morton, Lee Jack, *32:* 140
Morton, Marian, *3:* 185
Moses, Grandma, *18:* 228
Moskof, Martin Stephen, *27:* 152
Moss, Donald, *11:* 184
Moss, Geoffrey, *32:* 198
Most, Bernard, *48:* 173
Mowry, Carmen, *50:* 62
Moyers, William, *21:* 65
Moyler, Alan, *36:* 142
Mozley, Charles, *9:* 87; *20:* 176, 192,
193; *22:* 228; *25:* 205; *33:* 150;

43: 170, 171, 172, 173, 174;
   YABC 2: 89
Mueller, Hans Alexander, *26:* 64;
   27: 52, 53
Mugnaini, Joseph, *11:* 35; *27:* 52, 53;
   35: 62
Müller, Jörg, *35:* 215
Muller, Steven, *32:* 167
Mullins, Edward S., *10:* 101
Mullins, Patricia, *51:* 68
Munari, Bruno, *15:* 200
Munowitz, Ken, *14:* 148
Muñoz, William, *42:* 160
Munsinger, Lynn, *33:* 161; *46:* 126
Munson, Russell, *13:* 9
Murphy, Bill, *5:* 138
Murphy, Jill, *37:* 142
Murr, Karl, *20:* 62
Murray, Ossie, *43:* 176
Mussino, Attilio, *29:* 131
Mutchler, Dwight, *1:* 25
Myers, Bernice, *9:* 147; *36:* 75
Myers, Lou, *11:* 2

Nachreiner, Tom, *29:* 182
Nakai, Michael, *30:* 217
Nakatani, Chiyoko, *12:* 124
Nash, Linell, *46:* 175
Naso, John, *33:* 183
Nason, Thomas W., *14:* 68
Nasser, Muriel, *48:* 74
Nast, Thomas, *21:* 29; *28:* 23;
   51: 132, 133, 134, 135, 136, 137,
   138, 139, 141
Natti, Susanna, *20:* 146; *32:* 141, 142;
   35: 178; *37:* 143
Navarra, Celeste Scala, *8:* 142
Naylor, Penelope, *10:* 104
Nebel, M., *45:* 154
Neebe, William, *7:* 93
Needler, Jerry, *12:* 93
Neel, Alice, *31:* 23
Neely, Keith R., *46:* 124
Negri, Rocco, *3:* 213; *5:* 67; *6:* 91,
   108; *12:* 159
Neill, John R., *18:* 8, 10-11, 21, 30
Ness, Evaline, *1:* 164-165; *2:* 39; *3:* 8;
   10: 147; *12:* 53; *26:* 150, 151,
   152, 153; *49:* 30, 31, 32
Neville, Vera, *2:* 182
Newberry, Clare Turlay, *1:* 170
Newfeld, Frank, *14:* 121; *26:* 154
Newman, Ann, *43:* 90
Newsom, Carol, *40:* 159; *44:* 60;
   47: 189
Newsom, Tom, *49:* 149
Ng, Michael, *29:* 171
Nicholson, William, *15:* 33-34; *16:* 48
Nicklaus, Carol, *45:* 194
Nickless, Will, *16:* 139
Nicolas, *17:* 130, 132-133;
   YABC 2: 215
Niebrugge, Jane, *6:* 118
Nielsen, Jon, *6:* 100; *24:* 202
Nielsen, Kay, *15:* 7; *16:* 211-213, 215,
   217; *22:* 143; *YABC 1:* 32-33
Niland, Deborah, *25:* 191; *27:* 156

Niland, Kilmeny, *25:* 191
Ninon, *1:* 5; *38:* 101, 103, 108
Nissen, Rie, *44:* 35
Nixon, K., *14:* 152
Noble, Trinka Hakes, *39:* 162
Noguchi, Yoshie, *30:* 99
Nolan, Dennis, *42:* 163
Noonan, Julia, *4:* 163; *7:* 207; *25:* 151
Nordenskjold, Birgitta, *2:* 208
Norman, Mary, *36:* 138, 147
Norman, Michael, *12:* 117; *27:* 168
Numeroff, Laura Joffe, *28:* 161;
   30: 177
Nussbaumer, Paul, *16:* 219; *39:* 117
Nyce, Helene, *19:* 219
Nygren, Tord, *30:* 148

Oakley, Graham, *8:* 112; *30:* 164, 165
Oakley, Thornton, *YABC 2:* 189
Obligado, Lilian, *2:* 28, 66-67; *6:* 30;
   14: 179; *15:* 103; *25:* 84
Obrant, Susan, *11:* 186
O'Brien, Anne Sibley, *53:* 116, 117
O'Brien, John, *41:* 253
Odell, Carole, *35:* 47
O'Donohue, Thomas, *40:* 89
Oechsli, Kelly, *5:* 144-145; *7:* 115;
   8: 83, 183; *13:* 117; *20:* 94
Offen, Hilda, *42:* 207
Ogden, Bill, *42:* 59; *47:* 55
Ogg, Oscar, *33:* 34
Ohlsson, Ib, *4:* 152; *7:* 57; *10:* 20;
   11: 90; *19:* 217; *41:* 246
Ohtomo, Yasuo, *37:* 146; *39:* 212, 213
O'Kelley, Mattie Lou, *36:* 150
Oliver, Jenni, *23:* 121; *35:* 112
Olschewski, Alfred, *7:* 172
Olsen, Ib Spang, *6:* 178-179
Olugebefola, Ademola, *15:* 205
O'Neil, Dan IV, *7:* 176
O'Neill, Jean, *22:* 146
O'Neill, Rose, *48:* 30, 31
O'Neill, Steve, *21:* 118
Ono, Chiyo, *7:* 97
Orbaan, Albert, *2:* 31; *5:* 65, 171;
   9: 8; *14:* 241; *20:* 109
Orbach, Ruth, *21:* 112
Orfe, Joan, *20:* 81
Ormsby, Virginia H., *11:* 187
Orozco, José Clemente, *9:* 177
Orr, Forrest W., *23:* 9
Orr, N., *19:* 70
Osborne, Billie Jean, *35:* 209
Osmond, Edward, *10:* 111
O'Sullivan, Tom, *3:* 176; *4:* 55
Otto, Svend, *22:* 130, 141
Oudry, J. B., *18:* 167
Oughton, Taylor, *5:* 23
Övereng, Johannes, *44:* 36
Overlie, George, *11:* 156
Owens, Carl, *2:* 35; *23:* 521
Owens, Gail, *10:* 170; *12:* 157; *19:* 16;
   22: 70; *25:* 81; *28:* 203, 205;
   32: 221, 222; *36:* 132; *46:* 40;
   47: 57
Oxenbury, Helen, *3:* 150-151; *24:* 81

Padgett, Jim, *12:* 165
Page, Homer, *14:* 145
Paget, Sidney, *24:* 90, 91, 93, 95, 97
Pak, *12:* 76
Palazzo, Tony, *3:* 152-153
Palladini, David, *4:* 113; *40:* 176, 177,
   178-179, 181, 224-225; *50:* 138
Pallarito, Don, *43:* 36
Palmer, Heidi, *15:* 207; *29:* 102
Palmer, Jan, *42:* 153
Palmer, Juliette, *6:* 89; *15:* 208
Palmer, Lemuel, *17:* 25, 29
Palmquist, Eric, *38:* 133
Panesis, Nicholas, *3:* 127
Panton, Doug, *52:* 99
Papas, William, *11:* 223; *50:* 160
Papin, Joseph, *26:* 113
Papish, Robin Lloyd, *10:* 80
Paradis, Susan, *40:* 216
Paraquin, Charles H., *18:* 166
Paris, Peter, *31:* 127
Park, Seho, *39:* 110
Park, W. B., *22:* 189
Parker, Lewis, *2:* 179
Parker, Nancy Winslow, *10:* 113;
   22: 164; *28:* 47, 144; *52:* 7
Parker, Robert, *4:* 161; *5:* 74; *9:* 136;
   29: 39
Parker, Robert Andrew, *11:* 81;
   29: 186; *39:* 165; *40:* 25; *41:* 78;
   42: 123; *43:* 144; *48:* 182
Parks, Gordon, Jr., *33:* 228
Parnall, Peter, *5:* 137; *16:* 221; *24:* 70;
   40: 78; *51:* 130
Parnall, Virginia, *40:* 78
Parrish, Anne, *27:* 159, 160
Parrish, Dillwyn, *27:* 159
Parrish, Maxfield, *14:* 160, 161, 164,
   165; *16:* 109; *18:* 12-13;
   YABC 1: 149, 152, 267;
   YABC 2: 146, 149
Parry, David, *26:* 156
Parry, Marian, *13:* 176; *19:* 179
Partch, Virgil, *45:* 163, 165
Pascal, David, *14:* 174
Pasquier, J. A., *16:* 91
Paterson, Diane, *13:* 116; *39:* 163
Paterson, Helen, *16:* 93
Paton, Jane, *15:* 271; *35:* 176
Patterson, Robert, *25:* 118
Paul, James, *4:* 130; *23:* 161
Paull, Grace, *24:* 157
Payne, Joan Balfour, *1:* 118
Payson, Dale, *7:* 34; *9:* 151; *20:* 140;
   37: 22
Payzant, Charles, *21:* 147
Peake, Mervyn, *22:* 136, 149; *23:* 162,
   163, 164, *YABC 2:* 307
Pearson, Larry, *38:* 225
Peat, Fern B., *16:* 115
Peck, Anne Merriman, *18:* 241;
   24: 155
Pederson, Sharleen, *12:* 92
Pedersen, Vilhelm, *YABC 1:* 40
Peek, Merle, *39:* 168
Peet, Bill, *2:* 203; *41:* 159, 160, 161,
   162, 163
Peltier, Leslie C., *13:* 178

Pendle, Alexy, *7:* 159; *13:* 34; *29:* 161; *33:* 215
Pennington, Eunice, *27:* 162
Peppé, Mark, *28:* 142
Peppe, Rodney, *4:* 164-165
Perl, Susan, *2:* 98; *4:* 231; *5:* 44-45, 118; *6:* 199; *8:* 137; *12:* 88; *22:* 193; *34:* 54-55; *52:* 128; *YABC 1:* 176
Perry, Patricia, *29:* 137; *30:* 171
Perry, Roger, *27:* 163
Perske, Martha, *46:* 83; *51:* 108, 147
Pesek, Ludek, *15:* 237
Petersham, Maud, *17:* 108, 147-153
Petersham, Miska, *17:* 108, 147-153
Peterson, R. F., *7:* 101
Peterson, Russell, *7:* 130
Petie, Haris, *2:* 3; *10:* 41, 118; *11:* 227; *12:* 70
Petrides, Heidrun, *19:* 223
Peyo, *40:* 56, 57
Peyton, K. M., *15:* 212
Pfeifer, Herman, *15:* 262
Phillips, Douglas, *1:* 19
Phillips, F. D., *6:* 202
Phillips, Thomas, *30:* 55
"Phiz." *See* Browne, Hablot K.
Piatti, Celestino, *16:* 223
Picarella, Joseph, *13:* 147
Pickard, Charles, *12:* 38; *18:* 203; *36:* 152
Picken, George A., *23:* 150
Pickens, David, *22:* 156
Pienkowski, Jan, *6:* 183; *30:* 32
Pimlott, John, *10:* 205
Pincus, Harriet, *4:* 186; *8:* 179; *22:* 148; *27:* 164, 165
Pinkney, Jerry, *8:* 218; *10:* 40; *15:* 276; *20:* 66; *24:* 121; *33:* 109; *36:* 222; *38:* 200; *41:* 165, 166, 167, 168, 169, 170, 171, 173, 174; *44:* 198; *48:* 51; *53:* 20
Pinkwater, Daniel Manus, *46:* 180, 181, 182, 185, 188, 189, 190
Pinkwater, Manus, *8:* 156; *46:* 180
Pinto, Ralph, *10:* 131; *45:* 93
Pitz, Henry C., *4:* 168; *19:* 165; *35:* 128; *42:* 80; *YABC 2:* 95, 176
Pitzenberger, Lawrence J., *26:* 94
Plowden, David, *52:* 135, 136
Plummer, William, *32:* 31
Pogány, Willy, *15:* 46, 49; *19:* 222, 256; *25:* 214; *44:* 142, 143, 144, 145, 146, 147, 148
Poirson, V. A., *26:* 89
Polgreen, John, *21:* 44
Politi, Leo, *1:* 178; *4:* 53; *21:* 48; *47:* 173, 174, 176, 178, 179, 180, 181
Polonsky, Arthur, *34:* 168
Polseno, Jo, *1:* 53; *3:* 117; *5:* 114; *17:* 154; *20:* 87; *32:* 49; *41:* 245
Ponter, James, *5:* 204
Poortvliet, Rien, *6:* 212
Portal, Colette, *6:* 186; *11:* 203
Porter, George, *7:* 181
Potter, Beatrix, *YABC 1:* 208-210, 212, 213
Potter, Miriam Clark, *3:* 162

Powers, Richard M., *1:* 230; *3:* 218; *7:* 194; *26:* 186
Powledge, Fred, *37:* 154
Pratt, Charles, *23:* 29
Price, Christine, *2:* 247; *3:* 163, 253; *8:* 166
Price, Edward, *33:* 34
Price, Garrett, *1:* 76; *2:* 42
Price, Hattie Longstreet, *17:* 13
Price, Norman, *YABC 1:* 129
Price, Willard, *48:* 184
Primavera, Elise, *26:* 95
Primrose, Jean, *36:* 109
Prince, Leonora E., *7:* 170
Prittie, Edwin J., *YABC 1:* 120
Provensen, Alice, *37:* 204, 215, 222
Provensen, Martin, *37:* 204, 215, 222
Pucci, Albert John, *44:* 154
Pudlo, *8:* 59
Purdy, Susan, *8:* 162
Puskas, James, *5:* 141
Pyk, Jan, *7:* 26; *38:* 123
Pyle, Howard, *16:* 225-228, 230-232, 235; *24:* 27; *34:* 124, 125, 127, 128

Quackenbush, Robert, *4:* 190; *6:* 166; *7:* 175, 178; *9:* 86; *11:* 65, 221; *41:* 154; *43:* 157
Quennell, Marjorie (Courtney), *29:* 163, 164
Quidor, John, *19:* 82
Quirk, Thomas, *12:* 81

Rackham, Arthur, *15:* 32, 78, 214-227; *17:* 105, 115; *18:* 233; *19:* 254; *20:* 151; *22:* 129, 131, 132, 133; *23:* 175; *24:* 161, 181; *26:* 91; *32:* 118; *YABC 1:* 25, 45, 55, 147; *YABC 2:* 103, 142, 173, 210
Rafilson, Sidney, *11:* 172
Raible, Alton, *1:* 202-203; *28:* 193; *35:* 181
Ramsey, James, *16:* 41
Ramus, Michael, *51:* 171
Rand, Paul, *6:* 188
Ransome, Arthur, *22:* 201
Rao, Anthony, *28:* 126
Raphael, Elaine, *23:* 192
Rappaport, Eva, *6:* 190
Raskin, Ellen, *2:* 208-209; *4:* 142; *13:* 183; *22:* 68; *29:* 139; *36:* 134; *38:* 173, 174, 175, 176, 177, 178, 179, 180, 181
Ratzkin, Lawrence, *40:* 143
Rau, Margaret, *9:* 157
Raverat, Gwen, *YABC 1:* 152
Ravielli, Anthony, *1:* 198; *3:* 168; *11:* 143
Ray, Deborah. *See* Kogan, Deborah Ray.
Ray, Ralph, *2:* 239; *5:* 73
Raymond, Larry, *31:* 108
Rayner, Mary, *22:* 207; *47:* 140
Raynor, Dorka, *28:* 168

Raynor, Paul, *24:* 73
Razzi, James, *10:* 127
Read, Alexander D. "Sandy," *20:* 45
Reasoner, Charles, *53:* 33, 36, 37
Reed, Tom, *34:* 171
Reid, Stephen, *19:* 213; *22:* 89
Reinertson, Barbara, *44:* 150
Reiniger, Lotte, *40:* 185
Reiss, John J., *23:* 193
Relf, Douglas, *3:* 63
Relyea, C. M., *16:* 29; *31:* 153
Rémi, Georges, *13:* 184
Remington, Frederic, *19:* 188; *41:* 178, 179, 180, 181, 183, 184, 185, 186, 187, 188
Renlie, Frank, *11:* 200
Reschofsky, Jean, *7:* 118
Réthi, Lili, *2:* 153; *36:* 156
Reusswig, William, *3:* 267
Rey, H. A., *1:* 182; *26:* 163, 164, 166, 167, 169; *YABC 2:* 17
Reynolds, Doris, *5:* 71; *31:* 77
Rhead, Louis, *31:* 91
Rhodes, Andrew, *38:* 204; *50:* 163
Ribbons, Ian, *3:* 10; *37:* 161; *40:* 76
Rice, Elizabeth, *2:* 53, 214
Rice, James, *22:* 210
Rice, Eve, *34:* 174, 175
Richards, George, *40:* 116, 119, 121; *44:* 179
Richards, Henry, *YABC 1:* 228, 231
Richardson, Ernest, *2:* 144
Richardson, Frederick, *18:* 27, 31
Richman, Hilda, *26:* 132
Richmond, George, *24:* 179
Rieniets, Judy King, *14:* 28
Riger, Bob, *2:* 166
Riley, Kenneth, *22:* 230
Ringi, Kjell, *12:* 171
Rios, Tere. *See* Versace, Marie
Ripper, Charles L., *3:* 175
Ritz, Karen, *41:* 117
Rivkin, Jay, *15:* 230
Rivoche, Paul, *45:* 125
Roach, Marilynne, *9:* 158
Robbin, Jodi, *44:* 156, 159
Robbins, Frank, *42:* 167
Robbins, Ruth, *52:* 102
Roberts, Cliff, *4:* 126
Roberts, Doreen, *4:* 230; *28:* 105
Roberts, Jim, *22:* 166; *23:* 69; *31:* 110
Roberts, W., *22:* 2, 3
Robinson, Charles, *3:* 53; *5:* 14; *6:* 193; *7:* 150; *7:* 183; *8:* 38; *9:* 81; *13:* 188; *14:* 248-249; *23:* 149; *26:* 115; *27:* 48; *28:* 191; *32:* 28; *35:* 210; *36:* 37; *48:* 96; *52:* 33; *53:* 157
Robinson, Charles [1870-1937], *17:* 157, 171-173, 175-176; *24:* 207; *25:* 204; *YABC 2:* 308-310, 331
Robinson, Jerry, *3:* 262
Robinson, Joan G., *7:* 184
Robinson, T. H., *17:* 179, 181-183; *29:* 254
Robinson, W. Heath, *17:* 185, 187, 189, 191, 193, 195, 197, 199,

202; *23:* 167; *25:* 194; *29:* 150;
  YABC 1: 44; *YABC 2:* 183
Roche, Christine, *41:* 98
Rocker, Fermin, *7:* 34; *13:* 21; *31:* 40;
  40: 190, 191
Rockwell, Anne, *5:* 147; *33:* 171, 173
Rockwell, Gail, *7:* 186
Rockwell, Harlow, *33:* 171, 173, 175
Rockwell, Norman, *23:* 39, 196, 197,
  199, 200, 203, 204, 207; *41:* 140,
  143; *YABC 2:* 60
Rodegast, Roland, *43:* 100
Rodriguez, Joel, *16:* 65
Roever, J. M., *4:* 119; *26:* 170
Roffey, Maureen, *33:* 142, 176, 177
Rogasky, Barbara, *46:* 90
Rogers, Carol, *2:* 262; *6:* 164; *26:* 129
Rogers, Frances, *10:* 130
Rogers, Walter S., *31:* 135, 138
Rogers, William A., *15:* 151, 153-154;
  33: 35
Rojankovsky, Feodor, *6:* 134, 136;
  10: 183; *21:* 128, 129, 130;
  25: 110; *28:* 42
Rorer, Abigail, *43:* 222
Rosamilia, Patricia, *36:* 120
Rose, Carl, *5:* 62
Rose, David S., *29:* 109
Rosenbaum, Jonathan, *50:* 46
Rosenblum, Richard, *11:* 202; *18:* 18
Rosier, Lydia, *16:* 236; *20:* 104;
  21: 109; *22:* 125; *30:* 151, 158;
  42: 128; *45:* 214
Ross. *See* Thomson, Ross
Ross, Clare Romano, *3:* 123; *21:* 45;
  48: 199
Ross, Dave, *32:* 152
Ross, Herbert, *37:* 78
Ross, John, *3:* 123; *21:* 45
Ross, Johnny, *32:* 190
Ross, Larry, *47:* 168
Ross, Tony, *17:* 204
Rossetti, Dante Gabriel, *20:* 151, 153
Roth, Arnold, *4:* 238; *21:* 133
Rotondo, Pat, *32:* 158
Roughsey, Dick, *35:* 186
Rouille, M., *11:* 96
Rounds, Glen, *8:* 173; *9:* 171; *12:* 56;
  32: 194; *40:* 230; *51:* 161, 162,
  166; *YABC 1:* 1-3
Rowan, Evadne, *52:* 51
Rowe, Gavin, *27:* 144
Rowell, Kenneth, *40:* 72
Rowen, Amy, *52:* 143
Roy, Jeroo, *27:* 229; *36:* 110
Rubel, Nicole, *18:* 255; *20:* 59
Rubel, Reina, *33:* 217
Rud, Borghild, *6:* 15
Rudolph, Norman Guthrie, *17:* 13
Rue, Leonard Lee III, *37:* 164
Ruff, Donna, *50:* 173
Ruffins, Reynold, *10:* 134-135;
  41: 191, 192-193, 194-195, 196
Ruhlin, Roger, *34:* 44
Ruse, Margaret, *24:* 155
Rush, Peter, *42:* 75
Russell, E. B., *18:* 177, 182
Russell, Jim, *53:* 134
Russo, Susan, *30:* 182; *36:* 144

Ruth, Rod, *9:* 161
Rutherford, Meg, *25:* 174; *34:* 178,
  179
Rutland, Jonathan, *31:* 126
Ryden, Hope, *8:* 176
Rymer, Alta M., *34:* 181
Rystedt, Rex, *49:* 80

Saaf, Chuck, *49:* 179
Sabaka, Donna R., *21:* 172
Sabin, Robert, *45:* 35
Sacker, Amy, *16:* 100
Saffioti, Lino, *36:* 176; *48:* 60
Sagsoorian, Paul, *12:* 183; *22:* 154;
  33: 106
Saint Exupéry, Antoine de, *20:* 157
St. John, J. Allen, *41:* 62
Saldutti, Denise, *39:* 186
Sale, Morton, *YABC 2:* 31
Sambourne, Linley, *YABC 2:* 181
Sampson, Katherine, *9:* 197
Samson, Anne S., *2:* 216
Sancha, Sheila, *38:* 185
Sand, George X., *45:* 182
Sandberg, Lasse, *15:* 239, 241
Sanders, Beryl, *39:* 173
Sanderson, Ruth, *21:* 126; *24:* 53;
  28: 63; *33:* 67; *41:* 48, 198, 199,
  200, 201, 202, 203; *43:* 79;
  46: 36, 44; *47:* 102; *49:* 58
Sandin, Joan, *4:* 36; *6:* 194; *7:* 177;
  12: 145, 185; *20:* 43; *21:* 74;
  26: 144; *27:* 142; *28:* 224, 225;
  38: 86; *41:* 46; *42:* 35
Sandland, Reg, *39:* 215
Sandoz, Edouard, *26:* 45, 47
San Souci, Daniel, *40:* 200
Sapieha, Christine, *1:* 180
Sarg, Tony, *YABC 2:* 236
Sargent, Robert, *2:* 217
Saris, *1:* 33
Sarony, *YABC 2:* 170
Sasek, Miroslav, *16:* 239-242
Sassman, David, *9:* 79
Sätty, *29:* 203, 205
Sauber, Rob, *40:* 183
Savage, Steele, *10:* 203; *20:* 77; *35:* 28
Savitt, Sam, *8:* 66, 182; *15:* 278;
  20: 96; *24:* 192; *28:* 98
Say, Allen, *28:* 178
Scabrini, Janet, *13:* 191; *44:* 128
Scarry, Huck, *35:* 204-205
Scarry, Richard, *2:* 220-221; *18:* 20;
  35: 193, 194-195, 196, 197, 198,
  199, 200-201, 202
Schaeffer, Mead, *18:* 81, 94; *21:* 137,
  138, 139; *47:* 128
Scharl, Josef, *20:* 132; *22:* 128
Scheel, Lita, *11:* 230
Scheib, Ida, *29:* 28
Schermer, Judith, *30:* 184
Schick, Joel, *16:* 160; *17:* 167; *22:* 12;
  27: 176; *31:* 147, 148; *36:* 23;
  38: 64; *45:* 116, 117; *52:* 5, 85
Schindelman, Joseph, *1:* 74; *4:* 101;
  12: 49; *26:* 51; *40:* 146
Schindler, Edith, *7:* 22

Schindler, S. D., *38:* 107; *46:* 196
Schlesinger, Bret, *7:* 77
Schmid, Eleanore, *12:* 188
Schmiderer, Dorothy, *19:* 224
Schmidt, Elizabeth, *15:* 242
Schneider, Rex, *29:* 64; *44:* 171
Schoenherr, Ian, *32:* 83
Schoenherr, John, *1:* 146-147, 173;
  3: 39, 139; *17:* 75; *29:* 72; *32:* 83;
  37: 168, 169, 170; *43:* 164, 165;
  45: 160, 162; *51:* 127
Schomburg, Alex, *13:* 23
Schongut, Emanuel, *4:* 102; *15:* 186;
  47: 218, 219; *52:* 147, 148, 149,
  150
Schoonover, Frank, *17:* 107; *19:* 81,
  190, 233; *22:* 88, 129; *24:* 189;
  31: 88; *41:* 69; *YABC 2:* 282, 316
Schottland, Miriam, *22:* 172
Schramm, Ulrik, *2:* 16; *14:* 112
Schreiber, Elizabeth Anne, *13:* 193
Schreiber, Ralph W., *13:* 193
Schreiter, Rick, *14:* 97; *23:* 171;
  41: 247; *49:* 131
Schroeder, E. Peter, *12:* 112
Schroeder, Ted, *11:* 160; *15:* 189;
  30: 91; *34:* 43
Schrotter, Gustav, *22:* 212; *30:* 225
Schucker, James, *31:* 163
Schulz, Charles M., *10:* 137-142
Schwark, Mary Beth, *51:* 155
Schwartz, Amy, *47:* 191
Schwartz, Charles, *8:* 184
Schwartz, Daniel, *46:* 37
Schwartzberg, Joan, *3:* 208
Schweitzer, Iris, *2:* 137; *6:* 207
Schweninger, Ann, *29:* 172
Scott, Anita Walker, *7:* 38
Scott, Art, *39:* 41
Scott, Frances Gruse, *38:* 43
Scott, Julian, *34:* 126
Scott, Roszel, *33:* 238
Scott, Trudy, *27:* 172
Scribner, Joanne, *14:* 236; *29:* 78;
  33: 185; *34:* 208
Scrofani, Joseph, *31:* 65
Seaman, Mary Lott, *34:* 64
Searle, Ronald, *24:* 98; *42:* 172, 173,
  174, 176, 177, 179
Searle, Townley, *36:* 85
Sebree, Charles, *18:* 65
Sedacca, Joseph M., *11:* 25; *22:* 36
Ségur, Adrienne, *27:* 121
Seignobosc, Francoise, *21:* 145, 146
Sejima, Yoshimasa, *8:* 187
Selig, Sylvie, *13:* 199
Seltzer, Isadore, *6:* 18
Seltzer, Meyer, *17:* 214
Sempé, Jean-Jacques, *47:* 92;
  YABC 2: 109
Sendak, Maurice, *1:* 135, 190; *3:* 204;
  7: 142; *15:* 199; *17:* 210; *27:* 181,
  182, 183, 185, 186, 187, 189,
  190-191, 192, 193, 194, 195, 197,
  198, 199, 203; *28:* 181, 182;
  32: 108; *33:* 148, 149; *35:* 238;
  44: 180, 181; *45:* 97, 99; *46:* 174;
  YABC 1: 167
Sengler, Johanna, *18:* 256

Seredy, Kate, *1:* 192; *14:* 20-21;
   17: 210
Sergeant, John, *6:* 74
Servello, Joe, *10:* 144; *24:* 139; *40:* 91
Seton, Ernest Thompson, *18:* 260-269,
   271
Seuss, Dr. *See* Geisel, Theodor
Severin, John Powers, *7:* 62
Sewall, Marcia, *15:* 8; *22:* 170;
   37: 171, 172, 173; *39:* 73;
   45: 209
Seward, Prudence, *16:* 243
Sewell, Helen, *3:* 186; *15:* 308;
   33: 102; *38:* 189, 190, 191, 192
Shahn, Ben, *39:* 178; *46:* 193
Shalansky, Len, *38:* 167
Shanks, Anne Zane, *10:* 149
Sharp, Paul, *52:* 60
Sharp, William, *6:* 131; *19:* 241;
   20: 112; *25:* 141
Shaw, Charles, *21:* 135; *38:* 187;
   47: 124
Shaw, Charles G., *13:* 200
Shearer, Ted, *43:* 193, 194, 195, 196
Shecter, Ben, *16:* 244; *25:* 109;
   33: 188, 191; *41:* 77
Shefcik, James, *48:* 221, 222
Shefts, Joelle, *48:* 210
Shekerjian, Haig, *16:* 245
Shekerjian, Regina, *16:* 245; *25:* 73
Shenton, Edward, *45:* 187, 188, 189;
   YABC 1: 218-219, 221
Shepard, Ernest H., *3:* 193; *4:* 74;
   16: 101; *17:* 109; *25:* 148;
   33: 152, 199, 200, 201, 202, 203,
   204, 205, 206, 207; *46:* 194;
   YABC 1: 148, 153, 174, 176,
   180-181
Shepard, Mary, *4:* 210; *22:* 205;
   30: 132, 133
Sherman, Theresa, *27:* 167
Sherwan, Earl, *3:* 196
Shields, Charles, *10:* 150; *36:* 63
Shields, Leonard, *13:* 83, 85, 87
Shillabeer, Mary, *35:* 74
Shilston, Arthur, *49:* 61
Shimin, Symeon, *1:* 93; *2:* 128-129;
   3: 202; *7:* 85; *11:* 177; *12:* 139;
   13: 202-203; *27:* 138; *28:* 65;
   35: 129; *36:* 130; *48:* 151; *49:* 59
Shinn, Everett, *16:* 148; *18:* 229;
   21: 149, 150, 151; *24:* 218
Shore, Robert, *27:* 54; *39:* 192, 193;
   YABC 2: 200
Shortall, Leonard, *4:* 144; *8:* 196;
   10: 166; *19:* 227, 228-229, 230;
   25: 78; *28:* 66, 167; *33:* 127;
   52: 125
Shortt, T. M., *27:* 36
Shtainments, Leon, *32:* 161
Shulevitz, Uri, *3:* 198-199; *17:* 85;
   22: 204; *27:* 212; *28:* 184;
   50: 190, 191, 192, 193, 194-195,
   196, 197, 198, 199, 201
Shute, Linda, *46:* 59
Siberell, Anne, *29:* 193
Sibley, Don, *1:* 39; *12:* 196; *31:* 47
Sidjakov, Nicolas, *18:* 274
Siebel, Fritz, *3:* 120; *17:* 145

Siegl, Helen, *12:* 166; *23:* 216;
   34: 185, 186
Sills, Joyce, *5:* 199
Silverstein, Alvin, *8:* 189
Silverstein, Shel, *33:* 211
Silverstein, Virginia, *8:* 189
Simon, Eric M., *7:* 82
Simon, Hilda, *28:* 189
Simon, Howard, *2:* 175; *5:* 132;
   19: 199; *32:* 163, 164, 165
Simont, Marc, *2:* 119; *4:* 213; *9:* 168;
   13: 238, 240; *14:* 262; *16:* 179;
   18: 221; *26:* 210; *33:* 189, 194;
   44: 132
Sims, Blanche, *44:* 116
Singer, Edith G., *2:* 30
Singer, Gloria, *34:* 56; *36:* 43
Singer, Julia, *28:* 190
Sivard, Robert, *26:* 124
Skardinski, Stanley, *23:* 144; *32:* 84
Slackman, Charles B., *12:* 201
Slater, Rod, *25:* 167
Sloan, Joseph, *16:* 68
Sloane, Eric, *21:* 3; *52:* 153, 154, 155,
   156, 157, 158, 160
Slobodkin, Louis, *1:* 200; *3:* 232;
   5: 168; *13:* 251; *15:* 13, 88;
   26: 173, 174, 175, 176, 178, 179
Slobodkina, Esphyr, *1:* 201
Small, David, *50:* 204-205
Small, W., *33:* 113
Smalley, Janet, *1:* 154
Smedley, William T., *34:* 129
Smee, David, *14:* 78
Smith, A. G., Jr., *35:* 182
Smith, Alvin, *1:* 31, 229; *13:* 187;
   27: 216; *28:* 226; *48:* 149; *49:* 60
Smith, Anne Warren, *41:* 212
Smith, Carl, *36:* 41
Smith, Doris Susan, *41:* 139
Smith, E. Boyd, *19:* 70; *22:* 89;
   26: 63; *YABC 1:* 4-5, 240,
   248-249
Smith, Edward J., *4:* 224
Smith, Eunice Young, *5:* 170
Smith, Howard, *19:* 196
Smith, Jacqueline Bardner, *27:* 108;
   39: 197
Smith, Jessie Willcox, *15:* 91; *16:* 95;
   18: 231; *19:* 57, 242; *21:* 29, 156,
   157, 158, 159, 160, 161; *34:* 65;
   YABC 1: 6; *YABC 2:* 180, 185,
   191, 311, 325
Smith, Joseph A., *52:* 131
Smith, Kenneth R., *47:* 182
Smith, L. H., *35:* 174
Smith, Lee, *29:* 32
Smith, Linell Nash, *2:* 195
Smith, Maggie Kaufman, *13:* 205;
   35: 191
Smith, Moishe, *33:* 155
Smith, Philip, *44:* 134; *46:* 203
Smith, Ralph Crosby, *2:* 267; *49:* 203
Smith, Robert D., *5:* 63
Smith, Susan Carlton, *12:* 208
Smith, Terry, *12:* 106; *33:* 158
Smith, Virginia, *3:* 157; *33:* 72
Smith, William A., *1:* 36; *10:* 154;
   25: 65

Smollin, Mike, *39:* 203
Smyth, M. Jane, *12:* 15
Snyder, Andrew A., *30:* 212
Snyder, Jerome, *13:* 207; *30:* 173
Snyder, Joel, *28:* 163
Sofia, *1:* 62; *5:* 90; *32:* 166
Sokol, Bill, *37:* 178; *49:* 23
Sokolov, Kirill, *34:* 188
Solbert, Ronni, *1:* 159; *2:* 232; *5:* 121;
   6: 34; *17:* 249
Solonevich, George, *15:* 246; *17:* 47
Sommer, Robert, *12:* 211
Sorel, Edward, *4:* 61; *36:* 82
Sotomayor, Antonio, *11:* 215
Soyer, Moses, *20:* 177
Spaenkuch, August, *16:* 28
Spanfeller, James, *1:* 72, 149; *2:* 183;
   19: 230, 231, 232; *22:* 66;
   36: 160, 161; *40:* 75; *52:* 166
Sparks, Mary Walker, *15:* 247
Spence, Geraldine, *21:* 163; *47:* 196
Spence, Jim, *38:* 89; *50:* 102
Spiegel, Doris, *29:* 111
Spier, Jo, *10:* 30
Spier, Peter, *3:* 155; *4:* 200; *7:* 61;
   11: 78; *38:* 106
Spilka, Arnold, *5:* 120; *6:* 204; *8:* 131
Spivak, I. Howard, *8:* 10
Spollen, Christopher J., *12:* 214
Spooner, Malcolm, *40:* 142
Sprattler, Rob, *12:* 176
Spring, Bob, *5:* 60
Spring, Ira, *5:* 60
Springer, Harriet, *31:* 92
Spurrier, Steven, *28:* 198
Spy. *See* Ward, Leslie
Staffan, Alvin E., *11:* 56; *12:* 187
Stahl, Ben, *5:* 181; *12:* 91; *49:* 122
Stair, Gobin, *35:* 214
Stamaty, Mark Alan, *12:* 215
Stampnick, Ken, *51:* 142
Stanley, Diane, *3:* 45; *37:* 180
Stasiak, Krystyna, *49:* 181
Steadman, Ralph, *32:* 180
Steichen, Edward, *30:* 79
Steig, William, *18:* 275-276
Stein, Harve, *1:* 109
Steinberg, Saul, *47:* 193
Steinel, William, *23:* 146
Steiner, Charlotte, *45:* 196
Stephens, Charles H., *YABC 2:* 279
Stephens, William M., *21:* 165
Steptoe, John, *8:* 197
Stern, Simon, *15:* 249-250; *17:* 58;
   34: 192-193
Sterret, Jane, *53:* 27
Stevens, Janet, *40:* 126
Stevens, Mary, *11:* 193; *13:* 129;
   43: 95
Stevenson, James, *42:* 182, 183;
   51: 163
Stewart, Arvis, *33:* 98; *36:* 69
Stewart, Charles, *2:* 205
Stiles, Fran, *26:* 85
Stillman, Susan, *44:* 130
Stimpson, Tom, *49:* 171
Stinemetz, Morgan, *40:* 151
Stirnweis, Shannon, *10:* 164

Stobbs, William, *1:* 48-49; *3:* 68; *6:* 20; *17:* 117, 217; *24:* 150; *29:* 250
Stock, Catherine, *37:* 55
Stolp, Jaap, *49:* 98
Stone, David, *9:* 173
Stone, David K., *4:* 38; *6:* 124; *9:* 180; *43:* 182
Stone, Helen, *44:* 121, 122, 126
Stone, Helen V., *6:* 209
Stratton, Helen, *33:* 151
Stratton-Porter, Gene, *15:* 254, 259, 263-264, 268-269
Streano, Vince, *20:* 173
Strodl, Daniel, *47:* 95
Strong, Joseph D., Jr., *YABC 2:* 330
Ströyer, Poul, *13:* 221
Strugnell, Ann, *27:* 38
Stubis, Talivaldis, *5:* 182, 183; *10:* 45; *11:* 9; *18:* 304; *20:* 127
Stubley, Trevor, *14:* 43; *22:* 219; *23:* 37; *28:* 61
Stuecklen, Karl W., *8:* 34, 65; *23:* 103
Stull, Betty, *11:* 46
Suba, Susanne, *4:* 202-203; *14:* 261; *23:* 134; *29:* 222; *32:* 30
Sugarman, Tracy, *3:* 76; *8:* 199; *37:* 181, 182
Sugita, Yutaka, *36:* 180-181
Sullivan, Edmund J., *31:* 86
Sullivan, James F., *19:* 280; *20:* 192
Sumichrast, Jözef, *14:* 253; *29:* 168, 213
Sumiko, *46:* 57
Summers, Leo, *1:* 177; *2:* 273; *13:* 22
Svolinsky, Karel, *17:* 104
Swain, Su Zan Noguchi, *21:* 170
Swan, Susan, *22:* 220-221; *37:* 66
Swayne, Sam, *53:* 143, 145
Swayne, Zoa, *53:* 143, 145
Sweat, Lynn, *25:* 206
Sweet, Darryl, *1:* 163; *4:* 136
Sweet, Ozzie, *31:* 149, 151, 152
Sweetland, Robert, *12:* 194
Swope, Martha, *43:* 160
Sylvester, Natalie G., *22:* 222
Szafran, Gene, *24:* 144
Szasz, Susanne, *13:* 55, 226; *14:* 48
Szekeres, Cyndy, *2:* 218; *5:* 185; *8:* 85; *11:* 166; *14:* 19; *16:* 57, 159; *26:* 49, 214; *34:* 205

Taback, Simms, *40:* 207; *52:* 120
Tafuri, Nancy, *39:* 210
Tait, Douglas, *12:* 220
Takakjian, Portia, *15:* 274
Takashima, Shizuye, *13:* 228
Talarczyk, June, *4:* 173
Tallon, Robert, *2:* 228; *43:* 200, 201, 202, 203, 204, 205, 206, 207, 209
Tamas, Szecskó, *29:* 135
Tamburine, Jean, *12:* 222
Tandy, H. R., *13:* 69
Tannenbaum, Robert, *48:* 181
Tanobe, Miyuki, *23:* 221
Tarkington, Booth, *17:* 224-225
Taylor, Ann, *41:* 226

Taylor, Isaac, *41:* 228
Teale, Edwin Way, *7:* 196
Teason, James, *1:* 14
Teeple, Lyn, *33:* 147
Tee-Van, Helen Damrosch, *10:* 176; *11:* 182
Teicher, Dick, *50:* 211
Tempest, Margaret, *3:* 237, 238
Temple, Herbert, *45:* 201
Templeton, Owen, *11:* 77
Tenggren, Gustaf, *18:* 277-279; *19:* 15; *28:* 86; *YABC 2:* 145
Tenney, Gordon, *24:* 204
Tenniel, John, *YABC 2:* 99
Thacher, Mary M., *30:* 72
Thackeray, William Makepeace, *23:* 224, 228
Thamer, Katie, *42:* 187
Thelwell, Norman, *14:* 201
Theobalds, Prue, *40:* 23
Theurer, Marilyn Churchill, *39:* 195
Thistlethwaite, Miles, *12:* 224
Thollander, Earl, *11:* 47; *18:* 112; *22:* 224
Thomas, Allan, *22:* 13
Thomas, Art, *48:* 217
Thomas, Eric, *28:* 49
Thomas, Harold, *20:* 98
Thomas, Mark, *42:* 136
Thomas, Martin, *14:* 255
Thompson, Arthur, *34:* 107
Thompson, Ellen, *51:* 88, 151
Thompson, George, *22:* 18; *28:* 150; *33:* 135
Thompson, George, W., *33:* 135
Thompson, Julie, *44:* 158
Thomson, Arline K., *3:* 264
Thomson, Hugh, *26:* 88
Thomson, Ross, *36:* 179
Thorne, Diana, *25:* 212
Thorvall, Kerstin, *13:* 235
Thurber, James, *13:* 239, 242-245, 248-249
Tibbles, Paul, *45:* 23
Tichenor, Tom, *14:* 207
Tiegreen, Alan, *36:* 143; *43:* 55, 56, 58
Tilney, F. C., *22:* 231
Timbs, Gloria, *36:* 90
Timmins, Harry, *2:* 171
Tinkelman, Murray, *12:* 225; *35:* 44
Titherington, Jeanne, *39:* 90
Tolford, Joshua, *1:* 221
Tolkien, J. R. R., *2:* 243; *32:* 215
Tolmie, Ken, *15:* 292
Tomei, Lorna, *47:* 168, 171
Tomes, Jacqueline, *2:* 117; *12:* 139
Tomes, Margot, *1:* 224; *2:* 120-121; *16:* 207; *18:* 250; *20:* 7; *25:* 62; *27:* 78, 79; *29:* 81, 199; *33:* 82; *36:* 186, 187, 188, 189, 190; *46:* 129
Toner, Raymond John, *10:* 179
Toothill, Harry, *6:* 54; *7:* 49; *25:* 219; *42:* 192
Toothill, Ilse, *6:* 54
Topolski, Feliks, *44:* 48
Torbert, Floyd James, *22:* 226
Torrey, Marjorie, *34:* 105

Toschik, Larry, *6:* 102
Totten, Bob, *13:* 93
Travers, Bob, *49:* 100
Tremain, Ruthven, *17:* 238
Tresilian, Stuart, *25:* 53; *40:* 212
Trez, Alain, *17:* 236
Trier, Walter, *14:* 96
Trimby, Elisa, *47:* 199
Trinkle, Sally, *53:* 27
Tripp, F. J., *24:* 167
Tripp, Wallace, *2:* 48; *7:* 28; *8:* 94; *10:* 54, 76; *11:* 92; *31:* 170, 171; *34:* 203; *42:* 57
Trivas, Irene, *53:* 4
Trnka, Jiri, *22:* 151; *43:* 212, 213, 214, 215; *YABC 1:* 30-31
Troughton, Joanna, *37:* 186; *48:* 72
Troyer, Johannes, *3:* 16; *7:* 18
Trudeau, G. B., *35:* 220, 221, 222; *48:* 119, 123, 126, 127, 128-129, 133
Tsinajinie, Andy, *2:* 62
Tsugami, Kyuzo, *18:* 198-199
Tuckwell, Jennifer, *17:* 205
Tudor, Bethany, *7:* 103
Tudor, Tasha, *18:* 227; *20:* 185, 186, 187; *36:* 111; *YABC 2:* 46, 314
Tulloch, Maurice, *24:* 79
Tunis, Edwin, *1:* 218-219; *28:* 209, 210, 211, 212
Turkle, Brinton, *1:* 211, 213; *2:* 249; *3:* 226; *11:* 3; *16:* 209; *20:* 22; *50:* 23; *YABC 1:* 79
Turska, Krystyna, *12:* 103; *31:* 173, 174-175
Tusan, Stan, *6:* 58; *22:* 236-237
Tworkov, Jack, *47:* 207
Tzimoulis, Paul, *12:* 104

Uchida, Yoshiko, *1:* 220
Uderzo, *47:* 88
Ulm, Robert, *17:* 238
Unada. See Gliewe, Unada
Underhill, Liz, *53:* 159
Underwood, Clarence, *40:* 166
Ungerer, Tomi, *5:* 188; *9:* 40; *18:* 188; *29:* 175; *33:* 221, 222-223, 225
Unwin, Nora S., *3:* 65, 234-235; *4:* 237; *44:* 173, 174; *YABC 1:* 59; *YABC 2:* 301
Uris, Jill, *49:* 188, 197
Ursell, Martin, *50:* 51
Utpatel, Frank, *18:* 114
Utz, Lois, *5:* 190

Van Abbé, S., *16:* 142; *18:* 282; *31:* 90; *YABC 2:* 157, 161
Van Allsburg, Chris, *37:* 205, 206; *53:* 161, 162, 163, 165, 166, 167, 168, 169, 170-71
Vandivert, William, *21:* 175
Van Everen, Jay, *13:* 160; *YABC 1:* 121
Van Horn, William, *43:* 218

Van Loon, Hendrik Willem, *18:* 285, 289, 291
Van Sciver, Ruth, *37:* 162
Van Stockum, Hilda, *5:* 193
Van Wely, Babs, *16:* 50
Varga, Judy, *29:* 196
Vasiliu, Mircea, *2:* 166, 253; *9:* 166; *13:* 58
Vaughn, Frank, *34:* 157
Vavra, Robert, *8:* 206
Vawter, Will, *17:* 163
Veeder, Larry, *18:* 4
Velasquez, Eric, *45:* 217
Vendrell, Carme Solé, *42:* 205
Ver Beck, Frank, *18:* 16-17
Verney, John, *14:* 225
Verrier, Suzanne, *5:* 20; *23:* 212
Versace, Marie, *2:* 255
Vestal, H. B., *9:* 134; *11:* 101; *27:* 25; *34:* 158
Vickrey, Robert, *45:* 59, 64
Victor, Joan Berg, *30:* 193
Viereck, Ellen, *3:* 242; *14:* 229
Vigna, Judith, *15:* 293
Vilato, Gaspar E., *5:* 41
Villiard, Paul, *51:* 178
Vimnèra, A., *23:* 154
Vincent, Eric, *34:* 98
Vincent, Félix, *41:* 237
Vip, *45:* 164
Vivas, Julie, *51:* 67, 69
Vo-Dinh, Mai, *16:* 272
Vogel, Ilse-Margret, *14:* 230
Voigt, Erna, *35:* 228
Vojtech, Anna, *42:* 190
von Schmidt, Eric, *8:* 62; *50:* 209, 210
von Schmidt, Harold, *30:* 80
Vosburgh, Leonard, *1:* 161; *7:* 32; *15:* 295-296; *23:* 110; *30:* 214; *43:* 181
Voter, Thomas W., *19:* 3, 9
Vroman, Tom, *10:* 29

Waber, Bernard, *47:* 209, 210, 211, 212, 213, 214
Wagner, John, *8:* 200; *52:* 104
Wagner, Ken, *2:* 59
Waide, Jan, *29:* 225; *36:* 139
Wainwright, Jerry, *14:* 85
Wakeen, Sandra, *47:* 97
Waldman, Bruce, *15:* 297; *43:* 178
Waldman, Neil, *35:* 141; *50:* 163; *51:* 180
Walker, Charles, *1:* 46; *4:* 59; *5:* 177; *11:* 115; *19:* 45; *34:* 74
Walker, Dugald Stewart, *15:* 47; *32:* 202; *33:* 112
Walker, Gil, *8:* 49; *23:* 132; *34:* 42
Walker, Jim, *10:* 94
Walker, Mort, *8:* 213
Walker, Norman, *41:* 37; *45:* 58
Walker, Stephen, *12:* 229; *21:* 174
Wallace, Beverly Dobrin, *19:* 259
Wallace, Ian, *53:* 176, 177
Waller, S. E., *24:* 36
Wallner, Alexandra, *15:* 120

Wallner, John C., *9:* 77; *10:* 188; *11:* 28; *14:* 209; *31:* 56, 118; *37:* 64; *51:* 186, 187, 188-189, 190-191, 192-193, 194, 195; *52:* 96; *53:* 23, 26
Wallower, Lucille, *11:* 226
Walters, Audrey, *18:* 294
Walther, Tom, *31:* 179
Walton, Tony, *11:* 164; *24:* 209
Waltrip, Lela, *9:* 195
Waltrip, Mildred, *3:* 209; *37:* 211
Waltrip, Rufus, *9:* 195
Wan, *12:* 76
Ward, Fred, *52:* 19
Ward, John, *42:* 191
Ward, Keith, *2:* 107
Ward, Leslie, *34:* 126; *36:* 87
Ward, Lynd, *1:* 99, 132, 133, 150; *2:* 108, 158, 196, 259; *18:* 86; *27:* 56; *29:* 79, 187, 253, 255; *36:* 199, 200, 201, 202, 203, 204, 205, 206, 207, 209; *43:* 34
Ward, Peter, *37:* 116
Warner, Peter, *14:* 87
Warren, Betsy, *2:* 101
Warren, Marion Cray, *14:* 215
Warshaw, Jerry, *30:* 197, 198; *42:* 165
Washington, Nevin, *20:* 123
Washington, Phyllis, *20:* 123
Waterman, Stan, *11:* 76
Watkins-Pitchford, D. J., *6:* 215, 217
Watson, Aldren A., *2:* 267; *5:* 94; *13:* 71; *19:* 253; *32:* 220; *42:* 193, 194, 195, 196, 197, 198, 199, 200, 201; *YABC 2:* 202
Watson, Gary, *19:* 147; *36:* 68; *41:* 122; *47:* 139
Watson, J. D., *22:* 86
Watson, Karen, *11:* 26
Watson, Wendy, *5:* 197; *13:* 101; *33:* 116; *46:* 163
Watts, Bernadette, *4:* 227
Watts, John, *37:* 149
Webber, Helen, *3:* 141
Webber, Irma E., *14:* 238
Weber, Florence, *40:* 153
Weber, William J., *14:* 239
Webster, Jean, *17:* 241
Wegner, Fritz, *14:* 250; *20:* 189; *44:* 165
Weidenear, Reynold H., *21:* 122
Weihs, Erika, *4:* 21; *15:* 299
Weil, Lisl, *7:* 203; *10:* 58; *21:* 95; *22:* 188, 217; *33:* 193
Weiman, Jon, *50:* 162, 165; *52:* 103
Weiner, Sandra, *14:* 240
Weinhaus, Karen Ann, *53:* 90
Weisgard, Leonard, *1:* 65; *2:* 191, 197, 204, 264-265; *5:* 108; *21:* 42; *30:* 200, 201, 203, 204; *41:* 47; *44:* 125; *53:* 25; *YABC 2:* 13
Weiss, Ellen, *44:* 202
Weiss, Emil, *1:* 168; *7:* 60
Weiss, Harvey, *1:* 145, 223; *27:* 224, 227
Weiss, Nicki, *33:* 229
Weissman, Bari, *49:* 72
Wells, Frances, *1:* 183
Wells, H. G., *20:* 194, 200

Wells, Haru, *53:* 120, 121
Wells, Rosemary, *6:* 49; *18:* 297
Wells, Susan, *22:* 43
Wendelin, Rudolph, *23:* 234
Wengenroth, Stow, *37:* 47
Werenskiold, Erik, *15:* 6
Werner, Honi, *24:* 110; *33:* 41
Werth, Kurt, *7:* 122; *14:* 157; *20:* 214; *39:* 128
Westerberg, Christine, *29:* 226
Weston, Martha, *29:* 116; *30:* 213; *33:* 85, 100; *53:* 181, 182, 183, 184
Wetherbee, Margaret, *5:* 3
Wexler, Jerome, *49:* 73
Whalley, Peter, *50:* 49
Wheatley, Arabelle, *11:* 231; *16:* 276
Wheeler, Cindy, *49:* 205
Wheeler, Dora, *44:* 179
Wheelright, Rowland, *15:* 81; *YABC 2:* 286
Whistler, Rex, *16:* 75; *30:* 207, 208
White, David Omar, *5:* 56; *18:* 6
White, Martin, *51:* 197
Whitear, *32:* 26
Whithorne, H. S., *7:* 49
Whitney, George Gillett, *3:* 24
Whittam, Geoffrey, *30:* 191
Wiberg, Harald, *38:* 127
Wiese, Kurt, *3:* 255; *4:* 206; *14:* 17; *17:* 18-19; *19:* 47; *24:* 152; *25:* 212; *32:* 184; *36:* 211, 213, 214, 215, 216, 217, 218; *45:* 161
Wiesner, David, *33:* 47; *51:* 106
Wiesner, William, *4:* 100; *5:* 200, 201; *14:* 262
Wiggins, George, *6:* 133
Wikkelsoe, Otto, *45:* 25, 26
Wikland, Ilon, *5:* 113; *8:* 150; *38:* 124, 125, 130
Wilbur, C. Keith, M.D., *27:* 228
Wilburn, Kathy, *53:* 102
Wilcox, J.A.J., *34:* 122
Wilcox, R. Turner, *36:* 219
Wild, Jocelyn, *46:* 220-221, 222
Wilde, George, *7:* 139
Wildsmith, Brian, *16:* 281-282; *18:* 170-171
Wilkin, Eloise, *36:* 173; *49:* 208, 209, 210
Wilkinson, Barry, *50:* 213
Wilkinson, Gerald, *3:* 40
Wilkoń, Józef, *31:* 183, 184
Wilks, Mike, *34:* 24; *44:* 203
Williams, Ferelith Eccles, *22:* 238
Williams, Garth, *1:* 197; *2:* 49, 270; *4:* 205; *15:* 198, 302-304, 307; *16:* 34; *18:* 283, 298-301; *29:* 177, 178, 179, 232-233, 241-245, 248; *40:* 106; *YABC 2:* 15-16, 19
Williams, J. Scott, *48:* 28
Williams, Kit, *44:* 206-207, 208, 209, 211, 212
Williams, Maureen, *12:* 238
Williams, Patrick, *14:* 218
Williams, Richard, *44:* 93
Williams, Vera B., *53:* 186, 187, 188, 189

Wilson, Charles Banks, *17:* 92; *43:* 73
Wilson, Dagmar, *10:* 47
Wilson, Edward A., *6:* 24; *16:* 149;
    20: 220-221; *22:* 87; *26:* 67;
    38: 212, 214, 215, 216, 217
Wilson, Forrest, *27:* 231
Wilson, Gahan, *35:* 234; *41:* 136
Wilson, Jack, *17:* 139
Wilson, John, *22:* 240
Wilson, Maurice, *46:* 224
Wilson, Patten, *35:* 61
Wilson, Peggy, *15:* 4
Wilson, Rowland B., *30:* 170
Wilson, Sarah, *50:* 215
Wilson, Tom, *33:* 232
Wilson, W. N., *22:* 26
Wilwerding, Walter J., *9:* 202
Winchester, Linda, *13:* 231
Wind, Betty, *28:* 158
Windham, Kathryn Tucker, *14:* 260
Wing, Ron, *50:* 85
Winslow, Will, *21:* 124
Winsten, Melanie Willa, *41:* 41
Winter, Milo, *15:* 97; *19:* 221;
    21: 181, 203, 204, 205;
    YABC 2: 144
Winter, Paula, *48:* 227
Wise, Louis, *13:* 68
Wiseman, Ann, *31:* 187
Wiseman, B., *4:* 233
Wishnefsky, Phillip, *3:* 14
Wiskur, Darrell, *5:* 72; *10:* 50; *18:* 246
Wittman, Sally, *30:* 219
Woehr, Lois, *12:* 5
Wohlberg, Meg, *12:* 100; *14:* 197;
    41: 255
Woldin, Beth Weiner, *34:* 211
Wolf, J., *16:* 91
Wolf, Linda, *33:* 163
Wolff, Ashley, *50:* 217

Wondriska, William, *6:* 220
Wonsetler, John C., *5:* 168
Wood, Audrey, *50:* 221, 222, 223
Wood, Don, *50:* 220, 225, 226, 228-229
Wood, Grant, *19:* 198
Wood, Muriel, *36:* 119
Wood, Myron, *6:* 220
Wood, Owen, *18:* 187
Wood, Ruth, *8:* 11
Woodson, Jack, *10:* 201
Woodward, Alice, *26:* 89; *36:* 81
Wool, David, *26:* 27
Wooten, Vernon, *23:* 70; *51:* 170
Worboys, Evelyn, *1:* 166-167
Worth, Jo, *34:* 143
Worth, Wendy, *4:* 133
Wosmek, Frances, *29:* 251
Wrenn, Charles L., *38:* 96;
    YABC 1: 20, 21
Wright, Dare, *21:* 206
Wright, George, *YABC 1:* 268
Wright, Joseph, *30:* 160
Wronker, Lili Cassel, *3:* 247; *10:* 204;
    21: 10
Wyatt, Stanley, *46:* 210
Wyeth, Andrew, *13:* 40;
    YABC 1: 133-134
Wyeth, Jamie, *41:* 257
Wyeth, N. C., *13:* 41; *17:* 252-259,
    264-268; *18:* 181; *19:* 80, 191,
    200; *21:* 57, 183; *22:* 91; *23:* 152;
    24: 28, 99; *35:* 61; *41:* 65;
    YABC 1: 133, 223; *YABC 2:* 53,
    75, 171, 187, 317

Yang, Jay, *1:* 8; *12:* 239
Yap, Weda, *6:* 176

Yaroslava. *See* Mills, Yaroslava
    Surmach
Yashima, Taro, *14:* 84
Ylla. *See* Koffler, Camilla
Yohn, F. C., *23:* 128; *YABC 1:* 269
Young, Ed, *7:* 205; *10:* 206; *40:* 124;
    YABC 2: 242
Young, Noela, *8:* 221

Zacks, Lewis, *10:* 161
Zadig, *50:* 58
Zaffo, George, *42:* 208
Zaid, Barry, *50:* 127; *51:* 201
Zaidenberg, Arthur, *34:* 218, 219, 220
Zalben, Jane Breskin, *7:* 211
Zallinger, Jean, *4:* 192; *8:* 8, 129;
    14: 273
Zallinger, Rudolph F., *3:* 245
Zeck, Gerry, *40:* 232
Zeiring, Bob, *42:* 130
Zeldich, Arieh, *49:* 124
Zelinsky, Paul O., *14:* 269; *43:* 56;
    49: 218, 219, 220, 221, 222-223;
    53: 111
Zemach, Margot, *3:* 270; *8:* 201;
    21: 210-211; *27:* 204, 205, 210;
    28: 185; *49:* 22, 183, 224;
    53: 151
Zemsky, Jessica, *10:* 62
Zepelinsky, Paul, *35:* 93
Zimmer, Dirk, *38:* 195; *49:* 71
Zimnik, Reiner, *36:* 224
Zinkeisen, Anna, *13:* 106
Zoellick, Scott, *33:* 231
Zonia, Dhimitri, *20:* 234-235
Zweifel, Francis, *14:* 274; *28:* 187
Zwinger, Herman H., *46:* 227

Author Index

The following index gives the number of the volume in which an author's biographical sketch, Brief Entry, or Obituary appears.

This index includes references to all entries in the following series, which are also published by Gale Research Company.

YABC—*Yesterday's Authors of Books for Children: Facts and Pictures about Authors and Illustrators of Books for Young People from Early Times to 1960*, Volumes 1-2
CLR—*Children's Literature Review: Excerpts from Reviews, Criticism, and Commentary on Books for Children*, Volumes 1-14
SAAS—*Something about the Author Autobiography Series*, Volumes 1-6

A

Aardema, Verna 1911- *4*
Aaron, Chester 1923- *9*
Aaseng, Nate
    See Aaseng, Nathan
Aaseng, Nathan 1938- *51*
    Brief Entry *38*
Abbott, Alice
    See Borland, Kathryn Kilby
Abbott, Alice
    See Speicher, Helen Ross (Smith)
Abbott, Jacob 1803-1879 .... *22*
Abbott, Manager Henry
    See Stratemeyer, Edward L.
Abbott, Sarah
    See Zolotow, Charlotte S.
Abdul, Raoul 1929- *12*
Abel, Raymond 1911- *12*
Abell, Kathleen 1938- *9*
Abels, Harriette S(heffer)
    1926- *50*
Abercrombie, Barbara (Mattes)
    1939- *16*
Abernethy, Robert G. 1935- *5*
Abisch, Roslyn Kroop 1927- *9*
Abisch, Roz
    See Abisch, Roslyn Kroop
Abodaher, David J. (Naiph)
    1919- *17*
Abolafia, Yossi
    Brief Entry *46*
Abrahall, C. H.
    See Hoskyns-Abrahall, Clare
Abrahall, Clare Hoskyns
    See Hoskyns-Abrahall, Clare
Abrahams, Hilary (Ruth)
    1938- *29*
Abrahams, Robert D(avid)
    1905- *4*
Abrams, Joy 1941- *16*
Abrams, Lawrence F.
    Brief Entry *47*
Abrashkin, Raymond
    1911-1960 .... *50*
Achebe, Chinua 1930- *40*
    Brief Entry *38*
Ackerman, Eugene 1888-1974 .... *10*
Acs, Laszlo (Bela) 1931- *42*
    Brief Entry *32*
Acuff, Selma Boyd 1924- *45*
Ada, Alma Flor 1938- *43*

Adair, Ian 1942- *53*
Adair, Margaret Weeks
    (?)-1971 .... *10*
Adam, Cornel
    See Lengyel, Cornel Adam
Adams, Adrienne 1906- *8*
Adams, Andy
    1859-1935 .... *YABC 1*
Adams, Dale
    See Quinn, Elisabeth
Adams, Harriet S(tratemeyer)
    1893(?)-1982 .... *1*
    Obituary *29*
Adams, Harrison
    See Stratemeyer, Edward L.
Adams, Hazard 1926- *6*
Adams, Laurie 1941- *33*
Adams, Lowell
    See Joseph, James (Herz)
Adams, Richard 1920- *7*
Adams, Ruth Joyce *14*
Adams, William Taylor
    1822-1897 .... *28*
Adamson, Gareth 1925-1982 ...... *46*
    Obituary *30*
Adamson, George Worsley
    1913- *30*
Adamson, Graham
    See Groom, Arthur William
Adamson, Joy 1910-1980 .... *11*
    Obituary *22*
Adamson, Wendy Wriston
    1942- *22*
Addona, Angelo F. 1925- *14*
Addy, Ted
    See Winterbotham, R(ussell)
    R(obert)
Adelberg, Doris
    See Orgel, Doris
Adelson, Leone 1908- *11*
Adkins, Jan 1944- *8*
    See also CLR 7
Adler, C(arole) S(chwerdtfeger)
    1932- *26*
Adler, David A. 1947- *14*
Adler, Irene
    See Penzler, Otto
    See Storr, Catherine (Cole)
Adler, Irving 1913- *29*
    Earlier sketch in SATA 1
Adler, Larry 1939- *36*
Adler, Peggy *22*

Adler, Ruth 1915-1968 .... *1*
Adoff, Arnold 1935- *5*
    See also CLR 7
Adorjan, Carol 1934- *10*
Adrian, Mary
    See Jorgensen, Mary Venn
Adshead, Gladys L. 1896- *3*
Aesop 620(?)-564(?)B.C.
    See CLR 14
Aesop, Abraham
    See Newbery, John
Agapida, Fray Antonio
    See Irving, Washington
Agard, Nadema 1948- *18*
Agle, Nan Hayden 1905- *3*
Agnew, Edith J(osephine)
    1897- *11*
Ahern, Margaret McCrohan
    1921- *10*
Ahl, Anna Maria 1926- *32*
Ahlberg, Allan
    Brief Entry *35*
Ahlberg, Janet
    Brief Entry *32*
Aichinger, Helga 1937- *4*
Aiken, Clarissa (Lorenz)
    1899- *12*
Aiken, Conrad (Potter)
    1889-1973 .... *30*
    Earlier sketch in SATA 3
Aiken, Joan 1924- *30*
    Earlier sketch in SATA 2
    See also CLR 1
    See also SAAS 1
Ainsworth, Norma *9*
Ainsworth, Ruth 1908- *7*
Ainsworth, William Harrison
    1805-1882 .... *24*
Aistrop, Jack 1916- *14*
Aitken, Amy 1952-
    Brief Entry *40*
Aitken, Dorothy 1916- *10*
Akaba, Suekichi 1910- *46*
Akers, Floyd
    See Baum, L(yman) Frank
Alain
    See Brustlein, Daniel
Alajalov, Constantin 1900-1987
    Obituary *53*
Albert, Burton, Jr. 1936- *22*
Alberts, Frances Jacobs 1907- *14*
Albion, Lee Smith *29*

Albrecht, Lillie (Vanderveer)
1894- *12*
Alcock, Gudrun
Brief Entry *33*
Alcock, Vivien 1924- *45*
Brief Entry *38*
Alcorn, John 1935- *31*
Brief Entry *30*
Alcott, Louisa May
1832-1888 .... *YABC 1*
See also CLR 1
Alda, Arlene 1933- *44*
Brief Entry *36*
Alden, Isabella (Macdonald)
1841-1930 .... *YABC 2*
Alderman, Clifford Lindsey
1902- *3*
Alderson, Sue Ann 1940-
Brief Entry *48*
Aldis, Dorothy (Keeley)
1896-1966 .... *2*
Aldiss, Brian W(ilson) 1925- *34*
Aldon, Adair
See Meigs, Cornelia
Aldous, Allan (Charles) 1911- *27*
Aldrich, Ann
See Meaker, Marijane
Aldrich, Thomas Bailey
1836-1907 .... *17*
Aldridge, Alan 1943(?)-
Brief Entry *33*
Aldridge, Josephine Haskell *14*
Alegria, Ricardo E. 1921- *6*
Aleksin, Anatolii (Georgievich)
1924- *36*
Alex, Ben [a pseudonym]
1946- *45*
Alex, Marlee [a pseudonym]
1948- *45*
Alexander, Anna Cooke 1913- *1*
Alexander, Frances 1888- *4*
Alexander, Jocelyn (Anne) Arundel
1930- *22*
Alexander, Linda 1935- *2*
Alexander, Lloyd 1924- *49*
Earlier sketch in SATA 3
See also CLR 1, 5
Alexander, Martha 1920- *11*
Alexander, Rae Pace
See Alexander, Raymond Pace
Alexander, Raymond Pace
1898-1974 .... *22*
Alexander, Sue 1933- *12*
Alexander, Vincent Arthur 1925-1980
Obituary *23*
Alexeieff, Alexandre A.
1901- *14*
Alger, Horatio, Jr. 1832-1899 ..... *16*
Alger, Leclaire (Gowans)
1898-1969 .... *15*
Aliki
See Brandenberg, Aliki
See also CLR 9
Alkema, Chester Jay 1932- *12*
Allamand, Pascale 1942- *12*
Allan, Mabel Esther 1915- *32*
Earlier sketch in SATA 5
Allard, Harry
See Allard, Harry G(rover), Jr.

Allard, Harry G(rover), Jr.
1928- *42*
Allee, Marjorie Hill
1890-1945 .... *17*
Allen, Adam [Joint pseudonym]
See Epstein, Beryl and Epstein,
Samuel
Allen, Alex B.
See Heide, Florence Parry
Allen, Allyn
See Eberle, Irmengarde
Allen, Betsy
See Cavanna, Betty
Allen, Gertrude E(lizabeth)
1888- *9*
Allen, Jack 1899-
Brief Entry *29*
Allen, Jeffrey (Yale) 1948- *42*
Allen, Laura Jean
Brief Entry *53*
Allen, Leroy 1912- *11*
Allen, Linda 1925- *33*
Allen, Marjorie 1931- *22*
Allen, Maury 1932- *26*
Allen, Merritt Parmelee
1892-1954 .... *22*
Allen, Nina (Strömgren)
1935- *22*
Allen, Pamela 1934- *50*
Allen, Rodney F. 1938- *27*
Allen, Ruth
See Peterson, Esther (Allen)
Allen, Samuel (Washington)
1917- *9*
Allen, T. D. [Joint pseudonym]
See Allen, Terril Diener
Allen, Terril Diener 1908- *35*
Allen, Terry D.
See Allen, Terril Diener
Allen, Thomas B(enton)
1929- *45*
Allen, Tom
See Allen, Thomas B(enton)
Allerton, Mary
See Govan, Christine Noble
Alleyn, Ellen
See Rossetti, Christina (Georgina)
Allington, Richard L(loyd)
1947- *39*
Brief Entry *35*
Allison, Bob *14*
Allison, Linda 1948- *43*
Allmendinger, David F(rederick), Jr.
1938- *35*
Allred, Gordon T. 1930- *10*
Allsop, Kenneth 1920-1973 .... *17*
Almedingen, E. M.
1898-1971 .... *3*
Almedingen, Martha Edith von
See Almedingen, E. M.
Almond, Linda Stevens 1881(?)-1987
Obituary *50*
Almquist, Don 1929- *11*
Alsop, Mary O'Hara
1885-1980 .... *34*
Obituary *24*
Earlier sketch in SATA 5
Alter, Judith (MacBain) 1938- *52*

Alter, Judy
See Alter, Judith (MacBain)
Alter, Robert Edmond
1925-1965 .... *9*
Althea
See Braithwaite, Althea *23*
Altschuler, Franz 1923- *45*
Altsheler, Joseph A(lexander)
1862-1919 .... *YABC 1*
Alvarez, Joseph A. 1930- *18*
Alzada, Juan Sanchez
See Joseph, James (Herz)
Ambler, C(hristopher) Gifford 1886-
Brief Entry *29*
Ambrose, Stephen E(dward)
1936- *40*
Ambrus, Gyozo (Laszlo)
1935- *41*
Earlier sketch in SATA 1
Ambrus, Victor G.
See Ambrus, Gyozo (Laszlo)
See also SAAS 4
Amerman, Lockhart
1911-1969 .... *3*
Ames, Evelyn 1908- *13*
Ames, Gerald 1906- *11*
Ames, Lee J. 1921- *3*
Ames, Mildred 1919- *22*
Amon, Aline 1928- *9*
Amoss, Berthe 1925- *5*
Anastasio, Dina 1941- *37*
Brief Entry *30*
Anckarsvard, Karin
1915-1969 .... *6*
Ancona, George 1929- *12*
Andersdatter, Karla M(argaret)
1938- *34*
Andersen, Hans Christian
1805-1875 .... *YABC 1*
See also CLR 6
Andersen, Ted
See Boyd, Waldo T.
Andersen, Yvonne 1932- *27*
Anderson, Bernice G(oudy)
1894- *33*
Anderson, Brad(ley Jay)
1924- *33*
Brief Entry *31*
Anderson, C(larence) W(illiam)
1891-1971 .... *11*
Anderson, Clifford [Joint pseudonym]
See Gardner, Richard
Anderson, Ella
See MacLeod, Ellen Jane (Anderson)
Anderson, Eloise Adell 1927- *9*
Anderson, George
See Groom, Arthur William
Anderson, Grace Fox 1932- *43*
Anderson, J(ohn) R(ichard) L(ane)
1911-1981 .... *15*
Obituary *27*
Anderson, Joy 1928- *1*
Anderson, LaVere (Francis Shoenfelt)
1907- *27*
Anderson, Leone Castell
1923- *53*
Brief Entry *49*
Anderson, (John) Lonzo
1905- *2*

Anderson, Lucia (Lewis)
1922- *10*
Anderson, Madelyn Klein *28*
Anderson, Margaret J(ean)
1931- *27*
Anderson, Mary 1939- *7*
Anderson, Mona 1910- *40*
Anderson, Norman D(ean)
1928- *22*
Anderson, Poul (William) 1926-
Brief Entry *39*
Anderson, Rachel 1943- *34*
Andre, Evelyn M(arie) 1924- *27*
Andree, Louise
See Coury, Louise Andree
Andrews, Benny 1930- *31*
Andrews, F(rank) Emerson
1902-1978 .... *22*
Andrews, J(ames) S(ydney)
1934- *4*
Andrews, Jan 1942-
Brief Entry *49*
Andrews, Julie 1935- *7*
Andrews, Laura
See Coury, Louise Andree
Andrews, Roy Chapman
1884-1960 .... *19*
Andrews, V(irginia) C(leo) (?)-1986
Obituary *50*
Andrézel, Pierre
See Blixen, Karen (Christentze
Dinesen)
Andriola, Alfred J. 1912-1983
Obituary *34*
Andrist, Ralph K. 1914- *45*
Anfousse, Ginette 1944-
Brief Entry *48*
Angel, Marie (Felicity) 1923- *47*
Angeles, Peter A. 1931- *40*
Angell, Judie 1937- *22*
Angell, Madeline 1919- *18*
Angelo, Valenti 1897- *14*
Angelou, Maya 1928- *49*
Angier, Bradford *12*
Angle, Paul M(cClelland) 1900-1975
Obituary *20*
Anglund, Joan Walsh 1926- *2*
See also CLR 1
Angrist, Stanley W(olff)
1933- *4*
Anita
See Daniel, Anita
Annett, Cora
See Scott, Cora Annett
Annixter, Jane
See Sturtzel, Jane Levington
Annixter, Paul
See Sturtzel, Howard A.
Anno, Mitsumasa 1926- *38*
Earlier sketch in SATA 5
See also CLR 2, 14
Anrooy, Frans van
See Van Anrooy, Francine
Antell, Will D. 1935- *31*
Anthony, Barbara 1932- *29*
Anthony, C. L.
See Smith, Dodie
Anthony, Edward 1895-1971 ...... *21*
Anticaglia, Elizabeth 1939- *12*

Antolini, Margaret Fishback
1904-1985
Obituary *45*
Anton, Michael (James) 1940- *12*
Antonacci, Robert J(oseph)
1916- *45*
Brief Entry *37*
Aoki, Hisako 1942- *45*
Apfel, Necia H(alpern) 1930- *51*
Brief Entry *41*
Aphrodite, J.
See Livingston, Carole
Appel, Benjamin 1907-1977 .... *39*
Obituary *21*
Appel, Martin E(liot) 1948- *45*
Appel, Marty
See Appel, Martin E(liot)
Appiah, Peggy 1921- *15*
Apple, Margot
Brief Entry *42*
Applebaum, Stan 1929- *45*
Appleton, Victor [Collective
pseudonym] *1*
Appleton, Victor II [Collective
pseudonym] *1*
See also Adams, Harriet
S(tratemeyer)
Apsler, Alfred 1907- *10*
Aquillo, Don
See Prince, J(ack) H(arvey)
Aragonés, Sergio 1937- *48*
Brief Entry *39*
Arbuckle, Dorothy Fry 1910-1982
Obituary *33*
Arbuthnot, May Hill
1884-1969 .... *2*
Archer, Frank
See O'Connor, Richard
Archer, Jules 1915- *4*
See also SAAS 5
Archer, Marion Fuller 1917- *11*
Archibald, Joe
See Archibald, Joseph S(topford)
Archibald, Joseph S(topford)
1898-1986 .... *3*
Obituary *47*
Arden, Barbie
See Stoutenburg, Adrien
Arden, William
See Lynds, Dennis
Ardizzone, Edward 1900-1979 .... *28*
Obituary *21*
Earlier sketch in SATA 1
See also CLR 3
Ardley, Neil (Richard) 1937- *43*
Arehart-Treichel, Joan 1942- *22*
Arenella, Roy 1939- *14*
Arkin, Alan (Wolf) 1934-
Brief Entry *32*
Armer, Alberta (Roller) 1904- *9*
Armer, Laura Adams
1874-1963 .... *13*
Armitage, David 1943-
Brief Entry *38*
Armitage, Ronda (Jacqueline)
1943- *47*
Brief Entry *38*
Armour, Richard 1906- *14*
Armstrong, George D. 1927- *10*

Armstrong, Gerry (Breen)
1929- *10*
Armstrong, Louise *43*
Brief Entry *33*
Armstrong, Richard 1903- *11*
Armstrong, William H. 1914- *4*
See also CLR 1
Arndt, Ursula (Martha H.)
Brief Entry *39*
Arneson, D(on) J(on) 1935- *37*
Arnett, Carolyn
See Cole, Lois Dwight
Arno, Enrico 1913-1981 .... *43*
Obituary *28*
Arnold, Caroline 1944- *36*
Brief Entry *34*
Arnold, Elliott 1912-1980 .... *5*
Obituary *22*
Arnold, Emily 1939- *50*
Arnold, Oren 1900- *4*
Arnoldy, Julie
See Bischoff, Julia Bristol
Arnosky, Jim 1946- *22*
Arnott, Kathleen 1914- *20*
Arnov, Boris, Jr. 1926- *12*
Arnow, Harriette (Louisa Simpson)
1908-1986 .... *42*
Obituary *47*
Arnstein, Helene S(olomon)
1915- *12*
Arntson, Herbert E(dward)
1911- *12*
Aronin, Ben 1904-1980
Obituary *25*
Arora, Shirley (Lease) 1930- *2*
Arquette, Lois S(teinmetz)
1934- *1*
See also Duncan, Lois S(teinmetz)
Arrowood, (McKendrick Lee) Clinton
1939- *19*
Arthur, Robert
See Feder, Robert Arthur
Arthur, Ruth M(abel)
1905-1979 .... *7*
Obituary *26*
Artis, Vicki Kimmel 1945- *12*
Artzybasheff, Boris (Miklailovich)
1899-1965 .... *14*
Aruego, Ariane
See Dewey, Ariane
Aruego, Jose 1932- *6*
See also CLR 5
Arundel, Honor (Morfydd)
1919-1973 .... *4*
Obituary *24*
Arundel, Jocelyn
See Alexander, Jocelyn (Anne)
Arundel
Asbjörnsen, Peter Christen
1812-1885 .... *15*
Asch, Frank 1946- *5*
Ash, Jutta 1942- *38*
Ashabranner, Brent (Kenneth)
1921- *1*
Ashby, Gwynneth 1922- *44*
Ashe, Geoffrey (Thomas)
1923- *17*

Asher, Sandy (Fenichel)
  1942- 36
  Brief Entry 34
Ashey, Bella
  See Breinburg, Petronella
Ashford, Daisy
  See Ashford, Margaret Mary
Ashford, Margaret Mary
  1881-1972 10
Ashley, Bernard 1935- 47
  Brief Entry 39
  See also CLR 4
Ashley, Elizabeth
  See Salmon, Annie Elizabeth
Ashley, Ray
  See Abrashkin, Raymond
Ashton, Warren T.
  See Adams, William Taylor
Asimov, Issac 1920- 26
  Earlier sketch in SATA 1
  See also CLR 12
Asimov, Janet
  See Jeppson, J(anet) O(pal)
Asinof, Eliot 1919- 6
Astley, Juliet
  See Lofts, Nora (Robinson)
Aston, James
  See White, T(erence) H(anbury)
Atene, Ann
  See Atene, (Rita) Anna
Atene, (Rita) Anna 1922- 12
Atkinson, Allen
  Brief Entry 46
Atkinson, M. E.
  See Frankau, Mary Evelyn
Atkinson, Margaret Fleming 14
Atticus
  See Davies, (Edward) Hunter
  See Fleming, Ian (Lancaster)
Atwater, Florence (Hasseltine
  Carroll) 16
Atwater, Montgomery Meigs
  1904- 15
Atwater, Richard Tupper 1892-1948
  Brief Entry 27
Atwood, Ann 1913- 7
Atwood, Margaret (Eleanor)
  1939- 50
Aubry, Claude B. 1914-1984 29
  Obituary 40
Augarde, Steve 1950- 25
Augelli, John P(at) 1921- 46
Ault, Phillip H. 1914- 23
Ault, Rosalie Sain 1942- 38
Ault, Roz
  See Ault, Rosalie Sain
Aung, (Maung) Htin 1910- 21
Aung, U. Htin
  See Aung, (Maung) Htin
Auntie Deb
  See Coury, Louise Andree
Auntie Louise
  See Coury, Louise Andree
Austin, Elizabeth S. 1907- 5
Austin, Margot 11
Austin, Oliver L., Jr. 1903- 7
Austin, R. G.
  See Gelman, Rita Golden

Austin, Tom
  See Jacobs, Linda C.
Auth, Tony
  See Auth, William Anthony, Jr.
Auth, William Anthony, Jr.
  1942- 51
Averill, Esther 1902- 28
  Earlier sketch in SATA 1
Avery, Al
  See Montgomery, Rutherford
Avery, Gillian 1926- 7
  See also SAAS 6
Avery, Kay 1908- 5
Avery, Lynn
  See Cole, Lois Dwight
Avi
  See Wortis, Avi
Ayars, James S(terling) 1898- 4
Ayer, Jacqueline 1930- 13
Ayer, Margaret 15
Aylesworth, Jim 1943- 38
Aylesworth, Thomas G(ibbons)
  1927- 4
  See also CLR 6
Aymar, Brandt 1911- 22
Ayres, Carole Briggs
  See Briggs, Carole S(uzanne)
Ayres, Patricia Miller 1923-1985
  Obituary 46
Azaid
  See Zaidenberg, Arthur

                    B

B
  See Gilbert, W(illiam) S(chwenk)
B., Tania
  See Blixen, Karen (Christentze
  Dinesen)
BB
  See Watkins-Pitchford, D. J.
Baastad, Babbis Friis
  See Friis-Baastad, Babbis
Bab
  See Gilbert, W(illiam) S(chwenk)
Babbis, Eleanor
  See Friis-Baastad, Babbis
Babbitt, Natalie 1932- 6
  See also CLR 2
  See also SAAS 5
Babcock, Dennis Arthur
  1948- 22
Bach, Alice (Hendricks)
  1942- 30
  Brief Entry 27
Bach, Richard David 1936- 13
Bachman, Fred 1949- 12
Bacmeister, Rhoda W(arner)
  1893- 11
Bacon, Elizabeth 1914- 3
Bacon, Joan Chase
  See Bowden, Joan Chase
Bacon, Josephine Dodge (Daskam)
  1876-1961 48
Bacon, Margaret Frances 1895-1987
  Obituary 50
Bacon, Margaret Hope 1921- 6

Bacon, Martha Sherman
  1917-1981 18
  Obituary 27
  See also CLR 3
Bacon, Peggy 1895- 2
  See also Bacon, Margaret Frances
Bacon, R(onald) L(eonard)
  1924- 26
Baden-Powell, Robert (Stephenson
  Smyth) 1857-1941 16
Baerg, Harry J(ohn) 1909- 12
Bagnold, Enid 1889-1981 25
  Earlier sketch in SATA 1
Bahr, Robert 1940- 38
Bahti, Tom
  Brief Entry 31
Bailey, Alice Cooper 1890- 12
Bailey, Bernadine Freeman 14
Bailey, Carolyn Sherwin
  1875-1961 14
Bailey, Jane H(orton) 1916- 12
Bailey, John (Robert) 1940- 52
Bailey, Maralyn Collins (Harrison)
  1941- 12
Bailey, Matilda
  See Radford, Ruby L.
Bailey, Maurice Charles
  1932- 12
Bailey, Ralph Edgar 1893- 11
Baird, Bil 1904-1987 30
  Obituary 52
Baird, Thomas P. 1923- 45
  Brief Entry 39
Baity, Elizabeth Chesley
  1907- 1
Bakeless, John (Edwin) 1894- 9
Bakeless, Katherine Little
  1895- 9
Baker, Alan 1951- 22
Baker, Augusta 1911- 3
Baker, Betty (Lou) 1928- 5
Baker, Charlotte 1910- 2
Baker, Elizabeth 1923- 7
Baker, Eugene H.
  Brief Entry 50
Baker, Gayle C(unningham)
  1950- 39
Baker, James W. 1924- 22
Baker, Janice E(dla) 1941- 22
Baker, Jeannie 1950- 23
Baker, Jeffrey J(ohn) W(heeler)
  1931- 5
Baker, Jim
  See Baker, James W.
Baker, Laura Nelson 1911- 3
Baker, Margaret 1890- 4
Baker, Margaret J(oyce)
  1918- 12
Baker, Mary Gladys Steel
  1892-1974 12
Baker, (Robert) Michael
  1938- 4
Baker, Nina (Brown)
  1888-1957 15
Baker, Rachel 1904-1978 2
  Obituary 26
Baker, Samm Sinclair 1909- 12
Baker, Susan (Catherine)
  1942- 29

Balaam
See Lamb, G(eoffrey) F(rederick)
Balch, Glenn 1902- *3*
Baldridge, Cyrus LeRoy 1889-
   Brief Entry *29*
Balducci, Carolyn Feleppa
   1946- *5*
Baldwin, Anne Norris 1938- *5*
Baldwin, Clara *11*
Baldwin, Gordo
   See Baldwin, Gordon C.
Baldwin, Gordon C. 1908- *12*
Baldwin, James 1841-1925 .... *24*
Baldwin, James (Arthur)
   1924- *9*
Baldwin, Margaret
   See Weis, Margaret (Edith)
Baldwin, Stan(ley C.) 1929-
   Brief Entry *28*
Bales, Carol Ann 1940-
   Brief Entry *29*
Balet, Jan (Bernard) 1913- *11*
Balian, Lorna 1929- *9*
Ball, Zachary
   See Masters, Kelly R.
Ballantine, Lesley Frost
   See Frost, Lesley
Ballantyne, R(obert) M(ichael)
   1825-1894 .... *24*
Ballard, Lowell Clyne
   1904-1986 .... *12*
   Obituary *49*
Ballard, (Charles) Martin
   1929- *1*
Ballard, Mignon Franklin 1934-
   Brief Entry *49*
Balogh, Penelope 1916-1975 ...... *1*
   Obituary *34*
Balow, Tom 1931- *12*
Baltzer, Hans (Adolf) 1900- *40*
Bamfylde, Walter
   See Bevan, Tom
Bamman, Henry A. 1918- *12*
Bancroft, Griffing 1907- *6*
Bancroft, Laura
   See Baum, L(yman) Frank
Bandel, Betty 1912- *47*
Baner, Skulda V(anadis)
   1897-1964 .... *10*
Bang, Betsy (Garrett) 1912- *48*
   Brief Entry *37*
Bang, Garrett
   See Bang, Molly Garrett
Bang, Molly Garrett 1943- *24*
   See also CLR 8
Banks, Laura Stockton Voorhees
   1908(?)-1980
   Obituary *23*
Banks, Sara (Jeanne Gordon Harrell)
   1937- *26*
Banner, Angela
   See Maddison, Angela Mary
Bannerman, Helen (Brodie Cowan
   Watson) 1863(?)-1946 .... *19*
Banning, Evelyn I. 1903- *36*
Bannon, Laura (?)-1963 .... *6*
Barbary, James
   See Baumann, Amy (Brown)

Barbary, James
   See Beeching, Jack
Barbe, Walter Burke 1926- *45*
Barber, Antonia
   See Anthony, Barbara
Barber, Linda
   See Graham-Barber, Lynda
Barber, Richard (William)
   1941- *35*
Barbera, Joe
   See Barbera, Joseph Roland
Barbera, Joseph Roland 1911- *51*
Barbour, Ralph Henry
   1870-1944 .... *16*
Barclay, Isabel
   See Dobell, I.M.B.
Bare, Arnold Edwin 1920- *16*
Bare, Colleen Stanley *32*
Barish, Matthew 1907- *12*
Barker, Albert W. 1900- *8*
Barker, Carol (Minturn) 1938- *31*
Barker, Cicely Mary
   1895-1973 .... *49*
   Brief Entry *39*
Barker, Melvern 1907- *11*
Barker, S. Omar 1894- *10*
Barker, Will 1908- *8*
Barkhouse, Joyce 1913-
   Brief Entry *48*
Barkin, Carol 1944- *52*
Barkley, James Edward 1941- *6*
Barks, Carl 1901- *37*
Barnaby, Ralph S(tanton)
   1893- *9*
Barner, Bob 1947- *29*
Barnes, (Frank) Eric Wollencott
   1907-1962 .... *22*
Barnes, Malcolm 1909(?)-1984
   Obituary *41*
Barnett, Lincoln (Kinnear)
   1909-1979 .... *36*
Barnett, Moneta 1922-1976 .... *33*
Barnett, Naomi 1927- *40*
Barney, Maginel Wright
   1881-1966 .... *39*
   Brief Entry *32*
Barnhart, Clarence L(ewis)
   1900- *48*
Barnouw, Adriaan Jacob 1877-1968
   Obituary *27*
Barnouw, Victor 1915- *43*
   Brief Entry *28*
Barnstone, Willis 1927- *20*
Barnum, Jay Hyde
   1888(?)-1962 .... *20*
Barnum, Richard [Collective
   pseudonym] *1*
Baron, Virginia Olsen 1931- *46*
   Brief Entry *28*
Barr, Donald 1921- *20*
Barr, George 1907- *2*
Barr, Jene 1900-1985 .... *16*
   Obituary *42*
Barrer, Gertrude
   See Barrer-Russell, Gertrude
Barrer-Russell, Gertrude
   1921- *27*
Barrett, Ethel
   Brief Entry *44*

Barrett, Judith 1941- *26*
Barrett, Ron 1937- *14*
Barrett, William E(dmund) 1900-1986
   Obituary *49*
Barrie, J(ames) M(atthew)
   1860-1937 .... *YABC 1*
Barris, George 1925- *47*
Barrol, Grady
   See Bograd, Larry
Barry, James P(otvin) 1918- *14*
Barry, Katharina (Watjen)
   1936- *4*
Barry, Robert 1931- *6*
Barry, Scott 1952- *32*
Bartenbach, Jean 1918- *40*
Barth, Edna 1914-1980 .... *7*
   Obituary *24*
Barthelme, Donald 1931- *7*
Bartholomew, Barbara 1941-
   Brief Entry *42*
Bartlett, Philip A. [Collective
   pseudonym] *1*
Bartlett, Robert Merrill 1899- *12*
Barton, Byron 1930- *9*
Barton, Harriett
   Brief Entry *43*
Barton, May Hollis [Collective
   pseudonym] *1*
   See also Adams, Harriet
   S(tratemeyer)
Bartos-Hoeppner, Barbara
   1923- *5*
Bartsch, Jochen 1906- *39*
Baruch, Dorothy W(alter)
   1899-1962 .... *21*
Bas, Rutger
   See Rutgers van der Loeff, An(na)
   Basenau
Bashevis, Isaac
   See Singer, Isaac Bashevis
Baskin, Leonard 1922- *30*
   Brief Entry *27*
Bason, Lillian 1913- *20*
Bassett, Jeni 1960(?)-
   Brief Entry *43*
Bassett, John Keith
   See Keating, Lawrence A.
Batchelor, Joy 1914-
   Brief Entry *29*
Bate, Lucy 1939- *18*
Bate, Norman 1916- *5*
Bates, Barbara S(nedeker)
   1919- *12*
Bates, Betty 1921- *19*
Batey, Tom 1946- *52*
   Brief Entry *41*
Batherman, Muriel
   See Sheldon, Muriel
Batiuk, Thomas M(artin) 1947-
   Brief Entry *40*
Batson, Larry 1930- *35*
Battaglia, Aurelius 1910- *50*
   Brief Entry *33*
Batten, H(arry) Mortimer
   1888-1958 .... *25*
Batten, Mary 1937- *5*
Batterberry, Ariane Ruskin
   1935- *13*

Batterberry, Michael (Carver)
  1932- 32
Battles, Edith 1921- 7
Baudouy, Michel-Aime 1909- 7
Bauer, Caroline Feller 1935- 52
  Brief Entry 46
Bauer, Fred 1934- 36
Bauer, Helen 1900- 2
Bauer, Marion Dane 1938- 20
Bauernschmidt, Marjorie
  1926- 15
Baum, Allyn Z(elton) 1924- 20
Baum, L(yman) Frank
  1856-1919 18
Baum, Louis 1948-
  Brief Entry 52
Baum, Willi 1931- 4
Baumann, Amy (Brown)
  1922- 10
Baumann, Elwood D.
  Brief Entry 33
Baumann, Hans 1914- 2
Baumann, Kurt 1935- 21
Bawden, Nina
  See Kark, Nina Mary
  See also CLR 2
Bayer, Jane E. (?)-1985
  Obituary 44
Bayley, Nicola 1949- 41
Baylor, Byrd 1924- 16
  See also CLR 3
Baynes, Pauline (Diana)
  1922- 19
Beach, Charles
  See Reid, (Thomas) Mayne
Beach, Charles Amory [Collective
  pseudonym] 1
Beach, Edward L(atimer)
  1918- 12
Beach, Stewart Taft 1899- 23
Beachcroft, Nina 1931- 18
Bealer, Alex W(inkler III)
  1921-1980 8
  Obituary 22
Beals, Carleton 1893- 12
Beals, Frank Lee 1881-1972
  Obituary 26
Beame, Rona 1934- 12
Beamer, (G.) Charles, (Jr.)
  1942- 43
Beaney, Jan
  See Udall, Jan Beaney
Beard, Charles Austin
  1874-1948 18
Beard, Dan(iel Carter)
  1850-1941 22
Bearden, Romare (Howard)
  1914- 22
Beardmore, Cedric
  See Beardmore, George
Beardmore, George
  1908-1979 20
Bearman, Jane (Ruth) 1917- 29
Beatty, Elizabeth
  See Holloway, Teresa (Bragunier)
Beatty, Hetty Burlingame
  1907-1971 5
Beatty, Jerome, Jr. 1918- 5

Beatty, John (Louis)
  1922-1975 6
  Obituary 25
Beatty, Patricia (Robbins)
  1922- 30
  Earlier sketch in SATA 1
  See also SAAS 4
Bechtel, Louise Seaman
  1894-1985 4
  Obituary 43
Beck, Barbara L. 1927- 12
Becker, Beril 1901- 11
Becker, John (Leonard) 1901- 12
Becker, Joyce 1936- 39
Becker, May Lamberton
  1873-1958 33
Beckett, Sheilah 1913- 33
Beckman, Delores 1914- 51
Beckman, Gunnel 1910- 6
Beckman, Kaj
  See Beckman, Karin
Beckman, Karin 1913- 45
Beckman, Per (Frithiof) 1913- ... 45
Bedford, A. N.
  See Watson, Jane Werner
Bedford, Annie North
  See Watson, Jane Werner
Bedoukian, Kerop 1907-1981 53
Beebe, B(urdetta) F(aye)
  1920- 1
Beebe, (Charles) William
  1877-1962 19
Beeby, Betty 1923- 25
Beech, Webb
  See Butterworth, W. E.
Beeching, Jack 1922- 14
Beeler, Nelson F(rederick)
  1910- 13
Beers, Dorothy Sands 1917- 9
Beers, Lorna 1897- 14
Beers, V(ictor) Gilbert 1928- 9
Begley, Kathleen A(nne)
  1948- 21
Behn, Harry 1898-1973 2
  Obituary 34
Behnke, Frances L. 8
Behr, Joyce 1929- 15
Behrens, June York 1925- 19
Behrman, Carol H(elen) 1925- 14
Beiser, Arthur 1931- 22
Beiser, Germaine 1931- 11
Belair, Richard L. 1934- 45
Belaney, Archibald Stansfeld
  1888-1938 24
Belknap, B. H.
  See Ellis, Edward S(ylvester)
Bell, Corydon 1894- 3
Bell, Emily Mary
  See Cason, Mabel Earp
Bell, Gertrude (Wood) 1911- 12
Bell, Gina
  See Iannone, Jeanne
Bell, Janet
  See Clymer, Eleanor
Bell, Margaret E(lizabeth)
  1898- 2
Bell, Neill 1946-
  Brief Entry 50
Bell, Norman (Edward) 1899- 11

Bell, Raymond Martin 1907- 13
Bell, Robert S(tanley) W(arren)
  1871-1921
  Brief Entry 27
Bell, Thelma Harrington
  1896- 3
Bellairs, John 1938- 2
Bellingham, Brenda 1931-
  Brief Entry 51
Belloc, (Joseph) Hilaire (Pierre)
  1870-1953 ....*YABC* 1
Bellville, Cheryl Walsh 1944-
  Brief Entry 49
Bell-Zano, Gina
  See Iannone, Jeanne
Belpré, Pura 1899-1982 16
  Obituary 30
Belting, Natalie Maree 1915- 6
Belton, John Raynor 1931- 22
Beltran, Alberto 1923- 43
Belvedere, Lee
  See Grayland, Valerie
Bemelmans, Ludwig
  1898-1962 15
  See also CLR 6
Benary, Margot
  See Benary-Isbert, Margot
Benary-Isbert, Margot
  1889-1979 2
  Obituary 21
  See also CLR 12
Benasutti, Marion 1908- 6
Benchley, Nathaniel (Goddard)
  1915-1981 25
  Obituary 28
  Earlier sketch in SATA 3
Benchley, Peter 1940- 3
Bender, Lucy Ellen 1942- 22
Bendick, Jeanne 1919- 2
  See also CLR 5
  See also SAAS 4
Bendick, Robert L(ouis)
  1917- 11
Benedict, Dorothy Potter
  1889-1979 11
  Obituary 23
Benedict, Lois Trimble
  1902-1967 12
Benedict, Rex 1920- 8
Benedict, Stewart H(urd)
  1924- 26
Benét, Laura 1884-1979 3
  Obituary 23
Benét, Stephen Vincent
  1898-1943 ....*YABC* 1
Benet, Sula 1903(?)-1982 21
  Obituary 33
Benezra, Barbara 1921- 10
Benham, Leslie 1922- 48
Benham, Lois (Dakin) 1924- 48
Benjamin, Nora
  See Kubie, Nora (Gottheil) Benjamin
Bennett, Dorothea
  See Young, Dorothea Bennett
Bennett, Jay 1912- 41
  Brief Entry 27
  See also SAAS 4
Bennett, Jill (Crawford) 1934- .. 41
Bennett, John 1865-1956 .....*YABC* 1

Bennett, Rachel
  See Hill, Margaret (Ohler)
Bennett, Rainey 1907- *15*
Bennett, Richard 1899- *21*
Bennett, Russell H(oradley)
  1896- *25*
Benson, Sally 1900-1972 .... *35*
  Obituary *27*
  Earlier sketch in SATA 1
Bentley, Judith (McBride)
  1945- *40*
Bentley, Nicolas Clerihew 1907-1978
  Obituary *24*
Bentley, Phyllis (Eleanor)
  1894-1977 .... *6*
  Obituary *25*
Bentley, Roy 1947- *46*
Berelson, Howard 1940- *5*
Berends, Polly B(errien)
  1939- *50*
  Brief Entry *38*
Berenstain, Janice *12*
Berenstain, Michael 1951-
  Brief Entry *45*
Berenstain, Stan(ley) 1923- *12*
Beresford, Elisabeth *25*
Berg, Björn 1923-
  Brief Entry *47*
Berg, Dave
  See Berg, David
Berg, David 1920- *27*
Berg, Jean Horton 1913- *6*
Berg, Joan
  See Victor, Joan Berg
Berg, Ron 1952- *48*
Bergaust, Erik 1925-1978 .... *20*
Berger, Gilda
  Brief Entry *42*
Berger, Josef 1903-1971 .... *36*
Berger, Melvin H. 1927- *5*
  See also SAAS 2
Berger, Terry 1933- *8*
Bergey, Alyce (Mae) 1934- *45*
Berkebile, Fred D(onovan) 1900-1978
  Obituary *26*
Berkey, Barry Robert 1935- *24*
Berkowitz, Freda Pastor 1910- *12*
Berliner, Don 1930- *33*
Berliner, Franz 1930- *13*
Berlitz, Charles L. (Frambach)
  1913- *32*
Berman, Linda 1948- *38*
Berna, Paul 1910- *15*
Bernadette
  See Watts, Bernadette
Bernard, George I. 1949- *39*
Bernard, Jacqueline (de Sieyes)
  1921-1983 .... *8*
  Obituary *45*
Bernays, Anne
  See Kaplan, Anne Bernays
Bernstein, Joanne E(ckstein)
  1943- *15*
Bernstein, Theodore M(enline)
  1904-1979 .... *12*
  Obituary *27*
Berrien, Edith Heal
  See Heal, Edith

Berrill, Jacquelyn (Batsel)
  1905- *12*
Berrington, John
  See Brownjohn, Alan
Berry, B. J.
  See Berry, Barbara J.
Berry, Barbara J. 1937- *7*
Berry, Erick
  See Best, Allena Champlin
Berry, Jane Cobb 1915(?)-1979
  Obituary *22*
Berry, Joy Wilt
  Brief Entry *46*
Berry, William D(avid) 1926- *14*
Berson, Harold 1926- *4*
Berwick, Jean
  See Meyer, Jean Shepherd
Beskow, Elsa (Maartman)
  1874-1953 .... *20*
Best, (Evangel) Allena Champlin
  1892-1974 .... *2*
  Obituary *25*
Best, (Oswald) Herbert 1894- *2*
Bestall, Alfred (Edmeades) 1892-1986
  Obituary *48*
Betancourt, Jeanne 1941-
  Brief Entry *43*
Beth, Mary
  See Miller, Mary Beth
Bethancourt, T. Ernesto 1932- *11*
  See also CLR 3
Bethel, Dell 1929- *52*
Bethell, Jean (Frankenberry)
  1922- *8*
Bethers, Ray 1902- *6*
Bethune, J. G.
  See Ellis, Edward S(ylvester)
Betteridge, Anne
  See Potter, Margaret (Newman)
Bettina
  See Ehrlich, Bettina
Bettmann, Otto Ludwig 1903- *46*
Betts, James [Joint pseudonym]
  See Haynes, Betsy
Betz, Eva Kelly 1897-1968 .... *10*
Bevan, Tom
  1868-1930(?) .... *YABC 2*
Bewick, Thomas 1753-1828 .... *16*
Beyer, Audrey White 1916- *9*
Bezencon, Jacqueline (Buxcel)
  1924- *48*
Bhatia, June
  See Forrester, Helen
Bialk, Elisa *1*
Bianco, Margery (Williams)
  1881-1944 .... *15*
Bianco, Pamela 1906- *28*
Bibby, Violet 1908- *24*
Bible, Charles 1937- *13*
Bice, Clare 1909-1976 .... *22*
Bickerstaff, Isaac
  See Swift, Jonathan
Biegel, Paul 1925- *16*
Biemiller, Carl L(udwig)
  1912-1979 .... *40*
  Obituary *21*
Bienenfeld, Florence L(ucille)
  1929- *39*
Bierhorst, John 1936- *6*

Bileck, Marvin 1920- *40*
Bill, Alfred Hoyt 1879-1964 ...... *44*
Billings, Charlene W(interer)
  1941- *41*
Billington, Elizabeth T(hain) *50*
  Brief Entry *43*
Billout, Guy René 1941- *10*
Binkley, Anne
  See Rand, Ann (Binkley)
Binzen, Bill *24*
Binzen, William
  See Binzen, Bill
Birch, Reginald B(athurst)
  1856-1943 .... *19*
Birmingham, Lloyd 1924- *12*
Biro, Val 1921- *1*
Bischoff, Julia Bristol
  1909-1970 .... *12*
Bishop, Bonnie 1943- *37*
Bishop, Claire (Huchet) *14*
Bishop, Curtis 1912-1967 .... *6*
Bishop, Elizabeth 1911-1979
  Obituary *24*
Bisset, Donald 1910- *7*
Bitter, Gary G(len) 1940- *22*
Bixby, William (Courtney)
  1920-1986 .... *6*
  Obituary *47*
Bjerregaard-Jensen, Vilhelm Hans
  See Hillcourt, William
Bjorklund, Lorence F.
  1913-1978 .... *35*
  Brief Entry *32*
Black, Algernon David 1900- *12*
Black, Irma S(imonton)
  1906-1972 .... *2*
  Obituary *25*
Black, Mansell
  See Trevor, Elleston
Black, Susan Adams 1953- *40*
Blackburn, Claire
  See Jacobs, Linda C.
Blackburn, John(ny) Brewton
  1952- *15*
Blackburn, Joyce Knight
  1920- *29*
Blackett, Veronica Heath
  1927- *12*
Blackton, Peter
  See Wilson, Lionel
Blades, Ann 1947- *16*
Bladow, Suzanne Wilson
  1937- *14*
Blaine, John
  See Goodwin, Harold Leland
Blaine, John
  See Harkins, Philip
Blaine, Margery Kay 1937- *11*
Blair, Anne Denton 1914- *46*
Blair, Eric Arthur 1903-1950 ...... *29*
Blair, Helen 1910-
  Brief Entry *29*
Blair, Jay 1953- *45*
Blair, Ruth Van Ness 1912- *12*
Blair, Walter 1900- *12*
Blake, Olive
  See Supraner, Robyn
Blake, Quentin 1932- *52*
Blake, Robert 1949- *42*

Blake, Walker E.
 See Butterworth, W. E.
Blake, William 1757-1827 30
Bland, Edith Nesbit
 See Nesbit, E(dith)
Bland, Fabian [Joint pseudonym]
 See Nesbit, E(dith)
Blane, Gertrude
 See Blumenthal, Gertrude
Blassingame, Wyatt Rainey
 1909-1985 34
 Obituary 41
 Earlier sketch in SATA 1
Blauer, Ettagale 1940- 49
Bleeker, Sonia 1909-1971 2
 Obituary 26
Blegvad, Erik 1923- 14
Blegvad, Lenore 1926- 14
Blishen, Edward 1920- 8
Bliss, Corinne D(emas) 1947- 37
Bliss, Reginald
 See Wells, H(erbert) G(eorge)
Bliss, Ronald G(ene) 1942- 12
Bliven, Bruce, Jr. 1916- 2
Blixen, Karen (Christentze Dinesen)
 1885-1962 44
Bloch, Lucienne 1909- 10
Bloch, Marie Halun 1910- 6
Bloch, Robert 1917- 12
Blochman, Lawrence G(oldtree)
 1900-1975 22
Block, Irvin 1917- 12
Blocksma, Mary
 Brief Entry 44
Blood, Charles Lewis 1929- 28
Bloom, Freddy 1914- 37
Bloom, Lloyd
 Brief Entry 43
Blos, Joan W(insor) 1928- 33
 Brief Entry 27
Blough, Glenn O(rlando)
 1907- 1
Blue, Rose 1931- 5
Blumberg, Rhoda 1917- 35
Blume, Judy (Sussman) 1938- 31
 Earlier sketch in SATA 2
 See also CLR 2
Blumenthal, Gertrude 1907-1971
 Obituary 27
Blumenthal, Shirley 1943- 46
Blutig, Eduard
 See Gorey, Edward St. John
Bly, Janet Chester 1945- 43
Bly, Robert W(ayne) 1957-
 Brief Entry 48
Bly, Stephen A(rthur) 1944- 43
Blyton, Carey 1932- 9
Blyton, Enid (Mary)
 1897-1968 25
Boardman, Fon Wyman, Jr.
 1911- 6
Boardman, Gwenn R. 1924- 12
Boase, Wendy 1944- 28
Boatner, Mark Mayo III
 1921- 29
Bobbe, Dorothie 1905-1975 1
 Obituary 25
Bobri
 See Bobritsky, Vladimir

Bobri, Vladimir
 See Bobritsky, Vladimir
Bobritsky, Vladimir 1898- 47
 Brief Entry 32
Bock, Hal
 See Bock, Harold I.
Bock, Harold I. 1939- 10
Bock, William Sauts
 Netamux'we 14
Bodecker, N. M. 1922- 8
Boden, Hilda
 See Bodenham, Hilda Esther
Bodenham, Hilda Esther
 1901- 13
Bodie, Idella F(allaw) 1925- 12
Bodker, Cecil 1927- 14
Bodsworth, (Charles) Fred(erick)
 1918- 27
Boeckman, Charles 1920- 12
Boegehold, Betty (Doyle) 1913-1985
 Obituary 42
Boesch, Mark J(oseph) 1917- 12
Boesen, Victor 1908- 16
Boggs, Ralph Steele 1901- 7
Bograd, Larry 1953- 33
Bohdal, Susi 1951- 22
Boles, Paul Darcy 1916-1984 9
 Obituary 38
Bolian, Polly 1925- 4
Bollen, Roger 1941(?)-
 Brief Entry 29
Bolliger, Max 1929- 7
Bolognese, Don(ald Alan)
 1934- 24
Bolton, Carole 1926- 6
Bolton, Elizabeth
 See Johnston, Norma
Bolton, Evelyn
 See Bunting, Anne Evelyn
Bond, B. J.
 See Heneghan, James
Bond, Felicia 1954- 49
Bond, Gladys Baker 1912- 14
Bond, J. Harvey
 See Winterbotham, R(ussell)
 R(obert)
Bond, Michael 1926- 6
 See also CLR 1
 See also SAAS 3
Bond, Nancy (Barbara) 1945- 22
 See also CLR 11
Bond, Ruskin 1934- 14
Bonehill, Captain Ralph
 See Stratemeyer, Edward L.
Bonestell, Chesley 1888-1986
 Obituary 48
Bonham, Barbara 1926- 7
Bonham, Frank 1914- 49
 Earlier sketch in SATA 1
 See also SAAS 3
Bonn, Pat
 See Bonn, Patricia Carolyn
Bonn, Patricia Carolyn 1948- 43
Bonner, Mary Graham
 1890-1974 19
Bonners, Susan
 Brief Entry 48
Bonsall, Crosby (Barbara Newell)
 1921- 23

Bontemps, Arna 1902-1973 44
 Obituary 24
 Earlier sketch in SATA 2
 See also CLR 6
Bonzon, Paul-Jacques 1908- 22
Booher, Dianna Daniels 1948- 33
Bookman, Charlotte
 See Zolotow, Charlotte S.
Boone, Pat 1934- 7
Boorman, Linda (Kay) 1940- 46
Boorstin, Daniel J(oseph)
 1914- 52
Booth, Ernest Sheldon
 1915-1984 43
Booth, Graham (Charles)
 1935- 37
Bordier, Georgette 1924- 16
Boring, Mel 1939- 35
Borja, Corinne 1929- 22
Borja, Robert 1923- 22
Borland, Hal 1900-1978 5
 Obituary 24
Borland, Harold Glen
 See Borland, Hal
Borland, Kathryn Kilby 1916- 16
Born, Adolf 1930- 49
Bornstein, Ruth 1927- 14
Borski, Lucia Merecka 18
Borten, Helen Jacobson 1930- 5
Borton, Elizabeth
 See Treviño, Elizabeth B. de
Bortstein, Larry 1942- 16
Bosco, Jack
 See Holliday, Joseph
Boshell, Gordon 1908- 15
Boshinski, Blanche 1922- 10
Bosse, Malcolm J(oseph)
 1926- 35
Bossom, Naomi 1933- 35
Boston, Lucy Maria (Wood)
 1892- 19
 See also CLR 3
Bosworth, J. Allan 1925- 19
Bothwell, Jean 2
Botkin, B(enjamin) A(lbert)
 1901-1975 40
Botting, Douglas (Scott)
 1934- 43
Bottner, Barbara 1943- 14
Boulet, Susan Seddon 1941- 50
Boulle, Pierre (Francois Marie-Louis)
 1912- 22
Bourdon, David 1934- 46
Bourne, Leslie
 See Marshall, Evelyn
Bourne, Miriam Anne 1931- 16
Boutet De Monvel, (Louis) M(aurice)
 1850(?)-1913 30
Bova, Ben 1932- 6
 See also CLR 3
Bowden, Joan Chase 1925- 51
 Brief Entry 38
Bowen, Betty Morgan
 See West, Betty
Bowen, Catherine Drinker
 1897-1973 7
Bowen, David
 See Bowen, Joshua David
Bowen, Joshua David 1930- 22

Bowen, R(obert) Sidney
  1900(?)-1977 52
  Obituary 21
Bowie, Jim
  See Stratemeyer, Edward L.
Bowler, Jan Brett
  See Brett, Jan
Bowman, James Cloyd
  1880-1961 23
Bowman, John S(tewart)
  1931- 16
Bowman, Kathleen (Gill)
  1942- 52
  Brief Entry 40
Boyce, George A(rthur) 1898- 19
Boyd, Pauline
  See Schock, Pauline
Boyd, Selma
  See Acuff, Selma Boyd
Boyd, Waldo T. 1918- 18
Boyer, Robert E(rnst) 1929- 22
Boyle, Ann (Peters) 1916- 10
Boyle, Eleanor Vere (Gordon)
  1825-1916 28
Boylston, Helen (Dore)
  1895-1984 23
  Obituary 39
Boynton, Sandra 1953-
  Brief Entry 38
Boz
  See Dickens, Charles
Bradbury, Bianca 1908- 3
Bradbury, Ray (Douglas)
  1920- 11
Bradford, Ann (Liddell) 1917-
  Brief Entry 38
Bradford, Karleen 1936- 48
Bradford, Lois J(ean) 1936- 36
Bradley, Duane
  See Sanborn, Duane
Bradley, Virginia 1912- 23
Brady, Esther Wood
  1905-1987 31
  Obituary 53
Brady, Irene 1943- 4
Brady, Lillian 1902- 28
Bragdon, Elspeth 1897- 6
Bragdon, Lillian (Jacot) 24
Bragg, Mabel Caroline
  1870-1945 24
Bragg, Michael 1948- 46
Braithwaite, Althea 1940- 23
Bram, Elizabeth 1948- 30
Brancato, Robin F(idler)
  1936- 23
Brandenberg, Aliki (Liacouras)
  1929- 35
  Earlier sketch in SATA 2
Brandenberg, Franz 1932- 35
  Earlier sketch in SATA 8
Brandhorst, Carl T(heodore)
  1898- 23
Brandon, Brumsic, Jr. 1927- 9
Brandon, Curt
  See Bishop, Curtis
Brandreth, Gyles 1948- 28
Brandt, Catharine 1905- 40
Brandt, Keith
  See Sabin, Louis

Branfield, John (Charles)
  1931- 11
Branley, Franklyn M(ansfield)
  1915- 4
  See also CLR 13
Branscum, Robbie 1937- 23
Bransom, (John) Paul
  1885-1979 43
Bratton, Helen 1899- 4
Braude, Michael 1936- 23
Braymer, Marjorie 1911- 6
Brecht, Edith 1895-1975 6
  Obituary 25
Breck, Vivian
  See Breckenfeld, Vivian Gurney
Breckenfeld, Vivian Gurney
  1895- 1
Breda, Tjalmar
  See DeJong, David C(ornel)
Breinburg, Petronella 1927- 11
Breisky, William J(ohn) 1928- 22
Brennan, Gale Patrick 1927-
  Brief Entry 53
Brennan, Joseph L. 1903- 6
Brennan, Tim
  See Conroy, Jack (Wesley)
Brenner, Barbara (Johnes)
  1925- 42
  Earlier sketch in SATA 4
Brenner, Fred 1920- 36
  Brief Entry 34
Brent, Hope 1935(?)-1984
  Obituary 39
Brent, Stuart 14
Brett, Bernard 1925- 22
Brett, Grace N(eff) 1900-1975 23
Brett, Hawksley
  See Bell, Robert S(tanley) W(arren)
Brett, Jan 1949- 42
Brewer, Sally King 1947- 33
Brewster, Benjamin
  See Folsom, Franklin
Brewster, Patience 1952- 51
Brewton, John E(dmund)
  1898- 5
Brick, John 1922-1973 10
Bridgers, Sue Ellen 1942- 22
  See also SAAS 1
Bridges, Laurie
  See Bruck, Lorraine
Bridges, William (Andrew)
  1901- 5
Bridwell, Norman 1928- 4
Brier, Howard M(axwell)
  1903-1969 8
Briggs, Carole S(uzanne) 1950-
  Brief Entry 47
Briggs, Katharine Mary 1898-1980
  Obituary 25
Briggs, Peter 1921-1975 39
  Obituary 31
Briggs, Raymond (Redvers)
  1934- 23
  See also CLR 10
Bright, Robert 1902- 24
Brightfield, Richard 1927-
  Brief Entry 53
Brightfield, Rick
  See Brightfield, Richard

Brightwell, L(eonard) R(obert) 1889-
  Brief Entry 29
Brimberg, Stanlee 1947- 9
Brin, Ruth F(irestone) 1921- 22
Brinckloe, Julie (Lorraine)
  1950- 13
Brindel, June (Rachuy) 1919- 7
Brindze, Ruth 1903- 23
Brink, Carol Ryrie 1895-1981 31
  Obituary 27
  Earlier sketch in SATA 1
Brinsmead, H(esba) F(ay)
  1922- 18
  See also SAAS 5
Briquebec, John
  See Rowland-Entwistle, (Arthur)
  Theodore (Henry)
Brisco, Pat A.
  See Matthews, Patricia
Brisco, Patty
  See Matthews, Patricia
Briscoe, Jill (Pauline) 1935-
  Brief Entry 47
Brisley, Joyce Lankester
  1896- 22
Britt, Albert 1874-1969
  Obituary 28
Britt, Dell 1934- 1
Brittain, William 1930- 36
Britton, Kate
  See Stegeman, Janet Allais
Britton, Louisa
  See McGuire, Leslie (Sarah)
Bro, Margueritte (Harmon)
  1894-1977 19
  Obituary 27
Broadhead, Helen Cross
  1913- 25
Brochmann, Elizabeth (Anne)
  1938- 41
Brock, Betty 1923- 7
Brock, C(harles) E(dmund)
  1870-1938 42
  Brief Entry 32
Brock, Delia
  See Ephron, Delia
Brock, Emma L(illian)
  1886-1974 8
Brock, H(enry) M(atthew)
  1875-1960 42
Brockett, Eleanor Hall
  1913-1967 10
Brockman, C(hristian) Frank
  1902- 26
Broderick, Dorothy M. 1929- 5
Brodie, Sally
  See Cavin, Ruth (Brodie)
Broekel, Rainer Lothar 1923- 38
Broekel, Ray
  See Broekel, Rainer Lothar
Bröger, Achim 1944- 31
Brokamp, Marilyn 1920- 10
Bromhall, Winifred 26
Bromley, Dudley 1948-
  Brief Entry 51
Brommer, Gerald F(rederick)
  1927- 28
Brondfield, Jerome 1913- 22

Brondfield, Jerry
See Brondfield, Jerome
Bronson, Lynn
See Lampman, Evelyn Sibley
Bronson, Wilfrid Swancourt
1894-1985
Obituary 43
Brook, Judith Penelope 1926-
Brief Entry 51
Brook, Judy
See Brook, Judith Penelope
Brooke, L(eonard) Leslie
1862-1940 17
Brooke-Haven, P.
See Wodehouse, P(elham)
G(renville)
Brookins, Dana 1931- 28
Brooks, Anita 1914- 5
Brooks, Barbara
See Simons, Barbara B(rooks)
Brooks, Bruce
Brief Entry 53
Brooks, Charlotte K. 24
Brooks, Gwendolyn 1917- 6
Brooks, Jerome 1931- 23
Brooks, Lester 1924- 7
Brooks, Maurice (Graham)
1900- 45
Brooks, Polly Schoyer 1912- 12
Brooks, Ron(ald George) 1948-
Brief Entry 33
Brooks, Walter R(ollin)
1886-1958 17
Brosnan, James Patrick 1929- 14
Brosnan, Jim
See Brosnan, James Patrick
Broun, Emily
See Sterne, Emma Gelders
Brower, Millicent 8
Brower, Pauline (York) 1929- 22
Browin, Frances Williams
1898- 5
Brown, Alexis
See Baumann, Amy (Brown)
Brown, Bill
See Brown, William L.
Brown, Billye Walker
See Cutchen, Billye Walker
Brown, Bob
See Brown, Robert Joseph
Brown, Buck 1936- 45
Brown, Conrad 1922- 31
Brown, David
See Myller, Rolf
Brown, Dee (Alexander)
1908- 5
Brown, Drollene P. 1939- 53
Brown, Eleanor Frances 1908- 3
Brown, Elizabeth M(yers)
1915- 43
Brown, Fern G. 1918- 34
Brown, (Robert) Fletch 1923- 42
Brown, George Earl
1883-1964 11
Brown, George Mackay 1921- 35
Brown, Irene Bennett 1932- 3
Brown, Irving
See Adams, William Taylor

Brown, Ivor (John Carnegie)
1891-1974 5
Obituary 26
Brown, Joe David 1915-1976 44
Brown, Joseph E(dward) 1929-
Brief Entry 51
Brown, Judith Gwyn 1933- 20
Brown, Lloyd Arnold
1907-1966 36
Brown, Marc Tolon 1946- 53
Earlier sketch in SATA 10
Brown, Marcia 1918- 47
Earlier sketch in SATA 7
See also CLR 12
Brown, Margaret Wise
1910-1952 .... YABC 2
See also CLR 10
Brown, Margery 5
Brown, Marion Marsh 1908- 6
Brown, Myra Berry 1918- 6
Brown, Palmer 1919- 36
Brown, Pamela 1924- 5
Brown, Robert Joseph 1907- 14
Brown, Rosalie (Gertrude) Moore
1910- 9
Brown, Roswell
See Webb, Jean Francis (III)
Brown, Roy (Frederick)
1921-1982 51
Obituary 39
Brown, Vinson 1912- 19
Brown, Walter R(eed) 1929- 19
Brown, Will
See Ainsworth, William Harrison
Brown, William L(ouis)
1910-1964 5
Browne, Anthony (Edward Tudor)
1946- 45
Brief Entry 44
Browne, Dik
See Browne, Richard
Browne, Hablot Knight
1815-1882 21
Browne, Matthew
See Rands, William Brighty
Browne, Richard 1917-
Brief Entry 38
Browning, Robert
1812-1889 .... YABC 1
Brownjohn, Alan 1931- 6
Bruce, Dorita Fairlie 1885-1970
Obituary 27
Bruce, Mary 1927- 1
Bruchac, Joseph III 1942- 42
Bruck, Lorraine 1921-
Brief Entry 46
Bruemmer, Fred 1929- 47
Bruna, Dick 1927- 43
Brief Entry 30
See also CLR 7
Brunhoff, Jean de 1899-1937 24
See also CLR 4
Brunhoff, Laurent de 1925- 24
See also CLR 4
Brustlein, Daniel 1904- 40
Brustlein, Janice Tworkov 40
Bryan, Ashley F. 1923- 31
Bryan, Dorothy (Marie) 1896(?)-1984
Obituary 39

Bryant, Bernice (Morgan)
1908- 11
Brychta, Alex 1956- 21
Bryson, Bernarda 1905- 9
Buba, Joy Flinsch 1904- 44
Buchan, Bryan 1945- 36
Buchan, John 1875-1940 ..... YABC 2
Buchheimer, Naomi Barnett
See Barnett, Naomi
Buchwald, Art(hur) 1925- 10
Buchwald, Emilie 1935- 7
Buck, Lewis 1925- 18
Buck, Margaret Waring 1910- 3
Buck, Pearl S(ydenstricker)
1892-1973 25
Earlier sketch in SATA 1
Buckeridge, Anthony 1912- 6
Buckholtz, Eileen (Garber) 1949-
Brief Entry 47
Buckler, Ernest 1908-1984 47
Buckley, Helen E(lizabeth)
1918- 2
Buckmaster, Henrietta 6
Budd, Lillian 1897- 7
Buehr, Walter 1897-1971 3
Buff, Conrad 1886-1975 19
Buff, Mary Marsh 1890-1970 19
Bugbee, Emma 1888(?)-1981
Obituary 29
Bulfinch, Thomas 1796-1867 35
Bull, Angela (Mary) 1936- 45
Bull, Norman John 1916- 41
Bull, Peter (Cecil) 1912-1984
Obituary 39
Bulla, Clyde Robert 1914- 41
Earlier sketch in SATA 2
See also SAAS 6
Bumstead, Kathleen (Mary)
1918-1987 53
Bunin, Catherine 1967- 30
Bunin, Sherry 1925- 30
Bunting, A. E.
See Bunting, Anne Evelyn
Bunting, Anne Evelyn 1928- 18
Bunting, Eve
See Bunting, Anne Evelyn
Bunting, Glenn (Davison)
1957- 22
Burack, Sylvia K. 1916- 35
Burbank, Addison (Buswell)
1895-1961 37
Burch, Robert J(oseph) 1925- 1
Burchard, Peter D(uncan) 5
Burchard, Sue 1937- 22
Burchardt, Nellie 1921- 7
Burdick, Eugene (Leonard)
1918-1965 22
Burford, Eleanor
See Hibbert, Eleanor
Burger, Carl 1888-1967 9
Burgess, Anne Marie
See Gerson, Noel B(ertram)
Burgess, Em
See Burgess, Mary Wyche
Burgess, (Frank) Gelett
1866-1951 32
Brief Entry 30
Burgess, Mary Wyche 1916- 18

Burgess, Michael
  See Gerson, Noel B(ertram)
Burgess, Robert F(orrest)
  1927- *4*
Burgess, Thornton W(aldo)
  1874-1965 .... *17*
Burgess, Trevor
  See Trevor, Elleston
Burgwyn, Mebane H. 1914- *7*
Burke, David 1927- *46*
Burke, John
  See O'Connor, Richard
Burkert, Nancy Ekholm 1933- *24*
Burland, Brian (Berkeley)
  1931- *34*
Burland, C. A.
  See Burland, Cottie A.
Burland, Cottie A. 1905- *5*
Burlingame, (William) Roger
  1889-1967 .... *2*
Burman, Alice Caddy 1896(?)-1977
  Obituary *24*
Burman, Ben Lucien
  1896-1984 .... *6*
  Obituary *40*
Burn, Doris 1923- *1*
Burnett, Constance Buel
  1893-1975 .... *36*
Burnett, Frances (Eliza) Hodgson
  1849-1924 ....*YABC 2*
Burnford, S. D.
  See Burnford, Sheila
Burnford, Sheila 1918-1984 .... *3*
  Obituary *38*
  See also CLR 2
Burningham, John (Mackintosh)
  1936- *16*
  See also CLR 9
Burns, Marilyn
  Brief Entry *33*
Burns, Paul C. *5*
Burns, Raymond (Howard)
  1924- *9*
Burns, William A. 1909- *5*
Burr, Lonnie 1943- *47*
Burroughs, Edgar Rice
  1875-1950 .... *41*
Burroughs, Jean Mitchell
  1908- *28*
Burroughs, Polly 1925- *2*
Burroway, Janet (Gay) 1936- *23*
Burstein, John 1949-
  Brief Entry *40*
Burt, Jesse Clifton 1921-1976 ..... *46*
  Obituary *20*
Burt, Olive Woolley 1894- *4*
Burton, Hester 1913- *7*
  See also CLR 1
Burton, Leslie
  See McGuire, Leslie (Sarah)
Burton, Marilee Robin 1950- *46*
Burton, Maurice 1898- *23*
Burton, Robert (Wellesley)
  1941- *22*
Burton, Virginia Lee
  1909-1968 .... *2*
  See also CLR 11
Burton, William H(enry)
  1890-1964 .... *11*

Busby, Edith (?)-1964
  Obituary *29*
Busch, Phyllis S. 1909- *30*
Bushmiller, Ernie 1905-1982
  Obituary *31*
Busoni, Rafaello 1900-1962 .... *16*
Butler, Beverly 1932- *7*
Butler, Suzanne
  See Perreard, Suzanne Louise Butler
Butters, Dorothy Gilman
  1923- *5*
Butterworth, Emma Macalik
  1928- *43*
Butterworth, Oliver 1915- *1*
Butterworth, W(illiam) E(dmund III)
  1929- *5*
Byars, Betsy (Cromer) 1928- *46*
  Earlier sketch in SATA 4
  See also CLR 1
  See also SAAS 1
Byfield, Barbara Ninde 1930- *8*
Byrd, Elizabeth 1912- *34*
Byrd, Robert (John) 1942- *33*

C

C.3.3.
  See Wilde, Oscar (Fingal O'Flahertie
  Wills)
Cable, Mary 1920- *9*
Cabral, O. M.
  See Cabral, Olga
Cabral, Olga 1909- *46*
Caddy, Alice
  See Burman, Alice Caddy
Cadwallader, Sharon 1936- *7*
Cady, (Walter) Harrison
  1877-1970 .... *19*
Cagle, Malcolm W(infield)
  1918- *32*
Cahn, Rhoda 1922- *37*
Cahn, William 1912-1976 .... *37*
Cain, Arthur H. 1913- *3*
Cain, Christopher
  See Fleming, Thomas J(ames)
Caines, Jeanette (Franklin)
  Brief Entry *43*
Cairns, Trevor 1922- *14*
Caldecott, Moyra 1927- *22*
Caldecott, Randolph (J.)
  1846-1886 .... *17*
  See also CLR 14
Calder, Lyn
  See Calmenson, Stephanie
Caldwell, John C(ope) 1913- *7*
Calhoun, Mary (Huiskamp)
  1926- *2*
Calkins, Franklin
  See Stratemeyer, Edward L.
Call, Hughie Florence
  1890-1969 .... *1*
Callahan, Dorothy M. 1934- *39*
  Brief Entry *35*
Callahan, Philip S(erna) 1923- *25*
Callaway, Bernice (Anne)
  1923- *48*
Callaway, Kathy 1943- *36*

Callen, Larry
  See Callen, Lawrence Willard, Jr.
Callen, Lawrence Willard, Jr.
  1927- *19*
Calmenson, Stephanie 1952- *51*
  Brief Entry *37*
Calvert, John
  See Leaf, (Wilbur) Munro
Calvert, Patricia 1931- *45*
Cameron, Ann 1943- *27*
Cameron, Edna M. 1905- *3*
Cameron, Eleanor (Butler)
  1912- *25*
  Earlier sketch in SATA 1
  See also CLR 1
Cameron, Elizabeth
  See Nowell, Elizabeth Cameron
Cameron, Elizabeth Jane
  1910-1976 .... *32*
  Obituary *30*
Cameron, Ian
  See Payne, Donald Gordon
Cameron, Polly 1928- *2*
Camp, Charles Lewis 1893-1975
  Obituary *31*
Camp, Walter (Chauncey)
  1859-1925 ....*YABC 1*
Campbell, (Elizabeth) Andréa
  1963- *50*
Campbell, Ann R. 1925- *11*
Campbell, Bruce
  See Epstein, Samuel
Campbell, Camilla 1905- *26*
Campbell, Hope *20*
Campbell, Jane
  See Edwards, Jane Campbell
Campbell, Patricia J(ean)
  1930- *45*
Campbell, Patty
  See Campbell, Patricia J(ean)
Campbell, R. W.
  See Campbell, Rosemae Wells
Campbell, Rod 1945- *51*
  Brief Entry *44*
Campbell, Rosemae Wells
  1909- *1*
Campion, Nardi Reeder 1917- *22*
Campling, Elizabeth 1948- *53*
Candell, Victor 1903-1977
  Obituary *24*
Canfield, Dorothy
  See Fisher, Dorothy Canfield
Canfield, Jane White
  1897-1984 .... *32*
  Obituary *38*
Cannon, Cornelia (James) 1876-1969
  Brief Entry *28*
Cannon, Ravenna
  See Mayhar, Ardath
Canusi, Jose
  See Barker, S. Omar
Caplin, Alfred Gerald 1909-1979
  Obituary *21*
Capp, Al
  See Caplin, Alfred Gerald
Cappel, Constance 1936- *22*
Capps, Benjamin (Franklin)
  1922- *9*

Captain Kangaroo
See Keeshan, Robert J.
Carafoli, Marci
See Ridlon, Marci
Caras, Roger A(ndrew) 1928- *12*
Carbonnier, Jeanne 1894-1974 .... *3*
Obituary *34*
Care, Felicity
See Coury, Louise Andree
Carew, Jan (Rynveld) 1925- *51*
Brief Entry *40*
Carey, Bonnie 1941- *18*
Carey, Ernestine Gilbreth
1908- *2*
Carey, M. V.
See Carey, Mary (Virginia)
Carey, Mary (Virginia) 1925- *44*
Brief Entry *39*
Carigiet, Alois 1902-1985 .... *24*
Obituary *47*
Carini, Edward 1923- *9*
Carle, Eric 1929- *4*
See also CLR 10
See also SAAS 6
Carleton, Captain L. C.
See Ellis, Edward S(ylvester)
Carley, V(an Ness) Royal 1906-1976
Obituary *20*
Carlisle, Clark, Jr.
See Holding, James
Carlisle, Olga A(ndreyev)
1930- *35*
Carlsen, G(eorge) Robert
1917- *30*
Carlsen, Ruth C(hristoffer) *2*
Carlson, Bernice Wells 1910- *8*
Carlson, Dale Bick 1935- *1*
Carlson, Daniel 1960- *27*
Carlson, Nancy L(ee) 1953-
Brief Entry *45*
Carlson, Natalie Savage 1906- *2*
See also SAAS 4
Carlson, Vada F. 1897- *16*
Carlstrom, Nancy White
1948- *53*
Brief Entry *48*
Carmer, Carl (Lamson)
1893-1976 .... *37*
Obituary *30*
Carmer, Elizabeth Black
1904- *24*
Carmichael, Carrie *40*
Carmichael, Harriet
See Carmichael, Carrie
Carol, Bill J.
See Knott, William Cecil, Jr.
Caroselli, Remus F(rancis)
1916- *36*
Carpelan, Bo (Gustaf Bertelsson)
1926- *8*
Carpenter, Allan 1917- *3*
Carpenter, Frances 1890-1972 ..... *3*
Obituary *27*
Carpenter, Patricia (Healy Evans)
1920- *11*
Carr, Glyn
See Styles, Frank Showell
Carr, Harriett Helen 1899- *3*
Carr, Mary Jane *2*

Carrick, Carol 1935- *7*
Carrick, Donald 1929- *7*
Carrick, Malcolm 1945- *28*
Carrier, Lark 1947-
Brief Entry *50*
Carrighar, Sally *24*
Carris, Joan Davenport 1938- *44*
Brief Entry *42*
Carroll, Curt
See Bishop, Curtis
Carroll, Elizabeth
See Barkin, Carol
See James, Elizabeth
Carroll, Latrobe *7*
Carroll, Laura
See Parr, Lucy
Carroll, Lewis
See Dodgson, Charles Lutwidge
See also CLR 2
Carroll, Raymond
Brief Entry *47*
Carruth, Hayden 1921- *47*
Carse, Robert 1902-1971 .... *5*
Carson, Captain James
See Stratemeyer, Edward L.
Carson, John F. 1920- *1*
Carson, Rachel (Louise)
1907-1964 .... *23*
Carson, Rosalind
See Chittenden, Margaret
Carson, S. M.
See Gorsline, (Sally) Marie
Carter, Bruce
See Hough, Richard (Alexander)
Carter, Dorothy Sharp 1921- *8*
Carter, Forrest 1927(?)-1979 ...... *32*
Carter, Helene 1887-1960 .... *15*
Carter, (William) Hodding
1907-1972 .... *2*
Obituary *27*
Carter, Katharine J(ones)
1905- *2*
Carter, Nick
See Lynds, Dennis
Carter, Phyllis Ann
See Eberle, Irmengarde
Carter, Samuel III 1904- *37*
Carter, William E. 1926-1983 ..... *1*
Obituary *35*
Cartlidge, Michelle 1950- *49*
Brief Entry *37*
Cartner, William Carruthers
1910- *11*
Cartwright, Sally 1923- *9*
Carver, John
See Gardner, Richard
Carwell, L'Ann
See McKissack, Patricia (L'Ann)
C(arwell)
Cary
See Cary, Louis F(avreau)
Cary, Barbara Knapp 1912(?)-1975
Obituary *31*
Cary, Louis F(avreau) 1915- *9*
Caryl, Jean
See Kaplan, Jean Caryl Korn
Case, Marshal T(aylor) 1941- *9*
Case, Michael
See Howard, Robert West

Caseley, Judith 1951-
Brief Entry *53*
Casewit, Curtis 1922- *4*
Casey, Brigid 1950- *9*
Casey, Winifred Rosen
See Rosen, Winifred
Cason, Mabel Earp 1892-1965 .... *10*
Cass, Joan E(velyn) *1*
Cassedy, Sylvia 1930- *27*
Cassel, Lili
See Wronker, Lili Cassell
Cassel-Wronker, Lili
See Wronker, Lili Cassell
Castellanos, Jane Mollie (Robinson)
1913- *9*
Castellon, Federico 1914-1971 .... *48*
Castillo, Edmund L. 1924- *1*
Castle, Lee [Joint pseudonym]
See Ogan, George F. and Ogan,
Margaret E. (Nettles)
Castle, Paul
See Howard, Vernon (Linwood)
Caswell, Helen (Rayburn)
1923- *12*
Cate, Dick
See Cate, Richard (Edward Nelson)
Cate, Richard (Edward Nelson)
1932- *28*
Cather, Willa (Sibert)
1873-1947 .... *30*
Catherall, Arthur 1906- *3*
Cathon, Laura E(lizabeth)
1908- *27*
Catlin, Wynelle 1930- *13*
Catton, (Charles) Bruce
1899-1978 .... *2*
Obituary *24*
Catz, Max
See Glaser, Milton
Caudell, Marian 1930- *52*
Caudill, Rebecca 1899-1985 ...... *1*
Obituary *44*
Caulfield, Peggy F. 1926-1987
Obituary *53*
Cauley, Lorinda Bryan 1951- *46*
Brief Entry *43*
Cauman, Samuel 1910-1971 ...... *48*
Causley, Charles 1917- *3*
Cavallo, Diana 1931- *7*
Cavanagh, Helen (Carol)
1939- *48*
Brief Entry *37*
Cavanah, Frances 1899-1982 ...... *31*
Earlier sketch in SATA 1
Cavanna, Betty 1909- *30*
Earlier sketch in SATA 1
See also SAAS 4
Cavin, Ruth (Brodie) 1918- *38*
Cawley, Winifred 1915- *13*
Caxton, Pisistratus
See Lytton, Edward G(eorge) E(arle)
L(ytton) Bulwer-Lytton, Baron
Cazet, Denys 1938- *52*
Brief Entry *41*
Cebulash, Mel 1937- *10*
Ceder, Georgiana Dorcas *10*
Celestino, Martha Laing
1951- *39*
Cerf, Bennett 1898-1971 .... *7*

Cerf, Christopher (Bennett)
1941- 2
Cervon, Jacqueline
See Moussard, Jacqueline
Cetin, Frank (Stanley) 1921- 2
Chadwick, Lester [Collective·
pseudonym] 1
Chaffee, Allen 3
Chaffin, Lillie D(orton) 1925- 4
Chaikin, Miriam 1928- 24
Challans, Mary 1905-1983 23
Obituary 36
Chalmers, Mary 1927- 6
Chamberlain, Margaret 1954- 46
Chambers, Aidan 1934- 1
Chambers, Bradford 1922-1984
Obituary 39
Chambers, Catherine E.
See Johnston, Norma
Chambers, John W. 1933-
Brief Entry 46
Chambers, Margaret Ada Eastwood
1911- 2
Chambers, Peggy
See Chambers, Margaret Ada
Eastwood
Chandler, Caroline A(ugusta)
1906-1979 22
Obituary 24
Chandler, David Porter 1933- 28
Chandler, Edna Walker
1908-1982 11
Obituary 31
Chandler, Linda S(mith)
1929- 39
Chandler, Robert 1953- 40
Chandler, Ruth Forbes
1894-1978 2
Obituary 26
Channel, A. R.
See Catherall, Arthur
Chapian, Marie 1938- 29
Chapin, Alene Olsen Dalton
1915(?)-1986
Obituary 47
Chapman, Allen [Collective
pseudonym] 1
Chapman, (Constance) Elizabeth
(Mann) 1919- 10
Chapman, Gaynor 1935- 32
Chapman, Jean 34
Chapman, John Stanton Higham
1891-1972
Obituary 27
Chapman, Maristan [Joint pseudonym]
See Chapman, John Stanton Higham
Chapman, Vera 1898- 33
Chapman, Walker
See Silverberg, Robert
Chappell, Warren 1904- 6
Chardiet, Bernice (Kroll) 27
Charles, Donald
See Meighan, Donald Charles
Charles, Louis
See Stratemeyer, Edward L.
Charlip, Remy 1929- 4
See also CLR 8
Charlot, Jean 1898-1979 8
Obituary 31

Charlton, Michael (Alan)
1923- 34
Charmatz, Bill 1925- 7
Charosh, Mannis 1906- 5
Chase, Alice
See McHargue, Georgess
Chase, Emily
See Sachs, Judith
Chase, Mary (Coyle)
1907-1981 17
Obituary 29
Chase, Mary Ellen 1887-1973 10
Chastain, Madye Lee 1908- 4
Chauncy, Nan 1900-1970 6
See also CLR 6
Chaundler, Christine
1887-1972 1
Obituary 25
Chen, Tony 1929- 6
Chenault, Nell
See Smith, Linell Nash
Chenery, Janet (Dai) 1923- 25
Cheney, Cora 1916- 3
Cheney, Ted
See Cheney, Theodore Albert
Cheney, Theodore Albert
1928- 11
Cheng, Judith 1955- 36
Chermayeff, Ivan 1932- 47
Chernoff, Dorothy A.
See Ernst, (Lyman) John
Chernoff, Goldie Taub 1909- 10
Cherry, Lynne 1952- 34
Cherryholmes, Anne
See Price, Olive
Chess, Victoria (Dickerson)
1939- 33
Chessare, Michele
Brief Entry 42
Chesterton, G(ilbert) K(eith)
1874-1936 27
Chetin, Helen 1922- 6
Chetwin, Grace
Brief Entry 50
Chevalier, Christa 1937- 35
Chew, Ruth 7
Chidsey, Donald Barr
1902-1981 3
Obituary 27
Child, Philip 1898-1978 47
Childress, Alice 1920- 48
Earlier sketch in SATA 7
See also CLR 14
Childs, (Halla) Fay (Cochrane)
1890-1971 1
Obituary 25
Chimaera
See Farjeon, Eleanor
Chin, Richard (M.) 1946- 52
Chinery, Michael 1938- 26
Chipperfield, Joseph E(ugene)
1912- 2
Chittenden, Elizabeth F.
1903- 9
Chittenden, Margaret 1933- 28
Chittum, Ida 1918- 7
Choate, Judith (Newkirk)
1940- 30

Chorao, (Ann Mc)Kay (Sproat)
1936- 8
Chorpenning, Charlotte (Lee Barrows)
1872-1955
Brief Entry 37
Chrisman, Arthur Bowie
1889-1953 .... *YABC 1*
Christelow, Eileen 1943- 38
Brief Entry 35
Christensen, Gardell Dano
1907- 1
Christesen, Barbara 1940- 40
Christgau, Alice Erickson
1902- 13
Christian, Mary Blount 1933- 9
Christie, Agatha (Mary Clarissa)
1890-1976 36
Christopher, John
See Youd, (Christopher) Samuel
See also CLR 2
Christopher, Louise
See Hale, Arlene
Christopher, Matt(hew F.)
1917- 47
Earlier sketch in SATA 2
Christopher, Milbourne
1914(?)-1984 46
Christy, Howard Chandler
1873-1952 21
Chu, Daniel 1933- 11
Chukovsky, Kornei (Ivanovich)
1882-1969 34
Earlier sketch in SATA 5
Church, Richard 1893-1972 3
Churchill, E. Richard 1937- 11
Chute, B(eatrice) J(oy)
1913-1987 2
Obituary 53
Chute, Marchette (Gaylord)
1909- 1
Chwast, Jacqueline 1932- 6
Chwast, Seymour 1931- 18
Ciardi, John (Anthony)
1916-1986 1
Obituary 46
Clair, Andrée 19
Clampett, Bob
Obituary 38
See also Clampett, Robert
Clampett, Robert
1914(?)-1984 44
Clapp, Patricia 1912- 4
See also SAAS 4
Clare, Helen
See Hunter, Blair Pauline
Clark, Ann Nolan 1898- 4
Clark, Champ 1923- 47
Clark, David
See Hardcastle, Michael
Clark, David Allen
See Ernst, (Lyman) John
Clark, Frank J(ames) 1922- 18
Clark, Garel [Joint pseudonym]
See Garelick, May
Clark, Leonard 1905-1981 30
Obituary 29
Clark, Margaret Goff 1913- 8
Clark, Mary Higgins 46

Clark, Mavis Thorpe 8
See also SAAS 5
Clark, Merle
See Gessner, Lynne
Clark, Patricia (Finrow) 1929- 11
Clark, Ronald William
1916-1987 2
Obituary 52
Clark, Van D(eusen) 1909- 2
Clark, Virginia
See Gray, Patricia
Clark, Walter Van Tilburg
1909-1971 8
Clarke, Arthur C(harles)
1917- 13
Clarke, Clorinda 1917- 7
Clarke, Joan 1921- 42
Brief Entry 27
Clarke, John
See Laklan, Carli
Clarke, Mary Stetson 1911- 5
Clarke, Michael
See Newlon, Clarke
Clarke, Pauline
See Hunter Blair, Pauline
Clarkson, E(dith) Margaret
1915- 37
Clarkson, Ewan 1929- 9
Claverie, Jean 1946- 38
Clay, Patrice 1947- 47
Claypool, Jane
See Miner, Jane Claypool
Cleary, Beverly (Bunn) 1916- 43
Earlier sketch in SATA 2
See also CLR 2, 8
Cleaver, Bill 1920-1981 22
Obituary 27
See also CLR 6
Cleaver, Carole 1934- 6
Cleaver, Elizabeth (Mrazik)
1939-1985 23
Obituary 43
See also CLR 13
Cleaver, Hylton (Reginald)
1891-1961 49
Cleaver, Vera 22
See also CLR 6
Cleishbotham, Jebediah
See Scott, Sir Walter
Cleland, Mabel
See Widdemer, Mabel Cleland
Clemens, Samuel Langhorne
1835-1910 .... YABC 2
Clemens, Virginia Phelps
1941- 35
Clements, Bruce 1931- 27
Clemons, Elizabeth
See Nowell, Elizabeth Cameron
Clerk, N. W.
See Lewis, C. S.
Cleveland, Bob
See Cleveland, George
Cleveland, George 1903(?)-1985
Obituary 43
Cleven, Cathrine
See Cleven, Kathryn Seward
Cleven, Kathryn Seward 2
Clevin, Jörgen 1920- 7

Clewes, Dorothy (Mary)
1907- 1
Clifford, Eth
See Rosenberg, Ethel
Clifford, Harold B. 1893- 10
Clifford, Margaret Cort 1929- 1
Clifford, Martin
See Hamilton, Charles H. St. John
Clifford, Mary Louise (Beneway)
1926- 23
Clifford, Peggy
See Clifford, Margaret Cort
Clifton, Harry
See Hamilton, Charles H. St. John
Clifton, Lucille 1936- 20
See also CLR 5
Clifton, Martin
See Hamilton, Charles H. St. John
Climo, Shirley 1928- 39
Brief Entry 35
Clinton, Jon
See Prince, J(ack) H(arvey)
Clish, (Lee) Marian 1946- 43
Clive, Clifford
See Hamilton, Charles H. St. John
Cloudsley-Thompson, J(ohn) L(eonard)
1921- 19
Clymer, Eleanor 1906- 9
Clyne, Patricia Edwards 31
Coalson, Glo 1946- 26
Coates, Belle 1896- 2
Coates, Ruth Allison 1915- 11
Coats, Alice M(argaret) 1905- 11
Coatsworth, Elizabeth
1893-1986 2
Obituary 49
See also CLR 2
Cobb, Jane
See Berry, Jane Cobb
Cobb, Vicki 1938- 8
See also CLR 2
See also SAAS 6
Cobbett, Richard
See Pluckrose, Henry (Arthur)
Cober, Alan E. 1935- 7
Cobham, Sir Alan
See Hamilton, Charles H. St. John
Cocagnac, A(ugustin) M(aurice-Jean)
1924- 7
Cochran, Bobbye A. 1949- 11
Cockett, Mary 3
Coe, Douglas [Joint pseudonym]
See Epstein, Beryl and Epstein,
Samuel
Coe, Lloyd 1899-1976
Obituary 30
Coen, Rena Neumann 1925- 20
Coerr, Eleanor 1922- 1
Coffin, Geoffrey
See Mason, F. van Wyck
Coffman, Ramon Peyton
1896- 4
Coggins, Jack (Banham)
1911- 2
Cohen, Barbara 1932- 10
Cohen, Daniel 1936- 8
See also CLR 3
See also SAAS 4

Cohen, Jene Barr
See Barr, Jene
Cohen, Joan Lebold 1932- 4
Cohen, Miriam 1926- 29
Cohen, Peter Zachary 1931- 4
Cohen, Robert Carl 1930- 8
Cohn, Angelo 1914- 19
Coit, Margaret L(ouise) 2
Colbert, Anthony 1934- 15
Colby, C(arroll) B(urleigh)
1904-1977 35
Earlier sketch in SATA 3
Colby, Jean Poindexter 1909- 23
Cole, Annette
See Steiner, Barbara A(nnette)
Cole, Davis
See Elting, Mary
Cole, Jack
See Stewart, John (William)
Cole, Jackson
See Schisgall, Oscar
Cole, Jennifer
See Zach, Cheryl (Byrd)
Cole, Joanna 1944- 49
Brief Entry 37
See also CLR 5
Cole, Lois Dwight
1903(?)-1979 10
Obituary 26
Cole, Sheila R(otenberg)
1939- 24
Cole, William (Rossa) 1919- 9
Coleman, William L(eRoy)
1938- 49
Brief Entry 34
Coles, Robert (Martin) 1929- 23
Colin, Ann
See Ure, Jean
Collier, Christopher 1930- 16
Collier, Ethel 1903- 22
Collier, James Lincoln 1928- 8
See also CLR 3
Collier, Jane
See Collier, Zena
Collier, Zena 1926- 23
Collins, David 1940- 7
Collins, Hunt
See Hunter, Evan
Collins, Michael
See Lynds, Dennis
Collins, Pat Lowery 1932- 31
Collins, Ruth Philpott 1890-1975
Obituary 30
Collodi, Carlo
See Lorenzini, Carlo
See also CLR 5
Colloms, Brenda 1919- 40
Colman, Hila 53
Earlier sketch in SATA 1
Colman, Morris 1899(?)-1981
Obituary 25
Colombo, John Robert 1936- 50
Colonius, Lillian 1911- 3
Colorado (Capella), Antonio J(ulio)
1903- 23
Colt, Martin [Joint pseudonym]
See Epstein, Beryl and Epstein,
Samuel
Colum, Padraic 1881-1972 15

Columella
  See Moore, Clement Clarke
Colver, Anne 1908- *7*
Colwell, Eileen (Hilda) 1904- *2*
Combs, Robert
  See Murray, John
Comfort, Jane Levington
  See Sturtzel, Jane Levington
Comfort, Mildred Houghton
  1886- *3*
Comins, Ethel M(ae) *11*
Comins, Jeremy 1933- *28*
Commager, Henry Steele
  1902- *23*
Comus
  See Ballantyne, R(obert) M(ichael)
Conan Doyle, Arthur
  See Doyle, Arthur Conan
Condit, Martha Olson 1913- *28*
Cone, Ferne Geller 1921- *39*
Cone, Molly (Lamken) 1918- *28*
  Earlier sketch in SATA 1
Conford, Ellen 1942- *6*
  See also CLR 10
Conger, Lesley
  See Suttles, Shirley (Smith)
Conklin, Gladys (Plemon)
  1903- *2*
Conklin, Paul S. *43*
  Brief Entry *33*
Conkling, Hilda 1910- *23*
Conly, Robert Leslie
  1918(?)-1973 .... *23*
Connell, Kirk [Joint pseudonym]
  See Chapman, John Stanton Higham
Connelly, Marc(us Cook) 1890-1980
  Obituary *25*
Connolly, Jerome P(atrick)
  1931- *8*
Connolly, Peter 1935- *47*
Conover, Chris 1950- *31*
Conquest, Owen
  See Hamilton, Charles H. St. John
Conrad, Joseph 1857-1924 .... *27*
Conrad, Pam(ela) 1947- *52*
  Brief Entry *49*
Conroy, Jack (Wesley) 1899- *19*
Conroy, John
  See Conroy, Jack (Wesley)
Constant, Alberta Wilson
  1908-1981 .... *22*
  Obituary *28*
Conway, Gordon
  See Hamilton, Charles H. St. John
Cook, Bernadine 1924- *11*
Cook, Fred J(ames) 1911- *2*
Cook, Joseph J(ay) 1924- *8*
Cook, Lyn
  See Waddell, Evelyn Margaret
Cooke, Ann
  See Cole, Joanna
Cooke, David Coxe 1917- *2*
Cooke, Donald Ewin
  1916-1985 .... *2*
  Obituary *45*
Cookson, Catherine (McMullen)
  1906- *9*

Coolidge, Olivia E(nsor)
  1908- *26*
  Earlier sketch in SATA 1
Coombs, Charles I(ra) 1914- *43*
  Earlier sketch in SATA 3
Coombs, Chick
  See Coombs, Charles I(ra)
Coombs, Patricia 1926- *51*
  Earlier sketch in SATA 3
Cooney, Barbara 1917- *6*
Cooney, Caroline B. 1947- *48*
  Brief Entry *41*
Cooney, Nancy Evans 1932- *42*
Coontz, Otto 1946- *33*
Cooper, Elizabeth Keyser *47*
Cooper, Gordon 1932- *23*
Cooper, James Fenimore
  1789-1851 .... *19*
Cooper, James R.
  See Stratemeyer, Edward L.
Cooper, John R. [Collective
  pseudonym] *1*
Cooper, Kay 1941- *11*
Cooper, Lee (Pelham) *5*
Cooper, Lester (Irving)
  1919-1985 .... *32*
  Obituary *43*
Cooper, Lettice (Ulpha) 1897- *35*
Cooper, Susan 1935- *4*
  See also CLR 4
  See also SAAS 6
Copeland, Helen 1920- *4*
Copeland, Paul W. *23*
Copley, (Diana) Heather Pickering
  1918- *45*
Coppard, A(lfred) E(dgar)
  1878-1957 .... *YABC 1*
Corbett, Grahame *43*
  Brief Entry *36*
Corbett, Scott 1913- *42*
  Earlier sketch in SATA 2
  See also CLR 1
  See also SAAS 2
Corbett, W(illiam) J(esse)
  1938- *50*
  Brief Entry *44*
Corbin, Sabra Lee
  See Malvern, Gladys
Corbin, William
  See McGraw, William Corbin
Corby, Dan
  See Catherall, Arthur
Corcoran, Barbara 1911- *3*
Corcos, Lucille 1908-1973 .... *10*
Cordell, Alexander
  See Graber, Alexander
Coren, Alan 1938- *32*
Corey, Dorothy *23*
Corfe, Thomas Howell 1928- *27*
Corfe, Tom
  See Corfe, Thomas Howell
Corlett, William 1938- *46*
  Brief Entry *39*
Cormack, M(argaret) Grant
  1913- *11*
Cormack, Maribelle B.
  1902-1984 .... *39*

Cormier, Robert (Edmund)
  1925- *45*
  Earlier sketch in SATA 10
  See also CLR 12
Cornelius, Carol 1942- *40*
Cornell, J.
  See Cornell, Jeffrey
Cornell, James (Clayton, Jr.)
  1938- *27*
Cornell, Jean Gay 1920- *23*
Cornell, Jeffrey 1945- *11*
Cornish, Samuel James 1935- *23*
Cornwall, Nellie
  See Sloggett, Nellie
Correy, Lee
  See Stine, G. Harry
Corrigan, (Helen) Adeline
  1909- *23*
Corrigan, Barbara 1922- *8*
Corrin, Sara 1918-
  Brief Entry *48*
Corrin, Stephen
  Brief Entry *48*
Cort, M. C.
  See Clifford, Margaret Cort
Corwin, Judith Hoffman
  1946- *10*
Cosgrave, John O'Hara II 1908-1968
  Obituary *21*
Cosgrove, Margaret (Leota)
  1926- *47*
Cosgrove, Stephen E(dward)
  1945- *53*
  Brief Entry *40*
Coskey, Evelyn 1932- *7*
Cosner, Shaaron 1940- *43*
Costabel, Eva Deutsch 1924- *45*
Costello, David F(rancis)
  1904- *23*
Cott, Jonathan 1942- *23*
Cottam, Clarence 1899-1974 ...... *25*
Cottler, Joseph 1899- *22*
Cottrell, Leonard 1913-1974 ...... *24*
The Countryman
  See Whitlock, Ralph
Courlander, Harold 1908- *6*
Courtis, Stuart Appleton 1874-1969
  Obituary *29*
Coury, Louise Andree 1895(?)-1983
  Obituary *34*
Cousins, Margaret 1905- *2*
Cousteau, Jacques-Yves 1910- *38*
Coville, Bruce 1950- *32*
Cowen, Eve
  See Werner, Herma
Cowie, Leonard W(allace)
  1919- *4*
Cowles, Kathleen
  See Krull, Kathleen
Cowley, Joy 1936- *4*
Cox, Donald William 1921- *23*
Cox, Jack
  See Cox, John Roberts
Cox, John Roberts 1915- *9*
Cox, Palmer 1840-1924 .... *24*
Cox, Victoria
  See Garretson, Victoria Diane
Cox, Wally 1924-1973 .... *25*

Cox, William R(obert) 1901- 46
  Brief Entry 31
Coy, Harold 1902- 3
Craft, Ruth
  Brief Entry 31
Craig, A. A.
  See Anderson, Poul (William)
Craig, Alisa
  See MacLeod, Charlotte (Matilda
  Hughes)
Craig, Helen 1934- 49
  Brief Entry 46
Craig, John Eland
  See Chipperfield, Joseph
Craig, John Ernest 1921- 23
Craig, M. Jean 17
Craig, Margaret Maze
  1911-1964 9
Craig, Mary Francis 1923- 6
Craik, Dinah Maria (Mulock)
  1826-1887 34
Crane, Barbara J. 1934- 31
Crane, Caroline 1930- 11
Crane, M. A.
  See Wartski, Maureen (Ann Crane)
Crane, Roy
  See Crane, Royston Campbell
Crane, Royston Campbell 1901-1977
  Obituary 22
Crane, Stephen (Townley)
  1871-1900 ....YABC 2
Crane, Walter 1845-1915 18
Crane, William D(wight)
  1892- 1
Crary, Elizabeth (Ann) 1942-
  Brief Entry 43
Crary, Margaret (Coleman)
  1906- 9
Craven, Thomas 1889-1969 22
Crawford, Charles P. 1945- 28
Crawford, Deborah 1922- 6
Crawford, John E. 1904-1971 3
Crawford, Mel 1925- 44
  Brief Entry 33
Crawford, Phyllis 1899- 3
Craz, Albert G. 1926- 24
Crayder, Dorothy 1906- 7
Crayder, Teresa
  See Colman, Hila
Crayon, Geoffrey
  See Irving, Washington
Crecy, Jeanne
  See Williams, Jeanne
Credle, Ellis 1902- 1
Cresswell, Helen 1934- 48
  Earlier sketch in SATA 1
Cretan, Gladys (Yessayan)
  1921- 2
Crew, Helen (Cecilia) Coale
  1866-1941 ....YABC 2
Crews, Donald 1938- 32
  Brief Entry 30
  See also CLR 7
Crichton, (J.) Michael 1942- 9
Crofut, Bill
  See Crofut, William E. III
Crofut, William E. III 1934- 23
Croll, Carolyn 1945-
  Brief Entry 52

Croman, Dorothy Young
  See Rosenberg, Dorothy
Cromie, Alice Hamilton 1914- 24
Cromie, William J(oseph)
  1930- 4
Crompton, Anne Eliot 1930- 23
Crompton, Richmal
  See Lamburn, Richmal Crompton
Cronbach, Abraham
  1882-1965 11
Crone, Ruth 1919- 4
Cronin, A(rchibald) J(oseph)
  1896-1981 47
  Obituary 25
Crook, Beverly Courtney 38
  Brief Entry 35
Cros, Earl
  See Rose, Carl
Crosby, Alexander L.
  1906-1980 2
  Obituary 23
Crosher, G(eoffry) R(obins)
  1911- 14
Cross, Gilbert B. 1939-
  Brief Entry 51
Cross, Gillian (Clare) 1945- 38
Cross, Helen Reeder
  See Broadhead, Helen Cross
Cross, Wilbur Lucius III
  1918- 2
Crossley-Holland, Kevin 5
Crouch, Marcus 1913- 4
Crout, George C(lement)
  1917- 11
Crow, Donna Fletcher 1941- 40
Crowe, Bettina Lum 1911- 6
Crowe, John
  See Lynds, Dennis
Crowell, Grace Noll
  1877-1969 34
Crowell, Pers 1910- 2
Crowfield, Christopher
  See Stowe, Harriet (Elizabeth)
  Beecher
Crowley, Arthur M(cBlair)
  1945- 38
Crownfield, Gertrude
  1867-1945 ....YABC 1
Crowther, James Gerald 1899- 14
Cruikshank, George
  1792-1878 22
Crump, Fred H., Jr. 1931- 11
Crump, J(ames) Irving 1887-1979
  Obituary 21
Crunden, Reginald
  See Cleaver, Hylton (Reginald)
Crutcher, Chris(topher C.)
  1946- 52
Cruz, Ray 1933- 6
Ctvrtek, Vaclav 1911-1976
  Obituary 27
Cuffari, Richard 1925-1978 6
  Obituary 25
Cullen, Countee 1903-1946 18
Culliford, Pierre 1928- 40
Culp, Louanna McNary
  1901-1965 2
Cumming, Primrose (Amy)
  1915- 24

Cummings, Betty Sue 1918- 15
Cummings, Parke 1902-1987 2
  Obituary 53
Cummings, Pat 1950- 42
Cummings, Richard
  See Gardner, Richard
Cummins, Maria Susanna
  1827-1866 ....YABC 1
Cunliffe, John Arthur 1933- 11
Cunliffe, Marcus (Falkner)
  1922- 37
Cunningham, Captain Frank
  See Glick, Carl (Cannon)
Cunningham, Cathy
  See Cunningham, Chet
Cunningham, Chet 1928- 23
Cunningham, Dale S(peers)
  1932- 11
Cunningham, E.V.
  See Fast, Howard
Cunningham, Julia W(oolfolk)
  1916- 26
  Earlier sketch in SATA 1
  See also SAAS 2
Cunningham, Virginia
  See Holmgren, Virginia
  C(unningham)
Curiae, Amicus
  See Fuller, Edmund (Maybank)
Curie, Eve 1904- 1
Curley, Daniel 1918- 23
Curry, Jane L(ouise) 1932- 52
  Earlier sketch in SATA 1
  See also SAAS 6
Curry, Peggy Simson
  1911-1987 8
  Obituary 50
Curtis, Bruce (Richard) 1944- 30
Curtis, Patricia 1921- 23
Curtis, Peter
  See Lofts, Norah (Robinson)
Curtis, Richard (Alan) 1937- 29
Curtis, Wade
  See Pournelle, Jerry (Eugene)
Cushman, Jerome 2
Cutchen, Billye Walker 1930- 15
Cutler, (May) Ebbitt 1923- 9
Cutler, Ivor 1923- 24
Cutler, Samuel
  See Folsom, Franklin
Cutt, W(illiam) Towrie 1898- 16
Cuyler, Margery Stuyvesant
  1948- 39
Cuyler, Stephen
  See Bates, Barbara S(nedeker)

                    D

Dabcovich, Lydia
  Brief Entry 47
Dahl, Borghild 1890-1984 7
  Obituary 37
Dahl, Roald 1916- 26
  Earlier sketch in SATA 1
  See also CLR 1; 7
Dahlstedt, Marden 1921- 8
Dain, Martin J. 1924- 35

Dale, Jack
  See Holliday, Joseph
Dale, Margaret J(essy) Miller
  1911- *39*
Dale, Norman
  See Denny, Norman (George)
Dalgliesh, Alice 1893-1979 .... *17*
  Obituary *21*
Dalton, Alene
  See Chapin, Alene Olsen Dalton
Dalton, Anne 1948- *40*
Daly, Jim
  See Stratemeyer, Edward L.
Daly, Kathleen N(orah)
  Brief Entry *37*
Daly, Maureen *2*
  See also SAAS 1
Daly, Nicholas 1946- *37*
Daly, Niki
  See Daly, Nicholas
D'Amato, Alex 1919- *20*
D'Amato, Janet 1925- *9*
Damrosch, Helen Therese
  See Tee-Van, Helen Damrosch
Dana, Barbara 1940- *22*
Dana, Richard Henry, Jr.
  1815-1882 .... *26*
Danachair, Caoimhin O.
  See Danaher, Kevin
Danaher, Kevin 1913- *22*
D'Andrea, Kate
  See Steiner, Barbara A(nnette)
Dangerfield, Balfour
  See McCloskey, Robert
Daniel, Alan 1939-
  Brief Entry *53*
Daniel, Anita 1893(?)-1978 .... *23*
  Obituary *24*
Daniel, Anne
  See Steiner, Barbara A(nnette)
Daniel, Hawthorne 1890- *8*
Daniels, Guy 1919- *11*
Dank, Gloria Rand 1955-
  Brief Entry *46*
Dank, Leonard D(ewey)
  1929- *44*
Dank, Milton 1920- *31*
Danziger, Paula 1944- *36*
  Brief Entry *30*
Darby, J. N.
  See Govan, Christine Noble
Darby, Patricia (Paulsen) *14*
Darby, Ray K. 1912- *7*
Daringer, Helen Fern 1892- *1*
Darke, Marjorie 1929- *16*
Darley, F(elix) O(ctavius) C(arr)
  1822-1888 .... *35*
Darling, David J.
  Brief Entry *44*
Darling, Kathy
  See Darling, Mary Kathleen
Darling, Lois M. 1917- *3*
Darling, Louis, Jr. 1916-1970 ..... *3*
  Obituary *23*
Darling, Mary Kathleen 1943- *9*
Darrow, Whitney, Jr. 1909- *13*
Darwin, Len
  See Darwin, Leonard
Darwin, Leonard 1916- *24*

Dasent, Sir George Webbe 1817-1896
  Brief Entry *29*
Daskam, Josephine Dodge
  See Bacon, Josephine Dodge
  (Daskam)
Dauer, Rosamond 1934- *23*
Daugherty, Charles Michael
  1914- *16*
Daugherty, James (Henry)
  1889-1974 .... *13*
Daugherty, Richard D(eo)
  1922- *35*
Daugherty, Sonia Medwedeff (?)-1971
  Obituary *27*
d'Aulaire, Edgar Parin
  1898-1986 .... *5*
  Obituary *47*
d'Aulaire, Ingri (Maartenson Parin)
  1904-1980 .... *5*
  Obituary *24*
Daveluy, Paule Cloutier 1919- *11*
Davenport, Spencer
  See Stratemeyer, Edward L.
Daves, Michael 1938- *40*
David, Jonathan
  See Ames, Lee J.
Davidson, Alice Joyce 1932-
  Brief Entry *45*
Davidson, Basil 1914- *13*
Davidson, Jessica 1915- *5*
Davidson, Judith 1953- *40*
Davidson, Margaret 1936- *5*
Davidson, Marion
  See Garis, Howard R(oger)
Davidson, Mary R.
  1885-1973 .... *9*
Davidson, R.
  See Davidson, Raymond
Davidson, Raymond 1926- *32*
Davidson, Rosalie 1921- *23*
Davies, Andrew (Wynford)
  1936- *27*
Davies, Bettilu D(onna) 1942- *33*
Davies, (Edward) Hunter 1936-
  Brief Entry *45*
Davies, Joan 1934- *50*
  Brief Entry *47*
Davies, Peter 1937- *52*
Davies, Sumiko 1942- *46*
Davis, Bette J. 1923- *15*
Davis, Burke 1913- *4*
Davis, Christopher 1928- *6*
Davis, D(elbert) Dwight
  1908-1965 .... *33*
Davis, Daniel S(heldon) 1936- *12*
Davis, Gibbs 1953- *46*
  Brief Entry *41*
Davis, Grania 1943-
  Brief Entry *50*
Davis, Hubert J(ackson) 1904- *31*
Davis, James Robert 1945- *32*
Davis, Jim
  See Davis, James Robert
Davis, Julia 1904- *6*
Davis, Louise Littleton 1921- *25*
Davis, Marguerite 1889- *34*
Davis, Mary L(ee) 1935- *9*
Davis, Mary Octavia 1901- *6*
Davis, Paxton 1925- *16*

Davis, Robert
  1881-1949 .... *YABC 1*
Davis, Russell G. 1922- *3*
Davis, Verne T. 1889-1973 .... *6*
Dawson, Elmer A. [Collective
  pseudonym] *1*
Dawson, Mary 1919- *11*
Day, Beth (Feagles) 1924- *33*
Day, Maurice 1892-
  Brief Entry *30*
Day, Thomas 1748-1789 .....*YABC 1*
Dazey, Agnes J(ohnston) *2*
Dazey, Frank M. *2*
Deacon, Eileen
  See Geipel, Eileen
Deacon, Richard
  See McCormick, (George) Donald
  (King)
Dean, Anabel 1915- *12*
Dean, Karen Strickler 1923- *49*
de Angeli, Marguerite
  1889-1987 .... *27*
  Obituary *51*
  Earlier sketch in SATA 1
  See also CLR 1
DeArmand, Frances Ullmann
  1904(?)-1984 .... *10*
  Obituary *38*
Deary, Terry 1946- *51*
  Brief Entry *41*
deBanke, Cecile 1889-1965 .... *11*
De Bruyn, Monica 1952- *13*
de Camp, Catherine C(rook)
  1907- *12*
DeCamp, L(yon) Sprague
  1907- *9*
Decker, Duane 1910-1964 .... *5*
DeClements, Barthe 1920- *35*
Deedy, John 1923- *24*
Deegan, Paul Joseph 1937- *48*
  Brief Entry *38*
Defoe, Daniel 1660(?)-1731 .... *22*
deFrance, Anthony
  See Di Franco, Anthony (Mario)
Degen, Bruce
  Brief Entry *47*
DeGering, Etta 1898- *7*
De Grazia
  See De Grazia, Ted
De Grazia, Ted 1909-1982 .... *39*
De Grazia, Ettore
  See De Grazia, Ted
De Groat, Diane 1947- *31*
deGros, J. H.
  See Villiard, Paul
de Grummond, Lena Young *6*
Deiss, Joseph J. 1915- *12*
DeJong, David C(ornel)
  1905-1967 .... *10*
de Jong, Dola *7*
De Jong, Meindert 1906- *2*
  See also CLR 1
de Kay, Ormonde, Jr. 1923- *7*
de Kiriline, Louise
  See Lawrence, Louise de Kiriline
Dekker, Carl
  See Laffin, John (Alfred Charles)
Dekker, Carl
  See Lynds, Dennis

deKruif, Paul (Henry)
1890-1971 50
Earlier sketch in SATA 5
Delacre, Lulu 1957- 36
De Lage, Ida 1918- 11
de la Mare, Walter 1873-1956 16
Delaney, Harry 1932- 3
Delaney, Ned 1951- 28
Delano, Hugh 1933- 20
De La Ramée, (Marie) Louise
1839-1908 20
Delaune, Lynne 7
DeLaurentis, Louise Budde
1920- 12
Delderfield, Eric R(aymond)
1909- 14
Delderfield, R(onald) F(rederick)
1912-1972 20
De Leeuw, Adele Louise
1899- 30
Earlier sketch in SATA 1
Delessert, Etienne 1941- 46
Brief Entry 27
Delmar, Roy
See Wexler, Jerome (LeRoy)
Deloria, Vine (Victor), Jr.
1933- 21
Del Rey, Lester 1915- 22
Delton, Judy 1931- 14
Delulio, John 1938- 15
Delving, Michael
See Williams, Jay
Demarest, Chris(topher) L(ynn)
1951- 45
Brief Entry 44
Demarest, Doug
See Barker, Will
Demas, Vida 1927- 9
De Mejo, Oscar 1911- 40
de Messières, Nicole 1930- 39
Deming, Richard 1915- 24
Demuth, Patricia Brennan 1948-
Brief Entry 51
Dengler, Sandy 1939-
Brief Entry 40
Denmark, Harrison
See Zelazny, Roger (Joseph
Christopher)
Denney, Diana 1910- 25
Dennis, Morgan 1891(?)-1960 18
Dennis, Wesley 1903-1966 18
Denniston, Elinore 1900-1978
Obituary 24
Denny, Norman (George)
1901-1982 43
Denslow, W(illiam) W(allace)
1856-1915 16
Denzel, Justin F(rancis) 1917- 46
Brief Entry 38
Denzer, Ann Wiseman
See Wiseman, Ann (Sayre)
de Paola, Thomas Anthony
1934- 11
de Paola, Tomie
See de Paola, Thomas Anthony
See also CLR 4
DePauw, Linda Grant 1940- 24

deRegniers, Beatrice Schenk
(Freedman) 1914- 2
See also SAAS 6
Derleth, August (William)
1909-1971 5
Derman, Sarah Audrey 1915- 11
de Roo, Anne Louise 1931- 25
De Roussan, Jacques 1929-
Brief Entry 31
Derry Down Derry
See Lear, Edward
Derwent, Lavinia 14
Desbarats, Peter 1933- 39
De Selincourt, Aubrey
1894-1962 14
Desmond, Adrian J(ohn)
1947- 51
Desmond, Alice Curtis 1897- 8
Detine, Padre
See Olsen, Ib Spang
Deutsch, Babette 1895-1982 1
Obituary 33
De Valera, Sinead 1870(?)-1975
Obituary 30
Devaney, John 1926- 12
Devereux, Frederick L(eonard), Jr.
1914- 9
Devlin, Harry 1918- 11
Devlin, (Dorothy) Wende
1918- 11
DeWaard, E. John 1935- 7
DeWeese, Gene
See DeWeese, Thomas Eugene
DeWeese, Jean
See DeWeese, Thomas Eugene
DeWeese, Thomas Eugene
1934- 46
Brief Entry 45
Dewey, Ariane 1937- 7
Dewey, Jennifer (Owings)
Brief Entry 48
Dewey, Ken(neth Francis)
1940- 39
DeWit, Dorothy (May Knowles)
1916-1980 39
Obituary 28
Deyneka, Anita 1943- 24
Deyrup, Astrith Johnson
1923- 24
Diamond, Donna 1950- 35
Brief Entry 30
Diamond, Petra
See Sachs, Judith
Diamond, Rebecca
See Sachs, Judith
Dias, Earl Joseph 1916- 41
Dick, Cappy
See Cleveland, George
Dick, Trella Lamson
1889-1974 9
Dickens, Charles 1812-1870 15
Dickens, Frank
See Huline-Dickens, Frank William
Dickens, Monica 1915- 4
Dickerson, Roy Ernest 1886-1965
Obituary 26
Dickinson, Emily (Elizabeth)
1830-1886 29

Dickinson, Mary 1949- 48
Brief Entry 41
Dickinson, Peter 1927- 5
Dickinson, Susan 1931- 8
Dickinson, William Croft
1897-1973 13
Dickmeyer, Lowell A. 1939-
Brief Entry 51
Dickson, Helen
See Reynolds, Helen Mary
Greenwood Campbell
Dickson, Naida 1916- 8
Dietz, David H(enry)
1897-1984 10
Obituary 41
Dietz, Lew 1907- 11
Di Franco, Anthony (Mario)
1945- 42
Digges, Jeremiah
See Berger, Josef
D'Ignazio, Fred 1949- 39
Brief Entry 35
Di Grazia, Thomas (?)-1983 32
Dillard, Annie 1945- 10
Dillard, Polly (Hargis) 1916- 24
Dillon, Barbara 1927- 44
Brief Entry 39
Dillon, Diane 1933- 51
Earlier sketch in SATA 15
Dillon, Eilis 1920- 2
Dillon, Leo 1933- 51
Earlier sketch in SATA 15
Dilson, Jesse 1914- 24
Dinan, Carolyn
Brief Entry 47
Dines, Glen 1925- 7
Dinesen, Isak
See Blixen, Karen (Christentze
Dinesen)
Dinnerstein, Harvey 1928- 42
Dinsdale, Tim 1924- 11
Dirks, Rudolph 1877-1968
Brief Entry 31
Disney, Walt(er Elias)
1901-1966 28
Brief Entry 27
DiValentin, Maria 1911- 7
Divine, Arthur Durham 1904-1987
Obituary 52
Divine, David
See Divine, Arthur Durham
Dixon, Dougal 1947- 45
Dixon, Franklin W. [Collective
pseudonym] 1
See also Adams, Harriet
S(tratemeyer); McFarlane, Leslie;
Stratemeyer, Edward L.; Svenson,
Andrew E.
Dixon, Jeanne 1936- 31
Dixon, Peter L. 1931- 6
Doane, Pelagie 1906-1966 7
Dobell, I(sabel) M(arian) B(arclay)
1909- 11
Dobie, J(ames) Frank
1888-1964 43
Dobkin, Alexander 1908-1975
Obituary 30
Dobler, Lavinia G. 1910- 6
Dobrin, Arnold 1928- 4

Dobson, Julia 1941- *48*
Dockery, Wallene T. 1941- *27*
"Dr. A"
  See Silverstein, Alvin
Dr. X
  See Nourse, Alan E(dward)
Dodd, Ed(ward) Benton 1902- *4*
Dodd, Lynley (Stuart) 1941- *35*
Dodge, Bertha S(anford)
  1902- *8*
Dodge, Mary (Elizabeth) Mapes
  1831-1905 .... *21*
Dodgson, Charles Lutwidge
  1832-1898 ....*YABC 2*
Dodson, Kenneth M(acKenzie)
  1907- *11*
Dodson, Susan 1941- *50*
  Brief Entry *40*
Doerksen, Nan 1934-
  Brief Entry *50*
Doherty, C. H. 1913- *6*
Dolan, Edward F(rancis), Jr.
  1924- *45*
  Brief Entry *31*
Dolch, Edward William
  1889-1961 .... *50*
Dolch, Marguerite Pierce
  1891-1978 .... *50*
Dolson, Hildegarde 1908- *5*
Domanska, Janina *6*
Domino, John
  See Averill, Esther
Domjan, Joseph 1907- *25*
Donalds, Gordon
  See Shirreffs, Gordon D.
Donna, Natalie 1934- *9*
Donovan, Frank (Robert) 1906-1975
  Obituary *30*
Donovan, John 1928-
  Brief Entry *29*
  See also CLR 3
Donovan, William
  See Berkebile, Fred D(onovan)
Doob, Leonard W(illiam)
  1909- *8*
Dor, Ana
  See Ceder, Georgiana Dorcas
Doré, (Louis Christophe Paul) Gustave
  1832-1883 .... *19*
Doremus, Robert 1913- *30*
Dorian, Edith M(cEwen)
  1900- *5*
Dorian, Harry
  See Hamilton, Charles H. St. John
Dorian, Marguerite *7*
Dorin, Patrick C(arberry) 1939-
  Brief Entry *52*
Dorman, Michael 1932- *7*
Dorman, N. B. 1927- *39*
Dorson, Richard M(ercer)
  1916-1981 .... *30*
Doss, Helen (Grigsby) 1918- *20*
Doss, Margot Patterson *6*
dos Santos, Joyce Audy
  Brief Entry *42*
Dottig
  See Grider, Dorothy
Dotts, Maryann J. 1933- *35*
Doty, Jean Slaughter 1929- *28*

Doty, Roy 1922- *28*
Doubtfire, Dianne (Abrams)
  1918- *29*
Dougherty, Charles 1922- *18*
Douglas, James McM.
  See Butterworth, W. E.
Douglas, Kathryn
  See Ewing, Kathryn
Douglas, Marjory Stoneman
  1890- *10*
Douglass, Barbara 1930- *40*
Douglass, Frederick
  1817(?)-1895 .... *29*
Douty, Esther M(orris)
  1911-1978 .... *8*
  Obituary *23*
Dow, Emily R. 1904- *10*
Dowdell, Dorothy (Florence) Karns
  1910- *12*
Dowden, Anne Ophelia 1907- *7*
Dowdey, Landon Gerald
  1923- *11*
Dowdy, Mrs. Regera
  See Gorey, Edward St. John
Downer, Marion 1892(?)-1971 .... *25*
Downey, Fairfax 1893- *3*
Downie, Mary Alice 1934- *13*
Doyle, Arthur Conan
  1859-1930 .... *24*
Doyle, Donovan
  See Boegehold, Betty (Doyle)
Doyle, Richard 1824-1883 .... *21*
Drabble, Margaret 1939- *48*
Drackett, Phil(ip Arthur)
  1922- *53*
Draco, F.
  See Davis, Julia
Drager, Gary
  See Edens, Cooper
Dragonwagon, Crescent 1952- *41*
  Earlier sketch in SATA 11
Drake, Frank
  See Hamilton, Charles H. St. John
Drapier, M. B.
  See Swift, Jonathan
Drawson, Blair 1943- *17*
Dresang, Eliza (Carolyn Timberlake)
  1941- *19*
Drescher, Joan E(lizabeth)
  1939- *30*
Dreves, Veronica R. 1927-1986
  Obituary *50*
Drew, Patricia (Mary) 1938- *15*
Drewery, Mary 1918- *6*
Drial, J. E.
  See Laird, Jean E(louise)
Drucker, Malka 1945- *39*
  Brief Entry *29*
Drummond, V(iolet) H. 1911- *6*
Drummond, Walter
  See Silverberg, Robert
Drury, Roger W(olcott) 1914- *15*
Dryden, Pamela
  See Johnston, Norma
Duane, Diane (Elizabeth) 1952-
  Brief Entry *46*
du Blanc, Daphne
  See Groom, Arthur William

DuBois, Rochelle Holt
  See Holt, Rochelle Lynn
Du Bois, Shirley Graham
  1907-1977 .... *24*
Du Bois, W(illiam) E(dward)
  B(urghardt) 1868-1963 .... *42*
du Bois, William Pène 1916- *4*
  See also CLR 1
DuBose, LaRocque (Russ)
  1926- *2*
Du Chaillu, Paul (Belloni)
  1831(?)-1903 .... *26*
Duchesne, Janet 1930-
  Brief Entry *32*
Ducornet, Erica 1943- *7*
Dudley, Martha Ward 1909(?)-1985
  Obituary *45*
Dudley, Nancy
  See Cole, Lois Dwight
Dudley, Robert
  See Baldwin, James
Dudley, Ruth H(ubbell) 1905- *11*
Dueland, Joy V(ivian) *27*
Duff, Annis (James) 1904(?)-1986
  Obituary *49*
Duff, Maggie
  See Duff, Margaret K.
Duff, Margaret K. *37*
Dugan, Michael (Gray) 1947- *15*
Duggan, Alfred Leo
  1903-1964 .... *25*
Duggan, Maurice (Noel)
  1922-1974 .... *40*
  Obituary *30*
du Jardin, Rosamond (Neal)
  1902-1963 .... *2*
Dulac, Edmund 1882-1953 .... *19*
Dumas, Alexandre (the elder)
  1802-1870 .... *18*
Dumas, Philippe 1940- *52*
du Maurier, Daphne 1907- *27*
Dunbar, Paul Laurence
  1872-1906 .... *34*
Dunbar, Robert E(verett)
  1926- *32*
Duncan, Frances (Mary) 1942-
  Brief Entry *48*
Duncan, Gregory
  See McClintock, Marshall
Duncan, Jane
  See Cameron, Elizabeth Jane
Duncan, Julia K. [Collective
  pseudonym] *1*
Duncan, Lois S(teinmetz)
  1934- *36*
  Earlier sketch in SATA 1
  See also SAAS 2
Duncan, Norman
  1871-1916 ....*YABC 1*
Duncombe, Frances (Riker)
  1900- *25*
Dunlop, Agnes M.R. *3*
Dunlop, Eileen (Rhona) 1938- *24*
Dunn, Harvey T(homas)
  1884-1952 .... *34*
Dunn, Judy
  See Spangenberg, Judith Dunn
Dunn, Mary Lois 1930- *6*
Dunnahoo, Terry 1927- *7*

Author Index

Dunne, Mary Collins 1914- *11*
Dunnett, Margaret (Rosalind)
   1909-1977 .... *42*
Dunrea, Olivier 1953-
   Brief Entry *46*
Dupuy, T(revor) N(evitt)
   1916- *4*
Durant, John 1902- *27*
Durrell, Gerald (Malcolm)
   1925- *8*
Du Soe, Robert C.
   1892-1958 .... *YABC 2*
Dutz
   See Davis, Mary Octavia
Duval, Katherine
   See James, Elizabeth
Duvall, Evelyn Millis 1906- *9*
Duvoisin, Roger (Antoine)
   1904-1980 .... *30*
   Obituary *23*
   Earlier sketch in SATA 2
Dwiggins, Don 1913- *4*
Dwight, Allan
   See Cole, Lois Dwight
Dyer, James (Frederick) 1934- *37*
Dygard, Thomas J. 1931- *24*
Dyke, John 1935- *35*

                       E

E.V.B.
   See Boyle, Eleanor Vere (Gordon)
Eagar, Frances 1940- *11*
Eager, Edward (McMaken)
   1911-1964 .... *17*
Eagle, Mike 1942- *11*
Earle, Olive L. *7*
Earnshaw, Brian 1929- *17*
Eastman, Charles A(lexander)
   1858-1939 .... *YABC 1*
Eastman, P(hilip) D(ey)
   1909-1986 .... *33*
   Obituary *46*
Eastwick, Ivy O. *3*
Eaton, Anne T(haxter)
   1881-1971 .... *32*
Eaton, George L.
   See Verral, Charles Spain
Eaton, Jeanette 1886-1968 .... *24*
Eaton, Tom 1940- *22*
Ebel, Alex 1927- *11*
Eber, Dorothy (Margaret) Harley
   1930- *27*
Eberle, Irmengarde 1898-1979 .... *2*
   Obituary *23*
Eccles
   See Williams, Ferelith Eccles
Eckblad, Edith Berven 1923- *23*
Ecke, Wolfgang 1927-1983
   Obituary *37*
Eckert, Allan W. 1931- *29*
   Brief Entry *27*
Eckert, Horst 1931- *8*
Ede, Janina 1937- *33*
Edell, Celeste *12*
Edelman, Elaine
   Brief Entry *50*
Edelman, Lily (Judith) 1915- *22*

Edelson, Edward 1932- *51*
Edens, Cooper 1945- *49*
Edens, (Bishop) David 1926- *39*
Edey, Maitland A(rmstrong)
   1910- *25*
Edgeworth, Maria 1767-1849 .... *21*
Edmonds, I(vy) G(ordon)
   1917- *8*
Edmonds, Walter D(umaux)
   1903- *27*
   Earlier sketch in SATA 1
   See also SAAS 4
Edmund, Sean
   See Pringle, Laurence
Edsall, Marian S(tickney)
   1920- *8*
Edwards, Al
   See Nourse, Alan E(dward)
Edwards, Alexander
   See Fleischer, Leonore
Edwards, Anne 1927- *35*
Edwards, Audrey 1947- *52*
   Brief Entry *31*
Edwards, Bertram
   See Edwards, Herbert Charles
Edwards, Bronwen Elizabeth
   See Rose, Wendy
Edwards, Cecile (Pepin)
   1916- *25*
Edwards, Dorothy 1914-1982 ..... *4*
   Obituary *31*
Edwards, Gunvor *32*
Edwards, Harvey 1929- *5*
Edwards, Herbert Charles
   1912- *12*
Edwards, Jane Campbell
   1932- *10*
Edwards, Julie
   See Andrews, Julie
Edwards, Julie
   See Stratemeyer, Edward L.
Edwards, June
   See Forrester, Helen
Edwards, Linda Strauss 1948- *49*
   Brief Entry *42*
Edwards, Monica le Doux Newton
   1912- *12*
Edwards, Olwen
   See Gater, Dilys
Edwards, Sally 1929- *7*
Edwards, Samuel
   See Gerson, Noel B(ertram)
Egan, E(dward) W(elstead)
   1922- *35*
Eggenberger, David 1918- *6*
Eggleston, Edward 1837-1902 ..... *27*
Egielski, Richard 1952- *49*
   Earlier sketch in SATA 11
Egypt, Ophelia Settle
   1903-1984 .... *16*
   Obituary *38*
Ehlert, Lois (Jane) 1934- *35*
Ehrlich, Amy 1942- *25*
Ehrlich, Bettina (Bauer) 1903- *1*
Eichberg, James Bandman
   See Garfield, James B.
Eichenberg, Fritz 1901- *50*
   Earlier sketch in SATA 9
Eichler, Margrit 1942- *35*

Eichner, James A. 1927- *4*
Eifert, Virginia S(nider)
   1911-1966 .... *2*
Einsel, Naiad *10*
Einsel, Walter 1926- *10*
Einzig, Susan 1922- *43*
Eiseman, Alberta 1925- *15*
Eisenberg, Azriel 1903- *12*
Eisenberg, Lisa 1949-
   Brief Entry *50*
Eisenberg, Phyllis Rose 1924- *41*
Eisner, Vivienne
   See Margolis, Vivienne
Eisner, Will(iam Erwin) 1917- *31*
Eitzen, Allan 1928- *9*
Eitzen, Ruth (Carper) 1924- *9*
Elam, Richard M(ace, Jr.)
   1920- *9*
Elfman, Blossom 1925- *8*
Elgin, Kathleen 1923- *39*
Elia
   See Lamb, Charles
Eliot, Anne
   See Cole, Lois Dwight
Elisofon, Eliot 1911-1973
   Obituary *21*
Elkin, Benjamin 1911- *3*
Elkins, Dov Peretz 1937- *5*
Ellacott, S(amuel) E(rnest)
   1911- *19*
Elliott, Sarah M(cCarn) 1930- *14*
Ellis, Anyon
   See Rowland-Entwistle, (Arthur)
   Theodore (Henry)
Ellis, Edward S(ylvester)
   1840-1916 .... *YABC 1*
Ellis, Ella Thorp 1928- *7*
Ellis, Harry Bearse 1921- *9*
Ellis, Herbert
   See Wilson, Lionel
Ellis, Mel 1912-1984 .... *7*
   Obituary *39*
Ellison, Lucile Watkins
   1907(?)-1979 .... *50*
   Obituary *22*
Ellison, Virginia Howell
   1910- *4*
Ellsberg, Edward 1891- *7*
Elmore, (Carolyn) Patricia
   1933- *38*
   Brief Entry *35*
Elspeth
   See Bragdon, Elspeth
Elting, Mary 1906- *2*
Elwart, Joan Potter 1927- *2*
Elwood, Ann 1931-
   Brief Entry *52*
Emberley, Barbara A(nne) *8*
   See also CLR 5
Emberley, Ed(ward Randolph)
   1931- *8*
   See also CLR 5
Emberley, Michael 1960- *34*
Embry, Margaret (Jacob)
   1919- *5*
Emerson, Alice B. [Collective
   pseudonym] *1*
Emerson, William K(eith)
   1925- *25*

Emery, Anne (McGuigan)
1907- 33
Earlier sketch in SATA 1
Emmens, Carol Ann 1944- 39
Emmons, Della (Florence) Gould
1890-1983
Obituary 39
Emrich, Duncan (Black Macdonald)
1908- 11
Emslie, M. L.
See Simpson, Myrtle L(illias)
Ende, Michael 1930(?)-
Brief Entry 42
See also CLR 14
Enderle, Judith (Ann) 1941- 38
Enfield, Carrie
See Smith, Susan Vernon
Engdahl, Sylvia Louise 1933- 4
See also CLR 2
See also SAAS 5
Engle, Eloise Katherine 1923- 9
Englebert, Victor 1933- 8
English, James W(ilson)
1915- 37
Enright, D(ennis) J(oseph)
1920- 25
Enright, Elizabeth 1909-1968 9
See also CLR 4
Enright, Maginel Wright
See Barney, Maginel Wright
Enys, Sarah L.
See Sloggett, Nellie
Ephron, Delia 1944-
Brief Entry 50
Epp, Margaret A(gnes) 20
Epple, Anne Orth 1927- 20
Epstein, Anne Merrick 1931- 20
Epstein, Beryl (Williams)
1910- 31
Earlier sketch in SATA 1
Epstein, Perle S(herry) 1938- 27
Epstein, Samuel 1909- 31
Earlier sketch in SATA 1
Erdman, Loula Grace 1
Erdoes, Richard 1912- 33
Brief Entry 28
Erhard, Walter 1920-
Brief Entry 30
Erickson, Russell E(verett)
1932- 27
Erickson, Sabra R(ollins)
1912- 35
Ericson, Walter
See Fast, Howard
Erikson, Mel 1937- 31
Erlanger, Baba
See Trahey, Jane
Erlanger, Ellen (Louise) 1950-
Brief Entry 52
Erlich, Lillian (Feldman)
1910- 10
Ernest, William
See Berkebile, Fred D(onovan)
Ernst, (Lyman) John 1940- 39
Ernst, Kathryn (Fitzgerald)
1942- 25
Ernst, Lisa Campbell 1957-
Brief Entry 44
Ervin, Janet Halliday 1923- 4

Erwin, Will
See Eisner, Will(iam Erwin)
Esbensen, Barbara Juster
Brief Entry 53
Eshmeyer, R(einhart) E(rnst)
1898- 29
Espeland, Pamela (Lee) 1951- 52
Brief Entry 38
Espy, Willard R(ichardson)
1910- 38
Estep, Irene (Compton) 5
Estes, Eleanor 1906- 7
See also CLR 2
Estoril, Jean
See Allan, Mabel Esther
Etchemendy, Nancy 1952- 38
Etchison, Birdie L(ee) 1937- 38
Ets, Marie Hall 2
Eunson, Dale 1904- 5
Evans, Eva Knox 1905- 27
Evans, Hubert Reginald 1892-1986
Obituary 48
Evans, Katherine (Floyd)
1901-1964 5
Evans, Mari 10
Evans, Mark 19
Evans, Patricia Healy
See Carpenter, Patricia
Evarts, Esther
See Benson, Sally
Evarts, Hal G. (Jr.) 1915- 6
Everett, Gail
See Hale, Arlene
Evernden, Margery 1916- 5
Evslin, Bernard 1922- 45
Brief Entry 28
Ewen, David 1907-1985 4
Obituary 47
Ewing, Juliana (Horatia Gatty)
1841-1885 16
Ewing, Kathryn 1921- 20
Eyerly, Jeannette Hyde 1908- 4
Eyre, Dorothy
See McGuire, Leslie (Sarah)
Eyre, Katherine Wigmore
1901-1970 26
Eyvindson, Peter (Knowles) 1946-
Brief Entry 52
Ezzell, Marilyn 1937- 42
Brief Entry 38

F

Fabe, Maxene 1943- 15
Faber, Doris 1924- 3
Faber, Harold 1919- 5
Fabre, Jean Henri (Casimir)
1823-1915 22
Facklam, Margery Metz 1927- 20
Fadiman, Clifton (Paul) 1904- 11
Fair, Sylvia 1933- 13
Fairfax-Lucy, Brian (Fulke Cameron-
Ramsay) 1898-1974 6
Obituary 26
Fairlie, Gerard 1899-1983
Obituary 34
Fairman, Joan A(lexandra)
1935- 10

Faithfull, Gail 1936- 8
Falconer, James
See Kirkup, James
Falkner, Leonard 1900- 12
Fall, Thomas
See Snow, Donald Clifford
Falls, C(harles) B(uckles)
1874-1960 38
Brief Entry 27
Falstein, Louis 1909- 37
Fanning, Leonard M(ulliken)
1888-1967 5
Faralla, Dana 1909- 9
Faralla, Dorothy W.
See Faralla, Dana
Farb, Peter 1929-1980 12
Obituary 22
Farber, Norma 1909-1984 25
Obituary 38
Farge, Monique
See Grée, Alain
Farjeon, (Eve) Annabel 1919- 11
Farjeon, Eleanor 1881-1965 2
Farley, Carol 1936- 4
Farley, Walter 1920- 43
Earlier sketch in SATA 2
Farmer, Penelope (Jane)
1939- 40
Brief Entry 39
See also CLR 8
Farmer, Peter 1950- 38
Farnham, Burt
See Clifford, Harold B.
Farquhar, Margaret C(utting)
1905- 13
Farquharson, Alexander 1944- 46
Farquharson, Martha
See Finley, Martha
Farr, Finis (King) 1904- 10
Farrar, Susan Clement 1917- 33
Farrell, Ben
See Cebulash, Mel
Farrington, Benjamin 1891-1974
Obituary 20
Farrington, Selwyn Kip, Jr.
1904- 20
Farthing, Alison 1936- 45
Brief Entry 36
Fassler, Joan (Grace) 1931- 11
Fast, Howard 1914- 7
Fatchen, Max 1920- 20
Father Xavier
See Hurwood, Bernhardt J.
Fatigati, (Frances) Evelyn de Buhr
1948- 24
Fatio, Louise 6
Faulhaber, Martha 1926- 7
Faulkner, Anne Irvin 1906- 23
Faulkner, Nancy
See Faulkner, Anne Irvin
Fax, Elton Clay 1909- 25
Feagles, Anita MacRae 9
Feagles, Elizabeth
See Day, Beth (Feagles)
Feague, Mildred H. 1915- 14
Fecher, Constance 1911- 7
Feder, Paula (Kurzband)
1935- 26

Feder, Robert Arthur 1909-1969
  Brief Entry *35*
Feelings, Muriel (Grey) 1938- *16*
  See also CLR 5
Feelings, Thomas 1933- *8*
Feelings, Tom
  See Feelings, Thomas
  See also CLR 5
Fehrenbach, T(heodore) R(eed, Jr.)
  1925- *33*
Feiffer, Jules 1929- *8*
Feig, Barbara Krane 1937- *34*
Feikema, Feike
  See Manfred, Frederick F(eikema)
Feil, Hila 1942- *12*
Feilen, John
  See May, Julian
Feldman, Anne (Rodgers)
  1939- *19*
Félix
  See Vincent, Félix
Fellows, Muriel H. *10*
Felsen, Henry Gregor 1916- *1*
  See also SAAS 2
Felton, Harold William 1902- *1*
Felton, Ronald Oliver 1909- *3*
Felts, Shirley 1934- *33*
Fenderson, Lewis H.
  1907-1983 .... *47*
  Obituary *37*
Fenner, Carol 1929- *7*
Fenner, Phyllis R(eid)
  1899-1982 .... *1*
  Obituary *29*
Fenten, Barbara D(oris) 1935- *26*
Fenten, D. X. 1932- *4*
Fenton, Carroll Lane
  1900-1969 .... *5*
Fenton, Edward 1917- *7*
Fenton, Mildred Adams 1899- *21*
Fenwick, Patti
  See Grider, Dorothy
Feravolo, Rocco Vincent
  1922- *10*
Ferber, Edna 1887-1968 .... *7*
Ferguson, Bob
  See Ferguson, Robert Bruce
Ferguson, Cecil 1931- *45*
Ferguson, Robert Bruce 1927- *13*
Ferguson, Walter (W.) 1930- *34*
Fergusson, Erna 1888-1964 .... *5*
Fermi, Laura (Capon)
  1907-1977 .... *6*
  Obituary *28*
Fern, Eugene A. 1919- *10*
Ferrier, Lucy
  See Penzler, Otto
Ferris, Helen Josephine
  1890-1969 .... *21*
Ferris, James Cody [Collective
  pseudonym] *1*
  See also McFarlane, Leslie;
  Stratemeyer, Edward L.
Ferris, Jean 1939-
  Brief Entry *50*
Ferry, Charles 1927- *43*
Fetz, Ingrid 1915- *30*

Feydy, Anne Lindbergh
  Brief Entry *32*
  See Sapieyevski, Anne Lindbergh
Fiammenghi, Gioia 1929- *9*
Fiarotta, Noel 1944- *15*
Fiarotta, Phyllis 1942- *15*
Fichter, George S. 1922- *7*
Fidler, Kathleen (Annie)
  1899-1980 .... *3*
  Obituary *45*
Fiedler, Jean *4*
Field, Edward 1924- *8*
Field, Elinor Whitney 1889-1980
  Obituary *28*
Field, Eugene 1850-1895 .... *16*
Field, Gans T.
  See Wellman, Manly Wade
Field, Peter
  See Hobson, Laura Z(ametkin)
Field, Rachel (Lyman)
  1894-1942 .... *15*
Fife, Dale (Odile) 1910- *18*
Fighter Pilot, A
  See Johnston, H(ugh) A(nthony)
  S(tephen)
Figueroa, Pablo 1938- *9*
Fijan, Carol 1918- *12*
Fillmore, Parker H(oysted)
  1878-1944 .... *YABC 1*
Filstrup, Chris
  See Filstrup, E(dward) Christian
Filstrup, E(dward) Christian
  1942- *43*
Filstrup, Jane Merrill
  See Merrill, Jane
Filstrup, Janie
  See Merrill, Jane
Finder, Martin
  See Salzmann, Siegmund
Fine, Anne 1947- *29*
Finger, Charles J(oseph)
  1869(?)-1941 .... *42*
Fink, William B(ertrand)
  1916- *22*
Finke, Blythe F(oote) 1922- *26*
Finkel, George (Irvine)
  1909-1975 .... *8*
Finlay, Winifred 1910- *23*
Finlayson, Ann 1925- *8*
Finley, Martha 1828-1909 .... *43*
Firmin, Charlotte 1954- *29*
Firmin, Peter 1928- *15*
Fischbach, Julius 1894- *10*
Fischler, Stan(ley I.)
  Brief Entry *36*
Fishback, Margaret
  See Antolini, Margaret Fishback
Fisher, Aileen (Lucia) 1906- *25*
  Earlier sketch in SATA 1
Fisher, Barbara 1940- *44*
  Brief Entry *34*
Fisher, Clavin C(argill) 1912- *24*
Fisher, Dorothy Canfield
  1879-1958 .... *YABC 1*
Fisher, John (Oswald Hamilton)
  1909- *15*
Fisher, Laura Harrison 1934- *5*

Fisher, Leonard Everett 1924- *34*
  Earlier sketch in SATA 4
  See also SAAS 1
Fisher, Lois I. 1948- *38*
  Brief Entry *35*
Fisher, Margery (Turner)
  1913- *20*
Fisher, Robert (Tempest)
  1943- *47*
Fisk, Nicholas 1923- *25*
Fitch, Clarke
  See Sinclair, Upton (Beall)
Fitch, John IV
  See Cormier, Robert (Edmund)
Fitschen, Dale 1937- *20*
Fitzalan, Roger
  See Trevor, Elleston
FitzGerald, Cathleen 1932-1987
  Obituary *50*
Fitzgerald, Edward Earl 1919- *20*
Fitzgerald, F(rancis) A(nthony)
  1940- *15*
Fitzgerald, John D(ennis)
  1907- *20*
  See also CLR 1
Fitzgerald, Merni I(ngrassia)
  1955- *53*
Fitzhardinge, Joan Margaret
  1912- *2*
Fitzhugh, Louise (Perkins)
  1928-1974 .... *45*
  Obituary *24*
  Earlier sketch in SATA 1
  See also CLR 1
Fitz-Randolph, Jane (Currens)
  1915- *51*
Flack, Marjorie
  1899-1958 .... *YABC 2*
Flack, Naomi John (White) *40*
  Brief Entry *35*
Flash Flood
  See Robinson, Jan M.
Fleischer, Leonore 1934(?)-
  Brief Entry *47*
Fleischer, Max 1889-1972
  Brief Entry *30*
Fleischhauer-Hardt, Helga
  1936- *30*
Fleischman, Paul 1952- *39*
  Brief Entry *32*
Fleischman, (Albert) Sid(ney)
  1920- *8*
  See also CLR 1
Fleisher, Robbin 1951-1977 ...... *52*
  Brief Entry *49*
Fleishman, Seymour 1918-
  Brief Entry *32*
Fleming, Alice Mulcahey
  1928- *9*
Fleming, Elizabeth P. 1888-1985
  Obituary *48*
Fleming, Ian (Lancaster)
  1908-1964 .... *9*
Fleming, Susan 1932- *32*
Fleming, Thomas J(ames)
  1927- *8*
Fletcher, Charlie May 1897- *3*

Fletcher, Colin 1922- 28
Fletcher, Helen Jill 1911- 13
Fletcher, Richard E. 1917(?)-1983
  Obituary 34
Fletcher, Rick
  See Fletcher, Richard E.
Fleur, Anne 1901-
  Brief Entry 31
Flexner, James Thomas 1908- 9
Flitner, David P. 1949- 7
Floethe, Louise Lee 1913- 4
Floethe, Richard 1901- 4
Floherty, John Joseph
  1882-1964 25
Flood, Flash
  See Robinson, Jan M.
Flora, James (Royer) 1914- 30
  Earlier sketch in SATA 1
  See also SAAS 6
Florian, Douglas 1950- 19
Flory, Jane Trescott 1917- 22
Flowerdew, Phyllis 33
Floyd, Gareth 1940-
  Brief Entry 31
Fluchère, Henri A(ndré) 1914- 40
Flynn, Barbara 1928- 9
Flynn, Jackson
  See Shirreffs, Gordon D.
Flynn, Mary
  See Welsh, Mary Flynn
Fodor, Ronald V(ictor) 1944- 25
Foley, (Anna) Bernice Williams
  1902- 28
Foley, June 1944- 44
Foley, (Mary) Louise Munro 1933-
  Brief Entry 40
Foley, Rae
  See Denniston, Elinore
Folkard, Charles James 1878-1963
  Brief Entry 28
Follett, Helen (Thomas) 1884(?)-1970
  Obituary 27
Folsom, Franklin (Brewster)
  1907- 5
Folsom, Michael (Brewster)
  1938- 40
Fontenot, Mary Alice 1910- 34
Fooner, Michael 22
Foote, Timothy (Gilson)
  1926- 52
Forberg, Ati 1925- 22
Forbes, Bryan 1926- 37
Forbes, Cabot L.
  See Hoyt, Edwin P(almer), Jr.
Forbes, Esther 1891-1967 2
Forbes, Graham B. [Collective
  pseudonym] 1
Forbes, Kathryn
  See McLean, Kathryn (Anderson)
Ford, Albert Lee
  See Stratemeyer, Edward L.
Ford, Barbara
  Brief Entry 34
Ford, Brian J(ohn) 1939- 49
Ford, Elbur
  See Hibbert, Eleanor
Ford, George (Jr.) 31
Ford, Hilary
  See Youd, (Christopher) Samuel

Ford, Hildegarde
  See Morrison, Velma Ford
Ford, Marcia
  See Radford, Ruby L.
Ford, Nancy K(effer) 1906-1961
  Obituary 29
Foreman, Michael 1938- 2
Forest, Antonia 29
Forester, C(ecil) S(cott)
  1899-1966 13
Forman, Brenda 1936- 4
Forman, James Douglas 1932- 8
Forrest, Sybil
  See Markun, Patricia M(aloney)
Forrester, Frank H. 1919(?)-1986
  Obituary 52
Forrester, Helen 1919- 48
Forrester, Marian
  See Schachtel, Roger
Forrester, Victoria 1940- 40
  Brief Entry 35
Forsee, (Frances) Aylesa 1
Fort, Paul
  See Stockton, Francis Richard
Fortnum, Peggy 1919- 26
Foster, Brad W. 1955- 34
Foster, Doris Van Liew 1899- 10
Foster, E(lizabeth) C(onnell)
  1902- 9
Foster, Elizabeth 1905-1963 10
Foster, Elizabeth Vincent
  1902- 12
Foster, F. Blanche 1919- 11
Foster, G(eorge) Allen
  1907-1969 26
Foster, Genevieve (Stump)
  1893-1979 2
  Obituary 23
  See also CLR 7
Foster, Hal
  See Foster, Harold Rudolf
Foster, Harold Rudolf 1892-1982
  Obituary 31
Foster, John T(homas) 1925- 8
Foster, Laura Louise 1918- 6
Foster, Margaret Lesser 1899-1979
  Obituary 21
Foster, Marian Curtis
  1909-1978 23
Foulds, Elfrida Vipont 1902- 52
Fourth Brother, The
  See Aung, (Maung) Htin
Fowke, Edith (Margaret)
  1913- 14
Fowles, John 1926- 22
Fox, Charles Philip 1913- 12
Fox, Eleanor
  See St. John, Wylly Folk
Fox, Fontaine Talbot, Jr. 1884-1964
  Obituary 23
Fox, Fred 1903(?)-1981
  Obituary 27
Fox, Freeman
  See Hamilton, Charles H. St. John
Fox, Grace
  See Anderson, Grace Fox
Fox, Larry 30
Fox, Lorraine 1922-1975 11
  Obituary 27

Fox, Mary Virginia 1919- 44
  Brief Entry 39
Fox, Mem
  See Fox, Merrion Frances
Fox, Merrion Frances 1946- 51
Fox, Michael Wilson 1937- 15
Fox, Paula 1923- 17
  See also CLR 1
Fox, Petronella
  See Balogh, Penelope
Fox, Robert J. 1927- 33
Fradin, Dennis Brindel 1945- 29
Frame, Paul 1913-
  Brief Entry 33
Franchere, Ruth 18
Francis, Charles
  See Holme, Bryan
Francis, Dee
  See Haas, Dorothy F.
Francis, Dorothy Brenner
  1926- 10
Francis, Pamela (Mary) 1926- 11
Franco, Marjorie 38
Francois, André 1915- 25
Francoise
  See Seignobosc, Francoise
Frank, Anne 1929-1945(?)
  Brief Entry 42
Frank, Hélène
  See Vautier, Ghislaine
Frank, Josette 1893- 10
Frank, Mary 1933- 34
Frank, R., Jr.
  See Ross, Frank (Xavier), Jr.
Frankau, Mary Evelyn 1899- 4
Frankel, Bernice 9
Frankel, Edward 1910- 44
Frankel, Julie 1947- 40
  Brief Entry 34
Frankenberg, Robert 1911- 22
Franklin, Harold 1920- 13
Franklin, Max
  See Deming, Richard
Franklin, Steve
  See Stevens, Franklin
Franzén, Nils-Olof 1916- 10
Frascino, Edward 1938- 48
  Brief Entry 33
Frasconi, Antonio 1919- 53
  Earlier sketch in SATA 6
Fraser, Antonia (Pakenham) 1932-
  Brief Entry 32
Fraser, Betty
  See Fraser, Elizabeth Marr
Fraser, Elizabeth Marr 1928- 31
Fraser, Eric (George)
  1902-1983 38
Frazier, Neta Lohnes 7
Freed, Alvyn M. 1913- 22
Freedman, Benedict 1919- 27
Freedman, Nancy 1920- 27
Freedman, Russell (Bruce)
  1929- 16
Freeman, Barbara C(onstance)
  1906- 28
Freeman, Bill
  See Freeman, William Bradford
Freeman, Don 1908-1978 17

Freeman, Ira M(aximilian)
1905- 21
Freeman, Lucy (Greenbaum)
1916- 24
Freeman, Mae (Blacker)
1907- 25
Freeman, Peter J.
See Calvert, Patricia
Freeman, Tony
Brief Entry 44
Freeman, William Bradford 1938-
Brief Entry 48
Fregosi, Claudia (Anne Marie)
1946- 24
French, Allen 1870-1946 ..... YABC 1
French, Dorothy Kayser 1926- 5
French, Fiona 1944- 6
French, Kathryn
See Mosesson, Gloria R(ubin)
French, Michael 1944- 49
Brief Entry 38
French, Paul
See Asimov, Isaac
Freund, Rudolf 1915-1969
Brief Entry 28
Frewer, Glyn 1931- 11
Frick, C. H.
See Irwin, Constance Frick
Frick, Constance
See Irwin, Constance Frick
Friedlander, Joanne K(ohn)
1930- 9
Friedman, Estelle 1920- 7
Friedman, Frieda 1905- 43
Friedman, Ina R(osen) 1926- 49
Brief Entry 41
Friedman, Marvin 1930- 42
Brief Entry 33
Friedrich, Otto (Alva) 1929- 33
Friedrich, Priscilla 1927- 39
Friendlich, Dick
See Friendlich, Richard J.
Friendlich, Richard J. 1909- 11
Friermood, Elisabeth Hamilton
1903- 5
Friis, Babbis
See Friis-Baastad, Babbis
Friis-Baastad, Babbis
1921-1970 7
Frimmer, Steven 1928- 31
Friskey, Margaret Richards
1901- 5
Fritz, Jean (Guttery) 1915- 29
Earlier sketch in SATA 1
See also CLR 2, 14
See also SAAS 2
Froissart, Jean
1338(?)-1410(?) 28
Froman, Elizabeth Hull
1920-1975 10
Froman, Robert (Winslow)
1917- 8
Fromm, Lilo 1928- 29
Frommer, Harvey 1937- 41
Frost, A(rthur) B(urdett)
1851-1928 19
Frost, Erica
See Supraner, Robyn

Frost, Lesley 1899(?)-1983 14
Obituary 34
Frost, Robert (Lee) 1874-1963 14
Fry, Edward Bernard 1925- 35
Fry, Rosalie 1911- 3
Fuchs, Erich 1916- 6
Fuchs, Lucy 1935-
Brief Entry 52
Fuchshuber, Annegert 1940- 43
Fujikawa, Gyo 1908- 39
Brief Entry 30
Fujita, Tamao 1905- 7
Fujiwara, Michiko 1946- 15
Fuka, Vladimir 1926-1977
Obituary 27
Fuller, Catherine L(euthold)
1916- 9
Fuller, Edmund (Maybank)
1914- 21
Fuller, Iola
See McCoy, Iola Fuller
Fuller, Lois Hamilton 1915- 11
Fuller, Margaret
See Ossoli, Sarah Margaret (Fuller)
marchesa d'
Fults, John Lee 1932- 33
Funai, Mamoru (Rolland) 1932-
Brief Entry 46
Funk, Thompson
See Funk, Tom
Funk, Tom 1911- 7
Funke, Lewis 1912- 11
Furchgott, Terry 1948- 29
Furniss, Tim 1948- 49
Furukawa, Toshi 1924- 24
Fyleman, Rose 1877-1957 21
Fyson, J(enny) G(race) 1904- 42

G

Gackenbach, Dick 48
Brief Entry 30
Gaddis, Vincent H. 1913- 35
Gadler, Steve J. 1905- 36
Gaeddert, Lou Ann (Bigge)
1931- 20
Gàg, Flavia 1907-1979
Obituary 24
Gàg, Wanda (Hazel)
1893-1946 .... YABC 1
See also CLR 4
Gage, Wilson
See Steele, Mary Q(uintard Govan)
Gagliardo, Ruth Garver 1895(?)-1980
Obituary 22
Gál, László 1933- 52
Brief Entry 32
Galdone, Paul 1914-1986 17
Obituary 49
Galinsky, Ellen 1942- 23
Gallant, Roy (Arthur) 1924- 4
Gallico, Paul 1897-1976 13
Galt, Thomas Franklin, Jr.
1908- 5
Galt, Tom
See Galt, Thomas Franklin, Jr.
Gamerman, Martha 1941- 15
Gammell, Stephen 1943- 53

Gannett, Ruth Chrisman (Arens)
1896-1979 33
Gannett, Ruth Stiles 1923- 3
Gannon, Robert (Haines)
1931- 8
Gans, Roma 1894- 45
Gantos, Jack
See Gantos, John (Bryan), Jr.
Gantos, John (Bryan), Jr.
1951- 20
Ganz, Yaffa 1938-
Brief Entry 52
Garbutt, Bernard 1900-
Brief Entry 31
Gard, Joyce
See Reeves, Joyce
Gard, Robert Edward 1910- 18
Gard, (Sanford) Wayne 1899-1986
Obituary 49
Gardam, Jane 1928- 39
Brief Entry 28
See also CLR 12
Garden, Nancy 1938- 12
Gardner, Beau
Brief Entry 50
Gardner, Dic
See Gardner, Richard
Gardner, Hugh 1910-1986
Obituary 49
Gardner, Jeanne LeMonnier 5
Gardner, John (Champlin, Jr.)
1933-1982 40
Obituary 31
Gardner, Martin 1914- 16
Gardner, Richard 1931- 24
Gardner, Richard A. 1931- 13
Gardner, Robert 1929-
Brief Entry 43
Gardner, Sheldon 1934- 33
Garelick, May 19
Garfield, James B. 1881-1984 6
Obituary 38
Garfield, Leon 1921- 32
Earlier sketch in SATA 1
Garis, Howard R(oger)
1873-1962 13
Garner, Alan 1934- 18
Garnett, Eve C. R. 3
Garraty, John A. 1920- 23
Garret, Maxwell R. 1917- 39
Garretson, Victoria Diane
1945- 44
Garrett, Helen 1895- 21
Garrigue, Sheila 1931- 21
Garrison, Barbara 1931- 19
Garrison, Frederick
See Sinclair, Upton (Beall)
Garrison, Webb B(lack) 1919- 25
Garst, Doris Shannon 1894- 1
Garst, Shannon
See Garst, Doris Shannon
Garthwaite, Marion H. 1893- 7
Garton, Malinda D(ean) (?)-1976
Obituary 26
Gasperini, Jim 1952-
Brief Entry 49
Gater, Dilys 1944- 41

Gates, Doris 1901- *34*
    Earlier sketch in SATA 1
    See also SAAS 1
Gates, Frieda 1933- *26*
Gathorne-Hardy, Jonathan G.
    1933- *26*
Gatty, Juliana Horatia
    See Ewing, Juliana (Horatia Gatty)
Gatty, Margaret Scott 1809-1873
    Brief Entry *27*
Gauch, Patricia Lee 1934- *26*
Gault, Clare S. 1925- *36*
Gault, Frank 1926-1982 .... *36*
    Brief Entry *30*
Gault, William Campbell
    1910- *8*
Gaver, Becky
    See Gaver, Rebecca
Gaver, Rebecca 1952- *20*
Gay, Francis
    See Gee, H(erbert) L(eslie)
Gay, Kathlyn 1930- *9*
Gay, Zhenya 1906-1978 .... *19*
Gee, H(erbert) L(eslie) 1901-1977
    Obituary *26*
Gee, Maurice (Gough) 1931- *46*
Geer, Charles 1922- *42*
    Brief Entry *32*
Gehr, Mary *32*
Geipel, Eileen 1932- *30*
Geis, Darlene *7*
Geisel, Helen 1898-1967 .... *26*
Geisel, Theodor Seuss 1904- *28*
    Earlier sketch in SATA 1
    See also CLR 1
Geisert, Arthur (Frederick) 1941-
    Brief Entry *52*
Geldart, William 1936- *15*
Gelinas, Paul J. 1911- *10*
Gelman, Rita Golden 1937-
    Brief Entry *51*
Gelman, Steve 1934- *3*
Gemming, Elizabeth 1932- *11*
Gendel, Evelyn W. 1916(?)-1977
    Obituary *27*
Gennaro, Joseph F(rancis), Jr.
    1924- *53*
Gentle, Mary 1956- *48*
Gentleman, David 1930- *7*
George, Jean Craighead 1919- *2*
    See also CLR 1
George, John L(othar) 1916- *2*
George, S(idney) C(harles)
    1898- *11*
George, W(illiam) Lloyd 1900(?)-1975
    Obituary *30*
Georgiou, Constantine 1927- *7*
Gérard, Jean Ignace Isidore
    1803-1847 .... *45*
Geras, Adele (Daphne) 1944- *23*
Gergely, Tibor 1900-1978
    Obituary *20*
Geringer, Laura 1948- *29*
Gerler, William R(obert)
    1917- *47*
Gerrard, Jean 1933- *51*
Gerrard, Roy 1935- *47*
    Brief Entry *45*
Gerson, Corinne *37*

Gerson, Noel B(ertram) 1914- *22*
Gerstein, Mordicai 1935- *47*
    Brief Entry *36*
Gesner, Clark 1938- *40*
Gessner, Lynne 1919- *16*
Gevirtz, Eliezer 1950- *49*
Gewe, Raddory
    See Gorey, Edward St. John
Gibbons, Gail 1944- *23*
    See also CLR 8
Gibbs, Alonzo (Lawrence)
    1915- *5*
Gibbs, (Cecilia) May 1877-1969
    Obituary *27*
Gibbs, Tony
    See Gibbs, Wolcott, Jr.
Gibbs, Wolcott, Jr. 1935- *40*
Giblin, James Cross 1933- *33*
Gibson, Josephine
    See Joslin, Sesyle
Gidal, Sonia 1922- *2*
Gidal, Tim N(ahum) 1909- *2*
Giegling, John A(llan) 1935- *17*
Giff, Patricia Reilly 1935- *33*
Gifford, Griselda 1931- *42*
Gilbert, Ann
    See Taylor, Ann
Gilbert, Harriett 1948- *30*
Gilbert, (Agnes) Joan (Sewell)
    1931- *10*
Gilbert, John (Raphael) 1926- *36*
Gilbert, Miriam
    See Presberg, Miriam Goldstein
Gilbert, Nan
    See Gilbertson, Mildred
Gilbert, Sara (Dulaney) 1943- *11*
Gilbert, W(illiam) S(chwenk)
    1836-1911 .... *36*
Gilbertson, Mildred Geiger
    1908- *2*
Gilbreath, Alice (Thompson)
    1921- *12*
Gilbreth, Frank B., Jr. 1911- *2*
Gilfond, Henry *2*
Gilge, Jeanette 1924- *22*
Gill, Derek L(ewis) T(heodore)
    1919- *9*
Gill, Margery Jean 1925- *22*
Gillett, Mary *7*
Gillette, Henry Sampson
    1915- *14*
Gillham, Bill
    See Gillham, William Edwin Charles
Gillham, William Edwin Charles
    1936- *42*
Gilliam, Stan 1946- *39*
    Brief Entry *35*
Gilman, Dorothy
    See Butters, Dorothy Gilman
Gilman, Esther 1925- *15*
Gilmore, Iris 1900- *22*
Gilmore, Mary (Jean Cameron)
    1865-1962 .... *49*
Gilson, Barbara
    See Gilson, Charles James Louis
Gilson, Charles James Louis
    1878-1943 .... *YABC 2*
Gilson, Jamie 1933- *37*
    Brief Entry *34*

Ginsburg, Mirra *6*
Giovanni, Nikki 1943- *24*
    See also CLR 6
Giovanopoulos, Paul 1939- *7*
Gipson, Frederick B.
    1908-1973 .... *2*
    Obituary *24*
Girard, Linda Walvoord 1942- *41*
Girion, Barbara 1937- *26*
Gittings, Jo Manton 1919- *3*
Gittings, Robert 1911- *6*
Gladstone, Eve
    See Werner, Herma
Gladstone, Gary 1935- *12*
Gladstone, M(yron) J. 1923- *37*
Gladwin, William Zachary
    See Zollinger, Gulielma
Glanville, Brian (Lester)
    1931- *42*
Glanzman, Louis S. 1922- *36*
Glaser, Dianne E(lizabeth)
    1937- *50*
    Brief Entry *31*
Glaser, Milton 1929- *11*
Glaspell, Susan
    1882-1948 .... *YABC 2*
Glass, Andrew
    Brief Entry *46*
Glauber, Uta (Heil) 1936- *17*
Glazer, Tom 1914- *9*
Gleasner, Diana (Cottle)
    1936- *29*
Gleason, Judith 1929- *24*
Glendinning, Richard 1917- *24*
Glendinning, Sally
    See Glendinning, Sara W(ilson)
Glendinning, Sara W(ilson)
    1913- *24*
Glenn, Mel 1943- *51*
    Brief Entry *45*
Gles, Margaret Breitmaier
    1940- *22*
Glick, Carl (Cannon)
    1890-1971 .... *14*
Glick, Virginia Kirkus 1893-1980
    Obituary *23*
Gliewe, Unada 1927- *3*
Glines, Carroll V(ane), Jr.
    1920- *19*
Globe, Leah Ain 1900- *41*
Glovach, Linda 1947- *7*
Glubok, Shirley *6*
    See also CLR 1
Gluck, Felix 1924(?)-1981
    Obituary *25*
Glynne-Jones, William 1907- *11*
Gobbato, Imero 1923- *39*
Goble, Dorothy *26*
Goble, Paul 1933- *25*
Goble, Warwick (?)-1943 .... *46*
Godden, Rumer 1907- *36*
    Earlier sketch in SATA 3
Gode, Alexander
    See Gode von Aesch, Alexander
    (Gottfried Friedrich)
Gode von Aesch, Alexander (Gottfried
    Friedrich) 1906-1970 .... *14*
Godfrey, Jane
    See Bowden, Joan Chase

Godfrey, William
  See Youd, (Christopher) Samuel
Goettel, Elinor 1930- *12*
Goetz, Delia 1898- *22*
Goffstein, M(arilyn) B(rooke)
  1940- *8*
  See also CLR 3
Golann, Cecil Paige 1921- *11*
Golbin, Andrée 1923- *15*
Gold, Phyllis 1941- *21*
Gold, Sharlya *9*
Goldberg, Herbert S. 1926- *25*
Goldberg, Stan J. 1939- *26*
Goldfeder, Cheryl
  See Pahz, Cheryl Suzanne
Goldfeder, Jim
  See Pahz, James Alon
Goldfrank, Helen Colodny
  1912- *6*
Goldin, Augusta 1906- *13*
Goldsborough, June 1923- *19*
Goldsmith, Howard 1943- *24*
Goldsmith, John Herman Thorburn
  1903-1987
  Obituary *52*
Goldsmith, Oliver 1728-1774 ..... *26*
Goldstein, Ernest A. 1933-
  Brief Entry *52*
Goldstein, Nathan 1927- *47*
Goldstein, Philip 1910- *23*
Goldston, Robert (Conroy)
  1927- *6*
Goll, Reinhold W(eimar)
  1897- *26*
Gonzalez, Gloria 1940- *23*
Goodall, John S(trickland)
  1908- *4*
Goodbody, Slim
  See Burstein, John
Goode, Diane 1949- *15*
Goode, Stephen 1943-
  Brief Entry *40*
Goodenow, Earle 1913- *40*
Goodman, Deborah Lerme
  1956- *50*
  Brief Entry *49*
Goodman, Elaine 1930- *9*
Goodman, Joan Elizabeth
  1950- *50*
Goodman, Walter 1927- *9*
Goodrich, Samuel Griswold
  1793-1860 .... *23*
Goodwin, Hal
  See Goodwin, Harold Leland
Goodwin, Harold Leland
  1914- *51*
  Earlier sketch in SATA 13
Goor, Nancy (Ruth Miller)
  1944- *39*
  Brief Entry *34*
Goor, Ron(ald Stephen) 1940- *39*
  Brief Entry *34*
Goossen, Agnes
  See Epp, Margaret A(gnes)
Gordon, Bernard Ludwig
  1931- *27*
Gordon, Colonel H. R.
  See Ellis, Edward S(ylvester)

Gordon, Donald
  See Payne, Donald Gordon
Gordon, Dorothy 1893-1970 ...... *20*
Gordon, Esther S(aranga)
  1935- *10*
Gordon, Frederick [Collective
  pseudonym] *1*
Gordon, Hal
  See Goodwin, Harold Leland
Gordon, John 1925- *6*
Gordon, John
  See Gesner, Clark
Gordon, Lew
  See Baldwin, Gordon C.
Gordon, Margaret (Anna)
  1939- *9*
Gordon, Mildred 1912-1979
  Obituary *24*
Gordon, Selma
  See Lanes, Selma G.
Gordon, Shirley 1921- *48*
  Brief Entry *41*
Gordon, Sol 1923- *11*
Gordon, Stewart
  See Shirreffs, Gordon D.
Gordons, The [Joint pseudonym]
  See Gordon, Mildred
Gorelick, Molly C. 1920- *9*
Gorey, Edward St. John
  1925- *29*
  Brief Entry *27*
Gorham, Charles Orson
  1911-1975 .... *36*
Gorham, Michael
  See Folsom, Franklin
Gormley, Beatrice 1942- *39*
  Brief Entry *35*
Gorog, Judith (Allen) 1938- *39*
Gorsline, Douglas (Warner)
  1913-1985 .... *11*
  Obituary *43*
Gorsline, (Sally) Marie 1928- *28*
Gorsline, S. M.
  See Gorsline, (Sally) Marie
Goryan, Sirak
  See Saroyan, William
Goscinny, René 1926-1977 .... *47*
  Brief Entry *39*
Gottlieb, Bill
  See Gottlieb, William P(aul)
Gottlieb, Gerald 1923- *7*
Gottlieb, William P(aul) *24*
Goudey, Alice E. 1898- *20*
Goudge, Elizabeth 1900-1984 .... *2*
  Obituary *38*
Gough, Catherine 1931- *24*
Gough, Philip 1908- *45*
Goulart, Ron 1933- *6*
Gould, Chester 1900-1985 .... *49*
  Obituary *43*
Gould, Jean R(osalind) 1919- *11*
Gould, Lilian 1920- *6*
Gould, Marilyn 1923- *15*
Govan, Christine Noble 1898- *9*
Govern, Elaine 1939- *26*
Graaf, Peter
  See Youd, (Christopher) Samuel
Graber, Alexander *7*

Graber, Richard (Fredrick)
  1927- *26*
Grabiański, Janusz 1929-1976 ..... *39*
  Obituary *30*
Graboff, Abner 1919- *35*
Grace, F(rances Jane) *45*
Graeber, Charlotte Towner
  Brief Entry *44*
Graff, Polly Anne
  See Colver, Anne
Graff, (S.) Stewart 1908- *9*
Graham, Ada 1931- *11*
Graham, Brenda Knight 1942- *32*
Graham, Charlotte
  See Bowden, Joan Chase
Graham, Eleanor 1896-1984 ..... *18*
  Obituary *38*
Graham, Frank, Jr. 1925- *11*
Graham, John 1926- *11*
Graham, Kennon
  See Harrison, David Lee
Graham, Lorenz B(ell) 1902- *2*
  See also CLR 10
  See also SAAS 5
Graham, Margaret Bloy 1920- *11*
Graham, Robin Lee 1949- *7*
Graham, Shirley
  See Du Bois, Shirley Graham
Graham-Barber, Lynda 1944- *42*
Graham-Cameron, M.
  See Graham-Cameron, M(alcolm)
  G(ordon)
Graham-Cameron, M(alcolm) G(ordon)
  1931- *53*
  Brief Entry *45*
Graham-Cameron, Mike
  See Graham-Cameron, M(alcolm)
  G(ordon)
Grahame, Kenneth
  1859-1932 ....*YABC 1*
  See also CLR 5
Gramatky, Hardie 1907-1979 ..... *30*
  Obituary *23*
  Earlier sketch in SATA 1
Grand, Samuel 1912- *42*
Grandville, J. J.
  See Gérard, Jean Ignace Isidore
Grandville, Jean Ignace Isidore Gérard
  See Gérard, Jean Ignace Isidore
Grange, Peter
  See Nicole, Christopher Robin
Granger, Margaret Jane 1925(?)-1977
  Obituary *27*
Granger, Peggy
  See Granger, Margaret Jane
Granstaff, Bill 1925- *10*
Grant, Bruce 1893-1977 .... *5*
  Obituary *25*
Grant, Cynthia D. 1950- *33*
Grant, Eva 1907- *7*
Grant, Evva H. 1913-1977
  Obituary *27*
Grant, Gordon 1875-1962 .... *25*
Grant, Gwen(doline Ellen)
  1940- *47*
Grant, (Alice) Leigh 1947- *10*
Grant, Matthew C.
  See May, Julian

Grant, Maxwell
    See Lynds, Dennis
Grant, Myrna (Lois) 1934- *21*
Grant, Neil 1938- *14*
Gravel, Fern
    See Hall, James Norman
Graves, Charles Parlin
    1911-1972 .... *4*
Graves, Robert (von Ranke)
    1895-1985 .... *45*
Gray, Elizabeth Janet 1902- *6*
Gray, Genevieve S. 1920- *4*
Gray, Harold (Lincoln)
    1894-1968 .... *33*
    Brief Entry *32*
Gray, Jenny
    See Gray, Genevieve S.
Gray, Marian
    See Pierce, Edith Gray
Gray, Nicholas Stuart
    1922-1981 .... *4*
    Obituary *27*
Gray, Nigel 1941- *33*
Gray, (Lucy) Noel (Clervaux)
    1898-1983 .... *47*
Gray, Patricia *7*
Gray, Patsey
    See Gray, Patricia
Grayland, V. Merle
    See Grayland, Valerie
Grayland, Valerie *7*
Great Comte, The
    See Hawkesworth, Eric
Greaves, Margaret 1914- *7*
Grée, Alain 1936- *28*
Green, Adam
    See Weisgard, Leonard
Green, D.
    See Casewit, Curtis
Green, Hannah
    See Greenberg, Joanne (Goldenberg)
Green, Jane 1937- *9*
Green, Mary Moore 1906- *11*
Green, Morton 1937- *8*
Green, Norma B(erger) 1925- *11*
Green, Phyllis 1932- *20*
Green, Roger James 1944-
    Brief Entry *52*
Green, Roger (Gilbert) Lancelyn
    1918-1987 .... *2*
    Obituary *53*
Green, Sheila Ellen 1934- *8*
Greenaway, Kate
    1846-1901 .... *YABC 2*
    See also CLR 6
Greenbank, Anthony Hunt
    1933- *39*
Greenberg, Harvey R. 1935- *5*
Greenberg, Joanne (Goldenberg)
    1932- *25*
Greenberg, Polly 1932- *52*
    Brief Entry *43*
Greene, Bette 1934- *8*
    See also CLR 2
Greene, Carla 1916- *1*
Greene, Carol
    Brief Entry *44*
Greene, Constance C(larke)
    1924- *11*

Greene, Ellin 1927- *23*
Greene, Graham 1904- *20*
Greene, Laura 1935- *38*
Greene, Wade 1933- *11*
Greenfeld, Howard *19*
Greenfield, Eloise 1929- *19*
    See also CLR 4
Greenhaus, Thelma Nurenberg
    1903-1984 .... *45*
Greening, Hamilton
    See Hamilton, Charles H. St. John
Greenleaf, Barbara Kaye
    1942- *6*
Greenleaf, Peter 1910- *33*
Greenwald, Sheila
    See Green, Sheila Ellen
Gregg, Walter H(arold) 1919- *20*
Gregor, Arthur 1923- *36*
Gregori, Leon 1919- *15*
Gregorian, Joyce Ballou
    1946- *30*
Gregorowski, Christopher
    1940- *30*
Gregory, Diana (Jean) 1933- *49*
    Brief Entry *42*
Gregory, Jean
    See Ure, Jean
Gregory, Stephen
    See Penzler, Otto
Greisman, Joan Ruth 1937- *31*
Grendon, Stephen
    See Derleth, August (William)
Grenville, Pelham
    See Wodehouse, P(elham)
    G(renville)
Gretz, Susanna 1937- *7*
Gretzer, John *18*
Grey, Jerry 1926- *11*
Grey Owl
    See Belaney, Archibald Stansfeld
Gri
    See Denney, Diana
Grice, Frederick 1910- *6*
Grider, Dorothy 1915- *31*
Gridley, Marion E(leanor)
    1906-1974 .... *35*
    Obituary *26*
Grieder, Walter 1924- *9*
Griese, Arnold A(lfred) 1921- *9*
Grifalconi, Ann 1929- *2*
Griffin, Gillett Good 1928- *26*
Griffin, Judith Berry *34*
Griffith, Helen V(irginia)
    1934- *39*
Griffith, Jeannette
    See Eyerly, Jeanette
Griffiths, G(ordon) D(ouglas)
    1910-1973
    Obituary *20*
Griffiths, Helen 1939- *5*
    See also SAAS 5
Grimm, Cherry Barbara Lockett 1930-
    Brief Entry *43*
Grimm, Jacob Ludwig Karl
    1785-1863 .... *22*
Grimm, Wilhelm Karl
    1786-1859 .... *22*
Grimm, William C(arey)
    1907- *14*

Grimshaw, Nigel (Gilroy)
    1925- *23*
Grimsley, Gordon
    See Groom, Arthur William
Gringhuis, Dirk
    See Gringhuis, Richard H.
Gringhuis, Richard H.
    1918-1974 .... *6*
    Obituary *25*
Grinnell, George Bird
    1849-1938 .... *16*
Gripe, Maria (Kristina) 1923- *2*
    See also CLR 5
Groch, Judith (Goldstein)
    1929- *25*
Grode, Redway
    See Gorey, Edward St. John
Grohskopf, Bernice *7*
Grol, Lini Richards 1913- *9*
Grollman, Earl A. 1925- *22*
Groom, Arthur William
    1898-1964 .... *10*
Gross, Alan 1947-
    Brief Entry *43*
Gross, Ruth Belov 1929- *33*
Gross, Sarah Chokla
    1906-1976 .... *9*
    Obituary *26*
Grossman, Nancy 1940- *29*
Grossman, Robert 1940- *11*
Groth, John 1908- *21*
Groves, Georgina
    See Symons, (Dorothy) Geraldine
Gruelle, John (Barton)
    1880-1938 .... *35*
    Brief Entry *32*
Gruelle, Johnny
    See Gruelle, John
Gruenberg, Sidonie M(atsner)
    1881-1974 .... *2*
    Obituary *27*
Grummer, Arnold E(dward)
    1923- *49*
Guck, Dorothy 1913- *27*
Gugliotta, Bobette 1918- *7*
Guillaume, Jeanette G. (Flierl)
    1899- *8*
Guillot, Rene 1900-1969 .... *7*
Gundersheimer, Karen
    Brief Entry *44*
Gundrey, Elizabeth 1924- *23*
Gunn, James E(dwin) 1923- *35*
Gunston, Bill
    See Gunston, William Tudor
Gunston, William Tudor
    1927- *9*
Gunterman, Bertha Lisette
    1886(?)-1975
    Obituary *27*
Gunther, John 1901-1970 .... *2*
Gurko, Leo 1914- *9*
Gurko, Miriam *9*
Gustafson, Anita 1942-
    Brief Entry *45*
Gustafson, Sarah R.
    See Riedman, Sarah R.
Gustafson, Scott 1956- *34*
Guthrie, Anne 1890-1979 .... *28*

Gutman, Bill
  Brief Entry *43*
Gutman, Naham 1899(?)-1981
  Obituary *25*
Guy, Rosa (Cuthbert) 1928- *14*
  See also CLR 13
Guymer, (Wilhelmina) Mary
  1909- *50*
Gwynne, Fred(erick Hubbard)
  1926- *41*
  Brief Entry *27*

H

Haas, Carolyn Buhai 1926- *43*
Haas, Dorothy F. *46*
  Brief Entry *43*
Haas, Irene 1929- *17*
Haas, James E(dward) 1943- *40*
Haas, Merle S. 1896(?)-1985
  Obituary *41*
Habenstreit, Barbara 1937- *5*
Haber, Louis 1910- *12*
Hader, Berta (Hoerner)
  1891(?)-1976 .... *16*
Hader, Elmer (Stanley)
  1889-1973 .... *16*
Hadley, Franklin
  See Winterbotham, R(ussell)
  R(obert)
Hadley, Lee 1934- *47*
  Brief Entry *38*
Hafner, Marylin 1925- *7*
Hager, Alice Rogers 1894-1969
  Obituary *26*
Haggard, H(enry) Rider
  1856-1925 .... *16*
Haggerty, James J(oseph)
  1920- *5*
Hagon, Priscilla
  See Allan, Mabel Esther
Hague, (Susan) Kathleen
  1949- *49*
  Brief Entry *45*
Hague, Michael (Riley) 1948- *48*
  Brief Entry *32*
Hahn, Emily 1905- *3*
Hahn, Hannelore 1926- *8*
Hahn, James (Sage) 1947- *9*
Hahn, (Mona) Lynn 1949- *9*
Hahn, Mary Downing 1937- *50*
  Brief Entry *44*
Haig-Brown, Roderick (Langmere)
  1909-1976 .... *12*
Haight, Anne Lyon 1895-1977
  Obituary *30*
Haines, Gail Kay 1943- *11*
Haining, Peter 1940- *14*
Halacy, D(aniel) S(tephen), Jr.
  1919- *36*
Haldane, Roger John 1945- *13*
Hale, Arlene 1924-1982 .... *49*
Hale, Edward Everett
  1822-1909 .... *16*
Hale, Helen
  See Mulcahy, Lucille Burnett
Hale, Irina 1932- *26*
Hale, Kathleen 1898- *17*

Hale, Linda 1929- *6*
Hale, Lucretia Peabody
  1820-1900 .... *26*
Hale, Nancy 1908- *31*
Haley, Gail E(inhart) 1939- *43*
  Brief Entry *28*
Haley, Neale *52*
Hall, Adam
  See Trevor, Elleston
Hall, Adele 1910- *7*
Hall, Anna Gertrude
  1882-1967 .... *8*
Hall, Borden
  See Yates, Raymond F(rancis)
Hall, Brian P(atrick) 1935- *31*
Hall, Caryl
  See Hansen, Caryl (Hall)
Hall, Donald (Andrew, Jr.)
  1928- *23*
Hall, Douglas 1931- *43*
Hall, Elvajean *6*
Hall, James Norman
  1887-1951 .... *21*
Hall, Jesse
  See Boesen, Victor
Hall, Katy
  See McMullan, Kate (Hall)
Hall, Lynn 1937- *47*
  Earlier sketch in SATA 2
  See also SAAS 4
Hall, Malcolm 1945- *7*
Hall, Marjory
  See Yeakley, Marjory Hall
Hall, Rosalys Haskell 1914- *7*
Hallard, Peter
  See Catherall, Arthur
Hallas, Richard
  See Knight, Eric (Mowbray)
Hall-Clarke, James
  See Rowland-Entwistle, (Arthur)
  Theodore (Henry)
Haller, Dorcas Woodbury
  1946- *46*
Halliburton, Warren J. 1924- *19*
Halliday, William R(oss)
  1926- *52*
Hallin, Emily Watson 1919- *6*
Hallinan, P(atrick) K(enneth)
  1944- *39*
  Brief Entry *37*
Hallman, Ruth 1929- *43*
  Brief Entry *28*
Hall-Quest, (Edna) Olga W(ilbourne)
  1899-1986 .... *11*
  Obituary *47*
Hallstead, William F(inn) III
  1924- *11*
Hallward, Michael 1889- *12*
Halsell, Grace 1923- *13*
Halsted, Anna Roosevelt 1906-1975
  Obituary *30*
Halter, Jon C(harles) 1941- *22*
Hamalian, Leo 1920- *41*
Hamberger, John 1934- *14*
Hamblin, Dora Jane 1920- *36*
Hamerstrom, Frances 1907- *24*
Hamil, Thomas Arthur 1928- *14*
Hamil, Tom
  See Hamil, Thomas Arthur

Hamill, Ethel
  See Webb, Jean Francis (III)
Hamilton, Alice
  See Cromie, Alice Hamilton
Hamilton, Charles Harold St. John
  1875-1961 .... *13*
Hamilton, Clive
  See Lewis, C. S.
Hamilton, Dorothy 1906-1983 ..... *12*
  Obituary *35*
Hamilton, Edith 1867-1963 .... *20*
Hamilton, Elizabeth 1906- *23*
Hamilton, Morse 1943- *35*
Hamilton, Robert W.
  See Stratemeyer, Edward L.
Hamilton, Virginia 1936- *4*
  See also CLR 1, 11
Hamley, Dennis 1935- *39*
Hammer, Richard 1928- *6*
Hammerman, Gay M(orenus)
  1926- *9*
Hammond, Winifred G(raham)
  1899- *29*
Hammontree, Marie (Gertrude)
  1913- *13*
Hampson, (Richard) Denman
  1929- *15*
Hampson, Frank 1918(?)-1985
  Obituary *46*
Hamre, Leif 1914- *5*
Hamsa, Bobbie 1944- *52*
  Brief Entry *38*
Hancock, Mary A. 1923- *31*
Hancock, Sibyl 1940- *9*
Handforth, Thomas (Schofield)
  1897-1948 .... *42*
Handville, Robert (Tompkins)
  1924- *45*
Hane, Roger 1940-1974
  Obituary *20*
Haney, Lynn 1941- *23*
Hanff, Helene *11*
Hanlon, Emily 1945- *15*
Hann, Jacquie 1951- *19*
Hanna, Bill
  See Hanna, William
Hanna, Paul R(obert) 1902- *9*
Hanna, William 1910- *51*
Hannam, Charles 1925- *50*
Hano, Arnold 1922- *12*
Hansen, Caryl (Hall) 1929- *39*
Hansen, Joyce 1942- *46*
  Brief Entry *39*
Hanser, Richard (Frederick)
  1909- *13*
Hanson, Joan 1938- *8*
Hanson, Joseph E. 1894(?)-1971
  Obituary *27*
Harald, Eric
  See Boesen, Victor
Harcourt, Ellen Knowles 1890(?)-1984
  Obituary *36*
Hardcastle, Michael 1933- *47*
  Brief Entry *38*
Harding, Lee 1937- *32*
  Brief Entry *31*
Hardwick, Richard Holmes, Jr.
  1923- *12*

Hardy, Alice Dale [Collective
  pseudonym] *1*
Hardy, David A(ndrews)
  1936- *9*
Hardy, Jon 1958- *53*
Hardy, Stuart
  See Schisgall, Oscar
Hardy, Thomas 1840-1928 .... *25*
Hare, Norma Q(uarles) 1924- *46*
  Brief Entry *41*
Harford, Henry
  See Hudson, W(illiam) H(enry)
Hargrove, James 1947-
  Brief Entry *50*
Hargrove, Jim
  See Hargrove, James
Hark, Mildred
  See McQueen, Mildred Hark
Harkaway, Hal
  See Stratemeyer, Edward L.
Harkins, Philip 1912- *6*
Harlan, Elizabeth 1945- *41*
  Brief Entry *35*
Harlan, Glen
  See Cebulash, Mel
Harman, Fred 1902(?)-1982
  Obituary *30*
Harman, Hugh 1903-1982
  Obituary *33*
Harmelink, Barbara (Mary) *9*
Harmer, Mabel 1894- *45*
Harmon, Margaret 1906- *20*
Harnan, Terry 1920- *12*
Harnett, Cynthia (Mary)
  1893-1981 .... *5*
  Obituary *32*
Harper, Anita 1943- *41*
Harper, Mary Wood
  See Dixon, Jeanne
Harper, Wilhelmina
  1884-1973 .... *4*
  Obituary *26*
Harrah, Michael 1940- *41*
Harrell, Sara Gordon
  See Banks, Sara (Jeanne Gordon
  Harrell)
Harries, Joan 1922- *39*
Harrington, Lyn 1911- *5*
Harris, Aurand 1915- *37*
Harris, Christie 1907- *6*
Harris, Colver
  See Colver, Anne
Harris, Dorothy Joan 1931- *13*
Harris, Janet 1932-1979 .... *4*
  Obituary *23*
Harris, Joel Chandler
  1848-1908 ....*YABC 1*
Harris, Jonathan 1921- *52*
Harris, Lavinia
  See Johnston, Norma
Harris, Leon A., Jr. 1926- *4*
Harris, Lorle K(empe) 1912- *22*
Harris, Marilyn
  See Springer, Marilyn Harris
Harris, Mark Jonathan 1941- *32*
Harris, Robie H.
  Brief Entry *53*
Harris, Rosemary (Jeanne) *4*
Harris, Sherwood 1932- *25*

Harrison, C. William 1913- *35*
Harrison, David Lee 1937- *26*
Harrison, Deloris 1938- *9*
Harrison, Harry 1925- *4*
Harrison, Molly 1909- *41*
Harshaw, Ruth H(etzel)
  1890-1968 .... *27*
Hart, Bruce 1938-
  Brief Entry *39*
Hart, Carole 1943-
  Brief Entry *39*
Harte, (Francis) Bret(t)
  1836-1902 .... *26*
Hartley, Ellen (Raphael)
  1915- *23*
Hartley, Fred Allan III 1953- *41*
Hartley, William B(rown)
  1913- *23*
Hartman, Evert 1937- *38*
  Brief Entry *35*
Hartman, Jane E(vangeline)
  1928- *47*
Hartman, Louis F(rancis)
  1901-1970 .... *22*
Hartshorn, Ruth M. 1928- *11*
Harvey, Edith 1908(?)-1972
  Obituary *27*
Harwin, Brian
  See Henderson, LeGrand
Harwood, Pearl Augusta (Bragdon)
  1903- *9*
Haseley, Dennis
  Brief Entry *44*
Haskell, Arnold 1903- *6*
Haskins, James 1941- *9*
  See also CLR 3
Haskins, Jim
  See Haskins, James
  See also SAAS 4
Hasler, Joan 1931- *28*
Hassall, Joan 1906- *43*
Hassler, Jon (Francis) 1933- *19*
Hastings, Beverly
  See Barkin, Carol
  See James, Elizabeth
Hatch, Mary Cottam 1912-1970
  Brief Entry *28*
Hatlo, Jimmy 1898-1963
  Obituary *23*
Haugaard, Erik Christian
  1923- *4*
  See also CLR 11
Hauman, Doris 1898- *32*
Hauman, George 1890-1961 ...... *32*
Hauser, Margaret L(ouise)
  1909- *10*
Hausman, Gerald 1945- *13*
Hausman, Gerry
  See Hausman, Gerald
Hautzig, Deborah 1956- *31*
Hautzig, Esther 1930- *4*
Havenhand, John
  See Cox, John Roberts
Havighurst, Walter (Edwin)
  1901- *1*
Haviland, Virginia 1911- *6*
Hawes, Judy 1913- *4*
Hawk, Virginia Driving
  See Sneve, Virginia Driving Hawk

Hawkesworth, Eric 1921- *13*
Hawkins, Arthur 1903- *19*
Hawkins, Quail 1905- *6*
Hawkinson, John 1912- *4*
Hawkinson, Lucy (Ozone)
  1924-1971 .... *21*
Hawley, Mable C. [Collective
  pseudonym] *1*
Hawthorne, Captain R. M.
  See Ellis, Edward S(ylvester)
Hawthorne, Nathaniel
  1804-1864 ....*YABC 2*
Hay, John 1915- *13*
Hay, Timothy
  See Brown, Margaret Wise
Haycraft, Howard 1905- *6*
Haycraft, Molly Costain
  1911- *6*
Hayden, Gwendolen Lampshire
  1904- *35*
Hayden, Robert C(arter), Jr.
  1937- *47*
  Brief Entry *28*
Hayden, Robert E(arl)
  1913-1980 .... *19*
  Obituary *26*
Hayes, Carlton J. H.
  1882-1964 .... *11*
Hayes, Geoffrey 1947- *26*
Hayes, John F. 1904- *11*
Hayes, Sheila 1937- *51*
  Brief Entry *50*
Hayes, Will *7*
Hayes, William D(imitt)
  1913- *8*
Haynes, Betsy 1937- *48*
  Brief Entry *37*
Hays, H(offman) R(eynolds)
  1904-1980 .... *26*
Hays, Wilma Pitchford 1909- *28*
  Earlier sketch in SATA 1
  See also SAAS 3
Hayward, Linda 1943-
  Brief Entry *39*
Haywood, Carolyn 1898- *29*
  Earlier sketch in SATA 1
Hazen, Barbara Shook 1930- *27*
Head, Gay
  See Hauser, Margaret L(ouise)
Headley, Elizabeth
  See Cavanna, Betty
Headstrom, Richard 1902- *8*
Heady, Eleanor B(utler) 1917- *8*
Heal, Edith 1903- *7*
Healey, Brooks
  See Albert, Burton, Jr.
Healey, Larry 1927- *44*
  Brief Entry *42*
Heaps, Willard (Allison)
  1909- *26*
Hearn, Emily
  See Valleau, Emily
Hearne, Betsy Gould 1942- *38*
Heath, Charles D(ickinson)
  1941- *46*
Heath, Veronica
  See Blackett, Veronica Heath
Heaven, Constance
  See Fecher, Constance

Hecht, George J(oseph) 1895-1980
    Obituary 22
Hecht, Henri Joseph 1922- 9
Hechtkopf, Henryk 1910- 17
Heck, Bessie Holland 1911- 26
Hedderwick, Mairi 1939- 30
Hedges, Sid(ney) G(eorge)
    1897-1974 28
Hefter, Richard 1942- 31
Hegarty, Reginald Beaton
    1906-1973 10
Heide, Florence Parry 1919- 32
    See also SAAS 6
Heiderstadt, Dorothy 1907- 6
Heilman, Joan Rattner 50
Hein, Lucille Eleanor 1915- 20
Heinemann, George Alfred 1918-
    Brief Entry 31
Heinlein, Robert A(nson)
    1907- 9
Heins, Paul 1909- 13
Heintze, Carl 1922- 26
Heinz, W(ilfred) C(harles)
    1915- 26
Heinzen, Mildred
    See Masters, Mildred
Helfman, Elizabeth S(eaver)
    1911- 3
Helfman, Harry 1910- 3
Hellberg, Hans-Eric 1927- 38
Heller, Linda 1944- 46
    Brief Entry 40
Hellman, Hal
    See Hellman, Harold
Hellman, Harold 1927- 4
Helps, Racey 1913-1971 2
    Obituary 25
Helweg, Hans H. 1917- 50
    Brief Entry 33
Hemming, Roy 1928- 11
Hemphill, Martha Locke
    1904-1973 37
Henbest, Nigel 1951-
    Brief Entry 52
Henderley, Brooks [Collective
    pseudonym] 1
Henderson, Gordon 1950- 53
Henderson, Kathy 1949-
    Brief Entry 53
Henderson, LeGrand
    1901-1965 9
Henderson, Nancy Wallace
    1916- 22
Henderson, Zenna (Chlarson)
    1917- 5
Hendrickson, Walter Brookfield, Jr.
    1936- 9
Heneghan, James 1930- 53
Henkes, Kevin 1960- 43
Henriod, Lorraine 1925- 26
Henry, Joanne Landers 1927- 6
Henry, Marguerite 11
    See also CLR 4
Henry, O.
    See Porter, William Sydney
Henry, Oliver
    See Porter, William Sydney

Henry, T. E.
    See Rowland-Entwistle, (Arthur)
    Theodore (Henry)
Henson, James Maury 1936- 43
Henson, Jim
    See Henson, James Maury
Henstra, Friso 1928- 8
Hentoff, Nat(han Irving)
    1925- 42
    Brief Entry 27
    See also CLR 1
Herald, Kathleen
    See Peyton, Kathleen (Wendy)
Herbert, Cecil
    See Hamilton, Charles H. St. John
Herbert, Don 1917- 2
Herbert, Frank (Patrick)
    1920-1986 37
    Obituary 47
    Earlier sketch in SATA 9
Herbert, Wally
    See Herbert, Walter William
Herbert, Walter William
    1934- 23
Hergé
    See Rémi, Georges
    See also CLR 6
Herkimer, L(awrence) R(ussell)
    1925- 42
Herman, Charlotte 1937- 20
Hermanson, Dennis (Everett)
    1947- 10
Hermes, Patricia 1936- 31
Herriot, James
    See Wight, James Alfred
Herrmanns, Ralph 1933- 11
Herron, Edward A(lbert)
    1912- 4
Hersey, John (Richard) 1914- 25
Hertz, Grete Janus 1915- 23
Hess, Lilo 1916- 4
Hesse, Hermann 1877-1962 50
Heuer, Kenneth John 1927- 44
Heuman, William 1912-1971 21
Hewes, Agnes Danforth
    1874-1963 35
Hewett, Anita 1918- 13
Hext, Harrington
    See Phillpotts, Eden
Hey, Nigel S(tewart) 1936- 20
Heyduck-Huth, Hilde 1929- 8
Heyerdahl, Thor 1914- 52
    Earlier sketch in SATA 2
Heyliger, William
    1884-1955 .... YABC 1
Heyman, Ken(neth Louis)
    1930- 34
Heyward, Du Bose 1885-1940 21
Heywood, Karen 1946- 48
Hibbert, Christopher 1924- 4
Hibbert, Eleanor Burford
    1906- 2
Hickman, Janet 1940- 12
Hickman, Martha Whitmore
    1925- 26
Hickok, Lorena A.
    1892(?)-1968 20
Hickok, Will
    See Harrison, C. William

Hicks, Clifford B. 1920- 50
Hicks, Eleanor B.
    See Coerr, Eleanor
Hicks, Harvey
    See Stratemeyer, Edward L.
Hieatt, Constance B(artlett)
    1928- 4
Hiebert, Ray Eldon 1932- 13
Higdon, Hal 1931- 4
Higginbottom, J(effrey) Winslow
    1945- 29
Higham, David (Michael)
    1949- 50
Highet, Helen
    See MacInnes, Helen
Hightower, Florence Cole
    1916-1981 4
    Obituary 27
Highwater, Jamake 1942- 32
    Brief Entry 30
Hildebrandt, Greg 1939-
    Brief Entry 33
Hildebrandt, Tim 1939-
    Brief Entry 33
Hilder, Rowland 1905- 36
Hildick, E. W.
    See Hildick, Wallace
    See also SAAS 6
Hildick, (Edmund) Wallace
    1925- 2
Hill, Donna (Marie) 24
Hill, Douglas (Arthur) 1935- 39
Hill, Elizabeth Starr 1925- 24
Hill, Eric 1927-
    Brief Entry 53
    See also CLR 13
Hill, Grace Brooks [Collective
    pseudonym] 1
Hill, Grace Livingston
    1865-1947 .... YABC 2
Hill, Helen M(orey) 1915- 27
Hill, Kathleen Louise 1917- 4
Hill, Kay
    See Hill, Kathleen Louise
Hill, Lorna 1902- 12
Hill, Margaret (Ohler) 1915- 36
Hill, Meg
    See Hill, Margaret (Ohler)
Hill, Monica
    See Watson, Jane Werner
Hill, Robert W(hite)
    1919-1982 12
    Obituary 31
Hill, Ruth A.
    See Viguers, Ruth Hill
Hill, Ruth Livingston
    See Munce, Ruth Hill
Hillcourt, William 1900- 27
Hillerman, Tony 1925- 6
Hillert, Margaret 1920- 8
Hillman, Martin
    See Hill, Douglas (Arthur)
Hillman, Priscilla 1940- 48
    Brief Entry 39
Hills, C(harles) A(lbert) R(eis)
    1955- 39
Hilton, Irene (P.) 1912- 7
Hilton, James 1900-1954 34
Hilton, Ralph 1907- 8

Hilton, Suzanne 1922- *4*

Him, George 1900-1982
    Obituary *30*

Himler, Ann 1946- *8*

Himler, Ronald 1937- *6*

Himmelman, John (Carl)
    1959- *47*

Hinckley, Helen
    See Jones, Helen Hinckley

Hind, Dolores (Ellen) 1931- *53*
    Brief Entry *49*

Hines, Anna G(rossnickle)
    1946- *51*
    Brief Entry *45*

Hinton, S(usan) E(loise)
    1950- *19*
    See also CLR 3

Hinton, Sam 1917- *43*

Hintz, (Loren) Martin 1945- *47*
    Brief Entry *39*

Hirsch, Phil 1926- *35*

Hirsch, S. Carl 1913- *2*

Hirschmann, Linda (Ann)
    1941- *40*

Hirsh, Marilyn 1944- *7*

Hirshberg, Al(bert Simon)
    1909-1973 .... *38*

Hiser, Iona Seibert 1901- *4*

Hitchcock, Alfred (Joseph)
    1899-1980 .... *27*
    Obituary *24*

Hitte, Kathryn 1919- *16*

Hitz, Demi 1942- *11*

Hnizdovsky, Jacques 1915- *32*

Ho, Minfong 1951- *15*

Hoagland, Edward 1932- *51*

Hoare, Robert J(ohn)
    1921-1975 .... *38*

Hoban, Lillian 1925- *22*

Hoban, Russell C(onwell)
    1925- *40*
    Earlier sketch in SATA 1
    See also CLR 3

Hoban, Tana *22*
    See also CLR 13

Hobart, Lois *7*

Hoberman, Mary Ann 1930- *5*

Hobson, Burton (Harold)
    1933- *28*

Hobson, Laura Z(ametkin)
    1900-1986 .... *52*

Hochschild, Arlie Russell
    1940- *11*

Hockaby, Stephen
    See Mitchell, Gladys (Maude
    Winifred)

Hockenberry, Hope
    See Newell, Hope (Hockenberry)

Hodge, P(aul) W(illiam)
    1934- *12*

Hodgell, P(atricia) C(hristine)
    1951- *42*

Hodges, C(yril) Walter 1909- *2*

Hodges, Carl G. 1902-1964 .... *10*

Hodges, Elizabeth Jamison *1*

Hodges, Margaret Moore
    1911- *33*
    Earlier sketch in SATA 1

Hodgetts, Blake Christopher
    1967- *43*

Hoexter, Corinne K. 1927- *6*

Hoff, Carol 1900- *11*

Hoff, Syd(ney) 1912- *9*
    See also SAAS 4

Hoffman, Edwin D. *49*

Hoffman, Phyllis M. 1944- *4*

Hoffman, Rosekrans 1926- *15*

Hoffmann, E(rnst) T(heodor)
    A(madeus) 1776-1822 .... *27*

Hoffmann, Felix 1911-1975 .... *9*

Hoffmann, Margaret Jones
    1910- *48*

Hoffmann, Peggy
    See Hoffmann, Margaret Jones

Hofsinde, Robert 1902-1973 ...... *21*

Hogan, Bernice Harris 1929- *12*

Hogan, Inez 1895- *2*

Hogarth, Jr.
    See Kent, Rockwell

Hogarth, Paul 1917- *41*

Hogg, Garry 1902- *2*

Hogner, Dorothy Childs *4*

Hogner, Nils 1893-1970 .... *25*

Hogrogian, Nonny 1932- *7*
    See also CLR 2
    See also SAAS 1

Hoh, Diane 1937- *52*
    Brief Entry *48*

Hoke, Helen (L.) 1903- *15*

Hoke, John 1925- *7*

Holbeach, Henry
    See Rands, William Brighty

Holberg, Ruth Langland
    1889- *1*

Holbrook, Peter
    See Glick, Carl (Cannon)

Holbrook, Sabra
    See Erickson, Sabra R(ollins)

Holbrook, Stewart Hall
    1893-1964 .... *2*

Holden, Elizabeth Rhoda
    See Lawrence, Louise

Holding, James 1907- *3*

Holisher, Desider 1901-1972 ...... *6*

Holl, Adelaide (Hinkle) *8*

Holl, Kristi D(iane) 1951- *51*

Holland, Isabelle 1920- *8*

Holland, Janice 1913-1962 .... *18*

Holland, John L(ewis) 1919- *20*

Holland, Lys
    See Gater, Dilys

Holland, Marion 1908- *6*

Hollander, John 1929- *13*

Hollander, Phyllis 1928- *39*

Holldobler, Turid 1939- *26*

Holliday, Joe
    See Holliday, Joseph

Holliday, Joseph 1910- *11*

Holling, Holling C(lancy)
    1900-1973 .... *15*
    Obituary *26*

Hollingsworth, Alvin C(arl)
    1930- *39*

Holloway, Teresa (Bragunier)
    1906- *26*

Holm, (Else) Anne (Lise)
    1922- *1*

Holman, Felice 1919- *7*

Holme, Bryan 1913- *26*

Holmes, Marjorie 1910- *43*

Holmes, Oliver Wendell
    1809-1894 .... *34*

Holmes, Rick
    See Hardwick, Richard Holmes, Jr.

Holmgren, George Ellen
    See Holmgren, Helen Jean

Holmgren, Helen Jean 1930- *45*

Holmgren, Virginia C(unningham)
    1909- *26*

Holmquist, Eve 1921- *11*

Holt, Margaret 1937- *4*

Holt, Margaret Van Vechten
    (Saunders) 1899-1963 .... *32*

Holt, Michael (Paul) 1929- *13*

Holt, Rackham
    See Holt, Margaret Van Vechten
    (Saunders)

Holt, Rochelle Lynn 1946- *41*

Holt, Stephen
    See Thompson, Harlan H.

Holt, Victoria
    See Hibbert, Eleanor

Holton, Leonard
    See Wibberley, Leonard (Patrick
    O'Connor)

Holyer, Erna Maria 1925- *22*

Holyer, Ernie
    See Holyer, Erna Maria

Holz, Loretta (Marie) 1943- *17*

Homze, Alma C. 1932- *17*

Honig, Donald 1931- *18*

Honness, Elizabeth H. 1904- *2*

Hoobler, Dorothy *28*

Hoobler, Thomas *28*

Hood, Joseph F. 1925- *4*

Hood, Robert E. 1926- *21*

Hook, Frances 1912- *27*

Hook, Martha 1936- *27*

Hooker, Ruth 1920- *21*

Hooks, William H(arris)
    1921- *16*

Hooper, Byrd
    See St. Clair, Byrd Hooper

Hooper, Meredith (Jean)
    1939- *28*

Hoopes, Lyn L(ittlefield)
    1953- *49*
    Brief Entry *44*

Hoopes, Ned E(dward) 1932- *21*

Hoopes, Roy 1922- *11*

Hoople, Cheryl G.
    Brief Entry *32*

Hoover, H(elen) M(ary) 1935- *44*
    Brief Entry *33*

Hoover, Helen (Drusilla Blackburn)
    1910-1984 .... *12*
    Obituary *39*

Hope, Laura Lee [Collective
    pseudonym] *1*
    See also Adams, Harriet
    S(tratemeyer)

Hope Simpson, Jacynth 1930- *12*

Hopf, Alice L(ightner) 1904- *5*

Hopkins, A. T.
    See Turngren, Annette

Hopkins, Clark 1895-1976
  Obituary .... _34_
Hopkins, Joseph G(erard) E(dward)
  1909- .... _11_
Hopkins, Lee Bennett 1938- ...... _3_
  See also SAAS 4
Hopkins, Lyman
  See Folsom, Franklin
Hopkins, Marjorie 1911- .... _9_
Hoppe, Joanne 1932- .... _42_
Hopper, Nancy J. 1937- .... _38_
  Brief Entry .... _35_
Horgan, Paul 1903- .... _13_
Hornblow, Arthur (Jr.)
  1893-1976 .... _15_
Hornblow, Leonora (Schinasi)
  1920- .... _18_
Horne, Richard Henry
  1803-1884 .... _29_
Horner, Althea (Jane) 1926- ...... _36_
Horner, Dave 1934- .... _12_
Hornos, Axel 1907- .... _20_
Horvath, Betty 1927- .... _4_
Horwich, Frances R(appaport)
  1908- .... _11_
Horwitz, Elinor Lander .... _45_
  Brief Entry .... _33_
Hosford, Dorothy (Grant)
  1900-1952 .... _22_
Hosford, Jessie 1892- .... _5_
Hoskyns-Abrahall, Clare .... _13_
Houck, Carter 1924- .... _22_
Hough, (Helen) Charlotte
  1924- .... _9_
Hough, Judy Taylor 1932-
  Brief Entry .... _51_
Hough, Richard (Alexander)
  1922- .... _17_
Houghton, Eric 1930- .... _7_
Houlehen, Robert J. 1918- .... _18_
Household, Geoffrey (Edward West)
  1900- .... _14_
Houselander, (Frances) Caryll
  1900-1954
  Brief Entry .... _31_
Housman, Laurence
  1865-1959 .... _25_
Houston, James A(rchibald)
  1921- .... _13_
  See also CLR 3
Houton, Kathleen
  See Kilgore, Kathleen
Howard, Alan 1922- .... _45_
Howard, Alyssa
  See Buckholtz, Eileen (Garber)
Howard, Elizabeth
  See Mizner, Elizabeth Howard
Howard, Prosper
  See Hamilton, Charles H. St. John
Howard, Robert West 1908- ...... _5_
Howard, Vernon (Linwood)
  1918- .... _40_
Howarth, David 1912- .... _6_
Howe, Deborah 1946-1978 .... _29_
Howe, Fanny 1940-
  Brief Entry .... _52_
Howe, James 1946- .... _29_
  See also CLR 9
Howell, Pat 1947- .... _15_

Howell, S.
  See Styles, Frank Showell
Howell, Virginia Tier
  See Ellison, Virginia Howell
Howes, Barbara 1914- .... _5_
Howker, Janni
  Brief Entry .... _46_
  See also CLR 14
Hoy, Nina
  See Roth, Arthur J(oseph)
Hoyle, Geoffrey 1942- .... _18_
Hoyt, Edwin P(almer), Jr.
  1923- .... _28_
Hoyt, Olga (Gruhzit) 1922- ...... _16_
Hubbell, Patricia 1928- .... _8_
Hubley, Faith (Elliot) 1924- ...... _48_
Hubley, John 1914-1977 .... _48_
  Obituary .... _24_
Hudson, Jeffrey
  See Crichton, (J.) Michael
Hudson, (Margaret) Kirsty
  1947- .... _32_
Hudson, W(illiam) H(enry)
  1841-1922 .... _35_
Huffaker, Sandy 1943- .... _10_
Huffman, Tom .... _24_
Hughes, Dean 1943- .... _33_
Hughes, (James) Langston
  1902-1967 .... _33_
  Earlier sketch in SATA 4
Hughes, Matilda
  See MacLeod, Charlotte (Matilda
    Hughes)
Hughes, Monica 1925- .... _15_
  See also CLR 9
Hughes, Richard (Arthur Warren)
  1900-1976 .... _8_
  Obituary .... _25_
Hughes, Sara
  See Saunders, Susan
Hughes, Shirley 1929- .... _16_
Hughes, Ted 1930- .... _49_
  Brief Entry .... _27_
  See also CLR 3
Hughes, Thomas 1822-1896 ...... _31_
Hughes, Walter (Llewellyn)
  1910- .... _26_
Hugo, Victor (Marie)
  1802-1885 .... _47_
Huline-Dickens, Frank William
  1931- .... _34_
Hull, Eleanor (Means) 1913- ..... _21_
Hull, Eric Traviss
  See Harnan, Terry
Hull, H. Braxton
  See Jacobs, Helen Hull
Hull, Jesse Redding
  See Hull, Jessie Redding
Hull, Jessie Redding 1932- ...... _51_
Hull, Katharine 1921-1977 ...... _23_
Hülsmann, Eva 1928- .... _16_
Hults, Dorothy Niebrugge
  1898- .... _6_
Hume, Lotta Carswell .... _7_
Hume, Ruth (Fox) 1922-1980 ..... _26_
  Obituary .... _22_
Hummel, Berta 1909-1946 .... _43_
Hummel, Sister Maria Innocentia
  See Hummel, Berta

Humphrey, Henry (III) 1930- ..... _16_
Humphreys, Graham 1945-
  Brief Entry .... _32_
Hungerford, Pixie
  See Brinsmead, H(esba) F(ay)
Hunkin, Tim(othy Mark Trelawney)
  1950- .... _53_
Hunt, Francis
  See Stratemeyer, Edward L.
Hunt, Irene 1907- .... _2_
  See also CLR 1
Hunt, Joyce 1927- .... _31_
Hunt, Linda Lawrence 1940- ...... _39_
Hunt, Mabel Leigh 1892-1971 .... _1_
  Obituary .... _26_
Hunt, Morton 1920- .... _22_
Hunt, Nigel
  See Greenbank, Anthony Hunt
Hunter, Bernice Thurman 1922-
  Brief Entry .... _45_
Hunter, Clingham, M.D.
  See Adams, William Taylor
Hunter, Dawe
  See Downie, Mary Alice
Hunter, Edith Fisher 1919- .... _31_
Hunter, Evan 1926- .... _25_
Hunter, Hilda 1921- .... _7_
Hunter, Kristin (Eggleston)
  1931- .... _12_
  See also CLR 3
Hunter, Leigh
  See Etchison, Birdie L(ee)
Hunter, Mel 1927- .... _39_
Hunter, Mollie
  See McIllwraith, Maureen
Hunter, Norman (George Lorimer)
  1899- .... _26_
Hunter Blair, Pauline 1921- ...... _3_
Huntington, Harriet E(lizabeth)
  1909- .... _1_
Huntsberry, William E(mery)
  1916- .... _5_
Hurd, Clement 1908- .... _2_
Hurd, Edith Thacher 1910- .... _2_
Hurd, Thacher 1949- .... _46_
  Brief Entry .... _45_
Hürlimann, Bettina 1909-1983 ... _39_
  Obituary .... _34_
Hürlimann, Ruth 1939- .... _32_
  Brief Entry .... _31_
Hurwitz, Johanna 1937- .... _20_
Hurwood, Bernhardt J.
  1926-1987 .... _12_
  Obituary .... _50_
Hutchens, Paul 1902-1977 ...... _31_
Hutchins, Carleen Maley
  1911- .... _9_
Hutchins, Hazel J. 1952-
  Brief Entry .... _51_
Hutchins, Pat 1942- .... _15_
Hutchins, Ross E(lliott) 1906- .... _4_
Hutchmacher, J. Joseph 1929- .... _5_
Hutto, Nelson (Allen) 1904- ..... _20_
Hutton, Warwick 1939- .... _20_
Hyde, Dayton O(gden) .... _9_
Hyde, Hawk
  See Hyde, Dayton O(gden)

Hyde, Margaret Oldroyd
  1917- *42*
  Earlier sketch in SATA 1
Hyde, Shelley
  See Reed, Kit
Hyde, Wayne F. 1922- *7*
Hylander, Clarence J.
  1897-1964 .... *7*
Hyman, Robin P(hilip) 1931- *12*
Hyman, Trina Schart 1939- *46*
  Earlier sketch in SATA 7
Hymes, Lucia M. 1907- *7*
Hyndman, Jane Andrews
  1912-1978 .... *46*
  Obituary *23*
  Earlier sketch in SATA 1
Hyndman, Robert Utley
  1906(?)-1973 .... *18*

I

I.W.
  See Watts, Isaac
Iannone, Jeanne *7*
Ibbotson, Eva 1925- *13*
Ibbotson, M. C(hristine)
  1930- *5*
Ichikawa, Satomi 1949- *47*
  Brief Entry *36*
Ilowite, Sheldon A. 1931- *27*
Ilsley, Dent [Joint pseudonym]
  See Chapman, John Stanton Higham
Ilsley, Velma (Elizabeth)
  1918- *12*
Immel, Mary Blair 1930- *28*
Ingelow, Jean 1820-1897 .... *33*
Ingham, Colonel Frederic
  See Hale, Edward Everett
Ingman, Nicholas 1948- *52*
Ingraham, Leonard W(illiam)
  1913- *4*
Ingrams, Doreen 1906- *20*
Inyart, Gene 1927- *6*
Ionesco, Eugene 1912- *7*
Ipcar, Dahlov (Zorach) 1917- *49*
  Earlier sketch in SATA 1
Irvin, Fred 1914- *15*
Irving, Alexander
  See Hume, Ruth (Fox)
Irving, Robert
  See Adler, Irving
Irving, Washington
  1783-1859 .... *YABC 2*
Irwin, Ann(abelle Bowen)
  1915- *44*
  Brief Entry *38*
Irwin, Constance Frick 1913- *6*
Irwin, Hadley [Joint pseudonym]
  See Hadley, Lee and Irwin, Ann
Irwin, Keith Gordon
  1885-1964 .... *11*
Isaac, Joanne 1934- *21*
Isaacs, Jacob
  See Kranzler, George G(ershon)
Isadora, Rachel 1953(?)-
  Brief Entry *32*
  See also CLR 7

Isham, Charlotte H(ickox)
  1912- *21*
Ish-Kishor, Judith 1892-1972 ..... *11*
Ish-Kishor, Sulamith
  1896-1977 .... *17*
Ishmael, Woodi 1914- *31*
Israel, Elaine 1945- *12*
Israel, Marion Louise 1882-1973
  Obituary *26*
Iverson, Genie 1942-
  Brief Entry *52*
Iwamatsu, Jun Atsushi 1908- *14*

J

Jac, Lee
  See Morton, Lee Jack, Jr.
Jackson, Anne 1896(?)-1984
  Obituary *37*
Jackson, C. Paul 1902- *6*
Jackson, Caary
  See Jackson, C. Paul
Jackson, Geoffrey (Holt Seymour)
  1915-1987
  Obituary *53*
Jackson, Jesse 1908-1983 .... *29*
  Obituary *48*
  Earlier sketch in SATA 2
Jackson, O. B.
  See Jackson, C. Paul
Jackson, Robert B(lake) 1926- *8*
Jackson, Sally
  See Kellogg, Jean
Jackson, Shirley 1919-1965 .... *2*
Jacob, Helen Pierce 1927- *21*
Jacobi, Kathy
  Brief Entry *42*
Jacobs, Flora Gill 1918- *5*
Jacobs, Francine 1935- *43*
  Brief Entry *42*
Jacobs, Frank 1929- *30*
Jacobs, Helen Hull 1908- *12*
Jacobs, Joseph 1854-1916 .... *25*
Jacobs, Leland Blair 1907- *20*
Jacobs, Linda C. 1943- *21*
Jacobs, Lou(is), Jr. 1921- *2*
Jacobs, Susan 1940- *30*
Jacobs, William Jay 1933- *28*
Jacobson, Daniel 1923- *12*
Jacobson, Morris K(arl) 1906- *21*
Jacopetti, Alexandra 1939- *14*
Jacques, Robin 1920- *32*
  Brief Entry *30*
  See also SAAS 5
Jaffee, Al(lan) 1921-
  Brief Entry *37*
Jagendorf, Moritz (Adolf)
  1888-1981 .... *2*
  Obituary *24*
Jahn, (Joseph) Michael 1943- *28*
Jahn, Mike
  See Jahn, (Joseph) Michael
Jahsmann, Allan Hart 1916- *28*
James, Andrew
  See Kirkup, James
James, Dynely
  See Mayne, William

James, Edwin
  See Gunn, James E(dwin)
James, Elizabeth 1942- *52*
James, Harry Clebourne 1896- *11*
James, Josephine
  See Sterne, Emma Gelders
James, Robin (Irene) 1953- *50*
James, T. F.
  See Fleming, Thomas J(ames)
James, Will(iam Roderick)
  1892-1942 .... *19*
Jance, J. A.
  See Jance, Judith A(nn)
Jance, Judith A(nn) 1944-
  Brief Entry *50*
Jane, Mary Childs 1909- *6*
Janeczko, Paul B(ryan) 1945- *53*
Janes, Edward C. 1908- *25*
Janes, J(oseph) Robert 1935-
  Brief Entry *50*
Janeway, Elizabeth (Hall)
  1913- *19*
Janice
  See Brustlein, Janice Tworkov
Janosch
  See Eckert, Horst
Jansen, Jared
  See Cebulash, Mel
Janson, Dora Jane 1916- *31*
Janson, H(orst) W(oldemar)
  1913- *9*
Jansson, Tove (Marika) 1914- *41*
  Earlier sketch in SATA 3
  See also CLR 2
Janus, Grete
  See Hertz, Grete Janus
Jaques, Faith 1923- *21*
Jaques, Francis Lee 1887-1969
  Brief Entry *28*
Jaquith, Priscilla 1908- *51*
Jarman, Rosemary Hawley
  1935- *7*
Jarrell, Mary von Schrader
  1914- *35*
Jarrell, Randall 1914-1965 .... *7*
  See also CLR 6
Jarrett, Roxanne
  See Werner, Herma
Jauss, Anne Marie 1907- *10*
Jayne, Lieutenant R. H.
  See Ellis, Edward S(ylvester)
Jaynes, Clare [Joint pseudonym]
  See Mayer, Jane Rothschild
Jeake, Samuel, Jr.
  See Aiken, Conrad
Jefferds, Vincent H(arris) 1916-
  Brief Entry *49*
Jefferies, (John) Richard
  1848-1887 .... *16*
Jeffers, Susan *17*
Jefferson, Sarah
  See Farjeon, Annabel
Jeffries, Roderic 1926- *4*
Jenkins, Marie M. 1909- *7*
Jenkins, William A(twell)
  1922- *9*
Jenkyns, Chris 1924- *51*
Jennings, Gary (Gayne) 1928- *9*

Jennings, Robert
See Hamilton, Charles H. St. John
Jennings, S. M.
See Meyer, Jerome Sydney
Jennison, C. S.
See Starbird, Kaye
Jennison, Keith Warren 1911- 14
Jensen, Niels 1927- 25
Jensen, Virginia Allen 1927- 8
Jeppson, J(anet) O(pal) 1926-
Brief Entry 46
Jeschke, Susan 42
Brief Entry 27
Jessel, Camilla (Ruth) 1937- 29
Jewell, Nancy 1940-
Brief Entry 41
Jewett, Eleanore Myers
1890-1967 5
Jewett, Sarah Orne 1849-1909 15
Jezard, Alison 1919-
Brief Entry 34
Jiler, John 1946- 42
Brief Entry 35
Jobb, Jamie 1945- 29
Joerns, Consuelo 44
Brief Entry 33
John, Naomi
See Flack, Naomi John (White)
Johns, Avery
See Cousins, Margaret
Johnson, A. E. [Joint pseudonym]
See Johnson, Annabell and Johnson,
Edgar
Johnson, Annabell Jones
1921- 2
Johnson, Benj. F., of Boone
See Riley, James Whitcomb
Johnson, Charles R. 1925- 11
Johnson, Charlotte Buel
1918-1982 46
Johnson, Chuck
See Johnson, Charles R.
Johnson, Crockett
See Leisk, David (Johnson)
Johnson, D(ana) William
1945- 23
Johnson, Dorothy M(arie)
1905-1984 6
Obituary 40
Johnson, E(ugene) Harper 44
Johnson, Edgar Raymond
1912- 2
Johnson, Elizabeth 1911-1984 7
Obituary 39
Johnson, Eric W(arner) 1918- 8
Johnson, Evelyne 1932- 20
Johnson, Gaylord 1884- 7
Johnson, Gerald White
1890-1980 19
Obituary 28
Johnson, Harper
See Johnson, E(ugene) Harper
Johnson, Harriett 1908-1987
Obituary 53
Johnson, James Ralph 1922- 1
Johnson, James Weldon
See Johnson, James William
Johnson, James William
1871-1938 31

Johnson, Jane 1951- 48
Johnson, John E(mil) 1929- 34
Johnson, LaVerne B(ravo)
1925- 13
Johnson, Lois S(mith) 6
Johnson, Lois W(alfrid) 1936- 22
Johnson, Margaret S(weet)
1893-1964 35
Johnson, Mary Frances K.
1929(?)-1979
Obituary 27
Johnson, Maud Battle 1918(?)-1985
Obituary 46
Johnson, Milton 1932- 31
Johnson, Natalie
See Robison, Nancy L(ouise)
Johnson, (Walter) Ryerson
1901- 10
Johnson, Shirley K(ing) 1927- 10
Johnson, Siddie Joe 1905-1977
Obituary 20
Johnson, Spencer 1938-
Brief Entry 38
Johnson, Sylvia A.
Brief Entry 52
Johnson, William R. 38
Johnson, William Weber
1909- 7
Johnston, Agnes Christine
See Dazey, Agnes J.
Johnston, Annie Fellows
1863-1931 37
Johnston, H(ugh) A(nthony) S(tephen)
1913-1967 14
Johnston, Johanna
1914(?)-1982 12
Obituary 33
Johnston, Norma 29
Johnston, Portia
See Takakjian, Portia
Johnston, Tony 1942- 8
Jonas, Ann 1932- 50
Brief Entry 42
See also CLR 12
Jones, Adrienne 1915- 7
Jones, Charles M(artin) 1912- 53
Jones, Chuck
See Jones, Charles M(artin)
Jones, Diana Wynne 1934- 9
Jones, Douglas C(lyde) 1924- 52
Jones, Elizabeth Orton 1910- 18
Jones, Evan 1915- 3
Jones, Geraldine 1951- 43
Jones, Gillingham
See Hamilton, Charles H. St. John
Jones, Harold 1904- 14
Jones, Helen Hinckley 1903- 26
Jones, Helen L. 1904(?)-1973
Obituary 22
Jones, Hettie 1934- 42
Brief Entry 27
Jones, Hortense P. 1918- 9
Jones, Jessie Mae Orton 1887(?)-1983
Obituary 37
Jones, Margaret Boone
See Zarif, Margaret Min'imah
Jones, Mary Alice 6
Jones, McClure 34
Jones, Penelope 1938- 31

Jones, Rebecca C(astaldi)
1947- 33
Jones, Terry 1942- 51
Jones, Weyman 1928- 4
Jonk, Clarence 1906- 10
Joosse, Barbara M(onnot)
1949- 52
Jordan, Don
See Howard, Vernon (Linwood)
Jordan, E(mil) L(eopold) 1900-
Brief Entry 31
Jordan, Hope (Dahle) 1905- 15
Jordan, Jael (Michal) 1949- 30
Jordan, June 1936- 4
See also CLR 10
Jordan, Mildred 1901- 5
Jorgensen, Mary Venn 36
Jorgenson, Ivar
See Silverberg, Robert
Joseph, James (Herz) 1924- 53
Joseph, Joan 1939- 34
Joseph, Joseph M(aron)
1903-1979 22
Joslin, Sesyle 1929- 2
Joyce, J(ames) Avery
1902-1987 11
Obituary 50
Joyce, William 1959(?)-
Brief Entry 46
Joyner, Jerry 1938- 34
Jucker, Sita 1921- 5
Judd, Denis (O'Nan) 1938- 33
Judd, Frances K. [Collective
pseudonym] 1
Judson, Clara Ingram
1879-1960 38
Brief Entry 27
Jukes, Mavis
Brief Entry 43
Jumpp, Hugo
See MacPeek, Walter G.
Jupo, Frank J. 1904- 7
Juster, Norton 1929- 3
Justus, May 1898- 1
Juvenilia
See Taylor, Ann

K

Kabdebo, Tamas
See Kabdebo, Thomas
Kabdebo, Thomas 1934- 10
Kabibble, Osh
See Jobb, Jamie
Kadesch, Robert R(udstone)
1922- 31
Kahl, M(arvin) P(hilip) 1934- 37
Kahl, Virginia (Caroline)
1919- 48
Brief Entry 38
Kahn, Joan 1914- 48
Kahn, Roger 1927- 37
Kakimoto, Kozo 1915- 11
Kalashnikoff, Nicholas
1888-1961 16
Kalb, Jonah 1926- 23
Kaler, James Otis 1848-1912 15
Kalnay, Francis 1899- 7

Kalow, Gisela 1946- *32*
Kamen, Gloria 1923- *9*
Kamerman, Sylvia E.
  See Burack, Sylvia K.
Kamm, Josephine (Hart)
  1905- *24*
Kandell, Alice S. 1938- *35*
Kane, Henry Bugbee
  1902-1971 .... *14*
Kane, Robert W. 1910- *18*
Kanetzke, Howard W(illiam)
  1932- *38*
Kanzawa, Toshiko
  See Furukawa, Toshi
Kaplan, Anne Bernays 1930- *32*
Kaplan, Bess 1927- *22*
Kaplan, Boche 1926- *24*
Kaplan, Irma 1900- *10*
Kaplan, Jean Caryl Korn
  1926- *10*
Karageorge, Michael
  See Anderson, Poul (William)
Karasz, Ilonka 1896-1981
  Obituary *29*
Karen, Ruth 1922- *9*
Kark, Nina Mary 1925- *4*
Karl, Jean E(dna) 1927- *34*
Karlin, Eugene 1918- *10*
Karp, Naomi J. 1926- *16*
Kashiwagi, Isami 1925- *10*
Kassem, Lou
  Brief Entry *51*
Kästner, Erich 1899-1974 .... *14*
  See also CLR 4
Kasuya, Masahiro 1937- *51*
Katchen, Carole 1944- *9*
Kathryn
  See Searle, Kathryn Adrienne
Katona, Robert 1949- *21*
Katsarakis, Joan Harries
  See Harries, Joan
Katz, Bobbi 1933- *12*
Katz, Fred 1938- *6*
Katz, Jane 1934- *33*
Katz, Marjorie P.
  See Weiser, Marjorie P(hillis) K(atz)
Katz, William Loren 1927- *13*
Kaufman, Joe 1911- *33*
Kaufman, Mervyn D. 1932- *4*
Kaufmann, Angelika 1935- *15*
Kaufmann, John 1931- *18*
Kaula, Edna Mason 1906- *13*
Kavaler, Lucy 1930- *23*
Kay, Helen
  See Goldfrank, Helen Colodny
Kay, Mara *13*
Kaye, Danny 1913-1987
  Obituary *50*
Kaye, Geraldine 1925- *10*
Keane, Bil 1922- *4*
Keating, Bern
  See Keating, Leo Bernard
Keating, Lawrence A.
  1903-1966 .... *23*
Keating, Leo Bernard 1915- *10*
Keats, Ezra Jack 1916-1983 ...... *14*
  Obituary *34*
  See also CLR 1
Keegan, Marcia 1943- *9*

Keel, Frank
  See Keeler, Ronald F(ranklin)
Keeler, Ronald F(ranklin)
  1913-1983 .... *47*
Keen, Martin L. 1913- *4*
Keene, Carolyn [Collective
  pseudonym]
  See Adams, Harriet S.
Keeping, Charles (William James)
  1924- *9*
Keeshan, Robert J. 1927- *32*
Keir, Christine
  See Pullein-Thompson, Christine
Keith, Carlton
  See Robertson, Keith
Keith, Eros 1942- *52*
Keith, Hal 1934- *36*
Keith, Harold (Verne) 1903- *2*
Keith, Robert
  See Applebaum, Stan
Kelen, Emery 1896-1978 .... *13*
  Obituary *26*
Kelleam, Joseph E(veridge)
  1913-1975 .... *31*
Kelleher, Victor 1939-
  Brief Entry *52*
Keller, B(everly) L(ou) *13*
Keller, Charles 1942- *8*
Keller, Dick 1923- *36*
Keller, Gail Faithfull
  See Faithfull, Gail
Keller, Holly
  Brief Entry *42*
Keller, Irene (Barron) 1927- *36*
Keller, Mollie
  Brief Entry *50*
Kelley, Leo P(atrick) 1928- *32*
  Brief Entry *31*
Kelley, True Adelaide 1946- *41*
  Brief Entry *39*
Kellin, Sally Moffet 1932- *9*
Kelling, Furn L. 1914- *37*
Kellogg, Gene
  See Kellogg, Jean
Kellogg, Jean 1916- *10*
Kellogg, Steven 1941- *8*
  See also CLR 6
Kellow, Kathleen
  See Hibbert, Eleanor
Kelly, Eric P(hilbrook)
  1884-1960 .... *YABC 1*
Kelly, Martha Rose
  1914-1983 .... *37*
Kelly, Marty
  See Kelly, Martha Rose
Kelly, Ralph
  See Geis, Darlene
Kelly, Regina Z. *5*
Kelly, Rosalie (Ruth) *43*
Kelly, Walt(er Crawford)
  1913-1973 .... *18*
Kelsey, Alice Geer 1896- *1*
Kemp, Gene 1926- *25*
Kempner, Mary Jean
  1913-1969 .... *10*
Kempton, Jean Welch 1914- *10*
Kendall, Carol (Seeger) 1917- *11*
Kendall, Lace
  See Stoutenburg, Adrien

Kenealy, James P. 1927- *52*
  Brief Entry *29*
Kenealy, Jim
  See Kenealy, James P.
Kennedy, Dorothy M(intzlaff)
  1931- *53*
Kennedy, John Fitzgerald
  1917-1963 .... *11*
Kennedy, Joseph 1929- *14*
Kennedy, Paul E(dward)
  1929- *33*
Kennedy, (Jerome) Richard
  1932- *22*
Kennedy, T(eresa) A. 1953- *42*
  Brief Entry *35*
Kennedy, X. J.
  See Kennedy, Joseph
Kennell, Ruth E(pperson)
  1893-1977 .... *6*
  Obituary *25*
Kenny, Ellsworth Newcomb
  1909-1971
  Obituary *26*
Kenny, Herbert A(ndrew)
  1912- *13*
Kenny, Kathryn
  See Bowden, Joan Chase
  See Krull, Kathleen
Kenny, Kevin
  See Krull, Kathleen
Kent, Alexander
  See Reeman, Douglas Edward
Kent, David
  See Lambert, David (Compton)
Kent, Deborah Ann 1948- *47*
  Brief Entry *41*
Kent, Jack
  See Kent, John Wellington
Kent, John Wellington
  1920-1985 .... *24*
  Obituary *45*
Kent, Margaret 1894- *2*
Kent, Rockwell 1882-1971 .... *6*
Kent, Sherman 1903-1986 .... *20*
  Obituary *47*
Kenward, Jean 1920- *42*
Kenworthy, Leonard S. 1912- *6*
Kenyon, Kate
  See Ransom, Candice F.
Kenyon, Ley 1913- *6*
Kepes, Juliet A(ppleby) 1919- *13*
Kerigan, Florence 1896- *12*
Kerman, Gertrude Lerner
  1909- *21*
Kerr, Jessica 1901- *13*
Kerr, (Anne) Judith 1923- *24*
Kerr, M. E.
  See Meaker, Marijane
  See also SAAS 1
Kerry, Frances
  See Kerigan, Florence
Kerry, Lois
  See Duncan, Lois S(teinmetz)
Ker Wilson, Barbara 1929- *20*
Kessel, Joyce Karen 1937- *41*
Kessler, Ethel 1922- *44*
  Brief Entry *37*
Kessler, Leonard P. 1921- *14*

Kesteven, G. R.
See Crosher, G(eoffry) R(obins)
Ketcham, Hank
See Ketcham, Henry King
Ketcham, Henry King 1920- 28
Brief Entry 27
Kettelkamp, Larry 1933- 2
See also SAAS 3
Kevles, Bettyann 1938- 23
Key, Alexander (Hill)
1904-1979 8
Obituary 23
Keyes, Daniel 1927- 37
Keyes, Fenton 1915- 34
Keyser, Marcia 1933- 42
Keyser, Sarah
See McGuire, Leslie (Sarah)
Khanshendel, Chiron
See Rose, Wendy
Kherdian, David 1931- 16
Kidd, Ronald 1948- 42
Kiddell, John 1922- 3
Kidwell, Carl 1910- 43
Kiefer, Irene 1926- 21
Kiesel, Stanley 1925- 35
Kikukawa, Cecily H. 1919- 44
Brief Entry 35
Kilgore, Kathleen 1946- 42
Kilian, Crawford 1941- 35
Killilea, Marie (Lyons) 1913- 2
Kilreon, Beth
See Walker, Barbara K.
Kimball, Yeffe 1914-1978 37
Kimbrough, Emily 1899- 2
Kimmel, Eric A. 1946- 13
Kimmel, Margaret Mary
1938- 43
Brief Entry 33
Kindred, Wendy 1937- 7
Kines, Pat Decker 1937- 12
King, Adam
See Hoare, Robert J(ohn)
King, Arthur
See Cain, Arthur H.
King, Billie Jean 1943- 12
King, (David) Clive 1924- 28
King, Cynthia 1925- 7
King, Frank O. 1883-1969
Obituary 22
King, Marian 1900(?)-1986 23
Obituary 47
King, Martin
See Marks, Stan(ley)
King, Martin Luther, Jr.
1929-1968 14
King, Paul
See Drackett, Phil(ip Arthur)
King, Reefe
See Barker, Albert W.
King, Stephen 1947- 9
King, Tony 1947- 39
Kingman, Dong (Moy Shu)
1911- 44
Kingman, (Mary) Lee 1919- 1
See also SAAS 3
Kingsland, Leslie William
1912- 13
Kingsley, Charles
1819-1875 .... YABC 2

Kingsley, Emily Perl 1940- 33
King-Smith, Dick 1922- 47
Brief Entry 38
Kingston, Maxine (Ting Ting) Hong
1940- 53
Kinney, C. Cle 1915- 6
Kinney, Harrison 1921- 13
Kinney, Jean Stout 1912- 12
Kinsey, Elizabeth
See Clymer, Eleanor
Kipling, (Joseph) Rudyard
1865-1936 .... YABC 2
Kirk, Ruth (Kratz) 1925- 5
Kirkland, Will
See Hale, Arlene
Kirkup, James 1927- 12
Kirkus, Virginia
See Glick, Virginia Kirkus
Kirtland, G. B.
See Joslin, Sesyle
Kishida, Eriko 1929- 12
Kisinger, Grace Gelvin
1913-1965 10
Kissin, Eva H. 1923- 10
Kjelgaard, James Arthur
1910-1959 17
Kjelgaard, Jim
See Kjelgaard, James Arthur
Klagsbrun, Francine (Lifton) 36
Klaits, Barrie 1944- 52
Klaperman, Gilbert 1921- 33
Klaperman, Libby Mindlin
1921-1982 33
Obituary 31
Klass, Morton 1927- 11
Klass, Sheila Solomon 1927- 45
Kleberger, Ilse 1921- 5
Klein, Aaron E. 1930- 45
Brief Entry 28
Klein, Gerda Weissmann
1924- 44
Klein, H. Arthur 8
Klein, Leonore 1916- 6
Klein, Mina C(ooper) 8
Klein, Norma 1938- 7
See also CLR 2
See also SAAS 1
Klein, Robin 1936-
Brief Entry 45
Klemm, Edward G., Jr. 1910- 30
Klemm, Roberta K(ohnhorst)
1884- 30
Klevin, Jill Ross 1935- 39
Brief Entry 38
Kliban, B. 1935- 35
Klimowicz, Barbara 1927- 10
Kline, Suzy 1943-
Brief Entry 48
Klug, Ron(ald) 1939- 31
Knapp, Ron 1952- 34
Knebel, Fletcher 1911- 36
Knickerbocker, Diedrich
See Irving, Washington
Knifesmith
See Cutler, Ivor
Knigge, Robert (R.) 1921(?)-1987
Obituary 50
Knight, Anne (Katherine)
1946- 34

Knight, Damon 1922- 9
Knight, David C(arpenter) 14
Knight, Eric (Mowbray)
1897-1943 18
Knight, Francis Edgar 14
Knight, Frank
See Knight, Francis Edgar
Knight, Hilary 1926- 15
Knight, Mallory T.
See Hurwood, Bernhardt J.
Knight, Ruth Adams 1898-1974
Obituary 20
Knott, Bill
See Knott, William Cecil, Jr.
Knott, William Cecil, Jr.
1927- 3
Knotts, Howard (Clayton, Jr.)
1922- 25
Knowles, Anne 1933- 37
Knowles, John 1926- 8
Knox, Calvin
See Silverberg, Robert
Knox, (Mary) Eleanor Jessie
1909- 30
Knox, James
See Brittain, William
Knudsen, James 1950- 42
Knudson, Richard L(ewis)
1930- 34
Knudson, R. R.
See Knudson, Rozanne
Knudson, Rozanne 1932- 7
Koch, Dorothy Clarke 1924- 6
Kocsis, J. C.
See Paul, James
Koehn, Ilse
See Van Zwienen, Ilse (Charlotte
Koehn)
Koerner, W(illiam) H(enry) D(avid)
1878-1938 21
Koertge, Ronald 1940- 53
Kogan, Deborah 1940- 50
Kohl, Herbert 1937- 47
Kohler, Julilly H(ouse) 1908-1976
Obituary 20
Kohn, Bernice (Herstein)
1920- 4
Kohner, Frederick 1905-1986 10
Obituary 48
Koide, Tan 1938-1986 50
Kolba, Tamara 22
Komisar, Lucy 1942- 9
Komoda, Beverly 1939- 25
Komoda, Kiyo 1937- 9
Komroff, Manuel 1890-1974 2
Obituary 20
Konigsburg, E(laine) L(obl) 48
Earlier sketch in SATA 4
See also CLR 1
Koning, Hans
See Koningsberger, Hans
Koningsberger, Hans 1921- 5
Konkle, Janet Everest 1917- 12
Koob, Theodora (Johanna Foth)
1918- 23
Kooiker, Leonie
See Kooyker-Romijn, Johanna Maria
Kooyker-Romijn, Johanna Maria
1927- 48

Kopper, Lisa (Esther) 1950-
  Brief Entry *51*
Korach, Mimi 1922- *9*
Koren, Edward 1935- *5*
Korinetz, Yuri (Iosifovich)
  1923- *9*
  See also CLR 4
Korman, Gordon 1963- *49*
  Brief Entry *41*
Korty, Carol 1937- *15*
Kossin, Sandy (Sanford)
  1926- *10*
Kotzwinkle, William 1938- *24*
  See also CLR 6
Kouhi, Elizabeth 1917-
  Brief Entry *49*
Koutoukas, H. M.
  See Rivoli, Mario
Kouts, Anne 1945- *8*
Krahn, Fernando 1935- *49*
  Brief Entry *31*
  See also CLR 3
Kramer, Anthony
  Brief Entry *42*
Kramer, George
  See Heuman, William
Kramer, Nora 1896(?)-1984 .... *26*
  Obituary *39*
Krantz, Hazel (Newman)
  1920- *12*
Kranzler, George G(ershon)
  1916- *28*
Kranzler, Gershon
  See Kranzler, George G(ershon)
Krasilovsky, Phyllis 1926- *38*
  Earlier sketch in SATA 1
  See also SAAS 5
Kraske, Robert
  Brief Entry *36*
Kraus, Robert 1925- *4*
Krauss, Ruth (Ida) 1911- *30*
  Earlier sketch in SATA 1
Krautter, Elisa
  See Bialk, Elisa
Krauze, Andrzej 1947-
  Brief Entry *46*
Kredel, Fritz 1900-1973 .... *17*
Krementz, Jill 1940- *17*
  See also CLR 5
Krensky, Stephen (Alan)
  1953- *47*
  Brief Entry *41*
Kripke, Dorothy Karp *30*
Kristof, Jane 1932- *8*
Kroeber, Theodora (Kracaw)
  1897- *1*
Kroll, Francis Lynde
  1904-1973 .... *10*
Kroll, Steven 1941- *19*
Kropp, Paul (Stephen) 1948- *38*
  Brief Entry *34*
Krull, Kathleen 1952- *52*
  Brief Entry *39*
Krumgold, Joseph 1908-1980 .... *48*
  Obituary *23*
  Earlier sketch in SATA 1
Krupp, E(dwin) C(harles)
  1944- *53*
Krupp, Robin Rector 1946- *53*

Krush, Beth 1918- *18*
Krush, Joe 1918- *18*
Krüss, James 1926- *8*
  See also CLR 9
Kubie, Nora (Gottheil) Benjamin
  1899- *39*
Kubinyi, Laszlo 1937- *17*
Kuh, Charlotte 1892(?)-1985
  Obituary *43*
Kujoth, Jean Spealman 1935-1975
  Obituary *30*
Kullman, Harry 1919-1982 .... *35*
Kumin, Maxine (Winokur)
  1925- *12*
Kunhardt, Dorothy (Meserve)
  1901-1979 .... *53*
  Obituary *22*
Künstler, Morton 1927- *10*
Kunz, Roxane (Brown) 1932-
  Brief Entry *53*
Kupferberg, Herbert 1918- *19*
Kuratomi, Chizuko 1939- *12*
Kurelek, William 1927-1977 ...... *8*
  Obituary *27*
  See also CLR 2
Kurland, Gerald 1942- *13*
Kurland, Michael (Joseph)
  1938- *48*
Kushner, Donn 1927- *52*
Kuskin, Karla (Seidman)
  1932- *2*
  See also CLR 4
  See also SAAS 3
Kuttner, Paul 1931- *18*
Kuzma, Kay 1941- *39*
Kvale, Velma R(uth) 1898- *8*
Kyle, Elisabeth
  See Dunlop, Agnes M. R.
Kyte, Kathy S. 1946- *50*
  Brief Entry *44*

L

Lacy, Leslie Alexander 1937- *6*
Ladd, Veronica
  See Miner, Jane Claypool
Lader, Lawrence 1919- *6*
Lady, A
  See Taylor, Ann
Lady Mears
  See Tempest, Margaret Mary
Lady of Quality, A
  See Bagnold, Enid
La Farge, Oliver (Hazard Perry)
  1901-1963 .... *19*
La Farge, Phyllis *14*
Laffin, John (Alfred Charles)
  1922- *31*
La Fontaine, Jean de
  1621-1695 .... *18*
Lager, Marilyn 1939- *52*
Lagercrantz, Rose (Elsa)
  1947- *39*
Lagerlöf, Selma (Ottiliana Lovisa)
  1858-1940 .... *15*
  See also CLR 7
Laiken, Deirdre S(usan) 1948- *48*
  Brief Entry *40*

Laimgruber, Monika 1946- *11*
Laing, Martha
  See Celestino, Martha Laing
Laird, Jean E(louise) 1930- *38*
Laite, Gordon 1925- *31*
Lake, Harriet
  See Taylor, Paula (Wright)
Laklan, Carli 1907- *5*
la Mare, Walter de
  See de la Mare, Walter
Lamb, Beatrice Pitney 1904- *21*
Lamb, Charles 1775-1834 .... *17*
Lamb, Elizabeth Searle 1917- *31*
Lamb, G(eoffrey) F(rederick) *10*
Lamb, Harold (Albert)
  1892-1962 .... *53*
Lamb, Lynton 1907- *10*
Lamb, Mary Ann 1764-1847 ...... *17*
Lamb, Robert (Boyden) 1941- *13*
Lambert, David (Compton) 1932-
  Brief Entry *49*
Lambert, Janet (Snyder)
  1894-1973 .... *25*
Lambert, Saul 1928- *23*
Lamburn, Richmal Crompton
  1890-1969 .... *5*
Lamorisse, Albert (Emmanuel)
  1922-1970 .... *23*
Lampert, Emily 1951- *52*
  Brief Entry *49*
Lamplugh, Lois 1921- *17*
Lampman, Evelyn Sibley
  1907-1980 .... *4*
  Obituary *23*
Lamprey, Louise
  1869-1951 .... *YABC 2*
Lampton, Chris
  See Lampton, Christopher
Lampton, Christopher
  Brief Entry *47*
Lancaster, Bruce 1896-1963 .... *9*
Lancaster, Matthew 1973(?)-1983
  Obituary *45*
Land, Barbara (Neblett) 1923- *16*
Land, Jane [Joint pseudonym]
  See Borland, Kathryn Kilby and
  Speicher, Helen Ross (Smith)
Land, Myrick (Ebben) 1922- *15*
Land, Ross [Joint pseudonym]
  See Borland, Kathryn Kilby and
  Speicher, Helen Ross (Smith)
Landau, Elaine 1948- *10*
Landau, Jacob 1917- *38*
Landeck, Beatrice 1904- *15*
Landin, Les(lie) 1923- *2*
Landis, J(ames) D(avid) 1942-
  Brief Entry *52*
Landon, Lucinda 1950-
  Brief Entry *51*
Landon, Margaret (Dorothea
  Mortenson) 1903- *50*
Landshoff, Ursula 1908- *13*
Lane, Carolyn 1926- *10*
Lane, Jerry
  See Martin, Patricia Miles
Lane, John 1932- *15*
Lane, Margaret 1907-
  Brief Entry *38*

Lane, Rose Wilder 1886-1968 29
  Brief Entry 28
Lanes, Selma G. 1929- 3
Lang, Andrew 1844-1912 16
Lange, John
  See Crichton, (J.) Michael
Lange, Suzanne 1945- 5
Langley, Noel 1911-1980
  Obituary 25
Langner, Nola 1930- 8
Langone, John (Michael)
  1929- 46
  Brief Entry 38
Langstaff, John 1920- 6
  See also CLR 3
Langstaff, Launcelot
  See Irving, Washington
Langton, Jane 1922- 3
  See also SAAS 5
Lanier, Sidney 1842-1881 18
Lansing, Alfred 1921-1975 35
Lantz, Paul 1908- 45
Lantz, Walter 1900- 37
Lappin, Peter 1911- 32
Larom, Henry V. 1903(?)-1975
  Obituary 30
Larrecq, John M(aurice)
  1926-1980 44
  Obituary 25
Larrick, Nancy G. 1910- 4
Larsen, Egon 1904- 14
Larson, Eve
  See St. John, Wylly Folk
Larson, Norita D. 1944- 29
Larson, William H. 1938- 10
Larsson, Carl (Olof)
  1853-1919 35
Lasell, Elinor H. 1929- 19
Lasell, Fen H.
  See Lasell, Elinor H.
Lash, Joseph P. 1909- 43
Lasher, Faith B. 1921- 12
Lasker, David 1950- 38
Lasker, Joe 1919- 9
Lasky, Kathryn 1944- 13
  See also CLR 11
Lassalle, C. E.
  See Ellis, Edward S(ylvester)
Latham, Barbara 1896- 16
Latham, Frank B. 1910- 6
Latham, Jean Lee 1902- 2
Latham, Mavis
  See Clark, Mavis Thorpe
Latham, Philip
  See Richardson, Robert S(hirley)
Lathrop, Dorothy P(ulis)
  1891-1980 14
  Obituary 24
Lathrop, Francis
  See Leiber, Fritz
Lattimore, Eleanor Frances
  1904-1986 7
  Obituary 48
Lauber, Patricia (Grace) 1924- 33
  Earlier sketch in SATA 1
Laugesen, Mary E(akin)
  1906- 5
Laughbaum, Steve 1945- 12
Laughlin, Florence 1910- 3

Lauré, Ettagale
  See Blauer, Ettagale
Lauré, Jason 1940- 50
  Brief Entry 44
Laurence, Ester Hauser 1935- 7
Laurence, (Jean) Margaret (Wemyss)
  1926-1987
  Obituary 50
Laurin, Anne
  See McLaurin, Anne
Lauritzen, Jonreed 1902- 13
Lauscher, Hermann
  See Hesse, Hermann
Laux, Dorothy 1920- 49
Lavine, David 1928- 31
Lavine, Sigmund A. 1908- 3
Laviolette, Emily A. 1923(?)-1975
  Brief Entry 49
Lawford, Paula Jane 1960-
  Brief Entry 53
Lawrence, Ann (Margaret)
  1942- 41
Lawrence, Isabelle (Wentworth)
  Brief Entry 29
Lawrence, J. T.
  See Rowland-Entwistle, (Arthur)
  Theodore (Henry)
Lawrence, John 1933- 30
Lawrence, Josephine 1890(?)-1978
  Obituary 24
Lawrence, Linda
  See Hunt, Linda Lawrence
Lawrence, Louise 1943- 38
Lawrence, Louise de Kiriline
  1894- 13
Lawrence, Mildred 1907- 3
Lawson, Carol (Antell) 1946- 42
Lawson, Don(ald Elmer)
  1917- 9
Lawson, Marion Tubbs 1896- 22
Lawson, Robert
  1892-1957 ....YABC 2
  See also CLR 2
Laycock, George (Edwin)
  1921- 5
Lazare, Gerald John 1927- 44
Lazare, Jerry
  See Lazare, Gerald John
Lazarevich, Mila 1942- 17
Lazarus, Keo Felker 1913- 21
Lea, Alec 1907- 19
Lea, Richard
  See Lea, Alec
Leach, Maria 1892-1977 39
  Brief Entry 28
Leacroft, Helen 1919- 6
Leacroft, Richard 1914- 6
Leaf, (Wilbur) Munro
  1905-1976 20
Leaf, VaDonna Jean 1929- 26
Leakey, Richard E(rskine Frere)
  1944- 42
Leander, Ed
  See Richelson, Geraldine
Lear, Edward 1812-1888 18
  See also CLR 1
Leavitt, Jerome E(dward)
  1916- 23

LeBar, Mary E(velyn)
  1910-1982 35
LeCain, Errol 1941- 6
Leder, Jane Mersky 1945-
  Brief Entry 51
Lederer, Muriel 1929- 48
Lee, Amanda [Joint pseudonym]
  See Buckholtz, Eileen (Garber)
Lee, Benjamin 1921- 27
Lee, Betsy 1949- 37
Lee, Carol
  See Fletcher, Helen Jill
Lee, Dennis (Beynon) 1939- 14
  See also CLR 3
Lee, Doris (Emrick)
  1905-1983 44
  Obituary 35
Lee, (Nelle) Harper 1926- 11
Lee, John R(obert) 1923-1976 27
Lee, Manning de V(illeneuve)
  1894-1980 37
  Obituary 22
Lee, Marian
  See Clish, (Lee) Marian
Lee, Mary Price 1934- 8
Lee, Mildred 1908- 6
Lee, Robert C. 1931- 20
Lee, Robert J. 1921- 10
Lee, Roy
  See Hopkins, Clark
Lee, Tanith 1947- 8
Leedy, Loreen (Janelle) 1959-
  Brief Entry 50
Leekley, Thomas B(riggs)
  1910- 23
Leeming, Jo Ann
  See Leeming, Joseph
Leeming, Joseph 1897-1968 26
Leeson, R. A.
  See Leeson, Robert (Arthur)
Leeson, Robert (Arthur) 1928- 42
Lefler, Irene (Whitney) 1917- 12
Le Gallienne, Eva 1899- 9
Legg, Sarah Martha Ross Bruggeman
  (?)-1982
  Obituary 40
LeGrand
  See Henderson, LeGrand
Le Guin, Ursula K(roeber)
  1929- 52
  Earlier sketch in SATA 4
  See also CLR 3
Legum, Colin 1919- 10
Lehn, Cornelia 1920- 46
Lehr, Delores 1920- 10
Leiber, Fritz 1910- 45
Leibold, Jay 1957-
  Brief Entry 52
Leichman, Seymour 1933- 5
Leigh, Tom 1947- 46
Leigh-Pemberton, John 1911- 35
Leighton, Clare (Veronica Hope)
  1900(?)- 37
Leighton, Margaret 1896-1987 1
  Obituary 52
Leipold, L. Edmond 1902- 16
Leisk, David (Johnson)
  1906-1975 30
  Obituary 26
  Earlier sketch in SATA 1

Leister, Mary 1917- 29
Leitch, Patricia 1933- 11
LeMair, H(enriette) Willebeek
    1889-1966
    Brief Entry 29
Lemke, Horst 1922- 38
Lenanton, C.
    See Oman, Carola (Mary Anima)
Lenard, Alexander 1910-1972
    Obituary 21
L'Engle, Madeleine 1918- 27
    Earlier sketch in SATA 1
    See also CLR 1, 14
Lengyel, Cornel Adam 1915- 27
Lengyel, Emil 1895-1985 3
    Obituary 42
Lens, Sidney 1912-1986 13
    Obituary 48
Lenski, Lois 1893-1974 26
    Earlier sketch in SATA 1
Lent, Blair 1930- 2
Lent, Henry Bolles 1901-1973 17
Leodhas, Sorche Nic
    See Alger, Leclaire (Gowans)
Leokum, Arkady 1916(?)- 45
Leonard, Constance (Brink)
    1923- 42
    Brief Entry 40
Leonard, Jonathan N(orton)
    1903-1975 36
Leong Gor Yun
    See Ellison, Virginia Howell
Lerner, Aaron B(unsen) 1920- 35
Lerner, Carol 1927- 33
Lerner, Marguerite Rush
    1924-1987 11
    Obituary 51
Lerner, Sharon (Ruth)
    1938-1982 11
    Obituary 29
Leroe, Ellen W(hitney) 1949-
    Brief Entry 51
LeRoy, Gen 52
    Brief Entry 36
Lerrigo, Marion Olive 1898-1968
    Obituary 29
LeShan, Eda J(oan) 1922- 21
    See also CLR 6
LeSieg, Theo
    See Geisel, Theodor Seuss
Leslie, Robert Franklin 1911- 7
Leslie, Sarah
    See McGuire, Leslie (Sarah)
Lesser, Margaret 1899(?)-1979
    Obituary 22
Lesser, Rika 1953- 53
Lester, Alison 1952- 50
Lester, Helen 1936- 46
Lester, Julius B. 1939- 12
    See also CLR 2
Le Sueur, Meridel 1900- 6
Le Tord, Bijou 1945- 49
Leutscher, Alfred (George)
    1913- 23
Levai, Blaise 1919- 39
Levin, Betty 1927- 19
Levin, Marcia Obrasky 1918- 13
Levin, Meyer 1905-1981 21
    Obituary 27

Levine, Abby 1943-
    Brief Entry 52
Levine, David 1926- 43
    Brief Entry 35
Levine, Edna S(imon) 35
Levine, I(srael) E. 1923- 12
Levine, Joan Goldman 11
Levine, Joseph 1910- 33
Levine, Rhoda 14
Levinson, Nancy Smiler
    1938- 33
Levinson, Riki 52
    Brief Entry 49
Levitin, Sonia 1934- 4
    See also SAAS 2
Levoy, Myron 49
    Brief Entry 37
Levy, Elizabeth 1942- 31
Lewees, John
    See Stockton, Francis Richard
Lewin, Betsy 1937- 32
Lewin, Hugh (Francis) 1939-
    Brief Entry 40
    See also CLR 9
Lewin, Ted 1935- 21
Lewis, Alfred E. 1912-1968
    Brief Entry 32
Lewis, Alice C. 1936- 46
Lewis, Alice Hudson 1895(?)-1971
    Obituary 29
Lewis, (Joseph) Anthony
    1927- 27
Lewis, C(live) S(taples)
    1898-1963 13
    See also CLR 3
Lewis, Claudia (Louise) 1907- 5
Lewis, E. M. 20
Lewis, Elizabeth Foreman
    1892-1958 ....YABC 2
Lewis, Francine
    See Wells, Helen
Lewis, Hilda (Winifred) 1896-1974
    Obituary 20
Lewis, Lucia Z.
    See Anderson, Lucia (Lewis)
Lewis, Marjorie 1929- 40
    Brief Entry 35
Lewis, Paul
    See Gerson, Noel B(ertram)
Lewis, Richard 1935- 3
Lewis, Roger
    See Zarchy, Harry
Lewis, Shari 1934- 35
    Brief Entry 30
Lewis, Thomas P(arker) 1936- 27
Lewiton, Mina 1904-1970 2
Lexau, Joan M. 36
    Earlier sketch in SATA 1
Ley, Willy 1906-1969 2
Leydon, Rita (Flodén) 1949- 21
Leyland, Eric (Arthur) 1911- 37
L'Hommedieu, Dorothy K(easley)
    1885-1961
    Obituary 29
Libby, Bill
    See Libby, William M.
Libby, William M. 1927-1984 5
    Obituary 39
Liberty, Gene 1924- 3

Liebers, Arthur 1913- 12
Lieblich, Irene 1923- 22
Liers, Emil E(rnest)
    1890-1975 37
Lietz, Gerald S. 1918- 11
Lifton, Betty Jean 6
Lightner, A. M.
    See Hopf, Alice L.
Lignell, Lois 1911- 37
Lillington, Kenneth (James)
    1916- 39
Lilly, Charles
    Brief Entry 33
Lilly, Ray
    See Curtis, Richard (Alan)
Lim, John 1932- 43
Liman, Ellen (Fogelson)
    1936- 22
Limburg, Peter R(ichard)
    1929- 13
Lincoln, C(harles) Eric 1924- 5
Lindbergh, Anne
    See Sapieyevski, Anne Lindbergh
Lindbergh, Anne Morrow (Spencer)
    1906- 33
Lindbergh, Charles A(ugustus, Jr.)
    1902-1974 33
Lindblom, Steven (Winther)
    1946- 42
    Brief Entry 39
Linde, Gunnel 1924- 5
Lindgren, Astrid 1907- 38
    Earlier sketch in SATA 2
    See also CLR 1
Lindgren, Barbro 1937-
    Brief Entry 46
Lindman, Maj (Jan)
    1886-1972 43
Lindop, Edmund 1925- 5
Lindquist, Jennie Dorothea
    1899-1977 13
Lindquist, Willis 1908- 20
Lindsay, Norman (Alfred William)
    1879-1969
    See CLR 8
Lindsay, (Nicholas) Vachel
    1879-1931 40
Line, Les 1935- 27
Linfield, Esther 40
Lingard, Joan 8
    See also SAAS 5
Link, Martin 1934- 28
Lionni, Leo 1910- 8
    See also CLR 7
Lipinsky de Orlov, Lino S.
    1908- 22
Lipkind, William 1904-1974 15
Lipman, David 1931- 21
Lipman, Matthew 1923- 14
Lippincott, Bertram 1898(?)-1985
    Obituary 42
Lippincott, Joseph Wharton
    1887-1976 17
Lippincott, Sarah Lee 1920- 22
Lippman, Peter J. 1936- 31
Lipsyte, Robert 1938- 5
Lisker, Sonia O. 1933- 44
Lisle, Janet Taylor
    Brief Entry 47

Lisle, Seward D.
See Ellis, Edward S(ylvester)
Lisowski, Gabriel 1946- 47
Brief Entry 31
Liss, Howard 1922- 4
Lissim, Simon 1900-1981
Brief Entry 28
List, Ilka Katherine 1935- 6
Liston, Robert A. 1927- 5
Litchfield, Ada B(assett)
1916- 5
Litowinsky, Olga (Jean) 1936- 26
Littke, Lael J. 1929- 51
Little, A. Edward
See Klein, Aaron E.
Little, (Flora) Jean 1932- 2
See also CLR 4
Little, Lessie Jones 1906-1986
Obituary 50
Little, Mary E. 1912- 28
Littledale, Freya (Lota) 2
Lively, Penelope 1933- 7
See also CLR 7
Liversidge, (Henry) Douglas
1913- 8
Livingston, Carole 1941- 42
Livingston, Myra Cohn 1926- 5
See also CLR 7
See also SAAS 1
Livingston, Richard R(oland)
1922- 8
Llerena-Aguirre, Carlos Antonio
1952- 19
Llewellyn, Richard
See Llewellyn Lloyd, Richard
Dafydd Vyvyan
Llewellyn, T. Harcourt
See Hamilton, Charles H. St. John
Llewellyn Lloyd, Richard Dafydd
Vyvyan 1906-1983 11
Obituary 37
Lloyd, E. James
See James, Elizabeth
Lloyd, Errol 1943- 22
Lloyd, James
See James, Elizabeth
Lloyd, Norman 1909-1980
Obituary 23
Lloyd, (Mary) Norris 1908- 10
Lobel, Anita 1934- 6
Lobel, Arnold 1933- 6
See also CLR 5
Lobsenz, Amelia 12
Lobsenz, Norman M. 1919- 6
Lochak, Michèle 1936- 39
Lochlons, Colin
See Jackson, C. Paul
Locke, Clinton W. [Collective
pseudonym] 1
Locke, Lucie 1904- 10
Locker, Thomas 1937-
See CLR 14
Lockwood, Mary
See Spelman, Mary
Lodge, Bernard 1933- 33
Lodge, Maureen Roffey
See Roffey, Maureen
Loeb, Robert H., Jr. 1917- 21
Loeper, John J(oseph) 1929- 10

Loescher, Ann Dull 1942- 20
Loescher, Gil(burt Damian)
1945- 20
Loewenstein, Bernice
Brief Entry 40
Löfgren, Ulf 1931- 3
Lofting, Hugh 1886-1947 15
Lofts, Norah (Robinson)
1904-1983 8
Obituary 36
Logue, Christopher 1926- 23
Loken, Newton (Clayton)
1919- 26
Lomas, Steve
See Brennan, Joseph L.
Lomask, Milton 1909- 20
London, Jack 1876-1916 18
London, Jane
See Geis, Darlene
London, John Griffith
See London, Jack
Lonergan, (Pauline) Joy (Maclean)
1909- 10
Lonette, Reisie (Dominee)
1924- 43
Long, Earlene (Roberta)
1938- 50
Long, Helen Beecher [Collective
pseudonym] 1
Long, Judith Elaine 1953- 20
Long, Judy
See Long, Judith Elaine
Long, Laura Mooney 1892-1967
Obituary 29
Longfellow, Henry Wadsworth
1807-1882 19
Longman, Harold S. 1919- 5
Longsworth, Polly 1933- 28
Longtemps, Kenneth 1933- 17
Longway, A. Hugh
See Lang, Andrew
Loomis, Robert D. 5
Lopshire, Robert 1927- 6
Lord, Athena V. 1932- 39
Lord, Beman 1924- 5
Lord, (Doreen Mildred) Douglas
1904- 12
Lord, John Vernon 1939- 21
Lord, Nancy
See Titus, Eve
Lord, Walter 1917- 3
Lorenz, Lee (Sharp) 1932(?)-
Brief Entry 39
Lorenzini, Carlo 1826-1890 29
Loring, Emilie (Baker)
1864(?)-1951 51
Lorraine, Walter (Henry)
1929- 16
Loss, Joan 1933- 11
Lot, Parson
See Kingsley, Charles
Lothrop, Harriet Mulford Stone
1844-1924 20
Louie, Ai-Ling 1949- 40
Brief Entry 34
Louisburgh, Sheila Burnford
See Burnford, Sheila
Lourie, Helen
See Storr, Catherine (Cole)

Love, Katherine 1907- 3
Love, Sandra (Weller) 1940- 26
Lovelace, Delos Wheeler
1894-1967 7
Lovelace, Maud Hart
1892-1980 2
Obituary 23
Lovell, Ingraham
See Bacon, Josephine Dodge
(Daskam)
Lovett, Margaret (Rose) 1915- 22
Low, Alice 1926- 11
Low, Elizabeth Hammond
1898- 5
Low, Joseph 1911- 14
Lowe, Jay, Jr.
See Loper, John J(oseph)
Lowenstein, Dyno 1914- 6
Lowitz, Anson C.
1901(?)-1978 18
Lowitz, Sadyebeth (Heath)
1901-1969 17
Lowrey, Janette Sebring
1892- 43
Lowry, Lois 1937- 23
See also CLR 6
See also SAAS 3
Lowry, Peter 1953- 7
Lowther, George F. 1913-1975
Obituary 30
Lozier, Herbert 1915- 26
Lubell, Cecil 1912- 6
Lubell, Winifred 1914- 6
Lubin, Leonard B. 1943- 45
Brief Entry 37
Lucas, E(dward) V(errall)
1868-1938 20
Lucas, Jerry 1940- 33
Luce, Celia (Geneva Larsen)
1914- 38
Luce, Willard (Ray) 1914- 38
Luckhardt, Mildred Corell
1898- 5
Ludden, Allen (Ellsworth)
1918(?)-1981
Obituary 27
Ludlam, Mabel Cleland
See Widdemer, Mabel Cleland
Ludwig, Helen 33
Lueders, Edward (George)
1923- 14
Luenn, Nancy 1954- 51
Lufkin, Raymond H. 1897- 38
Lugard, Flora Louisa Shaw
1852-1929 21
Luger, Harriett M(andelay)
1914- 23
Luhrmann, Winifred B(ruce)
1934- 11
Luis, Earlene W. 1929- 11
Lum, Peter
See Crowe, Bettina Lum
Lund, Doris (Herold) 1919- 12
Lunn, Janet 1928- 4
Lurie, Alison 1926- 46
Lustig, Loretta 1944- 46
Luther, Frank 1905-1980
Obituary 25
Luttrell, Guy L. 1938- 22

Luttrell, Ida (Alleene) 1934- *40*
Brief Entry *35*
Lutzker, Edythe 1904- *5*
Luzzati, Emanuele 1912- *7*
Luzzatto, Paola (Caboara)
1938- *38*
Lydon, Michael 1942- *11*
Lyfick, Warren
See Reeves, Lawrence F.
Lyle, Katie Letcher 1938- *8*
Lynch, Lorenzo 1932- *7*
Lynch, Marietta 1947- *29*
Lynch, Patricia (Nora)
1898-1972 .... *9*
Lynds, Dennis 1924- *47*
Brief Entry *37*
Lyngseth, Joan
See Davies, Joan
Lynn, Mary
See Brokamp, Marilyn
Lynn, Patricia
See Watts, Mabel Pizzey
Lyon, Elinor 1921- *6*
Lyon, Lyman R.
See De Camp, L(yon) Sprague
Lyons, Dorothy 1907- *3*
Lyons, Grant 1941- *30*
Lystad, Mary (Hanemann)
1928- *11*
Lyttle, Richard B(ard) 1927- *23*
Lytton, Edward G(eorge) E(arle)
L(ytton) Bulwer-Lytton, Baron
1803-1873 .... *23*

M

Maar, Leonard (F., Jr.) 1927- *30*
Maas, Selve *14*
Mabery, D. L. 1953-
Brief Entry *53*
Mac
See MacManus, Seumas
Mac Aodhagáin, Eamon
See Egan, E(dward) W(elstead)
MacArthur-Onslow, Annette
(Rosemary) 1933- *26*
Macaulay, David (Alexander)
1946- *46*
Brief Entry *27*
See also CLR 3, 14
MacBeth, George 1932- *4*
MacClintock, Dorcas 1932- *8*
MacDonald, Anson
See Heinlein, Robert A(nson)
MacDonald, Betty (Campbell Bard)
1908-1958 ....*YABC 1*
Macdonald, Blackie
See Emrich, Duncan
Macdonald, Dwight
1906-1982 .... *29*
Obituary *33*
MacDonald, George
1824-1905 .... *33*
Mac Donald, Golden
See Brown, Margaret Wise
Macdonald, Marcia
See Hill, Grace Livingston

Macdonald, Mary
See Gifford, Griselda
Macdonald, Shelagh 1937- *25*
MacDonald, Suse 1940-
Brief Entry *52*
Macdonald, Zillah K(atherine)
1885- *11*
Mace, Elisabeth 1933- *27*
Mace, Varian 1938- *49*
MacEwen, Gwendolyn 1941- *50*
MacFarlan, Allan A.
1892-1982 .... *35*
MacFarlane, Iris 1922- *11*
MacGregor, Ellen 1906-1954 ..... *39*
Brief Entry *27*
MacGregor-Hastie, Roy 1929- *3*
Machetanz, Frederick 1908- *34*
Machin Goodall, Daphne
(Edith) *37*
MacInnes, Helen 1907-1985 ...... *22*
Obituary *44*
MacIntyre, Elisabeth 1916- *17*
Mack, Stan(ley) *17*
Mackay, Claire 1930- *40*
MacKaye, Percy (Wallace)
1875-1956 .... *32*
MacKellar, William 1914- *4*
Macken, Walter 1915-1967 .... *36*
Mackenzie, Dr. Willard
See Stratemeyer, Edward L.
MacKenzie, Garry 1921-
Brief Entry *31*
MacKinstry, Elizabeth
1879-1956 .... *42*
MacLachlan, Patricia 1938-
Brief Entry *42*
See also CLR 14
MacLean, Alistair (Stuart)
1923-1987 .... *23*
Obituary *50*
MacLeod, Beatrice (Beach)
1910- *10*
MacLeod, Charlotte (Matilda Hughes)
1922- *28*
MacLeod, Ellen Jane (Anderson)
1916- *14*
MacManus, James
See MacManus, Seumas
MacManus, Seumas
1869-1960 .... *25*
MacMaster, Eve (Ruth) B(owers)
1942- *46*
MacMillan, Annabelle
See Quick, Annabelle
MacPeek, Walter G.
1902-1973 .... *4*
Obituary *25*
MacPherson, Margaret 1908- *9*
See also SAAS 4
MacPherson, Thomas George
1915-1976
Obituary *30*
Macrae, Hawk
See Barker, Albert W.
MacRae, Travi
See Feagles, Anita (MacRae)
Macumber, Mari
See Sandoz, Mari
Madden, Don 1927- *3*

Maddison, Angela Mary
1923- *10*
Maddock, Reginald 1912- *15*
Madian, Jon 1941- *9*
Madison, Arnold 1937- *6*
Madison, Winifred *5*
Maestro, Betsy 1944-
Brief Entry *30*
Maestro, Giulio 1942- *8*
Magorian, James 1942- *32*
Maguire, Anne
See Nearing, Penny
Maguire, Gregory 1954- *28*
Maher, Ramona 1934- *13*
Mählqvist, (Karl) Stefan
1943- *30*
Mahon, Julia C(unha) 1916- *11*
Mahony, Elizabeth Winthrop
1948- *8*
Mahood, Kenneth 1930- *24*
Mahy, Margaret 1936- *14*
See also CLR 7
Maiden, Cecil (Edward)
1902-1981 .... *52*
Maidoff, Ilka List
See List, Ilka Katherine
Maik, Henri
See Hecht, Henri Joseph
Maiorano, Robert 1946- *43*
Maitland, Antony (Jasper)
1935- *25*
Major, Kevin 1949- *32*
See also CLR 11
Makie, Pam 1943- *37*
Malcolmson, Anne
See Storch, Anne B. von
Malcolmson, David 1899- *6*
Mali, Jane Lawrence 1937- *51*
Brief Entry *44*
Mallowan, Agatha Christie
See Christie, Agatha (Mary Clarissa)
Malmberg, Carl 1904- *9*
Malo, John 1911- *4*
Malory, (Sir) Thomas 1410(?)-1471(?)
Brief Entry *33*
Maltese, Michael 1908(?)-1981
Obituary *24*
Malvern, Corinne 1905-1956 ......*34*
Malvern, Gladys (?)-1962 ....*23*
Mama G.
See Davis, Grania
Manchel, Frank 1935- *10*
Manes, Stephen 1949- *42*
Brief Entry *40*
Manfred, Frederick F(eikema)
1912- *30*
Mangione, Jerre 1909- *6*
Mango, Karin N. 1936- *52*
Mangurian, David 1938- *14*
Maniscalco, Joseph 1926- *10*
Manley, Deborah 1932- *28*
Manley, Seon *15*
See also CLR 3
See also SAAS 2
Mann, Peggy *6*
Mannetti, Lisa 1953-
Brief Entry *51*
Mannheim, Grete (Salomon)
1909- *10*

Manniche, Lise 1943- 31
Manning, Rosemary 1911- 10
Manning-Sanders, Ruth 1895- 15
Manson, Beverlie 1945-
  Brief Entry 44
Manton, Jo
  See Gittings, Jo Manton
Manushkin, Fran 1942- 7
Mapes, Mary A.
  See Ellison, Virginia Howell
Mara, Barney
  See Roth, Arthur J(oseph)
Mara, Jeanette
  See Cebulash, Mel
Marais, Josef 1905-1978
  Obituary 24
Marasmus, Seymour
  See Rivoli, Mario
Marcellino
  See Agnew, Edith J.
Marchant, Bessie
  1862-1941 .... YABC 2
Marchant, Catherine
  See Cookson, Catherine (McMulen)
Marcher, Marion Walden
  1890- 10
Marcus, Rebecca B(rian)
  1907- 9
Margaret, Karla
  See Andersdatter, Karla M(argaret)
Margolis, Richard J(ules)
  1929- 4
Margolis, Vivienne 1922- 46
Mariana
  See Foster, Marian Curtis
Marino, Dorothy Bronson
  1912- 14
Maris, Ron
  Brief Entry 45
Mark, Jan 1943- 22
  See also CLR 11
Mark, Pauline (Dahlin) 1913- 14
Mark, Polly
  See Mark, Pauline (Dahlin)
Markins, W. S.
  See Jenkins, Marie M.
Markle, Sandra L(ee) 1946-
  Brief Entry 41
Marko, Katherine D(olores) 28
Marks, Burton 1930- 47
  Brief Entry 43
Marks, Hannah K.
  See Trivelpiece, Laurel
Marks, J
  See Highwater, Jamake
Marks, J(ames) M(acdonald)
  1921- 13
Marks, Margaret L. 1911(?)-1980
  Obituary 23
Marks, Mickey Klar 12
Marks, Peter
  See Smith, Robert Kimmel
Marks, Rita 1938- 47
Marks, Stan(ley) 1929- 14
Marks-Highwater, J
  See Highwater, Jamake
Markun, Patricia M(aloney)
  1924- 15

Marlowe, Amy Bell [Collective
  pseudonym] 1
Marokvia, Artur 1909- 31
Marokvia, Mireille (Journet)
  1918- 5
Marr, John S(tuart) 1940- 48
Marrin, Albert 1936- 53
  Brief Entry 43
Marriott, Alice Lee 1910- 31
Marriott, Pat(ricia) 1920- 35
Mars, W. T.
  See Mars, Witold Tadeusz J.
Mars, Witold Tadeusz J.
  1912- 3
Marsh, J. E.
  See Marshall, Evelyn
Marsh, Jean
  See Marshall, Evelyn
Marshall, Anthony D(ryden)
  1924- 18
Marshall, (Sarah) Catherine
  1914-1983 2
  Obituary 34
Marshall, Douglas
  See McClintock, Marshall
Marshall, Edward
  See Marshall, James (Edward)
Marshall, Evelyn 1897- 11
Marshall, James (Edward)
  1942- 51
  Earlier sketch in SATA 6
Marshall, James Vance
  See Payne, Donald Gordon
Marshall, Kim
  See Marshall, Michael (Kimbrough)
Marshall, Michael (Kimbrough)
  1948- 37
Marshall, Percy
  See Young, Percy M(arshall)
Marshall, S(amuel) L(yman) A(twood)
  1900-1977 21
Marsoli, Lisa Ann 1958-
  Brief Entry 53
Marsten, Richard
  See Hunter, Evan
Marston, Hope Irvin 1935- 31
Martchenko, Michael 1942- 50
Martignoni, Margaret E. 1908(?)-1974
  Obituary 27
Martin, Ann M(atthews)
  1955- 44
  Brief Entry 41
Martin, Bill, Jr.
  See Martin, William Ivan
Martin, David Stone 1913- 39
Martin, Dorothy 1921- 47
Martin, Eugene [Collective
  pseudonym] 1
Martin, Frances M(cEntee)
  1906- 36
Martin, Fredric
  See Christopher, Matt(hew F.)
Martin, J(ohn) P(ercival)
  1880(?)-1966 15
Martin, Jeremy
  See Levin, Marcia Obransky
Martin, Lynne 1923- 21
Martin, Marcia
  See Levin, Marcia Obransky

Martin, Nancy
  See Salmon, Annie Elizabeth
Martin, Patricia Miles
  1899-1986 43
  Obituary 48
  Earlier sketch in SATA 1
Martin, Peter
  See Chaundler, Christine
Martin, René 1891-1977 42
  Obituary 20
Martin, Rupert (Claude) 1905- ... 31
Martin, Stefan 1936- 32
Martin, Vicky
  See Storey, Victoria Carolyn
Martin, William Ivan 1916-
  Brief Entry 40
Martineau, Harriet
  1802-1876 .... YABC 2
Martini, Teri 1930- 3
Marx, Robert F(rank) 1936- 24
Marzani, Carl (Aldo) 1912- 12
Marzollo, Jean 1942- 29
Masefield, John 1878-1967 19
Mason, Edwin A. 1905-1979
  Obituary 32
Mason, F. van Wyck
  1901-1978 3
  Obituary 26
Mason, Frank W.
  See Mason, F. van Wyck
Mason, George Frederick
  1904- 14
Mason, Miriam (Evangeline)
  1900-1973 2
  Obituary 26
Mason, Tally
  See Derleth, August (William)
Mason, Van Wyck
  See Mason, F. van Wyck
Masselman, George
  1897-1971 19
Massie, Diane Redfield 16
Masters, Kelly R. 1897- 3
Masters, Mildred 1932- 42
Masters, William
  See Cousins, Margaret
Matchette, Katharine E. 1941- ... 38
Math, Irwin 1940- 42
Mathews, Janet 1914- 41
Mathews, Louise
  See Tooke, Louise Mathews
Mathiesen, Egon 1907-1976
  Obituary 28
Mathieu, Joe
  See Mathieu, Joseph P.
Mathieu, Joseph P. 1949- 43
  Brief Entry 36
Mathis, Sharon Bell 1937- 7
  See also CLR 3
  See also SAAS 3
Matson, Emerson N(els)
  1926- 12
Matsui, Tadashi 1926- 8
Matsuno, Masako 1935- 6
Matte, (Encarnacion) L'Enc
  1936- 22
Matthews, Ann
  See Martin, Ann M(atthews)
Matthews, Ellen 1950- 28

Matthews, Jacklyn Meek
  See Meek, Jacklyn O'Hanlon
Matthews, Patricia 1927- 28
Matthews, William Henry III
  1919- 45
  Brief Entry 28
Matthias, Catherine 1945-
  Brief Entry 41
Matthiessen, Peter 1927- 27
Mattingley, Christobel (Rosemary)
  1931- 37
Matulay, Laszlo 1912- 43
Matulka, Jan 1890-1972
  Brief Entry 28
Matus, Greta 1938- 12
Mauser, Patricia Rhoads
  1943- 37
Maves, Mary Carolyn 1916- 10
Maves, Paul B(enjamin)
  1913- 10
Mawicke, Tran 1911- 15
Max, Peter 1939- 45
Maxon, Anne
  See Best, Allena Champlin
Maxwell, Arthur S.
  1896-1970 11
Maxwell, Edith 1923- 7
May, Charles Paul 1920- 4
May, Julian 1931- 11
May, Robert Lewis 1905-1976
  Obituary 27
May, Robert Stephen 1929- 46
May, Robin
  See May, Robert Stephen
Mayberry, Florence V(irginia
  Wilson) 10
Mayer, Albert Ignatius, Jr. 1906-1960
  Obituary 29
Mayer, Ann M(argaret) 1938- 14
Mayer, Jane Rothschild 1903- 38
Mayer, Marianna 1945- 32
Mayer, Mercer 1943- 32
  Earlier sketch in SATA 16
  See also CLR 11
Mayerson, Charlotte Leon 36
Mayhar, Ardath 1930- 38
Maynard, Chris
  See Maynard, Christopher
Maynard, Christopher 1949-
  Brief Entry 43
Maynard, Olga 1920- 40
Mayne, William 1928- 6
Maynes, Dr. J. O. Rocky
  See Maynes, J. Oscar, Jr.
Maynes, J. O. Rocky, Jr.
  See Maynes, J. Oscar, Jr.
Maynes, J. Oscar, Jr. 1929- 38
Mayo, Margaret (Mary) 1935- 38
Mays, Lucinda L(a Bella)
  1924- 49
Mays, (Lewis) Victor, (Jr.)
  1927- 5
Mazer, Harry 1925- 31
Mazer, Norma Fox 1931- 24
  See also SAAS 1
Mazza, Adriana 1928- 19
McBain, Ed
  Hunter, Evan
  ry, Janet 1936- 38

McCaffrey, Anne 1926- 8
McCaffrey, Mary
  See Szudek, Agnes S(usan)
  P(hilomena)
McCain, Murray (David, Jr.)
  1926-1981 7
  Obituary 29
McCall, Edith S. 1911- 6
McCall, Virginia Nielsen
  1909- 13
McCallum, Phyllis 1911- 10
McCann, Gerald 1916- 41
McCannon, Dindga Fatima
  1947- 41
McCarter, Neely Dixon 1929- 47
McCarthy, Agnes 1933- 4
McCarty, Rega Kramer 1904- 10
McCaslin, Nellie 1914- 12
McCaughrean, Geraldine
  See Jones, Geraldine
McCay, Winsor 1869-1934 41
McClintock, Marshall
  1906-1967 3
McClintock, Mike
  See McClintock, Marshall
McClintock, Theodore
  1902-1971 14
McClinton, Leon 1933- 11
McCloskey, (John) Robert
  1914- 39
  Earlier sketch in SATA 2
  See also CLR 7
McClung, Robert M. 1916- 2
  See also CLR 11
McClure, Gillian Mary 1948- 31
McConnell, James Douglas
  (Rutherford) 1915- 40
McCord, Anne 1942- 41
McCord, David (Thompson Watson)
  1897- 18
  See also CLR 9
McCord, Jean 1924- 34
McCormick, Brooks
  See Adams, William Taylor
McCormick, Dell J.
  1892-1949 19
McCormick, (George) Donald (King)
  1911- 14
McCormick, Edith (Joan)
  1934- 30
McCourt, Edward (Alexander)
  1907-1972
  Obituary 28
McCoy, Iola Fuller 3
McCoy, J(oseph) J(erome)
  1917- 8
McCoy, Lois (Rich) 1941- 38
McCrady, Lady 1951- 16
McCrea, James 1920- 3
McCrea, Ruth 1921- 3
McCullers, (Lula) Carson
  1917-1967 27
McCulloch, Derek (Ivor Breashur)
  1897-1967
  Obituary 29
McCulloch, Sarah
  See Ure, Jean
McCullough, Frances Monson
  1938- 8

McCully, Emily Arnold 1939- 5
  See also Arnold, Emily
McCurdy, Michael 1942- 13
McDearmon, Kay 20
McDermott, Beverly Brodsky
  1941- 11
McDermott, Gerald 1941- 16
  See also CLR 9
McDole, Carol
  See Farley, Carol
McDonald, Gerald D.
  1905-1970 3
McDonald, Jamie
  See Heide, Florence Parry
McDonald, Jill (Masefield)
  1927-1982 13
  Obituary 29
McDonald, Lucile Saunders
  1898- 10
McDonnell, Christine 1949- 34
McDonnell, Lois Eddy 1914- 10
McEntee, Dorothy (Layng)
  1902- 37
McEwen, Robert (Lindley) 1926-1980
  Obituary 23
McFall, Christie 1918- 12
McFarland, Kenton D(ean)
  1920- 11
McFarlane, Leslie 1902-1977 31
McGaw, Jessie Brewer 1913- 10
McGee, Barbara 1943- 6
McGiffin, (Lewis) Lee (Shaffer)
  1908- 1
McGill, Marci
  See Ridlon, Marci
McGinley, Phyllis 1905-1978 44
  Obituary 24
  Earlier sketch in SATA 2
McGinnis, Lila S(prague)
  1924- 44
McGough, Elizabeth (Hemmes)
  1934- 33
McGovern, Ann 8
McGowen, Thomas E. 1927- 2
McGowen, Tom
  See McGowen, Thomas E.
McGrady, Mike 1933- 6
McGrath, Thomas 1916- 41
McGraw, Eloise Jarvis 1915- 1
  See also SAAS 6
McGraw, William Corbin
  1916- 3
McGregor, Craig 1933- 8
McGregor, Iona 1929- 25
McGuire, Edna 1899- 13
McGuire, Leslie (Sarah)
  1945- 52
  Brief Entry 45
McGurk, Slater
  See Roth, Arthur J(oseph)
McHargue, Georgess 4
  See also CLR 2
  See also SAAS 5
McHugh, (Berit) Elisabet 1941-
  Brief Entry 44
McIlwraith, Maureen 1922- 2
McInerney, Judith Whitelock
  1945- 49
  Brief Entry 46

McKay, Donald 1895- *45*
McKay, Robert W. 1921- *15*
McKeever, Marcia
   See Laird, Jean E(louise)
McKenzie, Dorothy Clayton
   1910-1981
   Obituary *28*
McKillip, Patricia A(nne)
   1948- *30*
McKim, Audrey Margaret
   1909- *47*
McKinley, (Jennifer Carolyn)
   Robin *50*
   Brief Entry *32*
   See also CLR 10
McKissack, Fredrick L(emuel) 1939-
   Brief Entry *53*
McKissack, Patricia (L'Ann) C(arwell)
   1944-
   Brief Entry *51*
McKown, Robin *6*
McLaurin, Anne 1953- *27*
McLean, Kathryn (Anderson)
   1909-1966 .... *9*
McLeish, Kenneth 1940- *35*
McLenighan, Valjean 1947- *46*
   Brief Entry *40*
McLeod, Emilie Warren
   1926-1982 .... *23*
   Obituary *31*
McLeod, Kirsty
   See Hudson, (Margaret) Kirsty
McLeod, Margaret Vail
   See Holloway, Teresa (Bragunier)
McLoughlin, John C. 1949- *47*
McMahan, Ian
   Brief Entry *45*
McManus, Patrick (Francis)
   1933- *46*
McMeekin, Clark
   See McMeekin, Isabel McLennan
McMeekin, Isabel McLennan
   1895- *3*
McMillan, Bruce 1947- *22*
McMullan, Kate (Hall) 1947- *52*
   Brief Entry *48*
McMullan, Katy Hall
   See McMullan, Kate (Hall)
McMullen, Catherine
   See Cookson, Catherine (McMullen)
McMurtrey, Martin A(loysius)
   1921- *21*
McNair, Kate *3*
McNamara, Margaret C(raig)
   1915-1981
   Obituary *24*
McNaught, Harry *32*
McNaughton, Colin 1951- *39*
McNeely, Jeannette 1918- *25*
McNeer, May *1*
McNeill, Janet 1907- *1*
McNickle, (William) D'Arcy
   1904-1977
   Obituary *22*
McNulty, Faith 1918- *12*
McPhail, David M(ichael)
   1940- *47*
   Brief Entry *32*

McPharlin, Paul 1903-1948
   Brief Entry *31*
McPhee, Richard B(yron)
   1934- *41*
McPherson, James M. 1936- *16*
McQueen, Lucinda
   Brief Entry *48*
McQueen, Mildred Hark
   1908- *12*
McShean, Gordon 1936- *41*
McSwigan, Marie 1907-1962 ..... *24*
McVicker, Charles (Taggart)
   1930- *39*
McVicker, Chuck
   See McVicker, Charles (Taggart)
McWhirter, Norris (Dewar)
   1925- *37*
McWhirter, (Alan) Ross
   1925-1975 .... *37*
   Obituary *31*
Mead, Margaret 1901-1978
   Obituary *20*
Mead, Russell (M., Jr.) 1935- *10*
Mead, Stella (?)-1981
   Obituary *27*
Meade, Ellen (Roddick) 1936- *5*
Meade, Marion 1934- *23*
Meader, Stephen W(arren)
   1892- *1*
Meadow, Charles T(roub)
   1929- *23*
Meadowcroft, Enid LaMonte
   See Wright, Enid Meadowcroft
Meaker, M. J.
   See Meaker, Marijane
Meaker, Marijane 1927- *20*
Means, Florence Crannell
   1891-1980 .... *1*
   Obituary *25*
Mearian, Judy Frank 1936- *49*
Medary, Marjorie 1890- *14*
Meddaugh, Susan 1944- *29*
Medearis, Mary 1915- *5*
Mee, Charles L., Jr. 1938- *8*
Meek, Jacklyn O'Hanlon
   1933- *51*
   Brief Entry *34*
Meek, S(terner St.) P(aul) 1894-1972
   Obituary *28*
Meeker, Oden 1918(?)-1976 ...... *14*
Meeks, Esther MacBain *1*
Meggendorfer, Lothar 1847-1925
   Brief Entry *36*
Mehdevi, Alexander 1947- *7*
Mehdevi, Anne (Marie)
   Sinclair *8*
Meighan, Donald Charles
   1929- *30*
Meigs, Cornelia Lynde
   1884-1973 .... *6*
Meilach, Dona Z(weigoron)
   1926- *34*
Melady, John 1938-
   Brief Entry *49*
Melcher, Daniel 1912-1985
   Obituary *43*
Melcher, Frederic Gershom 1879-1963
   Obituary *22*

Melcher, Marguerite Fellows
   1879-1969 .... *10*
Melin, Grace Hathaway
   1892-1973 .... *10*
Mellersh, H(arold) E(dward) L(eslie)
   1897- *10*
Meltzer, Milton 1915- *50*
   Earlier sketch in SATA 1
   See also SAAS 1
   See also CLR 13
Melville, Anne
   See Potter, Margaret (Newman)
Melwood, Mary
   See Lewis, E. M.
Melzack, Ronald 1929- *5*
Memling, Carl 1918-1969 .... *6*
Mendel, Jo [House pseudonym]
   See Bond, Gladys Baker
Mendonca, Susan
   Brief Entry *49*
   See also Smith, Susan Vernon
Mendoza, George 1934- *41*
   Brief Entry *39*
Meng, Heinz (Karl) 1924- *13*
Menotti, Gian Carlo 1911- *29*
Menuhin, Yehudi 1916- *40*
Mercer, Charles (Edward)
   1917- *16*
Meredith, David William
   See Miers, Earl Schenck
Meriwether, Louise 1923- *52*
   Brief Entry *31*
Merriam, Eve 1916- *40*
   Earlier sketch in SATA 3
   See also CLR 14
Merrill, Jane 1946- *42*
Merrill, Jean (Fairbanks)
   1923- *1*
Merrill, Phil
   See Merrill, Jane
Mertz, Barbara (Gross) 1927- *49*
Merwin, Decie 1894-1961
   Brief Entry *32*
Messick, Dale 1906-
   Brief Entry *48*
Messmer, Otto 1892(?)-1983 ...... *37*
Metcalf, Suzanne
   See Baum, L(yman) Frank
Metos, Thomas H(arry) 1932- *37*
Meyer, Carolyn 1935- *9*
Meyer, Edith Patterson 1895- *5*
Meyer, F(ranklyn) E(dward)
   1932- *9*
Meyer, Jean Shepherd 1929- *11*
Meyer, Jerome Sydney
   1895-1975 .... *3*
   Obituary *25*
Meyer, June
   See Jordan, June
Meyer, Kathleen Allan 1918- *51*
   Brief Entry *46*
Meyer, Louis A(lbert) 1942- *12*
Meyer, Renate 1930- *6*
Meyers, Susan 1942- *19*
Meynier, Yvonne (Pollet)
   1908- ....
Mezey, Robert 1935- ....

Mian, Mary (Lawrence Shipman)
1902-
  Brief Entry *47*
Micale, Albert 1913- *22*
Michaels, Barbara
  See Mertz, Barbara (Gross)
Michaels, Ski
  See Pellowski, Michael J(oseph)
Michel, Anna 1943- *49*
  Brief Entry *40*
Micklish, Rita 1931- *12*
Miers, Earl Schenck
  1910-1972 .... *1*
  Obituary *26*
Miklowitz, Gloria D. 1927- *4*
Mikolaycak, Charles 1937- *9*
  See also SAAS 4
Mild, Warren (Paul) 1922- *41*
Miles, Betty 1928- *8*
Miles, Miska
  See Martin, Patricia Miles
Miles, (Mary) Patricia 1930- *29*
Miles, Patricia A.
  See Martin, Patricia Miles
Milgrom, Harry 1912- *25*
Milhous, Katherine 1894-1977 .... *15*
Militant
  See Sandburg, Carl (August)
Millar, Barbara F. 1924- *12*
Miller, Albert G(riffith)
  1905-1982 .... *12*
  Obituary *31*
Miller, Alice P(atricia
  McCarthy) *22*
Miller, Don 1923- *15*
Miller, Doris R.
  See Mosesson, Gloria R(ubin)
Miller, Eddie
  See Miller, Edward
Miller, Edna (Anita) 1920- *29*
Miller, Edward 1905-1974 .... *8*
Miller, Elizabeth 1933- *41*
Miller, Eugene 1925- *33*
Miller, Frances A. 1937- *52*
  Brief Entry *46*
Miller, Helen M(arkley) *5*
Miller, Helen Topping 1884-1960
  Obituary *29*
Miller, Jane (Judith) 1925- *15*
Miller, John
  See Samachson, Joseph
Miller, Margaret J.
  See Dale, Margaret J(essy) Miller
Miller, Marilyn (Jean) 1925- *33*
Miller, Mary Beth 1942- *9*
Miller, Natalie 1917-1976 .... *35*
Miller, Ruth White
  See White, Ruth C.
Miller, Sandy (Peden) 1948- *41*
  Brief Entry *35*
Milligan, Spike
  See Milligan, Terence Alan
Milligan, Terence Alan 1918- *29*
Mills, Claudia 1954- *44*
  Brief Entry *41*
Mills, Yaroslava Surmach
  1925- *35*
Millstead, Thomas Edward *30*

Milne, A(lan) A(lexander)
  1882-1956 ....*YABC 1*
  See also CLR 1
Milne, Lorus J. *5*
Milne, Margery *5*
Milonas, Rolf
  See Myller, Rolf
Milotte, Alfred G(eorge)
  1904- *11*
Milton, Hilary (Herbert)
  1920- *23*
Milton, John R(onald) 1924- *24*
Milton, Joyce 1946- *52*
  Brief Entry *41*
Milverton, Charles A.
  See Penzler, Otto
Minarik, Else Holmelund
  1920- *15*
Miner, Jane Claypool 1933- *38*
  Brief Entry *37*
Miner, Lewis S. 1909- *11*
Minier, Nelson
  See Stoutenburg, Adrien
Mintonye, Grace *4*
Mirsky, Jeannette 1903-1987 ...... *8*
  Obituary *51*
Mirsky, Reba Paeff
  1902-1966 .... *1*
Miskovits, Christine 1939- *10*
Miss Francis
  See Horwich, Frances R.
Miss Read
  See Saint, Dora Jessie
Mister Rogers
  See Rogers, Fred (McFeely)
Mitchell, Cynthia 1922- *29*
Mitchell, (Sibyl) Elyne (Keith)
  1913- *10*
Mitchell, Gladys (Maude Winifred)
  1901-1983 .... *46*
  Obituary *35*
Mitchell, Joyce Slayton 1933- *46*
  Brief Entry *43*
Mitchell, Yvonne 1925-1979
  Obituary *24*
Mitchison, Naomi Margaret (Haldane)
  1897- *24*
Mitchnik, Helen 1901- *41*
  Brief Entry *35*
Mitsuhashi, Yoko *45*
  Brief Entry *33*
Mizner, Elizabeth Howard
  1907- *27*
Mizumura, Kazue *18*
Moché, Dinah (Rachel) L(evine)
  1936- *44*
  Brief Entry *40*
Mochi, Ugo (A.) 1889-1977 ...... *38*
Modell, Frank B. 1917- *39*
  Brief Entry *36*
Moe, Barbara 1937- *20*
Moeri, Louise 1924- *24*
Moffett, Martha (Leatherwood)
  1934- *8*
Mofsie, Louis B. 1936-
  Brief Entry *33*
Mohn, Peter B(urnet) 1934- *28*
Mohn, Viola Kohl 1914- *8*
Mohr, Nicholasa 1935- *8*

Molarsky, Osmond 1909- *16*
Moldon, Peter L(eonard)
  1937- *49*
Mole, John 1941- *36*
Molloy, Anne Baker 1907- *32*
Molloy, Paul 1920- *5*
Momaday, N(avarre) Scott
  1934- *48*
  Brief Entry *30*
Moncure, Jane Belk *23*
Monjo, F(erdinand) N.
  1924-1978 .... *16*
  See also CLR 2
Monroe, Lyle
  See Heinlein, Robert A(nson)
Monroe, Marion 1898-1983
  Obituary *34*
Monsell, Helen (Albee)
  1895-1971 .... *24*
Montana, Bob 1920-1975
  Obituary *21*
Montgomerie, Norah Mary
  1913- *26*
Montgomery, Constance
  See Cappell, Constance
Montgomery, Elizabeth Rider
  1902-1985 .... *34*
  Obituary *41*
  Earlier sketch in SATA 3
Montgomery, L(ucy) M(aud)
  1874-1942 ....*YABC 1*
  See also CLR 8
Montgomery, R(aymond) A., (Jr.)
  1936- *39*
Montgomery, Rutherford George
  1894- *3*
Montgomery, Vivian *36*
Montresor, Beni 1926- *38*
  Earlier sketch in SATA 3
  See also SAAS 4
Moody, Ralph Owen 1898- *1*
Moon, Carl 1879-1948 .... *25*
Moon, Grace 1877(?)-1947 .... *25*
Moon, Sheila (Elizabeth)
  1910- *5*
Mooney, Elizabeth C(omstock)
  1918-1986
  Obituary *48*
Moor, Emily
  See Deming, Richard
Moore, Anne Carroll
  1871-1961 .... *13*
Moore, Clement Clarke
  1779-1863 .... *18*
Moore, Don W. 1905(?)-1986
  Obituary *48*
Moore, Eva 1942- *20*
Moore, Fenworth
  See Stratemeyer, Edward L.
Moore, Jack (William) 1941- *46*
  Brief Entry *32*
Moore, Janet Gaylord 1905- *18*
Moore, Jim 1946- *42*
Moore, John Travers 1908- *12*
Moore, Lamont 1909-
  Brief Entry *29*
Moore, Lilian 1909- *52*
Moore, Margaret Rumberger
  1903- *12*

Moore, Marianne (Craig)
  1887-1972 20
Moore, Patrick (Alfred) 1923- 49
  Brief Entry 39
Moore, Ray (S.) 1905(?)-1984
  Obituary 37
Moore, Regina
  See Dunne, Mary Collins
Moore, Rosalie
  See Brown, Rosalie (Gertrude)
  Moore
Moore, Ruth 23
Moore, Ruth Nulton 1923- 38
Moore, S. E. 23
Moores, Dick
  See Moores, Richard (Arnold)
Moores, Richard (Arnold) 1909-1986
  Obituary 48
Mooser, Stephen 1941- 28
Mordvinoff, Nicolas
  1911-1973 17
More, Caroline [Joint pseudonym]
  See Cone, Molly Lamken and
  Strachan, Margaret Pitcairn
Morey, Charles
  See Fletcher, Helen Jill
Morey, Walt 1907- 51
  Earlier sketch in SATA 3
Morgan, Alfred P(owell)
  1889-1972 33
Morgan, Alison Mary 1930- 30
Morgan, Ellen
  See Bumstead, Kathleen (Mary)
Morgan, Geoffrey 1916- 46
Morgan, Helen (Gertrude Louise)
  1921- 29
Morgan, Helen Tudor
  See Morgan, Helen (Gertrude
  Louise)
Morgan, Jane
  See Cooper, James Fenimore
Morgan, Lenore 1908- 8
Morgan, Louise
  See Morgan, Helen (Gertrude
  Louise)
Morgan, Shirley 1933- 10
Morgan, Tom 1942- 42
Morgenroth, Barbara
  Brief Entry 36
Morrah, Dave
  See Morrah, David Wardlaw, Jr.
Morrah, David Wardlaw, Jr.
  1914- 10
Morressy, John 1930- 23
Morrill, Leslie H(olt) 1934- 48
  Brief Entry 33
Morris, Desmond (John)
  1928- 14
Morris, Robert A. 1933- 7
Morris, William 1913- 29
Morrison, Bill 1935-
  Brief Entry 37
Morrison, Dorothy Nafus 29
Morrison, Gert W.
  See Stratemeyer, Edward L.
Morrison, Lillian 1917- 3
Morrison, Lucile Phillips
  1896- 17

Morrison, Roberta
  See Webb, Jean Francis (III)
Morrison, Velma Ford 1909- 21
Morrison, William
  See Samachson, Joseph
Morriss, James E(dward)
  1932- 8
Morrow, Betty
  See Bacon, Elizabeth
Morse, Carol
  See Yeakley, Marjory Hall
Morse, Dorothy B(ayley) 1906-1979
  Obituary 24
Morse, Flo 1921- 30
Mort, Vivian
  See Cromie, Alice Hamilton
Mortimer, Mary H.
  See Coury, Louise Andree
Morton, (Eva) Jane 1931- 50
Morton, Lee Jack, Jr. 1928- 32
Morton, Miriam 1918(?)-1985 9
  Obituary 46
Moscow, Alvin 1925- 3
Mosel, Arlene 1921- 7
Moser, Don
  See Moser, Donald Bruce
Moser, Donald Bruce 1932- 31
Mosesson, Gloria R(ubin) 24
Moskin, Marietta D(unston)
  1928- 23
Moskof, Martin Stephen
  1930- 27
Moss, Don(ald) 1920- 11
Moss, Elaine Dora 1924-
  Brief Entry 31
Most, Bernard 1937- 48
  Brief Entry 40
Motz, Lloyd 20
Mountain, Robert
  See Montgomery, R(aymond) A.,
  (Jr.)
Mountfield, David
  See Grant, Neil
Moussard, Jacqueline 1924- 24
Mowat, Farley 1921- 3
Moyler, Alan (Frank Powell)
  1926- 36
Mozley, Charles 1915- 43
  Brief Entry 32
Mrs. Fairstar
  See Horne, Richard Henry
Mueller, Virginia 1924- 28
Muir, Frank 1920- 30
Mukerji, Dhan Gopal
  1890-1936 40
  See also CLR 10
Mulcahy, Lucille Burnett 12
Mulford, Philippa Greene
  1948- 43
Mulgan, Catherine
  See Gough, Catherine
Muller, Billex
  See Ellis, Edward S(ylvester)
Mullins, Edward S(wift)
  1922- 10
Mulock, Dinah Maria
  See Craik, Dinah Maria (Mulock)
Mulvihill, William Patrick
  1923- 8

Mun
  See Leaf, (Wilbur) Munro
Munari, Bruno 1907- 15
  See also CLR 9
Munce, Ruth Hill 1898- 12
Munowitz, Ken 1935-1977 14
Muñoz, William 1949- 42
Munro, Alice 1931- 29
Munro, Eleanor 1928- 37
Munsch, Robert N. 1945- 50
  Brief Entry 48
Munsinger, Lynn 1951- 33
Munson(-Benson), Tunie
  1946- 15
Munthe, Nelly 1947- 53
Munves, James (Albert) 1922- 30
Munzer, Martha E. 1899- 4
Murch, Mel and Starr, Ward [Joint
  double pseudonym]
  See Manes, Stephen
Murphy, Barbara Beasley
  1933- 5
Murphy, E(mmett) Jefferson
  1926- 4
Murphy, Jill 1949- 37
Murphy, Jim 1947- 37
  Brief Entry 32
Murphy, Pat
  See Murphy, E(mmett) Jefferson
Murphy, Robert (William)
  1902-1971 10
Murphy, Shirley Rousseau
  1928- 36
Murray, John 1923- 39
Murray, Marian 5
Murray, Michele 1933-1974 7
Murray, Ossie 1938- 43
Musgrave, Florence 1902- 3
Musgrove, Margaret W(ynkoop)
  1943- 26
Mussey, Virginia T. H.
  See Ellison, Virginia Howell
Mutz
  See Kunstler, Morton
Myers, Arthur 1917- 35
Myers, Bernice 9
Myers, Caroline Elizabeth (Clark)
  1887-1980 28
Myers, Elisabeth P(erkins)
  1918- 36
Myers, Hortense (Powner)
  1913- 10
Myers, Walter Dean 1937- 41
  Brief Entry 27
  See also CLR 4
  See also SAAS 2
Myller, Rolf 1926- 27
Myra, Harold L(awrence)
  1939- 46
  Brief Entry 42
Myrus, Donald (Richard)
  1927- 23

N

Nakatani, Chiyoko 1930-
  Brief Entry 40
Namioka, Lensey 1929- 27

Napier, Mark
  See Laffin, John (Alfred Charles)
Nash, Bruce M(itchell) 1947- *34*
Nash, Linell
  See Smith, Linell Nash
Nash, Mary (Hughes) 1925- *41*
Nash, (Frederic) Ogden
  1902-1971 .... *46*
  Earlier sketch in SATA 2
Nast, Elsa Ruth
  See Watson, Jane Werner
Nast, Thomas 1840-1902 .... *51*
  Brief Entry *33*
Nastick, Sharon 1954- *41*
Nathan, Adele (Gutman) 1900(?)-1986
  Obituary *48*
Nathan, Dorothy (Goldeen)
  (?)-1966 .... *15*
Nathan, Robert (Gruntal)
  1894-1985 .... *6*
  Obituary *43*
Natti, Susanna 1948- *32*
Navarra, John Gabriel 1927- *8*
Naylor, Penelope 1941- *10*
Naylor, Phyllis Reynolds
  1933- *12*
Nazaroff, Alexander I. 1898- *4*
Neal, Harry Edward 1906- *5*
Nearing, Penny 1916- *47*
  Brief Entry *42*
Nebel, Gustave E. *45*
  Brief Entry *33*
Nebel, Mimouca
  See Nebel, Gustave E.
Nee, Kay Bonner *10*
Needle, Jan 1943- *30*
Needleman, Jacob 1934- *6*
Negri, Rocco 1932- *12*
Neigoff, Anne *13*
Neigoff, Mike 1920- *13*
Neilson, Frances Fullerton (Jones)
  1910- *14*
Neimark, Anne E. 1935- *4*
Neimark, Paul G. 1934-
  Brief Entry *37*
Nelson, Cordner (Bruce) 1918-
  Brief Entry *29*
Nelson, Esther L. 1928- *13*
Nelson, Lawrence E(rnest) 1928-1977
  Obituary *28*
Nelson, Mary Carroll 1929- *23*
Nerlove, Miriam 1959- *53*
  Brief Entry *49*
Nesbit, E(dith)
  1858-1924 .... *YABC 1*
  See also CLR 3
Nesbit, Troy
  See Folsom, Franklin
Nespojohn, Katherine V.
  1912- *7*
Ness, Evaline (Michelow)
  1911-1986 .... *26*
  Obituary *49*
  Earlier sketch in SATA 1
  See also CLR 6
  See also SAAS 1
Nestor, William P(rodromos)
  1947- *49*

Neufeld, John 1938- *6*
  See also SAAS 3
Neumeyer, Peter F(lorian)
  1929- *13*
Neurath, Marie (Reidemeister)
  1898- *1*
Neusner, Jacob 1932- *38*
Neville, Emily Cheney 1919- *1*
  See also SAAS 2
Neville, Mary
  See Woodrich, Mary Neville
Nevins, Albert J. 1915- *20*
Newberry, Clare Turlay
  1903-1970 .... *1*
  Obituary *26*
Newbery, John 1713-1767 .... *20*
Newcomb, Ellsworth
  See Kenny, Ellsworth Newcomb
Newcombe, Jack *45*
  Brief Entry *33*
Newell, Crosby
  See Bonsall, Crosby (Barbara
  Newell)
Newell, Edythe W. 1910- *11*
Newell, Hope (Hockenberry)
  1896-1965 .... *24*
Newfeld, Frank 1928- *26*
Newlon, (Frank) Clarke
  1905(?)-1982 .... *6*
  Obituary *33*
Newman, Daisy 1904- *27*
Newman, Gerald 1939- *46*
  Brief Entry *42*
Newman, Robert (Howard)
  1909- *4*
Newman, Shirlee Petkin
  1924- *10*
Newsom, Carol 1948- *40*
Newton, James R(obert)
  1935- *23*
Newton, Suzanne 1936- *5*
Ney, John 1923- *43*
  Brief Entry *33*
Nic Leodhas, Sorche
  See Alger, Leclaire (Gowans)
Nichols, Cecilia Fawn 1906- *12*
Nichols, Peter
  See Youd, (Christopher) Samuel
Nichols, (Joanna) Ruth 1948- *15*
Nicholson, Joyce Thorpe
  1919- *35*
Nickelsburg, Janet 1893- *11*
Nickerson, Betty
  See Nickerson, Elizabeth
Nickerson, Elizabeth 1922- *14*
Nicklaus, Carol
  Brief Entry *33*
Nicol, Ann
  See Turnbull, Ann (Christine)
Nicolas
  See Mordvinoff, Nicolas
Nicolay, Helen
  1866-1954 .... *YABC 1*
Nicole, Christopher Robin
  1930- *5*
Nielsen, Kay (Rasmus)
  1886-1957 .... *16*
Nielsen, Virginia
  See McCall, Virginia Nielsen

Niland, Deborah 1951- *27*
Nixon, Hershell Howard
  1923- *42*
Nixon, Joan Lowery 1927- *44*
  Earlier sketch in SATA 8
Nixon, K.
  See Nixon, Kathleen Irene (Blundell)
Nixon, Kathleen Irene
  (Blundell) *14*
Noble, Iris 1922-1986 .... *5*
  Obituary *49*
Noble, Trinka Hakes
  Brief Entry *37*
Nodset, Joan L.
  See Lexau, Joan M.
Noguere, Suzanne 1947- *34*
Nolan, Dennis 1945- *42*
  Brief Entry *34*
Nolan, Jeannette Covert
  1897-1974 .... *2*
  Obituary *27*
Nolan, Paul T(homas) 1919- *48*
Nolan, William F(rancis) 1928-
  Brief Entry *28*
Noonan, Julia 1946- *4*
Norcross, John
  See Conroy, Jack (Wesley)
Nordhoff, Charles (Bernard)
  1887-1947 .... *23*
Nordlicht, Lillian *29*
Nordstrom, Ursula *3*
Norman, Charles 1904- *38*
Norman, James
  See Schmidt, James Norman
Norman, Mary 1931- *36*
Norman, Steve
  See Pashko, Stanley
Norris, Gunilla B(rodde)
  1939- *20*
North, Andrew
  See Norton, Alice Mary
North, Captain George
  See Stevenson, Robert Louis
North, Joan 1920- *16*
North, Robert
  See Withers, Carl A.
North, Sterling 1906-1974 .... *45*
  Obituary *26*
  Earlier sketch in SATA 1
Norton, Alice Mary 1912- *43*
  Earlier sketch in SATA 1
Norton, André
  See Norton, Alice Mary
Norton, Browning
  See Norton, Frank R(owland)
  B(rowning)
Norton, Frank R(owland) B(rowning)
  1909- *10*
Norton, Mary 1903- *18*
  See also CLR 6
Nöstlinger, Christine 1936-
  Brief Entry *37*
  See also CLR 12
Nourse, Alan E(dward) 1928- *48*
Novak, Matt 1962-
  Brief Entry *52*
Nowell, Elizabeth Cameron *12*
Numeroff, Laura Joffe 1953- *28*

Nurenberg, Thelma
See Greenhaus, Thelma Nurenberg
Nurnberg, Maxwell
1897-1984 27
Obituary 41
Nussbaumer, Paul (Edmond)
1934- 16
Nyce, (Nellie) Helene von Strecker
1885-1969 19
Nyce, Vera 1862-1925 19
Nye, Harold G.
See Harding, Lee
Nye, Robert 1939- 6

O

Oakes, Vanya 1909-1983 6
Obituary 37
Oakley, Don(ald G.) 1927- 8
Oakley, Graham 1929- 30
See also CLR 7
Oakley, Helen 1906- 10
Oana, Katherine D. 1929- 53
Brief Entry 37
Oana, Kay D.
See Oana, Katherine D.
Obligado, Lilian (Isabel) 1931-
Brief Entry 45
Obrant, Susan 1946- 11
O'Brien, Anne Sibley 1952- 53
Brief Entry 48
O'Brien, Esse Forrester 1895(?)-1975
Obituary 30
O'Brien, Robert C.
See Conly, Robert Leslie
See also CLR 2
O'Brien, Thomas C(lement)
1938- 29
O'Carroll, Ryan
See Markun, Patricia M(aloney)
O'Connell, Margaret F(orster)
1935-1977 49
Obituary 30
O'Connell, Peg
See Ahern, Margaret McCrohan
O'Connor, Jane 1947-
Brief Entry 47
O'Connor, Karen 1938- 34
O'Connor, Patrick
See Wibberley, Leonard (Patrick O'Connor)
O'Connor, Richard 1915-1975
Obituary 21
O'Daniel, Janet 1921- 24
O'Dell, Scott 1903- 12
See also CLR 1
Odenwald, Robert P(aul)
1899-1965 11
Odor, Ruth Shannon 1926-
Brief Entry 44
Oechsli, Kelly 1918- 5
Ofek, Uriel 1926- 36
Offit, Sidney 1928- 10
Ofosu-Appiah, L(awrence) H(enry)
1920- 13
Ogan, George F. 1912- 13

Ogan, M. G. [Joint pseudonym]
See Ogan, George F. and Ogan, Margaret E. (Nettles)
Ogan, Margaret E. (Nettles)
1923- 13
Ogburn, Charlton, Jr. 1911- 3
Ogilvie, Elisabeth May 1917- 40
Brief Entry 29
O'Hagan, Caroline 1946- 38
O'Hanlon, Jacklyn
See Meek, Jacklyn O'Hanlon
O'Hara, Mary
See Alsop, Mary O'Hara
Ohlsson, Ib 1935- 7
Ohtomo, Yasuo 1946- 37
O'Kelley, Mattie Lou 1908- 36
Okimoto, Jean Davies 1942- 34
Olcott, Frances Jenkins
1872(?)-1963 19
Old Boy
See Hughes, Thomas
Old Fag
See Bell, Robert S(tanley) W(arren)
Oldenburg, E(gbert) William
1936-1974 35
Olds, Elizabeth 1896- 3
Olds, Helen Diehl 1895-1981 9
Obituary 25
Oldstyle, Jonathan
See Irving, Washington
O'Leary, Brian 1940- 6
Oleksy, Walter 1930- 33
Olesky, Walter
See Oleksy, Walter
Oliver, John Edward 1933- 21
Olmstead, Lorena Ann 1890- 13
Olney, Ross R. 1929- 13
Olschewski, Alfred 1920- 7
Olsen, Ib Spang 1921- 6
Olson, Gene 1922- 32
Olson, Helen Kronberg 48
Olugebefola, Ademole 1941- 15
Oman, Carola (Mary Anima)
1897-1978 35
Ommanney, F(rancis) D(ownes)
1903-1980 23
O Mude
See Gorey, Edward St. John
Oneal, Elizabeth 1934- 30
Oneal, Zibby
See Oneal, Elizabeth
See also CLR 13
O'Neill, Judith (Beatrice)
1930- 34
O'Neill, Mary L(e Duc) 1908- 2
Onslow, John 1906-1985
Obituary 47
Opgenoorth, Winfried 1939-
Brief Entry 50
Opie, Iona 1923- 3
See also SAAS 6
Opie, Peter (Mason)
1918-1982 3
Obituary 28
Oppenheim, Joanne 1934- 5
Oppenheimer, Joan L(etson)
1925- 28
Optic, Oliver
See Adams, William Taylor

Orbach, Ruth Gary 1941- 21
Orczy, Emmuska, Baroness
1865-1947 40
O'Reilly, Sean
See Deegan, Paul Joseph
Orgel, Doris 1929- 7
Oriolo, Joe
See Oriolo, Joseph
Oriolo, Joseph 1913-1985
Obituary 46
Orleans, Ilo 1897-1962 10
Ormai, Stella
Brief Entry 48
Ormerod, Jan(ette Louise) 1946-
Brief Entry 44
Ormes, Jackie
See Ormes, Zelda J.
Ormes, Zelda J. 1914-1986
Obituary 47
Ormondroyd, Edward 1925- 14
Ormsby, Virginia H(aire) 11
Orris
See Ingelow, Jean
Orth, Richard
See Gardner, Richard
Orwell, George
See Blair, Eric Arthur
Osborne, Chester G. 1915- 11
Osborne, David
See Silverberg, Robert
Osborne, Leone Neal 1914- 2
Osborne, Mary Pope 1949-
Brief Entry 41
Osceola
See Blixen, Karen (Christentze Dinesen)
Osgood, William E(dward)
1926- 37
Osmond, Edward 1900- 10
Ossoli, Sarah Margaret (Fuller)
marchesa d' 1810-1850 25
Otis, James
See Kaler, James Otis
O'Trigger, Sir Lucius
See Horne, Richard Henry
Ottley, Reginald (Leslie) 26
Otto, Margaret Glover 1909-1976
Obituary 30
Ouida
See De La Ramée, (Marie) Louise
Ousley, Odille 1896- 10
Overton, Jenny (Margaret Mary)
1942- 52
Brief Entry 36
Owen, Caroline Dale
See Snedecker, Caroline Dale (Parke)
Owen, Clifford
See Hamilton, Charles H. St. John
Owen, Dilys
See Gater, Dilys
Owen, (Benjamin) Evan
1918-1984 38
Oxenbury, Helen 1938- 3

P

Pace, Mildred Mastin 1907- 46
Brief Entry 29

Packard, Edward 1931- *47*
Packer, Vin
 See Meaker, Marijane
Page, Eileen
 See Heal, Edith
Page, Eleanor
 See Coerr, Eleanor
Page, Lou Williams 1912- *38*
Paget-Fredericks, Joseph E. P. Rous-
 Marten 1903-1963
 Brief Entry *30*
Pahz, (Anne) Cheryl Suzanne
 1949- *11*
Pahz, James Alon 1943- *11*
Paice, Margaret 1920- *10*
Paige, Harry W. 1922- *41*
 Brief Entry *35*
Paine, Roberta M. 1925- *13*
Paisley, Tom
 See Bethancourt, T. Ernesto
Palazzo, Anthony D.
 1905-1970 .... *3*
Palazzo, Tony
 See Palazzo, Anthony D.
Palder, Edward L. 1922- *5*
Palladini, David (Mario)
 1946- *40*
 Brief Entry *32*
Pallas, Norvin 1918- *23*
Pallister, John C(lare) 1891-1980
 Obituary *26*
Palmer, Bernard 1914- *26*
Palmer, C(yril) Everard 1930- *14*
Palmer, (Ruth) Candida 1926- *11*
Palmer, Heidi 1948- *15*
Palmer, Helen Marion
 See Geisel, Helen
Palmer, Juliette 1930- *15*
Palmer, Robin 1911- *43*
Paltrowitz, Donna (Milman) 1950-
 Brief Entry *50*
Paltrowitz, Stuart 1946-
 Brief Entry *50*
Panetta, George 1915-1969 .... *15*
Panowski, Eileen Thompson
 1920- *49*
Pansy
 See Alden, Isabella (Macdonald)
Pantell, Dora (Fuchs) 1915- *39*
Panter, Carol 1936- *9*
Papas, William 1927- *50*
Papashvily, George
 1898-1978 .... *17*
Papashvily, Helen (Waite)
 1906- *17*
Pape, D(onna) L(ugg) 1930- *2*
Paperny, Myra (Green) 1932- *51*
 Brief Entry *33*
Paradis, Adrian A(lexis)
 1912- *1*
Paradis, Marjorie (Bartholomew)
 1886(?)-1970 .... *17*
Parenteau, Shirley (Laurolyn)
 1935- *47*
 Brief Entry *40*
Parish, Peggy 1927- *17*
Park, Barbara 1947- *40*
 Brief Entry *35*

Park, Bill
 See Park, W(illiam) B(ryan)
Park, Ruth *25*
Park, W(illiam) B(ryan) 1936- *22*
Parker, Elinor 1906- *3*
Parker, Lois M(ay) 1912- *30*
Parker, Margot M. 1937- *52*
Parker, Nancy Winslow 1930- *10*
Parker, Richard 1915- *14*
Parker, Robert
 See Boyd, Waldo T.
Parkinson, Ethelyn M(inerva)
 1906- *11*
Parks, Edd Winfield
 1906-1968 .... *10*
Parks, Gordon (Alexander Buchanan)
 1912- *8*
Parley, Peter
 See Goodrich, Samuel Griswold
Parlin, John
 See Graves, Charles Parlin
Parnall, Peter 1936- *16*
Parr, Letitia (Evelyn) 1906- *37*
Parr, Lucy 1924- *10*
Parrish, Anne 1888-1957 .... *27*
Parrish, Mary
 See Cousins, Margaret
Parrish, (Frederick) Maxfield
 1870-1966 .... *14*
Parry, Marian 1924- *13*
Parsons, Tom
 See MacPherson, Thomas George
Partch, Virgil Franklin II
 1916-1984 .... *45*
 Obituary *39*
Partridge, Benjamin W(aring), Jr.
 1915- *28*
Partridge, Jenny (Lilian)
 1947- *52*
 Brief Entry *37*
Pascal, David 1918- *14*
Pascal, Francine 1938- *51*
 Brief Entry *37*
Paschal, Nancy
 See Trotter, Grace V(iolet)
Pashko, Stanley 1913- *29*
Patent, Dorothy Hinshaw
 1940- *22*
Paterson, Diane (R. Cole) 1946-
 Brief Entry *33*
Paterson, Katherine (Womeldorf)
 1932- *53*
 Earlier sketch in SATA 13
 See also CLR 7
Paton, Alan (Stewart) 1903- *11*
Paton, Jane (Elizabeth) 1934- *35*
Paton Walsh, Gillian 1939- *4*
 See also SAAS 3
Patten, Brian 1946- *29*
Patterson, Geoffrey 1943-
 Brief Entry *44*
Patterson, Lillie G. *14*
Paul, Aileen 1917- *12*
Paul, Elizabeth
 See Crow, Donna Fletcher
Paul, James 1936- *23*
Paul, Robert
 See Roberts, John G(aither)

Pauli, Hertha (Ernestine)
 1909-1973 .... *3*
 Obituary *26*
Paull, Grace A. 1898- *24*
Paulsen, Gary 1939- *50*
 Earlier sketch in SATA 22
Paulson, Jack
 See Jackson, C. Paul
Pavel, Frances 1907- *10*
Payne, Donald Gordon 1924- *37*
Payne, Emmy
 See West, Emily G(ovan)
Payson, Dale 1943- *9*
Payzant, Charles *18*
Payzant, Jessie Mercer Knechtel
 See Shannon, Terry
Paz, A.
 See Pahz, James Alon
Paz, Zan
 See Pahz, Cheryl Suzanne
Peake, Mervyn 1911-1968 .... *23*
Peale, Norman Vincent 1898- *20*
Pearce, (Ann) Philippa 1920- *1*
 See also CLR 9
Peare, Catherine Owens 1911- *9*
Pears, Charles 1873-1958
 Brief Entry *30*
Pearson, Gayle 1947- *53*
Pearson, Susan 1946- *39*
 Brief Entry *27*
Pease, Howard 1894-1974 .... *2*
 Obituary *25*
Peck, Anne Merriman 1884- *18*
Peck, Richard 1934- *18*
 See also SAAS 2
Peck, Robert Newton III
 1928- *21*
 See also SAAS 1
Peek, Merle 1938- *39*
Peel, Norman Lemon
 See Hirsch, Phil
Peeples, Edwin A. 1915- *6*
Peet, Bill
 See Peet, William Bartlett
 See also CLR 12
Peet, Creighton B. 1899-1977 ..... *30*
Peet, William Bartlett 1915- *41*
 Earlier sketch in SATA 2
Peirce, Waldo 1884-1970
 Brief Entry *28*
Pelaez, Jill 1924- *12*
Pellowski, Anne 1933- *20*
Pellowski, Michael J(oseph) 1949-
 Brief Entry *48*
Pelta, Kathy 1928- *18*
Peltier, Leslie C(opus) 1900- *13*
Pembury, Bill
 See Gronon, Arthur William
Pemsteen, Hans
 See Manes, Stephen
Pendennis, Arthur, Esquire
 See Thackeray, William Makepeace
Pender, Lydia 1907- *3*
Pendery, Rosemary *7*
Pendle, Alexy 1943- *29*
Pendle, George 1906-1977
 Obituary *28*
Penn, Ruth Bonn
 See Rosenberg, Ethel

Pennage, E. M.
  See Finkel, George (Irvine)
Penney, Grace Jackson 1904- 35
Pennington, Eunice 1923- 27
Pennington, Lillian Boyer
  1904- 45
Penrose, Margaret
  See Stratemeyer, Edward L.
Penzler, Otto 1942- 38
Pepe, Phil(ip) 1935- 20
Peppe, Rodney 1934- 4
Percy, Charles Henry
  See Smith, Dodie
Perera, Thomas Biddle 1938- 13
Perez, Walter
  See Joseph, James (Herz)
Perkins, Al(bert Rogers)
  1904-1975 30
Perkins, Marlin 1905-1986 21
  Obituary 48
Perl, Lila 6
Perl, Susan 1922-1983 22
  Obituary 34
Perlmutter, O(scar) William
  1920-1975 8
Perrault, Charles 1628-1703 25
Perreard, Suzanne Louise Butler 1919-
  Brief Entry 29
Perrine, Mary 1913- 2
Perry, Barbara Fisher
  See Fisher, Barbara
Perry, Patricia 1949- 30
Perry, Roger 1933- 27
Pershing, Marie
  See Schultz, Pearle Henriksen
Peters, Caroline
  See Betz, Eva Kelly
Peters, Elizabeth
  See Mertz, Barbara (Gross)
Peters, S. H.
  See Porter, William Sydney
Petersen, P(eter) J(ames)
  1941- 48
  Brief Entry 43
Petersham, Maud (Fuller)
  1890-1971 17
Petersham, Miska 1888-1960 17
Peterson, Esther (Allen) 1934- 35
Peterson, Hans 1922- 8
Peterson, Harold L(eslie)
  1922- 8
Peterson, Helen Stone 1910- 8
Peterson, Jeanne Whitehouse
  See Whitehouse, Jeanne
Peterson, Lorraine 1940-
  Brief Entry 44
Petie, Haris 1915- 10
Petrides, Heidrun 1944- 19
Petrie, Catherine 1947- 52
  Brief Entry 41
Petroski, Catherine (Ann Groom)
  1939- 48
Petrovich, Michael B(oro)
  1922- 40
Petrovskaya, Kyra
  See Wayne, Kyra Petrovskaya
Petry, Ann (Lane) 1908- 5
  See also CLR 12
Pevsner, Stella 8

Peyo
  See Culliford, Pierre
Peyton, K. M.
  See Peyton, Kathleen (Wendy)
  See also CLR 3
Peyton, Kathleen (Wendy)
  1929- 15
Pfeffer, Susan Beth 1948- 4
  See also CLR 11
Phelan, Josephine 1905-
  Brief Entry 30
Phelan, Mary Kay 1914- 3
Phelps, Ethel Johnston 1914- 35
Philbrook, Clem(ent E.) 1917- 24
Phillips, Betty Lou
  See Phillips, Elizabeth Louise
Phillips, Elizabeth Louise
  Brief Entry 48
Phillips, Irv
  See Phillips, Irving W.
Phillips, Irving W. 1908- 11
Phillips, Jack
  See Sandburg, Carl (August)
Phillips, Leon
  See Gerson, Noel B(ertram)
Phillips, Loretta (Hosey)
  1893- 10
Phillips, Louis 1942- 8
Phillips, Mary Geisler
  1881-1964 10
Phillips, Prentice 1894- 10
Phillpotts, Eden 1862-1960 24
Phipson, Joan
  See Fitzhardinge, Joan M.
  See also CLR 5
  See also SAAS 3
Phiz
  See Browne, Hablot Knight
Phleger, Fred B. 1909- 34
Phleger, Marjorie Temple
  1908(?)-1986 1
  Obituary 47
Phypps, Hyacinthe
  See Gorey, Edward St. John
Piaget, Jean 1896-1980
  Obituary 23
Piatti, Celestino 1922- 16
Picard, Barbara Leonie 1917- 2
Pickard, Charles 1932- 36
Pickering, James Sayre
  1897-1969 36
  Obituary 28
Pienkowski, Jan 1936- 6
  See also CLR 6
Pierce, Edith Gray 1893-1977 45
Pierce, Katherine
  See St. John, Wylly Folk
Pierce, Meredith Ann 1958-
  Brief Entry 48
Pierce, Ruth (Ireland) 1936- 5
Pierce, Tamora 1954- 51
  Brief Entry 49
Pierik, Robert 1921- 13
Pig, Edward
  See Gorey, Edward St. John
Pike, E(dgar) Royston 1896- 22
Pilarski, Laura 1926- 13
Pilgrim, Anne
  See Allan, Mabel Esther

Pilkington, Francis Meredyth
  1907- 4
Pilkington, Roger (Windle)
  1915- 10
Pinchot, David 1914(?)-1983
  Obituary 34
Pincus, Harriet 1938- 27
Pine, Tillie S(chloss) 1897- 13
Pinkerton, Kathrene Sutherland
  (Gedney) 1887-1967
  Obituary 26
Pinkney, Jerry 1939- 41
  Brief Entry 32
Pinkwater, Daniel Manus
  1941- 46
  Earlier sketch in SATA 8
  See also CLR 4
  See also SAAS 3
Pinner, Joma
  See Werner, Herma
Pioneer
  See Yates, Raymond F(rancis)
Piowaty, Kim Kennelly 1957- 49
Piper, Roger
  See Fisher, John (Oswald Hamilton)
Piper, Watty
  See Bragg, Mabel Caroline
Piro, Richard 1934- 7
Pirsig, Robert M(aynard)
  1928- 39
Pitman, (Isaac) James 1901-1985
  Obituary 46
Pitrone, Jean Maddern 1920- 4
Pitz, Henry C(larence)
  1895-1976 4
  Obituary 24
Pizer, Vernon 1918- 21
Place, Marian T. 1910- 3
Plaidy, Jean
  See Hibbert, Eleanor
Plaine, Alfred R. 1898(?)-1981
  Obituary 29
Platt, Kin 1911- 21
Plimpton, George (Ames)
  1927- 10
Plomer, William (Charles Franklin)
  1903-1973 24
Plotz, Helen (Ratnoff) 1913- 38
Plowden, David 1932- 52
Plowhead, Ruth Gipson
  1877-1967 43
Plowman, Stephanie 1922- 6
Pluckrose, Henry (Arthur)
  1931- 13
Plum, J.
  See Wodehouse, P(elham)
  G(renville)
Plum, Jennifer
  See Kurland, Michael (Joseph)
Plumb, Charles P. 1900(?)-1982
  Obituary 29
Plume, Ilse
  Brief Entry 43
Plummer, Margaret 1911- 2
Podendorf, Illa E.
  1903(?)-1983 18
  Obituary 35
Poe, Edgar Allan 1809-1849 23

Pogány, William Andrew
  1882-1955 44
Pogány, Willy
  Brief Entry 30
  See Pogány, William Andrew
Pohl, Frederik 1919- 24
Pohlmann, Lillian (Grenfell)
  1902- 11
Pointon, Robert
  See Rooke, Daphne (Marie)
Pola
  See Watson, Pauline
Polatnick, Florence T. 1923- 5
Polder, Markus
  See Krüss, James
Polette, Nancy (Jane) 1930- 42
Polhamus, Jean Burt 1928- 21
Politi, Leo 1908- 47
  Earlier sketch in SATA 1
Polking, Kirk 1925- 5
Polland, Barbara K(ay) 1939- 44
Polland, Madeleine A. 1918- 6
Pollock, Bruce 1945- 46
Pollock, Mary
  See Blyton, Enid (Mary)
Pollock, Penny 1935- 44
  Brief Entry 42
Pollowitz, Melinda (Kilborn)
  1944- 26
Polonsky, Arthur 1925- 34
Polseno, Jo 17
Pomerantz, Charlotte 20
Pomeroy, Pete
  See Roth, Arthur J(oseph)
Pond, Alonzo W(illiam) 1894- 5
Pontiflet, Ted 1932- 32
Poole, Gray Johnson 1906- 1
Poole, Josephine 1933- 5
  See also SAAS 2
Poole, Lynn 1910-1969 1
Poole, Peggy 1925- 39
Poortvliet, Marien
  See Poortvliet, Rien
Poortvliet, Rien 1933(?)-
  Brief Entry 37
Pope, Elizabeth Marie 1917- 38
  Brief Entry 36
Portal, Colette 1936- 6
Porte, Barbara Ann
  Brief Entry 45
Porter, Katherine Anne
  1890-1980 39
  Obituary 23
Porter, Sheena 1935- 24
Porter, William Sydney
  1862-1910 .... YABC 2
Portteus, Eleanora Marie Manthei
  (?)-1983
  Obituary 36
Posell, Elsa Z. 3
Posten, Margaret L(ois) 1915- 10
Potok, Chaim 1929- 33
Potter, (Helen) Beatrix
  1866-1943 .... YABC 1
  See also CLR 1
Potter, Margaret (Newman)
  1926- 21
Potter, Marian 1915- 9

Potter, Miriam Clark
  1886-1965 3
Pournelle, Jerry (Eugene)
  1933- 26
Powell, A. M.
  See Morgan, Alfred P(owell)
Powell, Ann 1951-
  Brief Entry 51
Powell, Richard Stillman
  See Barbour, Ralph Henry
Powers, Anne
  See Schwartz, Anne Powers
Powers, Bill 1931- 52
  Brief Entry 31
Powers, Margaret
  See Heal, Edith
Powledge, Fred 1935- 37
Poynter, Margaret 1927- 27
Prager, Arthur 44
Preiss, Byron (Cary) 47
  Brief Entry 42
Prelutsky, Jack 22
  See also CLR 13
Presberg, Miriam Goldstein 1919-1978
  Brief Entry 38
Preston, Edna Mitchell 40
Preston, Lillian Elvira 1918- ... 47
Preussler, Otfried 1923- 24
Prevert, Jacques (Henri Marie)
  1900-1977
  Obituary 30
Price, Christine 1928-1980 3
  Obituary 23
Price, Garrett 1896-1979
  Obituary 22
Price, Jennifer
  See Hoover, Helen (Drusilla
  Blackburn)
Price, Jonathan (Reeve) 1941- 46
Price, Lucie Locke
  See Locke, Lucie
Price, Margaret (Evans) 1888-1973
  Brief Entry 28
Price, Olive 1903- 8
Price, Susan 1955- 25
Price, Willard 1887-1983 48
  Brief Entry 38
Prideaux, Tom 1908- 37
Priestley, Lee (Shore) 1904- 27
Prieto, Mariana B(eeching)
  1912- 8
Primavera, Elise 1954-
  Brief Entry 48
Prime, Derek (James) 1931- 34
Prince, Alison 1931- 28
Prince, J(ack) H(arvey) 1908- ... 17
Pringle, Laurence 1935- 4
  See also SAAS 6
  See also CLR 4
Pritchett, Elaine H(illyer)
  1920- 36
Proctor, Everitt
  See Montgomery, Rutherford
Professor Zingara
  See Leeming, Joseph
Provensen, Alice 1918- 9
  See also CLR 11

Provensen, Martin 1916-1987 9
  Obituary 51
  See also CLR 11
Pryor, Helen Brenton
  1897-1972 4
Pucci, Albert John 1920- 44
Pudney, John (Sleigh)
  1909-1977 24
Pugh, Ellen T. 1920- 7
Pullein-Thompson, Christine
  1930- 3
Pullein-Thompson, Diana 3
Pullein-Thompson, Josephine 3
Puner, Helen W(alker) 1915- 37
Purdy, Susan Gold 1939- 8
Purscell, Phyllis 1934- 7
Purtill, Richard L. 1931- 53
Putnam, Arthur Lee
  See Alger, Horatio, Jr.
Putnam, Peter B(rock) 1920- 30
Pyle, Howard 1853-1911 16
Pyne, Mable Mandeville
  1903-1969 9
Python, Monty
  See Jones, Terry

Q

Quackenbush, Robert M.
  1929- 7
Quammen, David 1948- 7
Quarles, Benjamin 1904- 12
Queen, Ellery, Jr.
  See Holding, James
Quennell, Marjorie (Courtney)
  1884-1972 29
Quick, Annabelle 1922- 2
Quigg, Jane (Hulda) (?)-1986
  Obituary 49
Quin-Harkin, Janet 1941- 18
Quinn, Elisabeth 1881-1962 22
Quinn, Susan
  See Jacobs, Susan
Quinn, Vernon
  See Quinn, Elisabeth

R

Rabe, Berniece 1928- 7
Rabe, Olive H(anson)
  1887-1968 13
Rabinowich, Ellen 1946- 29
Rabinowitz, Sandy 1954- 52
  Brief Entry 39
Raboff, Ernest Lloyd
  Brief Entry 37
Rachlin, Harvey (Brant) 1951- ... 47
Rachlis, Eugene (Jacob) 1920-1986
  Obituary 50
Rackham, Arthur 1867-1939 15
Radford, Ruby L(orraine)
  1891-1971 6
Radin, Ruth Yaffe 1938-
  Brief Entry 52
Radlauer, David 1952- 28
Radlauer, Edward 1921- 15
Radlauer, Ruth (Shaw) 1926- 15

Radley, Gail 1951- 25
Rae, Gwynedd 1892-1977 37
Raebeck, Lois 1921- 5
Raftery, Gerald (Bransfield)
  1905- 11
Rahn, Joan Elma 1929- 27
Raible, Alton (Robert) 1918- 35
Raiff, Stan 1930- 11
Rainey, W. B.
  See Blassingame, Wyatt Rainey
Ralston, Jan
  See Dunlop, Agnes M. R.
Ramal, Walter
  See de la Mare, Walter
Rame, David
  See Divine, Arthur Durham
Rana, J.
  See Forrester, Helen
Ranadive, Gail 1944- 10
Rand, Ann (Binkley) 30
Rand, Paul 1914- 6
Randall, Florence Engel 1917- 5
Randall, Janet [Joint pseudonym]
  See Young, Janet Randall and
  Young, Robert W.
Randall, Robert
  See Silverberg, Robert
Randall, Ruth Painter
  1892-1971 3
Randolph, Lieutenant J. H.
  See Ellis, Edward S(ylvester)
Rands, William Brighty
  1823-1882 17
Ranney, Agnes V. 1916- 6
Ransom, Candice F. 1952- 52
  Brief Entry 49
Ransome, Arthur (Michell)
  1884-1967 22
  See also CLR 8
Rapaport, Stella F(read) 10
Raphael, Elaine (Chionchio)
  1933- 23
Rappaport, Eva 1924- 6
Rarick, Carrie 1911- 41
Raskin, Edith (Lefkowitz)
  1908- 9
Raskin, Ellen 1928-1984 38
  Earlier sketch in SATA 2
  See also CLR 1, 12
Raskin, Joseph 1897-1982 12
  Obituary 29
Rasmussen, Knud Johan Victor
  1879-1933
  Brief Entry 34
Rathjen, Carl H(enry) 1909- 11
Rattray, Simon
  See Trevor, Elleston
Rau, Margaret 1913- 9
  See also CLR 8
Rauch, Mabel Thompson 1888-1972
  Obituary 26
Raucher, Herman 1928- 8
Ravielli, Anthony 1916- 3
Rawlings, Marjorie Kinnan
  1896-1953 ....YABC 1
Rawls, (Woodrow) Wilson
  1913- 22
Ray, Deborah
  See Kogan, Deborah

Ray, Deborah Kogan
  See Kogan, Deborah
Ray, Irene
  See Sutton, Margaret Beebe
Ray, JoAnne 1935- 9
Ray, Mary (Eva Pedder)
  1932- 2
Raymond, James Crossley 1917-1981
  Obituary 29
Raymond, Robert
  See Alter, Robert Edmond
Rayner, Mary 1933- 22
Rayner, William 1929-
  Brief Entry 36
Raynor, Dorka 28
Rayson, Steven 1932- 30
Razzell, Arthur (George)
  1925- 11
Razzi, James 1931- 10
Read, Elfreida 1920- 2
Read, Piers Paul 1941- 21
Ready, Kirk L. 1943- 39
Reaney, James 1926- 43
Reck, Franklin Mering 1896-1965
  Brief Entry 30
Redding, Robert Hull 1919- 2
Redway, Ralph
  See Hamilton, Charles H. St. John
Redway, Ridley
  See Hamilton, Charles H. St. John
Reed, Betty Jane 1921- 4
Reed, Gwendolyn E(lizabeth)
  1932- 21
Reed, Kit 1932- 34
Reed, Philip G. 1908-
  Brief Entry 29
Reed, Thomas (James) 1947- 34
Reed, William Maxwell
  1871-1962 15
Reeder, Colonel Red
  See Reeder, Russell P., Jr.
Reeder, Russell P., Jr. 1902- 4
Reeman, Douglas Edward 1924-
  Brief Entry 28
Rees, David Bartlett 1936- 36
  See also SAAS 5
Rees, Ennis 1925- 3
Reese, Bob
  See Reese, Robert A.
Reese, Robert A. 1938-
  Brief Entry 53
Reeve, Joel
  See Cox, William R(obert)
Reeves, James 1909- 15
Reeves, Joyce 1911- 17
Reeves, Lawrence F. 1926- 29
Reeves, Ruth Ellen
  See Ranney, Agnes V.
Regehr, Lydia 1903- 37
Reggiani, Renée 18
Reid, Alastair 1926- 46
Reid, Barbara 1922- 21
Reid, Dorothy M(arion) (?)-1974
  Brief Entry 29
Reid, Eugenie Chazal 1924- 12
Reid, John Calvin 21
Reid, (Thomas) Mayne
  1818-1883 24

Reid, Meta Mayne 1905-
  Brief Entry 36
Reid Banks, Lynne 1929- 22
Reiff, Stephanie Ann 1948- 47
  Brief Entry 28
Reig, June 1933- 30
Reigot, Betty Polisar 1924-
  Brief Entry 41
Reinach, Jacquelyn (Krasne)
  1930- 28
Reiner, William B(uck)
  1910-1976 46
  Obituary 30
Reinfeld, Fred 1910-1964 3
Reiniger, Lotte 1899-1981 40
  Obituary 33
Reiss, Johanna de Leeuw
  1932- 18
Reiss, John J. 23
Reit, Seymour 21
Reit, Sy
  See Reit, Seymour
Rémi, Georges 1907-1983 13
  Obituary 32
Remington, Frederic (Sackrider)
  1861-1909 41
Renault, Mary
  See Challans, Mary
Rendell, Joan 28
Rendina, Laura Cooper 1902- 10
Renick, Marion (Lewis) 1905- 1
Renken, Aleda 1907- 27
Renlie, Frank H. 1936- 11
Rensie, Willis
  See Eisner, Will(iam Erwin)
Renvoize, Jean 1930- 5
Resnick, Michael D(iamond)
  1942- 38
Resnick, Mike
  See Resnick, Michael D(iamond)
Resnick, Seymour 1920- 23
Retla, Robert
  See Alter, Robert Edmond
Reuter, Carol (Joan) 1931- 2
Revena
  See Wright, Betty Ren
Rey, H(ans) A(ugusto)
  1898-1977 26
  Earlier sketch in SATA 1
  See also CLR 5
Rey, Margret (Elizabeth)
  1906- 26
  See also CLR 5
Reyher, Becky
  See Reyher, Rebecca Hourwich
Reyher, Rebecca Hourwich
  1897-1987 18
  Obituary 50
Reynolds, Dickson
  See Reynolds, Helen Mary
  Greenwood Campbell
Reynolds, Helen Mary Greenwood
  Campbell 1884-1969
  Obituary 26
Reynolds, John
  See Whitlock, Ralph
Reynolds, Madge
  See Whitlock, Ralph

Reynolds, Malvina 1900-1978 ..... *44*
  Obituary *24*
Reynolds, Pamela 1923- *34*
Rhodes, Bennie (Loran) 1927- *35*
Rhodes, Frank H(arold Trevor)
  1926- *37*
Rhue, Morton
  See Strasser, Todd
Rhys, Megan
  See Williams, Jeanne
Ribbons, Ian 1924- *37*
  Brief Entry *30*
  See also SAAS 3
Ricciuti, Edward R(aphael)
  1938- *10*
Rice, Charles D(uane) 1910-1971
  Obituary *27*
Rice, Dale R(ichard) 1948- *42*
Rice, Edward 1918- *47*
  Brief Entry *42*
Rice, Elizabeth 1913- *2*
Rice, Eve (Hart) 1951- *34*
Rice, Inez 1907- *13*
Rice, James 1934- *22*
Rich, Elaine Sommers 1926- *6*
Rich, Josephine 1912- *10*
Rich, Mark J. 1948-
  Brief Entry *53*
Richard, Adrienne 1921- *5*
Richard, James Robert
  See Bowen, R(obert) Sydney
Richards, Curtis
  See Curtis, Richard (Alan)
Richards, Frank
  See Hamilton, Charles H. St. John
Richards, Hilda
  See Hamilton, Charles H. St. John
Richards, Kay
  See Baker, Susan (Catherine)
Richards, Laura E(lizabeth Howe)
  1850-1943 ....*YABC 1*
Richards, Norman 1932- *48*
Richards, R(onald) C(harles) W(illiam)
  1923-
  Brief Entry *43*
Richardson, Frank Howard 1882-1970
  Obituary *27*
Richardson, Grace Lee
  See Dickson, Naida
Richardson, Robert S(hirley)
  1902- *8*
Richelson, Geraldine 1922- *29*
Richler, Mordecai 1931- *44*
  Brief Entry *27*
Richoux, Pat 1927- *7*
Richter, Alice 1941- *30*
Richter, Conrad 1890-1968 .... *3*
Richter, Hans Peter 1925- *6*
Rico, Don(ato) 1917-1985
  Obituary *43*
Ridge, Antonia (Florence)
  (?)-1981 .... *7*
  Obituary *27*
Ridge, Martin 1923- *43*
Ridley, Nat, Jr.
  See Stratemeyer, Edward L.
Ridlon, Marci 1942- *22*
Riedman, Sarah R(egal) 1902- *1*

Riesenberg, Felix, Jr.
  1913-1962 .... *23*
Rieu, E(mile) V(ictor)
  1887-1972 .... *46*
  Obituary *26*
Riggs, Sidney Noyes 1892-1975
  Obituary *28*
Rikhoff, Jean 1928- *9*
Riley, James Whitcomb
  1849-1916 .... *17*
Riley, Jocelyn (Carol) 1949-
  Brief Entry *50*
Rinaldi, Ann 1934- *51*
  Brief Entry *50*
Rinard, Judith E(llen) 1947- *44*
Ringi, Kjell Arne Sörensen
  1939- *12*
Rinkoff, Barbara (Jean)
  1923-1975 .... *4*
  Obituary *27*
Riordan, James 1936- *28*
Rios, Tere
  See Versace, Marie Teresa
Ripley, Elizabeth Blake
  1906-1969 .... *5*
Ripper, Charles L. 1929- *3*
Rissman, Art
  See Sussman, Susan
Rissman, Susan
  See Sussman, Susan
Ritchie, Barbara (Gibbons) *14*
Ritts, Paul 1920(?)-1980
  Obituary *25*
Rivera, Geraldo 1943-
  Brief Entry *28*
Riverside, John
  See Heinlein, Robert A(nson)
Rivkin, Ann 1920- *41*
Rivoli, Mario 1943- *10*
Roach, Marilynne K(athleen)
  1946- *9*
Roach, Portia
  See Takakjian, Portia
Robbins, Frank 1917- *42*
  Brief Entry *32*
Robbins, Ken
  Brief Entry *53*
Robbins, Raleigh
  See Hamilton, Charles H. St. John
Robbins, Ruth 1917(?)- *14*
Robbins, Tony
  See Pashko, Stanley
Roberson, John R(oyster)
  1930- *53*
Roberts, Bruce (Stuart) 1930- *47*
  Brief Entry *39*
Roberts, Charles G(eorge) D(ouglas)
  1860-1943
  Brief Entry *29*
Roberts, David
  See Cox, John Roberts
Roberts, Elizabeth Madox
  1886-1941 .... *33*
  Brief Entry *27*
Roberts, Jim
  See Bates, Barbara S(nedeker)
Roberts, John G(aither) 1913- *27*
Roberts, Nancy Correll 1924- *52*
  Brief Entry *28*

Roberts, Terence
  See Sanderson, Ivan T.
Roberts, Willo Davis 1928- *21*
Robertson, Barbara (Anne)
  1931- *12*
Robertson, Don 1929- *8*
Robertson, Dorothy Lewis
  1912- *12*
Robertson, Jennifer (Sinclair)
  1942- *12*
Robertson, Keith 1914- *1*
Robinet, Harriette Gillem
  1931- *27*
Robins, Seelin
  See Ellis, Edward S(ylvester)
Robinson, Adjai 1932- *8*
Robinson, Barbara (Webb)
  1927- *8*
Robinson, C(harles) A(lexander), Jr.
  1900-1965 .... *36*
Robinson, Charles 1870-1937 ..... *17*
Robinson, Charles 1931- *6*
Robinson, Jan M. 1933- *6*
Robinson, Jean O. 1934- *7*
Robinson, Jerry 1922-
  Brief Entry *34*
Robinson, Joan (Mary) G(ale Thomas)
  1910- *7*
Robinson, Marileta 1942- *32*
Robinson, Maudie (Millian Oller)
  1914- *11*
Robinson, Maurice R. 1895-1982
  Obituary *29*
Robinson, Nancy K(onheim)
  1942- *32*
  Brief Entry *31*
Robinson, Ray(mond Kenneth)
  1920- *23*
Robinson, Shari
  See McGuire, Leslie (Sarah)
Robinson, T(homas) H(eath)
  1869-1950 .... *17*
Robinson, (Wanda) Veronica
  1926- *30*
Robinson, W(illiam) Heath
  1872-1944 .... *17*
Robison, Bonnie 1924- *12*
Robison, Nancy L(ouise)
  1934- *32*
Robottom, John 1934- *7*
Roche, A. K. [Joint pseudonym]
  See Abisch, Roslyn Kroop and
  Kaplan, Boche
Roche, P(atricia) K.
  Brief Entry *34*
Roche, Terry
  See Poole, Peggy
Rock, Gail
  Brief Entry *32*
Rocker, Fermin 1907- *40*
Rockwell, Anne F. 1934- *33*
Rockwell, Gail
  Brief Entry *36*
Rockwell, Harlow *33*
Rockwell, Norman (Percevel)
  1894-1978 .... *23*
Rockwell, Thomas 1933- *7*
  See also CLR 6
Rockwood, Joyce 1947- *39*

Rockwood, Roy [Collective
  pseudonym] *1*
  See also McFarlane, Leslie;
  Stratemeyer, Edward L.
Roddenberry, Eugene Wesley
  1921- *45*
Roddenberry, Gene
  See Roddenberry, Eugene Wesley
Rodgers, Mary 1931- *8*
Rodman, Emerson
  See Ellis, Edward S(ylvester)
Rodman, Maia
  See Wojciechowska, Maia
Rodman, Selden 1909- *9*
Rodowsky, Colby 1932- *21*
Roe, Harry Mason
  See Stratemeyer, Edward L.
Roever, J(oan) M(arilyn)
  1935- *26*
Rofes, Eric Edward 1954- *52*
Roffey, Maureen 1936- *33*
Rogers, (Thomas) Alan (Stinchcombe)
  1937- *2*
Rogers, Frances 1888-1974 .... *10*
Rogers, Fred (McFeely) 1928- *33*
Rogers, Jean 1919-
  Brief Entry *47*
Rogers, Matilda 1894-1976 .... *5*
  Obituary *34*
Rogers, Pamela 1927- *9*
Rogers, Robert
  See Hamilton, Charles H. St. John
Rogers, W(illiam) G(arland)
  1896-1978 .... *23*
Rojan
  See Rojankovsky, Feodor
  (Stepanovich)
Rojankovsky, Feodor (Stepanovich)
  1891-1970 .... *21*
Rokeby-Thomas, Anna E(lma)
  1911- *15*
Roland, Albert 1925- *11*
Rolerson, Darrell A(llen)
  1946- *8*
Roll, Winifred 1909- *6*
Rollins, Charlemae Hill
  1897-1979 .... *3*
  Obituary *26*
Romano, Clare
  See Ross, Clare (Romano)
Romano, Louis 1921- *35*
Rongen, Björn 1906- *10*
Rood, Ronald (N.) 1920- *12*
Rooke, Daphne (Marie) 1914- *12*
Roop, Constance Betzer 1951-
  Brief Entry *49*
Roop, Peter 1951-
  Brief Entry *49*
Roos, Stephen (Kelley) 1945- *47*
  Brief Entry *41*
Roosevelt, (Anna) Eleanor
  1884-1962 .... *50*
Root, Phyllis
  Brief Entry *48*
Root, Shelton L., Jr. 1923-1986
  Obituary *51*
Roote, Mike
  See Fleischer, Leonore
Roper, Laura Wood 1911- *34*

Roscoe, D(onald) T(homas)
  1934- *42*
Rose, Anna Perrot
  See Wright, Anna (Maria Louisa
  Perrot) Rose
Rose, Anne *8*
Rose, Carl 1903-1971
  Brief Entry *31*
Rose, Elizabeth Jane (Pretty) 1933-
  Brief Entry *28*
Rose, Florella
  See Carlson, Vada F.
Rose, Gerald (Hembdon Seymour)
  1935-
  Brief Entry *30*
Rose, Nancy A.
  See Sweetland, Nancy A(nn)
Rose, Wendy 1948- *12*
Roseman, Kenneth David 1939-
  Brief Entry *52*
Rosen, Michael (Wayne)
  1946- *48*
  Brief Entry *40*
Rosen, Sidney 1916- *1*
Rosen, Winifred 1943- *8*
Rosenbaum, Maurice 1907- *6*
Rosenberg, Dorothy 1906- *40*
Rosenberg, Ethel *3*
Rosenberg, Maxine B(erta) 1939-
  Brief Entry *47*
Rosenberg, Nancy Sherman
  1931- *4*
Rosenberg, Sharon 1942- *8*
Rosenblatt, Arthur S. 1938-
  Brief Entry *45*
Rosenbloom, Joseph 1928- *21*
Rosenblum, Richard 1928- *11*
Rosenburg, John M. 1918- *6*
Rosenthal, Harold 1914- *35*
Ross, Alan
  See Warwick, Alan R(oss)
Ross, Alex(ander) 1909-
  Brief Entry *29*
Ross, Clare (Romano) 1922- *48*
Ross, Dave 1949- *32*
Ross, David 1896-1975 .... *49*
  Obituary *20*
Ross, Diana
  See Denney, Diana
Ross, Frank (Xavier), Jr.
  1914- *28*
Ross, John 1921- *45*
Ross, Pat(ricia Kienzle) 1943- *53*
  Brief Entry *48*
Ross, Tony 1938- *17*
Ross, Wilda 1915- *51*
  Brief Entry *39*
Rossel, Seymour 1945- *28*
Rössel-Waugh, C. C. [Joint
  pseudonym]
  See Waugh, Carol-Lynn Rössel
Rossetti, Christiana (Georgina)
  1830-1894 .... *20*
Roth, Arnold 1929- *21*
Roth, Arthur J(oseph) 1925- *43*
  Brief Entry *28*
Roth, David 1940- *36*
Roth, Harold
  Brief Entry *49*

Rothkopf, Carol Z. 1929- *4*
Rothman, Joel 1938- *7*
Roueché, Berton 1911- *28*
Roughsey, Dick 1921(?)- *35*
Rounds, Glen (Harold) 1906- *8*
Rourke, Constance (Mayfield)
  1885-1941 .... *YABC 1*
Rowe, Viola Carson 1903-1969
  Obituary *26*
Rowland, Florence Wightman
  1900- *8*
Rowland-Entwistle, (Arthur) Theodore
  (Henry) 1925- *31*
Rowsome, Frank (Howard), Jr.
  1914-1983 .... *36*
Roy, Jessie Hailstalk 1895-1986
  Obituary *51*
Roy, Liam
  See Scarry, Patricia
Roy, Ron(ald) 1940- *40*
  Brief Entry *35*
Rubel, Nicole 1953- *18*
Rubin, Eva Johanna 1925- *38*
Rubinstein, Robert E(dward)
  1943- *49*
Ruby, Lois 1942- *35*
  Brief Entry *34*
Ruchlis, Hy 1913- *3*
Ruckman, Ivy 1931- *37*
Ruck-Pauquèt, Gina 1931- *40*
  Brief Entry *37*
Rudeen, Kenneth
  Brief Entry *36*
Rudley, Stephen 1946- *30*
Rudolph, Marguerita 1908- *21*
Rudomin, Esther
  See Hautzig, Esther
Rue, Leonard Lee III 1926- *37*
Ruedi, Norma Paul
  See Ainsworth, Norma
Ruffell, Ann 1941- *30*
Ruffins, Reynold 1930- *41*
Rugoff, Milton 1913- *30*
Ruhen, Olaf 1911- *17*
Rukeyser, Muriel 1913-1980
  Obituary *22*
Rumsey, Marian (Barritt)
  1928- *16*
Runyan, John
  See Palmer, Bernard
Rush, Alison 1951- *41*
Rush, Peter 1937- *32*
Rushmore, Helen 1898- *3*
Rushmore, Robert (William)
  1926-1986 .... *8*
  Obituary *49*
Ruskin, Ariane
  See Batterberry, Ariane Ruskin
Ruskin, John 1819-1900 .... *24*
Russell, Charlotte
  See Rathjen, Carl H(enry)
Russell, Don(ald Bert) 1899-1986
  Obituary *47*
Russell, Franklin 1926- *11*
Russell, Helen Ross 1915- *8*
Russell, James 1933- *53*
Russell, Jim
  See Russell, James

Russell, Patrick
See Sammis, John
Russell, Solveig Paulson
1904- *3*
Russo, Susan 1947- *30*
Rutgers van der Loeff, An(na) Basenau
1910- *22*
Ruth, Rod 1912- *9*
Rutherford, Douglas
See McConnell, James Douglas
(Rutherford)
Rutherford, Meg 1932- *34*
Ruthin, Margaret *4*
Rutz, Viola Larkin 1932- *12*
Ruzicka, Rudolph 1883-1978
Obituary *24*
Ryan, Betsy
See Ryan, Elizabeth (Anne)
Ryan, Cheli Durán *20*
Ryan, Elizabeth (Anne) 1943- *30*
Ryan, John (Gerald Christopher)
1921- *22*
Ryan, Peter (Charles) 1939- *15*
Rydberg, Ernest E(mil) 1901- *21*
Rydberg, Lou(isa Hampton)
1908- *27*
Rydell, Wendell
See Rydell, Wendy
Rydell, Wendy *4*
Ryden, Hope *8*
Ryder, Joanne
Brief Entry *34*
Rye, Anthony
See Youd, (Christopher) Samuel
Rylant, Cynthia 1954- *50*
Brief Entry *44*
Rymer, Alta May 1925- *34*

S

Saal, Jocelyn
See Sachs, Judith
Saberhagen, Fred (Thomas)
1930- *37*
Sabin, Edwin Legrand
1870-1952 ....*YABC 2*
Sabin, Francene *27*
Sabin, Louis 1930- *27*
Sabre, Dirk
See Laffin, John (Alfred Charles)
Sabuso
See Phillips, Irving W.
Sachar, Louis 1954-
Brief Entry *50*
Sachs, Elizabeth-Ann 1946- *48*
Sachs, Judith 1947- *52*
Brief Entry *51*
Sachs, Marilyn 1927- *52*
Earlier sketch in SATA 3
See also CLR 2
See also SAAS 2
Sackett, S(amuel) J(ohn)
1928- *12*
Sackson, Sid 1920- *16*
Saddler, Allen
See Richards, R(onald) C(harles)
W(illiam)

Saddler, K. Allen
See Richards, R(onald) C(harles)
W(illiam)
Sadie, Stanley (John) 1930- *14*
Sadler, Catherine Edwards
Brief Entry *45*
Sadler, Mark
See Lynds, Dennis
Sage, Juniper [Joint pseudonym]
See Brown, Margaret Wise and
Hurd, Edith
Sagsoorian, Paul 1923- *12*
Saida
See LeMair, H(enriette) Willebeek
Saint, Dora Jessie 1913- *10*
St. Briavels, James
See Wood, James Playsted
St. Clair, Byrd Hooper 1905-1976
Obituary *28*
Saint Exupéry, Antoine de
1900-1944 .... *20*
See also CLR 10
St. George, Judith 1931- *13*
St. John, Nicole
See Johnston, Norma
St. John, Philip
See Del Rey, Lester
St. John, Wylly Folk
1908-1985 .... *10*
Obituary *45*
St. Meyer, Ned
See Stratemeyer, Edward L.
St. Tamara
See Kolba, Tamara
Saito, Michiko
See Fujiwara, Michiko
Salassi, Otto R(ussell) 1939- *38*
Saldutti, Denise 1953- *39*
Salkey, (Felix) Andrew (Alexander)
1928- *35*
Salmon, Annie Elizabeth
1899- *13*
Salten, Felix
See Salzmann, Siegmund
Salter, Cedric
See Knight, Francis Edgar
Salvadori, Mario (George)
1907- *40*
Salzer, L. E.
See Wilson, Lionel
Salzman, Yuri
Brief Entry *42*
Salzmann, Siegmund
1869-1945 .... *25*
Samachson, Dorothy 1914- *3*
Samachson, Joseph 1906-1980 .... *3*
Obituary *52*
Sammis, John 1942- *4*
Sampson, Fay (Elizabeth)
1935- *42*
Brief Entry *40*
Samson, Anne S(tringer)
1933- *2*
Samson, Joan 1937-1976 .... *13*
Samuels, Charles 1902- *12*
Samuels, Gertrude *17*
Sanborn, Duane 1914- *38*
Sancha, Sheila 1924- *38*

Sanchez Alzada, Juan
See Joseph, James (Herz)
Sanchez, Sonia 1934- *22*
Sánchez-Silva, José María
1911- *16*
See also CLR 12
Sand, George X. *45*
Sandak, Cass R(obert) 1950- *51*
Brief Entry *37*
Sandberg, (Karin) Inger 1930- ... *15*
Sandberg, Karl C. 1931- *35*
Sandberg, Lasse (E. M.)
1924- *15*
Sandburg, Carl (August)
1878-1967 .... *8*
Sandburg, Charles A.
See Sandburg, Carl (August)
Sandburg, Helga 1918- *3*
Sanderlin, George 1915- *4*
Sanderlin, Owenita (Harrah)
1916- *11*
Sanders, Winston P.
See Anderson, Poul (William)
Sanderson, Ivan T. 1911-1973 .... *6*
Sanderson, Ruth (L.) 1951- *41*
Sandin, Joan 1942- *12*
Sandison, Janet
See Cameron, Elizabeth Jane
Sandoz, Mari (Susette)
1901-1966 .... *5*
Sanger, Marjory Bartlett
1920- *8*
Sankey, Alice (Ann-Susan)
1910- *27*
San Souci, Robert D. 1946- *40*
Santesson, Hans Stefan 1914(?)-1975
Obituary *30*
Sapieyevski, Anne Lindbergh
1940- *35*
Sarac, Roger
See Caras, Roger A(ndrew)
Sarasin, Jennifer
See Sachs, Judith
Sarg, Anthony Fredrick
See Sarg, Tony
Sarg, Tony 1880-1942 ....*YABC 1*
Sargent, Pamela *29*
Sargent, Robert 1933- *2*
Sargent, Sarah 1937- *44*
Brief Entry *41*
Sargent, Shirley 1927- *11*
Sari
See Fleur, Anne
Sarnoff, Jane 1937- *10*
Saroyan, William 1908-1981 ...... *23*
Obituary *24*
Sarton, Eleanore Marie
See Sarton, (Eleanor) May
Sarton, (Eleanor) May 1912- *36*
Sasek, Miroslav 1916-1980 .... *16*
Obituary *23*
See also CLR 4
Satchwell, John
Brief Entry *49*
Sattler, Helen Roney 1921- *4*
Sauer, Julia (Lina) 1891-1983 .... *32*
Obituary *36*
Saul, (E.) Wendy 1946- *42*

Saunders, Caleb
   See Heinlein, Robert A(nson)
Saunders, Keith 1910- 12
Saunders, Rubie (Agnes)
   1929- 21
Saunders, Susan 1945- 46
   Brief Entry 41
Savage, Blake
   See Goodwin, Harold Leland
Savery, Constance (Winifred)
   1897- 1
Saville, (Leonard) Malcolm
   1901-1982 23
   Obituary 31
Saviozzi, Adriana
   See Mazza, Adriana
Savitt, Sam 8
Savitz, Harriet May 1933- 5
Sawyer, Ruth 1880-1970 17
Saxon, Antonia
   See Sachs, Judith
Say, Allen 1937- 28
Sayers, Frances Clarke 1897- 3
Sazer, Nina 1949- 13
Scabrini, Janet 1953- 13
Scagnetti, Jack 1924- 7
Scanlon, Marion Stephany 11
Scarf, Maggi
   See Scarf, Maggie
Scarf, Maggie 1932- 5
Scarlett, Susan
   See Streatfeild, (Mary) Noel
Scarry, Huck
   See Scarry, Richard, Jr.
Scarry, Patricia (Murphy)
   1924- 2
Scarry, Patsy
   See Scarry, Patricia
Scarry, Richard (McClure)
   1919- 35
   Earlier sketch in SATA 2
   See also CLR 3
Scarry, Richard, Jr. 1953- 35
Schachtel, Roger (Bernard)
   1949- 38
Schaefer, Jack 1907- 3
Schaeffer, Mead 1898- 21
Schaller, George B(eals)
   1933- 30
Schatell, Brian
   Brief Entry 47
Schatzki, Walter 1899-
   Brief Entry 31
Schechter, Betty (Goodstein)
   1921- 5
Scheer, Julian (Weisel) 1926- 8
Scheffer, Victor B. 1906- 6
Scheier, Michael 1943- 40
   Brief Entry 36
Schell, Mildred 1922- 41
Schell, Orville H. 1940- 10
Schellie, Don 1932- 29
Schemm, Mildred Walker
   1905- 21
Scher, Paula 1948- 47
Scherf, Margaret 1908- 10
Schermer, Judith (Denise)
   1941- 30
Schertle, Alice 1941- 36

Schick, Alice 1946- 27
Schick, Eleanor 1942- 9
Schick, Joel 1945- 31
   Brief Entry 30
Schiff, Ken 1942- 7
Schiller, Andrew 1919- 21
Schiller, Barbara (Heyman)
   1928- 21
Schiller, Justin G. 1943-
   Brief Entry 31
Schindelman, Joseph 1923-
   Brief Entry 32
Schindler, S(tephen) D.
   Brief Entry 50
Schisgall, Oscar 1901-1984 12
   Obituary 38
Schlee, Ann 1934- 44
   Brief Entry 36
Schlein, Miriam 1926- 2
Schloat, G. Warren, Jr. 1914- 4
Schmid, Eleonore 1939- 12
Schmiderer, Dorothy 1940- 19
Schmidt, Elizabeth 1915- 15
Schmidt, James Norman
   1912- 21
Schneider, Herman 1905- 7
Schneider, Laurie
   See Adams, Laurie
Schneider, Nina 1913- 2
Schneider, Rex 1937- 44
Schnirel, James R(einhold)
   1931- 14
Schock, Pauline 1928- 45
Schoen, Barbara 1924- 13
Schoenherr, John (Carl) 1935- 37
Scholastica, Sister Mary
   See Jenkins, Marie M.
Scholefield, Edmund O.
   See Butterworth, W. E.
Scholey, Arthur 1932- 28
Scholz, Jackson (Volney) 1897-1986
   Obituary 49
Schone, Virginia 22
Schongut, Emanuel 52
   Brief Entry 36
Schoonover, Frank (Earle)
   1877-1972 24
Schoor, Gene 1921- 3
Schraff, Anne E(laine) 1939- 27
Schrank, Joseph 1900-1984
   Obituary 38
Schreiber, Elizabeth Anne (Ferguson)
   1947- 13
Schreiber, Georges 1904-1977
   Brief Entry 29
Schreiber, Ralph W(alter)
   1942- 13
Schroeder, Ted 1931(?)-1973
   Obituary 20
Schulman, Janet 1933- 22
Schulman, L(ester) M(artin)
   1934- 13
Schulte, Elaine L(ouise) 1934- 36
Schultz, Gwendolyn 21
Schultz, James Willard
   1859-1947 .... YABC 1
Schultz, Pearle Henriksen
   1918- 21

Schulz, Charles M(onroe)
   1922- 10
Schur, Maxine 1948- 53
   Brief Entry 49
Schurfranz, Vivian 1925- 13
Schutzer, A. I. 1922- 13
Schuyler, Pamela R(icka)
   1948- 30
Schwark, Mary Beth 1954- 51
Schwartz, Alvin 1927- 4
   See also CLR 3
Schwartz, Amy 1954- 47
   Brief Entry 41
Schwartz, Ann Powers 1913- 10
Schwartz, Charles W(alsh)
   1914- 8
Schwartz, Daniel (Bennet) 1929-
   Brief Entry 29
Schwartz, Elizabeth Reeder
   1912- 8
Schwartz, Joel L. 1940-
   Brief Entry 51
Schwartz, Julius 1907- 45
Schwartz, Sheila (Ruth) 1929- 27
Schwartz, Stephen (Lawrence)
   1948- 19
Schweitzer, Iris
   Brief Entry 36
Schweninger, Ann 1951- 29
Scoggin, Margaret C.
   1905-1968 47
   Brief Entry 28
Scoppettone, Sandra 1936- 9
Scott, Ann Herbert 1926-
   Brief Entry 29
Scott, Bill 1902(?)-1985
   Obituary 46
Scott, Cora Annett (Pipitone)
   1931- 11
Scott, Dan [House pseudonym]
   See Barker, S. Omar; Stratemeyer,
   Edward L.
Scott, Elaine 1940- 36
Scott, Jack Denton 1915- 31
Scott, John 1912-1976 14
Scott, John Anthony 1916- 23
Scott, John M(artin) 1913- 12
Scott, Sally (Elisabeth) 1948- 44
Scott, Sally Fisher 1909-1978 43
Scott, Tony
   See Scott, John Anthony
Scott, Sir Walter
   1771-1832 .... YABC 2
Scott, Warwick
   See Trevor, Elleston
Scribner, Charles, Jr. 1921- 13
Scribner, Joanne L. 1949- 33
Scrimsher, Lila Gravatt 1897-1974
   Obituary 28
Scuro, Vincent 1951- 21
Seabrooke, Brenda 1941- 30
Seaman, Augusta Huiell
   1879-1950 31
Seamands, Ruth (Childers)
   1916- 9
Searcy, Margaret Zehmer 1926-
   Brief Entry 39
Searight, Mary W(illiams)
   1918- 17

Searle, Kathryn Adrienne
  1942- *10*
Searle, Ronald (William Fordham)
  1920- *42*
Sears, Stephen W. 1932- *4*
Sebastian, Lee
  See Silverberg, Robert
Sebestyen, Igen
  See Sebestyen, Ouida
Sebestyen, Ouida 1924- *39*
Sechrist, Elizabeth Hough
  1903- *2*
Sedges, John
  See Buck, Pearl S.
Seed, Jenny 1930- *8*
Seed, Sheila Turner 1937(?)-1979
  Obituary *23*
Seeger, Elizabeth 1889-1973
  Obituary *20*
Seeger, Pete(r) 1919- *13*
Seever, R.
  See Reeves, Lawrence F.
Sefton, Catherine
  See Waddell, Martin
Segal, Joyce 1940- *35*
Segal, Lore 1928- *4*
Segovia, Andrés 1893(?)-1987
  Obituary *52*
Seidelman, James Edward
  1926- *6*
Seiden, Art(hur)
  Brief Entry *42*
Seidler, Tor 1952- *52*
  Brief Entry *46*
Seidman, Laurence (Ivan)
  1925- *15*
Seigel, Kalman 1917- *12*
Seignobosc, Francoise
  1897-1961 .... *21*
Seitz, Jacqueline 1931- *50*
Seixas, Judith S. 1922- *17*
Sejima, Yoshimasa 1913- *8*
Selden, George
  See Thompson, George Selden
  See also CLR 8
Self, Margaret Cabell 1902- *24*
Selig, Sylvie 1942- *13*
Selkirk, Jane [Joint pseudonym]
  See Chapman, John Stanton
  Higham
Sellers, Naomi John
  See Flack, Naomi John (White)
Selsam, Millicent E(llis)
  1912- *29*
  Earlier sketch in SATA 1
  See also CLR 1
Seltzer, Meyer 1932- *17*
Seltzer, Richard (Warren, Jr.)
  1946- *41*
Sendak, Jack *28*
Sendak, Maurice (Bernard)
  1928- *27*
  Earlier sketch in SATA 1
  See also CLR 1
Sengler, Johanna 1924- *18*
Senn, Steve 1950-
  Brief Entry *48*
Serage, Nancy 1924- *10*

Seredy, Kate 1899-1975 .... *1*
  Obituary *24*
  See also CLR 10
Seroff, Victor I(lyitch)
  1902-1979 .... *12*
  Obituary *26*
Serraillier, Ian (Lucien) 1912- *1*
  See also CLR 2
  See also SAAS 3
Servello, Joe 1932- *10*
Service, Robert W(illiam)
  1874(?)-1958 .... *20*
Serwadda, William Moses
  1931- *27*
Serwer, Blanche L. 1910- *10*
Seth, Marie
  See Lexau, Joan M.
Seton, Anya *3*
Seton, Ernest Thompson
  1860-1946 .... *18*
Seuling, Barbara 1937- *10*
Seuss, Dr.
  See Geisel, Theodor Seuss
  See also CLR 9
Severn, Bill
  See Severn, William Irving
Severn, David
  See Unwin, David S(torr)
Severn, William Irving 1914- *1*
Sewall, Marcia 1935- *37*
Seward, Prudence 1926- *16*
Sewell, Anna 1820-1878 .... *24*
Sewell, Helen (Moore)
  1896-1957 .... *38*
Sexton, Anne (Harvey)
  1928-1974 .... *10*
Seymour, Alta Halverson *10*
Shachtman, Tom 1942- *49*
Shackleton, C. C.
  See Aldiss, Brian W(ilson)
Shafer, Robert E(ugene)
  1925- *9*
Shahn, Ben(jamin) 1898-1969
  Obituary *21*
Shahn, Bernarda Bryson
  See Bryson, Bernarda
Shane, Harold Gray 1914- *36*
Shanks, Ann Zane (Kushner) *10*
Shannon, George (William Bones)
  1952- *35*
Shannon, Monica (?)-1965 .... *28*
Shannon, Terry *21*
Shapiro, Irwin 1911-1981 .... *32*
Shapiro, Milton J. 1926- *32*
Shapp, Martha 1910- *3*
Sharfman, Amalie *14*
Sharma, Partap 1939- *15*
Sharmat, Marjorie Weinman
  1928- *33*
  Earlier sketch in SATA 4
Sharmat, Mitchell 1927- *33*
Sharp, Margery 1905- *29*
  Earlier sketch in SATA 1
Sharp, Zerna A. 1889-1981
  Obituary *27*
Sharpe, Mitchell R(aymond)
  1924- *12*
Shaw, Arnold 1909- *4*

Shaw, Charles (Green)
  1892-1974 .... *13*
Shaw, Evelyn 1927- *28*
Shaw, Flora Louisa
  See Lugard, Flora Louisa Shaw
Shaw, Ray *7*
Shaw, Richard 1923- *12*
Shay, Arthur 1922- *4*
Shay, Lacey
  See Shebar, Sharon Sigmond
Shea, George 1940-
  Brief Entry *42*
Shearer, John 1947- *43*
  Brief Entry *27*
Shearer, Ted 1919- *43*
Shebar, Sharon Sigmond
  1945- *36*
Shecter, Ben 1935- *16*
Sheedy, Alexandra (Elizabeth)
  1962- *39*
  Earlier sketch in SATA 19
Sheedy, Ally
  See Sheedy, Alexandra (Elizabeth)
Sheehan, Ethna 1908- *9*
Sheffer, H. R.
  See Abels, Harriette S(heffer)
Sheffield, Janet N. 1926- *26*
Shefts, Joelle
  Brief Entry *49*
Shekerjian, Regina Tor *16*
Sheldon, Ann [Collective
  pseudonym] *1*
Sheldon, Aure 1917-1976 .... *12*
Sheldon, Muriel 1926- *45*
  Brief Entry *39*
Shelley, Mary Wollstonecraft
  (Godwin) 1797-1851 .... *29*
Shelton, William Roy 1919- *5*
Shemin, Margaretha 1928- *4*
Shenton, Edward 1895-1977 ...... *45*
Shepard, Ernest Howard
  1879-1976 .... *33*
  Obituary *24*
  Earlier sketch in SATA 3
Shepard, Mary
  See Knox, (Mary) Eleanor Jessie
Shephard, Esther 1891-1975 ...... *5*
  Obituary *26*
Shepherd, Elizabeth *4*
Sherburne, Zoa 1912- *3*
Sherman, D(enis) R(onald)
  1934- *48*
  Brief Entry *29*
Sherman, Diane (Finn) 1928- *12*
Sherman, Elizabeth
  See Friskey, Margaret Richards
Sherman, Harold (Morrow)
  1898- *37*
Sherman, Nancy
  See Rosenberg, Nancy Sherman
Sherrod, Jane
  See Singer, Jane Sherrod
Sherry, (Dulcie) Sylvia 1932- *8*
Sherwan, Earl 1917- *3*
Shiefman, Vicky *22*
Shields, Brenda Desmond (Armstrong)
  1914- *37*
Shields, Charles 1944- *10*
Shimin, Symeon 1902- *13*

Shinn, Everett 1876-1953 .... *21*
Shippen, Katherine B(inney)
  1892-1980 .... *1*
  Obituary *23*
Shipton, Eric 1907- *10*
Shirer, William L(awrence)
  1904- *45*
Shirreffs, Gordon D(onald)
  1914- *11*
Sholokhov, Mikhail A. 1905-1984
  Obituary *36*
Shore, June Lewis *30*
Shore, Robert 1924- *39*
Shortall, Leonard W. *19*
Shotwell, Louisa R. 1902- *3*
Showalter, Jean B(reckinridge) *12*
Showell, Ellen Harvey 1934- *33*
Showers, Paul C. 1910- *21*
  See also CLR 6
Shreve, Susan Richards 1939- *46*
  Brief Entry *41*
Shtainmets, Leon *32*
Shub, Elizabeth *5*
Shulevitz, Uri 1935- *50*
  Earlier sketch in SATA 3
  See also CLR 5
Shulman, Alix Kates 1932- *7*
Shulman, Irving 1913- *13*
Shumsky, Zena
  See Collier, Zena
Shura, Mary Francis
  See Craig, Mary Francis
Shuttlesworth, Dorothy *3*
Shyer, Marlene Fanta *13*
Siberell, Anne *29*
Sibley, Don 1922- *12*
Siculan, Daniel 1922- *12*
Sidjakov, Nicolas 1924- *18*
Sidney, Frank [Joint pseudonym]
  See Warwick, Alan R(oss)
Sidney, Margaret
  See Lothrop, Harriet Mulford Stone
Siebel, Fritz (Frederick) 1913-
  Brief Entry *44*
Siegal, Aranka 1930-
  Brief Entry *37*
Siegel, Beatrice *36*
Siegel, Helen
  See Siegl, Helen
Siegel, Robert (Harold) 1939- *39*
Siegl, Helen 1924- *34*
Silas
  See McCay, Winsor
Silcock, Sara Lesley 1947- *12*
Silver, Ruth
  See Chew, Ruth
Silverberg, Robert *13*
Silverman, Mel(vin Frank)
  1931-1966 .... *9*
Silverstein, Alvin 1933- *8*
Silverstein, Shel(by) 1932- *33*
  Brief Entry *27*
  See also CLR 5
Silverstein, Virginia B(arbara
  Opshelor) 1937- *8*
Silverthorne, Elizabeth 1930- *35*
Simon, Charlie May
  See Fletcher, Charlie May
Simon, Hilda (Rita) 1921- *28*

Simon, Howard 1903-1979 .... *32*
  Obituary *21*
Simon, Joe
  See Simon, Joseph H.
Simon, Joseph H. 1913- *7*
Simon, Martin P(aul William)
  1903-1969 .... *12*
Simon, Mina Lewiton
  See Lewiton, Mina
Simon, Norma 1927- *3*
Simon, Seymour 1931- *4*
  See also CLR 9
Simon, Shirley (Schwartz)
  1921- *11*
Simon, Solomon 1895-1970 .... *40*
Simonetta, Linda 1948- *14*
Simonetta, Sam 1936- *14*
Simons, Barbara B(rooks)
  1934- *41*
Simont, Marc 1915- *9*
Simpson, Colin 1908- *14*
Simpson, Harriette
  See Arnow, Harriette (Louisa)
  Simpson
Simpson, Myrtle L(illias)
  1931- *14*
Sinclair, Clover
  See Gater, Dilys
Sinclair, Emil
  See Hesse, Hermann
Sinclair, Upton (Beall)
  1878-1968 .... *9*
Singer, Isaac Bashevis 1904- *27*
  Earlier sketch in SATA 3
  See also CLR 1
Singer, Jane Sherrod
  1917-1985 .... *4*
  Obituary *42*
Singer, Julia 1917- *28*
Singer, Kurt D(eutsch) 1911- *38*
Singer, Marilyn 1948- *48*
  Brief Entry *38*
Singer, Susan (Mahler) 1941- *9*
Sirof, Harriet 1930- *37*
Sisson, Rosemary Anne 1923- *11*
Sitomer, Harry 1903- *31*
Sitomer, Mindel 1903- *31*
Sive, Helen R. 1951- *30*
Sivulich, Sandra (Jeanne) Stroner
  1941- *9*
Skelly, James R(ichard) 1927- *17*
Skinner, Constance Lindsay
  1882-1939 .... *YABC 1*
Skinner, Cornelia Otis 1901- *2*
Skipper, G. C. 1939- *46*
  Brief Entry *38*
Skofield, James
  Brief Entry *44*
Skold, Betty Westrom 1923- *41*
Skorpen, Liesel Moak 1935- *3*
Skurzynski, Gloria (Joan)
  1930- *8*
Slackman, Charles B. 1934- *12*
Slade, Richard 1910-1971 .... *9*
Slate, Joseph (Frank) 1928- *38*
Slater, Jim 1929-
  Brief Entry *34*
Slaughter, Jean
  See Doty, Jean Slaughter

Sleator, William 1945- *3*
Sleigh, Barbara 1906-1982 .... *3*
  Obituary *30*
Slepian, Jan(ice B.) 1921- *51*
  Brief Entry *45*
Slicer, Margaret O. 1920- *4*
Sloane, Eric 1910(?)-1985 .... *52*
  Obituary *42*
Slobodkin, Florence (Gersh)
  1905- *5*
Slobodkin, Louis 1903-1975 ...... *26*
  Earlier sketch in SATA 1
Slobodkina, Esphyr 1909- *1*
Sloggett, Nellie 1851-1923 .... *44*
Slote, Alfred 1926- *8*
  See also CLR 4
Small, David 1945- *50*
  Brief Entry *46*
Small, Ernest
  See Lent, Blair
Smallwood, Norah (Evelyn)
  1910(?)-1984
  Obituary *41*
Smaridge, Norah 1903- *6*
Smiley, Virginia Kester 1923- *2*
Smith, Anne Warren 1938- *41*
  Brief Entry *34*
Smith, Beatrice S(chillinger) *12*
Smith, Betsy Covington 1937-
  Brief Entry *43*
Smith, Betty 1896-1972 .... *6*
Smith, Bradford 1909-1964 .... *5*
Smith, Caesar
  See Trevor, Elleston
Smith, Datus C(lifford), Jr.
  1907- *13*
Smith, Dodie *4*
Smith, Doris Buchanan 1934- *28*
Smith, Dorothy Stafford
  1905- *6*
Smith, E(lmer) Boyd
  1860-1943 .... *YABC 1*
Smith, E(dric) Brooks 1917- *40*
Smith, Elva S(ophronia) 1871-1965
  Brief Entry *31*
Smith, Emma 1923- *52*
  Brief Entry *36*
Smith, Eunice Young 1902- *5*
Smith, Frances C. 1904- *3*
Smith, Fredrika Shumway 1877-1968
  Brief Entry *30*
Smith, Gary R(ichard) 1932- *14*
Smith, George Harmon 1920- *5*
Smith, H(arry) Allen 1907-1976
  Obituary *20*
Smith, Howard Everett, Jr.
  1927- *12*
Smith, Hugh L(etcher)
  1921-1968 .... *5*
Smith, Imogene Henderson
  1922- *12*
Smith, Jacqueline B. 1937- *39*
Smith, Jean
  See Smith, Frances C.
Smith, Jean Pajot 1945- *10*
Smith, Jessie Willcox
  1863-1935 .... *21*
Smith, Jim 1920-
  Brief Entry *36*

Smith, Joan 1933-
Brief Entry *46*
Smith, Johnston
See Crane, Stephen (Townley)
Smith, Lafayette
See Higdon, Hal
Smith, Lee
See Albion, Lee Smith
Smith, Lillian H(elena) 1887-1983
Obituary *32*
Smith, Linell Nash 1932- *2*
Smith, Lucia B. 1943- *30*
Smith, Marion Hagens 1913- *12*
Smith, Marion Jaques 1899- *13*
Smith, Mary Ellen *10*
Smith, Mike
See Smith, Mary Ellen
Smith, Nancy Covert 1935- *12*
Smith, Norman F. 1920- *5*
Smith, Pauline C(oggeshall)
1908- *27*
Smith, Philip Warren 1936- *46*
Smith, Robert Kimmel 1930- *12*
Smith, Robert Paul 1915-1977 .... *52*
Obituary *30*
Smith, Ruth Leslie 1902- *2*
Smith, Samantha 1972-1985
Obituary *45*
Smith, Sarah Stafford
See Smith, Dorothy Stafford
Smith, Susan Carlton 1923- *12*
Smith, Susan Mathias 1950- *43*
Brief Entry *35*
Smith, Susan Vernon 1950- *48*
Smith, Vian (Crocker)
1919-1969 .... *11*
Smith, Ward
See Goldsmith, Howard
Smith, William A. *10*
Smith, William Jay 1918- *2*
Smith, Winsome 1935- *45*
Smith, Z. Z.
See Westheimer, David
Smits, Teo
See Smits, Theodore R(ichard)
Smits, Theodore R(ichard)
1905- *45*
Brief Entry *28*
Smucker, Barbara (Claassen)
1915- *29*
See also CLR 10
Snedeker, Caroline Dale (Parke)
1871-1956 .... *YABC 2*
Snell, Nigel (Edward Creagh) 1936-
Brief Entry *40*
Snellgrove, L(aurence) E(rnest)
1928- *53*
Sneve, Virginia Driving Hawk
1933- *8*
See also CLR 2
Sniff, Mr.
See Abisch, Roslyn Kroop
Snodgrass, Thomas Jefferson
See Clemens, Samuel Langhorne
Snook, Barbara (Lillian)
1913-1976 .... *34*
Snow, Donald Clifford 1917- *16*
Snow, Dorothea J(ohnston)
1909- *9*

Snow, Richard F(olger) 1947- *52*
Brief Entry *37*
Snyder, Anne 1922- *4*
Snyder, Carol 1941- *35*
Snyder, Gerald S(eymour)
1933- *48*
Brief Entry *34*
Snyder, Jerome 1916-1976
Obituary *20*
Snyder, Zilpha Keatley 1927- *28*
Earlier sketch in SATA 1
See also SAAS 2
Snyderman, Reuven K. 1922- *5*
Soble, Jennie
See Cavin, Ruth (Brodie)
Sobol, Donald J. 1924- *31*
Earlier sketch in SATA 1
See also CLR 4
Sobol, Harriet Langsam 1936- *47*
Brief Entry *34*
Soderlind, Arthur E(dwin)
1920- *14*
Softly, Barbara (Frewin)
1924- *12*
Soglow, Otto 1900-1975
Obituary *30*
Sohl, Frederic J(ohn) 1916- *10*
Sokol, Bill
See Sokol, William
Sokol, William 1923- *37*
Sokolov, Kirill 1930- *34*
Solbert, Romaine G. 1925- *2*
Solbert, Ronni
See Solbert, Romaine G.
Solomon, Joan 1930(?)- *51*
Brief Entry *40*
Solomons, Ikey, Esquire, Jr.
See Thackeray, William Makepeace
Solonevich, George 1915- *15*
Solot, Mary Lynn 1939- *12*
Sommer, Elyse 1929- *7*
Sommer, Robert 1929- *12*
Sommerfelt, Aimee 1892- *5*
Sonneborn, Ruth (Cantor) A.
1899-1974 .... *4*
Obituary *27*
Sorche, Nic Leodhas
See Alger, Leclaire (Gowans)
Sorel, Edward 1929-
Brief Entry *37*
Sorensen, Virginia 1912- *2*
Sorley Walker, Kathrine *41*
Sorrentino, Joseph N. *6*
Sortor, June Elizabeth 1939- *12*
Sortor, Toni
See Sortor, June Elizabeth
Soskin, V. H.
See Ellison, Virginia Howell
Sotomayor, Antonio 1902- *11*
Soudley, Henry
See Wood, James Playsted
Soule, Gardner (Bosworth)
1913- *14*
Soule, Jean Conder 1919- *10*
Southall, Ivan 1921- *3*
See also CLR 2
See also SAAS 3
Spanfeller, James J(ohn)
1930- *19*

Spangenberg, Judith Dunn
1942- *5*
Spar, Jerome 1918- *10*
Sparks, Beatrice Mathews
1918- *44*
Brief Entry *28*
Sparks, Mary W. 1920- *15*
Spaulding, Leonard
See Bradbury, Ray
Speare, Elizabeth George
1908- *5*
See also CLR 8
Spearing, Judith (Mary Harlow)
1922- *9*
Specking, Inez 1890-196(?) *11*
Speicher, Helen Ross (Smith)
1915- *8*
Spellman, John W(illard)
1934- *14*
Spelman, Mary 1934- *28*
Spence, Eleanor (Rachel)
1927- *21*
Spence, Geraldine 1931- *47*
Spencer, Ann 1918- *10*
Spencer, Cornelia
See Yaukey, Grace S.
Spencer, Donald D(ean) 1931- *41*
Spencer, Elizabeth 1921- *14*
Spencer, William 1922- *9*
Spencer, Zane A(nn) 1935- *35*
Sperry, Armstrong W.
1897-1976 .... *1*
Obituary *27*
Sperry, Raymond, Jr. [Collective
pseudonym] *1*
Spicer, Dorothy (Gladys)
(?)-1975 .... *32*
Spiegelman, Judith M. *5*
Spielberg, Steven 1947- *32*
Spier, Peter (Edward) 1927- *4*
See also CLR 5
Spilhaus, Athelstan 1911- *13*
Spilka, Arnold 1917- *6*
Spinelli, Eileen 1942- *38*
Spinelli, Jerry 1941- *39*
Spink, Reginald (William)
1905- *11*
Spinner, Stephanie 1943- *38*
Spinossimus
See White, William
Splaver, Sarah 1921-
Brief Entry *28*
Spollen, Christopher 1952- *12*
Sprague, Gretchen (Burnham)
1926- *27*
Sprigge, Elizabeth 1900-1974 ..... *10*
Spring, (Robert) Howard
1889-1965 .... *28*
Springer, Marilyn Harris
1931- *47*
Springstubb, Tricia 1950- *46*
Brief Entry *40*
Spykman, E(lizabeth) C.
19(?)-1965 .... *10*
Spyri, Johanna (Heusser)
1827-1901 .... *19*
See also CLR 13
Squire, Miriam
See Sprigge, Elizabeth

Squires, Phil
  See Barker, S. Omar
S-Ringi, Kjell
  See Ringi, Kjell
Srivastava, Jane Jonas
  Brief Entry 37
Stadtler, Bea 1921- 17
Stafford, Jean 1915-1979
  Obituary 22
Stahl, Ben(jamin) 1910- 5
Stahl, Hilda 1938- 48
Stair, Gobin (John) 1912- 35
Stalder, Valerie 27
Stamaty, Mark Alan 1947- 12
Stambler, Irwin 1924- 5
Stanek, Muriel (Novella) 1915-
  Brief Entry 34
Stang, Judit 1921-1977 29
Stang, Judy
  See Stang, Judit
Stanhope, Eric
  See Hamilton, Charles H. St. John
Stankevich, Boris 1928- 2
Stanley, Diana 1909-
  Brief Entry 30
Stanley, Diane 1943- 37
  Brief Entry 32
Stanley, George Edward
  1942- 53
Stanley, Robert
  See Hamilton, Charles H. St. John
Stanli, Sue
  See Meilach, Dona Z(weigoron)
Stanovich, Betty Jo 1954-
  Brief Entry 51
Stanstead, John
  See Groom, Arthur William
Stapleton, Marjorie (Winifred)
  1932- 28
Stapp, Arthur D(onald)
  1906-1972 4
Starbird, Kaye 1916- 6
Stark, James
  See Goldston, Robert
Starkey, Marion L. 1901- 13
Starr, Ward and Murch, Mel [Joint
  double pseudonym]
  See Manes, Stephen
Starret, William
  See McClintock, Marshall
Stasiak, Krystyna 49
Stauffer, Don
  See Berkebile, Fred D(onovan)
Staunton, Schuyler
  See Baum, L(yman) Frank
Steadman, Ralph (Idris) 1936- 32
Stearns, Monroe (Mather)
  1913- 5
Steele, Chester K.
  See Stratemeyer, Edward L.
Steele, Mary Q(uintard Govan)
  1922- 51
  Earlier sketch in SATA 3
Steele, (Henry) Max(well)
  1922- 10
Steele, William O(wen)
  1917-1979 51
  Obituary 27
  Earlier sketch in SATA 1

Stegeman, Janet Allais 1923- 53
  Brief Entry 49
Steig, William 1907- 18
  See also CLR 2
Stein, Harvé 1904-
  Brief Entry 30
Stein, M(eyer) L(ewis) 6
Stein, Mini 2
Stein, R(ichard) Conrad 1937- 31
Stein, Sara Bonnett
  Brief Entry 34
Steinbeck, John (Ernst)
  1902-1968 9
Steinberg, Alfred 1917- 9
Steinberg, Fannie 1899- 43
Steinberg, Fred J. 1933- 4
Steinberg, Phillip Orso 1921- 34
Steinberg, Rafael (Mark)
  1927- 45
Steiner, Barbara A(nnette)
  1934- 13
Steiner, Charlotte 1900-1981 45
Steiner, Jörg 1930- 35
Steiner, Stan(ley) 1925-1987 14
  Obituary 50
Steiner-Prag, Hugo 1880-1945
  Brief Entry 32
Stephens, Mary Jo 1935- 8
Stephens, William M(cLain)
  1925- 21
Stephensen, A. M.
  See Manes, Stephen
Stepp, Ann 1935- 29
Steptoe, John (Lewis) 1950- 8
  See also CLR 2, 12
Sterling, Brett
  See Samachson, Joseph
Sterling, Dorothy 1913- 1
  See also CLR 1
  See also SAAS 2
Sterling, Helen
  See Hoke, Helen (L.)
Sterling, Philip 1907- 8
Stern, Ellen N(orman) 1927- 26
Stern, Madeleine B(ettina)
  1912- 14
Stern, Philip Van Doren
  1900-1984 13
  Obituary 39
Stern, Simon 1943- 15
Sterne, Emma Gelders
  1894-1971 6
Steurt, Marjorie Rankin 1888- 10
Stevens, Carla M(cBride)
  1928- 13
Stevens, Franklin 1933- 6
Stevens, Gwendolyn 1944- 33
Stevens, Kathleen 1936- 49
Stevens, Patricia Bunning
  1931- 27
Stevens, Peter
  See Geis, Darlene
Stevenson, Anna (M.) 1905- 12
Stevenson, Augusta
  1869(?)-1976 2
  Obituary 26
Stevenson, Burton E(gbert)
  1872-1962 25

Stevenson, James 1929- 42
  Brief Entry 34
Stevenson, Janet 1913- 8
Stevenson, Robert Louis
  1850-1894 .... YABC 2
  See also CLR 10, 11
Stewart, A(gnes) C(harlotte) 15
Stewart, Charles
  See Zurhorst, Charles (Stewart, Jr.)
Stewart, Elizabeth Laing
  1907- 6
Stewart, George Rippey
  1895-1980 3
  Obituary 23
Stewart, John (William) 1920- 14
Stewart, Mary (Florence Elinor)
  1916- 12
Stewart, Robert Neil
  1891-1972 7
Stewart, Scott
  See Zaffo, George J.
Stewart, W(alter) P. 1924- 53
Stewig, John Warren 1937- 26
Stiles, Martha Bennett 6
Stiles, Norman B. 1942-
  Brief Entry 36
Still, James 1906- 29
Stillerman, Robbie 1947- 12
Stilley, Frank 1918- 29
Stine, G(eorge) Harry 1928- 10
Stine, Jovial Bob
  See Stine, Robert Lawrence
Stine, Robert Lawrence 1943- 31
Stinetorf, Louise 1900- 10
Stirling, Arthur
  See Sinclair, Upton (Beall)
Stirling, Nora B. 3
Stirnweis, Shannon 1931- 10
Stobbs, William 1914- 17
Stockton, Francis Richard
  1834-1902 44
Stockton, Frank R(ichard)
  Brief Entry 32
  See Stockton, Francis Richard
Stoddard, Edward G. 1923- 10
Stoddard, Hope 1900- 6
Stoddard, Sandol
  See Warburg, Sandol Stoddard
Stoiko, Michael 1919- 14
Stoker, Abraham 1847-1912 29
Stoker, Bram
  See Stoker, Abraham
Stokes, Cedric
  See Beardmore, George
Stokes, Jack (Tilden) 1923- 13
Stokes, Olivia Pearl 1916- 32
Stolz, Mary (Slattery) 1920- 10
  See also SAAS 3
Stone, Alan [Collective
  pseudonym] 1
  See also Svenson, Andrew E.
Stone, D(avid) K(arl) 1922- 9
Stone, Eugenia 1879-1971 7
Stone, Gene
  See Stone, Eugenia
Stone, Helen V. 6
Stone, Irving 1903- 3
Stone, Jon 1931- 39

Stone, Josephine Rector
See Dixon, Jeanne
Stone, Raymond [Collective
pseudonym] *1*
Stone, Richard A.
See Stratemeyer, Edward L.
Stonehouse, Bernard 1926- *13*
Stong, Phil(ip Duffield)
1899-1957 .... *32*
Storch, Anne B. von
See von Storch, Anne B.
Storey, (Elizabeth) Margaret (Carlton)
1926- *9*
Storey, Victoria Carolyn
1945- *16*
Storme, Peter
See Stern, Philip Van Doren
Storr, Catherine (Cole) 1913- *9*
Story, Josephine
See Loring, Emilie (Baker)
Stoutenburg, Adrien 1916- *3*
Stover, Allan C(arl) 1938- *14*
Stover, Marjorie Filley 1914- *9*
Stowe, Harriet (Elizabeth) Beecher
1811-1896 .... *YABC 1*
Strachan, Margaret Pitcairn
1908- *14*
Strait, Treva Adams 1909- *35*
Strand, Mark 1934- *41*
Strange, Philippa
See Coury, Louise Andree
Stranger, Joyce
See Wilson, Joyce M(uriel Judson)
Strasser, Todd 1950- *45*
See also CLR 11
Stratemeyer, Edward L.
1862-1930 .... *1*
Stratford, Philip 1927- *47*
Stratton, Thomas [Joint pseudonym]
See DeWeese, Thomas Eugene
Stratton-Porter, Gene
1863-1924 .... *15*
Strauss, Joyce 1936- *53*
Strayer, E. Ward
See Stratemeyer, Edward L.
Streano, Vince(nt Catello)
1945- *20*
Streatfeild, Noel 1897-1985 .... *20*
Obituary *48*
Street, Julia Montgomery
1898- *11*
Stren, Patti 1949-
Brief Entry *41*
See also CLR 5
Strete, Craig Kee 1950- *44*
Stretton, Barbara (Humphrey)
1936- *43*
Brief Entry *35*
Strong, Charles [Joint pseudonym]
See Epstein, Beryl and Epstein,
Samuel
Strong, David
See McGuire, Leslie (Sarah)
Strong, J. J.
See Strong, Jeremy
Strong, Jeremy 1949- *36*
Ströyer, Poul 1923- *13*
Stuart, David
See Hoyt, Edwin P(almer), Jr.

Stuart, Forbes 1924- *13*
Stuart, Ian
See MacLean, Alistair (Stuart)
Stuart, (Hilton) Jesse
1907-1984 .... *2*
Obituary *36*
Stuart, Sheila
See Baker, Mary Gladys Steel
Stuart-Clark, Christopher
1940- *32*
Stubbs, Joanna 1940-
Brief Entry *53*
Stubis, Talivaldis 1926- *5*
Stubley, Trevor (Hugh) 1932- *22*
Stultifer, Morton
See Curtis, Richard (Alan)
Sture-Vasa, Mary
See Alsop, Mary O'Hara
Sturton, Hugh
See Johnston, H(ugh) A(nthony)
S(tephen)
Sturtzel, Howard A(llison)
1894- *1*
Sturtzel, Jane Levington
1903- *1*
Styles, Frank Showell 1908- *10*
Suba, Susanne *4*
Subond, Valerie
See Grayland, Valerie
Sudbery, Rodie 1943- *42*
Sugarman, Tracy 1921- *37*
Sugita, Yutaka 1930- *36*
Suhl, Yuri 1908-1986 .... *8*
Obituary *50*
See also CLR 2
See also SAAS 1
Suid, Murray 1942- *27*
Sullivan, George E(dward)
1927- *4*
Sullivan, Mary W(ilson)
1907- *13*
Sullivan, Thomas Joseph, Jr.
1947- *16*
Sullivan, Tom
See Sullivan, Thomas Joseph, Jr.
Sumichrast, Jözef 1948- *29*
Sumiko
See Davies, Sumiko
Summers, James L(evingston) 1910-
Brief Entry *28*
Sunderlin, Sylvia 1911- *28*
Sung, Betty Lee *26*
Supraner, Robyn 1930- *20*
Surge, Frank 1931- *13*
Susac, Andrew 1929- *5*
Sussman, Susan 1942- *48*
Sutcliff, Rosemary 1920- *44*
Earlier sketch in SATA 6
See also CLR 1
Sutherland, Efua (Theodora Morgue)
1924- *25*
Sutherland, Margaret 1941- *15*
Sutherland, Zena B(ailey)
1915- *37*
Suttles, Shirley (Smith) 1922- *21*
Sutton, Ann (Livesay) 1923- *31*
Sutton, Eve(lyn Mary) 1906- *26*
Sutton, Felix 1910(?)- *31*

Sutton, Jane 1950- *52*
Brief Entry *43*
Sutton, Larry M(atthew)
1931- *29*
Sutton, Margaret (Beebe)
1903- *1*
Sutton, Myron Daniel 1925- *31*
Svenson, Andrew E.
1910-1975 .... *2*
Obituary *26*
Swain, Su Zan (Noguchi)
1916- *21*
Swan, Susan 1944- *22*
Swarthout, Glendon (Fred)
1918- *26*
Swarthout, Kathryn 1919- *7*
Swayne, Sam(uel F.) 1907- *53*
Swayne, Zoa (Lourana) 1905- *53*
Sweeney, James B(artholomew)
1910- *21*
Sweeney, Karen O'Connor
See O'Connor, Karen
Sweetland, Nancy A(nn)
1934- *48*
Swenson, Allan A(rmstrong)
1933- *21*
Swenson, May 1919- *15*
Swift, David
See Kaufmann, John
Swift, Hildegarde Hoyt 1890(?)-1977
Obituary *20*
Swift, Jonathan 1667-1745 .... *19*
Swift, Merlin
See Leeming, Joseph
Swiger, Elinor Porter 1927- *8*
Swinburne, Laurence 1924- *9*
Swindells, Robert E(dward)
1939- *50*
Brief Entry *34*
Switzer, Ellen 1923- *48*
Sydney, Frank [Joint pseudonym]
See Warwick, Alan R(oss)
Sylvester, Natalie G(abry)
1922- *22*
Syme, (Neville) Ronald 1913- *2*
Symons, (Dorothy) Geraldine
1909- *33*
Symons, Stuart
See Stanley, George Edward
Synge, (Phyllis) Ursula 1930- *9*
Sypher, Lucy Johnston 1907- *7*
Szasz, Suzanne Shorr 1919- *13*
Szekeres, Cyndy 1933- *5*
Szudek, Agnes S(usan) P(hilomena)
Brief Entry *49*
Szulc, Tad 1926- *26*

T

Taback, Simms 1932- *40*
Brief Entry *36*
Taber, Gladys (Bagg) 1899-1980
Obituary *22*
Tabrah, Ruth Milander 1921- *14*
Tafuri, Nancy 1946- *39*
Tait, Douglas 1944- *12*
Takakjian, Portia 1930- *15*
Takashima, Shizuye 1928- *13*

Talbot, Charlene Joy 1928- *10*
Talbot, Toby 1928- *14*
Talker, T.
    See Rands, William Brighty
Tallcott, Emogene *10*
Tallon, Robert 1939- *43*
    Brief Entry *28*
Talmadge, Marian *14*
Tamarin, Alfred *13*
Tamburine, Jean 1930- *12*
Tang, You-Shan 1946- *53*
Tannen, Mary 1943- *37*
Tannenbaum, Beulah 1916- *3*
Tannenbaum, D(onald) Leb
    1948- *42*
Tanner, Louise S(tickney)
    1922- *9*
Tanobe, Miyuki 1937- *23*
Tapio, Pat Decker
    See Kines, Pat Decker
Tapp, Kathy Kennedy 1949-
    Brief Entry *50*
Tarkington, (Newton) Booth
    1869-1946 .... *17*
Tarry, Ellen 1906- *16*
Tarshis, Jerome 1936- *9*
Tarsky, Sue 1946- *41*
Tashjian, Virginia A. 1921- *3*
Tasker, James *9*
Tate, Eleanora E(laine) 1948- *38*
Tate, Ellalice
    See Hibbert, Eleanor
Tate, Joan 1922- *9*
Tate, Mary Anne
    See Hale, Arlene
Tatham, Campbell
    See Elting, Mary
Taves, Isabella 1915- *27*
Taylor, Ann 1782-1866 .... *41*
    Brief Entry *35*
Taylor, Barbara J. 1927- *10*
Taylor, Carl 1937- *14*
Taylor, David 1900-1965 .... *10*
Taylor, Elizabeth 1912-1975 ...... *13*
Taylor, Florence Walton *9*
Taylor, Florence M(arion Tompkins)
    1892- *9*
Taylor, Herb(ert Norman, Jr.)
    1942- *22*
Taylor, Jane 1783-1824 .... *41*
    Brief Entry *35*
Taylor, Jerry Duncan 1938- *47*
Taylor, Judy
    See Hough, Judy Taylor
Taylor, Kenneth N(athaniel)
    1917- *26*
Taylor, L(ester) B(arbour), Jr.
    1932- *27*
Taylor, Louise Todd 1939- *47*
Taylor, Mark 1927- *32*
    Brief Entry *28*
Taylor, Mildred D. *15*
    See also CLR 9
    See also SAAS 5
Taylor, Paula (Wright) 1942- *48*
    Brief Entry *33*
Taylor, Robert Lewis 1912- *10*

Taylor, Sydney (Brenner)
    1904(?)-1978 .... *28*
    Obituary *26*
    Earlier sketch in SATA 1
Taylor, Theodore 1924- *5*
    See also SAAS 4
Teague, Bob
    See Teague, Robert
Teague, Robert 1929- *32*
    Brief Entry *31*
Teal, Val 1903- *10*
Teale, Edwin Way 1899-1980 ..... *7*
    Obituary *25*
Teasdale, Sara 1884-1933 .... *32*
Tebbel, John (William) 1912- *26*
Tee-Van, Helen Damrosch
    1893-1976 .... *10*
    Obituary *27*
Teleki, Geza 1943- *45*
Telemaque, Eleanor Wong
    1934- *43*
Telescope, Tom
    See Newbery, John
Temkin, Sara Anne (Schlossberg)
    1913- *26*
Temko, Florence *13*
Tempest, Margaret Mary 1892-1982
    Obituary *33*
Templar, Maurice
    See Groom, Arthur William
Temple, Herbert 1919- *45*
Temple, Paul [Joint pseudonym]
    See McConnell, James Douglas
    (Rutherford)
Tenggren, Gustaf 1896-1970 ...... *18*
    Obituary *26*
Tennant, Kylie 1912- *6*
Tennant, Veronica 1946- *36*
Tenniel, Sir John 1820-1914
    Brief Entry *27*
Terban, Marvin
    Brief Entry *45*
ter Haar, Jaap 1922- *6*
Terhune, Albert Payson
    1872-1942 .... *15*
Terlouw, Jan (Cornelis) 1931- *30*
Terris, Susan 1937- *3*
Terry, Luther L(eonidas)
    1911-1985 .... *11*
    Obituary *42*
Terry, Walter 1913- *14*
Terzian, James P. 1915- *14*
Tester, Sylvia Root 1939-
    Brief Entry *37*
Tether, (Cynthia) Graham
    1950- *46*
    Brief Entry *36*
Thacher, Mary McGrath
    1933- *9*
Thackeray, William Makepeace
    1811-1863 .... *23*
Thaler, Michael C. 1936-
    Brief Entry *47*
Thaler, Mike
    See Thaler, Michael C.
Thamer, Katie 1955- *42*
Thane, Elswyth 1900- *32*
Tharp, Louise Hall 1898- *3*

Thayer, Jane
    See Woolley, Catherine
Thayer, Marjorie
    Brief Entry *37*
Thayer, Peter
    See Wyler, Rose
Thelwell, Norman 1923- *14*
Theroux, Paul 1941- *44*
Thieda, Shirley Ann 1943- *13*
Thiele, Colin (Milton) 1920- *14*
    See also SAAS 2
Thiry, Joan (Marie) 1926- *45*
Thistlethwaite, Miles 1945- *12*
Thollander, Earl 1922- *22*
Thomas, Allison
    See Fleischer, Leonore
Thomas, Andrea
    See Hill, Margaret (Ohler)
Thomas, Art(hur Lawrence)
    1952- *48*
    Brief Entry *38*
Thomas, Estelle Webb 1899- *26*
Thomas, H. C.
    See Keating, Lawrence A.
Thomas, Ianthe 1951-
    Brief Entry *42*
    See also CLR 8
Thomas, J. F.
    See Fleming, Thomas J(ames)
Thomas, Jane Resh 1936- *38*
Thomas, Joan Gale
    See Robinson, Joan G.
Thomas, Joyce Carol 1938- *40*
Thomas, Lowell (Jackson), Jr.
    1923- *15*
Thomas, Patricia J. 1934- *51*
Thomas, Victoria [Joint pseudonym]
    See DeWeese, Thomas Eugene
Thompson, Brenda 1935- *34*
Thompson, Christine Pullein
    See Pullein-Thompson, Christine
Thompson, David H(ugh)
    1941- *17*
Thompson, Diana Pullein
    See Pullein-Thompson, Diana
Thompson, Eileen
    See Panowski, Eileen Thompson
Thompson, George Selden
    1929- *4*
Thompson, Harlan H.
    1894-1987 .... *10*
    Obituary *53*
Thompson, Hilary 1943-
    Brief Entry *49*
Thompson, Josephine
    See Pullein-Thompson, Josephine
Thompson, Julian F(rancis) 1927-
    Brief Entry *40*
Thompson, Kay 1912- *16*
Thompson, Stith 1885-1976
    Obituary *20*
Thompson, Vivian L. 1911- *3*
Thomson, David (Robert Alexander)
    1914- *40*
Thomson, Peggy 1922- *31*
Thorburn, John
    See Goldsmith, John Herman
    Thorburn

Thorndyke, Helen Louise
  [Collective pseudonym] *1*
Thorne, Ian
  See May, Julian
Thornton, W. B.
  See Burgess, Thornton Waldo
Thorpe, E(ustace) G(eorge)
  1916- *21*
Thorvall, Kerstin 1925- *13*
Thrasher, Crystal (Faye)
  1921- *27*
Thum, Gladys 1920- *26*
Thum, Marcella *28*
  Earlier sketch in SATA 3
Thundercloud, Katherine
  See Witt, Shirley Hill
Thurber, James (Grover)
  1894-1961 .... *13*
Thurman, Judith 1946- *33*
Thwaite, Ann (Barbara Harrop)
  1932- *14*
Ticheburn, Cheviot
  See Ainsworth, William Harrison
Tichenor, Tom 1923- *14*
Tichy, William 1924- *31*
Tiegreen, Alan F. 1935-
  Brief Entry *36*
Tilton, Madonna Elaine 1929- *41*
Tilton, Rafael
  See Tilton, Madonna Elaine
Timmins, William F. *10*
Tiner, John Hudson 1944- *32*
Tinkelman, Murray 1933- *12*
Tinkle, (Julien) Lon
  1906-1980 .... *36*
Titler, Dale M(ilton) 1926- *35*
  Brief Entry *28*
Titmarsh, Michael Angelo
  See Thackeray, William Makepeace
Titus, Eve 1922- *2*
Tobias, Tobi 1938- *5*
  See also CLR 4
Todd, Anne Ophelia
  See Dowden, Anne Ophelia
Todd, Barbara K. 1917- *10*
Todd, H(erbert) E(atton)
  1908- *11*
Todd, Loreto 1942- *30*
Tolan, Stephanie S. 1942- *38*
Toland, John (Willard) 1912- *38*
Tolkien, J(ohn) R(onald) R(euel)
  1892-1973 .... *32*
  Obituary *24*
  Earlier sketch in SATA 2
Tolles, Martha 1921- *8*
Tolliver, Ruby C(hangos) 1922-
  Brief Entry *41*
Tolmie, Ken(neth Donald)
  1941- *15*
Tolstoi, Leo (Nikolaevich)
  1828-1910 .... *26*
Tomalin, Ruth *29*
Tomes, Margot (Ladd) 1917- *36*
  Brief Entry *27*
Tomfool
  See Farjeon, Eleanor
Tomkins, Jasper
  See Batey, Tom

Tomline, F. Latour
  See Gilbert, W(illiam) S(chwenk)
Tomlinson, Jill 1931-1976 .... *3*
  Obituary *24*
Tomlinson, Reginald R(obert)
  1885-1979(?)
  Obituary *27*
Tompert, Ann 1918- *14*
Toner, Raymond John 1908- *10*
Took, Belladonna
  See Chapman, Vera
Tooke, Louise Mathews 1950- *38*
Toonder, Martin
  See Groom, Arthur William
Toothaker, Roy Eugene 1928- *18*
Tooze, Ruth 1892-1972 .... *4*
Topping, Audrey R(onning)
  1928- *14*
Tor, Regina
  See Shekerjian, Regina Tor
Torbert, Floyd James 1922- *22*
Torgersen, Don Arthur 1934-
  Brief Entry *41*
Torrie, Malcolm
  See Mitchell, Gladys (Maude
   Winifred)
Totham, Mary
  See Breinburg, Petronella
Tournier, Michel 1924- *23*
Towne, Mary
  See Spelman, Mary
Townsend, John Rowe 1922- *4*
  See also CLR 2
  See also SAAS 2
Townsend, Sue 1946-
  Brief Entry *48*
Toye, Clive 1933(?)-
  Brief Entry *30*
Toye, William E(ldred) 1926- *8*
Traherne, Michael
  See Watkins-Pitchford, D. J.
Trahey, Jane 1923- *36*
Trapp, Maria (Augusta) von
  1905- *16*
Travers, P(amela) L(yndon)
  1906- *4*
  See also CLR 2
  See also SAAS 2
Treadgold, Mary 1910- *49*
Trease, (Robert) Geoffrey
  1909- *2*
  See also SAAS 6
Tredez, Alain 1926- *17*
Tredez, Denise (Laugier)
  1930- *50*
Treece, Henry 1911-1966 .... *2*
  See also CLR 2
Tregarthen, Enys
  See Sloggett, Nellie
Tregaskis, Richard 1916-1973 ..... *3*
  Obituary *26*
Trell, Max 1900- *14*
Tremain, Ruthven 1922- *17*
Trent, Robbie 1894- *26*
Trent, Timothy
  See Malmberg, Carl
Tresilian, (Cecil) Stuart
  1891-19(?) *40*
Tresselt, Alvin 1916- *7*

Treviño, Elizabeth B(orton) de
  1904- *29*
  Earlier sketch in SATA 1
  See also SAAS 5
Trevor, Elleston 1920- *28*
Trevor, Glen
  See Hilton, James
Trevor, (Lucy) Meriol 1919- *10*
Trez, Alain
  See Tredez, Alain
Trez, Denise
  See Tredez, Denise (Laugier)
Trimby, Elisa 1948- *47*
  Brief Entry *40*
Tripp, Eleanor B. 1936- *4*
Tripp, Paul *8*
Tripp, Wallace (Whitney)
  1940- *31*
Trivelpiece, Laurel 1926-
  Brief Entry *46*
Trivett, Daphne (Harwood)
  1940- *22*
Trnka, Jiri 1912-1969 .... *43*
  Brief Entry *32*
Trollope, Anthony 1815-1882 ... *22*
Trost, Lucille Wood 1938- *12*
Trotter, Grace V(iolet) 1900- *10*
Troughton, Joanna (Margaret)
  1947- *37*
Troyer, Johannes 1902-1969
  Brief Entry *40*
Trudeau, G(arretson) B(eekman)
  1948- *35*
Trudeau, Garry B.
  See Trudeau, G(arretson) B(eekman)
Truesdell, Sue
  See Truesdell, Susan G.
Truesdell, Susan G.
  Brief Entry *45*
Truss, Jan 1925- *35*
Tucker, Caroline
  See Nolan, Jeannette
Tudor, Tasha *20*
  See also CLR 13
Tully, John (Kimberley)
  1923- *14*
Tunis, Edwin (Burdett)
  1897-1973 .... *28*
  Obituary *24*
  Earlier sketch in SATA 1
  See also CLR 2
Tunis, John R(oberts)
  1889-1975 .... *37*
  Brief Entry *30*
Turkle, Brinton 1915- *2*
Turlington, Bayly 1919-1977 ...... *5*
  Obituary *52*
Turnbull, Agnes Sligh *14*
Turnbull, Ann (Christine)
  1943- *18*
Turner, Alice K. 1940- *10*
Turner, Ann W(arren) 1945- *14*
Turner, Elizabeth
  1774-1846 ....*YABC 2*
Turner, Josie
  See Crawford, Phyllis
Turner, Philip 1925- *11*
  See also SAAS 6

Turner, Sheila R.
    See Seed, Sheila Turner
Turngren, Annette 1902(?)-1980
    Obituary 23
Turngren, Ellen (?)-1964 3
Turska, Krystyna Zofia 1933- 31
    Brief Entry 27
Tusan, Stan 1936- 22
Tusiani, Joseph 1924- 45
Twain, Mark
    See Clemens, Samuel Langhorne
Tweedsmuir, Baron
    See Buchan, John
Tweton, D. Jerome 1933- 48
Tworkov, Jack 1900-1982 47
    Obituary 31
Tyler, Anne 1941- 7

U

Ubell, Earl 1926- 4
Uchida, Yoshiko 1921- 53
    Earlier sketch in SATA 1
    See also CLR 6
    See also SAAS 1
Udall, Jan Beaney 1938- 10
Uden, (Bernard Gilbert) Grant
    1910- 26
Udry, Janice May 1928- 4
Ulam, S(tanislaw) M(arcin)
    1909-1984 51
Ullman, James Ramsey
    1907-1971 7
Ulm, Robert 1934-1977 17
Ulmer, Louise 1943- 53
Ulyatt, Kenneth 1920- 14
Unada
    See Gliewe, Unada
Uncle Gus
    See Rey, H. A.
Uncle Mac
    See McCulloch, Derek (Ivor
    Breashur)
Uncle Ray
    See Coffman, Ramon Peyton
Uncle Shelby
    See Silverstein, Shel(by)
Underhill, Alice Mertie 1900-1971
Underhill, Liz 1948- 53
    Brief Entry 49
Ungerer, (Jean) Thomas 1931- 33
    Earlier sketch in SATA 5
Ungerer, Tomi
    See Ungerer, (Jean) Thomas
    See also CLR 3
Unkelbach, Kurt 1913- 4
Unnerstad, Edith 1900- 3
Unrau, Ruth 1922- 9
Unstead, R(obert) J(ohn)
    1915- 12
Unsworth, Walt 1928- 4
Untermeyer, Louis 1885-1977 37
    Obituary 26
    Earlier sketch in SATA 2
Unwin, David S(torr) 1918- 14
Unwin, Nora S. 1907-1982 3
    Obituary 49
Ure, Jean 48

Uris, Leon (Marcus) 1924- 49
Usher, Margo Scegge
    See McHargue, Georgess
Uttley, Alice Jane (Taylor)
    1884-1976 3
    Obituary 26
Uttley, Alison
    See Uttley, Alice Jane (Taylor)
Utz, Lois 1932-1986 5
    Obituary 50
Uzair, Salem ben
    See Horne, Richard Henry

V

Vaeth, J(oseph) Gordon 1921- 17
Valen, Nanine 1950- 21
Valencak, Hannelore 1929- 42
Valens, Evans G., Jr. 1920- 1
Valleau, Emily 1925- 51
Van Abbé, Salaman
    1883-1955 18
Van Allsburg, Chris 1949- 53
    Earlier sketch in SATA 37
    See also CLR 5
    See also CLR 13
Van Anrooy, Francine 1924- 2
Van Anrooy, Frans
    See Van Anrooy, Francine
Vance, Eleanor Graham 1908- 11
Vance, Marguerite 1889-1965 29
Vandenburg, Mary Lou 1943- 17
Vander Boom, Mae M. 14
Van der Veer, Judy
    1912-1982 4
    Obituary 33
Vandivert, Rita (Andre) 1905- 21
Van Duyn, Janet 1910- 18
Van Dyne, Edith
    See Baum, L(yman) Frank
Van Horn, William 1939- 43
Van Iterson, S(iny) R(ose) 26
Van Leeuwen, Jean 1937- 6
Van Lhin, Erik
    See Del Rey, Lester
Van Loon, Hendrik Willem
    1882-1944 18
Van Orden, M(erton) D(ick)
    1921- 4
Van Rensselaer, Alexander (Taylor
    Mason) 1892-1962 14
Van Riper, Guernsey, Jr.
    1909- 3
Van Steenwyk, Elizabeth Ann
    1928- 34
Van Stockum, Hilda 1908- 5
Van Tuyl, Barbara 1940- 11
Van Vogt, A(lfred) E(lton)
    1912- 14
Van Woerkom, Dorothy (O'Brien)
    1924- 21
Van Wormer, Joe
    See Van Wormer, Joseph Edward
Van Wormer, Joseph Edward
    1913- 35
Van-Wyck Mason, F.
    See Mason, F. van Wyck

Van Zwienen, Ilse (Charlotte Koehn)
    1929- 34
    Brief Entry 28
Varga, Judy
    See Stang, Judit
Varley, Dimitry V. 1906- 10
Vasiliu, Mircea 1920- 2
Vass, George 1927-
    Brief Entry 31
Vaughan, Carter A.
    See Gerson, Noel B(ertram)
Vaughan, Harold Cecil 1923- 14
Vaughan, Sam(uel) S. 1928- 14
Vaughn, Ruth 1935- 14
Vautier, Ghislaine 1932- 53
Vavra, Robert James 1944- 8
Vecsey, George 1939- 9
Veglahn, Nancy (Crary) 1937- 5
Velthuijs, Max 1923- 53
Venable, Alan (Hudson)
    1944- 8
Venn, Mary Eleanor
    See Jorgensen, Mary Venn
Ventura, Piero (Luigi) 1937-
    Brief Entry 43
Vequin, Capini
    See Quinn, Elisabeth
Verne, Jules 1828-1905 21
Verner, Gerald 1897(?)-1980
    Obituary 25
Verney, John 1913- 14
Vernon, (Elda) Louise A(nderson)
    1914- 14
Vernon, Rosemary
    See Smith, Susan Vernon
Vernor, D.
    See Casewit, Curtis
Verral, Charles Spain 1904- 11
Verrone, Robert J. 1935(?)-1984
    Obituary 39
Versace, Marie Teresa Rios
    1917- 2
Vesey, Paul
    See Allen, Samuel (Washington)
Vestly, Anne-Cath(arina)
    1920- 14
Vevers, (Henry) Gwynne
    1916- 45
Viator, Vacuus
    See Hughes, Thomas
Vicarion, Count Palmiro
    See Logue, Christopher
Vicker, Angus
    See Felsen, Henry Gregor
Vickery, Kate
    See Kennedy, T(eresa) A.
Victor, Edward 1914- 3
Victor, Joan Berg 1937- 30
Viereck, Ellen K. 1928- 14
Viereck, Phillip 1925- 3
Viertel, Janet 1915- 10
Vigna, Judith 1936- 15
Viguers, Ruth Hill 1903-1971 6
Villiard, Paul 1910-1974 51
    Obituary 20
Villiers, Alan (John) 1903- 10
Vincent, Eric Douglas 1953- 40
Vincent, Félix 1946- 41

Vincent, Gabrielle
  See CLR 13
Vincent, Mary Keith
  See St. John, Wylly Folk
Vinge, Joan D(ennison) 1948- *36*
Vining, Elizabeth Gray
  See Gray, Elizabeth Janet
Vinson, Kathryn 1911- *21*
Vinton, Iris *24*
Viorst, Judith *7*
  See also CLR 3
Vip
  See Partch, Virgil Franklin II
Vipont, Charles
  See Foulds, Elfrida Vipont
Vipont, Elfrida
  See Foulds, Elfrida Vipont
Visser, W(illiam) F(rederick)
  H(endrik) 1900-1968 .... *10*
Vlahos, Olivia 1924- *31*
Vlasic, Bob
  See Hirsch, Phil
Vo-Dinh, Mai 1933- *16*
Vogel, Ilse-Margret 1914- *14*
Vogel, John H(ollister), Jr.
  1950- *18*
Vogt, Esther Loewen 1915- *14*
Vogt, Gregory
  Brief Entry *45*
Vogt, Marie Bollinger 1921- *45*
Voight, Virginia Frances
  1909- *8*
Voigt, Cynthia 1942- *48*
  Brief Entry *33*
  See also CLR 13
Voigt, Erna 1925- *35*
Voigt-Rother, Erna
  See Voigt, Erna
Vojtech, Anna 1946- *42*
von Almedingen, Martha Edith
  See Almedingen, E. M.
Von Hagen, Victor Wolfgang
  1908- *29*
von Klopp, Vahrah
  See Malvern, Gladys
von Schmidt, Eric 1931- *50*
  Brief Entry *36*
von Storch, Anne B. 1910- *1*
Vosburgh, Leonard (W.)
  1912- *15*
Voyle, Mary
  See Manning, Rosemary

W

Waber, Bernard 1924- *47*
  Brief Entry *40*
Wachter, Oralee Roberts 1935-
  Brief Entry *51*
Waddell, Evelyn Margaret
  1918- *10*
Waddell, Martin 1941- *43*
Wade, Theodore E., Jr. 1936- *37*
Wagenheim, Kal 1935- *21*
Wagner, Jane *33*
Wagner, Sharon B. 1936- *4*
Wagoner, David (Russell)
  1926- *14*

Wahl, Jan 1933- *34*
  Earlier sketch in SATA 2
  See also SAAS 3
Waide, Jan 1952- *29*
Wainscott, John Milton
  1910-1981 .... *53*
Waitley, Douglas 1927- *30*
Wakefield, Jean L.
  See Laird, Jean E(louise)
Wakin, Edward 1927- *37*
Walck, Henry Z(eigler) 1908-1984
  Obituary *40*
Walden, Amelia Elizabeth *3*
Waldman, Bruce 1949- *15*
Waldman, Neil 1947- *51*
Waldron, Ann Wood 1924- *16*
Walker, Alice 1944- *31*
Walker, Barbara K. 1921- *4*
Walker, (James) Braz(elton)
  1934-1983 .... *45*
Walker, David Harry 1911- *8*
Walker, Diana 1925- *9*
Walker, Frank 1930- *36*
Walker, Holly Beth
  See Bond, Gladys Baker
Walker, Lou Ann 1952-
  Brief Entry *53*
Walker, Louise Jean 1891-1976
  Obituary *35*
Walker, Mildred
  See Schemm, Mildred Walker
Walker, (Addison) Mort
  1923- *8*
Walker, Pamela 1948- *24*
Walker, Stephen J. 1951- *12*
Wallace, Barbara Brooks *4*
Wallace, Beverly Dobrin
  1921- *19*
Wallace, Bill 1947-
  See Wallace, William Keith
  Brief Entry *47*
Wallace, Daisy
  See Cuyler, Margery Stuyvesant
Wallace, Ian 1950- *53*
Wallace, John A. 1915- *3*
Wallace, Nigel
  See Hamilton, Charles H. St. John
Wallace, Robert 1932- *47*
  Brief Entry *37*
Wallace, William Keith 1947- *53*
Wallace-Brodeur, Ruth 1941- *51*
  Brief Entry *41*
Waller, Leslie 1923- *20*
Wallis, G. McDonald
  See Campbell, Hope
Wallner, Alexandra 1946- *51*
  Brief Entry *41*
Wallner, John C. 1945- *51*
  Earlier sketch in SATA 10
Wallower, Lucille *11*
Walsh, Ellen Stoll 1942- *49*
Walsh, George Johnston
  1889-1981 .... *53*
Walsh, Jill Paton
  See Paton Walsh, Gillian
  See also CLR 2
Walter, Mildred Pitts
  Brief Entry *45*

Walter, Villiam Christian
  See Andersen, Hans Christian
Walters, Audrey 1929- *18*
Walters, Helen B. (?)-1987
  Obituary *50*
Walters, Hugh
  See Hughes, Walter (Llewellyn)
Walther, Thomas A. 1950- *31*
Walther, Tom
  See Walther, Thomas A.
Waltner, Elma 1912- *40*
Waltner, Willard H. 1909- *40*
Walton, Richard J. 1928- *4*
Waltrip, Lela (Kingston)
  1904- *9*
Waltrip, Mildred 1911- *37*
Waltrip, Rufus (Charles)
  1898- *9*
Walworth, Nancy Zinsser
  1917- *14*
Wangerin, Walter, Jr. 1944- *45*
  Brief Entry *37*
Wannamaker, Bruce
  See Moncure, Jane Belk
Warbler, J. M.
  See Cocagnac, A. M.
Warburg, Sandol Stoddard
  1927- *14*
Ward, John (Stanton) 1917- *42*
Ward, Lynd (Kendall)
  1905-1985 .... *36*
  Obituary *42*
  Earlier sketch in SATA 2
Ward, Martha (Eads) 1921- *5*
Ward, Melanie
  See Curtis, Richard (Alan)
Wardell, Dean
  See Prince, J(ack) H(arvey)
Ware, Leon (Vernon) 1909- *4*
Warner, Frank A. [Collective
  pseudonym] *1*
Warner, Gertrude Chandler
  1890- *9*
Warner, Lucille Schulberg *30*
Warner, Oliver 1903-1976 .... *29*
Warren, Betsy
  See Warren, Elizabeth Avery
Warren, Billy
  See Warren, William Stephen
Warren, Cathy
  Brief Entry *46*
Warren, Elizabeth
  See Supraner, Robyn
Warren, Elizabeth Avery
  1916- *46*
  Brief Entry *38*
Warren, Joyce W(illiams)
  1935- *18*
Warren, Mary Phraner 1929- *10*
Warren, Robert Penn 1905- *46*
Warren, William Stephen
  1882-1968 .... *9*
Warrick, Patricia Scott 1925- *35*
Warriner, John 1907(?)-1987
  Obituary *53*
Warsh
  See Warshaw, Jerry
Warshaw, Jerry 1929- *30*
Warshofsky, Fred 1931- *24*

Warshofsky, Isaac
See Singer, Isaac Bashevis
Wartski, Maureen (Ann Crane)
1940- *50*
Brief Entry *37*
Warwick, Alan R(oss)
1900-1973 ....*42*
Wa-sha-quon-asin
See Belaney, Archibald Stansfeld
Washburn, (Henry) Bradford (Jr.)
1910- *38*
Washburne, Heluiz Chandler
1892-1970 ....*10*
Obituary *26*
Washington, Booker T(aliaferro)
1858(?)-1915 ....*28*
Watanabe, Shigeo 1928- *39*
Brief Entry *32*
See also CLR 8
Waters, John F(rederick)
1930- *4*
Waterton, Betty (Marie) 1923- *37*
Brief Entry *34*
Watkins-Pitchford, D. J.
1905- *6*
See also SAAS 4
Watson, Aldren A(uld) 1917- *42*
Brief Entry *36*
Watson, Clyde 1947- *5*
See also CLR 3
Watson, Helen Orr 1892-1978
Obituary *24*
Watson, James 1936- *10*
Watson, Jane Werner 1915- *3*
Watson, Nancy Dingman *32*
Watson, Pauline 1925- *14*
Watson, Sally 1924- *3*
Watson, Wendy (McLeod)
1942- *5*
Watson Taylor, Elizabeth
1915- *41*
Watt, Thomas 1935- *4*
Watts, Bernadette 1942- *4*
Watts, Ephraim
See Horne, Richard Henry
Watts, Franklin (Mowry)
1904-1978 ....*46*
Obituary *21*
Watts, Isaac 1674-1748 ....*52*
Watts, Mabel Pizzey 1906- *11*
Waugh, Carol-Lynn Rössel
1947- *41*
Waugh, Dorothy *11*
Wayland, Patrick
See O'Connor, Richard
Wayne, (Anne) Jenifer
1917-1982 ....*32*
Wayne, Kyra Petrovskaya
1918- *8*
Wayne, Richard
See Decker, Duane
Waystaff, Simon
See Swift, Jonathan
Weales, Gerald (Clifford)
1925- *11*
Weary, Ogdred
See Gorey, Edward St. John
Weaver, John L. 1949- *42*

Weaver, Ward
See Mason, F. van Wyck
Webb, Christopher
See Wibberley, Leonard (Patrick
O'Connor)
Webb, Jean Francis (III)
1910- *35*
Webb, Sharon 1936- *41*
Webber, Irma E(leanor Schmidt)
1904- *14*
Weber, Alfons 1921- *8*
Weber, Lenora Mattingly
1895-1971 ....*2*
Obituary *26*
Weber, William John 1927- *14*
Webster, Alice (Jane Chandler)
1876-1916 ....*17*
Webster, David 1930- *11*
Webster, Frank V. [Collective
pseudonym] *1*
Webster, Gary
See Garrison, Webb B(lack)
Webster, James 1925-1981 ......*17*
Obituary *27*
Webster, Jean
See Webster, Alice (Jane Chandler)
Wechsler, Herman 1904-1976
Obituary *20*
Weddle, Ethel H(arshbarger)
1897- *11*
Wegen, Ron(ald)
Brief Entry *44*
Wegner, Fritz 1924- *20*
Weihs, Erika 1917- *15*
Weik, Mary Hays
1898(?)-1979 ....*3*
Obituary *23*
Weil, Ann Yezner 1908-1969 .....*9*
Weil, Lisl *7*
Weilerstein, Sadie Rose 1894- *3*
Weinberg, Larry
See Weinberg, Lawrence (E.)
Weinberg, Lawrence (E.)
Brief Entry *48*
Weiner, Sandra 1922- *14*
Weingarten, Violet (Brown)
1915-1976 ....*3*
Obituary *27*
Weingartner, Charles 1922- *5*
Weir, LaVada *2*
Weir, Rosemary (Green)
1905- *21*
Weis, Margaret (Edith) 1948- *38*
Weisberger, Bernard A(llen)
1922- *21*
Weiser, Marjorie P(hillis) K(atz)
1934- *33*
Weisgard, Leonard (Joseph)
1916- *30*
Earlier sketch in SATA 2
Weiss, Adelle 1920- *18*
Weiss, Ann E(dwards) 1943- *30*
Weiss, Ellen 1953- *44*
Weiss, Harvey 1922- *27*
Earlier sketch in SATA 1
See also CLR 4
Weiss, Leatie 1928-
Brief Entry *50*
Weiss, Malcolm E. 1928- *3*

Weiss, Miriam
See Schlein, Miriam
Weiss, Nicki 1954- *33*
Weiss, Renee Karol 1923- *5*
Weissenborn, Hellmuth 1898-1982
Obituary *31*
Welber, Robert *26*
Welch, D'Alte Aldridge 1907-1970
Obituary *27*
Welch, Jean-Louise
See Kempton, Jean Welch
Welch, Martha McKeen 1914-
Brief Entry *45*
Welch, Pauline
See Bodenham, Hilda Esther
Welch, Ronald
See Felton, Ronald Oliver
Weller, George (Anthony)
1907- *31*
Welles, Winifred 1893-1939
Brief Entry *27*
Wellman, Alice 1900-1984 ....*51*
Brief Entry *36*
Wellman, Manly Wade
1903-1986 ....*6*
Obituary *47*
Wellman, Paul I. 1898-1966 ......*3*
Wells, H(erbert) G(eorge)
1866-1946 ....*20*
Wells, Helen 1910-1986 ....*49*
Earlier sketch in SATA 2
Wells, J. Wellington
See DeCamp, L(yon) Sprague
Wells, Rosemary *18*
See also SAAS 1
Wels, Byron G(erald) 1924- *9*
Welsh, Mary Flynn 1910(?)-1984
Obituary *38*
Weltner, Linda R(iverly)
1938- *38*
Welty, S. F.
See Welty, Susan F.
Welty, Susan F. 1905- *9*
Wendelin, Rudolph 1910- *23*
Werner, Herma 1926- *47*
Brief Entry *41*
Werner, Jane
See Watson, Jane Werner
Werner, K.
See Casewit, Curtis
Wersba, Barbara 1932- *1*
See also CLR 3
See also SAAS 2
Werstein, Irving 1914-1971 ....*14*
Werth, Kurt 1896- *20*
West, Anna 1938- *40*
West, Barbara
See Price, Olive
West, Betty 1921- *11*
West, C. P.
See Wodehouse, P(elham)
G(renville)
West, Emily G(ovan) 1919- *38*
West, Emmy
See West, Emily G(ovan)
West, James
See Withers, Carl A.
West, Jerry
See Stratemeyer, Edward L.

West, Jerry
    See Svenson, Andrew E.
West, (Mary) Jessamyn 1902(?)-1984
    Obituary 37
West, Ward
    See Borland, Hal
Westall, Robert (Atkinson)
    1929- 23
    See also SAAS 2
    See also CLR 13
Westerberg, Christine 1950- 29
Westervelt, Virginia (Veeder)
    1914- 10
Westheimer, David 1917- 14
Westmacott, Mary
    See Christie, Agatha (Mary Clarissa)
Westman, Paul (Wendell)
    1956- 39
Weston, Allen [Joint pseudonym]
    See Norton, Alice Mary
Weston, John (Harrison)
    1932- 21
Weston, Martha 1947- 53
Westwood, Jennifer 1940- 10
Wexler, Jerome (LeRoy)
    1923- 14
Wharf, Michael
    See Weller, George (Anthony)
Wheatley, Arabelle 1921- 16
Wheeler, Captain
    See Ellis, Edward S(ylvester)
Wheeler, Cindy 1955- 49
    Brief Entry 40
Wheeler, Janet D. [Collective
    pseudonym] 1
Wheeler, Opal 1898- 23
Whelan, Elizabeth M(urphy)
    1943- 14
Whistler, Reginald John
    1905-1944 30
Whistler, Rex
    See Whistler, Reginald John
Whitcomb, Jon 1906- 10
White, Anne Hitchcock 1902-1970
    Brief Entry 33
White, Anne Terry 1896- 2
White, Bessie (Felstiner) 1892(?)-1986
    Obituary 50
White, Dale
    See Place, Marian T.
White, Dori 1919- 10
White, E(lwyn) B(rooks)
    1899-1985 29
    Obituary 44
    Earlier sketch in SATA 2
    See also CLR 1
White, Eliza Orne
    1856-1947 ....YABC 2
White, Florence M(eiman)
    1910- 14
White, Laurence B., Jr. 1935- 10
White, Martin 1943- 51
White, Ramy Allison [Collective
    pseudonym] 1
White, Robb 1909- 1
    See also CLR 3
    See also SAAS 1
White, Ruth C. 1942- 39

White, T(erence) H(anbury)
    1906-1964 12
White, William, Jr. 1934- 16
Whitehead, Don(ald) F. 1908- 4
Whitehouse, Arch
    See Whitehouse, Arthur George
Whitehouse, Arthur George
    1895-1979 14
    Obituary 23
Whitehouse, Elizabeth S(cott)
    1893-1968 35
Whitehouse, Jeanne 1939- 29
Whitinger, R. D.
    See Place, Marian T.
Whitlock, Pamela 1921(?)-1982
    Obituary 31
Whitlock, Ralph 1914- 35
Whitman, Walt(er) 1819-1892 20
Whitney, Alex(andra) 1922- 14
Whitney, David C(harles)
    1921- 48
    Brief Entry 29
Whitney, Phyllis A(yame)
    1903- 30
    Earlier sketch in SATA 1
Whitney, Thomas P(orter)
    1917- 25
Wibberley, Leonard (Patrick
    O'Connor) 1915-1983 45
    Obituary 36
    Earlier sketch in SATA 2
    See also CLR 3
Wiberg, Harald (Albin) 1908-
    Brief Entry 40
Widdemer, Mabel Cleland
    1902-1964 5
Widenberg, Siv 1931- 10
Wier, Ester 1910- 3
Wiese, Kurt 1887-1974 36
    Obituary 24
    Earlier sketch in SATA 3
Wiesner, Portia
    See Takakjian, Portia
Wiesner, William 1899- 5
Wiggin, Kate Douglas (Smith)
    1856-1923 ....YABC 1
Wight, James Alfred 1916-
    Brief Entry 44
Wikland, Ilon 1930-
    Brief Entry 32
Wilber, Donald N(ewton)
    1907- 35
Wilbur, C. Keith 1923- 27
Wilbur, Richard (Purdy)
    1921- 9
Wilcox, R(uth) Turner
    1888-1970 36
Wild, Jocelyn 1941- 46
Wild, Robin (Evans) 1936- 46
Wilde, D. Gunther
    See Hurwood, Bernhardt J.
Wilde, Oscar (Fingal O'Flahertie
    Wills) 1854-1900 24
Wilder, Cherry
    See Grimm, Cherry Barbara Lockett
Wilder, Laura Ingalls
    1867-1957 29
    See also CLR 2

Wildsmith, Brian 1930- 16
    See also CLR 2
    See also SAAS 5
Wilkie, Katharine E(lliott)
    1904-1980 31
Wilkin, Eloise (Burns) 1904- 49
Wilkins, Frances 1923- 14
Wilkins, Marilyn (Ruth)
    1926- 30
Wilkins, Marne
    See Wilkins, Marilyn (Ruth)
Wilkinson, (Thomas) Barry
    1923- 50
    Brief Entry 32
Wilkinson, Brenda 1946- 14
Wilkinson, Burke 1913- 4
Wilkinson, Sylvia (J.) 1940-
    Brief Entry 39
Wilkoń, Józef 1930- 31
Wilks, Michael Thomas 1947- 44
Wilks, Mike
    See Wilks, Michael Thomas
Will
    See Lipkind, William
Willard, Barbara (Mary)
    1909- 17
    See also CLR 2
    See also SAAS 5
Willard, Mildred Wilds 1911- 14
Willard, Nancy 1936- 37
    Brief Entry 30
    See also CLR 5
Willcox, Isobel 1907- 42
Willey, Robert
    See Ley, Willy
Williams, Barbara 1925- 11
Williams, Beryl
    See Epstein, Beryl
Williams, Charles
    See Collier, James Lincoln
Williams, Clyde C.
    1881-1974 8
    Obituary 27
Williams, Coe
    See Harrison, C. William
Williams, Eric (Ernest)
    1911-1983 14
    Obituary 38
Williams, Ferelith Eccles
    1920- 22
Williams, Frances B.
    See Browin, Frances Williams
Williams, Garth (Montgomery)
    1912- 18
Williams, Guy R. 1920- 11
Williams, Hawley
    See Heyliger, William
Williams, J. R.
    See Williams, Jeanne
Williams, J. Walker
    See Wodehouse, P(elham)
    G(renville)
Williams, Jay 1914-1978 41
    Obituary 24
    Earlier sketch in SATA 3
    See also CLR 8
Williams, Jeanne 1930- 5
Williams, Kit 1946(?)- 44
    See also CLR 4

Williams, Leslie 1941- *42*
Williams, Louise Bonino 1904(?)-1984
   Obituary *39*
Williams, Lynn
   See Hale, Arlene
Williams, Maureen 1951- *12*
Williams, Michael
   See St. John, Wylly Folk
Williams, Patrick J.
   See Butterworth, W. E.
Williams, Selma R(uth) 1925- *14*
Williams, Slim
   See Williams, Clyde C.
Williams, Ursula Moray
   1911- *3*
Williams, Vera B. 1927- *53*
   Brief Entry *33*
   See also CLR 9
Williams-Ellis, (Mary) Amabel
   (Nassau) 1894-1984 .... *29*
   Obituary *41*
Williamson, Henry 1895-1977 .... *37*
   Obituary *30*
Williamson, Joanne Small
   1926- *3*
Willson, Robina Beckles (Ballard)
   1930- *27*
Wilma, Dana
   See Faralla, Dana
Wilson, Beth P(ierre) *8*
Wilson, Budge
   See Wilson, Marjorie
Wilson, Carter 1941- *6*
Wilson, Charles Morrow
   1905-1977 .... *30*
Wilson, Christopher B. 1910(?)-1985
   Obituary *46*
Wilson, Dagmar 1916-
   Brief Entry *31*
Wilson, Dorothy Clarke 1904- *16*
Wilson, Edward A(rthur)
   1886-1970 .... *38*
Wilson, Ellen (Janet Cameron)
   (?)-1976 .... *9*
   Obituary *26*
Wilson, Eric H. 1940- *34*
   Brief Entry *32*
Wilson, Erica *51*
Wilson, Forrest 1918- *27*
Wilson, Gahan 1930- *35*
   Brief Entry *27*
Wilson, Gina 1943- *36*
   Brief Entry *34*
Wilson, (Leslie) Granville
   1912- *14*
Wilson, Hazel 1898- *3*
Wilson, Jacqueline 1945-
   Brief Entry *52*
Wilson, John 1922- *22*
Wilson, Joyce M(uriel Judson) *21*
Wilson, Lionel 1924- *33*
   Brief Entry *31*
Wilson, Marjorie 1927-
   Brief Entry *51*
Wilson, Maurice (Charles John)
   1914- *46*
Wilson, Ron(ald William) *38*
Wilson, Sarah 1934- *50*

Wilson, Tom 1931- *33*
   Brief Entry *30*
Wilson, Walt(er N.) 1939- *14*
Wilton, Elizabeth 1937- *14*
Wilwerding, Walter Joseph
   1891-1966 .... *9*
Winchester, James H(ugh)
   1917-1985 .... *30*
   Obituary *45*
Winders, Gertrude Hecker *3*
Windham, Basil
   See Wodehouse, P(elham)
   G(renville)
Windham, Kathryn T(ucker)
   1918- *14*
Windsor, Claire
   See Hamerstrom, Frances
Windsor, Patricia 1938- *30*
Winfield, Arthur M.
   See Stratemeyer, Edward L.
Winfield, Edna
   See Stratemeyer, Edward L.
Winn, Chris 1952- *42*
Winn, Janet Bruce 1928- *43*
Winn, Marie 1936- *38*
Winnick, Karen B(eth) B(inkoff)
   1946- *51*
Winston, Clara 1921-1983
   Obituary *39*
Winter, Milo (Kendall)
   1888-1956 .... *21*
Winter, Paula Cecelia 1929- *48*
Winter, R. R.
   See Winterbotham, R(ussell)
   R(obert)
Winterbotham, R(ussell) R(obert)
   1904-1971 .... *10*
Winters, Jon
   See Cross, Gilbert B.
Winterton, Gayle
   See Adams, William Taylor
Winthrop, Elizabeth
   See Mahony, Elizabeth Winthrop
Wirtenberg, Patricia Z. 1932- *10*
Wise, William 1923- *4*
Wise, Winifred E. *2*
Wiseman, Ann (Sayre) 1926- *31*
Wiseman, B(ernard) 1922- *4*
Wiseman, David 1916- *43*
   Brief Entry *40*
Wisler, G(ary) Clifton 1950-
   Brief Entry *46*
Wisner, Bill
   See Wisner, William L.
Wisner, William L.
   1914(?)-1983 .... *42*
Witham, (Phillip) Ross 1917- *37*
Withers, Carl A. 1900-1970 .... *14*
Witt, Shirley Hill 1934- *17*
Wittels, Harriet Joan 1938- *31*
Wittman, Sally (Anne Christensen)
   1941- *30*
Witty, Paul A(ndrew)
   1898-1976 .... *50*
   Obituary *30*
Wizard, Mr.
   See Herbert, Don
Wodehouse, P(elham) G(renville)
   1881-1975 .... *22*

Wodge, Dreary
   See Gorey, Edward St. John
Wohlberg, Meg 1905- *41*
Wohlrabe, Raymond A. 1900- *4*
Wojciechowska, Maia 1927- *28*
   Earlier sketch in SATA 1
   See also CLR 1
   See also SAAS 1
Wolcott, Patty 1929- *14*
Wold, Jo Anne 1938- *30*
Woldin, Beth Weiner 1955- *34*
Wolf, Bernard 1930-
   Brief Entry *37*
Wolfe, Burton H. 1932- *5*
Wolfe, Louis 1905- *8*
Wolfe, Rinna (Evelyn) 1925- *38*
Wolfenden, George
   See Beardmore, George
Wolff, (Jenifer) Ashley 1956- *50*
Wolff, Diane 1945- *27*
Wolff, Robert Jay 1905- *10*
Wolitzer, Hilma 1930- *31*
Wolkoff, Judie (Edwards)
   Brief Entry *37*
Wolkstein, Diane 1942- *7*
Wolny, P.
   See Janeczko, Paul B(ryan)
Wolters, Richard A. 1920- *35*
Wondriska, William 1931- *6*
Wood, Audrey *50*
   Brief Entry *44*
Wood, Catherine
   See Etchison, Birdie L(ee)
Wood, Don 1945- *50*
   Brief Entry *44*
Wood, Edgar A(llardyce)
   1907- *14*
Wood, Esther
   See Brady, Esther Wood
Wood, Frances Elizabeth *34*
Wood, James Playsted 1905- *1*
Wood, Kerry
   See Wood, Edgar A(llardyce)
Wood, Laura N.
   See Roper, Laura Wood
Wood, Nancy 1936- *6*
Wood, Phyllis Anderson
   1923- *33*
   Brief Entry *30*
Wood, Wallace 1927-1981
   Obituary *33*
Woodard, Carol 1929- *14*
Woodburn, John Henry 1914- *11*
Woodford, Peggy 1937- *25*
Woodrich, Mary Neville
   1915- *2*
Woods, George A(llan) 1926- *30*
Woods, Geraldine 1948-
   Brief Entry *42*
Woods, Harold 1945-
   Brief Entry *42*
Woods, Margaret 1921- *2*
Woods, Nat
   See Stratemeyer, Edward L.
Woodson, Jack
   See Woodson, John Waddie, Jr.
Woodson, John Waddie, Jr. *10*

Woodward, Cleveland
　1900-1986 .... *10*
　Obituary *48*
Woody, Regina Jones 1894- *3*
Wooldridge, Rhoda 1906- *22*
Woolley, Catherine 1904- *3*
Woolsey, Janette 1904- *3*
Worcester, Donald Emmet
　1915- *18*
Work, Virginia 1946-
　Brief Entry *45*
Worline, Bonnie Bess 1914- *14*
Wormser, Sophie 1896- *22*
Worth, Richard
　Brief Entry *46*
Worth, Valerie 1933- *8*
Worthington, Phoebe 1910-
　Brief Entry *52*
Wortis, Avi 1937- *14*
Wosmek, Frances 1917- *29*
Wriggins, Sally Hovey 1922 ...... *17*
Wright, Anna (Maria Louisa Perrot)
　Rose 1890-1968
　Brief Entry *35*
Wright, Betty Ren
　Brief Entry *48*
Wright, Dare 1926(?)- *21*
Wright, Enid Meadowcroft
　1898-1966 .... *3*
Wright, Esmond 1915- *10*
Wright, Frances Fitzpatrick
　1897- *10*
Wright, Judith 1915- *14*
Wright, Katrina
　See Gater, Dilys
Wright, Kenneth
　See Del Rey, Lester
Wright, Nancy Means *38*
Wright, R(obert) H. 1906- *6*
Wrightson, Patricia 1921- *8*
　See also CLR 4, 14
　See also SAAS 4
Wronker, Lili Cassel 1924- *10*
Wulffson, Don L. 1943- *32*
Wuorio, Eva-Lis 1918- *34*
　Brief Entry *28*
Wyeth, Betsy James 1921- *41*
Wyeth, N(ewell) C(onvers)
　1882-1945 .... *17*
Wyler, Rose 1909- *18*
Wylie, Betty Jane *48*
Wylie, Laura
　See Matthews, Patricia
Wymer, Norman George
　1911- *25*
Wynants, Miche 1934-
　Brief Entry *31*
Wyndham, Lee
　See Hyndman, Jane Andrews
Wyndham, Robert
　See Hyndman, Robert Utley
Wynter, Edward (John) 1914- *14*
Wynyard, Talbot
　See Hamilton, Charles H. St. John
Wyss, Johann David Von
　1743-1818 .... *29*
　Brief Entry *27*
Wyss, Thelma Hatch 1934- *10*

Y

Yaffe, Alan
　See Yorinks, Arthur
Yamaguchi, Marianne 1936- *7*
Yang, Jay 1941- *12*
Yarbrough, Ira 1910(?)-1983
　Obituary *35*
Yaroslava
　See Mills, Yaroslava Surmach
Yashima, Taro
　See Iwamatsu, Jun Atsushi
　See also CLR 4
Yates, Elizabeth 1905- *4*
　See also SAAS 6
Yates, Raymond F(rancis)
　1895-1966 .... *31*
Yaukey, Grace S(ydenstricker)
　1899- *5*
Yeakley, Marjory Hall 1908- *21*
Yeatman, Linda 1938- *42*
Yensid, Retlaw
　See Disney, Walt(er Elias)
Yeo, Wilma (Lethem) 1918- *24*
Yeoman, John (Brian) 1934- *28*
Yep, Laurence M. 1948- *7*
　See also CLR 3
Yerian, Cameron John *21*
Yerian, Margaret A. *21*
Yolen, Jane H. 1939- *40*
　Earlier sketch in SATA 4
　See also CLR 4
　See also SAAS 1
Yonge, Charlotte Mary
　1823-1901 .... *17*
Yorinks, Arthur 1953- *49*
　Earlier sketch in SATA 33
York, Andrew
　See Nicole, Christopher Robin
York, Carol Beach 1928- *6*
York, Rebecca [Joint pseudonym]
　See Buckholtz, Eileen (Garber)
Yost, Edna 1889-1971
　Obituary *26*
Youd, C. S. 1922-
　See SAAS 6
Youd, (Christopher) Samuel
　1922- *47*
　Brief Entry *30*
　See also SAAS 6
Young, Bob
　See Young, Robert W.
Young, Clarence [Collective
　pseudonym] *1*
Young, Dorothea Bennett
　1924- *31*
Young, Ed 1931- *10*
Young, Edward
　See Reinfeld, Fred
Young, Elaine L.
　See Schulte, Elaine L(ouise)
Young, Jan
　See Young, Janet Randall
Young, Janet Randall 1919- *3*
Young, Lois Horton
　1911-1981 .... *26*
Young, Margaret B(uckner)
　1922- *2*

Young, Miriam 1913-1934 .... *7*
Young, (Rodney Lee) Patrick (Jr.)
　1937- *22*
Young, Percy M(arshall)
　1912- *31*
Young, Robert W. 1916-1969 ..... *3*
Young, Scott A(lexander)
　1918- *5*
Young, Vivien
　See Gater, Dilys
Youngs, Betty 1934-1985 .... *53*
　Obituary *42*

Z

Zach, Cheryl (Byrd) 1947-
　Brief Entry *51*
Zaffo, George J. (?)-1984 .... *42*
Zaid, Barry 1938- *51*
Zaidenberg, Arthur 1908(?)- *34*
Zalben, Jane Breskin 1950- *7*
Zallinger, Jean (Day) 1918- *14*
Zallinger, Peter Franz 1943- *49*
Zappler, Lisbeth 1930- *10*
Zarchy, Harry 1912- *34*
Zarif, Margaret Min'imah
　(?)-1983 .... *33*
Zaring, Jane (Thomas) 1936- *51*
　Brief Entry *40*
Zaslavsky, Claudia 1917- *36*
Zeck, Gerald Anthony 1939- *40*
Zeck, Gerry
　See Zeck, Gerald Anthony
Zei, Alki *24*
　See also CLR 6
Zelazny, Roger (Joseph Christopher)
　1937-
　Brief Entry *39*
Zelinsky, Paul O. 1953- *49*
　Brief Entry *33*
Zellan, Audrey Penn 1950- *22*
Zemach, Harve 1933- *3*
Zemach, Kaethe 1958- *49*
　Brief Entry *39*
Zemach, Margot 1931- *21*
Zens, Patricia Martin 1926-1972
　Brief Entry *50*
Zerman, Melvyn Bernard
　1930- *46*
Ziemienski, Dennis 1947- *10*
Zillah
　See Macdonald, Zillah K.
Zim, Herbert S(pencer) 1909- *30*
　Earlier sketch in SATA 1
　See also CLR 2
　See also SAAS 2
Zim, Sonia Bleeker
　See Bleeker, Sonia
Zimelman, Nathan
　Brief Entry *37*
Zimmerman, Naoma 1914- *10*
Zimnik, Reiner 1930- *36*
　See also CLR 3
Zindel, Bonnie 1943- *34*
Zindel, Paul 1936- *16*
　See also CLR 3

Ziner, (Florence) Feenie
 1921- *5*
Zion, (Eu)Gene 1913-1975 .... *18*
Zollinger, Gulielma 1856-1917
 Brief Entry *27*
Zolotow, Charlotte S. 1915- *35*
 Earlier sketch in SATA 1
 See also CLR 2
Zonia, Dhimitri 1921- *20*
Zubrowski, Bernard 1939- *35*
Zupa, G. Anthony
 See Zeck, Gerald Anthony
Zurhorst, Charles (Stewart, Jr.)
 1913- *12*
Zuromskis, Diane
 See Stanley, Diane
Zweifel, Frances 1931- *14*
Zwinger, Ann 1925- *46*